DB2 UNIVERSAL DATABASE
CALL-LEVEL INTERFACE (CLI)
DEVELOPER'S GUIDE

McGraw-Hill Enterprise Computing Series

DB2 Universal Database Developer's Guide for Call Level Interface by Sanders
ISBN 0-07-134572-8

Enterprise Java Developer's Guide by Narayanan/Liu
ISBN 0-07-134673-2

Web Warehousing and Knowledge Management by Mattison
ISBN 0-07-0041103-4

ODBC 3.5 Developer's Guide by Sanders
ISBN 0-07-058087-1

Data Warehousing, Data Mining & OLAP by Berson/Smith
ISBN 0-07-006272-2

Data Stores, Data Warehousing and the Zachman Framework by Inman
ISBN 0-07-031429-2

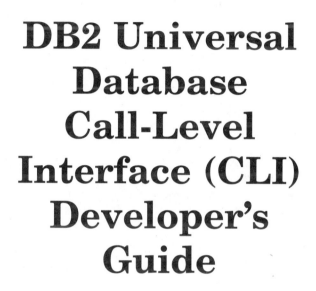

DB2 Universal Database Call-Level Interface (CLI) Developer's Guide

Roger E. Sanders

McGraw-Hill
New York • San Francisco • Washington, D.C. • Auckland
Bogotá • Caracas • Lisbon • London • Madrid • Mexico City
Milan • Montreal • New Delhi • San Juan • Singapore
Sydney • Tokyo • Toronto

McGraw-Hill

A Division of The McGraw-Hill Companies

1 2 3 4 5 6 7 8 9 0   AGM/AGM   9 0 4 3 2 1 0 9

ISBN: 0–07–134572–8

The sponsoring editor for this book was Simon Yates, and the production supervisor was Clare Stanley. It was set in Century Schoolbook by D&G Limited, LLC.

Printed and bound by Quebecor / Martinsburg

DEDICATION

To my daughter, Kristen Marie Sanders.

ACKNOWLEDGMENTS

A project of this magnitude requires both a great deal of time and the support of many different people. I would like to express my gratitude to the following people for their contributions:

- Paul Rivot—IBM
  Worldwide Brand Manager, Database Servers
  Paul provided me with DB2 Universal Database, Version 5.2 software, coordinated the delivery of the DB2 Universal Database documentation, and provided me with a key contact at the DB2 development lab in Toronto, Canada.

- Sheila Richardson—IBM Toronto Lab
  IBM Consulting Editor
  Sheila was my key contact at IBM Toronto. She was instrumental in providing me with DB2 Universal Database documentation and in getting me technical help when I needed it.

- Rick Swaggerman—IBM Toronto Lab
  DB2 Language Architect
  Rick provided me with information about upcoming SQL changes in DB2 Universal Database, Version 6.0.

- Robert Begg—IBM Toronto Lab
  Software Developer
  Robert provided me with information about upcoming CLI changes in DB2 Universal Database, Version 6.0, and he provided technical support about CLI cursor support and the `SQLSetPos()` function.

- Matthew Huras—IBM Toronto Lab
  Senior Technical Staff Member
  Matthew provided me with information about upcoming API changes in DB2 Universal Database, Version 6.0.

- Roger Zheng—IBM Toronto Lab
  Advisory Software Developer
  Roger tested the in-doubt transaction API examples for me and provided additional information about in-doubt transaction processing.

- Hershel Harris—IBM
  Director, Database Technology
  Mr. Harris was one of the behind-the-scenes authorizers that made it possible to include an evaluation copy of DB2 Universal Database in this book.

I would also like to thank my editor, Simon Yates; my project manager, Alan Harris, who worked with the production staff; and the staff at McGraw-Hill for their help and support.

Most of all, I would like to thank my wife, Beth, for all of her help and encouragement, and for once again overlooking the things that did not get done while I worked on this book.

CONTENTS

Contents

FOREWORD

Relational database technology was invented in IBM research more than 20 years ago. In 1983, IBM shipped the first version of DB2 for MVS. In 1997, IBM delivered its flagship relational technology on the AS/400 and OS/2. As we enter the 21st century, IBM has continued to extend its award winning database technology with additional function and support for additional platforms. Today, DB2 Universal Database is the most modern database on the planet, supporting the world's most popular system platforms (IBM OS/390, IBM OS/400, IBM RS/6000, IBM OS/2, Sun Solaris, HP-UX, Microsoft Windows NT, SCO OpenServer, and Linux).

DB2 Universal Database, which first shipped in 1997, has evolved to meet the rapid-fire changes within corporations around the world. Traditional companies are transforming their core business processes around the Internet. New e-companies are being formed, and a new generation of Web-based applications are being written. You might ask, "What is an e-business anyway?" e-business is buying and selling on the Internet. e-business is being open 24-hours-a-day, seven-days-a-week, without having to be there at the company. e-business is about reaching new customers, and e-business means working together in different ways. Some have said that e-business changes everything—or does it?

e-business demands highly scalable, available, secure, and reliable systems. e-business demands industrial strength database technology—the kind that DB2 has delivered to more than 40 million users over the last 15 years. IBM's DB2 Universal Database team has been hard at work delivering enhancements to DB2 Universal Database to make it the foundation for e-business. Today, users can access DB2 Universal Database from the Web. Application developers can write DB2 applications and stored procedures using Java or JDBC. Database administrators can administer DB2 databases from Web browsers, and DB2 is the most highly scalable, available, robust database in the world.

e-business poses a number of new requirements on the database, as well—access from any type of device. New, pervasive devices will be used to access DB2 databases. e-businesses will have a growing need to leverage information and knowledge, which will drive business intelligence and knowledge-based applications which require support for multi-terabyte databases to grow to petabytes. These applications will require advanced analytical functions to be supported in the database engine. They will also require access to rich content—documents, images, text, video, and spatial data. DB2 Universal Database has been extended to deliver this rich content today.

The next millennium will bring with it enormous change. The next millennium also will bring with it incredible opportunity for information technology professionals and those who support database systems. The new economy will be based on information exchange, and database professionals will be the stewards of this critical corporate asset. I encourage you to take advantage of the opportunity that Roger Sanders is providing to learn more about DB2 Universal Database. I also encourage you to obtain a certification in DB2 Universal Database. Your time will be well spent. DB2 Universal Database is the foundation for e-business for thousands of companies today, and we have only begun.

Janet Perna
General Manager, Data Management Solutions
IBM Corporation

INTRODUCTION

DB2 Universal Database is a robust database management system that is designed to be used for a variety of purposes in a variety of operating system environments.

DB2 Universal Database is not a new product; it has existed in some form or another since 1989. The earliest version was called Database Manager, and that version was bundled with OS/2 in a product called OS/2 Extended Edition. This product was IBM's first attempt to put its popular Database 2 product (which had been available for MVS operating systems on IBM mainframes since 1983) on a PC. Through the years, IBM's PC version of DB2 has matured to the point where the program is now one of the most powerful database products available for a wide variety of platforms.

DB2 Universal Database provides a rich set of programming interfaces (Structured Query Language, a Call-Level Interface, and numerous Application Programming Interface function calls) that can be used to develop several different kinds of applications. This book, one of a series of books that describe each of these programming interfaces in detail, is designed to provide you with a conceptual overview of DB2 Universal Database—as well as a comprehensive reference that covers DB2 Universal Database's Call-Level Interface.

Why I Wrote This Book

Although DB2 Universal Database has been available since 1989, only a handful of books have been written about the product. And, as the DB2 product evolved, many of the books that were written were not revised to reflect the differences in the product. Eventually, they went out of print. By 1993, when the DB2/2 GA product was released (with DB2/6000 following shortly after), no book existed that focused on DB2 application development. Robert Orfali and Dan Harkey's *Client/Server Programming with OS/2 2.1* contained four chapters covering the Extended Services 1.0 database manager and later DB2/2. However, because this book addressed client/server programming rather than DB2 application programming, its information about DB2 was limited. This situation meant that IBM's product manuals and online help were the only resources available to application developers writing applications for DB2/2.

In the summer of 1992, while developing a specialized DB2 application (then called the Extended Services 1.0 Database Manager) that used many of DB2's *Application Programming Interface* (API) calls, I discovered how lacking (particularly in the area of examples) some of the IBM manuals for this product really were. Because there were no other reference books available, I had to spend a considerable amount of trial-and-error programming to complete my DB2 application. I immediately saw the need for a good DB2 programming reference guide.

This inspiration ultimately led to the writing of my first book, *The Developer's Handbook to DB2 for Common Servers*.

Since that book was written, DB2 has undergone two more revisions, and several new features have been added to an already rich application development toolset. As I began revising my original book, I discovered that it would be impossible to put a thorough reference for this toolset in a single book. My editor, Simon Yates, decided to do the next best thing: to put this information in a series of books, where each book addressed a specific aspect of DB2 Universal Database's rich development toolset.

Who Is This Book For?

This book is for anyone who is interested in creating DB2 Universal Database applications using DB2's *Call Level Interface* (CLI). The book is written primarily for database application programmers and analysts who are familiar with SQL and are designing and/or coding software applications that access one or more DB2 databases. Experienced C/C++ programmers with little experience developing DB2 database applications will benefit most from the material covered in this book. Experienced DB2 database application developers who are familiar with earlier versions of the DB2 product will also benefit from this book, because the book describes in detail new features that are only available in the latest release of DB2 Universal Database. In either case, this book is meant to be a single resource that provides you with almost everything you need to know in order to design and develop DB2 database applications using DB2 CLI.

To get the most out of this book, you should have a working knowledge of the C++ programming language. An understanding of relational database concepts and *Structured Query Language* (SQL) will also be helpful, although not crucial.

How This Book Is Organized

This book is divided into three major parts. Part 1 discusses basic relational database concepts. Before you can successfully develop a DB2 database application, you must first have a good understanding of DB2's underlying database architecture and data consistency mechanisms. Two chapters in this section are designed to provide you with that understanding: Chapter 1 and Chapter 2.

Chapter 1 explains relational database concepts and describes the components of a DB2 Universal Database. This chapter also describes the internal file structures used by DB2 for data and database object storage. Chapter 2 discusses the mechanisms that DB2 provides for maintaining data integrity. These mechanisms include transactions, isolation levels, row- and table-level locking, and transaction logging. Together, these two chapters lay the groundwork for the rest of this book.

Part 2 discusses DB2 CLI database application development fundamentals. Once you have a good understanding of DB2's underlying database architecture and consistency mechanisms, you also need to understand general database application development as it applies to DB2. The four chapters in this section, Chapters 3 through 6, describe the different types of applications that can be developed for DB2 and provide you with an understanding of the methods used to develop applications using DB2 CLI.

Chapter 3 discusses the application development process as it applies to DB2. This chapter describes basic DB2 application design and identifies the main elements of a DB2 application. The chapter also explains how the database application development and testing environment are established before the application development process begins.

Chapter 4 explains how to write *Call-Level Interface* (CLI) applications and identifies the main components of a CLI application. This chapter also describes the steps you must take to convert CLI application source-code files into executable programs.

Chapter 5 introduces the major components used in almost all CLI applications to interact with data sources. This chapter introduces the concept of *handles* and explains how they are used. The chapter also describes how data buffers and length/indicator buffers are used to transfer data between CLI applications and databases.

Chapter 6 examines the basic SQL syntax and grammar recognized and used by DB2 Universal Database. This chapter describes the basic SQL statements used for data manipulation and data definition, along with the special clauses and predicates that can be used with them, and the escape sequences used by ODBC to process data source specific SQL statements. This chapter also describes the various ways that SQL statements can be constructed in a DB2 CLI application.

Part 3 contains information about each DB2 CLI API function that can be used in an application. This section is designed to be a detailed CLI function reference. The nine chapters in this section group the CLI functions according to their functionality.

Chapter 7 describes the steps an CLI application must take to initialize the CLI environment and establish a connection to a data source or driver. This chapter also contains a detailed reference section covering each CLI function that can be used to initialize the CLI/ODBC environment and establish a connection to a database. Each CLI function described in this chapter is accompanied by a Visual C++ example that illustrates how to code the CLI API in an application program.

Chapter 8 shows how a CLI application can obtain detailed information about, and to a lesser extent control, the capabilities of a particular data source or driver with which the CLI application is working. This chapter also contains a detailed reference section that covers each CLI function that can be used to obtain information about or control a data source or driver's capabilities. Each CLI function described in this chapter is accompanied by a Visual C++ example that illustrates how to code the CLI API in an application program.

Chapter 9 describes the process used by a CLI application to prepare and execute an SQL statement. This chapter also contains a detailed reference section that covers each CLI function that can be used to prepare, associate application variables to (bind), and submit SQL statements for execution. Each CLI function described in this chapter is accompanied by a Visual C++ example that illustrates how to code the CLI API in an application program.

Chapter 10 examines the *metadata* used to describe a result data set and shows how an application can use this metadata to retrieve (fetch) results produced when an SQL statement that produces a result data set (such as a **SELECT SQL** statement) is executed. This chapter also contains a detailed reference section that covers each CLI function that can be used to obtain result data set metadata, associate application variables to (bind) columns in a result data set, and perform basic data retrieval operations. Each CLI function described in this chapter is accompanied by a Visual C++ example that illustrates how to code the CLI API in an application program.

Chapter 11 introduces the *extended* cursors (that is, block cursors and scrollable cursors) used by CLI to perform advanced data retrieval operations and to determine how many rows were actually affected by an insert, update, or delete operation. This chapter also contains a detailed reference section covering each CLI function that can be used to perform advanced data retrieval operations using CLI's extended cursor set.

Each CLI function described in this chapter is accompanied by a Visual C++ example that illustrates how to code the CLI API in an application program.

Chapter 12 introduces the concept of descriptors. Although they have been "behind the scenes" for quite some time, with Version 5.0 descriptors were brought out of hiding. This chapter is designed to introduce CLI descriptors and show how they can be used to streamline application processing. This chapter also contains a detailed reference section that covers each CLI function that can be used to retrieve information from, modify, and copy descriptor records. Each CLI function described in this chapter is accompanied by a Visual C++ example that illustrates how to code the CLI API in an application program.

Chapter 13 describes the mechanisms used by CLI to report the success or failure of a CLI function to the calling application. This chapter also contains a detailed reference section that covers each CLI function that can be used to retrieve error/warning information from a diagnostic record and return the information to an application. Each CLI function described in this chapter is accompanied by a Visual C++ example that illustrates how to code the CLI API in an application program.

Chapter 14 describes the system catalog of a data source and explains how the information stored in the system catalog can be used by an application. This chapter also contains a detailed reference section that covers each CLI function that can be used to retrieve information from the system catalog of a specified data source. Each CLI function described in this chapter is accompanied by a Visual C++ example that illustrates how to code the CLI API in an application program.

Chapter 15 describes the mechanisms used by CLI to work with *Large Object* (LOB) data. This chapter contains a detailed reference section that covers each CLI function that can be used to manipulate LOBs. Each CLI function described in this chapter is accompanied by a Visual C++ example that illustrates how to code the CLI API in an application program.

NOTE: *The concepts covered in Chapters 1–3 are repeated in each book in this series. If you have another book in this series and are already familiar with this information, you may want to skip these three chapters.*

Syntax Conventions Used In This Book

SQL statement syntax is presented throughout this book to show the basic format to use when coding a particular SQL statement (that is to be used in conjunction with a DB2 CLI function). Wherever SQL statement syntax is presented, the following conventions are used:

■ [*parameter*]   Parameters shown inside brackets are required parameters and must be specified.

- *<parameter>*   Parameters shown inside angle brackets are optional parameters and do not have to be specified.
- *parameter | parameter*   Parameters, or other items separated by vertical bars, indicate that you must select one item from the list of items presented.
- *parameter,...*   If a parameter is followed by a comma and three periods (ellipsis), then multiple instances of that parameter can be included in the statement.

The following examples illustrate these syntax conventions:

- Example 1:

```
CONNECT TO [server-name] <connection-mode> <USER
[authorization-ID] USING [password]>
```

In this example, both **connection-mode** and **USER [authorization-ID] USING [password]** are optional parameters, as indicated by the angle brackets. The *server-name, authorization-ID*, and *password* parameters are required, as indicated by the brackets. However, *authorization-ID* and *password* are only required parameters if the **USER [authorization-ID] USING [password]** option is specified.

- Example 2:

```
RELEASE [server-name | CURRENT | ALL <SQL> ]
```

In this example, either *server-name*, **CURRENT**, or **ALL <SQL>** can be specified, as indicated by the vertical bar. One of these items must be specified, as indicated by the brackets. If **ALL** is selected, **SQL** can be added (that is, **ALL SQL**); however, it is not required, as indicated by the angle brackets.

- Example 3:

```
CREATE <UNIQUE> INDEX [index-name] ON [table-name] ( [column-name <ASC
| DESC>,...] )
```

In this example, *index-name, table-name*, and at least one *column-name* must be specified, as indicated by the brackets. **UNIQUE, ASC**, and **DESC** are options, as indicated by the angle brackets. Either **ASC**, or **DESC** can be specified as an option, but not both (as indicated by the vertical bar). More than one **column-name <ASC | DESC>** option can be specified, as indicated by the **,...** that follows the **column-name <ASC | DESC>** option.

CLI API Conformance

A header similar to the following one is provided with each DB2 CLI API function:

COMPATIBILITY				
X/OPEN 95 CLI	ISO/IEC 92 CLI	DB2 CLI 5.2	DB2 CLI 2.0	ODBC 3.x
☒	☑	☑	☑	☐

ODBC API CONFORMANCE LEVEL	**CORE**

Each standards specification that the DB2 CLI API function conforms to will be checked ✓. If the API conformed to an earlier version of a particular standard specification but is no longer supported by the latest version of that specification, the box under the specification will contain a ✗.

A Word About Unicode Support

Unicode is a method of software character encoding that treats all characters as having a fixed width of two bytes. This method is used as an alternative to the ANSI character encoding method that is normally used by Windows, which treats all characters as having a fixed width of one byte and limits to only 256 characters. Because Unicode can represent more than 65,000 characters, Unicode accommodates many languages whose characters are not represented in ANSI encoding.

Unicode does not require the use of codepages, which ANSI uses to accommodate a limited set of languages. This characteristic is an improvement over the *Double-Byte Character Set* (DBCS), which uses a mixture of 8-bit and 16-bit characters and requires the use of codepages.

One of the major differences between DB2 CLI Version 5.0 and DB2 CLI Version 2.0 is that DB2 CLI Version 5.0 is Unicode-enabled. This feature means that when using DB2 CLI Version 5.0, the CLI library or the ODBC 3.5 Driver Manager maps function string arguments and string data to either Unicode or ANSI characters, as required by the application and/or driver. This characteristic also means that the ODBC 3.5 Driver Manager supports the use of a Unicode driver with both a Unicode application and an ANSI application—and the use of an ANSI driver with an ANSI application. The Driver Manager also provides limited Unicode-to-ANSI mapping for a Unicode application that is working with an ANSI driver.

I have tried to document cases where Unicode support has an effect or imposes a limitation on DB2 CLI API function being used; however, for the sake of saving space, I have not gone into great detail about Unicode application development. If you are developing applications that need to provide full Unicode support, consult the "On-Line Help" for more information.

You can find out more information about the Unicode standard by visiting the Web site `http://www.cam.spyglass.com/unicode.html`.

About the Examples

The example programs provided are an essential part of this book; therefore, it is imperative that they are accurate. To make the use of each DB2 CLI API function call clear, I included only the required overhead in each example and provided limited error-checking. I have also tried to design the example programs so they verify that the CLI API function call being demonstrated actually executed as expected. For instance, an example program illustrating statement attribute modification might retrieve and display a value before and after the modification, to verify that the CLI API function used to modify the data worked correctly.

I compiled and tested all the examples in this book with Visual C++ 6.0, running against the SAMPLE database that is provided with DB2 Universal Database, Version 5.2. Appendix D shows the steps I used to create the test environment and the steps I used to reproduce and test all of the examples provided in this book.

A Word About CLI API Parameter and Return Code Data Types

As you examine the CLI API Syntax conventions and examples provided, you may notice that in many cases the **Syntax** section may indicate that a parameter in an API function call is one data type and the actual data type used in the example program is another. For example, the **Syntax** section for the **SQLConnect()** function shows that the first parameter has the data type **SQLHDBC**, but the data type used for the first parameter in the **SQLConnect()** function call shown in example **CH7EX1.CPP** is **SQLHANDLE**.

Although at first glance these differences may appear to be errors, they are not. An examination of the header file *SQLCLI.H* will show that many data types that appear to be different are actually the same. For example, the following excerpt from the *SQLCLI.H* header file shows that although different data types exist for environment, connection, statement, and descriptor handles, they are all really the same.

```
/*******************************************************************
 *
 * Source File Name = sqlcli.h
 *
 * (C) COPYRIGHT International Business Machines Corp. 1993, 1998
 * All Rights Reserved
 * Licensed Materials - Property of IBM
 *
 * US Government Users Restricted Rights - Use, duplication or
 * disclosure restricted by GSA ADP Schedule Contract with IBM
 * Corp.
 *
 * Function = Include File defining:
 *             DB2 CLI Interface - Constants
 *             DB2 CLI Interface - Data Structures
 *             DB2 CLI Interface - Function Prototypes
 *
 * Operating System = Common C Include File
 *
 *******************************************************************
  . . .
#ifdef DB2WIN
typedef  SQLINTEGER          SQLHANDLE;
typedef  HENV                SQLHENV;
typedef  HDBC                SQLHDBC;
typedef  HSTMT               SQLHSTMT;
typedef  HWND                SQLHWND;
#else
#ifndef __SQLTYPES
typedef  SQLINTEGER          SQLHANDLE;
typedef  SQLINTEGER          SQLHENV;
```

```
typedef    SQLINTEGER          SQLHDBC;
typedef    SQLINTEGER          SQLHSTMT;
#endif
. . .
```

Feedback and Source Code on the CD

I have tried to make sure that all the information and examples provided in this book are accurate; however, I am not perfect. If you happen to find a problem with some of the information in this book or with one of the example programs, please send me the correction so I can make the appropriate changes in future printings. In addition, I welcome any comments you might have about this book. The best way to communicate with me is via e-mail at **r-bsanders@mindspring.com**.

As mentioned earlier, all the example programs provided in this book have been tested for accuracy. Thus, if you type them in exactly as they appear in the book, they should compile and execute successfully. To help you avoid all that typing, electronic copies of these programs have been provided on the CD accompanying this book.

Limits of Liability and Warranty Disclaimer

Both the publisher and I have used our best efforts in preparing the material in this book. These efforts include obtaining technical information from IBM, as well as developing and testing the example programs to determine their effectiveness and accuracy. We make no warranty of any kind, expressed or implied, with regard to the documentation and example programs provided in this book. We shall not be liable in any event for incidental or consequential damages in connection with or arising out of the furnishing, performance, or use of either this documentation or these example programs.

Basic Database Concepts

DB2 Database Architecture

Before you begin developing DB2 database applications, you need to understand the underlying architecture of DB2 *Universal Database* (UDB), Version 5.2. This chapter is designed to introduce you to the architecture used by DB2 UDB. This chapter begins with a description of the relational database model and its data-handling operations. This is followed by an introduction to the data objects and support objects that make up a DB2 database. Finally, the directory, subdirectory, and file-naming conventions used by DB2 for storing these data and system objects are discussed. Let's begin by defining a relational database management system.

The Relational Database

DB2 UDB, Version 5.2, is a 32-bit relational database management system. A *relational database management system* is a database management system that is designed around a set of powerful mathematical concepts known as *relational algebra*. The first relational database model was introduced in the early 1970s by Mr. E. F. Codd at the IBM San Jose Research Center. This model is based on the following operations that are identified in relational algebra:

SELECTION—This operation selects one or more records from a table based on a specified condition.

PROJECTION—This operation returns a column or columns from a table based on some condition.

JOIN—This operation enables you to paste two or more tables together. Each table must have a common column before a JOIN operation can work.

UNION—This operation combines two like tables to produce a set of all records found in both tables. Each table must have compatible columns before a UNION operation can work. In other words, each field in the first table must match each field in the second table. Essentially, a UNION of two tables is the same as the mathematical addition of two tables.

DIFFERENCE—This operation tells you which records are unique to one table when two tables are compared. Again, each table must have identical columns before a DIFFERENCE operation can work. Essentially, a DIFFERENCE of two tables is the same as the mathematical subtraction of two tables.

INTERSECTION—This operation tells you which records are common to two or more tables when they are compared. This operation involves performing the UNION and DIFFERENCE operations twice.

PRODUCT—This operation combines two dissimilar tables to produce a set of all records found in both tables. Essentially, a PRODUCT of two tables is the same as the mathematical multiplication of two tables. The PRODUCT operation can often produce unwanted side effects, however, requiring you to use the PROJECTION operation to clean them up.

As you can see, in a relational database data is perceived to exist in one or more two-dimensional tables. These tables are made up of rows and columns, where each record (row) is divided into fields (columns) that contain individual pieces of information. Although data is not actually stored this way, visualizing the data as a collection of two-dimensional tables makes it easier to describe data needs in easy-to-understand terms.

Relational Database Objects

A relational database system is more than just a collection of two-dimensional tables. Additional objects exist that aid in data storage and retrieval, database structure control, and database disaster recovery. In general, *objects* are defined as items about which DB2 retains information. With DB2, two basic types of objects exist: *data objects* and *support objects*.

Data objects are the database objects that are used to store and manipulate data. Data objects also control how user data (and some system data) is organized. Data objects include

■ Databases

■ Table Spaces

■ Tables

■ User-Defined Data Types (UDTs)

■ User-Defined Functions (UDFs)

■ Check Constraints

■ Indexes

■ Views

■ Packages (access plans)

■ Triggers

■ Aliases

■ Event Monitors

Databases

A *database* is simply a set of all DB2-related objects. When you create a DB2 database, you are establishing an administrative entity that provides an underlying structure for an eventual collection of tables, views, associated indexes, etc.—as well as the table spaces in which these items exist. Figure 1–1 illustrates a simple database object. The database structure also includes items such as system catalogs, transaction recovery logs, and disk storage directories. Data (or user) objects are always accessed from within the underlying structure of a database.

Table Spaces

A *table space* logically groups (or partitions) data objects such as tables, views, and indexes based on their data types. Up to three table spaces can be used per table. Typically, the first table space is used for table data (by default), while a second table space is used as a temporary storage area for *Structured Query Language* (SQL) operations (such as sorting, reorganizing tables, joining tables, and creating indexes). The third table space is typically used for *large object* (LOB) fields. Table spaces are designed to provide a level of indirection between user tables and the database in which they exist. Two basic types of table spaces exist: *database managed spaces* (DMSs) and *system managed spaces* (SMSs). For SMS-managed spaces, each storage space is a directory that is managed by the operating system's file manager system. For DMS-managed spaces, each storage space is either a fixed-size, pre-allocated file or a specific physical device (such as a disk) that is managed by the DB2 Database Manager. As mentioned earlier, table spaces can also allocate storage areas for LOBs and can control the device, file, or directory where both LOBs and table data are to be stored. Table spaces can span

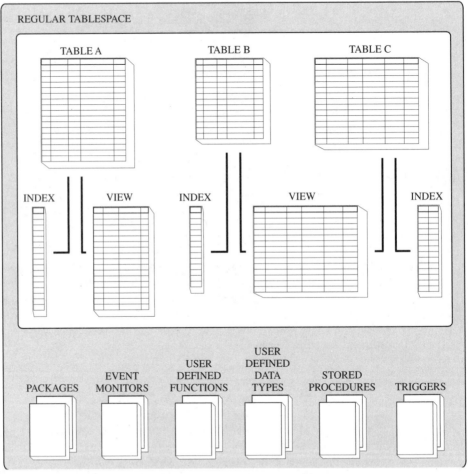

Figure 1–1 Database object and its related data objects

multiple physical disk drives, and their size can be extended at any time (stopping and restarting the database is not necessary). Figure 1–2 illustrates how you can use table spaces to direct a database object to store its table data on one physical disk drive—and store the table's corresponding indexes on another physical disk drive.

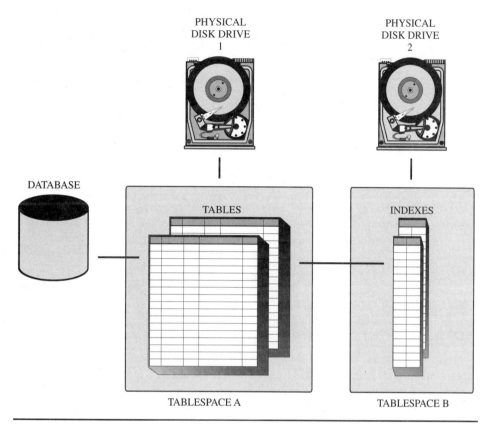

PHYSICAL DISK DRIVE 1

PHYSICAL DISK DRIVE 2

DATABASE

TABLES

INDEXES

TABLESPACE A

TABLESPACE B

Figure 1–2   Using table spaces to separate the physical storage of tables and indexes

NOTE: *You should recognize that the table space concept implemented by DB2 Universal Database is different from the table space concept used by DB2 for OS/390.*

Tables

The *table* is the most fundamental data object of a DB2 database. All user data is stored in and retrieved from one or more tables in a database. Two types of tables can exist in a DB2 database: *base tables* and *result tables*. Tables that are created by the user to store user data are known as *base tables*. Temporary tables that are created (and deleted) by DB2 from one or more base tables to satisfy the result of a query are known as *result tables*. Each table contains an unordered collection of rows, and a fixed number of columns. The definition of the columns in the table makes up the table structure, and the rows contain the actual table data. The storage representation of a row is called a *record*, and the storage representation of a column is called a *field*. At each intersection of a row and column in a database table is a specific data item called a *value*. Figure 1–3 shows the structure of a simple database table.

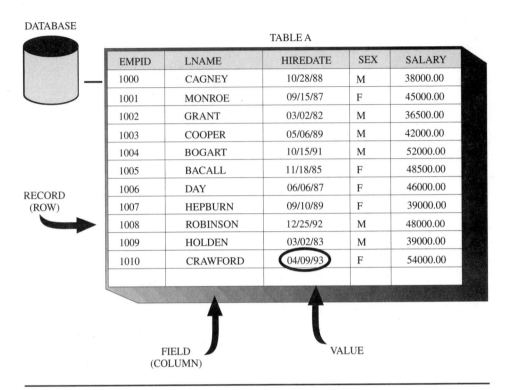

DATABASE

TABLE A

RECORD
(ROW)

EMPID	LNAME	HIREDATE	SEX	SALARY
1000	CAGNEY	10/28/88	M	38000.00
1001	MONROE	09/15/87	F	45000.00
1002	GRANT	03/02/82	M	36500.00
1003	COOPER	05/06/89	M	42000.00
1004	BOGART	10/15/91	M	52000.00
1005	BACALL	11/18/85	F	48500.00
1006	DAY	06/06/87	F	46000.00
1007	HEPBURN	09/10/89	F	39000.00
1008	ROBINSON	12/25/92	M	48000.00
1009	HOLDEN	03/02/83	M	39000.00
1010	CRAWFORD	04/09/93	F	54000.00

FIELD
(COLUMN)

VALUE

Figure 1–3 Simple database table

DATA TYPES   Each column in a table is assigned a specific data type during its creation. This action ensures that only data of the correct type is stored in the table's columns. The following data types are available in DB2:

SMALLINT—A small integer is a binary integer with a precision of 15 bits. The range of a small integer is –32,768 to +32,767.

INTEGER (INT)—An integer is a large binary integer with a precision of 31 bits. The range of an integer is –2,147,483,648 to +2,147,483,647.

BIGINT—A big integer is a large binary integer with a precision of 63 bits.

FLOAT (REAL)—A single-precision, floating-point number is a 32-bit approximation of a real number. The range of a single-precision, floating-point number is $10.0 E^{-38}$ to $10.0 E^{+38}$.

DOUBLE—A double-precision, floating-point number is a 64-bit approximation of a real number. The number can be zero or can range from $-1.79769E^{+308}$ to $-2.225E^{-307}$ and $2.225E^{-307}$ to $1.79769E^{+308}$.

DECIMAL (DEC, NUMERIC, NUM)—A decimal value is a packed decimal number with an implicit decimal point. The position of the decimal point is determined by the precision and scale of the number. The range of a decimal variable or the numbers in a decimal column is $-n$ to $+n$, where the absolute value of n is the largest number that can be represented with the applicable precision and scale.

CHARACTER (CHAR)—A character string is a sequence of bytes. The length of the string is the number of bytes in the sequence and must be between 1 and 254.

VARCHAR—A varying-length character string is a sequence of bytes in varying lengths, up to 4,000 bytes.

LONG VARCHAR—A long, varying-length character string is a sequence of bytes in varying lengths, up to 32,700 bytes.

GRAPHIC—A graphic string is a sequence of bytes that represents double-byte character data. The length of the string is the number of double-byte characters in the sequence and must be between 1 and 127.

VARGRAPHIC—A varying-length graphic string is a sequence of bytes in varying lengths, up to 2,000 double-byte characters.

LONG VARGRAPHIC—A long, varying-length graphic string is a sequence of bytes in varying lengths, up to 16,350 double-byte characters.

BLOB—A binary large object string is a varying-length string, measured in bytes, that can be up to 2GB (2,147,483,647 bytes) long. A BLOB is primarily intended to hold nontraditional data, such as pictures, voice, and mixed media. BLOBs can also hold structured data for user-defined types and functions.

CLOB—A character large object string is a varying-length string measured in bytes that can be up to 2GB long. A CLOB can store large, single-byte character strings or multibyte, character-based data, such as documents written with a single character set.

DBCLOB—A double-byte character large object string is a varying-length string of double-byte characters that can be up to 1,073,741,823 characters long. A DBCLOB can store large, double-byte, character-based data, such as documents written with a single character set. A DBCLOB is considered to be a graphic string.

DATE—A date is a three-part value (year, month, and day) designating a calendar date. The range of the year part is 0001 to 9999, the range of the month part is one to 12, and the range of the day part is one to n (28, 29, 30, or 31), where n depends on the month and whether the year value corresponds to a leap year.

TIME—A time is a three-part value (hour, minutes, and seconds) designating a time of day under a 24-hour clock. The range of the hour part is zero to 24, the range of the minutes part is 0 to 59, and the range of the seconds part is also 0 to 59. If the hour part is set to 24, the minutes and seconds must be 0.

TIMESTAMP—A timestamp is a seven-part value (year, month, day, hour, minutes, seconds, and microseconds) that designates a calendar date and time-of-day under a 24-hour clock. The ranges for each part are the same as defined for the previous two data types, while the range for the fractional specification of microseconds is 0 to 999,999.

DISTINCT TYPE—A distinct type is a user-defined data type that shares its internal representation (source type) with one of the previous data types—but is considered to be a separate, incompatible type for most SQL operations. For example, a user can define an AUDIO data type for referencing external .WAV files that use the BLOB data type for their internal source type. Distinct types do not automatically acquire the functions and operators of their source types, because these items might no longer be meaningful. However, user-defined functions and operators can be created and applied to distinct types to replace this lost functionality.

For more information about DB2 data types, refer to the *IBM DB2 Universal Database SQL Reference, Version 5.2* product manual.

CHECK CONSTRAINTS When you create or alter a table, you can also establish restrictions on data entry for one or more columns in the table. These restrictions, known as *check constraints*, exist to ensure that none of the data entered (or changed) in a table violates predefined conditions. Three types of check constraints exist, as shown in the following list:

Unique Constraint—A rule that prevents duplicate values from being stored in one or more columns within a table

Referential Constraint—A rule that ensures that values stored in one or more columns in a table can be found in a column of another table

Table Check Constraint—A rule that sets restrictions on all data that is added to a specific table

The conditions defined for a check constraint cannot contain any SQL queries, and they cannot refer to columns within another table. Tables can be defined with or without check constraints, and check constraints can define multiple restrictions on the data in a table. Check constraints are defined in the CREATE TABLE and ALTER TABLE SQL statements. If you define a check constraint in the ALTER TABLE SQL statement for a table that already contains data, the existing data will usually be checked against the new condition before the ALTER TABLE statement can be successfully completed. You can, however, place the table in a check-pending state with the SET CONSTRAINTS SQL statement, which enables the ALTER TABLE SQL statement to execute without checking existing data. If you place a table in a check-pending state, you must execute the SET CONSTRAINTS SQL statement again after the table has been altered to check the existing data and return the table to a normal state.

Indexes

An *index* is an ordered set of pointers to the rows of a base table. Each index is based on the values of data in one or more columns (refer to the definition of *key*, later in this section), and more than one index can be defined for a table. An index uses a balanced *binary tree* (a hierarchical data structure in which each element has at most one predecessor but can have many successors) to order the values of key columns in a table. When you index a table by one or more of its columns, DB2 can access data directly and more efficiently because the index is ordered by the columns to be retrieved. Also, because an index is stored separately from its associated table, the index provides a way to define keys outside of the table definition. Once you create an index, the DB2 Database Manager automatically builds the appropriate binary tree structure and maintains that structure. Figure 1–4 shows a simple table and its corresponding index.

DB2 uses indexes to quickly locate specific rows (records) in a table. If you create an index of frequently used columns in a table, you will see improved performance on row access and updates. A unique index (refer to the following paragraph) helps maintain data integrity by ensuring that each row of data in a table is unique. Indexes also provide greater concurrency when more than one transaction accesses the same table. Because row retrieval is faster, locks do not last as long. These benefits, however, are not without a price. Indexes increase actual disk-space requirements and cause a slight decrease in performance whenever an indexed table's data is updated, because all indexes defined for the table must also be updated.

A *key* is a column (or set of columns) in a table or index that is used to identify or access a particular row (or rows) of data. A key that is composed of more than one column is called a *composite key*. A column can be part of several composite keys. A key that is defined in such a way that the key identifies a single row of data within a table is called a *unique key*. A unique key that is part of the definition of a table is called a *primary key*. A table can have only one primary key, and the columns of a primary key cannot contain null (missing) values. A key that references (or points to) a primary key in another table is called a *foreign key*. A foreign key establishes a referential link to a primary key, and the columns defined in each key must match. In Figure 1–4, the EMPID column is the primary key for Table A.

TABLE A

EMPID	LNAME	HIREDATE
1004	CAGNEY	10/28/88
1001	MONROE	09/15/87
1007	GRANT	03/02/82
1010	COOPER	05/06/89
1002	BOGART	10/15/91
1005	BACALL	11/18/85
1003	DAY	06/06/87
1000	HEPBURN	09/10/89
1008	ROBINSON	12/25/92
1006	HOLDEN	03/02/83
1009	CRAWFORD	03/02/83

ROW 1, ROW 2, ROW 3, ROW 4, ROW 5, ROW 6, ROW 7, ROW 8, ROW 9, ROW 10, ROW 11

INDEX A

KEY	ROW
1000	8
1001	2
1002	5
1003	7
1004	1
1005	6
1006	10
1007	3
1008	9
1009	11
1010	4

Figure 1–4 *Simple database table and its corresponding index, where the EMPID column is the primary key*

Views

A *view* is an alternative way of representing data that exists in one or more tables. Essentially, a view is a named specification of a result table. The specification is a pre-defined data selection that occurs whenever the view is referenced in an SQL statement. For this reason, you can picture a view as having columns and rows, just like a base table. In fact, a view can be used just like a base table in most cases. Although a view looks like a base table, a view does not exist as a table in physical storage—so a view does not contain data. Instead, a view refers to data stored in other base tables. (Although a view might refer to another view, the reference is ultimately to data stored in one or more base tables.) Figure 1–5 illustrates the relationship between two base tables and a view.

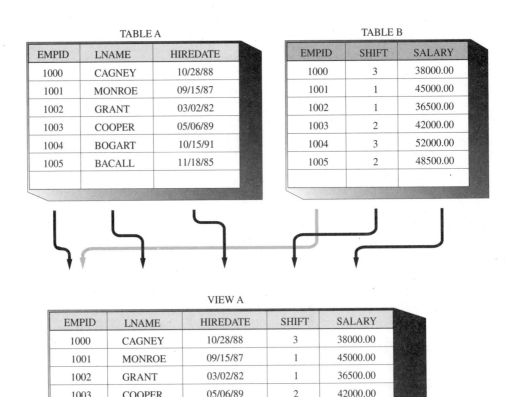

TABLE A

EMPID	LNAME	HIREDATE
1000	CAGNEY	10/28/88
1001	MONROE	09/15/87
1002	GRANT	03/02/82
1003	COOPER	05/06/89
1004	BOGART	10/15/91
1005	BACALL	11/18/85

TABLE B

EMPID	SHIFT	SALARY
1000	3	38000.00
1001	1	45000.00
1002	1	36500.00
1003	2	42000.00
1004	3	52000.00
1005	2	48500.00

VIEW A

EMPID	LNAME	HIREDATE	SHIFT	SALARY
1000	CAGNEY	10/28/88	3	38000.00
1001	MONROE	09/15/87	1	45000.00
1002	GRANT	03/02/82	1	36500.00
1003	COOPER	05/06/89	2	42000.00
1004	BOGART	10/15/91	3	52000.00
1005	BACALL	11/18/85	2	48500.00

Figure 1–5 In this figure, a view is created from two separate tables. Because the EMPID column is common in both tables, the EMPID column joins the tables to create a single view.

A view can include any number of columns from one or more base tables. A view can also include any number of columns from other views, so a view can be a combination of columns from both views and tables. When the column of a view comes from a column of a base table, that column inherits any constraints that apply to the column of the base table. For example, if a view includes a column that is a unique key for its base table, operations performed against that view are subject to the same constraint as operations performed against the underlying base table.

Packages (Access Plans)

A *package* (or *access plan*) is an object that contains control structures (known as *sections*) that are used to execute SQL statements. If an application program intends to access a database using static SQL, the application developer must embed the appropriate SQL statements in the program source code. When the program source code is converted to an executable object (static SQL) or executed (dynamic SQL), the strategy for executing each embedded SQL statement is stored in a package as a single section. Each section is the bound (or operational) form of the embedded SQL statement, and this form contains information such as which index to use and how to use the index.

When developing DB2 UDB database applications, you should hide package creation from users whenever possible. Packages and binding are discussed in more detail in Chapter 3, "Getting Started with DB2 Application Development."

Triggers

A *trigger* is a set of actions that are automatically executed (or triggered) when an **INSERT**, **UPDATE**, or **DELETE** SQL statement is executed against a specified table. Whenever the appropriate SQL statement is executed, the trigger is activated—and a set of predefined actions begin execution. You can use triggers along with foreign keys (referential constraints) and check constraints to enforce data integrity rules. You can also use triggers to apply updates to other tables in the database, to automatically generate and/or transform values for inserted or updated rows, and to invoke user-defined functions.

When creating a trigger, in order to determine when the trigger should be activated, you must first define and then later use the following criteria:

Subject table—The table for which the trigger is defined

Trigger event—A specific SQL operation that updates the subject table (could be an **INSERT**, **UPDATE**, or **DELETE** operation)

Activation time—Indicates whether the trigger should be activated before or after the trigger event is performed on the subject table

Set of affected rows—The rows of the subject table on which the **INSERT**, **UPDATE**, or **DELETE** SQL operation is performed

Trigger granularity—Defines whether the actions of the trigger will be performed once for the whole SQL operation or once for each of the rows in the set of affected rows

Triggered action—Triggered action is an optional search condition and a set of SQL statements that are to be executed whenever the trigger is activated. The triggered action is executed only if the search condition evaluates to TRUE.

At times, triggered actions might need to refer to the original values in the set of affected rows. This reference can be made with transition variables and/or transition tables. Transition variables are temporary storage variables that use the names of the columns in the subject table and are qualified by a specified name that identifies whether the reference is to the old value (prior to the SQL operation) or the new value (after the SQL operation). Transition tables also use the names of the columns of the subject table, but they have a specified name that enables the complete set of affected rows to be treated as a single table. As with transition variables, transition tables can be defined for both the old values and the new values.

Multiple triggers can be specified for a single table. The order in which the triggers are activated is based on the order in which they were created, so the most recently created trigger will be the last trigger to be activated. Activating a trigger that executes SQL statements may cause other triggers to be activated (or even the same trigger to be reactivated). This event is referred to as *trigger cascading*. When trigger cascading occurs, referential integrity delete rules can also be activated, thus a single operation can significantly change a database. Therefore, whenever you create a trigger, make sure to thoroughly examine the effects that the trigger's operation will have on all other triggers and referential constraints defined for the database.

Aliases

An *alias* is an alternate name for a table or view. Aliases can be referenced in the same way the original table or view is referenced. An alias can also be an alternate name for another alias. This process of aliases referring to each other is known as *alias chaining*. Because aliases are publicly referenced names, no special authority or privilege is needed to use them—unlike tables and views.

Event Monitors

An *event monitor* observes each event that happens to another specified object and records all selected events to either a named pipe or to an external file. Essentially, event monitors are "tracking" devices that inform other applications (either via named pipes or files) whenever specified event conditions occur. Event monitors allow you to observe the events that take place in a database whenever database applications are executing against it. Once defined, event monitors can automatically be started each time a database is opened.

Schemas

All data objects are organized (by the database administrator) into *schemas*, which provide a logical classification of the objects in the database. Object names consist of two parts. The first (leftmost) part is called the *qualifier*, or *schema*, and the second (rightmost) part is called the *simple* (or *unqualified*) *name*. Syntactically, these two parts are concatenated as a single string of characters separated by a period. When an object such as a table space, table, index, view, alias, user-defined data type, user-defined function, package, event monitor, or trigger is created, that object is assigned to an appropriate schema based on its name. Figure 1–6 illustrates how a table is assigned to a particular schema during the table creation process.

NOTE: *If no schema is specified when an object is created, the DB2 Database Manager uses the creator's user ID as the default schema.*

This section completes the discussion of data objects. Now let's examine DB2 support objects. Support objects are database objects that contain descriptions of all objects in the database, provide transaction and failure support, and control system resource usage. Support objects include the following items:

- System catalog tables/views
- Log files and the Recovery History file
- DB2 Database Manager configuration files
- Database configuration files

System Catalog Views

DB2 creates and maintains a set of views and base tables for each database created. These views and base tables are collectively known as the *system catalog*. The system

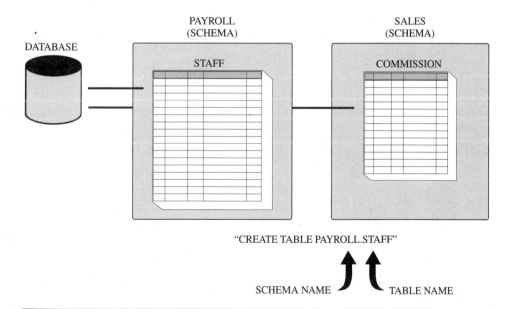

Figure 1–6   *Implementing schemas with the CREATE SQL statement*

catalog consists of tables that contain accurate descriptions of all objects in the database at all times. DB2 automatically updates the system catalog tables in response to SQL data definition statements, environment routines, and certain utility routines. The catalog views are similar to any other database views, with the exception that they cannot be explicitly created, updated (with the exception of some specific updateable views), or dropped. You can retrieve data in the catalog views in the same way that you retrieve data from any other view in the database. For a complete listing of the DB2 catalog views, refer to the *IBM DB2 Universal Database SQL Reference, Version 5.2* product manual.

Recovery Log Files and the Recovery History File

Database *recovery log files* keep a running record of all changes made to tables in a database, and these files serve two important purposes. First, they provide necessary support for transaction processing. Because an independent record of all database changes is written to the recovery log files, the sequence of changes making up a transaction can be removed from the database if the transaction is rolled back. Second, recovery log files ensure that a system power outage or application error will not leave the database in an inconsistent state. In the event of a failure, the changes that have been made, but that have not been made permanent (committed) are rolled back. Furthermore, all committed transactions, which might not have been physically written to disk, are redone. Database recovery logging is always active and cannot be deactivated. These actions ensure that the integrity of the database is always maintained.

You can also keep additional recovery log files to provide forward recovery in the event of disk (media) failure. The roll-forward database recovery utility uses these additional database recovery logs, called *archived logs*, to enable a database to be rebuilt to a specific point in time. In addition to using the information in the active database recovery log to rebuild a database, archived logs are used to reapply previous changes. For roll-forward database recovery to work correctly, you are required to have both a previous backup version of the database and a recovery log containing changes made to the database since that backup was made. The following list describes the types of database recovery logs that can exist:

Active log files—Active log files contain information for transactions whose changes have not yet been written to the database files. Active log files contain information necessary to roll back any active transaction not committed during normal processing. Active log files also contain transactions that are committed but are not yet physically written from memory (buffer pool) to disk (database files).

Online archived log files—An activity parallel to logging exists that automatically dumps the active transaction log file to an archive log file whenever transaction activity ceases, when the active log file is closed, or when the active log file gets full. An archived log is said to be "online" when the archived log is stored in the database log path directory.

Offline archived log files—Archived log files can be stored in locations other than the database log path directory. An archived log file is said to be "offline" when it is not stored in the database log path directory.

If you delete an active log file, the database becomes unusable and must be restored before the database can be used again. If you delete an archived log file (either online or offline) roll-forward recovery will only be possible up to the point in time covered by the log file that was written to before the deleted log file was created.

The *recovery history file* contains a summary of the backup information that is used to recover part or all of the database to a specific point in time. A recovery history file is automatically created when a database is created, and the file is automatically updated whenever the database is backed up, restored, or populated with the LOAD operation.

Configuration Files

Similar to all computer software applications, DB2 UDB uses system resources both when it is installed and when it is running. In most cases, run time resource management (RAM and shared control blocks, for example) are managed by the *operating system* (OS). If, however, an application is greedy for system resources, problems can occur for both the application and for other concurrently running applications.

DB2 provides two sets of configuration parameters that can be used to control its consumption of system resources. One set of parameters that is used for the DB2 Database Manager itself exists in a DB2 Database Manager configuration file. This file contains values that are to be used to control resource usage when creating databases (database code page, collating sequence, and DB2 release level, for example). This file also controls system resources that are used by all database applications (as total shared RAM, for example).

A second set of parameters exists for each DB2 database created and is stored in a database configuration file. This file contains parameter values that are used to indicate the current state of the database (backup pending flag, database consistency flag, or roll-forward pending flag, for example) and parameter values that define the amount of system resources the database can use (buffer pool size, database logging, or sort memory size, for example). A database configuration file exists for each database, so a change to one database configuration does not have a corresponding effect on other databases. By fine-tuning these two configuration files, you can tailor DB2 for optimum performance in any number of OS environments. For more information about DB2 configuration file parameters, refer to the *IBM DB2 Universal Database Administration Guide, Version 5.2* product manual.

DB2 Database Directories

DB2 UDB uses a set of directories for establishing an environment, storing data objects, and enabling data access to both local and other remote workstations (nodes) and databases. The set of directories used by DB2 contain the following items:

- One or more physical database directories
- One or more volume directories

■ A system directory
■ A workstation (node) directory
■ A database connection services directory

These directories define the overall DB2 Database Manager operating environment. Figure 1–7 illustrates DB2's directory structure.

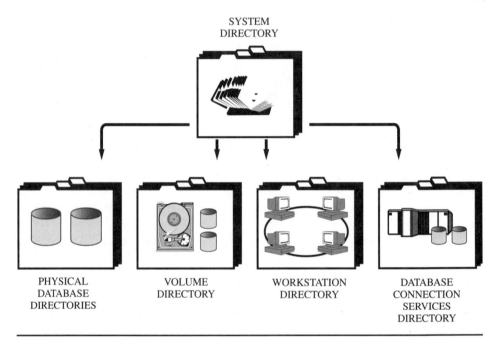

Figure 1–7 *DB2's directory structure*

Physical Database Directory

Each time a database is created, the DB2 Database Manager creates a separate subdirectory in which to store control files (such as log header files) and to allocate containers in which default table spaces are stored. Objects associated with the database are usually stored in the database subdirectory, but they can be stored in other various locations —including system devices. All database subdirectories are created within the instance defined in the **DB2INSTANCE** environment variable or within the instance to which the user application has been explicitly attached. The naming scheme used for a DB2 instance or UNIX Platforms is ***install_ path/*$DB2INSTANCE/NODE*nnnn*. The naming scheme used on Intel platforms is ***drive_letter:*\$DB2INSTANCE\NODE*nnnn*. In both cases, **NODE*nnnn*** is the node identifier in a partitioned database environment where **NODE0000** is the first node, **NODE0001** is the second node, and so on. The naming scheme for database subdirectories created within an instance is **SQL00001** through **SQL*nnnnn***, where the number for *nnnnn* increases each time a new database is created. For example, directory **SQL00001** contains all objects associated with the first database created, **SQL00002** contains all objects for the second database created, and so on. DB2 automatically creates and maintains these subdirectories.

Volume Directory

In addition to physical database directories, a volume directory exists on every logical disk drive available (on a single workstation) that contains one or more DB2 databases. This directory contains one entry for each database that is physically stored on that particular logical disk drive. The volume directory is automatically created when the first database is created on the logical disk drive, and DB2 updates its contents each time a database creation or deletion event occurs. Each entry in the volume directory contains the following information:

- The database name, as provided with the **CREATE DATABASE** command
- The database alias name (which is the same as the database name)
- The database comment, as provided with the **CREATE DATABASE** command
- The name of the root directory in which the database exists
- The product name and release number associated with the database
- Other system information, including the code page the database was created under and entry type (which is always **HOME**)
- The actual number of volume database directories that exist on the workstation, which is the number of logical disk drives on that workstation that contain one or more DB2 databases

System Directory

The system database directory is the master directory for a DB2 workstation. This directory contains one entry for each local and remote cataloged database that can be accessed by the DB2 Database Manager from a particular workstation. Databases are implicitly cataloged when the **CREATE DATABASE** command or API function is issued and can also be explicitly cataloged with the **CATALOG DATABASE** command or API function. The system directory exists on the logical disk drive where the DB2 product software is installed. Each entry in the system directory contains the following information:

- The database name provided with the **CREATE DATABASE** or **CATALOG DATABASE** command or API function
- The database alias name (which is usually the same as the database name)
- The database comment, as provided with the **CREATE DATABASE** or **CATALOG DATABASE** command or API function
- The logical disk drive on which the database exists, if it is local
- The node name on which the database exists, if it is remote
- Other system information, including where validation of authentication names (user IDs) and passwords will be performed

Workstation Directory

The workstation or node directory contains one entry for each remote database server workstation that can be accessed. The workstation directory also exists on the logical disk drive where the DB2 product software is installed. Entries in the workstation directory are used in conjunction with entries in the system directory to make connections to remote DB2 UDB database servers. Entries in the workstation directory are also used in conjunction with entries in the database connection services directory to make connections to hosts (OS/390, AS/400, etc.) database servers. Each entry in the workstation directory contains the following information:

- The node name of the remote server workstation where a DB2 database exists
- The node name comment
- The protocol that will be used to communicate with the remote server workstation
- The type of security checking that will be performed by the remote server workstation
- The hostname or address of the remote server
- The service name or port number for the remote server

Database Connection Services Directory

A database connection services directory only exists if the DB2 Connect product has been installed on the workstation. This directory exists on the logical disk drive where the DB2 Connect product software is installed. The database connection services directory contains one entry for each host (OS/390, AS/400, etc.) database that DB2 can access via the *distributed relational database architecture* (DRDA) services. Each entry in the connection services directory contains the following information:

- The local database name
- The target database name
- The database comment
- The application requester library file that executes the DRDA protocol to communicate with the host database
- The user-defined name or nickname for the remote server database
- The database system used on the remote server workstation
- Other system information, including a defaults override parameter string that defines SQLCODE mapping requirements, date and time formatting to use, etc.

NOTE: *To avoid potential problems, do not create directories that use the same naming scheme as the physical database directories, and do not manipulate the volume, system, node, and database connection services directories that have been created by DB2.*

SUMMARY

The goal of this chapter is to provide you with an overview of the underlying architecture of a DB2 *Universal Database* (UDB), Version 5.2 database. You should now understand the relational database model and be familiar with the following data objects and support objects:

- Data objects
    - Databases
    - Table spaces
    - Tables
    - User-Defined Data Types (UDTs)
    - User-Defined Functions (UDFs)
- Check constraints
    - Indexes
    - Views
    - Packages (access plans)
    - Triggers
    - Aliases
    - Event monitors
- Support objects
    - System catalog views
    - Recovery log files and the Recovery History file
    - DB2 Database Manager configuration file
    - Database configuration files

Finally, you should be aware of how DB2 UDB creates and uses the following directories and subdirectories on your storage media:

- Physical database directories
- Volume directories
- System directory
- Workstation directory
- Database Connection Services directory

You should be comfortable with these basic DB2 database concepts before you begin your database application design work (and especially before you actually begin writing the source code for your application). The next chapter continues to present these concepts by discussing the database consistency mechanisms available in DB2 Universal Database, Version 5.2.

2

Database Consistency Mechanisms

Once you understand the underlying architecture of DB2 Universal Database, you should become familiar with the mechanisms DB2 uses to provide and maintain data consistency. This chapter is designed to introduce you to the concepts of data consistency and to the three mechanisms DB2 uses to enforce consistency: *transactions*, *locking*, and *transaction logging*. The first part of this chapter defines database consistency and examines some of the requirements a database management system must meet to provide and maintain consistency. This part is followed by a close look at the heart of all data manipulation: the transaction. Next, DB2's locking mechanism is described and how that mechanism is used by multiple transactions working concurrently to maintain data integrity is discussed. Finally, this chapter concludes with a discussion of transaction logging and the data recovery process used by DB2 to restore data consistancy if application or system failure occurs.

What Is Data Consistency?

The best way to define data consistency is by example. Suppose your company owns a chain of restaurants, and you have a database designed to keep track of supplies stored in each of those restaurants. To facilitate the supplies purchasing process, your database contains an inventory table for each restaurant in the chain. Whenever supplies are received or used by a restaurant, the inventory table for that restaurant is updated. Now, suppose some bottles of ketchup are physically moved from one restaurant to another. The ketchup bottle count value in the donating restaurant's inventory table needs to be lowered, and the ketchup bottle count value in the receiving restaurant's inventory table needs to be raised to accurately represent this inventory move. If a user lowers the ketchup bottle count from the donating restaurant's inventory table but fails to raise the ketchup bottle count in the receiving restaurant's inventory table, the data has become inconsistent. Now, the total ketchup bottle count for the entire chain of restaurants is incorrect.

Data can become inconsistent if a user fails to make all necessary changes (as in the previous example), if the system crashes while the user is in the middle of making changes, or if an application accessing data stops prematurely for some reason. Inconsistency can also occur when several users are accessing the same data at the same time. For example, one user might read another user's changes before the data has been properly updated and take some inappropriate action—or make an incorrect change based on the premature data values read.

To properly maintain data consistency, solutions must be provided for the following questions:

- How can you maintain generic consistency of data if you do not know what each individual data owner or user wants?
- How can you keep a single application from accidentally destroying data consistency?
- How can you ensure that multiple applications accessing the same data at the same time will not destroy data consistency?
- If the system fails while a database is in use, how can the database be returned to a consistent state?

DB2 provides solutions to these questions with its transaction support, locking, and logging mechanisms.

Transactions

A *transaction*, or a *unit of work*, is a recoverable sequence of one or more SQL operations grouped together as a single unit within an application process. The initiation and termination of a transaction define the points of data consistency within an application process. Either all SQL operations within a transaction are applied to the data source, or the effects of all SQL operations within a transaction are completely "undone."

Transactions and commitment control are relational database concepts that have been around for quite some time. They provide the capability to commit or recover from pending changes made to a database in order to enforce data consistency and integrity. With embedded SQL applications, transactions are automatically initiated when the application process is started. With *Open Database Connectivity* (ODBC) and *Call-Level Interface* (CLI), transactions are implicitly started whenever the application begins working with a data source.

Regardless of how transactions are initiated, they are terminated when they are either committed or rolled back. When a transaction is committed, all changes made to the data source since the transaction was initiated are made permanent. When a transaction is rolled back, all changes made to the data source since the transaction was initiated are removed, and the data in the data source is returned to its previous state (before the transaction began). In either case, the data source is guaranteed to be in a consistent state at the completion of each transaction.

A commit or roll back operation only affects the data changes made within the transaction they end. As long as data changes remain uncommitted, other application processes are usually unable to see them, and they can be removed with the roll back operation. However, once data changes are committed, they become accessible to other application processes and can no longer be removed by a roll back operation.

A database application program can do all of its work in a single transaction or spread its work over several sequential transactions. Data used within a transaction is protected from being changed or seen by other transactions through various isolation levels.

Transactions provide generic database consistency by ensuring that changes become permanent only when you issue a COMMIT SQL statement or via API calls defined within a Transaction Manager. Your responsibility, however, is to ensure that the sequence of SQL operations in each transaction results in a consistent database. DB2 then ensures that each transaction is either completed (committed) or removed (rolled back) as a single unit of work. If a failure occurs before the transaction is complete, DB2 will back out all uncommitted changes to restore the database consistency that DB2 assumes existed when the transaction was initiated. Figure 2–1 shows the effects of both a successful transaction and a transaction that failed.

Concurrency and Transaction Isolation Levels

So far, we have only looked at transactions from a single-user data source point-of-view. With single-user data sources, each transaction occurs serially and does not have to contend with interference from other transactions. With multi-user data sources, however, transactions can occur simultaneously, and each transaction has the potential to interfere with another transaction. Transactions that have the potential of interfering with one another are said to be *interleaved*, or parallel, transactions. Transactions that run isolated from each other are said to be *serializable*, which means that the results of running them

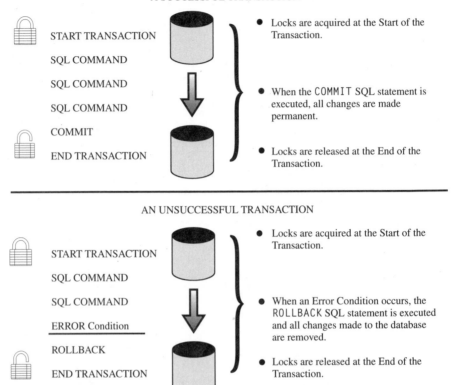

Figure 2–1   Events that take place during the execution of a successful and an unsuccessful transaction

simultaneously are the same as the results of running them one right after another (serially). Ideally, all transactions should be serializable.

So why should transactions be serializable? Consider the following problem. Suppose a salesman is entering orders on a database system at the same time a clerk is sending out bills. Now, suppose the salesman enters an order from Company X but does not commit the order (the salesman is still talking to the representative from Company X). While the salesman is on the phone, the clerk queries the database for a list of all outstanding orders, sees the order for Company X, and sends Company X a bill. Now, suppose the representative from Company X decides to cancel the order. The salesman rolls back the transaction, because the representative changed his mind and the order information was never committed. A week later, Company X receives a bill for a part it never ordered. If the salesman's transaction and the clerk's transaction had been isolated from each other (serialized), this problem would never have occurred. Either the salesman's transaction would have finished before the clerk's transaction started, or the clerk's transaction would have finished before the salesman's transaction started. In either case, Company X would not have received a bill.

When transactions are not isolated from each other in multi-user environments, the following three types of events (or phenomena) can occur as a result:

- **Dirty reads**—This event occurs when a transaction reads data that has not yet been committed. For example: Transaction 1 changes a row of data, and Transaction 2 reads the changed row before Transaction 1 commits the change. If Transaction 1 rolls back the change, then Transaction 2 will have read data that is considered never to have existed.

- **Nonrepeatable reads**—This event occurs when a transaction reads the same row of data twice but receives different data values each time. For example: Transaction 1 reads a row of data, and Transaction 2 changes or deletes that row and commits the change. If Transaction 1 attempts to reread the row, Transaction 1 retrieves different data values (if the row was updated) or discovers that the row no longer exists (if the row was deleted).

- **Phantoms**—This event occurs when a row of data matches a search criteria but initially is not seen. For example: Transaction 1 reads a set of rows that satisfy some search criteria, and Transaction 2 inserts a new row matching Transaction 1's search criteria. If Transaction 1 re-executes the query statement that produced the original set of rows, a different set of rows will be retrieved.

Maintaining database consistency and data integrity while enabling more than one application to access the same data at the same time is known as *concurrency*. DB2 enforces concurrency by using four different transaction isolation levels. An isolation level determines how data is locked or isolated from other processes while the data is being accessed. DB2 supports the following isolation levels:

- Repeatable read
- Read stability
- Cursor stability
- Uncommitted read

Repeatable Read

The *repeatable read* isolation level locks all the rows an application retrieves within a single transaction. If you use the repeatable read isolation level, **SELECT** SQL statements issued multiple times within the same transaction will yield the same result. A transaction running under the repeatable read isolation level can retrieve and operate on the same rows as many times as needed until the transaction completes. However, no other transactions can update, delete, or insert a row (which would affect the result table being accessed) until the isolating transaction terminates. Transactions running under the repeatable read isolation level cannot see uncommitted changes of other transactions. The repeatable read isolation level does not allow phantom rows to be seen.

Read Stability

The *read stability* isolation level locks only those rows that an application retrieves within a transaction. This feature ensures that any row read by a transaction is not changed by other transactions until the transaction holding the lock is terminated. Unfortunately, if a transaction using the read stability isolation level issues the same query more than once, the transaction can retrieve new rows that were entered by other transactions that now meet the search criteria. This event occurs because the read stability isolation level ensures that all data retrieved remains unchanged until the time that the transaction sees the data, even when temporary tables or row blocking is used. Thus, the read stability isolation level allows phantom rows to be seen and non-repeatable reads to occur.

Cursor Stability

The *cursor stability* isolation level locks any row being accessed by a transaction, as long as the cursor is positioned on that row. This lock remains in effect until the next row is retrieved (fetched)—or until the transaction is terminated. If a transaction running under the cursor stability isolation level has retrieved a row from a table, no other transactions can update or delete that row as long as the cursor is positioned on that row. Additionally, if a transaction running under the cursor stability isolation level changes the row it retrieved, no other application can update or delete that row until the isolating transaction is terminated. When a transaction has locked a row with the cursor stability isolation level, other transactions can insert, delete, or change rows on either side of the locked row—as long as the locked row is not accessed via an index. Therefore, the same **SELECT** SQL statement issued twice within a single transaction might not always yield the same results. Transactions running under the cursor stability isolation level cannot see uncommitted changes made by other transactions. With the cursor stability isolation level, both nonrepeatable reads and phantom reads are possible.

Uncommitted Read

The *uncommitted read* isolation level allows a transaction to access uncommitted changes made by other transactions (in either the same or in different applications). A transaction running under the uncommitted read isolation level does not lock other applications out of the row it is reading—unless another transaction attempts to drop or alter the table. If a transaction running under the uncommitted read isolation level accesses a read-only cursor, the transaction can access most uncommitted changes made by other transactions. The transaction cannot access tables, views, and indexes that are being created or dropped by other transactions, however, until those transactions are complete. All other changes made by other transactions can be read before they are committed or rolled back. If a transaction running under the uncommitted read isolation level accesses an updateable cursor, the transaction will behave as if the cursor stability isolation level were in effect. With the uncommitted read isolation level, both nonrepeatable reads and phantom reads are possible.

Table 2–1 shows the four transaction isolation levels that are supported by DB2 Universal Database, as well as the types of phenomena that can occur when each one is used.

Table 2–1 Transaction isolation levels supported by DB2 and the phenomena that can occur when each is used

DB2 Transaction Isolation Level	Dirty Reads	Nonrepeatable Reads	Phantoms
Uncommitted Read	Yes	Yes	Yes
Cursor Stability	No	Yes	Yes
Read Stability	No	No	Yes
Repeatable Read	No	No	No

Specifying the Isolation Level

You specify the isolation level for an embedded SQL application either at precompile time or when binding the application to a database. In most cases, you set the isolation level for embedded SQL applications with the ISOLATION option of the command line processor PREP or BIND commands. In other cases, you can set an embedded SQL application's isolation level by using the PREP or BIND API functions. The isolation level for a CLI application is set by CLI statement handle attributes. The default isolation level used for all applications is the cursor stability isolation level.

Locking

Along with isolation levels, DB2 uses locks to provide concurrency control and to control data access. A *lock* is a mechanism that associates a data resource with a single transaction, with the purpose of controlling how other transactions interact with that resource while the resource is associated with the transaction that acquired the lock. The transaction with which the resource is associated is said to "hold" or "own" the lock. When a data resource in the database is accessed by a transaction, that resource is locked according to the previously specified isolation level. This lock prevents other transactions from accessing the resource in a way that would interfere with the owning transaction. Once the owning transaction is terminated (either committed or rolled back), changes made to the resource are either made permanent or are removed, and the data resource is unlocked so it can be used by other transactions. Figure 2–2 illustrates the principles of data resource locking.

If one transaction tries to access a data resource in a way that is incompatible with a lock held by another transaction, that transaction must wait until the owning transaction has ended. This situation is known as a *lock wait*. When this event occurs, the transaction attempting to access the resource simply stops execution until the owning transaction has terminated and the incompatible lock is released. Locks are automatically provided by DB2 for each transaction, so applications do not need to explicitly request data resource locks.

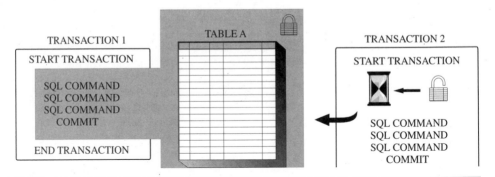

Figure 2–2 *DB2 prevents uncontrolled concurrent table access by using locks. In this example, Transaction 1 has locked table A, and Transaction 2 must wait until the lock is released before it can execute.*

Lock Attributes

All locks used by DB2 have the following basic attributes:

Object—The object attribute identifies the data resource being locked. Tables are the only data resource objects that can be explicitly locked by an application. DB2 can set locks on other types of resources, such as rows, tables, etc., but these locks are used for internal purposes only.

Size—The size attribute specifies the physical size of the portion of the data resource that is being locked. A lock does not always have to control an entire data resource. For example, rather than giving an application exclusive control over an entire table, DB2 can only give the lock exclusive control over the row that needs to be changed.

Duration—The duration attribute specifies the length of time a lock is held. The isolation levels described earlier control the duration of a lock.

Mode—The mode attribute specifies the type of access permitted for the lock owner, as well as the type of access permitted for concurrent users of the locked data resource. Mode is sometimes referred to as the "state" of the lock.

Lock States

As a transaction performs its operations, DB2 automatically acquires locks on the data resources it references. These locks are placed on a table, a row (or multiple rows), or both a table and a row (or rows). The only object a transaction can explicitly acquire a lock for is a table, and a transaction can only change the state of row locks by issuing a **COMMIT** or a **ROLLBACK** SQL statement. The locks that are placed on a data resource by a transaction can have one of the following states:

Next Key Share (NS)—If a lock is set in the Next Key Share state, the lock owner and all concurrent transactions can read—but cannot change—data in the locked row. Only individual rows can be locked in the Next Key Share state. This lock is acquired in place of a Share lock on data that is read using the read stability or cursor stability transaction isolation level.

Share (S)—If a lock is set in the Share state, the lock owner and any other concurrent transactions can read—but cannot change—data in the locked table or row. As long as a table is not Share locked, individual rows in that table can be Share locked. If, however, a table is Share locked, no row Share locks can be set in that table by the lock owner. If either a table or a row is Share locked, other concurrent transactions can read the data, but they cannot change the data.

Update (U)—If a lock is set in the Update state, the lock owner can update data in the locked data table. Furthermore, the Update operation automatically acquires Exclusive locks on the rows it updates. Other concurrent transactions can read—but not update—data in the locked table.

Next Key Exclusive (NX)—If a lock is set in the Next Key Exclusive state, the lock owner can read—but not change—the locked row. Only individual rows can be locked in the Next Key Exclusive state. This lock is acquired on the next row in a table when a row is deleted from or inserted into the index for a table.

Next Key Weak Exclusive (NW)—If a lock is set in the Next Key Weak Exclusive state, the lock owner can read—but not change—the locked row. Only individual rows can be locked in the Next Key Weak Exclusive state. This lock is acquired on the next row in a table when a row is inserted into the index of a non-catalog table.

Exclusive (X)—If a table or row lock is set in the Exclusive state, the lock owner can both read and change data in the locked table, but only transactions using the uncommitted read isolation level can access the locked table or row(s). Exclusive locks are best used with data resources that are to be manipulated with the **INSERT**, **UPDATE**, and/or **DELETE** SQL statements.

Weak Exclusive (W)—If a lock is set in the Weak Exclusive state, the lock owner can read and change the locked row. Only individual rows can be locked in the Weak Exclusive state. This lock is acquired on a row when the row is inserted into a non-catalog table.

Super Exclusive (Z)—If a lock is set in the Super Exclusive state, the lock owner can alter a table, drop a table, create an index, or drop an index. This lock is automatically acquired on a table whenever a transaction performs any one of these operations. No other concurrent transactions can read or update the table until this lock is removed.

In addition to these eight primary locks, there are four more special locks that are only used on tables. They are called intention locks and are used to signify that rows within the table may eventually become locked. These locks are always placed on the table before any rows within the table are locked. Intention locks can have one of the following states:

Intent None (IN)—If an intention lock is set in the Intent None state, the lock owner can read data in the locked data table, including uncommitted data, but cannot change this data. In this mode, no row locks are acquired by the lock owner, so other concurrent transactions can read and change data in the table.

Intent Share (IS)—If an intention lock is set in the Intent Share state, the lock owner can read data in the locked data table but cannot change the data. Again, because the lock owner does not acquire row locks, other concurrent transactions can both read and change data in the table. When a transaction owns an Intent Share lock on a table, the transaction acquires a Share lock on each row it reads. This intention lock is acquired when a transaction does not convey the intent to update any rows in the table.

Intent Exclusive (IX)—If an intention lock is set in the Intent Exclusive state, the lock owner and any other concurrent transactions can read and change data in the locked table. When the lock owner reads data from the data table, the lock owner acquires a Share lock on each row it reads and an Update and Exclusive lock on each row it updates. Other concurrent transactions can both read and update the locked table. This intent lock is acquired when a transaction conveys the intent to update rows in the table. The **SELECT FOR UPDATE**, **UPDATE WHERE**, and **INSERT** SQL statements convey the intent to update.

Share with Intent Exclusive (SIX)—If an intention lock is set in the Share with Intent Exclusive state, the lock owner can both read and change data in the locked table. The lock owner acquires Exclusive locks on the rows it updates but not on the rows it reads, so other concurrent transactions can read but not update data in the locked table.

As a transaction performs its operations, DB2 automatically acquires appropriate locks as data objects are referenced. Figure 2–3 illustrates the logic DB2 uses to determine the type of lock to acquire on a referenced data object.

Locks and Application Performance

When developing DB2 applications, you must be aware of several factors concerning the uses of locks and the effect they have on the performance of an application. The following factors can affect application performance:

- Concurrency versus lock size
- Deadlocks
- Lock compatibility
- Lock conversion
- Lock escalation

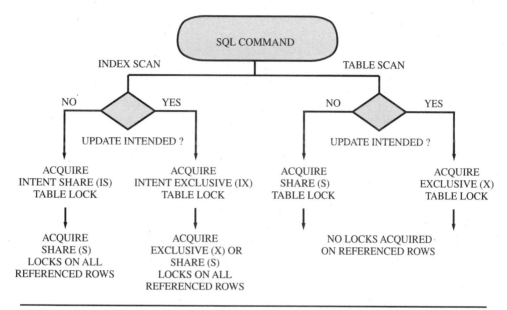

Figure 2–3   *Logic used by DB2 to determine which type of lock(s) to acquire*

CONCURRENCY VERSUS LOCK SIZE   As long as multiple transactions access tables for the purpose of reading data, concurrency should be only a minor concern. What becomes more of an issue is the situation in which at least one transaction writes to a table. Unless an appropriate index is defined on a table, there is almost no concurrent write access to that table. Concurrent updates are only possible with Intent Share or Intent Exclusive locks. If no index exists for the locked table, the entire table must be scanned for the appropriate data row (table scan). In this case, the transaction must hold either a Share or an Exclusive lock on the table. Simply creating indexes on all tables does not guarantee concurrency. DB2's optimizer decides for you whether indexes are used in processing your SQL statements, so even if you have defined indexes, the optimizer might choose to perform a table scan for any of several reasons:

■ No index is defined for your search criteria (**WHERE** clause). The index key must match the columns used in the **WHERE** clause in order for the optimizer to use the index to help locate the desired rows. If you choose to optimize for high concurrency, make sure your table design includes a primary key for each table that will be updated. These primary keys should then be used whenever these tables are referenced with an **UPDATE** SQL statement.

■ Direct access might be faster than via an index. The table must be large enough so the optimizer thinks it is worthwhile to take the extra step of going through the index, rather than just searching all the rows in the table. For example, the optimizer would probably not use any index defined on a table with only four rows of data.

■ A large number of row locks will be acquired. If many rows in a table will be accessed by a transaction, the optimizer will probably acquire a table lock.

Any time one transaction holds a lock on a table or row, other transactions might be denied access until the owner transaction has terminated. To optimize for maximum concurrency, a small, row-level lock is usually better than a large table lock. Because locks require storage space (to keep) and processing time (to manage), you can minimize both of these factors by using one large lock—rather than many small ones.

DEADLOCKS When two or more transactions are contending for locks, a situation known as a *deadlock* can occur. Consider the following example. Transaction 1 locks Table A with an Exclusive lock, and Transaction 2 locks Table B with an Exclusive lock. Now, suppose Transaction 1 attempts to lock Table B with an Exclusive lock, and Transaction 2 attempts to lock Table A with an Exclusive lock. Both transactions will be suspended until their second lock request is granted. Because neither lock request can be granted until one of the transactions performs a COMMIT or ROLLBACK operation—and because neither transaction can perform a COMMIT or ROLLBACK operation because they are both suspended (waiting on locks)—a deadlock situation has occurred. Figure 2–4 illustrates this scenario.

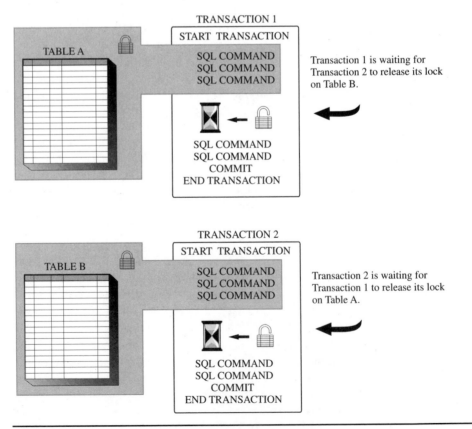

Figure 2–4 *Deadlock cycle between two transactions*

A deadlock is more precisely referred to as a "deadlock cycle," because the transactions involved in a deadlock form a circle of wait states. Each transaction in the circle is waiting for a lock held by one of the other transactions in the circle. When a deadlock cycle occurs, all the transactions involved in the deadlock will wait indefinitely—unless an outside agent performs some action to end the deadlock cycle. Because of this, DB2 contains an asynchronous system background process associated with each active database that is responsible for finding and resolving deadlocks in the locking subsystem. This background process is called the *deadlock detector*. When a database becomes active, the deadlock detector is started as part of the process that initializes the database for use. The deadlock detector stays "asleep" most of the time but "wakes up" at preset intervals to look for the presence of deadlocks between transactions using the database. Normally, the deadlock detector sees that there are no deadlocks on the database and goes back to sleep. If, however, the deadlock detector discovers a deadlock on the database, the detector selects one of the transactions in the cycle to roll back and terminate. The transaction that is rolled back receives an SQL error code, and all of its locks are released. The remaining transaction can then proceed, because the deadlock cycle is broken. The possibility exists (although unlikely) that more than one deadlock cycle exists on a database. If this is the case, the detector will find each remaining cycle and terminate one of the offending transactions in the same manner until all deadlock cycles are broken.

Because at least two transactions are involved in a deadlock cycle, you might assume that two data objects are always involved in the deadlock. This is not true. A certain type of deadlock, known as a *conversion deadlock*, can occur on a single data object. A conversion deadlock occurs when two or more transactions already hold compatible locks on an object, and then each transaction requests new, incompatible lock modes on that same object. A conversion deadlock usually occurs between two transactions searching for rows via an index (index scan). Using an index scan, each transaction acquires Share and Exclusive locks on rows. When each transaction has read the same row and then attempts to update that row, a conversion deadlock situation occurs.

Application designers need to watch out for deadlock scenarios when designing high-concurrency applications that are to be run by multiple concurrent users. In situations where the same set of rows will likely be read and then updated by multiple copies of the same application program, that program should be designed to roll back and retry any transactions that might be terminated as a result of a deadlock situation. As a general rule, the shorter the transaction, the less likely the transaction will be to get into a deadlock cycle. Setting the proper interval for the deadlock detector (in the database configuration file) is also necessary to ensure good concurrent application performance. An interval that is too short will cause unnecessary overhead, and an interval that is too long will enable a deadlock cycle to delay a process for an unacceptable amount of time. You must balance the possible delays in resolving deadlocks with the overhead of detecting the possible delays.

LOCK COMPATIBILITY   If the state of one lock placed on a data resource enables another lock to be placed on the same resource, the two locks (or states) are said to be *compatible*. Whenever one transaction holds a lock on a data resource and a second transaction requests a lock on the same resource, DB2 examines the two lock states

Part 1: Basic Database Concepts

to determine whether they are compatible. If the locks are compatible, the lock is granted to the second transaction (as long as no other transaction is waiting for the data resource). If the locks are incompatible, however, the second transaction must wait until the first transaction releases its lock. (In fact, the second transaction must wait until all existing incompatible locks are released.) Table 2–2 shows a lock compatibility matrix that identifies which locks are compatible and which are not.

Table 2–2 Lock compatibility matrix

	Lock Held By First Transaction												
Lock Type	none	IN	IS	NS	S	IX	SIX	U	NX	NW	X	W	Z
none	YES	YES	YES	YES	YES	YES	YES	YES	YES	YES	YES	YES	YES
IN	YES	YES	YES	YES	YES	YES	YES	YES	YES	YES	YES	YES	NO
IS	YES	YES	YES	YES	YES	YES	YES	YES	NO	NO	NO	NO	NO
NS	YES	YES	YES	YES	YES	NO	NO	YES	YES	YES	NO	NO	NO
S	YES	YES	YES	YES	YES	NO	NO	YES	NO	NO	NO	NO	NO
IX	YES	YES	YES	NO	NO	YES	NO	NO	NO	NO	NO	NO	NO
SIX	YES	YES	YES	NO	NO	NO	NO	NO	NO	NO	NO	NO	NO
U	YES	YES	YES	YES	YES	NO	NO	NO	NO	NO	NO	NO	NO
NX	YES	YES	NO	YES	NO	NO	NO	NO	NO	NO	NO	NO	NO
NW	YES	YES	NO	YES	NO	NO	NO	NO	NO	NO	NO	YES	NO
X	YES	YES	NO	NO	NO	NO	NO	NO	NO	NO	NO	NO	NO
W	YES	YES	NO	NO	NO	NO	NO	NO	NO	YES	NO	NO	NO
Z	YES	NO	NO	NO	NO	NO	NO	NO	NO	NO	NO	NO	NO

Lock Requested By Second Transaction

Adapted from *IBM DB2 Universal Database Embedded SQL Programming Guide*, page 143.

YES	Locks are compatible, therefore the lock requested is granted
NO	Locks are not compatible; therefore, the requesting transaction must wait for the held lock to be released or for a timeout to occur.

Lock Types

IN	Intent None
IS	Intent Share
NS	Next Key Share
S	Share
IX	Intent Exclusive
SIX	Share With Intent Exclusive
U	Update
NX	Next Key Exclusive
NW	Next Key Weak Exclusive
X	Exclusive
W	Weak Exclusive
Z	Super Exclusive

LOCK CONVERSION   When a transaction accesses a data resource on which the transaction already holds a lock—and the mode of access requires a more restrictive lock than the one the transaction already holds—the state of the lock is changed to the more restrictive state. The operation of changing the state of a lock already held to a more restrictive state is called a *lock conversion*. Lock conversion occurs because a transaction can only hold one lock on a data resource at a time. The conversion case for row locks is simple. A conversion only occurs if an Exclusive lock is needed and a Share or Update lock is held.

More distinct lock conversions exist for tables than for rows. In most cases, conversions result in the requested lock state becoming the new state of the lock currently held whenever the requested state is the higher state. Intent Exclusive and Share locks, however, are special cases, because neither is considered to be more restrictive than the other. If one of these locks is held and the other is requested, the resulting conversion is to a Share with Intent Exclusive lock. Lock conversion can cause locks only to increase restriction. Once a lock has been converted, the lock stays at the highest level obtained until the transaction is terminated.

LOCK ESCALATION   All locks require space for storage, and because this space is finite, DB2 limits the amount of space the system can use for locks. Furthermore, a limit is placed on the space each transaction can use for its own locks. A process known as lock escalation occurs when too many record locks are issued in the database and one of these space limitations is exceeded. *Lock escalation* is the process of converting several locks on individual rows in a table into a single, table-level lock. When a transaction requests a lock after the lock space is full, one of its tables is selected—and lock escalation takes place to create space in the lock list data structure. If enough space is not freed, another table is selected for escalation, and so on, until enough space has been freed for the transaction to continue. If there is still not enough space in the lock list after all the transaction's tables have been escalated, the transaction is asked to either commit or roll back all changes made since its initiation (i.e., the transaction receives an SQL error code, and the transaction is terminated).

An important point to remember is that an attempted escalation only occurs to the transaction that encounters a limit. This situation happens because, in most cases, the lock storage space will be filled when that transaction reaches its own transaction lock limit. If the system storage lock space limit is reached, however, a transaction that does not hold many locks might try to escalate, fail, and then be terminated. This event means that offending transactions holding many locks over a long period of time can cause other transactions to terminate prematurely. If escalation becomes objectionable, there are two ways to solve the problem:

▨ Increase the number of locks enabled in the database configuration file (with a corresponding increase in memory). This solution might be the best if concurrent access to the table by other processes is important. A point of diminishing returns exists on index access and record locking, even when concurrency is the primary concern. The overhead of obtaining record-level locks can impose more delays to other processes, which negates the benefits of concurrent access to the table.

▨ Locate and adjust the offending transaction(s), which might be the one(s) terminating prematurely, and explicitly issue **LOCK TABLE** SQL statements within the transaction(s). This choice might be the best if memory size is crucial, or if an extremely high percentage of rows are being locked.

■ Change the degree of transaction isolation being used.

■ Increase the frequency of commit operations.

Transaction Logging

Transaction logging is simply a method of keeping track of what changes have been made to a database. Every change made to a row of data in a database table is recorded in the active log file as an individual log record. Each log record enables DB2 to either remove or apply the data change to the database. To fully understand transaction logging operations, you should know what the transaction log contains, how transaction logging works, how the transaction log gets synchronized, and how to manage log file space.

HOW TRANSACTION LOGGING WORKS   Each change to a row in a table is made with an INSERT, UPDATE, or DELETE SQL statement. If you use the INSERT SQL statement, a transaction record containing the new row is written to the log file. If you use the UPDATE SQL statement, transaction records containing the old row information and the new row information are written to the log file (two separate records are written). If you use the DELETE SQL statement, a transaction record containing the old row information is written to the log file. These types of transaction log records make up the majority of the records in the transaction log file. Other transaction records also exist, which indicate whether a ROLLBACK or a COMMIT SQL statement was used to end a transaction. These records end a sequence of data log records for a single transaction.

Whenever a ROLLBACK or a COMMIT log record is written, the record is immediately forced out to the active log file. This action ensures that all the log records of a completed transaction are in the log file and will not be lost due to a system failure. Because more than one transaction might be using a database at any given time, the active log file contains the changes made by multiple transactions. To keep everything straight in the log, each log record contains an identifier of the transaction that created the record. In addition, all the log records for a single transaction are chained together.

Once a transaction is committed, all log records for that transaction are no longer needed (after all changes made by that transaction are physically written to the disk). If a ROLLBACK occurs, DB2 processes each log record written by the transaction in reverse order and backs out all changes made. Both "before" and "after" image UPDATE records are written to the log file for this reason.

LOG FILE AND DATABASE SYNCHRONIZATION   DB2 can maintain consistency only by keeping the log file and database synchronized. This synchronization is achieved with a write-ahead logging technique. When a transaction changes a row in a table, that change is actually made in a memory buffer contained in the database buffer pool and is written to the disk later. As a result, the most current data changes made to a working database are in the buffer pool, not on the disk. Write-ahead logging preserves consistency by writing the log record of a row change to the disk before the change itself is written from the memory buffer to the disk. Log records are written to disk whenever a transaction terminates—or whenever the buffer pool manager writes the memory buffer to the disk database.

If the system crashes, the log file and database will no longer be synchronized. Fortunately, the log file contains a record of every uncommitted change made to the database, because the log record of the change is forced to disk before the actual change is written. This event enables the recovery process to restore the database to a consistent state. The recovery process is discussed in more detail in the Database Recovery section later in this chapter.

MANAGING LOG FILE SPACE   It was mentioned earlier that DB2 writes records sequentially to the log file in order to support transactions. Because the log file grows until the file is reset, if no limits were imposed on the log file size, all free space on the system disk would eventually become full of log records. DB2's Log Manager controls the size of the log file, and whenever possible, the Log Manager resets the log to an empty state. The growth of the log is controlled by the initial size of the primary log files, the size limit for each secondary log file, and the number of primary and secondary log files being used. When the primary log file is filled, the Log Manager allocates space for a secondary log file, and the overflow is stored in that secondary file.

Whenever the primary log file becomes empty due to transaction inactivity (i.e., no transactions have uncommitted records in the log), the primary log file is reset and any secondary log files that have been allocated are released. If a transaction runs out of log space, either because the maximum primary log file size was reached and a secondary file was not used, or because there was too little disk space to allocate the next secondary log file, a roll back occurs and the transaction is terminated. Regardless of cause, this process continues until the log's inactive state is reached and the log is reset to its minimum size.

If two or more continuously overlapping transactions (e.g., high volume and high activity rate) are running, the primary log file might never be reset. Continuously overlapping transactions are not likely, but they can happen when two or more transactions starting at close intervals use the same database. When designing a database system in which the transaction arrival rate is high, you should increase the log file size to reduce the probability of transactions being rolled back due to insufficient log file space.

You can also prevent the primary log file from being reset if a lengthy transaction (one that causes many log records to be written before they are committed) is running. But first, you must consider how these transactions are used, as well as the amount of log file space needed to support them, when designing the database system. If other transactions are running concurrently with a lengthy transaction, the log file space requirement will increase. A lengthy transaction should probably run by itself, and the transaction should probably open the database for exclusive usage and fill up the log file before committing its changes. Any transaction that never ends execution (i.e., never performs a ROLLBACK or COMMIT) is a faulty application, because the transaction will eventually cause itself and possibly other transactions to fail.

DATABASE RECOVERY *Database recovery* is the process of returning the data in a database to a consistent state after a system failure (such as a power failure in the middle of a work session) occurs. If a DB2 database is active when a system failure occurs, that database is left in an inconsistent state until the database is accessed again. At that time, a special recovery process is executed that restores the database to a new, consistent state. This new, consistent state is defined by the transaction boundaries of any applications that were using the database when the system failure occurred. This recovery process is made possible by the database log file (see *Recovery Log File* in Chapter 1, "DB2 Database Architecture"). Because the log file contains both a "before" and "after" image of every change made to a row, all transaction records stored in the log file can be either removed from or added to the database as necessary.

DB2 determines whether database recovery is needed by examining the recovery log file the first time a database is opened after a system failure occurs. If the log file shows that the database was not shut down normally, the disk image of the database could be inconsistent. That's because changes made by completed transactions (still in the memory buffers) might have been lost. To restore the database to a consistent state, DB2 does the following actions:

- Any change made by a transaction that was in flight (had not been committed or rolled back) is removed from the database. DB2 works backward through the log file; if an uncommitted change is found, the record is restored to the "before" image retrieved from the log file.

- Any change made by a committed transaction that is not found in the database is written to the database. As DB2 scans the log file, any committed log records found that are not in the database are written to the database.

- If a transaction was in the process of being rolled back, the roll back operation is completed so that all changes made to the database by that transaction are removed.

Because DB2 knows that changes are only consistent when they are explicitly committed, all work done by in-flight transactions is considered inconsistent and must be backed out of the database to preserve database consistency.

As described previously, during the recovery process DB2 must scan the log file to restore the database to a consistent state. While scanning the log file, DB2 reads the database to determine whether the database contains the committed or uncommitted changes. If the log file is large, you could spend quite a while scanning the whole log and reading associated rows from the database. Fortunately, scanning the whole log is usually unnecessary, because the actions recorded at the beginning of the log file have been in the log file longer than the other actions. The chance is greater, then, that their transactions have been completed and that the data has already been written to the database; therefore, no recovery actions are required for the log records generated by these transactions.

If some way existed to skip these log records during the recovery process, the length of time necessary to recover the entire database could be shortened. This is the purpose of the *soft checkpoint*, which establishes a pointer in the log at which to begin database recovery. All log file records recorded before this checkpoint are the result of completed transactions, and their changes have already been written to the database. A soft checkpoint is most useful when log files are large, because the checkpoint can reduce the number of log records that are examined during database recovery; the more often the soft checkpoint is updated, the faster the database can be recovered.

SUMMARY

You will find it extremely important to understand the mechanisms DB2 uses to ensure database consistency before designing your database application. Unfortunately, this aspect is one of the more complicated topics of database application design. This chapter was designed to provide you with an overview of the database consistency mechanisms found in DB2 Universal Database, Version 5.2. You should now know what database consistency is and how to maintain it. You should also be familiar with transactions and how your application uses them to maintain data integrity. Furthermore, you should be familiar with the following transaction isolation levels:

- Repeatable read
- Read stability
- Cursor stability
- Uncommitted read

You should also understand the following lock attributes:

- Object
- Size
- Duration
- Mode

And you should understand the difference between the following lock states:

- Intent None (IN)
- Intent Share (IS)
- Next Key Share (NS)
- Share (S)
- Intent Exclusive (IX)
- Share with Intent Exclusive (SIX)
- Update (U)
- Next Key Exclusive (NX)
- Next Key Weak Exclusive (NW)
- Exclusive (X)

- Weak Exclusive (W)
- Super Exclusive (Z)

You should also be familiar with lock size, deadlocks, lock compatibility, lock conversion, and lock escalation. Finally, you should be aware of how transaction logging works and how transaction logs are used to restore database consistency in the event of a system failure.

As you build your database application, you will need to understand most of the information covered in this chapter. Incorporating this information in your application during the design and development process will help you catch and hopefully avoid potential problems in your application design.

PART

2

Application Development Fundamentals

3

Getting Started with DB2 Application Development

The DB2 database application development process begins with the application design and continues with the actual source code development. This chapter is designed to introduce you to the elements that can be used to drive your application's design. The first part of this chapter defines a simple application program and explains how a DB2 database application differs. This is followed by an introduction to the four main elements that are used to develop DB2 applications. Next, directions for establishing a DB2 database application development and testing environment are discussed. Finally, a brief overview of transaction management and source code creation and preparation is provided. We will begin by answering the question, "What is a DB2 database application?"

What Is a DB2 Database Application?

Before identifying the basic elements of a DB2 database application, let's examine the basic elements of a simple application. Most simple applications contain five essential parts:

- Input
- Logic (decision control)
- Memory (data storage and retrieval)
- Arithmetic (calculation)
- Output

Input is defined as the way an application receives the information it needs in order to produce solutions for the problems that it was designed to solve. Once input has been received, *logic* takes over and determines what information should be placed in or taken out of *memory* (data storage) and what *arithmetic* operations should be performed. Non-database applications use functions supplied by the operating system to store data in (and retrieve data from) simple, byte-oriented files. Once the application has produced a solution to the problem that it was designed to solve, it provides appropriate *output* in the form of either an answer or a specific action.

A DB2 database application contains these same five elements. The only real difference between a simple application program and a DB2 application program is the method of data storage/retrieval and decision control used. In DB2 applications, operating system file *input / output* (I/O) is replaced with DB2 database I/O, which provides more than just data storage and retrieval. DB2 database applications also require less decision control (logic); thanks to the nonprocedural nature of SQL, you can have DB2 applications retrieve only the data they need by restricting SELECT SQL statements with WHERE, GROUP BY, and HAVING clauses. In addition, you can eliminate data sorting routines by using the ORDER BY clause. Figure 3–1 illustrates the essential parts of both a simple application program and a DB2 database application program.

Designing a DB2 Database Application

Designing an efficient database application program requires a good understanding of how the production database is organized. If no written database design document exists, it is a good idea to produce one before you begin designing the actual database application. A good database design document should provide answers to the following questions:

- What data will be stored in the database?
- How will the data be stored?
- What are the functional dependencies in the database?
- How can the functional dependencies in the database be isolated?

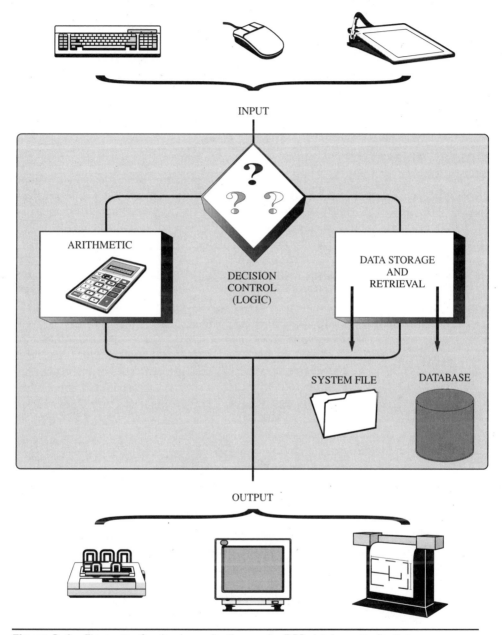

INPUT

? ? ?

ARITHMETIC

DECISION
CONTROL
(LOGIC)

DATA STORAGE
AND
RETRIEVAL

SYSTEM FILE

DATABASE

OUTPUT

Figure 3–1 Elements of a simple application and a DB2 database application

■ How can data redundancy be reduced or eliminated?

■ What keys need to be created in order to establish referential data integrity?

Ideally, the best database design document will evolve around the requirements of the database applications that will access the database. Once the database design document has been prepared, the application designing process can begin. Application design considerations should include the following items:

- Transaction definitions
- Transaction management and logging
- Volatility and volume of data
- Security considerations
- *Remote Units of Work* (RUOW)
- *Distributed Units of Work* (DUOW)

Because DB2 provides you with a variety of application development capabilities, one of the most important design decisions that an application designer can make is, "Which capabilities of DB2 should be used in my application?" This question can be difficult to answer, because the capabilities that can be chosen and the extent to which they can be used can vary greatly.

The first and most fundamental decision to be made before this question can be answered is the determination of how much data logic (logic that is used to enforce business rules) to move into the database itself—and how much to keep in the application. The key advantage of transferring data logic from the application to the database is that the application becomes more independent from the data. This feature is beneficial when several applications access the same data. Data or data logic maintenance can be performed at one location—the database—and all applications accessing the database see the effects immediately. Although this advantage is powerful, you must take into consideration that when data logic is stored in a database, *all* users of that database are affected. If the data logic rules and constraints that you wish to impose should only apply to the users of your application, it is probably more appropriate to keep the data logic in the application and out of the database.

Elements of a DB2 Database Application

Now that you know the basic requirements of a DB2 database application design, let's examine the specific elements of a DB2 database application. The following elements are the major building blocks of DB2 database applications:

- A high-level programming language
- SQL statements
- CLI function calls (optional)
- *Application Programming Interface* (API) calls (optional)

Each of these elements accomplishes specific tasks in the overall design of a DB2 database application. You can accomplish almost any DB2 task by using a high-level programming language in conjunction with an SQL statement, a CLI function call, or an API call, although some tasks require several of these elements.

High-Level Programming Language

A *high-level programming language* provides the framework within which all .SQL statements, CLI function calls, and API calls are contained. This framework enables you to control the sequence of your application's tasks (logic) and provides a way for your application to collect user input and produce appropriate output. A high-level programming language also enables you to use operating system calls and DB2 application elements (SQL statements, CLI function calls, and API calls) within the same application program. In essence, the high-level programming language can take care of everything except data storage and retrieval.

By combining OS calls and DB2 elements, you can develop DB2 database applications that incorporate OS-specific file I/O for referencing external data files. You can also use the high-level programming language to incorporate Presentation Manager functions, User Interface class library routines, and/or *Microsoft Foundation Class* (MFC) library routines in the application for both collecting user input and displaying application output. Additionally, by building a DB2 database application with a high-level language, you can exploit the capabilities of the computer hardware to enhance application performance (i.e., optimizing for high-level processors such as the Pentium III processor) and simplify user interaction (i.e., using special I/O devices such as light pens and scanners). DB2 Universal Database, Version 5.2, provides support for the following high-level languages:

- C
- C++
- COBOL
- FORTRAN
- REXX
- Visual BASIC (through the DB2 Stored Procedure Builder)

SQL Statements

SQL is a standardized language that is used to define, store, manipulate, and retrieve data in a relational database management system. SQL statements are executed by DB2, not by the operating system. Because SQL is nonprocedural by design, it is not an actual programming language; therefore, most database applications are a combination of the decision and sequence control of a high-level programming language and the data storage, manipulation, and retrieval capabilities of SQL statements. Two types of SQL statements can be embedded in an application program: *static* SQL statements and *dynamic* SQL statements. Each has its advantages and disadvantages.

STATIC SQL A static SQL statement is an SQL statement that is hard-coded in an application program when a source code file is written. Because high-level programming language compilers cannot interpret SQL statements, all source code files containing static SQL statements must be processed by an SQL *precompiler* before they can be compiled. Likewise, DB2 cannot work directly with high-level programming language variables. Instead, DB2 must work with host variables that are defined in a special place within an embedded SQL source code file (so the SQL precompiler can recognize them). The SQL precompiler is responsible for translating all SQL statements found in a source code file into their appropriate host-language function calls and for converting the actual SQL statements into host-language comments. The SQL precompiler is also responsible for evaluating the declared data types of host variables and determining which data conversion methods to use when moving data to-and-from the database. Additionally, the SQL precompiler performs error checking on each coded SQL statement and ensures that appropriate host-variable data types are used for their respective table column values.

Static SQL has one distinct advantage over dynamic SQL. Because the structure of the SQL statements used is known at precompile time, the work of analyzing the statement and creating a package containing a data access plan is done during the development phase. Thus, static SQL executes quickly, because its operational form already exists in the database at application run time. The down side to this property is that all static SQL statements must be prepared (i.e., their access plan must be stored in the database) before they can be executed, and they cannot be altered at run time. Because of this characteristic, if an application uses static SQL, its operational package(s) must be "bound" to each database the application will work with before the static SQL statements can be executed.

NOTE: *Because static SQL applications require prior knowledge of database, table, schema, and field names, changes made to these objects after the application is developed could produce undesirable results.*

DYNAMIC SQL   Although static SQL statements are fairly easy to use, they are limited because their format must be known in advance by the precompiler, and they can only use host variables. A dynamic SQL statement does not have a precoded, fixed format, so the data objects the statement uses can change each time the statement is executed. This feature is useful for an application that has an SQL requirement in which the format and syntax of the SQL statement is not known at the time the source code is written. Dynamic SQL statements do not have to be precompiled (although the overhead for dynamic SQL statements sometimes has to) and bound to the database they will access. Instead, they are combined with high-level programming language statements to produce an executable program, and all binding takes place at run time, rather than during compilation.

Because dynamic SQL statements are dynamically created according to the flow of application logic at execution time, they are more powerful than static SQL statements. Unfortunately, dynamic SQL statements are also more complicated to implement. Additionally, because dynamic SQL statements must be prepared at application run time, most will execute more slowly than their equivalent static SQL counterparts. However, because dynamic SQL statements use the most current database statistics during execution, there are some cases in which a dynamic SQL statement will execute faster than an equivalent static SQL statement. Dynamic SQL statements also enable the optimizer to see the real values of arguments, so they are not confined to the use of host variables. Figure 3–2 shows how both static SQL and dynamic SQL applications interact with a DB2 database.

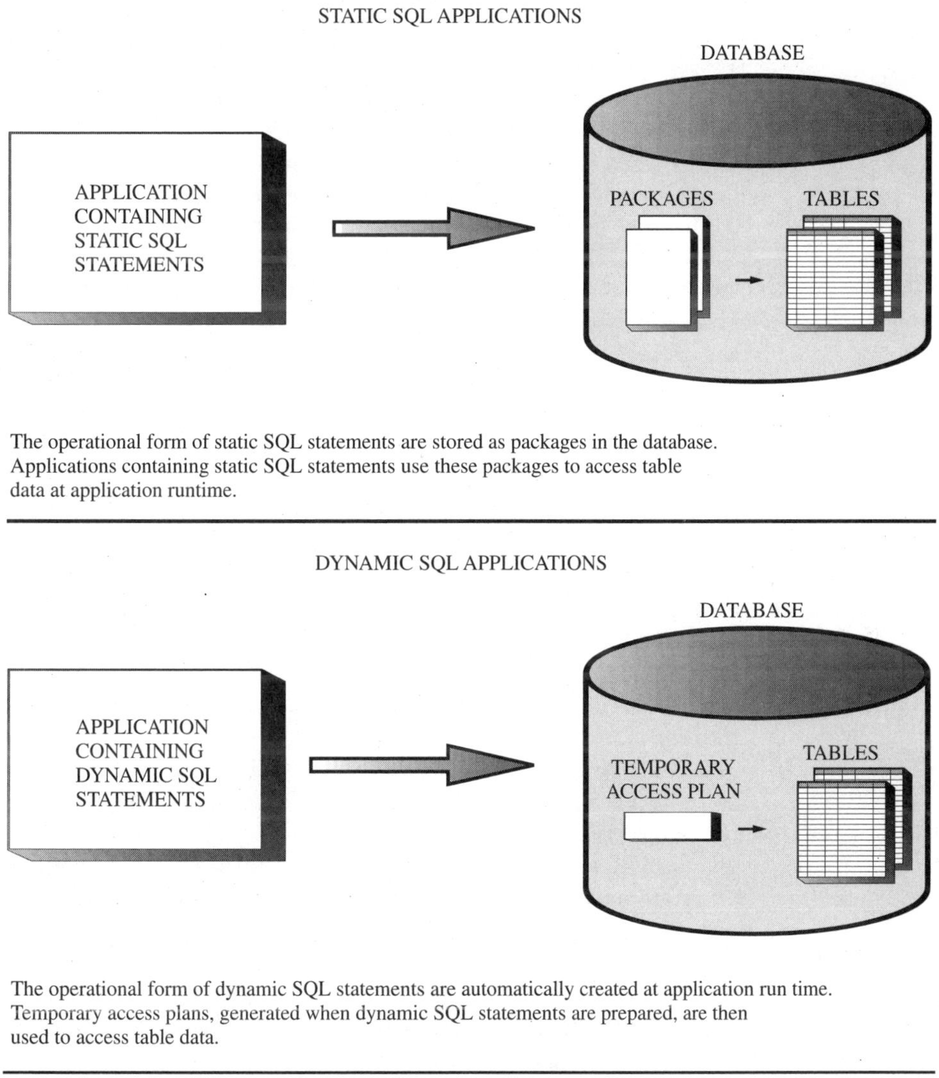

STATIC SQL APPLICATIONS

DATABASE

APPLICATION
CONTAINING
STATIC SQL
STATEMENTS

PACKAGES

TABLES

The operational form of static SQL statements are stored as packages in the database.
Applications containing static SQL statements use these packages to access table
data at application runtime.

DYNAMIC SQL APPLICATIONS

DATABASE

APPLICATION
CONTAINING
DYNAMIC SQL
STATEMENTS

TEMPORARY
ACCESS PLAN

TABLES

The operational form of dynamic SQL statements are automatically created at application run time.
Temporary access plans, generated when dynamic SQL statements are prepared, are then
used to access table data.

Figure 3–2   How SQL applications interact with a DB2 database

CLI Function Calls

DB2's *Call Level Interface* (CLI) is a collection of API function calls that were developed
specifically for database access.

To understand the call level interface, you need to understand the basis of DB2's CLI
and how it compares with existing, callable, SQL interfaces. In the early 1990s, the
X/Open Company and the *SQL Access Group* (SAG), now a part of X/Open, jointly developed a standard specification for a callable SQL interface called the *X/Open Call-Level
Interface*, or *X/Open CLI*. The goal of the X/Open CLI was to increase the portability of

database applications by enabling them to become independent of any one database management system's programming interface. Most of the X/Open CLI specifications were later accepted as part of a new ISO CLI international standard. DB2's CLI is based on this ISO CLI standard interface specification.

In 1992, Microsoft Corporation developed a callable SQL interface, ODBC, for the Microsoft Windows operating system. ODBC is based on the X/Open CLI standards specification but provides extended functions that support additional capability. The ODBC specification also defines an operating environment where database-specific ODBC drivers are dynamically loaded (based on the database name provided with the connection request) at application run time by an ODBC Driver Manager. This Driver Manager provides a central point of control for each datasource-specific library (driver) that implements ODBC function calls and interacts with a specific *database management system* (DBMS). By using drivers, an application can be linked directly to a single ODBC driver library, rather than to each DBMS itself. When the application runs, the ODBC Driver Manager mediates its function calls and ensures that they are directed to the appropriate driver. Figure 3–3 shows how CLI applications interact with a DB2 database via the ODBC Driver Manager and the DB2 CLI driver.

Applications that incorporate DB2's CLI are linked directly to the DB2 CLI load library. The DB2 CLI load library can then be loaded as an ODBC driver by any ODBC Driver Manager or it can be used independently. DB2's CLI provides support for all ODBC 3.X Level 1 functions except `SQLBulkOperations()`; all ODBC Level 2 functions except `SQLDrivers()`; some X/Open CLI functions, and some DB2-specific functions. The CLI specifications defined for ISO, X/Open, ODBC, and DB2 are continually evolving in a cooperative manner to produce new functions that provide additional capabilities.

The important difference between embedded dynamic SQL statements and CLI function calls lies in how the actual SQL statements are invoked. With dynamic SQL, an application prepares and executes SQL for a single DBMS—in this case, DB2. For a dynamic SQL application to work with a different DBMS, the application would have to be precompiled and recompiled for that DBMS. With CLI, an application uses procedure calls at execution time to perform SQL operations. Because CLI applications do not have to be precompiled, they can be executed on a variety of database systems without undergoing any alteration.

API Function Calls

Application Programming Interface (API) function calls are a collection of DB2 product-specific function calls that provide services other than the data storage, manipulation, and retrieval services that are provided by SQL statements and CLI function calls. API calls are embedded within a high-level programming language and operate in a fashion similar to other host-language function calls. Each API function has both a call and a return interface, and the calling application must wait until a requested API function completes before it can continue. The services provided by DB2 API function calls can be divided into the following categories:

■ Database manager control APIs

■ Database manager configuration APIs

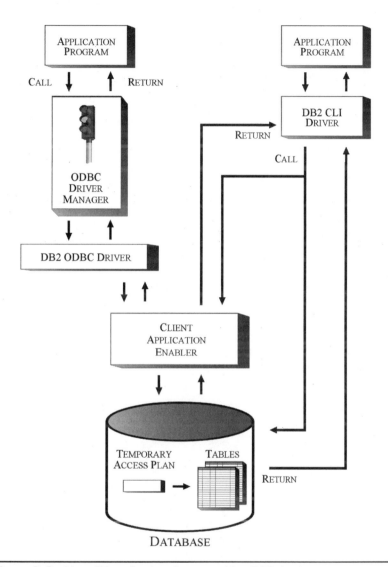

Figure 3–3   How CLI applications interact with a DB2 database

- Database control APIs
- Database configuration APIs
- Database directory management APIs
- Client/server directory management APIs
- Node management APIs
- Network support APIs
- Backup/recovery APIs

- Operational utility APIs
- Database monitoring APIs
- Data utility APIs
- General application programming APIs
- Application preparation APIs
- Remote server APIs
- Table space management APIs
- Transaction APIs
- Miscellaneous APIs

An application can use APIs to access DB2 facilities that are not available via SQL statements or CLI function calls. In addition, you can write applications containing only APIs that will perform the following functions:

- Manipulate the DB2 environment by cataloging and uncataloging databases and workstations (nodes), by scanning system database and workstation directories, and by creating, deleting, and migrating databases
- Perform routine database maintenance by backing up and restoring databases— and by exporting data to and importing data from external data files
- Manipulate the DB2 database manager configuration file and other DB2 database configuration files
- Perform specific client/server operations
- Provide a run-time interface for precompiled SQL statements
- Precompile embedded SQL applications
- Bulk load tables by importing data from external data files

Figure 3–4 illustrates how an application containing the **BACKUP** API interacts with the DB2 Database Manager to back up a DB2 database.

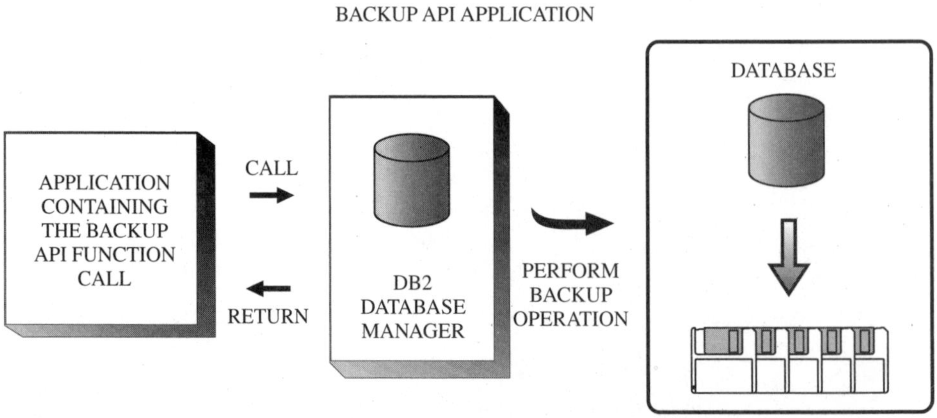

BACKUP API APPLICATION

Figure 3–4   How a BACKUP API call is processed by DB2

Establishing the DB2 Database Application Development Environment

Before you can begin developing DB2 database applications, you must establish the appropriate application development/operating system environment by performing the following steps:

1. Install the appropriate DB2 Universal Database software product on the workstation that will be used for application development. If the application will be developed in a client-server environment, you must install the DB2 Universal Database server software on the workstation that will act as the server and install the appropriate DB2 Universal Database *Client Application Enabler* (CAE) software on all client workstations. You also must install a communication protocol that is common to both client and server workstations.

2. Install and properly configure the DB2 Universal Database *Software Developer's Kit* (SDK) software on all workstations that will be used for application development.

3. Install and properly configure a high-level language compiler on all workstations that will be used for application development.

4. Make sure you can establish a connection to the appropriate database(s).

For additional information on how to accomplish these tasks, refer to the installation documentation for DB2 Universal Database, DB2 Universal Database SDK, the compiler being used, and the appropriate communications package.

You can develop DB2 database applications on any workstation that has the DB2 SDK installed. You can run DB2 database applications either at a DB2 server workstation or on any client workstation that has the appropriate DB2 CAE software installed. You can even develop applications in such a way that one part of the application runs on the client workstation and another part runs on the server workstation. When a DB2 database application is divided across workstations in this manner, the part that resides on the server workstation is known as a *stored procedure*.

To precompile, compile, and link DB2 database applications, your environment paths need to be properly set. If you follow the installation instructions that come with the DB2 Universal Database SDK and the supported high-level language compiler, your environment should automatically support application development. If, however, after installing the DB2 Universal Database SDK and your high-level language compiler you are unable to precompile, compile, and link your application, check the environment paths and make sure they point to the correct drives and directories.

NOTE: *Although environment paths are usually set appropriately during the installation process, the compiler/development interface being used may require that these paths are explicitly provided.*

Establishing the DB2 Database Application Testing Environment

As with any other application, the best way to ensure that a DB2 database application performs as expected is to thoroughly test it. You must perform this testing during both the actual development of the application and after the application coding phase has been completed. To thoroughly test your application, establish an appropriate testing environment that includes the following items:

■ A testing database

■ Appropriate testing tables

■ Valid test data

Creating a Testing Database

If your application creates, alters, or drops tables, views, indexes, or any other data objects, you should create a temporary database for testing purposes. If your application inserts, updates, or deletes data from tables and views, you should also use a testing database to prevent your application from corrupting production-level data while it is being tested. You can create a testing database in any of the following ways:

■ By writing a small application that calls the **CREATE DATABASE** API call, either with a high-level programming language (such as C) or as a command file with REXX

■ By issuing the **CREATE DATABASE** command from the DB2 command-line processor

■ By backing up the production database and restoring it on a dedicated application development and/or testing workstation

Creating Testing Tables and Views

To determine which testing tables and views you will need in the test database, you must first analyze the data needs of the application (or part of the application) being tested. You can perform this analysis by preparing a list of all data needed by the application and then describing how each data item in the list is going to be accessed. When the analysis is complete, you can construct the test tables and views that are necessary for testing the application in any of the following ways:

■ By writing a small application in a high-level programming language that executes the **CREATE TABLE** or **CREATE VIEW** SQL statement and creates all necessary tables and views. (This application could be the same application that creates the testing database—provided static SQL is not used.)

■ By issuing the **CREATE TABLE** or **CREATE VIEW** SQL statement from the DB2 command-line processor

■ By backing up the production database and restoring it on a dedicated application development and/or testing workstation

If you are developing the database schema along with the application, you may need to refine the definitions of the test tables repeatedly throughout the development process. Data objects such as tables and views usually cannot be created and accessed within the same database application, because the DB2 Database Manager cannot bind SQL statements to data objects that do not exist. To make the process of creating and changing data objects less time-consuming, and to avoid this type of binding problem, you can create a separate application that constructs all necessary data objects as you are developing the main application. When the main application development is complete, you can then use the application that creates the data objects to construct production databases. If appropriate, this application can then be incorporated into the main application's installation program.

Generating Test Data

The data an application uses during testing should represent all possible data input conditions. If the application is designed to check the validity of input data, the test data should include both valid and invalid data. This feature is necessary to verify that the valid data is processed appropriately—and the invalid data is detected and handled correctly. You can insert test data into tables in any of the following ways:

■ By writing a small application that executes the **INSERT** SQL statement. This statement will insert one or more rows into the specified table each time the statement is issued.

■ By writing a small application that executes the **INSERT . . . SELECT** SQL statement. This statement will obtain data from an existing table and insert the data into the specified table each time the statement is issued.

■ By writing a small application that calls the **IMPORT** API. You can use this API to load large amounts of new or existing data, or you can use this API in conjunction with the **EXPORT** API to duplicate one or more tables that have already been populated in a production database.

■ By writing a small application that calls the **LOAD** API. You can also use this API to bulk load large amounts of new or existing data into a database.

■ By backing up the production database and restoring it on a dedicated application development and/or testing workstation.

Managing Transactions

You might recall in Chapter 2, "Database Consistency Mechanisms," that transactions were described as the basic building blocks that DB2 uses to maintain database consistency. All data storage, manipulation, and retrieval must be performed within one or more transactions, and any application that successfully connects to a database automatically initiates a transaction. The application, therefore, must end the transaction by issuing either a **COMMIT** or a **ROLLBACK** SQL statement (or by calling the SQL **EndTrans()** CLI function), or by disconnecting from the database (which causes the DB2 Database Manager to automatically perform a **COMMIT** operation).

NOTE: *You should not disconnect from a database and allow the DB2 Database Manager to automatically end the transaction, because some database management systems behave differently than others (for example, DB2/400 will perform a* **ROLLBACK** *instead of a* **COMMIT**).

The **COMMIT** SQL statement makes all changes in the transaction permanent, while the **ROLLBACK** SQL statement removes all these changes from the database. Once a transaction has ended, all locks held by the transaction are freed—and another transaction can access the previously locked data. (Refer to Chapter 2, "Database Consistency Mechanisms," for more information.)

Applications should be developed in such a way that they end transactions on a timely basis, so other applications (or other transactions within the same application) are not denied access to necessary data resources for long periods of time. Applications should also be developed in such a way that their transactions do not inadvertently cause deadlock situations to occur. During the execution of an application program, you can issue explicit **COMMIT** or **ROLLBACK** SQL statements to ensure that transactions are terminated on a timely basis. Keep in mind, however, that once a **COMMIT** or **ROLLBACK** SQL statement has been issued, its processing cannot be stopped—and its effects cannot easily be reversed.

Creating and Preparing Source Code Files

The high-level programming language statements in an application program are usually written to a standard ASCII text file, known as a *source code file*, which can be edited with any text or source code editor. The source code files must have the proper file extension for the host language in which the code is written (i.e., C source files have a .C extension, and COBOL source files have a .COB extension) for the high-level language compiler to know what to do with them.

If your application is written in an interpreted language such as REXX, you can execute the application directly from the operating system command prompt by entering the program name after connecting to the required database. Applications written in interpreted host languages do not need to be precompiled, compiled, or linked. However, if your application was written in a compiled host language such as C, you must perform additional steps to build your application. Before you can compile your program, you must precompile it if it contains embedded SQL. Simply stated, *precompiling* is the process of converting embedded SQL statements into DB2 run-time API calls that a host compiler can process. The SQL calls are then stored in a package, in a bind file, or in both, depending upon the precompiler options specified. After the program is precompiled, compiled, and linked, the program must then be bound to the test or the production database. *Binding* is the process of creating a package from the source code or bind file and storing the package in the database for later use. If your application accesses more than one database, and if it contains embedded SQL, it must be bound to each database used before it can be executed. Precompiling and binding are only required if the source files contain embedded SQL statements; if they contain only CLI function calls and/or API calls, precompiling and binding are not necessary.

SUMMARY

The goal of this chapter was to provide you with an overview of the DB2 database application development process. You should now understand what a DB2 database application is, and you should be familiar with some of the issues that affect database application design.

You should also be familiar with the following application development building blocks:

- A high-level programming language
- SQL statements
- CLI function calls
- API calls

You should also be able to establish a DB2 database application development environment and create testing databases, testing tables, and test data. Finally, you should have some understanding about the way source code files are created and converted into executable programs. Chapter 4 continues to present DB2 database application development fundamentals by focusing on the development of CLI applications for DB2 Universal Database, Version 5.2.

4

Writing CLI Applications

DB2 Universal Database CLI applications are similar to embedded SQL applications, with the exception that CLI applications use function calls to pass dynamic SQL statements to DB2—rather than executing the SQL statements themselves. This chapter is designed to introduce you to CLI application development and to the steps required to convert a CLI source-code file to an executable DB2 database application. This chapter begins by describing the differences between embedded SQL statements and CLI function calls. This description is followed by an introduction to the three main parts of a CLI application: initialization, transaction processing, and termination. Next, the design and implementation of common error-handling routines, focusing on the retrieval and analysis of return codes and SQLSTATE values, is discussed. Finally, this chapter concludes with a brief discussion on how to use the compiler and linker to convert CLI application source-code files to an executable program.

A Word About Prototyping CLI Function Calls

As you design and code a DB2 CLI application program, you should take advantage of DB2's Interactive CLI tool to prototype your CLI function calls. Interactive CLI enables you to test CLI function calls before you place them into a high-level language application program. With Interactive CLI, commands can be submitted either interactively or via an input file. Likewise, the results of Interactive CLI commands can either be displayed on the terminal or written to an output file. In addition, the Interactive CLI command driver can capture all commands entered during a session and write them to a file, creating a "command script" file that can be edited and rerun later. Prototyping CLI function calls before coding them in a source-code file can help reduce the amount of errors generated—both during the compilation process and when the final application is tested. For more information about the DB2 Interactive CLI application, refer to the *Interactive CLI (Applet) Documentation* manual.

NOTE: *Because Interactive CLI is a testing tool provided for application developers who want to use the program, IBM makes no guarantees about its performance. Also, because Interactive CLI is not intended for end users, it does not have extensive error-checking built into it. Therefore, Interactive CLI can crash over something as simple as a missing closing delimiter at the end of a string parameter.*

The Main Parts of a CLI Source-Code File

DB2 CLI application programs are organized so that they perform three distinct tasks:

- Initialization
- Transaction processing
- Termination

One or more CLI function calls may be required to perform each of these tasks, and many of these functions must also be called in the appropriate order or an error condition will occur. Besides the three distinct tasks listed, there are also general tasks such as error handling that can be incorporated throughout a CLI application's source code file(s).

The Initialization Task

In the *initialization task*, the DB2 CLI library (or the ODBC Driver Manager) is loaded, and resources needed by the transaction processing task are allocated and initialized. These resources generally consist of data areas that are identified by unique handles. A *handle* is simply a pointer variable that refers to a data object controlled by DB2 CLI and is referenced by CLI function calls. By using handles, the application is freed from the responsibility of having to allocate and manage global variables and/or data structures (such as the SQLCA, SQLDA, and SQLCHAR data structures that are used in embedded SQL applications). The four types of handles used by CLI function calls are as follows:

Environment handle   The environment handle refers to the data storage area that contains global information about the current state of the application.

Connection handle   The connection handle refers to a data storage area that contains information associated with a database connection that is being managed by either DB2 or by the ODBC Driver Manager. This data storage area includes general status information, transaction status information, and diagnostic information.

Statement handle   The statement handle refers to a data storage area that contains information about an SQL statement that is being managed by DB2. Statement handles are usually not allocated in the initialization task; rather, they are allocated in the transaction processing task.

Descriptor handle   The descriptor handle is a pointer to a data storage area that contains a collection of metadata that describes either the parameters of an SQL statement or the columns of a result data set.

At a minimum, a CLI application must allocate one environment data storage area and at least one connection data storage area. Once these data storage areas have been allocated and their corresponding handles have been initialized, one or both handle(s) are passed to either the DB2 CLI Library or to the ODBC Driver Manager (as arguments) whenever a CLI API function call is made. During the initialization task, an application also tells the DB2 CLI Library or ODBC Driver Manager which ODBC specification it plans to follow.

ALLOCATING RESOURCES   The `SQLAllocHandle()` function must always be the first function called in the initialization task, and this function must be called with the `SQL_HANDLE_ENV` option specified. Once an environment storage area is established, the `SQLAllocHandle()` function must then be called with the `SQL_HANDLE_DBC` option specified to establish a communications area for the data source connection that will soon be established. If an application intends to connect concurrently to more than one data source (or to connect concurrently multiple times to the same data source), the application must call the `SQLAllocHandle()` function for each connection it plans to establish. The handles returned from these calls are then used with the `SQLConnect()`, `SQLDriverConnect()`, or the `SQLBrowseConnect()` function to establish the desired data source connections. Figure 4–1 illustrates how a connection data storage area is allocated during the initialization task of an application—and how its handle is then passed to the CLI Library ODBC Driver Manager with subsequent CLI API function calls.

The use of separate connection handles ensures that multi-threaded applications can use one connection per thread without encountering concurrency problems.

Declaring the Application's CLI/ODBC Version

A special set of CLI API function calls can be used to control the attributes associated with an environment and/or a connection. Some of these attributes must be set before a connection to a data source is made, while others can only be set afterwards.

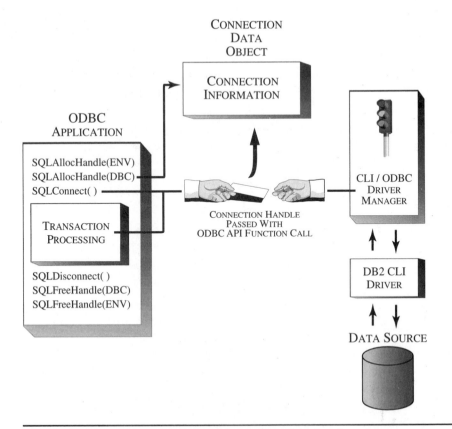

Figure 4–1 How CLI connection handles are established and used

Before an application allocates a connection handle, it must set the **SQL_ATTR_ODBC_ VERSION** environment attribute to either **SQL_OV_ODBC3** or **SQL_OV_ODBC2**. This attribute tells the ODBC Driver Manager that the application follows either the CLI 5.0 (ODBC 3.X) or the CLI 2.0 (ODBC 2.0 or earlier) specification when using the following items:

- SQLSTATEs—Many SQLSTATE values are different between versions.
- The *CatalogName* argument in **SQLTables()**—In CLI 2.0 (ODBC 2.0), if the wild card characters % and _ are used in the *CatalogName* argument of the **SQLTables()** API function, they are treated literally. In CLI 5.0 (ODBC 3.X), they are treated as wild cards. Thus, an application that follows the CLI 2.0 (ODBC 2.0) specification cannot use wild cards with this argument.

The ODBC 3.X Driver Manager checks the version of the CLI/ODBC specification to which an application is written and responds accordingly.

The Transaction Processing Task

The *transaction processing task* follows the initialization task and makes up the bulk of a CLI application. This is where the SQL statements that query and/or modify data are passed to DB2 by various CLI API function calls. In the transaction processing task, an application performs the following five steps, in the order shown:

1. Allocates statement handles
2. Prepares and executes SQL statements
3. Processes the results
4. Commits or rolls back the transaction
5. Frees statement handles

Figure 4–2 illustrates these five steps and identifies the CLI 5.0 (ODBC 3.X) API function calls that are used to perform them.

ALLOCATING STATEMENT HANDLES As mentioned earlier, a statement handle refers to a data object that contains information about a single SQL statement. This information includes the SQL statement text, any dynamic SQL statement arguments, cursor information, bindings for dynamic SQL statement parameter marker arguments, result data set columns, result values, and status information. Statement handles are allocated by calling the `SQLAllocHandle()` function with the `SQL_HANDLE_STMT` option specified. A statement handle must be allocated for an SQL statement before that statement can be executed. Also, each statement handle allocated must be associated with a specific connection handle.

PREPARING AND EXECUTING SQL STATEMENTS Once a statement handle has been allocated, there are two methods that can be used to prepare and execute an actual SQL statement:

■ Prepare then Execute—This method separates the preparation of the SQL statement from its actual execution and is typically used when an SQL statement is to be executed repeatedly (usually with different parameter values). This method is also used when the application needs information about the columns in the result data set that will be produced before the SQL statement can be executed.

■ Execute Direct—This method combines the prepare step and the execute step into a single step and is usually used when an SQL statement is executed only once. This method is also used when the application does not need additional information about the columns in the result data set produced before the SQL statement can be executed.

Both of these preparation and execution methods enable the use of parameter markers in place of expressions in an SQL statement. Parameter markers are represented by the question mark (?) character, and they indicate the position in the SQL statement where the contents of application variables are to be substituted when the SQL statement is actually executed. Parameter markers are referenced sequentially, from left to

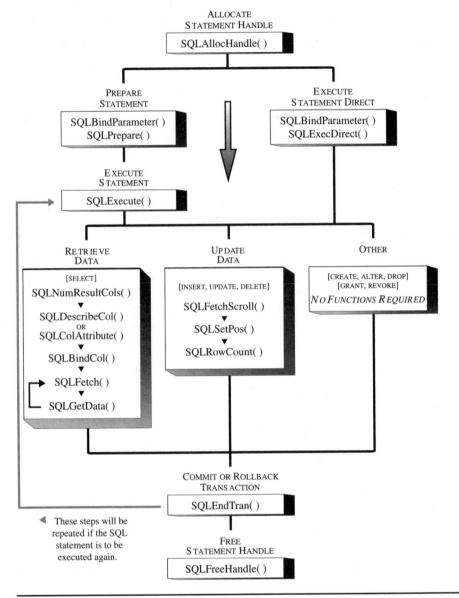

Figure 4–2 The typical order of ODBC API function calls in the transaction processing task

right, starting at number one. When an application variable is associated with a parameter marker in an SQL statement, the application variable is said to be "bound" to that parameter marker. Binding is carried out by calling the `SQLBindParameter()` function. Once a parameter marker is bound to an application variable, the information about that variable remains in effect until it is overridden—or until the application unbinds it or frees its corresponding statement handle. Whenever possible, the C data type of the application variable being bound should be the same as the SQL data type required by the SQL statement. If you bind a variable of a C data type that is different from the SQL data type required by the SQL statement to a parameter marker, DB2 automatically attempts to convert the contents of the bound variable to the required data type.

No data is read from a bound variable until the actual SQL statement is executed. By using bound variables, an application can execute the same SQL statement many times and obtain different results simply by modifying the contents of the bound parameter variables.

PROCESSING THE RESULTS After an SQL statement has been prepared and executed, the results of the execution must be retrieved and processed. SQL statement execution result information is obtained from the data storage areas to which the connection and statement handles point. If the SQL statement was not a **SELECT** statement, then the only additional processing required after the SQL statement has been executed is the regular check of the CLI API function return code, to ensure that no error occurred. If, however, the SQL statement was a **SELECT** statement, the following steps are generally needed to retrieve each row data in the result data set produced:

1. Determine the structure (i.e., the number of columns, column data types, and data lengths) of the result data set returned.

2. Bind application variables to the columns in the result data set (optional).

3. Repeatedly fetch the next row of data from the result data set into the bound application variables. Values for columns that were not bound to application variables in Step 2 can be retrieved by calling the **SQLGetData()** function after each successful fetch.

The first step analyzes the prepared or executed SQL statement to determine the structure of the result data set produced. If the SQL statement was hard-coded into the application, this step is not necessary because the structure of the result data set is already known. If, however, the SQL statement was generated at run time (that is, entered by a user), then the application needs to query the result data set to obtain this information. Result data set structure information can be obtained by calling the **SQLNumResultsCol()**, the **SQLDescribeCol()**, and/or the **SQLColAttribute()** function immediately after the SQL statement has been either prepared or executed.

The second step binds application variables to columns in the result data set so that the application program can retrieve data directly into them. Columns in a result data set are bound to application variables much like the way that application variables are bound to SQL statement parameter markers. This time, however, the variables are used as output arguments and data is written to them whenever the **SQLFetch()** function call is used. Because the **SQLGetData()** function call can also be used to retrieve data, application variable binding is optional.

The third step actually retrieves the data stored in the result data set by repeatedly calling the **SQLFetch()** function until no more data exists. If any application variables have been bound to columns in the result data set, their values will automatically be updated each time **SQLFetch()** is called. The **SQLGetData()** function call can be used to retrieve data from any columns that were not previously bound. This CLI function is also useful for retrieving variable length column data in smaller pieces, which cannot be done when bound application variables are used. All column data in the result data set can be retrieved by using any combination of these two methods. If any data conversion is necessary, the data conversion occurs automatically when the **SQLFetch()** function is called (if bound variables are used), or the conversion can be specified when the **SQLGetData()** function call is invoked. While performing these steps, the application should always check the return code each time a CLI API function call is made to ensure that no errors have occurred.

If the SQL statement specified was a positioned **UPDATE** or **DELETE** statement, you must use a cursor (a moveable pointer to a row within a result data set). Unlike embedded SQL, where cursor names are used to retrieve, update, or delete rows, in CLI a cursor name is needed only for positioned **UPDATE** and **DELETE** SQL statements, because they reference a cursor by name. A cursor name is automatically generated, if appropriate, when a statement handle is allocated.

ENDING THE TRANSACTION (ROLLBACK OR COMMIT)   Transactions enable a group of SQL statements to be processed as a single operation. This characteristic means that all SQL statements within the operation are guaranteed to be completed (committed) or undone (rolled back) as if they were a single SQL statement. CLI applications can contain multiple data source connections, and each connection to a data source constitutes a separate transaction boundary. Figure 4–3 shows the two transaction boundaries that could exist in a CLI application that communicates with two separate databases.

CLI applications can be configured to run in either auto-commit or manual-commit mode. In auto-commit mode, each SQL statement is treated as a complete transaction, and each transaction is automatically committed if the SQL statement was successfully executed. For non-query SQL statements, this commit takes place immediately after the statement is executed. For query SQL statements, this commit takes place immediately after the cursor being used is closed. (Remember that CLI automatically declares and opens a cursor if a cursor is needed.) In manual-commit mode, transactions are started implicitly the first time the application accesses the data source (that is, upon the first occurrence of any CLI function call that returns a result data set). Transactions are ended when the **SQLEndTrans()** function is called. This CLI function call is used to either roll back or commit the changes made to the database by the current transaction. Therefore, all SQL statements executed between the time the data source was first accessed and the time the **SQLEndTrans()** function call is made are treated as a single transaction.

The auto-commit mode is the default commit mode used and is usually sufficient for simple CLI applications. Larger applications, however, particularly applications that need to perform updates, should switch to manual-commit mode as soon as the data source connection is established.

All transactions must be ended before the connection to the data source is terminated; that is, before the **SQLDisconnect()** function is called. You should not wait this long before you commit or roll back a transaction, however, because of the concurrency and locking problems that can arise. Likewise, it is not always a good idea to use the

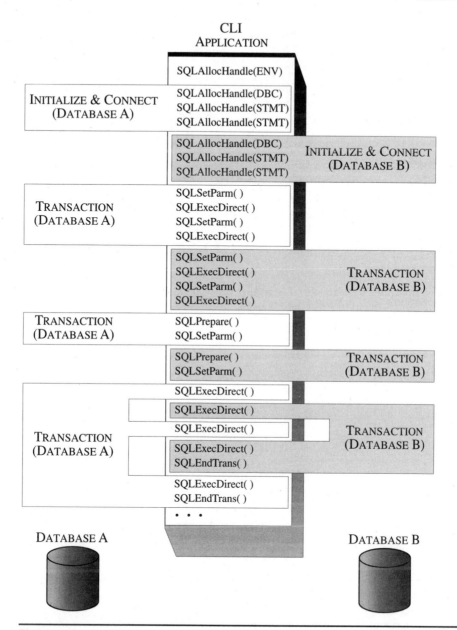

Figure 4–3 Transaction boundaries in a CLI application that works simultaneously with two different databases

auto-commit mode or to call the **SQLEndTrans()** function after each SQL statement is executed, because this action increases overhead and reduces application performance. When trying to decide the best time to end a transaction, consider the following points:

- Only the current transaction can be committed or rolled back; therefore, all dependent SQL statements should be kept within the same transaction.

- Various table and row locks can be held by the current transaction. When the transaction is ended, these locks are released and other applications are given access to the data.

- Once a transaction has been successfully committed or rolled back, it is fully recoverable from the system log files. Any transaction that is open at the time of a system failure or application program failure is not recoverable. Therefore, transactions should be ended as soon as reasonably possible.

NOTE: *DB2 guarantees that successfully committed or rolled-back transactions are fully recoverable from the system log files. However, this might not be true for other database products. When developing applications for multiple database products, refer to their documentation to determine when transactions are recoverable.*

When defining transaction boundaries, keep in mind that all resources associated with the transaction, except those associated with a held cursor, are released. Prepared SQL statements, cursor names, bound parameters, and column bindings, however, are maintained from one transaction to the next. This means that once an SQL statement has been prepared, the statement does not need to be reprepared—even after a commit or roll back occurs—as long as it remains associated with the same statement handle. Also, by default, cursors are preserved after a transaction is committed and are emptied after a transaction is rolled back.

FREEING SQL STATEMENT HANDLES   After the results of an executed SQL statement have been processed, the SQL statement handle data storage area that was allocated when the transaction processing began needs to be freed. SQL statement handles are freed by calling the **SQLFreeHandle()** function with the **SQL_HANDLE_STMT** option specified. When used, this CLI API function performs one or more of the following tasks:

- Unbinds all previously bound column application variables
- Unbinds all previously bound parameter application variables
- Closes any open cursors and discards their results
- Drops the SQL statement handle and releases all associated resources

NOTE: *If an SQL statement handle is not dropped, it can be used to process another SQL statement. However, when an SQL statement handle is reused, any cached access plan for the SQL statement associated with that handle will be discarded.*

The Termination Task

The termination task takes place just before the CLI application terminates. This is where all data source connections are ended and all resources allocated by the initialization task are freed and are returned to the operating system. Usually, these resources consist of an environment data storage area and one or more connection data storage areas. After all existing database connections are terminated with the **SQLDisconnect()** function, their corresponding connection data storage areas are freed by calling the **SQLFreeHandle()** function with the **SQL_HANDLE_DBC** option specified. When all connection data storage areas are freed, the environment data storage area is freed by calling the **SQLFreeHandle()** function with the **SQL_HANDLE_ENV** option specified. Once the termination task has completed, the application can return control to the operating system.

Error Handling

In the last chapter, you saw that error handling is an important part of every DB2 database application program. The best way to handle error conditions is with a common error-handling routine. Whenever a CLI function call is executed, a special value known as a *return code* is returned to the calling application. A common error-handling routine should first determine whether an error or warning condition has occurred by checking this return-code value. If the error-handling routine discovers that an error or warning has occurred, it should examine the SQLSTATE value that is also returned and process the error accordingly. At a minimum, an error-handling routine should notify users that an error or warning has occurred—and provide enough information so the problem can be corrected.

Evaluating Return Codes

As mentioned earlier, whenever a CLI function call is executed, a return-code value is returned to the calling application. Table 4–1 lists all possible return codes that can be generated by a CLI function.

The return code **SQL_INVALID_HANDLE** always indicates a programming error and should never be encountered at run time. All the other return codes provide run-time information about the overall success or failure of the CLI API function, although the **SQL_ERROR** return code can sometimes indicate a programming error.

Evaluating SQLSTATEs (Diagnostic Messages)

Although the CLI function return code notifies the application program if an error or warning condition prevented the CLI function from executing properly, the return code does not provide the application (or the developer or user) with specific information about what caused the error or warning condition to occur. Because information about an error or warning condition is usually necessary, DB2 (as well as other relational database products) uses a set of diagnostic error message codes that are referred to as

Table 4–1   Return codes generated by CLI API functions

Return Code	Meaning
SQL_SUCCESS	The CLI API function completed successfully. With CLI 5.0 drivers, the application can call the **SQLGetDiagField()** function to obtain additional information from the diagnostic header record. With CLI 2.0 no additional information is available.
SQL_SUCCESS_WITH_INFO	The CLI API function completed successfully, however a warning or a nonfatal error was generated. The application can call the **SQLGetDiagRec()** function or the **SQLGetDiagField()** function to obtain additional information.
SQL_NO_DATA	The CLI API function completed successfully, but no relevant data was found. The application can call the **SQLGetDiagRec()** function or the **SQLGetDiagField()** function to obtain additional information.
SQL_INVALID_HANDLE	The CLI API function failed to execute because an invalid environment, connection, statement, or descriptor handle was specified. This code is only returned when the specified handle is either a NULL pointer or the wrong handle type (for example, when a statement handle is specified for a connection handle parameter). Because this is a programming error, no additional information is available.
SQL_NEED_DATA	The application tried to execute an SQL statement, but the CLI API function failed because data the application had indicated would be available at execution time was missing—such as when parameter data is sent at execution time or when additional connection information is needed. The application can call the **SQLGetDiagRec()** function or the **SQLGetDiagField()** function to obtain additional information.
SQL_STILL_EXECUTING	An CLI API function that was started asynchronously is still executing. The application can call the **SQLGetDiagRec()** function or the **SQLGetDiagField()** function to obtain additional information.
SQL_ERROR	The CLI API function failed to complete. The application can call the **SQLGetDiagRec()** function or the **SQLGetDiagField()** function to obtain additional information.

SQLSTATEs. SQLSTATEs can help determine exactly what went wrong whenever a CLI function call fails. Because different database servers often have different diagnostic message codes, DB2 supports the standard set of SQLSTATEs that are defined by the X/Open CLI standard specification. This standardization of SQLSTATE values enables application developers to use consistent error and warning message routines across different relational database product platforms.

SQLSTATEs are alphanumeric strings that are five characters (bytes) in length and have the format *ccsss*, where *cc* indicates the error message class and *sss* indicates the error message subclass. Any SQLSTATE with a class of **01** is a warning; any SQLSTATE with a class of **HY** is an error that was generated by DB2 CLI; and any SQLSTATE with a class of **IM** is an error that was generated only by the ODBC Driver Manager.

Either the **SQLGetDiagRec()** or the **SQLGetDiagField()** CLI function can be used to retrieve SQLSTATE values from the database server. These functions can also return native error codes if such codes were also returned. When connected to DB2 Universal Database, the native error code will always be the same as the SQLCODE value. If the error code was generated by the DB2 CLI driver instead of the database server, the native error code will be set to –99999. SQLSTATE values include both additional IBM-defined values that are returned by the database server and DB2 CLI-defined values that are returned for conditions that are not defined in the X/Open CLI standard specification. This characteristic exists so that the maximum amount of diagnostic information is available for the calling application. When executing CLI database application programs on the Windows operating system with ODBC, you can also receive ODBC-defined SQLSTATE values.

The following is a set of guidelines that should be considered whenever you examine SQLSTATE values in your application:

- Always check the CLI function return code before calling the **SQLGetDiagRec()** or **SQLGetDiagField()** CLI functions to determine whether diagnostic information is available.

- Use the standard set of SQLSTATE values, rather than the native error codes, to increase application portability.

- Build dependencies only on the subset of DB2 CLI SQLSTATEs that are defined by the X/Open CLI standard specification, and return any additional ones as information only. (Dependencies occur when the application makes logic-flow decisions based on specific SQLSTATEs).

- For maximum diagnostic information, return the text message along with the SQLSTATE value. (If applicable, the text message will also include the IBM-defined SQLSTATE.) You will also find it useful if the application prints out the name of the function that returned the error.

Evaluating SQLCA Return Codes

As a general rule, embedded SQL applications rely on the *SQL Communications Area* (SQLCA) data structure for information about the success or failure of an SQL statement's execution. Although CLI applications can retrieve much of the same information by evaluating the SQLSTATEs, they might still have a need to examine the SQLCA data structure. You can use the **SQLGetSQLCA()** CLI function call, if needed, to retrieve information about the last SQL statement executed. You should remember that the SQLCA structure will only contain meaningful information if the last SQL statement executed interacted with the database (i.e., if the last SQL statement executed was a **CONNECT**, **PREPARE**, **EXECUTE**, **FETCH**, or **DISCONNECT** SQL statement).

Creating Executable Applications

Once CLI source-code files have been written, the next step is to convert them into an executable DB2 database application program. This conversion process involves the following two steps:

1. Compile the source-code files to create object modules.
2. Link the object modules to create an executable program.

After an application source code file has been written, the file must be compiled by a high-level language compiler (such as Visual C++, Visual Basic, and so on). The high-level language compiler converts the source code file into an object module the linker uses to create the executable program. Once the source file has been compiled without errors, the resulting object module is used as input to the linker. The linker combines specified object modules and high-level language libraries to produce an executable application (provided no errors or unresolved external references occur). For most operating systems, this executable application can be either an *executable load module* (EXE), a *shared library*, or a *dynamic link library* (DLL). Figure 4–4 illustrates this source code file-to-executable application conversion process.

Running, Testing, and Debugging CLI Applications

Once your application program has been successfully compiled and linked, you can run the program and determine whether the program performs as expected. You should be able to run your CLI application program just like you would run any other application program on your particular operating system. If problems occur, you can use the following checklist to help test and debug your code:

■ When compiling and linking, specify the proper compiler and linker options so that the executable program produced can be used with a symbolic debugger (usually provided with the high-level language compiler).

■ Make full use of the **SQLGetDiagRec()** and/or **SQLGetDiagField()** API function calls. Display all diagnostic error messages and return codes generated whenever a CLI API function call fails.

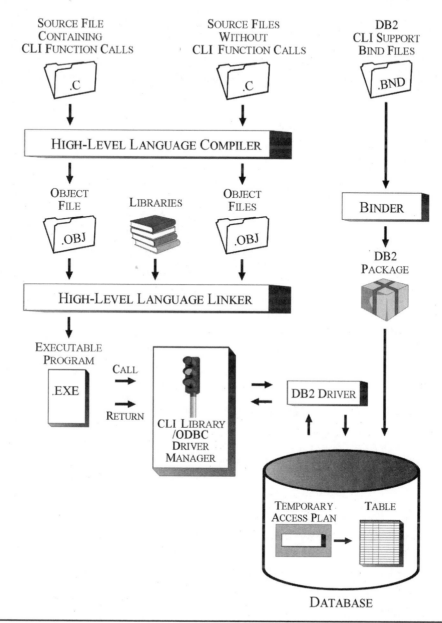

Figure 4–4 Process to convert CLI source-code files into executable DB2 application programs

SUMMARY

The goal of this chapter was to provide you with an overview of how DB2 CLI application source-code files are structured and to describe the processes involved in converting CLI application source-code files into executable database application programs. You should now understand how to use the IBM Interactive CLI application to prototype your CLI function call. You should also know that a CLI application source-code file is divided into the following three tasks:

- Initialization
- Transaction processing
- Termination

In addition, you should know that the transaction processing task is responsible for performing the following five steps:

1. Locating statement handles
2. Preparing and executing SQL statements
3. Processing the results
4. Committing or rolling back the transaction
5. Freeing all allocated statement handles

You should understand how to process errors with a common error-handling routine by evaluating CLI function call return codes, SQLSTATE values, and SQLCA values. You should also be familiar with the following steps for converting embedded SQL source-code files to executable database applications:

- Compiling
- Linking

5

Components that DB2 CLI Uses to Interact with Applications

DB2 CLI uses a set of special components to help applications communicate with one or more databases. This chapter is designed to introduce you to these major components, which can be found in almost all DB2 CLI applications. The first part of this chapter introduces the concept of handles and describes how they are used to access and/or update information about the environment, a connection to a database, an SQL statement, and a descriptor. This description is followed by a short discussion about environment, connection, and SQL statement handle states and state transitions. Next, the data buffers and length/indicator buffers that are used with many DB2 CLI functions are described. Finally, the C and SQL data types used by DB2 CLI are discussed, along with information about how one data type is converted to the other.

Handles

One of the first fundamental issues that CLI designers had to address was how to allow applications to access multiple data sources simultaneously, yet free them from having to allocate and manage global variables and/or data structures (such as the SQLCA and SQLDA data structures that are used with embedded SQL) for each data source used. Their solution was to use (with some modifications) the handle concept that was already being used by the Microsoft Windows operating system. In Windows, a *handle* is simply an application pointer variable that refers to a data object the operating system uses to store context information. In a Windows application, handles are used to access data structures for which only Windows knows the details. The same function is true with DB2 CLI: applications never look "inside" a handle, nor can they directly manipulate the data stored in the storage area to which the handle points (this concept is known as *information hiding*).

The handle concept also makes it easier for application developers to obtain and process error information when an DB2 CLI function call fails. Without handles, it would be difficult to return error information to applications. DB2 CLI would have to either return all error information as an API function return code value, or it would have to store error information in a local or global memory storage area that could only be accessed by the application. Either of these two approaches would add complexity to CLI application development, and this complexity would increase each time a new thread was used. The handle approach in a multithreaded environment always makes it clear to both the application and the CLI Library or the ODBC Driver Manager where context and error information should be stored. Additionally, when an error occurs, there is never a question about what the application is supposed to do—the application should pass the handle used in the API function that generated the error to the appropriate CLI error-handling function.

The context information kept in handles can also be used to expose additional features that are supported by a driver, such as synchronous cancel. *Synchronous cancel* allows an application to start executing an SQL statement on one thread and cancel its execution on another thread. Again, handles make this type of functionality possible, because the handle used to execute the SQL statement in one thread can be used in any other thread to cancel the statement. The handle lets the CLI Library or the ODBC Driver Manager know that both actions are to be performed for the same SQL statement.

DB2 CLI uses the following four types of handles:

- Environment handles
- Connection handles
- Statement handles
- Descriptor handles

The Environment Handle

An *environment handle* is a pointer to a data storage area that contains CLI specific information that is global in nature. This information includes the following:

- The current state of the environment
- The current value of each environment attribute
- The handle for each connection data storage area currently allocated within the environment
- The number of connections currently available in the environment and their current state ("Connected" or "Disconnected")
- Diagnostic information about the current environment

Every application program that intends to use CLI must begin by allocating an environment handle. Usually only one environment handle can be allocated per application, and that handle must be allocated before any other handles are allocated. All other handles (that is, all connection, statement, and descriptor handles for an application) are managed within the context of an environment handle.

In addition to being an application's global placeholder for all other handles and for context information, the environment handle is used in a limited number of CLI functions for the following purposes:

- To pass any errors occurring at the environment level (such as an attempt to free the environment handle while connections are still active, or an attempt to use an invalid environment handle during connection handle allocation) to the appropriate CLI error-handling function
- To serve as the context handle for the CLI function that enumerates the data sources that are currently installed (**SQLDataSources()**)
- To manage transactions when the **SQLEndTran()** function is used to commit or roll back all open transactions on all connections (rather than having an application commit or roll back outstanding transactions on each connection, the environment handle can be used to force the CLI Library or the ODBC Driver Manager to commit or roll back outstanding transactions on *all* connections)

The Connection Handle

A *connection handle* is a pointer to a data structure that contains information about a data source connection that is being managed by the CLI Library or by the ODBC Driver Manager. This information includes the following:

- The current state of the connection
- The current value of each connection attribute
- The handle for each SQL statement data storage area currently allocated within the connection
- The handle for each descriptor data storage area currently allocated within the connection
- Diagnostic information about the connection

When a connection handle is allocated, the CLI Library or the ODBC Driver Manager stores the handle inside the data storage area that the environment handle points to. Once a connection handle is allocated, the handle can be used to establish a connection to a data source. When a connection is made to a data source via a connection handle, the appropriate driver is loaded into memory, an array of pointers to the CLI API functions in that driver are stored in the connection handle, and the data source is made available to the application. At this point, the connection handle is said to be in an "Active" or a "Connected" state to distinguish the handle from a connection handle that is in an "Allocated" state. Thereafter, each time a DB2 CLI function is called with the connection handle specified as an argument, the CLI Library or the ODBC Driver Manager looks up the corresponding API function entry point in the array of function pointers stored in the connection handle and routes the call to the appropriate function in the driver.

In addition to storing connection information and establishing connections to data sources, connection handles are also used in a number of CLI functions for the following purposes:

- To terminate (break) a connection to a data source
- To pass any errors occurring at the connection level (such as the failure to load a driver, the failure to connect to the server across the network, a network communication error, an attempt to use a connection already in use, and so on) to the appropriate CLI error-handling function
- To set connection options such as time-outs, transaction isolation levels, and so on
- As the main transaction management handle. The context of a transaction is determined by the connection handle; that is, the set of all SQL statements that are associated with a connection handle constitutes the scope of a transaction.
- As an argument of the CLI informational functions that return information about a data source and/or a connection associated with a connection handle
- To return SQL strings to an application with all escape sequences and/or clauses translated to data source-specific syntax

The Statement Handle

A *statement handle* is a pointer to a data structure that contains information about a single SQL statement. This information includes the following:

- The current state of the SQL statement
- The current value of each SQL statement attribute
- The addresses of all application variables bound to the SQL statement's parameter markers
- The addresses of all application variables bound to columns in the SQL statement's result data set
- Diagnostic information about the SQL statement

The statement handle is the real workhorse of DB2 CLI. The statement handle is used to process all SQL statements contained in an application—both application-defined SQL statements and the SQL statements performed behind-the-scenes when a CLI data source catalog query function is called. Notably, statement handles are used in CLI function calls to bind parameter markers and result data set columns to application variables, to prepare and execute SQL statements, to retrieve metadata about result data sets, to retrieve (fetch) results from result data sets, and to retrieve diagnostic information.

Each SQL statement used in an application must have its own statement handle, and each statement handle used can only be associated with one connection handle. However, multiple statement handles can be associated with a single connection handle. When a CLI function is called with a statement handle specified as an argument, the CLI Library or the ODBC Driver Manager uses the connection handle stored within the statement handle to route the function call to the appropriate data source driver. The data source then uses the statement handle to obtain the information it needs to execute the SQL statement for the application—and to store result data sets created (if any) after the statement is executed.

The Descriptor Handle

A *descriptor handle* is a pointer to a data storage area that contains a collection of metadata that describes either the parameters of an SQL statement or the columns of a result data set, as seen by the application or data source.

Four types of descriptors are recognized by DB2 CLI:

■ *Application Parameter Descriptors* (APD)—Contain information about the application variables (buffers) bound to the parameter markers used in an SQL statement, such as their addresses, lengths, and C data types

■ *Implementation Parameter Descriptors* (IPD)—Contain information about the parameters used in an SQL statement, such as their SQL data types, lengths, and nullability

■ *Application Row Descriptors* (ARD)—Contain information about the application variables (buffers) bound to the columns in a result data set, such as their addresses, lengths, and C data types

■ *Implementation Row Descriptors* (IRD)—Contain information about the columns in a result data set, such as their SQL data types, lengths, and nullability

Four descriptor handles (one for each type of descriptor described) are automatically allocated when a statement handle is allocated. These descriptor handles remain associated with the statement handle that allocated them for the life of that handle.

DB2 CLI applications can explicitly allocate additional descriptor handles for a specific connection handle. Once allocated, these descriptor handles can be associated with one or more statement handles that are associated with the same connection handle to fulfill the role of an implicitly allocated APD or ARD descriptor.

Most CLI operations can be performed without the use of explicitly defined descriptor handles. However, explicitly defined descriptor handles can provide a convenient shortcut for some operations.

State Transitions

DB2 CLI defines discrete states for each environment, connection, and SQL statement handle. For example, an environment handle has three possible states:

- **Unallocated**—No environment handle is allocated.
- **Allocated**—An environment handle is allocated, but no connection handles are allocated.
- **Connection**—An environment handle and one or more connection handles are allocated.

A connection handle has seven possible states:

- **No Environment**—No environment handle or connection handle is allocated.
- **Unallocated**—An environment handle is allocated, but no connection handle is allocated.
- **Allocated**—An environment handle and a connection handle is allocated.
- **Need Data**—Connection function needs data
- **Connected**—Connected to a data source
- **Statement**—Connected to a data source, and a statement handle has been allocated
- **Transaction**—Connected to a data source, and a transaction is in progress

A statement handle has 13 states:

- **Unallocated**—No statement handle is allocated.
- **Allocated**—A statement handle is allocated.
- **No Results**—A statement has been prepared, and no result data set will be created.
- **Results**—A statement has been prepared, and a result data set will be created; however, the data set may be empty.
- **Executed**—A statement has been executed, and no result data set was created.
- **Opened**—A statement has been executed, and a result data set was created; however, the data set may be empty. The cursor has been opened and is positioned before the first row of data in the result data set.
- **SQLFetch**—The cursor has been positioned by `SQLFetch()` or `SQLFetchScroll()`.
- **SQLExtendedFetch**—The cursor has been positioned by `SQLExtendedFetch()`.
- **Need Data**—A function needs data, and `SQLParamData()` has not been called.
- **Must Put**—A function needs data, and `SQLPutData()` has not been called.
- **Can Put**—A function needs data, and `SQLPutData()` has been called.
- **Still Executing**—A statement is still executing. A statement is left in this state after a function that was executed asynchronously returns the value `SQL_`

STILL_EXECUTING. A statement handle is temporarily placed into this state while any function that uses a statement handle as an argument is executing.

- **Async Canceled**—Asynchronous execution has been canceled.

An environment, a connection, or a statement handle moves from one state to another whenever an application calls a CLI function with the handle specified as an argument. This movement is known as *state transition*. For example, allocating an environment handle with the CLI function **SQLAllocHandle()** moves the environment handle from the "Unallocated" state to the "Allocated" state. Freeing the environment handle with the CLI function **SQLFreeHandle()** moves the environment from the "Allocated" state back to the "Unallocated" state.

Some CLI functions do not affect states at all (for example, the functions that retrieve environment, connection, and statement attributes). Other CLI functions only affect the state of a single item (for example, the function that disconnects from a data source can change a connection handle from the "Connected" state to the "Allocated" state). Other CLI API functions, however, affect the state of more than one item (for example, the functions that allocate a connection handle, change both a connection handle from the "Unallocated" state to the "Allocated" state, and change the environment handle from the "Allocated" state to the "Connection" state).

Because CLI defines a limited number of legal state transitions for environment handles, connection handles, and statement handles, most CLI functions must be called in a certain order. For example, an application must call the CLI function that executes an SQL statement that generates a result data set before the application can call the CLI function that retrieves data from the result data set created. If an application calls a CLI function out of order, the function returns the following state transition error: SQLSTATE **HY**010 (function sequence error). Some state transitions are inherent in the design of CLI. For example, it is not possible to allocate a connection handle without first allocating an environment handle, because the CLI function that allocates a connection handle requires an environment handle as one of its arguments.

From the application's point of view, state transitions are generally straight-forward because well-written applications tend to call CLI functions in their proper order.

Buffers

A *buffer* is any portion of application memory (either stack or heap) that is used to pass data between an application and a data source (via a driver). *Input buffers* are used to pass data from the application to the data source, and *output buffers* are used to return data from the data source to the application.

NOTE: *If a CLI function returns SQL_ERROR, the contents of any output buffers that would have been filled by that function are undefined.*

To make DB2 CLI interoperable with various high-level programming languages, most buffers used have an indeterminate data type. The addresses of these buffers appear as arguments of type **SQLPOINTER** in most CLI API function references, and the buffers themselves generally come in pairs. One buffer in the pair is the actual data buffer, and the other is a length/indicator buffer. The data buffer in this pair is used to pass the data itself, while the length/indicator buffer is used to pass either the length of the data stored in the data buffer or a special predefined value that provides additional information about the data stored in the data buffer (for example, **SQL_NULL_DATA** is an indicator value that indicates the data is NULL). The length of the actual data in a data buffer is usually different from the length (or size) of the data buffer itself. Figure 5–1 shows the relationship between a data buffer and the length/indicator buffer.

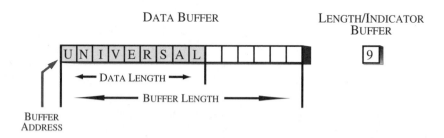

Figure 5–1   The relationship between a data buffer and its corresponding length/indicator buffer

NOTE: *The length of both the data buffer and the data it contains is measured in bytes, as opposed to characters. This distinction is unimportant for applications using ANSI strings, because bytes and characters are essentially the same size. This distinction becomes more important for applications using character systems in which bytes and characters are different sizes. An example of such a character system is the double-byte character system (DBCS) used throughout most of Asia.*

A length/indicator buffer must be provided any time the data buffer contains variable-length data, such as character or binary data. If a data buffer contains fixed-length data, such as an integer or a data structure, a length/indicator buffer is only needed if one or more special indicator values are to be passed to a CLI function; the length of the data in the data buffer is already known. In fact, if an application uses a length/indicator buffer with fixed-length data, the driver ignores any length values passed in that data buffer.

When a data buffer is used to represent a driver-defined descriptor record field, a diagnostic record field, or an environment, connection, or statement attribute, the application should inform the CLI Library or the ODBC Driver Manager about the nature of the data in the buffer. The application can complete this task by setting the length argument in any CLI function call that sets/retrieves field or attribute values as follows;

■ If the CLI function argument that the value for the field or attribute is (or is to be) stored in is a pointer to a character string, the length argument should contain either the length of the string or **SQL_NTS** (indicating that the string is NULL-terminated).

- If the CLI function argument that the value for the field or attribute is (or is to be) stored in is a pointer to a binary buffer, the length argument should contain the result of the **SQL_LEN_BINARY_ATTR(*length*)** macro.

- If the CLI function argument that the value for the field or attribute is (or is to be) stored in is a pointer to a value other than a character string or a binary string, the length argument should contain the value **SQL_IS_POINTER**.

- If the CLI function argument that the value for the field or attribute is (or is to be) stored in contains a fixed-length value, the length argument should contain either **SQL_IS_INTEGER, SQL_IS_UINTEGER, SQL_SMALLINT,** or **SQL_USMALLINT**.

Deferred Buffers

A *deferred buffer* is a buffer whose contents are used at some point after the buffer is specified in a CLI function call. For example, when a buffer is bound to a parameter marker in an SQL statement with a CLI function call, the data source driver saves information about the buffer itself—but the driver does not examine the buffer's contents. Later, when the application executes the SQL statement, the driver retrieves the information it saved about the buffer and uses that information to retrieve a value from the buffer and send the value to the data source. Thus, the input of data in the buffer is deferred.

Both input and output buffers can be deferred. Table 5–1 summarizes the common uses of deferred buffers and the CLI functions that specify and use them.

Table 5–1   Deferred Buffer Usage

Buffer Use	Type	Specified With	Used by
Sending data for input parameters	Deferred input	SQLBindParameter( )	SQLExecute( ) SQLExecDirect( )
Sending data to insert or update a row in a result data set	Deferred input	SQLBindCol( )	SQLSetPos( )
Returning data for output and input/ output parameters	Deferred output	SQLBindParameter( )	SQLExecute( ) SQLExecDirect( )
Returning data from a result data set	Deferred output	SQLBindCol( )	SQLFetch( ) SQLFetchScroll( ) SQLSetPos( )

Adapted from *Microsoft ODBC 3.0 Programmer's Reference, Volume 1, and SDK Guide*, page 59.

Allocating and Freeing Buffers

All buffers are allocated and freed by the application. Stack buffers are allocated when they are declared, and heap buffers are allocated by calling the appropriate high-level language memory allocation function. If a buffer is not going to be used as a deferred buffer, it only needs to exist for the duration of the call to the CLI function that references it. On the other hand, because deferred buffers are specified in one CLI function call and are used in another, they must exist from the time they are specified in the first CLI function call until they are either used or unspecified by another CLI function call. The same is true for deferred length/indicator buffers. An application programming error can occur if a deferred buffer is freed while the driver still expects the buffer to exist. Such errors are easily made if a deferred buffer is declared or allocated locally within an application-specific function. By design, the buffer is freed when application control leaves the function.

Describing Data Buffers

Data buffers are described to CLI functions by three pieces of information:

- Data Type—The C data type of the buffer
- Address—The physical memory address of the data buffer
- Length (in bytes)—The length or size, in bytes, of the data buffer

Often one, two, or even all three of these pieces of information about a buffer are passed to a data source/driver as CLI function arguments.

DATA BUFFER TYPE   The C data type of a buffer is automatically specified by an application written in C or C++ when the data type is declared, or when memory for the data type is allocated. In the case of generic memory—that is, memory pointed to by a pointer of type **void**—the C data type is provided when the memory is typecast by the application.

Regardless of how a buffer's C data type is specified, a driver discovers buffer data types in one of two ways:

- Buffer Data Type Arguments—Some CLI functions that have an argument for a data buffer also have an argument for an associated C data type. This situation is usually the case for buffers used to transfer parameter marker and result data set values between an application and a data source.

- Predefined Data Types—Some CLI functions automatically assume that a data buffer is a specific C data type. This situation is usually the case for buffers used to retrieve options or attributes from a data source. In this case, the application is responsible for declaring or allocating a buffer of the appropriate C data type.

DATA BUFFER ADDRESS   An address is automatically assigned to a buffer when the address is declared or when memory for the address is allocated (provided that the memory allocation was successful). CLI functions that work with buffers often have an argument that is used to specify the buffer's address. Unless it is strictly prohibited by the CLI function, a buffer's address can be a NULL pointer value. If a NULL pointer buffer address is specified for an input argument, the driver ignores the information stored in the buffer. If a NULL pointer buffer address is specified for an output argument, the driver does not return a value to that buffer. In both cases, the driver ignores any corresponding C data type and length/indicator arguments.

DATA BUFFER LENGTH The length of a buffer is specified when it is declared or when memory for the buffer is allocated (in applications written in C or C++). CLI functions that work with buffers often have an argument that is used to specify the buffer's length in bytes. Data buffer lengths are only required for output buffers. The driver uses them to avoid writing past the end of the buffer. However, the driver only checks a data buffer's length when it is writing variable-length data, such as character or binary data, to the buffer. If the driver is writing fixed-length data such as integer or data structure data to the buffer, it ignores the value in the data buffer length argument and assumes that the buffer is large enough to hold the data. Therefore, when working with fixed-length data, it is important for an application to declare/allocate a buffer that is large enough.

A driver always returns the number of bytes (not the number of characters) written to the buffer in the buffer length argument if the buffer length argument is associated with an output buffer argument that receives a string value. If the data buffer is not large enough to hold the string value returned, the string is truncated and the length returned in the buffer length argument is the maximum byte length needed to store the complete string value. Fixed-length data is never truncated.

Using Length/Indicator Buffers

Earlier in this text, I mentioned that the length/indicator buffer is used to pass either the byte length of the data in the data buffer or a special indicator value to the data source. Depending on the CLI function used, a length/indicator buffer is defined to be either an **SQLINTEGER** or an **SQLSMALLINT** data type. Because it is a fixed-length buffer, only one argument is needed to describe the buffer. If the data buffer to which the length/indicator buffer refers is a non-deferred input buffer, this argument contains the byte length of the data itself or an indicator value. If the data buffer to which the length/indicator buffer refers is a deferred input buffer, a non-deferred output buffer, or an output buffer, this argument contains the address of the length/indicator buffer.

Unless it is specifically prohibited, the value specified in a length/indicator buffer CLI function argument can be 0 (if a non-deferred input buffer is used) or a NULL pointer (if a output or deferred input buffer is used). If either value is specified for an input buffer, the byte length of the data is ignored. If either value is specified for an output buffer, neither the byte length of the data written to the buffer nor an indicator value are returned.

The following length/indicator values are valid:

- 0—Ignore (input)/do not return (output) the byte length of the data in the corresponding data buffer.

■ *n*, where *n* > 0—The size, in bytes, of the data in the corresponding data buffer

■ `SQL_NTS`—A NULL-terminated string is in the corresponding data buffer. This method is convenient for C/C++ programmers to pass strings without having to calculate their byte length. This value is legal only when the data buffer is an input buffer.

■ `SQL_NULL_DATA`—The data in the corresponding data buffer is a NULL data value and should be ignored. This value is only legal for SQL data sent to or retrieved from the data source.

■ `SQL_DATA_AT_EXEC`—The corresponding data buffer does not contain any data. Instead, the data is sent by calling the `SQLPutData()` CLI function after an SQL statement is executed, or when the `SQLSetPos()` CLI function is called. This value is legal only for SQL data sent to the data source.

■ Result of the `SQL_LEN_DATA_AT_EXEC(length)` macro—Similar to `SQL_DATA_AT_EXEC`

■ `SQL_NO_TOTAL`—The driver cannot determine the number of bytes of long data still available to be returned in the corresponding output buffer. This value is only legal for SQL data retrieved from the data source.

■ `SQL_DEFAULT_PARAM`—A stored procedure is to use the default value for a parameter, instead of the value in the corresponding data buffer.

■ `SQL_COLUMN_IGNORE`—The `SQLSetPos()` CLI function is to ignore the value in the corresponding data buffer. When updating a row of data by a call to this function, the column value is not changed. When inserting a new row of data by a call to this function, the column value is set to its default value or, if the column does not have a default, to NULL.

Data Length, Buffer Length, and Truncation

It is important to realize that the data length value stored in a length/indicator buffer is the byte length of the data as it is (or as it will be) stored in the corresponding data buffer, not as it is (or as it will be) stored in the data source. This distinction is important, often because data stored as one data type in a data buffer is stored as a different data type in the data source. Thus, for data being sent to the data source, the byte length specifies the size of the data before it is converted to the data source's data type. For data being returned from the data source, the byte length value specifies the size of the data after it has been converted to the data buffer's data type—and before any truncation is done.

For fixed-length data such as an integer or a data structure, the byte length of the data is always the size of the data type of the buffer. For variable-length data such as character or binary data, it is important to recognize that the byte length of the data is separate and is often different from the byte length of the buffer. For example, suppose an application allocates 20 bytes for a character data buffer. Now, suppose the data source has 10 bytes of character data to return. The data source returns those 10 bytes in the data buffer and sets the length/indicator buffer to 10. The byte length of the data is 10, and the byte length of the buffer is 20. Now, suppose the data source has 30 bytes of character data to return. The data source truncates the data to 20 bytes, returns those 20 bytes in the data buffer, sets the length/indicator buffer, and returns **SQL_SUCCESS_ WITH_INFO**.

Whenever data is truncated, a diagnostic record containing detailed information about the truncation is created. Because it takes time to create and process this diagnostic record, data truncation can reduce overall performance. In most cases, data truncation can be avoided simply by allocating data buffers that are large enough; although, this option may not always be possible—especially when working with long data. When data truncation occurs, the application can sometimes allocate a larger buffer and retrieve (fetch) the data again; however, this approach will not work in all cases and should usually be avoided.

A Word about Character Data and C/C++ Strings

If an application terminates strings with the NULL character, as is the standard practice in C and C++, then the length/indicator buffer can contain either the length (in bytes) of the string (excluding the NULL-terminator) or the value **SQL_NTS** (to indicate that the data is a NULL-terminated string). The length/indicator buffer can also contain the value **0** to specify a zero-length string, which is different from a NULL value. When NULL-terminated strings are used to hold character data, the NULL-termination character is not considered to be part of the data. Therefore, the character is not counted as part of the string's byte length. When the value **SQL_NTS** is used, the driver attempts to determine the length of the string by locating the position of the NULL-termination character.

When character data is returned from a data source to an application, the data is always NULL-terminated. This practice allows application developers to choose whether they want to handle character data as strings or as character arrays. If an output buffer is not large enough to hold all the character data returned, the data source truncates the data to the byte length of the buffer minus the number of bytes needed for the NULL-termination character (usually 1 byte), NULL-terminates the truncated data, and stores the data in the appropriate data buffer. This means that applications must take into account the space needed for the NULL-termination character when allocating memory for output buffers that receive character data from a data source. For example, a 51-byte output buffer is needed to hold 50 bytes of character data.

Special care must be taken by both the application and the data source when sending or receiving long character data in parts. In these situations, if the data is passed as a series of NULL-terminated strings, the NULL-termination characters on all strings except the last one must be stripped off before the data can be reassembled.

 NOTE: *Because character data can be stored in a non-NULL-terminated array with its byte length stored in a length/indicator buffer, it is possible to embed NULL characters within character data. However, the behavior of CLI functions when this type of data is used is undefined. Applications should always treat character data that contains embedded NULL characters as binary data.*

Data Types

When the X/Open CLI specification was originally designed, a set of data types had to be defined so that no information would be lost between applications and data sources. To provide interoperability, these data types had to be defined in such a way that data source-specific information would not have to be encoded in application logic. Specifically, X/Open CLI had to provide a precise definition of the type of data being placed into application memory buffers; otherwise, the data would not have any meaning.

Other characteristics of the data, however, did not have to be defined so precisely. For example, the maximum length of character data types varies widely, but there is no reason to enforce a length limit in CLI as long as an application can determine the limits from the data source. However, this means that if an application copies data from one data source to another, the application cannot assume that the length limits of the two data sources are the same.

In order to build robustness and reliability into CLI, the SQL-92 standard was carefully reviewed along with the top ten (in terms of market share) database products, and a list of data types, including type names, length limits, and all behavioral characteristics was compiled. Then, using this list, a second list of C data types to which every data type on the first list could be mapped without losing information was created. Ultimately, this creation led to the development of two sets of data types for CLI: SQL data types, which are used in the data source, and C data types, which are used in application programs. DB2 CLI supports this SQL type/C type distinction by providing a set of SQL data type names that begin with the prefix **SQL_** and a similar set of C data type names that begin with the prefix **SQL_C_**.

SQL Data Type Identifiers

DB2 CLI defines type identifiers for and describes the general characteristics of several SQL data types that might be mapped to a corresponding data type within a DB2 database.

For example, **SQL_CHAR** is the CLI SQL type identifier for a character column with a fixed length: typically between one and 254 characters. These characteristics correspond to the **CHAR** data type found in DB2 databases. Thus, when an application discovers that the CLI SQL type identifier for a column is **SQL_CHAR**, the application can assume it is dealing with a column that has a **CHAR** data type. This is also the case when working with other drivers. However, the byte length of the column should always be checked. The application should not assume that its length is between one and 254 characters.

C Data Type Identifiers

DB2 CLI also defines type identifiers for the C data types that might be mapped to a corresponding data type in a DB2 database. Among other things, these type identifiers are used to describe the application variables and/or buffers that are bound to SQL statement parameter markers and result data set columns. For example, suppose an application wants to retrieve data from a result data set column in character format. First, the application declares a variable with the **SQLCHAR** * data type, then it binds this variable to the result data set column with a C data type identifier of **SQL_C_CHAR**.

DB2 CLI also defines a default C data type mapping for each SQL data type identifier. For example, a 2-byte **INTEGER** data type in a DB2 database is, by default, mapped to a 2-byte integer in an application. To use the default mapping, an application simply specifies **SQL_C_DEFAULT** as the C data type identifier.

Data Type Conversions

Data can be converted from one data type to another at any of the following times:

- When data is transferred from one application variable to another (C to C)
- When data in an application variable is sent to an SQL statement parameter (C to SQL)
- When data in a result data set column is returned in an application variable (SQL to C)
- When data is transferred from one data source column to another (SQL to SQL)

When an application binds a variable to a parameter marker in an SQL statement or to a column in a result data set, the application implicitly specifies a data type conversion between an SQL data type and the C data type of the application variable. For example, suppose a column in a result data set contains integer data. If the application binds an integer variable to the column, the application implicitly specifies that no conversion is necessary. If, however, the application binds a character variable to the column, the application implicitly specifies that the data is to be converted from an integer to a character.

DB2 CLI contains an internal set of rules that define how data is converted between each SQL and C data type. Basically, all reasonable conversions such as character to integer and integer to float are supported. Ill-defined conversions, such as float to date, are not.

In addition, ODBC defines a scalar function that CLI can take advantage of for converting data from one SQL data type to another. This scalar function (**CONVERT()**) is mapped by the driver to any underlying scalar function(s) that are designed to perform conversions in the data source.

SUMMARY

A handle is simply an application pointer variable that refers to a data object in which DB2 CLI can store context information. DB2 CLI uses four types of handles:

- Environment handles
- Connection handles

■ Statement handles

■ Descriptor handles

An environment handle is a pointer to a data storage area containing CLI-specific information that is global in nature. Every application program using CLI must begin by allocating an environment handle, and only one environment handle can be allocated per application. An environment handle must be allocated before any other handle is allocated.

A connection handle is a pointer to a data structure containing information about a data source connection being managed by the CLI Library or by the ODBC Driver Manager.

A statement handle is a pointer to a data structure containing information about a single SQL statement. The statement handle is the real workhorse of DB2 CLI and is used to process all SQL statements contained in an application. Each SQL statement must have its own statement handle, and each statement handle used can only be associated with one connection handle.

A descriptor handle is a pointer to a data storage area containing a collection of metadata describing either the parameters of an SQL statement or the columns of a result data set, as seen by the application or driver.

DB2 CLI recognizes four types of descriptors:

■ Application Parameter Descriptor (APD)

■ Implementation Parameter Descriptor (IPD)

■ Application Row Descriptor (ARD)

■ Implementation Row Descriptor (IRD)

One descriptor handle is automatically allocated for each type of descriptor described when a statement handle is allocated. In addition to these descriptor handles, DB2 CLI applications can explicitly allocate additional application descriptor handles.

DB2 CLI defines three discrete states for each environment handle, seven discrete states for each connection handle, and thirteen discrete states for each SQL statement handle. An environment, connection, or statement handle moves from one state to another when an application calls CLI functions with a handle as an argument. This movement is known as *state transition*.

A buffer is any portion of application memory (either stack or heap) that is used to pass data between an application and a data source. Input buffers are used to pass data from the application to the data source, and output buffers are used to return data from the data source to the application. A deferred buffer is a buffer whose contents are used at some point after the buffer is specified in a CLI function call. All buffers are allocated and are freed by the application.

Data buffers are described to CLI functions by three pieces of information:

■ The C data type of the buffer

■ The physical memory address of the buffer

■ The length or size, in bytes, of the buffer

Length/indicator buffers are often used to pass either the byte length of the data in a data buffer or a special indicator to the data source. The following are valid length/indicator values:

- 0
- n, where $n > 0$
- `SQL_NTS`
- `SQL_NULL_DATA`
- `SQL_DATA_AT_EXEC`
- Result of the `SQL_LEN_DATA_AT_EXEC(length)` macro
- `SQL_NO_TOTAL`
- `SQL_DEFAULT_PARAM`
- `SQL_COLUMN_IGNORE`

Two sets of data types are used by DB2 CLI: SQL data types and C data types. CLI defines type identifiers for and describes the general characteristics of the SQL data types that might be mapped to a corresponding data type in a DB2 database. DB2 CLI also defines type identifiers for the C data types that might be mapped to a corresponding data type in a DB2 database. Among other things, these type identifiers are used to describe the application variables/buffers that are bound to SQL statement parameters and result data set columns.

Data can be converted from one data type to another at any of the following times:

- When data is transferred from one application variable to another (C to C)
- When data in an application variable is sent to an SQL statement parameter (C to SQL)
- When data in a result data set column is returned in an application variable (SQL to C)
- When data is transferred from one data source column to another (SQL to SQL)

SQL Statements and DB2 CLI

DB2 CLI applications perform almost all data retrieval and manipulation by submitting SQL statements to a data source for processing. This chapter is designed to introduce you to some of the SQL syntax and grammar that is recognized by DB2 CLI. The first part of this chapter describes the basic SQL statements that are used for data manipulation and data definition, along with the special clauses and predicates that can be used with them. This is followed by a close look at DB2-specific SQL statements and ODBC escape sequences. Next, the various ways SQL statements can be constructed in a DB2 CLI application are described. Finally, techniques that can be used to construct interoperable SQL statements are discussed.

This chapter is not designed to teach you how to write complex and clever SQL statements. Instead, the chapter is designed to present a basic overview of the SQL statements typically used in a DB2 CLI application.

Types of SQL Statements

Because SQL's primary function is to support the definition, manipulation, and control of data in a relational database, most SQL statements fall under one of the following classifications:

- Data Manipulation Language (DML) statements
- Data Definition Language (DDL) statements
- Data Control statements

Data Manipulation Language (DML) statements are used to retrieve data from, add data to, and otherwise manipulate data in a relational database. *Data Definition Language* (DDL) statements are used to define the data objects (that is, tables, views, indexes, and so on) that make up a relational database. *Data control* statements control the execution of DML and DDL SQL statements to ensure that data stored in a relational database remains consistent and secure in a multi-user environment. Of these three, data manipulation language statements are used the most in CLI applications, followed by data definition language statements.

Data Manipulation Language (DML) Statements

Four basic SQL statements can be used for data manipulation in a CLI application:

- The **SELECT** statement
- The **INSERT** statement
- The **UPDATE** statement
- The **DELETE** statement

THE SELECT SQL STATEMENT AND ITS CLAUSES   Eventually, almost every database application needs to retrieve specific data from the database with which it is interacting. In both embedded SQL and CLI applications, the **SELECT** SQL statement is used to perform all data retrieval operations. When a **SELECT** statement is sent to a DB2 database for processing, the DB2 Database Manager gathers or *selects* the data that meet the precise specifications defined by the **SELECT** statement and returns that data to the application.

In an embedded SQL application, data retrieved by a **SELECT** statement can be moved directly into a result data set (which is then accessed by a cursor that the application defines) or into one or more application host variables. However, in a CLI application, data retrieved by a **SELECT** statement is not actually moved directly into the application. Instead, data is moved into a special storage buffer, and other CLI API functions are responsible for moving the data from the storage buffer to the application.

Because the **SELECT** statement is the primary SQL statement used to retrieve data, it can be the most complex and the most complicated SQL statement used. Six different clauses can be used with a **SELECT** statement, and each of these clauses has its own set of predicates. Although some commercial implementations of SQL may support other SQL statement clauses, only the following **SELECT** statement clauses are recognized by DB2 CLI:

- FROM
- WHERE
- GROUP BY
- HAVING
- UNION
- ORDER BY

THE FROM CLAUSE   The **FROM** clause is used in conjunction with a table reference list to tell the database which table(s) from which to retrieve data. The following line shows the syntax for the simplest form of a **SELECT** SQL statement, which by design must always contain a **FROM** clause:

```
SELECT [item_list] FROM [table_list]
```

Column names (specified alone or with an alias), literals, expressions, ODBC scalar functions, or DB2-specific functions can be included in the *item_list*. The *table_list* can contain table names, table names with correlation names (that is, user-created aliases to be used as a more meaningful qualifier to column names elsewhere in the query or in a subquery), or an outer join specification that specifies the table names and condition to use for the outer join.

OUTER JOINS   The basic idea behind an outer join is as follows: Suppose Table A and Table B are joined by an ordinary (inner) join. Any row in either Table A or Table B that does not match a row in the other table (under the rules of the join condition) is left out of the result data set. By contrast, if Table A and Table B are joined by an outer join, any row in either Table A or Table B not containing a matching row in the other table is included in the result data set (exactly once). Columns in that row that would have contained matching values from the other table are empty. Thus, an outer join adds non-matching rows to a result data set, where an inner join would exclude them. A *left* outer join of Table A with Table B preserves non-matching rows from Table A; a *right* outer join of Table A with Table B preserves non-matching rows from Table B; and a *full* outer join preserves non-matching rows from both Table A and Table B.

The following line shows the syntax for the simplest form of a **SELECT** SQL statement using an outer join:

```
SELECT [item_list] FROM {oj [table_reference_1] [LEFT | RIGHT | FULL]
        OUTER JOIN [table_reference_2 | outer_join] ON [join_condition] }
```

NOTE: *{ oj } is the ODBC escape sequence for outer joins. Escape sequences are discussed later in this chapter.*

THE WHERE CLAUSE The **WHERE** clause is used to tell the database how to search one or more tables for specific data. The **WHERE** clause is always followed by a search condition containing one or more predicates that define how the data source is to choose the information to return in the result data set produced. Six types of **WHERE** clause predicates are supported by DB2 CLI:

- Relational Predicates (Comparisons)
- **BETWEEN**
- **LIKE**
- **IN**
- **EXISTS**
- **NULL**

Relational Predicates The relational predicates (otherwise known as comparisons) are the operators that can be used to define a comparison relationship between two values. The following comparison operators are recognized by CLI:

- < (less than)
- > (greater than)
- <= (less than or equal to)
- >= (greater than or equal to)
- = (equal to)
- <> (not equal to)

Relational predicates are used to include or exclude rows from the final result data set produced. Therefore, they are typically used to specify a condition in which the value of a column is less than, greater than, equal to, or not equal to a specified literal value. For example, the SQL statement

```
SELECT LastName FROM Employees WHERE Salary > 50000
```

produces a result data set containing the last name of all employees whose salary is greater than $50,000.

The application has the responsibility to ensure that the data type of the comparison column and the data type of the literal (or other value being checked) are compatible. If necessary, scalar functions can be embedded in the **SELECT** statement to achieve this result.

The BETWEEN Predicate The **BETWEEN** predicate is used to define a comparison relationship in which a value is checked, to see whether the value falls within a range of values. For example, the SQL statement

```
SELECT LastName FROM Employees WHERE EmpID BETWEEN 100 AND 120
```

produces a result data set containing the last name of all employees whose employee number is greater than or equal to 100 and is less than or equal to 120.

If the **NOT** negation operator is applied to the **BETWEEN** predicate, a value is checked to see whether or not it falls outside a range of values. For example, the SQL statement

```
SELECT LastName FROM Employees WHERE EmpID NOT BETWEEN 100 AND 120
```

produces a result data set containing the last name of all employees whose employee number is less than 100 or greater than 120.

The LIKE Predicate   The **LIKE** predicate is used to define a comparison relationship in which a character value is checked, to see whether or not it contains a prescribed pattern. The prescribed pattern is any arbitrary character string. Characters in the pattern string are interpreted as follows:

■ The underscore character (_) is treated as a wild card that stands for any single character.

■ The percent character (%) is treated as a wild card that stands for any sequence of characters.

■ All other characters are treated as regular characters (that is, they stand for themselves).

For example, the SQL statement

```
SELECT LastName, FirstName FROM Employees WHERE LastName LIKE "La%"
```

produces a result data set containing the last name and first name of all employees whose last name begins with the letters "La" (for example, Larson, Layton, Lawson, and so on).

When using wild card characters, care must be taken to ensure that they are placed in the appropriate location in the pattern string. Note that in the preceding example, only records for employees whose last name begins with the characters "La" would be returned. If the pattern specified had been "%La%", records for employees whose last name contains the characters "La" (anywhere in the name) would have been returned.

Likewise, you must also be careful about using uppercase and lowercase letters in pattern strings. If the data source processing the **SELECT** statement is configured to sort data in a case-sensitive manner, the characters used in a pattern string must match the case used to store the data in the column being searched.

*NOTE: Although the **LIKE** predicate can be an appealingly easy method to use to search for needed data, it should be used with caution. In most relational database management systems, processing a **LIKE** predicate is the slowest type of operation that can be performed, and this action can be extremely resource-intensive. For this reason, **LIKE** predicates should only be used when there is no other way to locate the data needed.*

The IN Predicate   The **IN** predicate is used to define a comparison relationship in which a value is checked to see whether it matches a value in a finite list of values. **IN** predicates come in two different formats: one simple and the other quite complex.

In its simplest form, the **IN** predicate can compare a value against a finite set of literal values. For example, the SQL statement

```
SELECT LastName FROM Customers WHERE State IN ("CA", "NY", "IL")
```

produces a result data set containing the last name of all customers living in California, New York, and Illinois.

In its more complex form, the **IN** predicate can compare a value against a finite set of values generated by a subquery. For example, the SQL statement

```
SELECT CustID FROM Customers WHERE State IN (SELECT State FROM Regions
    WHERE RegionID = 1)
```

produces a result data set containing the customer ID of all customers living in any state considered part of Region 1. In this example, the subquery **SELECT State FROM Regions WHERE RegionID = 1** produces a list of all states found in the territory the company has identified as "Region 1." Then the outer or main query checks each state value in the customers table to see if it exists in the set of state values returned from the subquery.

The EXISTS Predicate   The **EXISTS** predicate is used to determine whether a particular row of data exists in á table. The **EXISTS** predicate is always followed by a subquery; therefore, it returns a TRUE or FALSE value indicating whether a particular row of data is found in the result data set generated by the subquery. For example, the SQL statement

```
SELECT CompanyName FROM Suppliers WHERE EXISTS (SELECT * FROM
    AcountsPayable WHERE AmtDue > 10000 AND AcountsPayable.CustID =
    Suppliers.CustID)
```

produces a result data set containing the name of all supplier companies owed $10,000 or more.

EXISTS predicates are often ANDed with other conditions to determine final row selection.

The NULL Predicate   The **NULL** predicate is used to determine whether a particular column in a row of data contains a value. For example, the SQL statement

```
SELECT EmpID FROM Employees WHERE MiddleInitial IS NULL
```

produces a result data set containing the employee IDs of all employees whose record does not contain a middle initial (as part of their name).

NOTE: NULL *and zero (0) or blank (" ") are not the same.* NULL *is a special marker used to represent missing information. On the other hand, zero or blank (empty string) are actual values that can be placed in a column to indicate a specific value (or lack thereof).*

Some data sources do not recognize **NULL** *values, while others allow the user to decide whether each individual column in a table supports* **NULL** *values. Before writing SQL statements that check for* **NULL** *values, make sure the data source supports them and that the NULL value is valid for the column(s) specified.*

THE GROUP BY CLAUSE The **GROUP BY** clause is used to organize the rows of data in a result data set by the values contained in the column(s) specified. The **GROUP BY** clause is also used to specify which column to use for control breaks when using aggregate functions such as **SUM()** and **AVG()**. For example, the SQL statement

```
SELECT DeptName, SUM(SalesAmt) FROM Departments D, SalesHistory S WHERE
        D.DeptID = S.DeptID GROUP BY DeptName
```

produces a result data set containing one row for each department with rows in the sales history table. Each row in the result data set produced contains the department name and the total sales amount for that department.

A common mistake often made with this type of query is the addition of other non-aggregate columns to the **GROUP BY** clause. Because grouping is performed by combining all the non-aggregate columns together into a single, concatenated key and breaking whenever that key value changes, extraneous columns can cause unexpected breaks.

NOTE: *Some data sources do not allow non-aggregate columns to be specified in the* **GROUP BY** *clause.*

THE HAVING CLAUSE The **HAVING** clause is used to apply further selection criteria to columns referenced in a **GROUP BY** clause. The **HAVING** clause uses the same syntax as the **WHERE** clause, except that it refers to grouped data, rather than raw data. Like the **WHERE** clause, the **HAVING** clause is commonly used to tell the database how to search one or more tables for specific data. For example, if a **HAVING** clause were added to the previous example as follows,

```
SELECT DeptName, SUM(SalesAmt) FROM Departments D, SalesHistory S WHERE
        D.DeptID = S.DeptID GROUP BY DeptName HAVING SUM(SalesAmt) >
        1000000
```

the result data set produced would contain one row for each department, with rows in the sales history table whose total sales amount exceeds one million dollars.

THE UNION CLAUSE The **UNION** clause is used to combine two separate and individual result data sets to produce one single result data set. For two result data sets to be combined with a **UNION** clause, each must have the same number of columns. Each of those columns also must have the same data types assigned to them.

For example, suppose a company keeps employee information in a special table that is archived at the end of each year. Just before the table is archived, a new table is created, and the records for all employees still employed by the company are copied to the table. Throughout the year, as new employees are hired, they are added to the new table. To obtain a list of all employees employed by the company in 1996 and 1997, each archived table would have to be queried, and the results would have to be combined. This operation could be performed by using the **UNION** clause in an SQL statement. For example:

```
SELECT LastName, EmpID FROM Employees96 UNION SELECT LastName, EmpID
     FROM Employees97
```

When executed, this SQL statement produces a result data set containing the last name and the employee ID of all employees that worked for the company in 1996 and 1997.

By default, when two result data sets are combined, all duplicate rows are removed. However, if the keyword **ALL** follows the **UNION** clause (for example: **UNION ALL**), all rows of data in each result data set (including duplicates) are copied to the combined result data.

THE ORDER BY CLAUSE   The **ORDER BY** clause is used to sort and order the rows of data in a result data set by the values contained in the column(s) specified. Multiple columns can be used for ordering, and each column used can be ordered in either ascending or descending order. If the keyword **ASC** follows the column name, ascending order is used; if the keyword **DESC** follows the column name, descending order is used. When more than one column is specified for the **ORDER BY** clause, the result data set produced is sorted by the first column specified (the primary sort), then the sorted data is sorted again by the next column specified, and so on. For example, the SQL statement

```
SELECT LastName, FirstName, DeptID FROM Employees ORDER BY DeptID ASC,
     LastName ASC
```

produces a result data set containing employee last names, first names, and department IDs ordered by department ID and employee last name (the department IDs would be in ascending order, and the employee last names associated with each department would be in ascending alphabetical order).

If a column (in the result data set) to be sorted is a summary column or a result column that cannot be specified by name, an integer value corresponding to the column number can be used in place of the column name. When integer values are used, the first or leftmost column in the result data set is treated as column 1, the next is column 2, and so on. Although integer values are primarily used in the **ORDER BY** clause to specify columns that cannot be specified by name, they can be used in place of almost any column name. For example, the previous SQL statement could also have been coded as:

```
SELECT LastName, FirstName, DeptID FROM Employees ORDER BY 3 ASC, 1 ASC
```

THE INSERT STATEMENT   In some cases, an application may need to add specific data to the database with which it is interacting. In both embedded SQL and DB2 CLI applications, the **INSERT** SQL statement is used to add one or more rows of data to a data source. The **INSERT** statement is easier to use than the **SELECT** statement, because it does not have as many optional clauses and predicates.

The following line shows the syntax for the simplest form of an **INSERT** SQL statement:

```
INSERT INTO [table_name] < ( [columns_list] ) > VALUES ( [values_list] )
```

If values are provided for all columns in the table (in *values_list*), column names do not have to be provided (in *columns_list*). However, if the number of values in the *values_ list* does not match the number of columns in the table, or if values in the *values_list* are to be placed in specific columns in the table, column names must be explicitly stated (in the *columns_list*). Depending on how a table was defined, NULL or some predefined default value may be inserted into columns for which no corresponding value is provided.

Literal values for columns can be hard-coded directly into an **INSERT** statement, or they can be placed in variables that are to be populated at application run time. The **INSERT** statement expects values to be provided at run time if dynamic parameter markers (question marks) are coded into the **VALUES** clause in place of literal values. The following line is an example of such an **INSERT** statement:

```
INSERT INTO Employees VALUES (?, ?, ?, ?, ?)
```

The **INSERT** statement can also contain a subselect in place of literal values in the **VALUES** clause. This format of the **INSERT** statement creates a type of "cut and paste" action in which values are retrieved from one table and are inserted into another.

THE UPDATE STATEMENT   Sometimes, an application may need to change data that already exists in the database with which it is interacting. In both embedded SQL and DB2 CLI applications, the **UPDATE** SQL statement is used to change specific data values in a database. An **UPDATE** statement can change the value of one, many, or all the columns in a row of data.

Like the **INSERT** statement, the **UPDATE** statement is easier to use than the **SELECT** statement—even though the **UPDATE** statement optionally uses the **WHERE** clause and its predicates.

The following line shows the syntax for the simplest form of an **UPDATE** SQL statement:

```
UPDATE [table_name] SET [column] = [value] <WHERE [where_condition] >
```

In DB2 CLI, the **UPDATE** statement must always contain a **WHERE** clause, unless it is a positioned **UPDATE** statement.

THE DELETE STATEMENT   Occasionally, an application may need to remove existing data from the database with which it is interacting. In both embedded SQL and DB2 CLI applications, the **DELETE** SQL statement is used to remove one or more rows of data from a database. The following line shows the syntax for the simplest form of a **DELETE** SQL statement:

```
DELETE FROM [table_name] <WHERE [where_condition] >
```

Omitting the **WHERE** clause in a **DELETE** statement causes the delete operation to be applied to all rows in the specified table. Therefore, it is important to always provide a **WHERE** clause with a **DELETE** statement, unless you explicitly want to discard all data stored in a table.

Data Definition Language (DDL) Statements

In addition to the data manipulation language statements just described, DB2 CLI also supports several data definition language statements.

Although some of these statements are almost self-explanatory, others can be quite complex. For this reason, syntax is not provided for data definition language statements, and they are not discussed in detail.

DB2 Universal Database SQL Statements Supported By CLI

Usually, any SQL statement that can be dynamically prepared in embedded SQL can be used with DB2 CLI. However, there are some exceptions to this rule when working with DB2 databases. In some cases, specific DB2 CLI functions must be called in place of an SQL statement, and in other cases, some statements that can only be statically prepared in embedded SQL can be dynamically executed with DB2 CLI. Table 6–1 lists the SQL statements supported by DB2 Universal Database, Version 5.2 that can be issued with DB2 CLI.

Table 6–1   DB2 Universal Database SQL statements that are supported by CLI

SQL Statement	Description
ALTER BUFFERPOOL	Changes the definition of an existing buffer pool
ALTER NODEGROUP	Changes the definition of an existing nodegroup
ALTER TABLE	Changes the definition of an existing table
ALTER TABLESPACE	Changes the definition of a *Database-Managed* (DMS) table space
CALL	Invokes a stored procedure
COMMENT ON	Adds or replaces the comment (in the system catalog tables) that describes an object
Compound SQL (BEGIN COMPOUND ... END COMPOUND)	Combines one or more SQL sub-statements into an executable block that is treated as a single SQL statement. BEGIN COMPOUND and END COMPOUND define the beginning and end of a compound SQL statement block.
CREATE ALIAS	Defines and creates an alias for a table, view, or another alias
CREATE BUFFERPOOL	Defines and creates a new buffer pool
CREATE DISTINCT TYPE	Defines and creates a distinct user-defined data type

Table 6–1   *DB2 Universal Database SQL statements that are supported by CLI*   (Continued)

SQL Statement	Description
CREATE EVENT MONITOR	Defines and creates a new event monitor (identifies events in the database to monitor)
CREATE FUNCTION	Registers an external, user-defined table or scalar function
CREATE INDEX	Defines and creates an index for a table
CREATE NODEGROUP	Defines and creates a nodegroup
CREATE PROCEDURE	Registers a user-defined stored procedure
CREATE SCHEMA	Defines and creates a schema
CREATE TABLE	Defines and creates a table
CREATE TABLESPACE	Defines and creates a table space
CREATE TRIGGER	Defines and creates an SQL trigger
CREATE VIEW	Defines and creates a view of one or more tables and/or views
DELETE	Removes one or more rows of data from a table
DROP	Deletes an object (table, index, view, etc.) and removes its definition from the database
EXPLAIN	Captures information about the access plan chosen for an SQL statement
FREE LOCATOR	Removes the association between a LOB locator variable and its value
GRANT	Gives a user or a group of users one or more specific authorizations
INSERT	Inserts one or more rows of data into a table
LOCK TABLE	Prevents concurrent processes from either changing or accessing a database table
RENAME TABLE	Renames an existing table
REVOKE	Removes specific authorizations previously given to a user or a group of users
SELECT	Retrieves data from one or more tables and/or views
SET CONSTRAINTS	Toggles on and off the "Check-Pending" state of a table and checks entered data for constraint violations
SET CURRENT DEGREE	Changes the value of the CURRENT DEGREE special register, which is used to specify the degree to which the execution of an SQL statement can use intra-partition parallelism
SET CURRENT EXPLAIN MODE	Changes the value of the CURRENT EXPLAIN MODE special register, which is used to specify whether or not the Explain facility is to be enabled or disabled
SET CURRENT EXPLAIN SNAPSHOT	Changes the value of the CURRENT EXPLAIN SNAPSHOT special register, which is used to specify whether or not Explain snapshot information should be captured for SQL statements

Table 6–1   DB2 Universal Database SQL statements that are supported by CLI   (Continued)

SQL Statement	Description
SET CURRENT FUNCTION PATH	Changes the value of the CURRENT FUNCTION PATH special register, which is used to locate the definitions of both internal and user-defined functions
SET CURRENT QUERY OPTIMIZATION	Changes the value of the CURRENT QUERY OPTIMIZATION special register, which is used to specify the amount of optimization techniques to use when selecting a package for processing subsequent SQL statements
SET EVENT MONITOR STATE	Activates or deactivates an event monitor
SET	Assigns values to NEW transition variables within a trigger
SIGNAL SQLSTATE	Signals an error condition from within a trigger
UPDATE	Modifies the values of one or more columns in one or more rows of data in a table

ODBC Escape Sequences

When the X/Open Company and the SQL Access Group developed the 1992 SQL CAE specification, they recognized that some data sources would need a way to process exceptions and additions to the standard SQL language. Thus, the SQL CAE specification defines a special "escape clause" method that can be used to send SQL language extensions directly to the data source.

A number of SQL language features, such as outer joins and scalar function calls, are implemented by almost every DBMS. Unfortunately, the SQL syntax for these features are usually data source-specific—even when standard SQL syntaxes have been defined for them by the various SQL standards specifications. For this reason, ODBC provides several predefined escape sequences that provide applications with a standardized SQL grammar that can be used to invoke these features. ODBC escape sequences use the "escape clause" method defined in the 1992 SQL CAE specification to send data source-specific SQL grammar to a data source (via the driver) for processing.

ODBC escape sequences are recognized and are parsed by drivers. When a driver receives an escape sequence, the driver replaces the sequence with the appropriate data source-specific SQL grammar before sending it to the data source for processing.

ODBC provides escape sequences (and corresponding standardized SQL syntax) for the following SQL language features:

- Date, time, and timestamp literals
- Datetime interval literals
- Scalar functions such as numeric, string, and data type conversion functions
- **LIKE** predicate escape characters
- Outer joins
- Stored procedure calls

To increase portability and its own flexibility, DB2 CLI provides support for each of these ODBC escape sequences.

Date, Time, and Timestamp Literals

The ODBC escape sequence for date, time, and timestamp literals is

```
{literal_type 'value'}
```

where *literal_type* is one of the values shown in Table 6–2, and *value* is a valid date, time, or timestamp value specified using the appropriate value in Table 6–2.

Table 6–2   ODBC date, time, and timestamp escape sequence literals and formats

Data Type	*literal_type* Value	*value* Format
Date	d	yyyy-mm-dd
Time	t	hh:mm:ss[1]
Timestamp	ts	yyyy-mm-dd hh:mm:ss[.f...][1]

Adapted from *Microsoft ODBC 3.0 Programmer's Reference, Volume 1, and SDK Guide*, page 130.

[1] The number of digits to the right of the decimal point in a time or timestamp literal containing a seconds component is dependent on the seconds precision supported by the descriptor.

If the data source supports date, time, or timestamp data types, its driver must support the corresponding ODBC escape sequence. In drivers that support ODBC, the data, time, and timestamp literals escape sequence may also support the datetime literals defined in the ANSI SQL-92 specification, which are different from the ODBC escape sequences.

Datetime Interval Literals

The following line shows the ODBC escape sequence for a datetime interval literal:

```
{interval < + | - > 'value' < interval_qualifier >}
```

where *value* is the value to be converted, and *interval_qualifier* is either a single date-time field or a value composed of two datetime fields, in the following form:

```
<leadingfield> to <trailingfield>
```

For example, the following ODBC escape sequence

```
{interval '163-11' YEAR(3) to Month}
```

specifies an interval of 163 years and 11 months. The interval leading precision is 3.

All interval literals begin with the word `"interval"`. This keyword, along with the opening brace, is sufficient to indicate that it is an interval literal. If the data source supports a date/time interval data type, its driver must also support the corresponding ODBC escape sequence. Data sources drivers can also support the datetime literals defined in the ANSI SQL92 specification, which are different from the ODBC escape sequences for datetime interval literals.

Scalar Function Calls

The following line shows the ODBC escape sequence for calling a scalar function:

```
{fn scalar_function}
```

where *scalar_function* is one of the functions listed in Appendix A.

Scalar functions return a value for each row in a database table. For example, the **ABS()** (absolute value) scalar function takes a numeric column as an argument and returns the absolute value of each value in that column.

For maximum interoperability, applications should use the **CONVERT()** scalar function to make sure the output of a scalar function is the required data type. The **CONVERT()** function converts data from one SQL data type to another. The following line shows the syntax of the **CONVERT()** function:

```
CONVERT(value_exp, data_type)
```

where *value_exp* is a column name, the result of another scalar function, or a literal value, and *data_type* is a keyword that matches a valid SQL data type identifier.

LIKE Predicate Escape Character

The following line shows the ODBC escape sequence that defines the **LIKE** predicate escape character:

```
{escape 'escape_character'}
```

where *escape_character* is any character that is supported by the data source.

In a **LIKE** predicate, the percent sign character (%) and the underscore character (_) are used as wild card characters. In order to use an actual percent sign or underscore character in a **LIKE** predicate, it must be preceded by an escape character that has been previously defined with the **LIKE** predicate escape character ODBC escape sequence.

Outer Joins

The following line shows the ODBC escape sequence that defines an outer join:

```
{oj outer_join}
```

where *outer_join* is an outer join statement in the following format:

```
table_reference [LEFT | RIGHT | FULL] OUTER JOIN [table_reference |
        outer_join] ON search_condition
```

where *table_reference* specifies a table name, *outer_join* specifies a secondary outer join, and *search_condition* specifies the join condition between the table references. An outer join request must appear after the **FROM** clause of a **SELECT** statement and before the **WHERE** clause (if one exists). ODBC supports SQL-92 left, right, and full outer join syntax.

Stored Procedure Calls

The following line shows the ODBC escape sequence for calling a stored procedure:

```
{<?=> call procedure_name < (<parameter, ...> ) >}
```

where *procedure_name* specifies the name of a stored procedure and *parameter* specifies one or more stored procedure parameters values.

A stored procedure is an executable object (usually containing one or more precompiled SQL statements) that is stored in the data source. A stored procedure can have zero or more parameters, and it can also return a value as indicated by the optional parameter marker "?=" at the beginning of the escape sequence syntax. If the parameter is an input or an input/output parameter, its value can be either a literal value or a parameter marker (interoperable applications should always use parameter markers). If a parameter is an output parameter, its value must always be a parameter marker.

If an input or input/output parameter is omitted, the stored procedure uses the default value of the parameter. If an input/output parameter is omitted, or if a literal value is supplied for the parameter, the driver discards the output value. Similarly, if the parameter marker for the return value of a procedure is omitted, the driver discards the return value. Finally, if an application specifies a return value parameter for a stored procedure that does not return a value, the driver sets the value of the length/indicator buffer bound to the parameter to **SQL_NULL_DATA**.

Input and input/output parameters can be omitted from stored procedure calls. If a stored procedure is called without parentheses (that is, **{call procedure_name}**), the driver calls the procedure without sending it any parameter values. If a stored procedure is called with parentheses but without any parameters (that is **{call procedure_name ()}**), the driver instructs the data source to use the default value for the first parameter. All other parameters are ignored.

NOTE: *If a stored procedure does not have parameters and if it is called with parenthesis (that is,* **{call procedure_name ()}**), *the procedure fails.*

Constructing SQL Statements

In a DB2 CLI application, SQL statements can be constructed in one of three ways: they can be hard-coded during application development, they can be dynamically constructed at application run time, or they can be entered directly by the user at application run time. Although applications generally use only one of these methods, any combination can be used.

Hard-Coded SQL Statements

Applications designed to perform one or more fixed tasks usually contain hard-coded SQL statements. There are several advantages to using this approach:

- Hard-coded SQL statements can be prototyped and tested before the application is written.
- Hard-coded SQL statements are simple to implement.
- Hard-coded SQL statements simplify the application.

Hard-coded SQL statements become more dynamic when they contain parameter markers instead of literal values. Additionally, it is usually easier to construct a parameterized SQL statement, because the data values it uses can be sent to the database in their native types, such as integers and floating point numbers, instead of having to be converted into strings.

If a hard-coded SQL statement is to be executed repeatedly, it can be prepared for even greater efficiency. Additionally, if parameterized SQL statements are prepared, they can be treated as if they were multiple statements by simply changing the parameter values each time the statements are executed. In this case, the SQL statement only has to be re-executed. There is no need to rebuild (reprepare) the statement.

Another way to use hard-coded SQL statements is to put them in special stored procedures. Because stored procedures are constructed at application development time and are stored on the data source, the SQL statements in them do not have to be prepared at application run time. The drawback with using this method is that the syntax for creating stored procedures is usually data source-specific; therefore, stored procedures must be constructed separately for each data source against which an application using them will run.

Run-Time-Constructed (Dynamic) SQL Statements

Applications designed to perform an ad-hoc analysis usually build their SQL statements at application run time. The same is true for most *interactive development environments* (IDEs) such as Visual Age C++ and Visual C++. However, the SQL statements IDEs construct are typically hard-coded in the application the IDE is being used to develop, where they can be optimized and tested.

Applications that build their SQL statements at run time provide tremendous flexibility to the user. Unfortunately, constructing and using SQL statements at application run time is vastly more complex than using hard-coded SQL statements. Furthermore, testing such applications can be difficult, because they can construct an arbitrary number of SQL statements. Another disadvantage of this approach is that it takes far more processing time to dynamically construct and execute an SQL statement than it does to use a hard-coded SQL statement. Fortunately, this situation is rarely a concern, because such applications tend to be user interface-intensive. Thus, the time the application spends constructing SQL statements is generally small compared to the time the user spends entering information.

User-Supplied SQL Statements

Some applications that are designed to perform ad-hoc analyses allow the user to enter SQL statements directly into the application. This approach simplifies application coding, because the user is responsible for building the SQL statement—and the data source is responsible for checking the statement's validity. Because writing a *graphical user interface* (GUI) that adequately exposes the intricacies of SQL is a difficult task, simply asking the user to enter SQL statement text may be a preferable alternative. However, this action requires the user to be knowledgeable about both SQL and the underlying schema of the database being queried.

Differences Between Embedded SQL and CLI Function Calls

In Chapter 3, you saw that DB2 database applications that use embedded SQL require a precompiler to convert the SQL statements into high-level language source code that is then compiled, bound to the database, and executed. In contrast, DB2 database applications that use CLI function calls do not require precompilation or binding. Instead, they use a standardized set of function calls to execute dynamic SQL statements (and related services) at application run time. At first glance, this difference seems important only because it eliminates two steps in the process used to convert source code files to executable applications (subsequently reducing application development time). You will soon see, however, that the difference between embedded SQL and CLI applications is much greater.

Normally, SQL precompilers are designed specifically for the database product with which they are packaged, which means that precompilers essentially tie embedded SQL applications to a single DBMS product. Thus, if you want an embedded SQL application to work with other database products, you must rebuild it using the other database product's precompiler. Additionally, if the other database product uses access plans (packages), you will also have to bind the application to the new database(s). Because DB2 CLI applications do not require precompilation, they do not have to be recompiled or rebound to work with other database products. Instead, once a DB2 CLI application is written and successfully compiled, it can immediately be run against other database products that support ODBC or CLI. CLI function calls and embedded SQL statements also differ in the following ways:

- CLI function calls do not require the explicit declaration of host variables. Instead, any variable defined in a CLI application source-code file can send data to or retrieve data from a DB2 database.

- CLI function calls do not require the explicit declaration of cursors. Instead, cursors are automatically generated by DB2 as needed.

- The OPEN SQL statement is unnecessary in CLI applications. When cursors are generated by DB2 for CLI function calls that need them, they are automatically opened.

- Unlike embedded SQL, CLI function calls allow parameter markers to be used in their SQL statements.

- CLI function calls manage the information related to an SQL statement by using statement handles that treat the data as an abstract object. This use of handles means that CLI applications do not need to use database-specific data structures such as the SQLCA, SQLDA, and SQLCHAR data structures.

- Unlike embedded SQL, CLI can support two or more concurrent transactions on different database servers. CLI can also support two or more connections to the same database server simultaneously.

Despite these differences between CLI function calls and embedded SQL statements, there is an important common concept between the two. CLI applications can execute any SQL statement that can be dynamically prepared and executed in embedded SQL applications. This is guaranteed, because a CLI application passes all of its SQL statements directly to DB2 for dynamic execution—instead of attempting to execute them itself.

NOTE: *CLI can also accept some SQL statements that cannot be dynamically prepared in embedded SQL, such as compound SQL statements. In addition, CLI will process any SQL statement that can be dynamically prepared by the DBMS product against which the CLI application is running, because some DBMS products support SQL statements that other DBMS products do not.*

By allowing the database product—in this case, DB2—to execute all SQL statements, the portability of CLI applications is guaranteed. This guarantee is not always the case with embedded SQL statements, because their dynamic preparation can vary with each relational database product. Also, because COMMIT and ROLLBACK SQL statements can be dynamically prepared by some database products but not by others, they are not used in CLI applications. Instead, CLI applications use the SQLEndTrans() function call to perform rollback and commit operations. This function ensures that CLI applications can successfully end their transactions, regardless of which database product is being used.

Advantages and Disadvantages of Using CLI Function Calls

DB2 CLI offers the following key advantages over embedded SQL:

- CLI provides a consistent interface for executing SQL statements, regardless of which database server to which the application is connected.

- CLI increases the portability of applications by removing the dependence on database-specific precompilers. Applications can be distributed as ready-to-run executable programs or as run time libraries, but they do not have to be distributed as source code. (Source code does not have to be precompiled and rebuilt for each database product.)

- CLI applications do not have to be bound to each database they connect to. Instead, only the bind files shipped with DB2 CLI need to be bound to a database (once) in order for many CLI applications to run against the database.

- CLI applications can connect to multiple databases, and they can establish multiple connections to the same database within a single application. In order to connect concurrently to one or more database servers, the application must allocate a connection handle for each connection it needs. You can then use the allocated connection handles to request database connections via the **SQLConnect()** CLI function call.

- CLI is better-suited for client-server environments in which the target database product is not known at the time the application is built.

- CLI eliminates the need for application-controlled global data storage areas, such as the SQLCA, SQLDA, and SQLCHAR data structures that are needed by embedded SQL. By replacing these global data storage areas with allocated storage areas that the application can reference via handles, CLI enables the development of multithreaded applications in which each thread can have its own connection and separate commit scope area.

- CLI provides enhanced parameter input and data fetching capability by enabling you to specify arrays of data on input by retrieving multiple rows of data directly into an array and executing an SQL statement multiple times. This functionality produces different result sets (through the use of parameter markers). CLI also allows you to retrieve multiple rows generated from a stored procedure call.

- CLI provides a consistent interface that can be used to obtain system catalog information contained in the catalog tables of various database products. This interface shields the application from catalog changes across different releases of database servers, as well as differences among different database products.

- CLI provides extended data conversion, resulting in fewer application code requirements when converting information between various SQL and high-level language data types.

■ CLI incorporates both the ODBC and the X/Open CLI function calls, both of which are accepted industry-standard specifications. CLI is also aligned with the ISO/IEC CLI standard, which means you can apply any time already spent learning these specifications to CLI application development.

CLI applications, however, cannot take advantage of the API calls offered by DB2 (e.g., **GET ERROR MESSAGE**, **BACKUP**, and **RESTORE**) and still remain portable. DB2's APIs can still be called from a CLI application, but the CLI application can no longer execute on other database platforms without first being modified, recompiled, or both. Another disadvantage of CLI is shown in a performance comparison between dynamic and static SQL. As described in Chapter 3, dynamic SQL is prepared at run time, and static SQL is written directly into the source-code file and is prepared when the source-code file is precompiled. Because preparing SQL statements requires additional processing time, static SQL is usually more efficient. Because DB2 CLI adds additional overhead to dynamic SQL, performance can be reduced even farther. If your application requires optimum performance, then using DB2 CLI might not be an option.

You can take advantage of both CLI and embedded SQL by creating static SQL stored procedures and invoking them from within a CLI application. You can also write key modules with embedded SQL and link them to CLI applications. This approach, however, complicates the application design and should be considered only if static SQL stored procedures for some reason cannot be used.

SUMMARY

DB2 CLI applications perform almost all their data retrieval and manipulation by submitting SQL statements to a specific data source for processing. Because the primary function of SQL is to support the definition, manipulation, and control of data in a relational database, most SQL statements fall into one of the following classifications:

■ Data Manipulation Language (DML) Statements

■ Data Definition Language (DDL) Statements

■ Data Control Statements

Data manipulation language statements are used to retrieve data from, add data to, and manipulate data stored in a relational database. Data definition language statements are used to define the data objects (that is, tables, views, indexes, and so on) that make up a relational database. Data control statements control the execution of DML and DDL SQL statements to ensure that a relational database remains consistent and secure in a multi-user environment.

DB2 CLI recognizes four basic data manipulation language SQL statements:

■ The **SELECT** statement

■ The **INSERT** statement

■ The **UPDATE** statement

■ The **DELETE** statement

Different clauses can be used with a **SELECT** statement, and each clause has its own set of predicates. The following **SELECT** statement clauses are recognized by DB2 CLI:

- **FROM**
- **WHERE**
- **GROUP BY**
- **HAVING**
- **UNION**
- **ORDER BY**

In addition to these six clauses, six types of **WHERE** clause predicates are also supported by DB2 CLI:

- Relational Predicates (Comparisons)
- **BETWEEN**
- **LIKE**
- **IN**
- **EXISTS**
- **NULL**

In addition to the DML statements described previously, DB2 CLI also supports several DDL statements.

A number of SQL language features, such as outer joins and scalar function calls, are implemented by almost every DBMS. Unfortunately, the SQL syntax for these features is usually data source-specific. Because of this fact, ODBC provides a set of escape sequences that provide a standardized SQL grammar for invoking the following SQL language features:

- Date, time, and timestamp literals
- Datetime interval literals
- Scalar functions such as numeric, string, and data type conversion functions
- **LIKE** predicate escape characters
- Outer joins
- Stored procedure calls

To increase portability and its own flexibility, DB2 CLI provides support for each of these ODBC escape sequences.

SQL statements can be constructed in DB2 CLI applications in one of three ways:

- They can be hard-coded during application development.
- They can be dynamically constructed at application run time.
- They can be entered directly by the user at application run time.

Applications designed to perform a fixed task usually contain hard-coded SQL statements. Applications designed to perform ad-hoc analyses usually build their SQL statements at application run time. However, some applications designed to perform an ad-hoc analysis allow the user to enter SQL statements directly into the application. This approach simplifies application development, because the application relies on the user to build the SQL statement and relies on the database to check the statement's validity.

As with everything else in life, there are advantages and disadvantages of using CLI function calls in place of embedded SQL. CLI functions allow an application to work with multiple data sources without undergoing any modifications. However, this increase in portability comes with a slight decrease in overall performance. If performance is an issue, CLI may not be the best programming tool to use.

3

Call Level
Interface
(CLI)
Functions

CHAPTER 7

Initializing CLI/ODBC and Connecting to a Data Source

CLI provides several API functions that are used to initialize the CLI/ODBC environment and establish a connection to a data source or driver. This chapter is designed to introduce you to these API functions. The first part of this chapter introduces the environment and connection handle allocation function and describes how it is used to initialize the CLI Library or the ODBC Driver Manager. This is followed by a detailed discussion about the data source/driver connection functions available. Next, the function used to free environment and connection handles previously allocated is described. Finally, a detailed reference section covering each CLI API function that can be used to initialize the CLI/ODBC environment and establish a connection to a data source or driver is provided.

Initializing the CLI/ODBC Environment

What is a Data Source?

A data source consists of a DBMS, along with the platform on which the DBMS resides and the network (if any) used to access that platform. In order for a data source to be accessible to a DB2 CLI application, some type of CLI load library or ODBC driver must exist. This load library/driver provides special information to the application when attempting to establish a connection.

Before a CLI application can access data in any data source, the application must connect to that data source. An application connects to a data source by sending a connection request to the CLI Library or to the ODBC Driver Manager. However, before the CLI Library or the ODBC Driver Manager can process any type of requests, it must first be loaded and initialized by the application. The process by which an application physically loads the CLI Library or sends a request to the ODBC Driver Manager is operating system-dependent. On the Windows NT Server, Windows NT Workstation, or Windows 95 operating system, an application can either statically link directly to the CLI Library or to the ODBC Driver Manager library at compile time, or it can dynamically load and link to the Driver Manager *Dynamic Link Library* (DLL) at application run time. Once the CLI Library or the ODBC Driver Manager is loaded, an application initializes it by allocating memory for one environment and one or more connection handles.

Allocating an Environment Handle

Regardless of how the CLI Library or the ODBC Driver Manager is loaded, an application must initialize it by allocating an environment handle. To do this task, an application does the following:

1. Creates (declares) an environment handle variable.
2. Calls the **SQLAllocHandle()** function and passes it the address of the environment handle variable.

When this function is called, the CLI Library or the ODBC Driver Manager allocates a structure in which to store information about the environment and stores the handle to this structure in the environment handle variable specified.

Allocating a Connection Handle

After an application allocates an environment handle, it must allocate a connection handle before it can connect to a specific data source or driver. To perform this task, the application does the following:

1. Creates (declares) a connection handle variable.

2. Calls the **SQLAllocHandle()** function and passes it the previously allocated environment handle, along with the address of the connection handle variable.

When this function is called, the CLI Library or the ODBC Driver Manager allocates a structure in which to store information about the connection in the environment handle specified—and stores the handle to this structure in the connection handle variable specified.

You should realize that allocating a connection handle is not the same as physically connecting to the data source. Thus, after an application allocates a connection handle, the only CLI API functions the application can legitimately call before connecting to a data source or driver are the following:

▦ **SQLGetConnectAttr()**

▦ **SQLSetConnectAttr()**

▦ **SQLGetInfo()** with the **SQL_ODBC_VER** information type specified

If any other CLI API functions are called, SQLSTATE **08**003 (Connection not open) is returned.

Connecting to a Data Source

Once a connection handle has been allocated and its attributes have been set, an application uses the handle to physically connect to a data source. Three different CLI API functions can be used to establish a connection:

▦ **SQLConnect()**

▦ **SQLDriverConnect()**

▦ **SQLBrowseConnect()**

Applications can use any combination of these functions to connect to any number of data sources and drivers—at the same time, if necessary. Additionally, an application's connections can consist of a variety of drivers and data sources, a single driver and a variety of data sources, or even multiple connections to the same driver and data source.

NOTE: *Some data sources limit the number of active connections they support. An application can call the* **SQLGetInfo()** *function with the* **SQL_MAX_DRIVER_CONNECTIONS** *information type specified to determine how many active connections a particular data source supports.*

Connecting with SQLConnect( )

The simplest CLI connection function available, **SQLConnect()**, assumes that the only information needed to establish a connection is a data source name—and, optionally, a user (authorization) ID and password. This function works well for applications that need to connect to data sources that might require a user ID and/or password. This function also works well for applications that want to control their own connection interface or that have no user interface at all. The **SQLConnect()** function is the only connection function supported by both the X/Open 95 and the ISO/IEC 92 CLI standards.

Connecting with SQLDriverConnect( )

The **SQLConnect()** function assumes that any information needed to establish a connection to a data source, other than data source name, user ID, and password, is stored in the ODBC section of the system information storage area. This information will be stored in either the [COMMON] section of the *DB2CLI.INF* file, the [ODBC] section of the *ODBC.INI* file, or the ODBC subkey in the system registry. However, storing additional connection information in the system information storage area can sometimes produce undesirable side effects. For example, suppose a driver needs one user ID/password to log on to a server workstation and a different user ID/password to log on to a relational DBMS residing on the server. Because the **SQLConnect()** function accepts only one user ID and password, the second user ID and password would have to be stored in the system information storage area. This situation has the potential to cause a breach in security, particularly if the password stored in the system information storage area is not encrypted.

The **SQLDriverConnect()** function eliminates this problem by enabling an application to send connection information to the driver via a connection string, as opposed to storing the data in the information storage area. A connection string is simply a series of keyword/value pairs, separated by semicolons, that contains information used to establish the connection. Using the previous example, a custom program that always uses the "Payroll" data source might prompt the user for user IDs and passwords and build the following connection string to pass to the driver with the **SQLDriverConnect()** function:

```
DSN=Payroll;UID=Sanders;PWD=Cat;UIDDBMS=Sanders;PWDDBMS=Dog;
```

The **DSN** keyword specifies the data source name, while the **UID** and **PWD** keywords specify the user ID and password for the server—and the **UIDDBMS** and **PWDDBMS** keywords specify the user ID and password for the relational DBMS on the server (the final semicolon is optional). When called, the **SQLDriverConnect()** function parses this string and uses the "Payroll" data source name to retrieve additional connection information from the system (for example, the server address). Then, the function logs on to the server and DBMS using the user IDs and passwords specified.

All keyword-value pairs specified in a connection string must adhere to the following syntax rules:

- The keywords and their values can not contain the [] {} () , ; ? * = ! or @ characters.

- Because of the registry grammar, key words and data source names cannot contain the backslash (\) character.

- The value of the **DSN** keyword cannot consist only of blanks and cannot contain leading blanks.

- Spaces are not permitted around the equal sign (=) in the keyword-value pair.

PROMPTING THE USER FOR CONNECTION INFORMATION   If an application using the **SQLConnect()** function needs to prompt the user for connection information, such as a user ID and password, it must provide and process its own user interface. Applications using the **SQLDriverConnect()** function can avoid this extra work by letting the driver prompt the user for any connection information needed.

The **SQLDriverConnect()** function can also be used to prompt the user for a data source. For example, when the **SQLDriverConnect()** function receives an empty connection string, the DB2 CLI Library displays the dialog box shown in Figure 7–1.

This dialog prompts the user to select a data source from a list of data sources recognized by DB2 CLI. Once the user selects a data source from the list, CLI constructs a connection string specifying that data source and uses the string to connect to the appropriate data source.

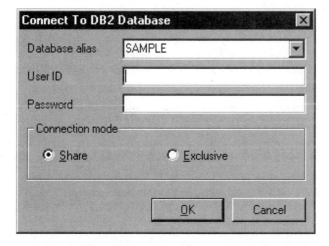

Figure 7–1   The DB2 CLI connection information dialog used by SQLDriverConnect( ) to obtain connection information from a user

Connecting with SQLBrowseConnect( )

Like the SQLDriverConnect() function, the SQLBrowseConnect() function uses a connection string to send connection information to a driver. Unlike the SQLDriverConnect() function, however, the SQLBrowseConnect() function can be used to construct a complete connection string at application run time. This difference enables an application to do two tasks:

■ Build its own dialog boxes to prompt a user for connection information, thereby retaining control over its "look and feel"

■ Search (browse) the system for data sources that can be used by a particular driver, possibly in several steps. For example, an application might first browse the network for servers, and after choosing a server it can browse the server for databases that are accessible by a specific driver.

Here is how the SQLBrowseConnect() function is typically used:

1. An application calls the SQLBrowseConnect() function and passes it a connection string, known as the browse request connection string, containing a keyword/value pair that specifies a particular driver or data source to use.

2. The driver returns a connection string, known as the browse result connection string, containing keywords, possible values (if the keyword accepts a discrete set of values) for each keyword, and a user-friendly name for each keyword to the calling application.

3. The application displays a dialog box listing the user-friendly names and prompts the user for specific keyword values (using the information returned in the browse result connection string).

4. After the user has provided the appropriate information, the application builds a new browse request connection string. This string is built using the keywords obtained from the browse result connection string and the values provided by the user. The connection string is then returned to the driver with another call to the SQLBrowseConnect() function.

5. If enough information was provided to establish a connection, a connection is made to the data source—and the connection string used is returned to the application. If not, a new browse result connection string is returned to the application, and steps 3 and 4 are repeated.

Because connection strings are passed back and forth between an application and a driver, the driver can provide several levels of browsing by returning a new browse result connection string each time the application returns the old one (see step 5). For example, the first time an application calls the SQLBrowseConnect() function, the driver might return keywords that prompt the user for a server name. When the application returns the server name to the driver with a second SQLBrowseConnect() call, the driver might return keywords that prompt the user for a database name. The browsing process would be complete after the application returned the database name to the driver with another SQLBrowseConnect() function call.

Each time the **SQLBrowseConnect()** function returns a new browse result connection string, **SQL_NEED_DATA** is returned as the function's return code. This information lets the application know that the connection process is not complete. Until the **SQLBrowseConnect()** function returns **SQL_SUCCESS**, the connection is in a "Need Data" state, and its handle cannot be used for any other purposes (for example, to set a connection attribute). An application can terminate the connection browsing process at any time by calling the **SQLDisconnect()** function.

Connection Pooling

The whole connection process adds a certain amount of processing requirements to an application. Thus, applications that repeatedly connect and disconnect from a data source (for example, some Internet applications) and middle-tier applications that connect to a data source over a network can require a significant amount of overhead. With these types of applications, connection pooling can be used to provide substantial performance gains and reduce application overhead. When connection pooling is enabled, each time a new connection is established, that connection is placed in a common *pool*. Any application can then use or reuse the connection without having to perform the complete connection process. Each connection in a connection pool can be used repeatedly by multiple applications.

Connection pooling is enabled by setting the **SQL_ATTR_CONNECTION_POOLING** environment attribute to **SQL_CP_ONE_PER_DRIVER** (which specifies a maximum of one pool per driver) or to **SQL_CP_ONE_PER_HENV** (which specifies a maximum of one pool per environment) before an environment handle is allocated. The **SQLSetEnvAttr()** function is used to set the **SQL_ATTR_CONNECTION_POOLING** attribute). If the **SQL_CP_ONE_PER_DRIVER** environment attribute is set to **SQL_CP_ONE_PER_DRIVER**, a single connection pool is supported for each driver. When this setting is used, a user cannot share connections between environments. If an application works with many drivers and few environments, this option may be more efficient. If the **SQL_CP_ONE_PER_DRIVER** environment attribute is set to **SQL_CP_ONE_PER_HENV**, a single connection pool is supported for each environment. When this setting is used, a user can share connections between environments. If an application works with many environments and few drivers, this option may be more efficient. If the **SQL_CP_ONE_PER_DRIVER** environment attribute is set to **SQL_CP_OFF**, connection pooling is disabled.

When an environment handle is allocated after connection pooling has been enabled, the environment (known as a *shared environment*) to which the environment handle refers can be used by all applications that use one or more of the connections in the pool. By allowing an environment and its associated connections to be used (shared) by multiple components in a single process, standalone components that are part of the same process can interact with each other without being aware of each other's existence.

The actual shared environment to be used by all applications is not determined until a connection handle is allocated. At that time, the CLI Library or the ODBC Driver Manager attempts to find an existing shared environment that matches the environment attributes set by the application. If no such environment exists, one is created with a reference count (maintained by the CLI Library or the ODBC Driver Manager) of one, and its handle is returned to the application. If, however, a matching shared environment is found, the environment handle is returned to the application—and its reference count is incremented by one.

When connection pooling is used, the pool is automatically maintained by the CLI Library or the ODBC Driver Manager. Each time an application calls the **SQLConnect()** or **SQLDriverConnect()** functions, the CLI Library or the ODBC Driver Manager attempts to find an existing connection in the pool matching the criteria specified. This criteria includes the connection options passed to the **SQLConnect()** function (the data source name, user ID, and password), the keyword/value pairs specified in the connection string used with the **SQLDriverConnect()** function, and any connection attributes set since the connection handle was allocated. The CLI Library or ODBC Driver Manager checks this criteria against the corresponding connection keywords and attributes of each connection in the pool. If a match is found, that connection is used. However, if a match is not found, a new connection is created. When an application calls the **SQLDisconnect()** function, the connection is returned to the connection pool and is made available for reuse. The actual size of the pool grows dynamically as resource allocations are requested, and the pool shrinks as resource allocations are freed. Resource deallocation is based on inactivity timeout; if a connection is inactive for a period of time (has not been used recently in a CLI API function call), it is removed from the pool. The size of the pool is limited only by memory constraints and by any limits imposed by the server.

NOTE: *Connection pooling can be used by a DB2 CLI 5.2 application exhibiting DB2 CLI 2.0 behavior, as long as the application can call the* **SQLSetEnvAttr()** *function. When using connection pooling, the application must not execute SQL statements that change the database or the context of the database, such as changing the database name—which changes the catalog used by a data source.*

Disconnecting from a Data Source or Driver

When a CLI application has finished using a data source, the application can call the **SQLDisconnect()** function to free any SQL statement handles allocated for the connection and to terminate the connection. Once a connection to a data source is terminated, the connection handle associated with the connection can be reused to either connect to a different data source/driver or to reconnect to the same data source/driver. However, when deciding whether to remain connected or to disconnect and reconnect later, the relative costs of each option must be weighed. This consideration must be made because connecting to a data source and remaining connected can be relatively costly, depending on the connection medium being used. To properly evaluate the tradeoffs, assumptions sometimes have to be made about the likelihood of performing further operations on the same data source and about the time frame in which further operations will be performed.

Freeing Environment and Connection Handles

When an application has finished using a connection to a particular data source or driver, the application can call the **SQLFreeHandle()** function to free the connection handle associated with the connection. When a connection handle is freed, the memory used to store the structure that contained information about the connection is released, and the handle can no longer be used.

When an application has finished using CLI, it can call the **SQLFreeHandle()** function to free the environment handle that was first allocated during the initialization process. When an environment handle is freed, the memory used to store the structure containing information about the environment is released, and most CLI functions can no longer be used. All connection handles associated with an environment handle must be freed before the environment handle itself can be freed.

Using any freed handle in a CLI API function call is an application programming error. Doing so has undefined, but probably fatal, consequences.

The CLI/ODBC Initialization and Data Source/Driver Connection Control Functions

Table 7–1 lists the CLI API functions used to allocate or free resources and establish connections to specified data sources.

Each of these functions are described in detail in the remaining portion of this chapter.

Table 7–1 The CLI/ODBC initialization and data source/driver connection control functions

Function Name	Description
SQLAllocHandle()	Allocates an environment, connection, SQL statement, or descriptor handle and its associated resources
SQLConnect()	Establishes a connection to a specified data source using a specific user ID and password
SQLDriverConnect()	Establishes a connection to a specified data source or driver using a connection string, or optionally requests that the DB2 CLI Library or the ODBC Driver Manager and/or driver display the CLI connection dialog so that the end user can provide connection information
SQLBrowseConnect()	Returns successive levels of connection attributes and corresponding valid values to an application. When all connection attributes have been specified, a connection to the data source is established.
SQLSetConnection()	Sets the current active connection in CLI applications that support multiple concurrent connections and contain embedded SQL statements
SQLDisconnect()	Closes a data source connection
SQLFreeHandle()	Releases an environment, connection, SQL statement or descriptor handle and its associated resources

SQLAllocHandle

COMPATIBILITY

X/OPEN 95 CLI	ISO/IEC 92 CLI	DB2 CLI 5.2	DB2 CLI 2.0	ODBC 3.x
☑	☑	☑	☐	☑

ODBC API CONFORMANCE LEVEL   CORE

Purpose   The `SQLAllocHandle()` function is used to allocate memory for an environment, connection, SQL statement, or descriptor handle.

Syntax
```
SQLRETURN  SQLAllocHandle  (SQLSMALLINT    HandleType,
                            SQLHANDLE      InputHandle,
                            SQLHANDLE      *OutputHandle);
```

Parameters   *HandleType*   Specifies the type of handle to allocate memory for. This parameter must be set to one of the following values:

- **SQL_HANDLE_ENV**
  Allocate memory for an environment handle

- **SQL_HANDLE_DBC**
  Allocate memory for a connection handle

- **SQL_HANDLE_STMT**
  Allocate memory for an SQL statement handle

- **SQL_HANDLES_DESC**
  Allocate memory for a descriptor handle

InputHandle   Specifies the existing handle in the context that the environment, connection, statement, or descriptor handle is to be allocated. If *HandleType* is set to **SQL_HANDLE_ENV**, this parameter must be set to **SQL_NULL_HANDLE**; otherwise, if *HandleType* is set to **SQL_HANDLE_DBC**, this parameter must contain a previously allocated environment handle. If *HandleType* is set to **SQL_HANDLE_STMT** or **SQL_HANDLE_DESC**, this parameter must contain a previously allocated connection handle.

OutputHandle   A pointer to a location in memory where this function is to store the starting address of the allocated handle's information storage buffer (data structure).

Description   The **SQLAllocHandle()** function is used to allocate handles (and their associated resources) for environments, connections, SQL statements, and descriptors.

To allocate an environment handle, an application calls this function with the *HandleType* parameter set to **SQL_HANDLE_ENV** and the *InputHandle* parameter set to **SQL_NULL_HANDLE**. During execution, the CLI Library or the ODBC Driver Manager allocates memory for the environment information storage buffer and passes the starting address of that buffer (the environment handle) back to the application in the *OutputHandle* parameter. The environment handle returned by this function can then be passed to all subsequent CLI function calls requiring an environment handle as an input parameter. The environment handle is used by other CLI functions to reference global information related to the environment, including information about available connection handles and about whether a specific connection handle is active.

To allocate a connection handle, an application calls this function with the *HandleType* parameter set to **SQL_HANDLE_DBC** and the *InputHandle* parameter set to a previously allocated environment handle. During execution, the CLI Library or the ODBC Driver Manager allocates memory for the connection information storage buffer and passes the starting address of that buffer (the connection handle) back to the application in the *OutputHandle* parameter. The connection handle returned by this function can then be passed to all subsequent CLI function calls requiring a connection handle as an input parameter. The connection handle is used by other CLI functions to reference information related to a specific data source connection, including general status information, the current transaction state, and connection error information.

To allocate a SQL statement handle, an application calls this function with the *HandleType* parameter set to **SQL_HANDLE_STMT** and the *InputHandle* parameter set to a previously allocated connection handle. During execution, the CLI Library or the ODBC Driver Manager allocates memory for the SQL statement information storage buffer and passes the starting address of the buffer (the SQL statement handle) back to the application in the *OutputHandle* parameter. The SQL statement handle returned by this function can then be passed to all subsequent CLI function calls that require a statement handle as an input parameter. The statement handle is used by other CLI functions to reference information related to a specific SQL statement, including cursor information, result data set information, status information for SQL statement processing, and statement processing error information.

To allocate a descriptor handle, an application calls this function with the *HandleType* parameter set to **SQL_HANDLE_DESC** and the *InputHandle* parameter set to a previously allocated connection handle. During execution, the CLI Library or the ODBC Driver Manager explicitly allocates memory for a descriptor information storage buffer and passes the starting address of the buffer (the descriptor handle) back to the application in the *OutputHandle* parameter. An application can direct a driver to use an explicitly allocated application descriptor in place of an automatically allocated descriptor when processing SQL statements for a specific data source connection. The driver completes this task by calling the **SQLSetStmtAttr()** function with the **SQL_ATTR_APP_ROW_DESC** or **SQL_ATTR_APP_PARAM_DESC** attribute and the descriptor handle returned by this function.

> **NOTE:** *This function replaces the DB2 CLI 2.0 functions* **SQLAllocEnv()** *(for allocating environment handles),* **SQLAllocConnect()** *(for allocating connection handles), and* **SQLAllocStmt()** *(for allocating SQL statement handles).*

Return Codes   SQL_SUCCESS, SQL_SUCCESS_WITH_INFO, SQL_INVALID_HANDLE, or SQL_ERROR

SQLSTATEs   If this function returns **SQL_SUCCESS_WITH_INFO** or **SQL_ERROR**, one of the following SQLSTATE values may be obtained by calling the **SQLGetDiagRec()** function:

01000, **08**003, **HY**000, **HY**001, **HY**010, **HY**013, **HY**014, **HY**092, or **HYC**00

Refer to Appendix B for detailed information about each SQLSTATE value that can be returned.

Comments
- If memory cannot be allocated for the handle pointer stored in the *OutputHandle* parameter, or if a NULL pointer is specified for the *OutputHandle* parameter, when this function is called, **SQL_ERROR** is returned. When this function is called with the *HandleType* parameter set to **SQL_HANDLE_ENV**, the *OutputHandle* parameter is set to **SQL_NULL_HENV**—unless a NULL pointer was specified. In this case, because there is no handle with which to associate additional diagnostic information, the **SQLGetDiagRec()** function cannot be used to obtain additional information about why the error occurred.

- If **SQL_ERROR** is returned by this function when a handle other than an environment handle is allocated, the values **SQL_NULL_HDBC**, **SQL_NULL_HSTMT**, or **SQL_NULL_HDESC** are stored in the *OutputHandle* parameter. The actual value stored is dependent upon the value stored in the *HandleType* parameter, provided that the *OutputHandle* parameter did not refer to a NULL pointer when this function was called.

- More than one environment, connection, or statement handle can be allocated at a time by an application.

- If an existing environment, connection, statement, or descriptor handle (allocated by a previous call to this function) is specified in the *OutputHandle* parameter, the address of the information storage buffer (data structure) to which the object points is overwritten when this function executes. Consequently, memory used by the information storage buffer to which the environment, connection, statement, or descriptor handle originally pointed can no longer be freed, because its starting address is no longer available. Programming errors of this type cannot be detected by CLI; therefore, no associated return code or SQLSTATE is generated when this kind of error occurs.

- This function does not automatically set the **SQL_ATTR_ODBC_VERSION** environment attribute when it is used to allocate an environment handle. Instead, an explicit call to the **SQLSetEnvAttr()** function must be made.

- Descriptors were introduced in DB2 CLI 5.0, and they are not supported by DB2 CLI 2.0 (or earlier) libraries. Therefore, when working with an DB2 CLI 2.0 (or earlier) library, this function can not be used to allocate a descriptor handle.

■ When a statement handle is allocated, a set of four descriptor handles are automatically (implicitly) allocated.

■ An implementation descriptor handle cannot be explicitly allocated by this function.

■ Applications can use the same environment, connection, statement, or descriptor handle in several different threads on operating systems that support multiple threads.

■ When the CLI Library or the Driver Manager processes this function with the *HandleType* parameter set to **SQL_HANDLE_ENV**—and the *InputHandle* parameter set to **SQL_NULL_HANDLE**—the program checks the **Trace** keyword. **Trace** is located in the ODBC section of the system information storage area (either the [COMMON] section of the *DB2CLI.INI* file, the [ODBC] section of the *ODBC.INI* file, or the ODBC subkey in the registry). If its value is set to **1**, the CLI Library or ODBC Driver Manager enables tracing for the current application. The computer must be running Windows 95, Windows NT Server, or Windows NT Workstation.

If enabled, tracing begins when an environment handle is allocated—and ends when an environment handle is freed.

Prerequisites   The **SQL_ATTR_ODBC_VERSION** environment attribute must be set before this function is used to allocate a connection handle.

Restrictions   If an existing handle is to be specified in the *OutputHandle* parameter, the **SQLFreeHandle()** function must first be used to free the handle before this function is used to reallocate it. Overwriting CLI handles without freeing them first may lead to inconsistent behavior or errors.

See Also   **SQLFreeHandle()**, **SQLGetEnvAttr()**, **SQLSetEnvAttr()**

Example   The following Visual C++ program illustrates how to allocate an environment handle and a connection handle and how to establish a connection to a data source.

```
/*------------------------------------------------------------------*/
/* NAME: CH7EX1.CPP                                                 */
/* PURPOSE: Illustrate How To Use The Following CLI API Function    */
/*          In A C++ Program:                                       */
/*                                                                  */
/*              SQLAllocHandle()                                    */
/*              SQLConnect()                                        */
/*              SQLDisconnect()                                     */
/*              SQLFreeHandle()                                     */
/*                                                                  */
/* OTHER CLI APIs SHOWN:                                            */
/*          SQLSetEnvAttr()                                         */
/*                                                                  */
/*------------------------------------------------------------------*/

// Include The Appropriate Header Files
#include <windows.h>
#include <sqlcli1.h>
#include <iostream.h>
```

```cpp
// Define The CLI_Class Class
class CLI_Class
{
    // Attributes
    public:
        SQLHANDLE    EnvHandle;
        SQLHANDLE    ConHandle;
        SQLRETURN    rc;

    // Operations
    public:
        CLI_Class();                              // Constructor
        ~CLI_Class();                             // Destructor
};

// Define The Class Constructor
CLI_Class:CLI_Class()
{
    // Initialize The Return Code Variable
    rc = SQL_SUCCESS;

    // Allocate An Environment Handle
    rc = SQLAllocHandle(SQL_HANDLE_ENV, SQL_NULL_HANDLE, &EnvHandle);

    // Set The ODBC Application Version To 3.x
    if (rc == SQL_SUCCESS)
        rc = SQLSetEnvAttr(EnvHandle, SQL_ATTR_ODBC_VERSION,
                (SQLPOINTER) SQL_OV_ODBC3, SQL_IS_UINTEGER);

    // Allocate A Connection Handle
    if (rc == SQL_SUCCESS)
        rc = SQLAllocHandle(SQL_HANDLE_DBC, EnvHandle, &ConHandle);
}

// Define The Class Destructor
CLI_Class:~CLI_Class()
{
    // Free The Connection Handle
    if (ConHandle != NULL)
        SQLFreeHandle(SQL_HANDLE_DBC, ConHandle);

    // Free The Environment Handle
    if (EnvHandle != NULL)
        SQLFreeHandle(SQL_HANDLE_ENV, EnvHandle);
}

/*-----------------------------------------------------------*/
/* The Main Function                                         */
/*-----------------------------------------------------------*/
int main()
{
    // Declare The Local Memory Variables
    SQLRETURN rc = SQL_SUCCESS;

    // Create An Instance Of The CLI_Class Class
```

```
CLI_Class Example;

// Connect To The DB2 Sample Database-If Successful,
// Display An Appropriate Message
if (Example.ConHandle != NULL)
{
    rc = SQLConnect(Example.ConHandle, (SQLCHAR *) "SAMPLE",
            SQL_NTS, (SQLCHAR *) "userid", SQL_NTS,
            (SQLCHAR *) "password", SQL_NTS);

    if (rc == SQL_SUCCESS || rc == SQL_SUCCESS_WITH_INFO)
        cout << "Connected to DB2 Sample database." << endl;

    // Disconnect From The DB2 Sample Database
    rc = SQLDisconnect(Example.ConHandle);
}

// Return To The Operating System
return(rc);

}
```

SQLConnect

COMPATIBILITY

X/OPEN 95 CLI	ISO/IEC 92 CLI	DB2 CLI 5.2	DB2 CLI 2.0	ODBC 3.x
✓	✓	✓	✓	✓

ODBC API CONFORMANCE LEVEL   **CORE**

Purpose   The **SQLConnect()** function is used to establish a connection to a specified data source.

Syntax

```
SQLRETURN  SQLConnect  (SQLHDBC        ConnectionHandle,
                        SQLCHAR        *DSName,
                        SQLSMALLINT    DSNameSize,
                        SQLCHAR        *UserID,
                        SQLSMALLINT    UserIDSize,
                        SQLCHAR        *Password,
                        SQLSMALLINT    PasswordSize);
```

Parameters   *ConnectionHandle*   A data source connection handle that refers to a previously allocated connection information storage buffer (data structure).

DSName   A pointer to a location in memory where the name or alias of the data source to connect to is stored.

DSNameSize   The length of the data source name value stored in the *DSName* parameter.

UserID	A pointer to a location in memory where the user's authorization name (user identifier) is stored.
UserIDSize	The length of the user authorization name value stored in the *UserID* parameter.
Password	A pointer to a location in memory where the password for the specified authorization name is stored.
PasswordSize	The length of the password value stored in the *Password* parameter.

Description The `SQLConnect()` function is used to establish a connection to a specified data source. When using this function, an application must supply the name of a target data source, a user ID (authorization name), and a corresponding password (authorization string). When a connection to the target data source is established, the connection handle specified with this function call can be used to reference all information about the connection, including status, transaction state, and error information.

Return Codes `SQL_SUCCESS`, `SQL_SUCCESS_WITH_INFO`, `SQL_INVALID_HANDLE,` or `SQL_ERROR`

SQLSTATE If this function returns `SQL_SUCCESS_WITH_INFO` or `SQL_ERROR`, one of the following SQLSTATE values may be obtained by calling the `SQLGetDiagRec()` function:

08001, **08**002, **08**004, **28**000, **58**004, **HY**001, **HY**009, **HY**013, **HY**090, **HY**501, or **HYT**00

Refer to Appendix B for detailed information about each SQLSTATE value that can be returned.

Comments ■ The input length parameters (*DSNameSize*, *UserIDSize*, and *PasswordSize*) can be set to either the actual length of their associated data values (not including a NULL-terminating character) or to the value `SQL_NTS`, to indicate that the associated data is a NULL-terminated string.

■ The length of the data source name specified in the *DSName* parameter must not exceed 128 characters.

■ An application can connect to more than one data source at the same time; however, only one connection can be current at a time.

■ You can obtain a list of available data sources to which an application can connect by calling the `SQLDataSources()` function. However, before an IBM database alias can be returned by the `SQLDataSources()` function, its corresponding database must first be cataloged. Under the Windows operating system (using the ODBC driver manager), the user must catalog the database twice: once to the IBM RDBMS, and once to the ODBC Driver Manager. You can accomplish this task in a single step by using the DB2 Client Setup program included with IBM's DB2 Client Application Enabler products. Although the methods of cataloging a database are different between the ODBC Driver Manager and an IBM RDBMS, DB2 CLI applications are shielded from this. (One of the strengths of call-level interface is that the application does not have to know about the target data source until the `SQLConnect()` function is invoked at application runtime.) Mapping the data source name to an actual DBMS is outside the scope and responsibility of the CLI application.

- The *DSName* and *UserID* parameter values specified cannot contain blanks.
- Either this function, the **SQLDriverConnect()** function, or the **SQLBrowseConnect()** function must be performed before any SQL statements can be executed.
- Do not use this function to establish a data source connection if the application needs to do the following:
  - Require the end user to specify more than just the data source name, user ID, and password arguments to establish the connection
  - Display a graphical dialog box to prompt the user for connection information
- The end user can specify various connection options in either the *DB2CLI.INI* or the *ODBC.INI* configuration file. You can also set connection options by calling the **SQLSetConnectAttr()** function after a connection has been established. Or, you can pass the connection options to the data source as part of the connection string that is supplied to the **SQLDriverConnect()** function (when that function is used instead of this one to establish the data source connection).
- Stored procedures that contain DB2 CLI function calls must make a NULL **SQLConnect()** function call during their initialization. A NULL **SQLConnect()** function call is a **SQLConnect()** function call in which the data source name, user ID, and password are set to NULL—and their corresponding length arguments are set to zero.

Prerequisites   A connection handle must be allocated with the **SQLAllocHandle()** function before this function is called.

Restrictions   The implicit connection (or default database) option available for IBM Relational Database Management Systems is not supported by DB2 CLI.

See Also   **SQLAllocHandle(), SQLDriverConnect(), SQLBrowseConnect(), SQLDisconnect(), SQLDataSources(), SQLGetConnectAttr(), SQLSetConnectAttr()**

Example   See the example provided for the **SQLAllocHandle()** function on page 128.

SQLDriverConnect

COMPATIBILITY

X/OPEN 95 CLI	ISO/IEC 92 CLI	DB2 CLI 5.2	DB2 CLI 2.0	ODBC 3.x
☐	☐	☑	☑	☑

ODBC API CONFORMANCE LEVEL   CORE*

*IN ODBC 2.0, THIS FUNCTION WAS A LEVEL 1 API CONFORMANCE LEVEL FUNCTION

Purpose   The `SQLDriverConnect()` function is used to establish a connection to a specified data source that requires additional information not provided by the `SQLConnect()` function—or to enable a data source driver to prompt the user for required connection information.

Syntax

```
SQLRETURN  SQLDriverConnect  (SQLHDBC       ConnectionHandle,
                              SQLHWND       WindowHandle,
                              SQLCHAR       *ConnectIn,
                              SQLSMALLINT   ConnectInSize,
                              SQLCHARU      *ConnectOut,
                              SQLSMALLINT   ConnectOutMaxSize,
                              SQLSMALLINT   *ConnectOutSize,
                              SQLUSMALLINT  DriverCompletion);
```

Parameters

ConnectionHandle	A data source connection handle that refers to a previously allocated connection information storage buffer (data structure).
WindowHandle	The platform-dependent window handle used for displaying the DB2 CLI connection information dialog, if additional prompting is necessary to obtain all mandatory connection information. On Windows, this handle is the parent Windows handle; on OS/2, this handle is the parent PM window handle; and on AIX, this handle is the parent MOTIF Widget window handle. If this parameter contains a NULL pointer, the DB2 CLI connection dialog is not displayed.
ConnectIn	A pointer to a location in memory where a full, partial, or empty (NULL pointer) connection string is stored. This connection string is used to pass one or more values needed to establish a connection to a data source to a driver for processing.
ConnectInSize	The length of the connection string value stored in the *ConnectIn* parameter.
ConnectOut	A pointer to a location in memory where this function is to store the complete connection string used to connect to the data source (provided a connection was successfully established).
ConnectOutMaxSize	The maximum size of the memory storage buffer where this function is to store the complete data source connection string used to connect to the data source.
ConnectOutSize	A pointer to a location in memory where this function is to store the actual number of bytes written to the complete data source connection string memory storage buffer (*ConnectOut*).

DriverCompletion   Specifies whether (and when) DB2 CLI is to display the connection information dialog used to prompt the user for additional connection information. This parameter must be set to one of the following values:

- **SQL_DRIVER_PROMPT**
  The DB2 CLI connection information dialog is always displayed. Information from both the connection string and the data source specification in the system information storage area (the [COMMON] section of the *DB2CLI.INI* file) is used for initial values, which can be overridden or supplemented by data input via the DB2 CLI connection dialog.

- **SQL_DRIVER_COMPLETE**
  The DB2 CLI connection information dialog is displayed only if there is not enough information in the connection string provided to establish a connection to the specified data source. Information from the connection string is used as initial values, which can be overridden or supplemented by data input via the DB2 CLI connection information dialog.

- **SQL_DRIVER_COMPLETE_REQUIRED**
  The DB2 CLI connection information dialog is displayed only if there is not enough mandatory information in the connection string provided to establish a connection to the specified data source. Information from the connection string is used as initial values, which can be overridden or supplemented by data input via the DB2 CLI connection information dialog. The end user is only prompted for mandatory information. The controls for information that is not required to connect to the specified data source are disabled.

- **SQL_DRIVER_NOPROMPT**
  The DB2 CLI connection information dialog is not displayed, and the user is not prompted for connection information. The DB2 CLI attempts to establish a connection to the specified data source by using the connection string provided. If there is not enough information in the connection string to establish a connection to the specified data source, **SQL_ERROR** is returned.

Description   The **SQLDriverConnect()** function is used as an alternative to the **SQLConnect()** function to establish a connection to a specified data source. Both functions are used to establish a connection to a specific data source, but the **SQLDriverConnect()** function provides the following additional capabilities:

■ It allows an application to establish a connection to a data source by using a connection string containing the data source name, one or more user IDs, one or more corresponding passwords, and any other information needed by the data source.

■ It allows an application to establish a connection to a data source by using a partial connection string or no additional information. In this case, DB2 CLI can prompt the user for additional connection information.

■ It allows an application to establish a connection to a data source that is not defined in the system information storage area. If the application supplies a partial connection string, the driver can prompt the user for any required connection information.

Once a connection is established by the **SQLDriverConnect()** function, the complete connection string used to connect to the data source is returned to the calling application. The application can store this string and use it later if necessary, to make subsequent connections to the same data source (for a given user ID).

Return Codes SQL_SUCCESS, SQL_SUCCESS_WITH_INFO, SQL_NO_DATA, SQL_INVALID_HANDLE, or SQL_ERROR

SQLSTATEs If this function returns **SQL_SUCCESS_WITH_INFO** or **SQL_ERROR**, one of the following SQLSTATE values may be obtained by calling the **SQLGetDiagRec()** function:

01004, **01**S00, **HY**000, **HY**090, or **HY**110

Refer to Appendix B for detailed information about each SQLSTATE value that can be returned.

Comments ■ Applications should allocate at least 1,024 bytes of memory for the buffer in which this function is to store the complete connection string used to connect to the data source (*ConnectOut*).

■ If the complete connection string used is a Unicode string, the *ConnectOutMaxSize* parameter must contain an even number.

■ If the complete connection string's actual length is greater than or equal to the maximum string size value specified in the *ConnectOutMaxSize* parameter, the complete connection string is truncated to *ConnectOutMaxSize*–1 characters (the length of a NULL-termination character).

■ The connection string stored in the *ConnectIn* parameter must have the following format:

`keyword=attribute; . . .`

The `keyword=attribute` combination can be any of the following:

■ `DSN=Data Source Name`—Specifies the name of a data source as returned by the **SQLDataSources()** function or the data source's child-dialog of the DB2 CLI connection information dialog

- **UID=User ID**—Specifies the user ID (authorization name) of the user attempting to establish the connection

- **PWD=Password**—Specifies the password corresponding to the user ID (authorization name) specified. If a password is not required for the specified user ID, an empty password string should be used (**PWD=;**).

- **APPENDAPINAME=0|1**—Specifies whether the DB2 CLI function (API) name that generated an error is to be appended to the error message information retrieved by the **SQLGetDiagRec()** function. By default, DB2 CLI function names are not displayed as part of the error message information returned by the **SQLGetDiagRec()** function (**APPENDAPINAME=0**). If the function name is appended to the error message, the name will be enclosed in curly braces ({ }).

- **ASYNCENABLE=1|0**—Specifies whether queries can be executed asynchronously. By default, queries can be executed asynchronously (**ASYNCENABLE=1**).

- **BITDATA=1|0**—Specifies whether binary "SQL" data types (i.e., SQL_BINARY, SQL_VARBINARY, SQL_LONGVARBINARY, and SQL_BLOB) are reported as binary-type data. IBM DBMSs support columns with binary data types by defining those columns as either BLOB or CHAR, VARCHAR, and LONG VARCHAR data types with the FOR BIT DATA attribute set. By default, FOR BIT DATA and BLOB data types are treated as binary data types (**BITDATA=1**). Only specify **BITDATA=0** if you are sure that all columns defined as FOR BIT DATA or BLOB contain only character data—and that the application is incapable of displaying binary data columns.

- **CONNECTTYPE=1|2**—Specifies the default connection type to use. This keyword accepts the following attribute values:

  1 Use multiple concurrent connections, each with its own commit scope. Concurrent transactions are not coordinated (the default value).

  2 Use coordinated connections where multiple databases participate under the same distributed unit of work. This setting works in conjunction with the **SYNCPOINT** setting to determine whether a Transaction Manager should be used.

- **CURRENTFUNCTIONPATH=Current Function Path**—Specifies the schema name path to be used to resolve function and data type references used in dynamic SQL statements. The default value for this keyword is "SYSIBM," "SYSFUN", "X," where X is the value of the USER special register (i.e., the current user ID).

- **CURRENTPACKAGESET=Schema Name**—Specifies the schema name (collection identifier) that will be used to select the package to use for processing subsequent embedded SQL statements

- **CURRENTSQLID=Current SQLID**—Enables the end user and the application to name SQL objects without having to qualify them by schema name. This keyword is only valid for DB2 DBMSs that support the **SET CURRENT SQLID** SQL statement (such as DB2 for MVS/ESA). If this keyword is present when a connection is established, a **SET CURRENT SQLID** SQL statement will be sent to the DBMS.

- **CURSORHOLD=1|0**—Controls how the completion of a transaction affects open cursors. This keyword accepts the following attribute values:

  1 Open cursors are preserved from one transaction to the next (the default value).

  0 Open cursors are destroyed from one transaction to the next.

- **DB2DEGREE=0|*Positive Number* (1 to 32767)|ANY**—Specifies the degree of parallelism to use when executing SQL statements. The DB2 Database Manager will determine the degree of parallelism to use if the attribute **ANY** is specified.

- **DB2ESTIMATE=0|*Large Positive Number***—Determines whether DB2 CLI will pop up a graphic display window to report estimates returned by the DB2 optimizer at the end of SQL query statement preparation. By default, estimate values are not returned (**DB2ESTIMATE=0**). If a large, positive number is specified, that number will be used as the threshold value above which DB2 CLI displays the window to report estimates. The recommended value for **DB2ESTIMATE** is 60,000. This keyword is only valid if connecting to a DB2 Version 2.0 or later database. In order for the graphic display window to appear, the application using this keyword must have a *graphical user interface* (GUI).

- **DB2EXPLAIN=0|1|2|3**—This keyword determines whether Explain snapshot and/or Explain table information is to be generated by DB2. This keyword accepts the following attribute values:

  0 Do not generate Explain information (the default value).

  1 Generate Explain snapshot information.

  2 Generate Explain table information.

  3 Generate Explain snapshot and Explain table information.

  Before Explain information can be generated, the Explain tables must be created.

- **DB2OPTIMIZATION=*Positive Number* (0 to 9)**—Specifies the query optimization level at which the optimizer should process SQL queries. If this keyword is specified, DB2 CLI will issue the following SQL statement after a successful connection is established:

  SET CURRENT QUERY OPTIMIZATION *Positive_Number*

- **DBALIAS=Database Alias**—Specifies a data source alias name that contains more than eight characters

- **DBNAME=Database Name**—Specifies an MVS database name. This keyword is only used when connecting to DB2 for MVS/ESA—and only if (base) table catalog information is requested by the application.

■ **DEFAULTPROCLIBRARY=Full Path Name**—Specifies the location that is to be used to locate a stored procedure library when no library name is specified. Because the attribute for this keyword specifies a physical location on a server workstation, the path provided must be in the format that is used by the server's operating system. This keyword should only be used on a temporary basis.

■ **DEFERREDPREPARE=0|1**—Specifies that **PREPARE** requests are not to be processed until an **EXECUTE** request is sent. The two commands are then combined into a single-step process. By default, DB2 CLI defers the processing of **PREPARE** requests (**DEFERREDPREPARE=1**).

■ **DISABLEMULTITHREAD=0|1**—Enables or disables multi-thread processing. By default, DB2 CLI enables multi-thread processing (**DISABLEMULTITHREAD=0**).

■ **EARLYCLOSE=1|0**—Specifies whether the cursor associated with the connection should be closed early (when the end of the result data set is encountered). By default, DB2 CLI closes cursors when the end of the result data set is reached (**EARLYCLOSE=1**).

■ **GATEWAYVERSION=5|2**—Specifies that either the DB2 Connect (Version 5.0) or the DB2 DDCS (Version 2.0) software product is being used to communicate with the gateway.

■ **GRANTEELIST="'UserID1', 'UserID2', ... "**—Specifies one or more user authorization IDs that have been granted privileges needed to access tables in a database or columns in a table.

■ **GRANTORLIST="'UserID1', 'UserID2', ... "**—Specifies one or more user authorization IDs that have granted privileges needed to access tables in a database or columns in a table.

■ **GRAPHIC=0|1|2|3**—Controls whether DB2 CLI reports the IBM GRAPHIC (double-byte character support) data type as one of the supported data types when the **SQLGetTypeInfo()** function is called. By default, DB2 CLI does not report GRAPHIC data types (**GRAPHIC=0**). This keyword accepts the following attribute values:

   0   Do not report the IBM GRAPHIC data type as being supported; return length of GRAPHIC columns as number of DBCS characters used (the default value)

   1   Report the IBM GRAPHIC data type as being supported; return length of GRAPHIC columns as number of DBCS characters used

   2   Do not report the IBM GRAPHIC data type as being supported; return length of GRAPHIC columns as number of bytes used

   3   Report the IBM GRAPHIC data type as being supported; return length of GRAPHIC columns as number of bytes used

■ **IGNOREWARNINGS=0|1**—Specifies whether warnings from the DB2 Database Manager are to be reported (0) or ignored (1). By default, DB2 CLI reports warnings generated by the DB2 Database Manager (**IGNOREWARNINGS=0**).

- **KEEPCONNECT=0** | *Positive Number*—Specifies the number of connections to keep open (with the connection information cached) at one time. By default, DB2 CLI does not keep connections open and cached (**KEEPCONNECT=0**).

- **KEEPSTATEMENT=***Positive Number*—Specifies the number of statement handles to keep open and cached at one time. By default, DB2 CLI keeps five statement handles open and cached at one time. When a statement handle is closed, the memory used by that statement handle is not deallocated; instead, the memory is reused when the next statement handle is allocated.

- **LOBMAXCOLUMNSIZE=LOB** *Size*—This keyword enables you to override the 2GB (1GB for DBCLOB) value returned by the **SQLGetTypeInfo()** function for the column size of SQL_CLOB, SQL_BLOB, and SQL_DBCLOB data types.

- **LONGDATACOMPAT=0|1**—Specifies whether the application expects CLOB, BLOB, and DBCLOB data types to be reported as SQL_LONGVARCHAR, SQL_LONGVARBINARY, and SQL_LONGVARGRAPHIC data types (respectively), or to be reported as their native data type. By default, LOB data types are reported as SQL_CLOB, SQL_BLOB, and SQL_DBCLOB (**LONGDATACOMPAT=0**).

- **MAXCONN=0** | *Positive Number*—Specifies the maximum number of connections allowed for each CLI application program. By default, an application can open as many connections as permitted by the system resources (**MAXCONN=0**).

- **MODE=SHARE|EXCLUSIVE**—This keyword sets the CONNECT mode to either SHARE or EXCLUSIVE. By default, the CONNECT mode is set to SHARE (**MODE=SHARE**). If a mode is set by the application at connect time, this value is ignored.

- **MULTICONNECT=0|1**—Specifies how **SQLConnect()** requests are mapped to physical database connections. This keyword accepts the following attribute values:

  0   Each **SQLConnect()** request will produce a different physical database connection (the default value).

  1   Each **SQLConnect()** request will be mapped to the same physical database connection.

- **OPTIMIZEFORNROWS=***Positive Number*—Specifies that the "**OPTIMIZE FOR** *n* **ROWS**" clause (where *n* = *Positive Number*) is to be added to each **SELECT** SQL statement.

- **PATCH1={0|1|2|4|8|16|** ... **}**—Specifies work-around patches for known ODBC applications. If you want the work-arounds to be additive, add the values together to form the keyword value. For example, if you want patches 1, 4, and 8, then specify PATCH1 = 13. By default, no ODBC work-around patches are used (**PATCH1=0**).

■ **PATCH2=0|"Patch Value 1, Patch Value 2, ... "**—Specifies work-around patches for known problems with CLI/ODBC applications. By default, no CLI/ODBC work-around patches are used (**PATCH2=0**). For an updated list of available CLI/ODBC patches, refer to the README file that is shipped with the DB2/product Universal Database.

■ **POPUPMESSAGE=0|1**—Specifies that a message box is to pop up every time DB2 CLI generates an error. This keyword is useful for debugging applications that do not report messages to users. By default, no message box is displayed (**POPUPMESSAGE=0**).

■ **SCHEMALIST="'schema1', 'schema2', ... "**—Specifies a list of schemas in the database that are to be used when CLI/ODBC catalog function calls are issued to obtain system catalog information. If a large number of tables are defined in the database, you can specify a schema list to reduce the time it takes for the application to query table information—and to reduce the number of tables listed by the application. Each schema name must be delimited with single quotes, be separated by commas, and be in uppercase. The entire string must also be enclosed in double quotes.

■ **SQLSTATEFILTER="'xxxxx', 'xxxxx', ... "**—This keyword is used in conjunction with the **POPUPMESSAGE=1** keyword to prevent DB2 CLI from displaying errors associated with specific SQLSTATES states.

■ **SYNCPOINT=1|2**—This keyword enables you to specify how commits and rollbacks are coordinated among multiple database (DUOW) connections. This keyword accepts the following attribute values:

  1 A Transaction Manager is not used to perform two-phase commits; instead, a one-phase commit commits the work done by each database in a multiple database transaction (the default value).

  2 A Transaction Manager is required to coordinate two-phase commits among databases.

■ **SYSSCHEMA=schema**—Specifies an alternative schema to be searched in place of the SYSIBM (or SYSTEM or RSYS2) schemas when DB2 CLI/ODBC catalog function calls are issued to obtain system catalog information. If no value is specified, the default system schemas are as follows:

SYSCAT or SYSIBM—DB2 Universal Database

SYSIBM—DB2 for Common Servers, Versions 2.1 and earlier; DB2 for MVS/ESA; and DB2 for OS/400

SYSTEM—DB2 for VSE and DB2 for VM

QSYS2—DB2 for OS/400

■ **TABLETYPE="'TABLE'|,'ALIAS'|,'VIEW'|,'INOPERATIVEVIEW'|,'SYSTEM TABLE'|,'SYNONYM'"**—Specifies one or more table types to access when CLI/ODBC catalog function calls are issued to obtain table information. If a large number of tables are defined in the database, you can specify a table type string to reduce the time it takes for the application to query table information—and to reduce the number of tables listed by the application.

Any number of the values can be specified, but each type must be delimited with single quotes, be separated by commas, and be in uppercase. The entire string must also be enclosed in double quotes.

■ **TEMPDIR=Full Path Name**—Specifies the directory that is to be used for storing temporary files associated with LOB fields. Because the attribute for this keyword specifies a physical location on a server workstation, the path provided must be in the format that is used by the server's operating system.

■ **TRACE=0|1**—Specifies whether CLI/ODBC trace records are to be appended to the file specified in the **TRACEFILENAME** setting or to the files stored in the subdirectory specified in the **TRACEPATHNAME** setting. By default, DB2 CLI does not capture and store CLI/ODBC trace records (**TRACE=0**).

■ **TRACEFILENAME=File Name**—Specifies the name of the file that is to be used to store CLI/ODBC trace information.

■ **TRACEFLUSH=0|1**—Specifies whether to force a disk write each time a CLI/ODBC trace record is captured and stored. By default, a disk write is not forced each time a CLI/ODBC trace record is written (**TRACEFLUSH=0**). This attribute is only used when the **TRACE** option is activated.

■ **TRACEPATHNAME=Path Name**—Specifies the name of the subdirectory that is to be used to store CLI/ODBC trace files. Because the attribute for this keyword specifies a physical location on a server workstation, the path provided must be in the format that is used by the server's operating system. This attribute is only used when the **TRACE** option is activated.

■ **TRANSLATEDLL=X:\Path Name\DB2TRANS.DLL**—This keyword is used in Windows when connecting to DB2/2 Version 1 or when using a version of DDCS for OS/2 prior to Version 2.3. This keyword is used to provide proper mapping of NLS SBCS characters (such as the Umlaut characters in German, which are non-ASCII characters) to the corresponding characters in the Windows code page **1004**. **x:** is the directory where the DB2 Client Application Enabler for Windows or the DB2 SDK for Windows product has been installed. **DB2TRANS.DLL** contains the code page mapping tables.

■ **TRANSLATEOPTION=Database Codepage Number**—Specifies the code page number to use when translating characters to the Windows **1004** code page. Only two code page values are currently supported: numbers **437** and **850**. If any other value is specified, a warning will be returned on the connect request —indicating that translation is not possible.

■ **TXNISOLATION=1|2|4|8|32**—This keyword sets the transaction isolation level to one of the following values. The DB2 equivalents for SQL92 isolation levels are shown in brackets.

1   Read Uncommitted [Uncommitted Read]

2   Read Committed [Cursor Stability] (the default value)

4   Repeatable Read [Read Stability]

  8   Serializable [Repeatable Read]

  32   No commit (DB2 for OS/400 only)

- **UNDERSCORE=1|0**—Specifies whether the underscore character (_) acts as a wild card character (to match any one character, including no character) or whether the underscore is used as is. This parameter affects only catalog function calls that accept search pattern strings. By default, the underscore is treated as a wild card for pattern matching (**UNDERSCORE=**1).

- **WARNINGLIST="'xxxxx', 'xxxxx', ... "**—Specifies which SQLSTATE values (that are normally returned as errors) to downgrade to warnings. Each SQLSTATE provided must be delimited with single quotes, be separated by commas, and be in uppercase.

The connection string may also include any number of driver-defined keywords and their corresponding attribute values.

- Data source names cannot contain leading spaces (blanks) or the backslash (\ ) character. Likewise, data source names cannot consist only of spaces.

- If any **keyword=attribute** combination is repeated in the connection string, only the attribute value associated with the first occurrence of the keyword is used.

- An application can connect to more than one data source at the same time; however, only one connection can be current at a time.

- If any keywords exist in either the *DB2CLI.INI* or the *ODBC.INI* configuration files, their respective attributes (values) will augment the information passed to DB2 CLI in the connection string. If a keyword's attribute in either of these configuration files is different from the keyword attribute specified in the connection string, the attribute supplied in the connection string will take precedence.

- If the value of the *DriverCompletion* parameter is set to **SQL_DRIVER_NOPROMPT**, the **DSN=Data Source Name** keyword=attribute combination must be specified in the connection string.

- If the user exits the DB2 CLI connection information dialog without entering the required connection information, the **SQL_NO_DATA** return code will be returned.

- The following restrictions apply when this function is used to connect to a pooled connection:

    - If connection pooling is enabled, this function can only be called with the *DriverCompletion* parameter set to **SQL_DRIVER_NOPROMPT**. If the *DriverCompletion* parameter is set to any other value, **SQL_ERROR** and SQLSTATE **HY**110 (Invalid driver completion) is returned.

Prerequisites   A connection handle must be allocated with the **SQLAllocHandle()** function before this function is called.

Restrictions   There are no restrictions associated with this function call.

See Also   SQLAllocHandle(), SQLConnect(), SQLBrowseConnect(), SQLDisconnect()

Example   The following Visual C++ program illustrates how to establish a connection to a data source using the SQLDriverConnect() function:

```
/*------------------------------------------------------------*/
/* NAME:     CH7EX2.CPP                                       */
/* PURPOSE: Illustrate How To Use The Following CLI API Function */
/*          In A C++ Program:                                 */
/*                                                            */
/*               SQLDriverConnect()                           */
/*                                                            */
/* OTHER CLI APIs SHOWN:                                      */
/*          SQLAllocHandle()              SQLSetEnvAttr()     */
/*          SQLDisconnect()               SQLFreeHandle()     */
/*                                                            */
/*------------------------------------------------------------*/

// Include The Appropriate Header Files
#include <windows.h>
#include <sqlcli1.h>
#include <iostream.h>

// Define The CLI_Class Class
class CLI_Class
{
    // Attributes
    public:
        SQLHANDLE    EnvHandle;
        SQLHANDLE    ConHandle;
        SQLRETURN    rc;

    // Operations
    public:
        CLI_Class();                            // Constructor
        ~CLI_Class();                           // Destructor
};

// Define The Class Constructor
CLI_Class::CLI_Class()
{
    // Initialize The Return Code Variable
    rc = SQL_SUCCESS;

    // Allocate An Environment Handle
    rc = SQLAllocHandle(SQL_HANDLE_ENV, SQL_NULL_HANDLE, &EnvHandle);

    // Set The ODBC Application Version To 3.x
    if (rc == SQL_SUCCESS)
        rc = SQLSetEnvAttr(EnvHandle, SQL_ATTR_ODBC_VERSION,
                (SQLPOINTER) SQL_OV_ODBC3, SQL_IS_UINTEGER);

    // Allocate A Connection Handle
    if (rc == SQL_SUCCESS)
```

```cpp
        rc = SQLAllocHandle(SQL_HANDLE_DBC, EnvHandle, &ConHandle);
}


// Define The Class Destructor
CLI_Class::~CLI_Class()
{
    // Free The Connection Handle
    if (ConHandle != NULL)
        SQLFreeHandle(SQL_HANDLE_DBC, ConHandle);

    // Free The Environment Handle
    if (EnvHandle != NULL)
        SQLFreeHandle(SQL_HANDLE_ENV, EnvHandle);
}

/*————————————————————————————————————————*/
/* The Main Function                                       */
/*————————————————————————————————————————*/
int main()
{
    // Declare The Local Memory Variables
    SQLRETURN   rc = SQL_SUCCESS;
    SQLCHAR     ConnectIn[62];

    // Create An Instance Of The CLI_Class Class
    CLI_Class   Example;

    // Build A Connection String
    memcpy(ConnectIn, "DSN=SAMPLE;UID=userid;PWD=password;
           AUTOCOMMIT=0;CONNECTTYPE=1;", 61);

    // Connect To The DB2 Sample Database - If Successful,
    // Display An Appropriate Message
    if (Example.ConHandle != NULL)
    {
        rc = SQLDriverConnect(Example.ConHandle, NULL, ConnectIn,
                SQL_NTS, NULL, 0, NULL, SQL_DRIVER_PROMPT);

        if (rc == SQL_SUCCESS || rc == SQL_SUCCESS_WITH_INFO)
            cout << "Connected to DB2 Sample database." << endl;

        // Disconnect From The DB2 Sample Database
        rc = SQLDisconnect(Example.ConHandle);
    }

    // Return To The Operating System
    return(rc);
}
```

SQLBrowseConnect

COMPATIBILITY

X/OPEN 95 CLI	ISO/IEC 92 CLI	DB2 CLI 5.2	DB2 CLI 2.0	ODBC 3.x
☐	☐	☑	☐	☑

ODBC API CONFORMANCE LEVEL   LEVEL 1*

*IN ODBC 2.0, THIS FUNCTION WAS A LEVEL 2 API CONFORMANCE LEVEL FUNCTION

Purpose The SQLBrowseConnect() function is used to establish a connection to a specified data source by discovering and enumerating the keywords and the corresponding attribute values that are required to connect to that data source.

Syntax
```
SQLRETURN SQLBrowseConnect    (SQLHDBC        ConnectionHandle,
                               SQLCHAR        *BrowseRequest,
                               SQLSMALLINT    BrowseRequestSize,
                               SQLCHAR        *BrowseResult,
                               SQLSMALLINT    BrowseResultMaxSize,
                               SQLSMALLINT    *BrowseResultSize);
```

Parameters

ConnectionHandle A data source connection handle that refers to a previously allocated connection information storage buffer (data structure).

BrowseRequest A pointer to a location in memory where a browse request connection string is stored. This string is used to pass one or more values needed for a connection request to the specified data source for processing.

BrowseRequestSize The length of the browse request connection string value stored in the *BrowseRequest* parameter.

BrowseResult A pointer to a location in memory where this function is to store the browse result connection string—provided additional information is needed to establish a connection to the specified data source.

BrowseResultMaxSize The maximum size of the memory storage buffer where this function is to store the browse result connection string returned.

BrowseResultSize A pointer to a location in memory where this function is to store the actual number of bytes written to the browse result connection string memory storage buffer (*BrowseResult*).

Description   The **SQLBrowseConnect()** function is used to establish a connection to a specified data source by discovering and enumerating the keywords and their corresponding attribute values that are required to connect to that data source.

The first time the **SQLBrowseConnect()** function is called, the browse request connection string specified in the *BrowseRequest* parameter must contain the **DSN** keyword, along with a corresponding attribute value (see **SQLDriverConnect()** for more information). Depending on which of these keywords is stored in the browse request connection string, the events that take place are as follows:

■ If the browse request connection string contains the **DSN** keyword, the CLI Library or the ODBC Driver Manager tries to locate a corresponding data source specification in the system information storage area (the [COMMON] section of the *DB2CLI.INI* file, the [ODBC] section of *ODBC.INI* file or the ODBC subkey in the registry).

■ If the CLI Library or the ODBC Driver Manager finds the corresponding data source specification, it loads the associated driver. The driver can then retrieve information about the data source from the system information storage area.

■ If the CLI Library or the ODBC Driver Manager cannot find the corresponding data source specification, and if there is no default data source specification, the CLI Library or the ODBC Driver Manager returns **SQL_ERROR** with SQLSTATE **IM**002 (data source name not found and no default driver specified) to the calling application.

After the appropriate driver is loaded, an attempt is made to connect to its underlying data source. If additional connection attributes are required (but were not provided in the browse request connection string), the driver returns **SQL_NEED_DATA** to the application. In this case, a connection string identifying the next connection attribute (or set of attributes) needed is stored in the browse result connection string memory storage buffer (*BrowseResult*).

The application uses the contents of the browse result connection string returned to build the browse request connection string for the next call to the **SQLBrowseConnect()** function. All mandatory attributes (those not preceded by an asterisk) identified in the browse result connection string must be included in the next **SQLBrowseConnect()** function call. When all connection attributes have been enumerated, the driver returns **SQL_SUCCESS**, a connection to the data source is established, and the complete connection string used to connect to the data source is returned to the calling application. The application can store this string and use it later if subsequent connections to the same data source (for a given user ID) are needed. The complete connection string can be used with the **SQLDriverConnect()** function to establish another connection; however, the complete string cannot be used in another call to the **SQLBrowseConnect()** function. If **SQLBrowseConnect()** is called after it returns **SQL_SUCCESS**, the entire sequence of calls must be repeated.

Return Codes   **SQL_SUCCESS, SQL_SUCCESS_WITH_INFO, SQL_NEED_DATA, SQL_INVALID_HANDLE**, or **SQL_ERROR**

SQLSTATEs   If this function returns **SQL_SUCCESS_WITH_INFO**, **SQL_NEED_DATA**, or **SQL_ERROR**, one of the following SQLSTATE values may be obtained by calling the **SQLGetDiagRec()** function:

01000, **01**004, **01**S00, **01**S02, **08**001, **08**002, **08**004, **08**S01, **28**000, **HY**000, **HY**001, **HY**013, or **HY**090

Refer to Appendix B for detailed information about each SQLSTATE value that can be returned.

Comments   ■ Applications should allocate at least 1,024 bytes of memory for the buffer in which this function is to store the browse result connection string and the complete connection string used to connect to the data source (*BrowseResult*).

■ If the browse result/complete connection string's actual length is greater than or equal to the maximum string size value specified in the *BrowseResultMaxSize* parameter, the browse result/complete connection string is truncated to *BrowseResultMaxSize*–1 characters (the length of a NULL-termination character).

■ The browse request connection string stored in the *BrowseRequest* parameter must have the following format:

```
keyword=attribute; . . .
```

or

```
DRIVER=<[>attribute<]>; . . .
```

The **keyword**=attribute combination can be any of the following:

■ **DSN=Data Source Name**—Specifies the name of a data source as returned by the **SQLDataSources()** function or the data sources child-dialog of the ODBC connection dialog

■ **UID=User ID**—Specifies the user ID (authorization name) of the user attempting to establish the connection

■ **PWD=Password**—Specifies the password that corresponds to the user ID (authorization name) specified. If a password is not required for the specified user ID, an empty password string should be used (**PWD=;**).

■ **DRIVER=Driver Name**—Specifies the name of an ODBC driver

The browse request connection string may also include any number of the DB2 defined **keyword=attribute** pairs that can be used with the **SQLDriverConnect()** function.

■ If any **keyword=attribute** combination is repeated in the browse request connection string, the driver uses the attribute value associated with the first occurrence of the keyword.

■ The **DSN** keyword and the **DRIVER** keyword are mutually exclusive. If both are used in the same browse request connection string, the keyword that appears first is the one that is used. The keyword that appears second is ignored.

■ The browse result connection string stored in the *BrowseResult* parameter should be used according to the following semantic rules:

- If an asterisk (*) precedes a **keyword=attribute** combination, the attribute is optional and may be omitted in the next **SQLBrowseConnect()** function call.

- A driver-defined keyword names the kind of attribute for which an attribute value may be supplied (for example, **HOST**, **SERVER**, **DATABASE**, and **DBMS**).

- ODBC-defined keywords and driver-defined keywords include a localized (user-friendly) version of the keyword (for example, "Host," "Server," "Database Name," and "Database Management System"). However, the keyword itself, not the description, must be used in the browse request string that is passed in the next **SQLBrowseConnect()** function call.

- An attribute value list may be included with ODBC-defined keywords and driver-defined keywords. An attribute value list is an enumeration of actual values that are valid for the corresponding attribute keyword (for example, the list may be a list of server names or database names). Attribute value lists are enclosed in curly braces, { }.

- If an attribute keyword is followed by a single question mark (?), a single value corresponds to the attribute keyword.

- Each call to **SQLBrowseConnect()** only returns the attribute information needed to satisfy the next level of the connection process. The driver associates connection state information with the connection handle so that the context can always be determined on each function call.

- Attribute values containing the characters [] {} () , ; ? * = ! and @ should be avoided.

- Data source names cannot contain leading spaces (blanks) or the backslash (\ ) character. Likewise, data source names can not consist only of spaces.

- This function does not support connection pooling. If **SQLBrowseConnect()** is called while connection pooling is enabled, **SQL_ERROR** and SQLSTATE **HY**000 (General error) is returned.

- An application cannot use the contents of previous browse result connection strings to build the current browse request connection string. In other words, the application cannot specify different values for attributes that were set in previous levels.

- This function also returns **SQL_NEED_DATA** if recoverable, nonfatal errors occurred during the browse process (for example, if an invalid password or attribute keyword was supplied by the application). When **SQL_NEED_DATA** is returned and the browse result connection string is unchanged, an error has occurred—and the application can call the **SQLGetDiagRec()** function to return SQLSTATE information about browse-time errors. This function permits an application to correct the attribute value and continue the browse connect operation.

Part 3: Call Level Interface (CLI) Functions

- An application can terminate the browse process at any time by calling the SQLDisconnect() function.
- If this function returns SQL_ERROR, outstanding connections are terminated—and the connection handle specified is returned to the "Unconnected" state.

Prerequisites A connection handle must be allocated with the SQLAllocHandle() function before this function is called.

Restrictions There are no restrictions associated with this function call.

See Also SQLAllocHandle(), SQLConnect(), SQLDriverConnect(), SQLDisconnect()

Example The following Visual C++ program illustrates how to establish a connection to a data source using the SQLBrowseConnect() function:

```
/*───────────────────────────────────────────────*/
/* NAME:     CH7EX3.CPP                            */
/* PURPOSE: Illustrate How To Use The Following CLI API Function */
/*          In A C++ Program:                      */
/*                                                 */
/*                SQLBrowseConnect()               */
/*                                                 */
/* OTHER CLI APIs SHOWN:                           */
/*          SQLAllocHandle()        SQLSetEnvAttr()*/
/*          SQLDisconnect()         SQLFreeHandle()*/
/*                                                 */
/*───────────────────────────────────────────────*/

// Include The Appropriate Header Files
#include <windows.h>
#include <sqlcli1.h>
#include <iostream.h>

// Define The CLI_Class Class
class CLI_Class
{
    // Attributes
    public:
        SQLHANDLE      EnvHandle;
        SQLHANDLE      ConHandle;
        SQLRETURN      rc;

    // Operations
    public:
        CLI_Class();                            // Constructor
        ~CLI_Class();                           // Destructor
};

// Define The Class Constructor
CLI_Class::CLI_Class()
{
    // Initialize The Return Code Variable
    rc = SQL_SUCCESS;
```

```
                    // Allocate An Environment Handle
                    rc = SQLAllocHandle(SQL_HANDLE_ENV, SQL_NULL_HANDLE, &EnvHandle);

                    // Set The ODBC Application Version To 3.x
                    if (rc == SQL_SUCCESS)
                        rc = SQLSetEnvAttr(EnvHandle, SQL_ATTR_ODBC_VERSION,
                                (SQLPOINTER) SQL_OV_ODBC3, SQL_IS_UINTEGER);

                    // Allocate A Connection Handle
                    if (rc == SQL_SUCCESS)
                        rc = SQLAllocHandle(SQL_HANDLE_DBC, EnvHandle, &ConHandle);
                }

                // Define The Class Destructor
                CLI_Class::~CLI_Class()
                {
                    // Free The Connection Handle
                    if (ConHandle != NULL)
                        SQLFreeHandle(SQL_HANDLE_DBC, ConHandle);

                    // Free The Environment Handle
                    if (EnvHandle != NULL)
                        SQLFreeHandle(SQL_HANDLE_ENV, EnvHandle);
                }

                /*-------------------------------------------------------------------*/
                /* The Main Function                                                 */
                /*-------------------------------------------------------------------*/
                int main()
                {
                    // Declare The Local Memory Variables
                    SQLRETURN     rc = SQL_NEED_DATA;
                    SQLCHAR       BrowseRequest[1024];
                    SQLCHAR       BrowseResult[1024];
                    SQLSMALLINT   BrowseResultLen;

                    // Create An Instance Of The CLI_Class Class
                    CLI_Class     Example;

                    // Build The Initial Connection String
                    strcpy((char *) BrowseRequest, "DSN=SAMPLE;");

                    // Connect To The DB2 Sample Database - If Successful,
                    // Display An Appropriate Message
                    if (Example.ConHandle != NULL)
                    {
                        while (rc == SQL_NEED_DATA)
                        {
                            // Initiate The Browse Connect Request
                            rc = SQLBrowseConnect(Example.ConHandle, BrowseRequest,
                                    SQL_NTS, BrowseResult, sizeof(BrowseResult),
                                    &BrowseResultLen);
```

```cpp
    // If More Connection Information Is Needed ..
    if (rc == SQL_NEED_DATA)
    {
        // Display The Next Request
        cout << BrowseResult << endl << endl;

        /*-----------------------------------------------------*/
        /* The First Time Through This Loop, The Following */
        /* Might Be Displayed:                             */
        /*                                                 */
        /*   UID:UID=?;PWD:PWD=?;                          */
        /*                                                 */
        /*-----------------------------------------------------*/

        // Prompt The User For The Next Portion Of The
        // Connection String
        cin >> BrowseRequest;

        /*-----------------------------------------------------*/
        /* The First Time Through This Loop, The User      */
        /* Response Might Be:                              */
        /*                                                 */
        /*   UID=userid;PWD=password;                      */
        /*                                                 */
        /*-----------------------------------------------------*/
    }

    // If Successful, Print A Success Message And The Connection
    // String Used
    if (rc == SQL_SUCCESS || rc == SQL_SUCCESS_WITH_INFO)
    {
        cout << "Connected to DB2 Sample Database." << endl;
        cout << "   Connection String Used : DSN=SAMPLE;";
        cout << BrowseResult << endl;
    }

    // Disconnect From The DB2 Sample Database
    rc = SQLDisconnect(Example.ConHandle);
}

// Return To The Operating System
return(rc);
}
```

SQLSetConnection

COMPATIBILITY

X/OPEN 95 CLI	ISO/IEC 92 CLI	DB2 CLI 5.2	DB2 CLI 2.0	ODBC 3.x
☐	☐	☑	☑	☐

ODBC API CONFORMANCE LEVEL **NONE**

Purpose The **SQLSetConnection()** function is used to switch from one data source connection to another in an application that supports multiple connections and contains embedded SQL statements.

Syntax `SQLRETURN SQLSetConnection (SQLHDBC ConnectionHandle);`

Parameters *ConnectionHandle* A data source connection handle that refers to a previously allocated connection information storage buffer that is associated with the connection to which the application wants to switch.

Description In DB2 CLI Version 1.x, you could mix CLI API function calls with calls to routines containing embedded SQL—as long as the data source connection requests were issued via a CLI connect function (and not through the **CONNECT** SQL statement). Thus, embedded SQL routines would use existing DB2 CLI data source connections. Although this scenario still holds true, with DB2 CLI Version 2.0 and later a new complication exists. Multiple concurrent data source connections are now supported, which means you cannot be sure which data source connection an embedded SQL routine should use when it is invoked. In practice, the embedded SQL routine should use the data source connection associated with the most recent network activity. From the application's perspective, however, this connection cannot always be determined—and it is difficult to keep track of.

The **SQLSetConnection()** function is used whenever an application needs to switch from one data source connection to another before an embedded SQL routine is invoked. This function should only be used when an application mixes DB2 CLI function calls with embedded SQL routines in situations where multiple data source connections are involved.

Return Codes SQL_SUCCESS, SQL_INVALID_HANDLE, or SQL_ERROR

SQLSTATEs If this function returns SQL_ERROR, one of the following SQLSTATE values may be obtained by calling the **SQLGetDiagRec()** function:

08003 or **HY**000

Refer to Appendix B for detailed information about each SQLSTATE value that can be returned.

Comments   The `SQLSetConnection()` function is not needed if an application only uses DB2 CLI
function calls. With DB2 CLI, each statement handle is implicitly associated with a data
source connection handle, so there is never any confusion about the data source
connection to which a particular DB2 CLI function is applied.

Restrictions There are no restrictions associated with this function call.

See Also   `SQLConnect()`, `SQLDriverConnect()`, `SQLBrowseConnect()`

Examples   The following Visual C++ program illustrates how to use the `SQLSetConnection()`
function to switch between two active data source connections before executing an
embedded SQL function:

```cpp
/*-----------------------------------------------------------*/
/* NAME:      CH7EX4.CPP                                     */
/* PURPOSE: Illustrate How To Use The Following CLI API Function  */
/*          In A C++ Program:                               */
/*                                                           */
/* OTHER CLI APIs SHOWN:                                     */
/*          SQLSetEnvAttr()                                  */
/*               SQLAllocHandle()                            */
/*               SQLConnect()                                */
/*               SQLDisconnect()                             */
/*               SQLFreeHandle()                             */
/*               SQLSetConnection()                          */
/*                                                           */
/*-----------------------------------------------------------*/

// Include The Appropriate Header Files
#include <windows.h>
#include <sqlcli1.h>
#include <iostream.h>

// Define The CLI_Class Class
class CLI_Class
{
    // Attributes
    public:
        SQLHANDLE    EnvHandle;
        SQLHANDLE    ConHandle1;
        SQLHANDLE    ConHandle2;
        SQLRETURN    rc;

    // Operations
    public:
        CLI_Class();                              // Constructor
        ~CLI_Class();                             // Destructor
};

// Define The Class Constructor
CLI_Class::CLI_Class()
{
    // Initialize The Return Code Variable
```

```
    rc = SQL_SUCCESS;

    // Allocate An Environment Handle
    rc = SQLAllocHandle(SQL_HANDLE_ENV, SQL_NULL_HANDLE, &EnvHandle);

    // Set The ODBC Application Version To 3.x
    if (rc == SQL_SUCCESS)
        rc = SQLSetEnvAttr(EnvHandle, SQL_ATTR_ODBC_VERSION,
                    (SQLPOINTER) SQL_OV_ODBC3, SQL_IS_UINTEGER);

    // Allocate A Connection Handle For The DB2 Sample Database
    if (rc == SQL_SUCCESS)
        rc = SQLAllocHandle(SQL_HANDLE_DBC, EnvHandle, &ConHandle1);

    // Allocate A Connection Handle For The BOOKSAMP Sample Database
    if (rc == SQL_SUCCESS)
        rc = SQLAllocHandle(SQL_HANDLE_DBC, EnvHandle, &ConHandle2);
}

// Define The Class Destructor
CLI_Class::~CLI_Class()
{
    // Free The Connection Handles
    if (ConHandle1 != NULL)
        SQLFreeHandle(SQL_HANDLE_DBC, ConHandle1);

    if (ConHandle2 != NULL)
        SQLFreeHandle(SQL_HANDLE_DBC, ConHandle2);

    // Free The Environment Handle
    if (EnvHandle != NULL)
        SQLFreeHandle(SQL_HANDLE_ENV, EnvHandle);
}


/*-------------------------------------------------------------*/
/* The Main Function                                           */
/*-------------------------------------------------------------*/

int main()
{
    // Declare The Local Memory Variables
    SQLRETURN  rc = SQL_SUCCESS;

    // Create An Instance Of The CLI_Class Class
    CLI_Class  Example;

    // Connect To The DB2 Sample Database - If Successful,
    // Display An Appropriate Message
    if (Example.ConHandle1 != NULL)
    {
        rc = SQLConnect(Example.ConHandle1, (SQLCHAR *) "SAMPLE",
                    SQL_NTS, (SQLCHAR *) "userid", SQL_NTS,
                        (SQLCHAR *) "password", SQL_NTS);
```

```
        if (rc == SQL_SUCCESS || rc == SQL_SUCCESS_WITH_INFO)
            cout << "Connected to DB2 Sample database." << endl;
}

// Connect To The BOOKSAMP Sample Database - If Successful,
// Display An Appropriate Message
if (Example.ConHandle2 != NULL)
{
    rc = SQLConnect(Example.ConHandle2, (SQLCHAR *) "SAMPLE",
                SQL_NTS, (SQLCHAR *) "userid", SQL_NTS,
                (SQLCHAR *) "password", SQL_NTS);

    if (rc == SQL_SUCCESS || rc == SQL_SUCCESS_WITH_INFO)
        cout << "Connected to BOOKSAMP Sample database." << endl;
}

// Make The Connection To The DB2 Sample Database The Current
// Connection
rc = SQLSetConnection(Example.ConHandle1);
if (rc == SQL_SUCCESS)
{
    cout << endl << endl;
    cout << "Using Connection To DB2 Sample Database." << endl;

    /*————————————————————————————————————*/
    /* At This Point, Embedded SQL Statements (Coded In A        */
    /* Separate Function That Has Been Precompiled, Compiled,    */
    /* Linked To This File, And Bound To The Database) Can       */
    /* Be Executed Against The DB2 Sample Database               */
    /*————————————————————————————————————*/
}

// Make The Connection To The BOOKSAMP Database The Current
// Connection
rc = SQLSetConnection(Example.ConHandle2);
if (rc == SQL_SUCCESS)
{
    cout << endl << endl;
    cout << "Using Connection To BOOKSAMP Sample Database.";
    cout << endl;

    /*————————————————————————————————————*/
    /* At This Point, Embedded SQL Statements (Coded In A        */
    /* Separate Function That Has Been Precompiled, Compiled,    */
    /* Linked To This File, And Bound To The Database) Can       */
    /* Be Executed Against The BOOKSAMP Sample Database          */
    /*————————————————————————————————————*/
}

// Disconnect From The DB2 Sample Database
rc = SQLDisconnect(Example.ConHandle1);

// Disconnect From The BOOKSAMP Sample Database
rc = SQLDisconnect(Example.ConHandle2);
```

```
            // Return To The Operating System
            return(rc);
    }
```

SQLDisconnect

COMPATIBILITY

X/OPEN 95 CLI	ISO/IEC 92 CLI	DB2 CLI 5.2	DB2 CLI 2.0	ODBC 3.x
☑	☑	☑	☑	☑

ODBC API CONFORMANCE LEVEL   **CORE**

Purpose   The **SQLDisconnect()** function is used to close the data source connection associated with a specific connection handle.

Syntax   `SQLRETURN SQLDisconnect     (SQLHDBC ConnectionHandle);`

Parameters   *ConnectionHandle*   A data source connection handle that refers to a previously allocated connection information storage buffer (data structure).

Description The **SQLDisconnect()** function is used to close the data source connection associated with a specific connection handle. If an application calls the **SQLDisconnect()** function before it has freed all SQL statement handles associated with the specified connection handle, the driver automatically frees them—along with any descriptor handles that were implicitly or explicitly allocated for the connection. The driver does this task after it successfully disconnects from the data source, provided that none of the SQL statements associated with the connection are still executing asynchronously. When this function is called, the connection handle itself remains valid—and the **SQLConnect()**, **SQLDriverConnect()**, or **SQLBrowseConnect()** functions can be called again to establish a connection to another data source or to re-establish a connection to the same data source.

Return Codes SQL_SUCCESS, SQL_SUCCESS_WITH_INFO, SQL_INVALID_HANDLE, or SQL_ERROR

SQLSTATE   If this function returns SQL_SUCCESS_WITH_INFO or SQL_ERROR, one of the following SQLSTATE values may be obtained by calling the SQLGetDiagRec() function:

01002, **08**003, **25**000, **25**501*, **58**004, **HY**001, **HY**010, or **HY**013

Refer to Appendix B for detailed information about each SQLSTATE value that can be returned.

*The SQLSTATE **25**501 does not apply to stored procedures that contain DB2 CLI functions.

Comments
- If this function is called while one or more SQL statements associated with the specified connection handle are still executing asynchronously, **SQL_ERROR** is returned along with SQLSTATE **HY**010.
- If this function is called while there is an incomplete transaction associated with the specified connection handle, **SQL_ERROR** is returned along with SQLSTATE **25**000 and the transaction remains unchanged and open. An incomplete transaction is a transaction that has not been committed or rolled back.
- If this function is called after the **SQLBrowseConnect()** function returns **SQL_NEED_DATA** and before the function returns a different return code, the browse connect process is terminated and the connection is returned to the "Unconnected" state.
- If connection pooling is enabled, and this function is called to terminate a connection that is part of a shared environment, the connection is returned to the connection pool and remains available to other components that are using the same shared environment.
- If the **SQL_SUCCESS_WITH_INFO** return code is returned, it implies that even though the disconnect from the data source was successful, additional error or implementation specific diagnostic information is available.

Prerequisites   All outstanding transactions associated with the specified data source connection must be terminated with the **SQLEndTran()** function before this function is called.

Restrictions   There are no restrictions associated with this function call.

See Also   **SQLConnect()**, **SQLDriverConnect()**, **SQLBrowseConnect()**, **SQLEndTran()**

Example   See the example provided on page 131 for the **SQLAllocHandle()/SQLConnect()** function, on page 146 for the **SQLDriverConnect()** function, and on page 152 for the **SQLBrowseConnect()** function.

SQLFreeHandle

COMPATIBILITY

X/OPEN 95 CLI	ISO/IEC 92 CLI	DB2 CLI 5.2	DB2 CLI 2.0	ODBC 3.x
☑	☑	☑	☐	☑

ODBC API CONFORMANCE LEVEL   **CORE**

Purpose   The **SQLFreeHandle()** function is used to release an environment, connection, statement, or descriptor handle and free all memory associated with that object.

Syntax
```
SQLRETURN SQLFreeHandle      (SQLSMALLINT  HandleType,
                             SQLHANDLE    Handle);
```

Parameters   *HandleType*   Specifies the type of handle that the memory to be freed is associated with. This parameter must contain one of the following values:

- **SQL_HANDLE_ENV**
  Free memory associated with an environment handle

- **SQL_HANDLE_DBC**
  Free memory associated with a connection handle

- **SQL_HANDLE_STMT**
  Free memory associated with an SQL statement handle

- **SQL_HANDLES_DESC**
  Free memory associated with a descriptor handle

Handle   An environment, connection, statement, or descriptor handle that refers to a previously allocated environment, connection, statement, or descriptor information storage buffer (data structure).

Description   The **SQLFreeHandle()** function is used to release an environment, connection, statement, or descriptor handle and free memory associated with that object.

To free an environment handle, an application calls this function with the *HandleType* parameter set to **SQL_HANDLE_ENV** and the *Handle* parameter set to a previously allocated environment handle.

To free a connection handle, an application calls this function with the *HandleType* parameter set to **SQL_HANDLE_DBC** and the *Handle* parameter set to a previously allocated connection handle.

To free a SQL statement handle, an application calls this function with the *HandleType* parameter set to **SQL_HANDLE_STMT** and the *Handle* parameter set to a previously allocated SQL statement handle.

To free a descriptor handle, an application calls this function with the *HandleType* parameter set to **SQL_HANDLE_DESC** and the *Handle* parameter set to a previously allocated descriptor handle.

NOTE: *This function replaces the DB2 CLI 2.0 functions* **SQLFreeEnv()** *(for freeing environment handles),* **SQLFreeConnect()** *(for freeing connection handles), and* **SQLFreeStmt()** *with the* **SQL_DROP** *option specified (for freeing SQL statement handles).*

Return Codes   SQL_SUCCESS, SQL_INVALID_HANDLE, or SQL_ERROR

SQLSTATEs   If this function returns **SQL_ERROR**, one of the following SQLSTATE values may be obtained by calling the **SQLGetDiagRec()** function:

01000, **08**S01, **HY**000, **HY**001, **HY**010, **HY**013, or **HY**017

Refer to Appendix B for detailed information about each SQLSTATE value that can be returned.

Comments

- Descriptors were introduced in DB2 CLI 5.0, and they are not supported by DB2 CLI 2.0. Therefore, when working with DB2 CLI 2.0, this function cannot be used to free a descriptor handle.

- The CLI Library and the ODBC Driver Manager does not check the validity of a handle when it is used in a CLI function call. Therefore, an application should not use a handle once the handle has been freed.

- If **SQL_ERROR** is returned when this function is called, the handle that was supposed to be freed remains valid.

- If a shared environment is being used, the application calling this function to free an environment handle no longer has access to the environment once this function is executed. However, the environment's resources are not necessarily freed at that time. In a shared environment, each time this function is called to free an environment handle, the environment reference count maintained by the CLI Library or the ODBC Driver Manager is decremented by one. As long as the reference count does not equal zero, the shared environment is not freed—because the environment is still being used by another component. However, when the reference count equals zero, the shared environment's resources are freed.

- When an application frees a connection handle, all SQL statements and descriptors that are open on the specified connection are dropped.

- When an application frees an SQL statement handle that has results pending, the pending results are discarded.

- When an application frees an SQL statement handle, all implicitly allocated descriptors associated with that handle are automatically freed.

- When an application frees an explicitly allocated descriptor handle, memory being referenced by a pointer field of a result data set's column attribute (that is, the **SQL_DESC_DATA_PTR**, **SQL_DESC_INDICATOR_PTR**, and **SQL_DESC_OCTET_LENGTH_PTR** fields) is not released. Otherwise, all memory allocated for column attribute fields of a result data set is freed when the descriptor handle is freed.

- When an explicitly allocated descriptor handle is freed, all statement handles that the freed handle had been associated with revert to their respective implicitly allocated descriptor handles.

- When the CLI Library or the ODBC Driver Manager processes this function with the *HandleType* parameter set to **SQL_HANDLE_ENV** and the *Handle* parameter set to **SQL_NULL_HANDLE**, it checks the TraceAutoStop keyword in the ODBC section of the system information storage area. This keyword is located in either the [COMMON] section of the *DB2CLI.INI* file, the [ODBC] section of *ODBC.INI*, file or the ODBC subkey in the registry). If its value is set to **1**, the CLI Library or the ODBC Driver Manager disables tracing for all applications on a computer running Windows 95, Windows NT Server, or Windows NT Workstation. The program also sets the value of the **Trace** keyword in the ODBC section of the system information storage area to **0**.

Prerequisites An application must free all connection handles associated with an environment handle before this function is called to free an environment handle. Otherwise, **SQL_ERROR** is returned and the environment handle and any active connection handles associated with it remain valid. The **SQLDisconnect()** function must be called to terminate any connection that might be associated with the connection handle specified before this function is called to free a connection handle. Otherwise, **SQL_ERROR** is returned, and the connection handle remains valid.

Restrictions This function cannot be used to free an implicitly allocated descriptor.

See Also **SQLAllocHandle()**

Example See the example provided for the **SQLAllocHandle()** function on page 128.

CHAPTER 8

Data Source and Driver Capabilities

All data sources and drivers are not created equal. Because of this, DB2 CLI provides several functions that can be used to obtain detailed information about, and to a lesser extent, control the capabilities of a particular data source or driver. This chapter is designed to introduce you to these functions. The first part of this chapter introduces the function that can be used to determine what data sources are available. This is followed by a brief discussion about the functions that can be used to determine exactly what functionality a data source or driver provides. Next, the functions used to obtain or change the values of different driver attributes that control environment, connection, and SQL statement processing are described. Finally, a detailed reference section covering each CLI API function that can be used to obtain information about or control a data source or driver's capabilities is provided.

Finding Out What Data Sources Are Available

When an application is designed to work with only one or two specific data sources or drivers, information about those data source(s) is usually hard-coded directly into the application. Applications that are more generic in design often allow the user to select and use a particular data source at run time. This type of application usually provides the user with a list of available data sources and allows them to select the one they want to work with.

A list of available data sources can be obtained in one of two ways.

1. An application can call the **SQLDriverConnect()** function with a connection string that contains the **DSN** keyword and no associated value. In this case the DB2 CLI connection information dialog is displayed along with a list of available data source names.

2. An application can call the **SQLDataSources()** function to retrieve a list of available data source names (and corresponding descriptions), one at a time.

Obtaining Information About a Data Source

Because a CLI application can connect to a variety of data sources, it needs to be able to obtain information about the data source it is connected to. By design, all CLI/ODBC drivers must support three specific API functions that provide information about the capabilities of the driver itself and the capabilities of the driver's underlying data source. By knowing the capabilities and limitations of a particular data source, an application can adjust its behavior accordingly without having to incorporate tremendous amounts of conditional code that evaluates every data source available.

The first of these three functions, the **SQLGetInfo()** function, can be used to obtain information about the various characteristics of a data source. Of the three functions, this one is probably the most powerful—over 165 different pieces of information can be obtained.

The second of these functions, the **SQLGetFunctions()** function, tells an application whether a particular CLI function is supported by a data source. An application can use this function to find out whether a particular CLI function is supported, or it can tell this function to return a list of all CLI functions available, along with flags that indicate whether each function in the list is supported.

The last function, the **SQLGetTypeInfo()** function, provides an application with information about the native data types used by the data source. When this function is called, the driver builds a result data set in which each row describes a single data type that is recognized by the data source.

Retrieving and Setting Driver Attributes

The information returned about a data source by the **SQLGetInfo()**, **SQLGetFunctions()**, and **SQLGetTypeInfo()** functions is static—that is it can not be changed by an application. Most data source drivers also contain dynamic information about their capabilities, which can be changed to meet an application's needs. Each individual piece of dynamic driver information is classified as one of the following:

- An Environment attribute
- A Connection attribute
- An SQL statement attribute

These classifications are used to identify the behavior that each piece of dynamic information affects.

Environment Attributes

Environment attributes affect the behavior of CLI functions that operate under a specified environment. An application can retrieve the value of an environment attribute at any time by calling the **SQLGetEnvAttr()** function and it can set an environment attribute by calling the **SQLSetEnvAttr()** function. Environment attributes can be changed as long as no connection handle has been allocated for the environment.

DECLARING THE APPLICATION'S ODBC VERSION A DB2 CLI application is not required to set most environment attributes because all attributes have a default value. However, a DB2 CLI application working with ODBC must always set the **SQL_ATTR_ODBC_VERSION** environment attribute immediately after an environment handle is allocated. This attribute tells the ODBC Driver Manager that the application follows either the ODBC 3.x specification or the ODBC 2.0 (or earlier) specification when using the following items:

- SQLSTATEs—Many SQLSTATE values are different between ODBC 2.0 and ODBC 3.x. Also, more SQLSTATEs can be returned for CLI functions that are working with ODBC 3.x drivers.
- Date, Time, and Timestamp Type Identifiers—Date, Time, and Timestamp SQL and C data type identifiers are different between ODBC 2.0 and ODBC 3.x. Table 8–1 shows the date, time, and timestamp data type identifiers for both versions.

■ *CatalogName* argument in the **SQLTables()** function—In ODBC 2.0, wild card characters ('%' and '_') used in the *CatalogName* argument of the **SQLTables()** ODBC API function are treated literally. In ODBC 3.x, they are treated as wild cards. Thus, an application that follows the ODBC 2.0 specification cannot use these characters as wild card characters in the *CatalogName* argument of the **SQLTables()** function.

The ODBC 3.x Driver Manager and ODBC 3.x drivers check the version of the ODBC specification to which an application is written and respond accordingly. For example, if an application following the ODBC 2.0 specification calls the **SQLExecute()** function before calling the **SQLPrepare()** function, the ODBC 3.x Driver Manager returns SQLSTATE **S1**010 (Function sequence error). If same application follows the ODBC 3.x specification, the Driver Manager returns SQLSTATE **HY**010 (Function sequence error).

Connection Attributes

Connection attributes affect the behavior of data source and driver connections. An application can retrieve the value of a connection attribute at any time by calling the **SQLGetConnectAttr()** function, and it can set a connection attribute by calling the **SQLSetConnectAttr()** function. An application is not required to set any connection attribute—all connection attributes have default values.

Table 8–1   The Date, Time, and Timestamp Type Identifiers Used by ODBC 2.0 and ODBC 3.x

ODBC 2.0	OCBC 3.x
SQL Type Identifiers	
SQL_DATE	SQL_TYPE_DATE
SQL_TIME	SQL_TYPE_TIME
SQL_TIMESTAMP	SQL_TYPE_TIMESTAMP
C Type Identifiers	
SQL_C_DATE	SQL_C_TYPE_DATE
SQL_C_TIME	SQL_C_TYPE_TIME
SQL_C_TIMESTAMP	SQL_C_TYPE_TIMESTAMP

Adapted from table on page 92 of *Microsoft ODBC 3.0 Software Development Kit & Programmer's Reference.*

Timing becomes a very important element when setting connection attributes because:

- some connection attributes can be set any time after the connection handle is allocated.

- some connection attributes can be set after the connection handle is allocated, but not after the actual connection to the data source is established.

- some connection attributes can only be set after the connection handle is allocated and the connection to the data source is established.

- some connection attributes can only be set after the connection handle is allocated and the connection to the data source is established and only when there are no outstanding transactions or open cursors associated with the connection.

For example, the login timeout (**SQL_ATTR_LOGIN_TIMEOUT**) attribute applies to the connection process and is only effective if it is set before a connection is established.

The **SQLSetConnectAttr()** function can also be used to set statement attributes for all statement handles currently associated with a data source connection, as well as for all future statement handles that are to be allocated under the same connection handle.

SQL Statement Attributes

SQL statement attributes affect the behavior of CLI functions that are executed using a specific SQL statement handle. An application can retrieve the value of an SQL statement attribute at any time by calling the **SQLGetStmtAttr()** function and it can set an SQL statement attribute by calling the **SQLSetStmtAttr()** function. As with connection attributes, timing becomes a very important element when setting SQL statement attributes:

- The **SQL_ATTR_CONCURRENCY**, **SQL_ATTR_CURSOR_TYPE**, and **SQL_ATTR_USE_BOOKMARKS** statement attributes must be set before the SQL statement associated with the statement handle is executed.

- The **SQL_ATTR_ASYNC_ENABLE** and **SQL_ATTR_NOSCAN** statement attributes can be set at any time but are not applied until the SQL statement associated with the statement handle is used again.

- The **SQL_ATTR_MAX_LENGTH**, **SQL_ATTR_MAX_ROWS**, and **SQL_ATTR_QUERY_TIMEOUT** statement attributes can be set at any time, but it is driver-specific whether they are applied before the SQL statement associated with the statement handle is used again.

- All other statement attributes can be set at any time.

An application is not required to set any SQL statement attribute because all attributes have a default value.

NOTE: *In DB2 CLI 2.0 and earlier, some SQL statement attributes could be set at the connection level. However, this was changed in DB2 CLI 5.0; applications should never set SQL statement attributes at the connection level. The only exception to this rule are the* **SQL_ATTR_METADATA_ID** *and* **SQL_ATTR_ASYNC_ENABLE** *attributes, which are both connection attributes and statement attributes, and can be set at either the connection level or the statement level.*

The CLI Data Source Driver Information and Attribute Control Functions

Table 8–2 lists the CLI functions that can be used to obtain information about available data sources and their drivers and to set environment, connection, and SQL statement processing attributes.

Each of these functions are described, in detail, in the remaining portion of this chapter.

Table 8–2   The CLI Data Source Driver Information and Attribute Control Functions

Function Name	Description
SQLDataSources()	Generates a list of data sources that an application can connect to.
SQLGetInfo()	Retrieves information about a specific driver and its underlying data source.
SQLGetFunctions()	Retrieves information about whether a specific CLI/ODBC function is supported by a driver (and its underlying data source).
SQLGetTypeInfo()	Retrieves information about the native data types supported by a data source.
SQLGetEnvAttr()	Retrieves the current value of a specific environment attribute.
SQLSetEnvAttr()	Changes the value of a specific environment attribute.
SQLGetConnectAttr()	Retrieves the current value of a specific data source connection attribute.
SQLSetConnectAttr()	Changes the value of a specific data source connection attribute.
SQLGetStmtAttr()	Retrieves the current value of a specific SQL statement attribute.
SQLSetStmtAttr()	Changes the value of a specific SQL statement attribute.

SQLDataSources

COMPATIBILITY

X/OPEN 95 CLI	ISO/IEC 92 CLI	DB2 CLI 5.2	DB2 CLI 2.0	ODBC 3.x
✓	✓	✓	✓	✓

ODBC API CONFORMANCE LEVEL   CORE*

*IN ODBC 2.0, THIS FUNCTION WAS A LEVEL 2 API CONFORMANCE LEVEL FUNCTION

Purpose   The `SQLDataSources()` function is used to obtain information about one or more data sources that are available for an application to connect to.

Syntax

```
SQLRETURN  SQLDataSources  (SQLHENV        EnvironmentHandle,
                            SQLUSMALLINT   Selection,
                            SQLCHAR        *DSName,
                            SQLSMALLINT    DSNameMaxSize,
                            SQLSMALLINT    *DSNameSize,
                            SQLCHAR        *Description,
                            SQLSMALLINT    DescriptionMaxSize,
                            SQLSMALLINT    *DescriptionSize);
```

Parameters

EnvironmentHandle An environment handle that refers to a previously allocated environment information storage buffer (data structure).

Selection Specifies which data source, among a list of data sources, this function is to retrieve information for. This parameter must be set to one of the following values:

■ `SQL_FETCH_FIRST`
Retrieve information about the first data source in the list.

■ `SQL_FETCH_NEXT`
Retrieve information about the next data source in the list.

DSName A pointer to a location in memory where this function is to store the data source name retrieved.

DSNameMaxSize The maximum size of the memory storage buffer where this function is to store the data source name retrieved.

DSNameSize A pointer to a location in memory where this function is to store the actual number of bytes written to the data source name memory storage buffer (*DSName*).

Description A pointer to a location in memory where this function is to store the description that is associated with the data source name retrieved.

DescriptionMaxSize The maximum size of the memory storage buffer where this function is to store the data source description retrieved.

DescriptionSize A pointer to a location in memory where this function is to store the actual number of bytes written to the data source description memory storage buffer (*Description*).

Description The `SQLDataSources()` function is used to produce a list of data source (database) names that an application can connect to. The CLI Library or the ODBC Driver Manager retrieves this information from the system information storage area (either the [COMMON] section of the DB2CLI.INI file, the [ODBC] section of the ODBC.INI file, or the ODBC subkey in the registry).

Return Codes `SQL_SUCCESS`, `SQL_SUCCESS_WITH_INFO`, `SQL_NO_DATA`, `SQL_INVALID_HANDLE`, or `SQL_ERROR`

SQLSTATEs If this function returns `SQL_SUCCESS_WITH_INFO` or `SQL_ERROR`, one of the following SQLSTATE values may be obtained by calling the `SQLGetDiagRec()` function:

01004, **58**004, **HY**000, **HY**001, **HY**013, **HY**090, or **HY**103

Refer to Appendix B for detailed information about each SQLSTATE value that can be returned.

Comments
- If the data source name string's actual length is greater than or equal to the maximum string size value specified in the *DSNameMaxSize* parameter, the data source name string is truncated to *DSNameMaxSize–1* (the length of a NULL-termination character) characters.

- If the data source description string's actual length is greater than or equal to the maximum string size value specified in the *DescriptionMaxSize* parameter, the description is truncated to *DescriptionMaxSize–1* (the length of a NULL-termination character) characters.

- When this function is called with the *Selection* parameter set to `SQL_FETCH_FIRST`, subsequent calls to this function with the *Selection* parameter set to `SQL_FETCH_NEXT` return the remaining data source names.

- If the *Selection* parameter is set to `SQL_FETCH_NEXT`, the first time this function is called the first data source name found is returned.

- This function is usually called before a connection to a data source is established.

- An application can call this function multiple times to retrieve all data source names available.

- If this function is called when there are no more data source names to be retrieved, `SQL_NO_DATA` is returned. If this function is called with the *Selection* parameter set to `SQL_FETCH_NEXT` immediately after it returns `SQL_NO_DATA`, the first data source name in the list will be returned.

- The list of data sources returned by this function may not contain all the data sources an application can connect to. Furthermore, there is no guarantee that an application can successfully connect to every data source that is returned by this function; for example, a data source may require authentication information the application does not provide.

Prerequisites   There are no prerequisites for using this function call.

Restrictions   There are no restrictions associated with this function call.

See Also   SQLConnect(), SQLDriverConnect(), SQLBrowseConnect()

Example   The following Visual C++ program illustrates how the SQLDataSources() function can be used to produce a list of data sources that an application can connect to.

```cpp
/*------------------------------------------------------------*/
/* NAME:      CH8EX1.CPP                                      */
/* PURPOSE: Illustrate How To Use The Following CLI API Function */
/*          In A C++ Program:                                 */
/*                                                            */
/*              SQLDataSources()                              */
/*                                                            */
/* OTHER CLI APIs SHOWN:                                      */
/*              SQLAllocHandle()           SQLSetEnvAttr()    */
/*              SQLFreeHandle()                               */
/*                                                            */
/*------------------------------------------------------------*/

// Include The Appropriate Header Files
#include <windows.h>
#include <sqlcli1.h>
#include <iostream.h>

// Define The CLI_Class Class
class CLI_Class
{
    // Attributes
    public:
        SQLHANDLE   EnvHandle;
        SQLRETURN   rc;

    // Operations
    public:
        CLI_Class();                            // Constructor
        ~CLI_Class();                           // Destructor
        SQLRETURN   ShowDataSources();
};

// Define The Class Constructor
CLI_Class::CLI_Class()
{
    // Initialize The Return Code Variable
    rc = SQL_SUCCESS;

    // Allocate An Environment Handle
```

```cpp
    rc = SQLAllocHandle(SQL_HANDLE_ENV, SQL_NULL_HANDLE, &EnvHandle);

    // Set The ODBC Application Version To 3.x
    if (rc == SQL_SUCCESS)
        rc = SQLSetEnvAttr(EnvHandle, SQL_ATTR_ODBC_VERSION,
                    (SQLPOINTER) SQL_OV_ODBC3, SQL_IS_UINTEGER);
}

// Define The Class Destructor
CLI_Class::~CLI_Class()
{
    // Free The Environment Handle
    if (EnvHandle != NULL)
        SQLFreeHandle(SQL_HANDLE_ENV, EnvHandle);
}

// Define The ShowDataSources() Member Function
SQLRETURN CLI_Class::ShowDataSources()
{
    // Declare The Local Memory Variables
    SQLCHAR       DataSource[31];
    SQLCHAR       Description[255];
    SQLSMALLINT   DS_Size;
    SQLSMALLINT   DescSize;

    // Print The Information Header
    cout.setf(ios::left);
    cout.width(24);
    cout << "Data Source" << "Description (Comment)" << endl;
    for (int i = 0; i < 60; i++)
        cout << "-";
    cout << endl;

    // List All CLI Data Sources Available
    while (rc != SQL_NO_DATA)
    {
        // Retrieve A Data Source Name
        rc = SQLDataSources(EnvHandle, SQL_FETCH_NEXT, DataSource,
                sizeof(DataSource), &DS_Size, Description,
                sizeof(Description), &DescSize);

        // Print The Data Source Name Retrieved
        if (rc != SQL_NO_DATA)
        {
            cout.setf(ios::left);
            cout.width(24);
            cout << DataSource << Description << endl;
        }
    }

    // Return The CLI API Return Code To The Calling Function
    if (rc == SQL_NO_DATA)
        rc = SQL_SUCCESS;
    return(rc);
```

```
}

/*----------------------------------------------------------*/
/* The Main Function                                        */
/*----------------------------------------------------------*/
int main()
{
    // Declare The Local Memory Variables
    SQLRETURN  rc = SQL_SUCCESS;

    // Create An Instance Of The CLI_Class Class
    CLI_Class  Example;

    // List The Data Sources That Are Available To The Application
    rc = Example.ShowDataSources();

    // Return To The Operating System
    return(rc);
}
```

SQLGetInfo

COMPATIBILITY

X/OPEN 95 CLI	ISO/IEC 92 CLI	DB2 CLI 5.2	DB2 CLI 2.0	ODBC 3.x
✓	✓	✓	✓	✓

ODBC API CONFORMANCE LEVEL   CORE*

*IN ODBC 2.0, THIS FUNCTION WAS A LEVEL 1 API CONFORMANCE LEVEL FUNCTION

Purpose   The **SQLGetInfo()** function is used to retrieve general information about the data source an application is currently connected to.

Syntax
```
SQLRETURN  SQLGetInfo        (SQLHDBC        ConnectionHandle,
                             SQLUSMALLINT   InfoType,
                             SQLPOINTER     InfoValue,
                             SQLSMALLINT    InfoValueMaxSize,
                             SQLSMALLINT    *InfoValueSize);
```

Parameters   *ConnectionHandle*   A data source connection handle that refers to a previously allocated connection information storage buffer (data structure).

InfoType   A value that identifies the type of data source information to be retrieved. This parameter must be set to one of the values shown in Appendix C.

InfoValue	A pointer to a location in memory where this function is to store the information retrieved from the data source. Depending on the type of information being retrieved, the following can be returned:

- an **SQLUSMALLINT** (16-bit) value
- an **SQLUINTEGER** (32-bit) bitmask
- an **SQLUINTEGER** (32-bit) flag
- an **SQLUINTEGER** (32-bit) binary value
- a NULL-terminated character string

InfoValueMaxSize	The maximum size of the memory storage buffer where this function is to store the data source information retrieved.
InfoValueSize	A pointer to a location in memory where this function is to store the actual number of bytes written to the data source information memory storage buffer (*InfoValue*). If the value returned in the data source information memory storage buffer is not a NULL-terminated string, or if a NULL pointer is specified in the *InfoValue* parameter, this parameter is ignored.

Description The **SQLGetInfo()** function is used to retrieve general information about the data source an application is currently connected to. Appendix C alphabetically lists each value that can be specified for the *InfoType* parameter along with a description of the information returned for that value when this function is executed.

Return Code SQL_SUCCESS, SQL_SUCCESS_WITH_INFO, SQL_INVALID_HANDLE, or SQL_ERROR

SQLSTATEs If this function returns **SQL_SUCCESS_WITH_INFO** or **SQL_ERROR**, one of the following SQLSTATE values may be obtained by calling the **SQLGetDiagRec()** function:

01004, **08**003, **08**S01, **40**003, **58**004, **HY**001, **HY**009, **HY**090, **HY**096, or **HYC**00

Refer to Appendix B for detailed information about each SQLSTATE value that can be returned.

Comments
- In an ODBC environment, if **SQL_DRIVER_HDESC** or **SQL_DRIVER_HSTMT** is specified in the *InfoType* parameter, the *InfoValue* parameter is treated as both an input and an output parameter for this function. (See the **SQL_DRIVER_HDESC** and/or the **SQL_DRIVER_HSTMT** description in Appendix C for more information.)
- If the value returned for the information type specified in the *InfoType* parameter is a string, and if that string's actual length is greater than or equal to the maximum string size value specified in the *InfoValueMaxSize* parameter, the value will be truncated to *InfoValueMaxSize–1* (the length of a NULL-termination character) characters.

■ If the value returned for the information type specified in the *InfoType* parameter is a Unicode string, the *InfoValueMaxSize* parameter must contain an even number.

■ If the value returned to the *InfoValue* buffer is not a character string, or if *InfoValue* is a NULL pointer, the *InfoValueMaxSize* parameter is ignored. In this case, the DB2 CLI assumes that the size of *InfoValue* is **SQLUSMALLINT** or **SQLUINTEGER**, based on the *InfoType* specified.

Prerequisites There are no prerequisites for using this function call.

Restrictions All calls to this function require an open connection, except when the *InfoType* parameter is set to **SQL_ODBC_VER** (which returns the version of the ODBC Driver Manager).

See Also SQLGetFunctions(), SQLGetTypeInfo(), SQLGetEnvAttr(), SQLGetConnectAttr(), SQLGetStmtAttr()

Example The following Visual C++ program illustrates how the **SQLGetInfo()** function can be used to obtain information about the data source that an application is connected to.

```
/*———————————————————————————————————*/
/* NAME:     CH8EX2.CPP                                      */
/* PURPOSE: Illustrate How To Use The Following CLI API Function */
/*          In A C++ Program:                               */
/*                                                          */
/*                 SQLGetInfo()                             */
/*                                                          */
/* OTHER CLI APIs SHOWN:                                    */
/*          SQLAllocHandle()              SQLSetEnvAttr()   */
/*          SQLConnect()                  SQLDisconnect()   */
/*          SQLFreeHandle()                                 */
/*                                                          */
/*———————————————————————————————————*/

// Include The Appropriate Header Files
#include <windows.h>
#include <sqlcli1.h>
#include <iostream.h>

// Define The CLI_Class Class
class CLI_Class
{
    // Attributes
    public:
        SQLHANDLE    EnvHandle;
        SQLHANDLE    ConHandle;
        SQLRETURN    rc;

    // Operations
    public:
        CLI_Class();                    // Constructor
        ~CLI_Class();                   // Destructor
```

```
        SQLRETURN   ShowConnectionInfo();
};

// Define The Class Constructor
CLI_Class::CLI_Class()
{
    // Initialize The Return Code Variable
    rc = SQL_SUCCESS;

    // Allocate An Environment Handle
    rc = SQLAllocHandle(SQL_HANDLE_ENV, SQL_NULL_HANDLE, &EnvHandle);

    // Set The ODBC Application Version To 3.x
    if (rc == SQL_SUCCESS)
        rc = SQLSetEnvAttr(EnvHandle, SQL_ATTR_ODBC_VERSION,
                (SQLPOINTER) SQL_OV_ODBC3, SQL_IS_UINTEGER);

    // Allocate A Connection Handle
    if (rc == SQL_SUCCESS)
        rc = SQLAllocHandle(SQL_HANDLE_DBC, EnvHandle, &ConHandle);
}

// Define The Class Destructor
CLI_Class::~CLI_Class()
{
    // Free The Connection Handle
    if (ConHandle != NULL)
        SQLFreeHandle(SQL_HANDLE_DBC, ConHandle);

    // Free The Environment Handle
    if (EnvHandle != NULL)
        SQLFreeHandle(SQL_HANDLE_ENV, EnvHandle);
}

// Define The ShowConnectionInfo() Member Function
SQLRETURN CLI_Class::ShowConnectionInfo(void)
{
    // Declare The Local Memory Variables
    SQLCHAR       Buffer[255];
    SQLSMALLINT   InfoSize;

    // Obtain And Display Information About The Current Connection
    rc = SQLGetInfo(ConHandle, SQL_DATABASE_NAME,
            (SQLPOINTER) &Buffer, sizeof(Buffer), &InfoSize);
    if (rc == SQL_SUCCESS)
        cout << "Database Name : " << Buffer << endl;

    rc = SQLGetInfo(ConHandle, SQL_DRIVER_NAME,
            (SQLPOINTER) &Buffer, sizeof(Buffer), &InfoSize);
    if (rc == SQL_SUCCESS)
        cout << "Driver Name   : " << Buffer << endl;

    // Return The CLI API Return Code To The Calling Function
    return(rc);
```

```
}

/*————————————————————————————————*/
/* The Main Function                                              */
/*————————————————————————————————*/
int main()
{
    // Declare The Local Memory Variables
    SQLRETURN  rc = SQL_SUCCESS;

    // Create An Instance Of The CLI_Class Class
    CLI_Class  Example;

    // Connect To The DB2 Sample Database
    if (Example.ConHandle != NULL)
    {
        rc = SQLConnect(Example.ConHandle, (SQLCHAR *) "SAMPLE",
                    SQL_NTS, (SQLCHAR *) "userid", SQL_NTS,
                    (SQLCHAR *) "password", SQL_NTS);

        // Obtain And Display Information About The Current
        // Connection
        if (rc == SQL_SUCCESS || rc == SQL_SUCCESS_WITH_INFO)
            rc = Example.ShowConnectionInfo();

        // Disconnect From The DB2 Database
        rc = SQLDisconnect(Example.ConHandle);
    }

    // Return To The Operating System
    return(rc);
}
```

SQLGetFunctions

COMPATIBILITY

X/OPEN 95 CLI	ISO/IEC 92 CLI	DB2 CLI 5.2	DB2 CLI 2.0	ODBC 3.x
☑	☑	☑	☑	☑

ODBC API CONFORMANCE LEVEL   **CORE***

*IN ODBC 2.0, THIS FUNCTION WAS A LEVEL 2 API CONFORMANCE LEVEL FUNCTION

Purpose   The SQLGetFunctions() function is used to determine whether a specific CLI function is supported by the driver an application is currently connected to.

Syntax

```
SQLRETURN SQLGetFunctions    (SQLHDBC        ConnectionHandle,
                              SQLUSMALLINT    Function,
                              SQLUSMALLINT   *Supported);
```

Parameters

ConnectionHandle   A data source connection handle that refers to a previously allocated connection information storage buffer (data structure).

Function   A value that identifies the CLI function of interest. This parameter must be set to one of the values shown in Table 8–3.

Supported   A pointer to a location in memory where this function is to store the value **SQL_TRUE** or **SQL_FALSE** depending on whether the specified function is supported by the driver the application is currently connected to. In some cases this is a single value; in other cases it can be an array of **SQL_TRUE** and/or **SQL_FALSE** values.

Description   The **SQLGetFunctions()** function is used to determine whether a specific CLI function is supported by the driver an application is currently connected to. This information allows an application to adapt to varying levels of CLI function support as it connects to and executes against various data sources. Table 8–3 alphabetically lists each value that can be specified for the *Function* parameter, along with information about the DB2 CLI versions that are able to recognize that particular value.

Table 8–3   CLI API Function Values

Function Value	Recognized By
SQL_API_ALL_FUNCTIONS	All versions
SQL_API_SQLALLOCCONNECT	DB2 CLI 2.0 only
SQL_API_SQLALLOCENV	DB2 CLI 2.0 only
SQL_API_SQLALLOCHANDLE	DB2 CLI 5.2 only
SQL_API_SQLALLOCSTMT	DB2 CLI 2.0 only
SQL_API_SQLBINDCOL	All versions
SQL_API_SQLBINDFILETOCOL	All versions
SQL_API_SQLBINDFILETOPARAM	All versions
SQL_API_SQLBINDPARAMETER	All versions
SQL_API_SQLBROWSECONNECT	All versions
SQL_API_SQLBULKOPERATIONS	DB2 CLI 5.2 only
SQL_API_SQLCANCEL	All versions
SQL_API_SQLCLOSECURSOR	DB2 CLI 5.2 only
SQL_API_SQLCOLATTRIBUTE	DB2 CLI 5.2 only
SQL_API_SQLCOLATTRIBUTES	DB2 CLI 2.0 only
SQL_API_SQLCOLUMNPRIVILEGES	All versions

Table 8–3   CLI API Function Values (Continued)

Function Value	Recognized By
SQL_API_SQLCOLUMNS	All versions
SQL_API_SQLCONNECT	All versions
SQL_API_SQLCOPYDESC	DB2 CLI 5.2 only
SQL_API_SQLDATASOURCES	All versions
SQL_API_SQLBESCRIBECOL	All versions
SQL_API_SQLDESCRIBEPARAM	All versions
SQL_API_SQLDISCONNECT	All versions
SQL_API_SQLDRIVERCONNECT	All versions
SQL_API_SQLDRIVERS	All versions
SQL_API_SQLENDTRAN	DB2 CLI 5.2 only
SQL_API_SQLERROR	DB2 CLI 2.0 only
SQL_API_SQLEXECDIRECT	All versions
SQL_API_SQLEXECUTE	All versions
SQL_API_SQLEXTENDEDFETCH	DB2 CLI 2.0 only
SQL_API_SQLFETCH	All versions
SQL_API_SQLFETCHSCROLL	DB2 CLI 5.2only
SQL_API_SQLFOREIGNKEYS	All versions
SQL_API_SQLFREECONNECT	DB2 CLI 2.0 only
SQL_API_SQLFREEENV	DB2 CLI 2.0 only
SQL_API_SQLFREEHANDLE	DB2 CLI 5.2 only
SQL_API_SQLFREESTMT	All versions
SQL_API_SQLGETCONNECTATTR	DB2 CLI 5.2 only
SQL_API_SQLGETCONNECTOPTION	DB2 CLI 2.0 only
SQL_API_SQLGETCURSORNAME	All versions
SQL_API_SQLGETDATA	All versions
SQL_API_SQLGETDESCFIELD	DB2 CLI 5.2 only
SQL_API_SQLGETDESCREC	DB2 CLI 5.2 only
SQL_API_SQLGETDIAGFIELD	DB2 CLI 5.2 only
SQL_API_SQLGETDIAGREC	DB2 CLI 5.2 only
SQL_API_SQLGETENVATTR	DB2 CLI 5.2 only
SQL_API_SQLGETFUNCTIONS	All versions
SQL_API_SQLGETINFO	All versions
SQL_API_SQLGETLENGTH	All Versions
SQL_API_SQLGETPOSITION	All Versions

Table 8–3   CLI API Function Values (Continued)

Function Value	Recognized By
SQL_API_SQLGETSTMTATTR	DB2 CLI 5.2 only
SQL_API_SQLGETSTMTOPTION	DB2 CLI 2.0 only
SQL_API_SQLGETSUBSTRING	All Versions
SQL_API_SQLGETTYPEINFO	All versions
SQL_API_SQLMORERESULTS	All versions
SQL_API_SQLNATIVESQL	All versions
SQL_API_SQLNUMPARAMS	All versions
SQL_API_SQLNUMRESULTCOLS	All versions
SQL_API_SQLPARAMDATA	All versions
SQL_API_SQLPARAMOPTIONS	DB2 CLI 2.0 only
SQL_API_SQLPREPARE	All versions
SQL_API_SQLPRIMARYKEYS	All versions
SQL_API_SQLPROCEDURECOLUMNS	All versions
SQL_API_SQLPROCEDURES	All versions
SQL_API_SQLPUTDATA	All versions
SQL_API_SQLROWCOUNT	All versions
SQL_API_SQLSETCONNECTATTR	DB2 CLI 5.2 only
SQL_API_SQLSETCONNECTOPTION	DB2 CLI 2.0 only
SQL_API_SQLSETCURSORNAME	All versions
SQL_API_SQLSETDESCFIELD	DB2 CLI 5.2 only
SQL_API_SQLSETDESCREC	DB2 CLI 5.2 only
SQL_API_SQLSETENVATTR	DB2 CLI 5.2 only
SQL_API_SQLSETPARAM	DB2 CLI 2.0 only
SQL_API_SQLSETPOS	All versions
SQL_API_SQLSETSCROLLOPTIONS	DB2 CLI 2.0 only
SQL_API_SQLSETSTMTATTR	DB2 CLI 5.2 only
SQL_API_SQLSETSTMTOPTION	DB2 CLI 2.0 only
SQL_API_SQLSPECIALCOLUMNS	All versions
SQL_API_SQLSTATISTICS	All versions
SQL_API_SQLTABLEPRIVILEGES	All versions
SQL_API_SQLTABLES	All versions
SQL_API_SQLTRANSACT	DB2 CLI 2.0 only
SQL_API_SQLSETCOLATTRIBUTES	All versions
SQL_API_SQLSETCONNECTION	All versions

NOTE: *The DB2 CLI Library or the ODBC Driver Manager will map an ANSI function to the corresponding Unicode function if the Unicode function exists, and it will map a Unicode function to the corresponding ANSI function if the ANSI function exists.*

Return Codes   SQL_SUCCESS, SQL_SUCCESS_WITH_INFO, SQL_INVALID_HANDLE, or SQL_ERROR

SQLSTATEs   If this function returns SQL_SUCCESS_WITH_INFO or SQL_ERROR, one of the following SQLSTATE values may be obtained by calling the SQLGetDiagRec() function:

40003, 08S01, 58004, HY001, **HY**009, **HY**010, or **HY**013

Refer to Appendix B for detailed information about each SQLSTATE value that can be returned.

Comments   ■ If the value specified in the *Function* parameter is SQL_API_ALL_FUNCTIONS, the *Supported* parameter must point to a SQLSMALLINT array of 100 elements. This array, once populated, can be indexed by the same *Function* values that are used to identify many of the functions. Some elements of this array will be unused and other elements are reserved. Because some *Function* values are greater than 100, you cannot use this method to obtain a list of all available functions because functions whose value is greater than 100 will not be included in the list. Therefore, the SQLGetFunction() function must be explicitly called for all *Function* values greater than or equal to 100. The complete set of *Function* values are defined in sqlcli1.h.

■ The large object (LOB) support functions—SQLGetLength(), SQLGetPosition(), SQLGetSubString(), SQLBindFileToCol(), and SQLBindFileToParam()—are not supported when you are connected to an IBM RDBMS that does not support LOB data types.

Prerequisites   A connection to a data source or driver must exist before this function is called.

Restrictions   There are no restrictions associated with this function call.

See Also   SQLGetInfo(), SQLGetTypeInfo(), SQLGetEnvAttr(), SQLGetConnectAttr(), SQLGetStmtAttr()

Example   The following Visual C++ program illustrates how the SQLGetFunctions() function can be used to determine whether or not a specific CLI API function is supported by the data source that an application is connected to.

```
/*------------------------------------------------------------------*/
/* NAME:      CH8EX3.CPP                                            */
/* PURPOSE: Illustrate How To Use The Following CLI API Function    */
/*          In A C++ Program:                                       */
/*                                                                  */
/*                SQLGetFunctions()                                 */
/*                                                                  */
/* OTHER CLI APIs SHOWN:                                            */
/*                SQLAllocHandle()            SQLSetEnvAttr()       */
```

```
/*              SQLConnect()                 SQLDisconnect()              */
/*              SQLFreeHandle()                                          */
/*                                                                       */
/*----------------------------------------------------------------------*/

// Include The Appropriate Header Files
#include <windows.h>
#include <sqlcli1.h>
#include <iostream.h>

// Define The CLI_Class Class
class CLI_Class
{
    // Attributes
    public:
        SQLHANDLE   EnvHandle;
        SQLHANDLE   ConHandle;
        SQLRETURN   rc;

    // Operations
    public:
        CLI_Class();                          // Constructor
        ~CLI_Class();                         // Destructor
};

// Define The Class Constructor
CLI_Class::CLI_Class()
{
    // Initialize The Return Code Variable
    rc = SQL_SUCCESS;

    // Allocate An Environment Handle
    rc = SQLAllocHandle(SQL_HANDLE_ENV, SQL_NULL_HANDLE, &EnvHandle);

    // Set The ODBC Application Version To 3.x
    if (rc == SQL_SUCCESS)
        rc = SQLSetEnvAttr(EnvHandle, SQL_ATTR_ODBC_VERSION,
                (SQLPOINTER) SQL_OV_ODBC3, SQL_IS_UINTEGER);

    // Allocate A Connection Handle
    if (rc == SQL_SUCCESS)
        rc = SQLAllocHandle(SQL_HANDLE_DBC, EnvHandle, &ConHandle);
}

// Define The Class Destructor
CLI_Class::~CLI_Class()
{
    // Free The Connection Handle
    if (ConHandle != NULL)
        SQLFreeHandle(SQL_HANDLE_DBC, ConHandle);

    // Free The Environment Handle
    if (EnvHandle != NULL)
        SQLFreeHandle(SQL_HANDLE_ENV, EnvHandle);
```

```
    }

/*———————————————————————————————*/
/* The Main Function                                               */
/*———————————————————————————————*/
int main()
{
    // Declare The Local Memory Variables
    SQLRETURN       rc = SQL_SUCCESS;
    SQLUSMALLINT    Supported;

    // Create An Instance Of The CLI_Class Class
    CLI_Class       Example;

    // Connect To The DB2 Sample Database
    if (Example.ConHandle != NULL)
    {
        rc = SQLConnect(Example.ConHandle, (SQLCHAR *) "SAMPLE",
                SQL_NTS, (SQLCHAR *) "userid", SQL_NTS,
                (SQLCHAR *) "password", SQL_NTS);

        // Determine Whether Or Not The Current Data Source Supports
        // The SQLBrowseConnect() Function
        if (rc != SQL_SUCCESS || rc != SQL_SUCCESS_WITH_INFO)
        {
            rc = SQLGetFunctions(Example.ConHandle,
                    SQL_API_SQLBROWSECONNECT, &Supported);

            // Retrieve And Display The Results
            if (rc == SQL_SUCCESS || rc == SQL_SUCCESS_WITH_INFO)
            {
                cout << "SQLBrowseConnect() is ";
                if (Supported == TRUE)
                    cout << "supported ";
                else
                    cout << "not supported ";
                cout << "by the current data source." << endl;
            }
        }

        // Disconnect From The DB2 Sample Database
        rc = SQLDisconnect(Example.ConHandle);
    }

    // Return To The Operating System
    return(rc);
}
```

SQLGetTypeInfo

COMPATIBILITY

X/OPEN 95 CLI	ISO/IEC 92 CLI	DB2 CLI 5.2	DB2 CLI 2.0	ODBC 3.x
☑	☑	☑	☑	☑

ODBC API CONFORMANCE LEVEL   CORE*

*IN ODBC 2.0, THIS FUNCTION WAS A LEVEL 1 API CONFORMANCE LEVEL FUNCTION

Purpose   The SQLGetTypeInfo() function is used to retrieve information about the data types that are supported by the data source an application is currently connected to.

Syntax
```
SQLRETURN SQLGetTypeInfo      (SQLHSTMT      StatementHandle,
                               SQLSMALLINT   SQLDataType);
```

Parameters   *StatementHandle*   An SQL statement handle that refers to a previously allocated SQL statement information storage buffer (data structure).

SQLDataType   The SQL data type that information is to be retrieved for. This parameter must be set to a data source-specific data type or to one of the following values:

- SQL_CHAR
- SQL_VARCHAR
- SQL_LONGVARCHAR
- SQL_DECIMAL
- SQL_NUMERIC
- SQL_SMALLINT
- SQL_INTEGER
- SQL_REAL
- SQL_FLOAT
- SQL_DOUBLE
- SQL_BLOB
- SQL_CLOB
- SQL_DBCLOB
- SQL_BINARY
- SQL_VARBINARY
- SQL_LONGVARBINARY
- SQL_DATE
- SQL_TIME

- SQL_TIMESTAMP
- SQL_GRAPHIC
- SQL_VARGRAPHIC
- SQL_LONGVARGRAPHIC
- SQL_ALL_TYPES

NOTE: *The* SQL_ALL_TYPES *value causes information about all SQL data types to be returned.*

Description   The SQLGetTypeInfo() function is used to retrieve information about the data types that are supported by the data source an application is currently connected to. The information returned by this function is placed in a result data set and can be processed by using the same functions that are used to process a result data set generated by an SQL query. Table 8–4 describes this result data set.

One or more driver-defined columns may be added to this result data set. When that is the case, applications should gain access to each driver-specific column by counting down from column 19 (**INTERVAL_PRECISION**) of the result data set rather than by specifying an explicit ordinal position.

NOTE: *Depending on the driver being used,* SQLGetTypeInfo() *may or may not return information for all valid data types. However, an application can use any valid data type regardless of whether it is returned in the result data set produced by this function.*

Table 8–4   Result Data Set Returned By **SQLGetTypeInfo()**

Column Number	Column Name	Data Type	Description
1	**TYPE_NAME**	**VARCHAR(128) NOT NULL**	The data source-specific character representation of the SQL data type identified in the **DATA_TYPE** column. Valid values for this column include:

CHAR	VARCHAR
LONG VARCHAR	DECIMAL
NUMERIC	SMALLINT
INTEGER	REAL
FLOAT	DOUBLE PRECISION
BLOB	CLOB
DBCLOB	GRAPHIC
VAR-GRAPHIC	LONG VARGRAPHIC
TINYINT	BIGINT
BINARY	VARBINARY
LONG VARBINARY	DATE
TIME	TIMESTAMP

Table 8–4 Result Data Set Returned By **SQLGetTypeInfo()** (Continued)

Column Number	Column Name	Data Type	Description
2	DATA_TYPE	SMALLINT NOT NULL	An ODBC or driver-specific SQL data type that is supported by the data source. Valid values for this column include:
			SQL_CHAR SQL_VARCHAR SQL_LONGVARCHAR SQL_DECIMAL SQL_NUMERIC SQL_SMALLINT SQL_INTEGER SQL_REAL SQL_FLOAT SQL_DOUBLE SQL_BLOB SQL_CLOB SQL_DBCLOB SQL_BINARY SQL_VARBINARY SQL_LONGVARBINARY SQL_DATE SQL_TIME SQL_TIMESTAMP SQL_GRAPHIC SQL_VARGRAPHIC SQL_LONGVARGRAPHIC
3	COLUMN_SIZE	INTEGER	The maximum number of bytes needed to display the column data in character form. For numeric data types, this is either the total number of digits, or the total number of bits allowed in the column, depending on the value in the **NUM_PREC_RADIX** column. For character or binary string data types, this is the size of the string (string length), in bytes. For date, time, and timestamp data types, this is the total number of characters required to display the value when it is converted to a character string.
4	LITERAL_PREFIX	VARCHAR(128)	One or more characters used as a prefix for a literal representation of the SQL data type identified in the **DATA_TYPE** column. For example, a single quotation mark (') might be used for character data types, or '0x' might be used for binary data types. For data types where a literal prefix is not applicable, this column is set to NULL.
5	LITERAL_SUFFIX	VARCHAR(128)	One or more characters used as a suffix to terminate a literal representation of the SQL data type identified in the **DATA_TYPE** column. For example, a single quotation mark (') might be used for character data types. For data types in which a literal prefix is not applicable, this column is set to NULL.
6	CREATE_PARAMS	VARCHAR(128)	A list of keywords, separated by commas, corresponding to each parameter an application may specify in parentheses when using the name returned in the **TYPE_NAME** column as a data type in SQL (for example, **LENGTH**, **PRECISION**, **SCALE**, etc.). The keywords appear in the

Table 8–4　Result Data Set Returned By **SQLGetTypeInfo()** (Continued)

Column Number	Column Name	Data Type	Description
			list in the order required by the SQL syntax. For example, **CREATE_PARAMS** for **DECIMAL** would be **"PRECISION, SCALE"**; **CREATE_PARAMS** for **VARCHAR** would be **"LENGTH"**. If no parameters are specified for the data type are returned (for example: **INTEGER**), this column is set to NULL.
			Note: The intent of **CREATE_PARAMS** is to enable an application to customize the interface for a Data Definition Language (DDL) builder. An application using this column should expect to only to be able to determine the number of arguments required to define the data type.
7	**NULLABLE**	**SMALLINT NOT NULL**	Indicates whether the data type accepts a NULL value. Valid values for this column are:
			SQL_NO_NULLS: The data type does not accept NULL values.
			SQL_NULLABLE: The data type accepts NULL values.
			SQL_NULLABLE_UNKNOWN: It is not known whether the data type accepts NULL values.
8	**CASE_ SENSITIVE**	**SMALLINT NOT NULL**	Indicates whether the data type can be treated as case-sensitive for collation and comparison purposes. Valid values for this column are:
			SQL_TRUE: The data type is a character data type and is case-sensitive.
			SQL_FALSE: The data type is a character data type that is not case-sensitive, the data type is not a character data type.
9	**SEARCHABLE**	**SMALLINT NOT NULL**	Indicates how the data type is used in an SQL **WHERE** clause. Valid values for this column are:
			SQL_PRED_CHAR: The data type can only be used in a **WHERE** clause **LIKE** predicate.
			SQL_PRED_BASIC: The data type can be used with all comparison operators in a **WHERE** clause except a **LIKE** predicate.
			SQL_PRED_NONE: The data type can not be used in a **WHERE** clause.
10	**UNSIGNED_ ATTRIBUTE**	**SMALLINT**	Indicates whether the data type is unsigned. Valid values for this column are:
			SQL_TRUE: The data type is unsigned.

Table 8–4   Result Data Set Returned By **SQLGetTypeInfo()** (Continued)

Column Number	Column Name	Data Type	Description
			SQL_FALSE: The data type is signed.
			NULL: This attribute is not applicable to the data type or the data type is not numeric.
11	FIXED_PREC_ SCALE	SMALLINT NOT NULL	Indicates whether the data type is an exact numeric data type that always has the same precision and scale (that is, the same width and number of decimal places). Valid values for this column are:
			SQL_TRUE: The data type has a predefined fixed precision and scale.
			SQL_FALSE: The data type does not have a predefined fixed precision and scale.
12	AUTO_ INCREMENT	SMALLINT	Indicates whether a column of this data type is automatically set to a unique value whenever a new row is inserted. Valid values for this column are:
			SQL_TRUE: The data type is auto-incrementing.
			SQL_FALSE: The data type is not auto-incrementing or this attribute is not applicable to the data type or the data type is not numeric.
			An application can insert values into a column that has this attribute, but typically it cannot update the values in the column. When an **INSERT** operation is performed on an auto-increment column, a unique value is inserted into the column. The increment used is data-source specific— an application should not assume that an auto-increment column starts at any particular point or increments by any particular value.
13	LOCAL_TYPE_ NAME	VARCHAR(128)	Character representation of any localized (native language) name for the data type that is different from the regular data type name stored in the **TYPE_NAME** column.
			If there is no localized name for the data type, this column is set to NULL.
			This column is intended to be used for display purposes only. The character set of the string is locale-dependent and usually defaults to the character set used by the data source.

Table 8–4   Result Data Set Returned By **SQLGetTypeInfo()** (Continued)

Column Number	Column Name	Data Type	Description
14	MINIMUM_SCALE	INTEGER	The minimum scale value of the SQL data type. If the data type has a fixed scale, both the **MINIMUM_SCALE** column and the **MAXIMUM_SCALE** column contain the same value. For example, an **SQL_TYPE_TIMESTAMP** data type might have a fixed scale for fractional seconds.
			This column is set to NULL for data types where scale is not applicable.
15	MAXIMUM_SCALE	INTEGER	The maximum scale value of the SQL data type. If the maximum scale is not defined separately in the data source, but is defined instead to be the same as the maximum length of the column, then this column contains the same value as the **COLUMN_SIZE** column.
			This column is set to NULL for data types where scale is not applicable.
16	SQL_DATA_TYPE	SMALLINT NOT NULL	The SQL data type of the column identified in the **COLUMN_NAME** column, as it would appear in the **SQL_DESC_TYPE** field of an implementation row descriptor record.
			This column usually contains the same value as the **DATA_TYPE** column, with the following exception:
17	SQL_DATETIME_ SUB	SMALLINT	The subtype code for datetime and interval data types. This column is always set to NULL. (DB2 CLI does not support datetime and interval data types.)
18	NUM_PREC_RADIX	INTEGER	The radix value of the data type.
			For approximate numeric data types, this column contains the value **2** and the **COLUMN_SIZE** column contains the number of bits allowed in the column.
			For exact numeric data types, this column contains the value **10**, and the **COLUMN_SIZE** column contains the number of decimal digits allowed for the column.
			For numeric data types, this column can contain either **10** or **2**.
			For data types where radix is not applicable, this column is set to NULL.
19	INTERVAL_ PRECISION	SMALLINT	For interval data types this column contains the interval leading precision value. This column is always set to NULL. (DB2 CLI does not support interval data types.)

(Adapted from table 163 on pages 573-577 of *IBM DB2 Universal Database Call Level Interface Guide and Reference*.)

The data types returned by **SQLGetTypeInfo()** are the SQL-specific data types supported by the data source. These data types are intended to be used in Data Definition Language (DDL) statements.

Return Codes **SQL_SUCCESS**, **SQL_INVALID_HANDLE**, or **SQL_ERROR**

SQLSTATEs If this function returns **SQL_ERROR**, one of the following SQLSTATE values may be obtained by calling the **SQLGetDiagRec()** function:

08S01, **24**000, **40**003, **HY**001, **HY**004, **HY**010, or **HYT**00

Refer to Appendix B for detailed information about each SQLSTATE value that can be returned.

Comments
- Applications must use the type names returned in the **TYPE_NAME** column of the result data set produced by this function in **ALTER TABLE** and **CREATE TABLE** SQL statements.

- One or more rows in the result data set produced by this function can contain the same value in the **DATA_TYPE** column.

- If there is more than one name by which a data type can be specified, the result data set produced by this function may contain one row for each name. For example, for the data type **SQL_VARCHAR**, there might be one row for **VARCHAR** and one row for **CHARACTER VARYING**.

- If the value specified in the *SQLDataType* parameter is **SQL_ALL_TYPES**, information about all supported data types will be returned, (in ascending order, by **TYPE_NAME**). Unsupported data types will not be returned.

- Since this function generates a result data set (i.e. it is equivalent to executing a query) it automatically generates a cursor and begins a transaction. Before another SQL statement can be prepared and executed against the same SQL statement handle, the cursor created by this function must first be closed.

- If the value specified in the *SQLDataType* parameter is invalid, an empty result data set will be returned.

- If the **LONGDATACOMPAT** keyword was used to establish the connection or if the **SQL_LONGDATA_COMPAT** connection attribute has been set, **SQL_LONGVARBINARY**, **SQL_LONGVARCHAR**, and **SQL_LONGVARGRAPHIC** values will be returned in the **DATA_TYPE** column of the result data set in place of **SQL_BLOB**, **SQL_CLOB**, and **SQL_DBCLOB** respectively. (Refer to the **SQLDriverConnect()** and **SQLSetConnectAttr()** functions for more information.)

- Nonpersistent data type values, such as locator and user-defined data types, are not returned as part of the result data set.

- Although new columns may be added and the names of the existing columns in the result data set produced by this function might be changed in future releases of DB2 CLI, the positions of the current columns in this result data set will not change.

Prerequisites A connection to a data source must exist before this function is called.

Restrictions   The following ODBC-supported SQL data types (and their corresponding SQL-data type identifiers) are not supported by any IBM RDBMS:

TINY INT	SQL_TINYINT
BIG INT	SQL_BIGINT
BIT	SQL_BIT

See Also   SQLGetInfo(), SQLGetStmtAttr(), SQLBindCol(), SQLColAttribute(), SQLFetch(), SQLFetchScroll(), SQLCancel()

Example   The following Visual C++ program illustrates how the SQLGetTypeInfo() function can be used to obtain information about a specific data type.

```
/*-----------------------------------------------------------*/
/* NAME:     CH8EX4.CPP                                      */
/* PURPOSE: Illustrate How To Use The Following CLI API Function */
/*          In A C++ Program:                                */
/*                                                           */
/*                SQLGetTypeInfo()                           */
/*                                                           */
/* OTHER CLI APIs SHOWN:                                     */
/*          SQLAllocHandle()           SQLSetEnvAttr()       */
/*          SQLConnect()               SQLBindCol()          */
/*          SQLFetch()                 SQLDisconnect()       */
/*          SQLFreeHandle()                                  */
/*                                                           */
/*-----------------------------------------------------------*/

// Include The Appropriate Header Files
#include <windows.h>
#include <sqlcli1.h>
#include <iostream.h>

// Define The CLI_Class Class
class CLI_Class
{
    // Attributes
    public:
        SQLHANDLE   EnvHandle;
        SQLHANDLE   ConHandle;
        SQLHANDLE   StmtHandle;
        SQLRETURN   rc;

    // Operations
    public:
        CLI_Class();                              // Constructor
        ~CLI_Class();                             // Destructor
        SQLRETURN   ShowTypeInfo(SQLSMALLINT DataType);
};

// Define The Class Constructor
CLI_Class::CLI_Class()
{
    // Initialize The Return Code Variable
```

```
    rc = SQL_SUCCESS;

    // Allocate An Environment Handle
    rc = SQLAllocHandle(SQL_HANDLE_ENV, SQL_NULL_HANDLE, &EnvHandle);

    // Set The ODBC Application Version To 3.x
    if (rc == SQL_SUCCESS)
        rc = SQLSetEnvAttr(EnvHandle, SQL_ATTR_ODBC_VERSION,
                (SQLPOINTER) SQL_OV_ODBC3, SQL_IS_UINTEGER);

    // Allocate A Connection Handle
    if (rc == SQL_SUCCESS)
        rc = SQLAllocHandle(SQL_HANDLE_DBC, EnvHandle, &ConHandle);
}

// Define The Class Destructor
CLI_Class::~CLI_Class()
{
    // Free The Connection Handle
    if (ConHandle != NULL)
        SQLFreeHandle(SQL_HANDLE_DBC, ConHandle);

    // Free The Environment Handle
    if (EnvHandle != NULL)
        SQLFreeHandle(SQL_HANDLE_ENV, EnvHandle);
}

// Define The ShowTypeInfo() Member Function
SQLRETURN CLI_Class::ShowTypeInfo(SQLSMALLINT DataType)
{
    // Declare The Local Memory Variables
    SQLCHAR      TypeName[129];
    SQLSMALLINT  ColumnSize;

    // Allocate An SQL Statement Handle
    rc = SQLAllocHandle(SQL_HANDLE_STMT, ConHandle, &StmtHandle);

    // Retrieve Information About The Specified Data Type
    if (rc == SQL_SUCCESS)
    {
        rc = SQLGetTypeInfo(StmtHandle, DataType);
        if (rc == SQL_SUCCESS)
        {
            // Bind Columns In The Result Data Set Returned To
            // Application Variables
            rc = SQLBindCol(StmtHandle, 1, SQL_C_CHAR,
                    (SQLPOINTER) &TypeName, sizeof(TypeName), NULL);

            rc = SQLBindCol(StmtHandle, 3, SQL_C_DEFAULT,
                    (SQLPOINTER) &ColumnSize, sizeof(ColumnSize),
                    NULL);

            // Retrieve And Display The Results
            SQLFetch(StmtHandle);
```

```
                    cout << "SQL Data Type                 : SQL_CHAR" << endl;
                    cout << "Data-Source Data Type Name : ";
                    cout << TypeName << endl;
                    cout << "Column Size Supported       : ";
                    cout << ColumnSize << endl;
            }

            // Free The SQL Statement Handle
            if (StmtHandle != NULL)
                SQLFreeHandle(SQL_HANDLE_STMT, StmtHandle);
        }

        // Return The CLI API Return Code To The Calling Function
        return(rc);
}


/*----------------------------------------------------------------*/
/* The Main Function                                              */
/*----------------------------------------------------------------*/
int main()
{
        // Declare The Local Memory Variables
        SQLRETURN   rc = SQL_SUCCESS;

        // Create An Instance Of The CLI_Class Class
        CLI_Class  Example;

        // Connect To The DB2 Sample Database
        if (Example.ConHandle != NULL)
        {
            rc = SQLConnect(Example.ConHandle, (SQLCHAR *) "SAMPLE",
                        SQL_NTS, (SQLCHAR *) "userid", SQL_NTS,
                        (SQLCHAR *) "password", SQL_NTS);

            // Call The ShowTypeInfo() Member Function
            if (rc == SQL_SUCCESS || rc == SQL_SUCCESS_WITH_INFO)
                Example.ShowTypeInfo(SQL_CHAR);

            // Disconnect From The DB2 Sample Database
            rc = SQLDisconnect(Example.ConHandle);
        }

        // Return To The Operating System
        return(rc);
}
```

SQLGetEnvAttr

COMPATIBILITY

X/OPEN 95 CLI	ISO/IEC 92 CLI	DB2 CLI 5.2	DB2 CLI 2.0	ODBC 3.x
☑	☑	☑	☑	☑

ODBC API CONFORMANCE LEVEL   CORE

Purpose   The SQLGetEnvAttr() function is used to retrieve the current setting of a specified environment attribute.

Syntax
```
SQLRETURN SQLGetEnvAttr    (SQLHENV      EnvironmentHandle,
                            SQLINTEGER   Attribute,
                            SQLPOINTER   Value,
                            SQLINTEGER   ValueMaxSize,
                            SQLINTEGER   *StringLength);
```

Parameters   *EnvironmentHandle*   An environment handle that refers to a previously allocated environment information storage buffer (data structure).

Attribute   The environment attribute whose value is to be retrieved. This parameter must be set to one of the following values:

- SQL_ATTR_CONNECTION_POOLING
- SQL_ATTR_CONNECTTYPE
- SQL_ATTR_CP_MATCH
- SQL_ATTR_MAXCONN
- SQL_ATTR_ODBC_VERSION
- SQL_ATTR_OUTPUT_NTS
- SQL_ATTR_SYNC_POINT

Value   A pointer to a location in memory where this function is to store the current value of the specified environment attribute.

ValueMaxSize   The maximum size of the memory storage buffer where this function is to store the current value of the specified environment attribute. If the attribute value retrieved is not a character string value, this parameter is ignored.

StringLength   A pointer to a location in memory where this function returns the actual number of bytes written to the attribute value memory storage buffer (*Value*). If the attribute value retrieved is not a character string value, this parameter is ignored.

Description   The **SQLGetEnvAttr()** function is used to retrieve the current setting of a specified environment attribute. This function can be called at any time after an environment handle is allocated, as long as that environment handle has not been freed. Table 8–5 alphabetically lists each value that can be specified for the *Attribute* parameter, along with a description of the information returned for that value when this function is executed.

Table 8–5   Environment Attributes

Attribute	Data Type	Description
SQL_ATTR_CONNECTION_POOLING	32-bit SQLUINTEGER	Enables or disables connection pooling at the environment level.
		Valid values for this attribute are:
		SQL_CP_OFF: Connection pooling is turned off. This is the default value for this attribute.
		SQL_CP_ONE_PER_DRIVER: A single connection pool is supported for each DB2 CLI application (that is, every connection in a pool is associated with one application).
		SQL_CP_ONE_PER_HENV: A single connection pool is supported for each environment (that is, every connection in a pool is associated with one environment).
		Connection pooling is enabled by setting the **SQL_ATTR_CONNECTION_POOLING** attribute to **SQL_CP_ONE_PER_DRIVER** or **SQL_CP_ONE_PER_HENV**. This call must be made before the application allocates the shared environment for which connection pooling is to be enabled. The environment handle in the call to **SQLSetEnvAttr()** is set to NULL, which makes **SQL_ATTR_CONNECTION_POOLING** a process-level attribute. After connection pooling is enabled, the application then allocates an implicit shared environment by calling the **SQLAllocHandle()** function with the *InputHandle* parameter set to **SQL_HANDLE_ENV**.
		After connection pooling has been enabled and a shared environment has been selected for an application, the **SQL_ATTR_CONNECTION_POOLING** attribute cannot be changed for that environment because a NULL environment handle was used to set this attribute initially.

Table 8–5 *Environment Attributes (Continued)*

Attribute	Data Type	Description
		If this attribute is set while connection pooling is already enabled on a shared environment, the attribute only affects subsequent shared environment allocations.
`SQL_ATTR_CP_MATCH`	32-bit `SQLUINTEGER`	Determines how a connection is chosen from a connection pool. When `SQLConnect()` or `SQLDriverConnect()` is called, in order to determine which connection is to be reused from the pool, the the CLI Library or the ODBC Driver Manager attempts to match the connection options specified in the call and the connection attributes set by the application to the keywords and connection attributes of the connections in the pool. The value of this attribute determines the level of precision used to match the two. Valid values for this attribute are: `SQL_CP_STRICT_MATCH`: Only connections exactly matching the connection options in the call and the connection attributes set by the application are reused. This is the default value for this attribute. `SQL_CP_RELAXED_MATCH`: Connections with matching connection string keywords can be used. Keywords must match, but not all connection attributes must match.
`SQL_ATTR_CONNECTTYPE`	32-bit `INTEGER`	Specifies whether this application is to operate in a coordinated or uncoordinated distributed environment. If processing needs to be coordinated, then this attribute must be taken into consideration, along with the `SQL_SYNC_POINT` environment attribute. Valid values for this attribute are: `SQL_CONCURRENT_TRANS`: The application can have concurrent multiple connections to any one data source or to multiple data sources at any given time. Each data source connection has its own commit scope. No effort is made to enforce coordination of transactions. If an application issues a commit

Table 8–5 Environment Attributes (Continued)

Attribute	Data Type	Description
		using the environment handle with the **SQLEndTrans()** function and not all of the connections get committed successfully, the application is responsible for handling recovery. This value corresponds to the specification of the Type 1 **CONNECT** SQL statement.
		When this value is specified, the current setting of the **SQL_ATTR_SYNC_POINT** attribute is ignored. This is the default value for this attribute.
		SQL_COORDINATED_TRANS: The application wishes to have commits and rollbacks coordinated among multiple data source connections. This value corresponds to the specification of the Type 2 **CONNECT** SQL statement and must be considered in conjunction with the **SQL_ATTR_SYNC_POINT** environment attribute. In contrast to the **SQL_CONCURRENT_TRANS** value described above, the application is permitted only one open connection per data source.
		This attribute can only be changed when there are no connection handles allocated under this environment. All data source connections within an application must have the same **SQL_ATTR_CONNECTTYPE** and **SQL_ATTR_SYNC_POINT** values. This attribute can also be changed by calling the **SQLSetConnectAttr()** function. However, it is recommended that an application set this attribute at the environment level (with the **SQLSetEnvAttr()** function) rather than on a per connection basis (with the **SQLSetConnectAttr()** function). ODBC applications that are designed to take advantage of coordinated DB2 transaction processing must set this attribute at the connection level for each connection, using the **SQLSetConnectAttr()** function, since this attribute is not supported by ODBC's **SQLSetEnvAttr()** function.
		This is an IBM defined attribute.
SQL_ATTR_MAXCONN	32-bit **INTEGER**	Specifies the maximum number of concurrent data source connections that an application can have open at one time.

Table 8–5   Environment Attributes (Continued)

Attribute	Data Type	Description
		This attribute can be used to control the maximum number of connections allowed on a per application basis. The value specified for this attribute must be **0** or a positive number. The default value for this attribute is **0**, which means that an application can establish as many data source connections as system resources permit.
		On OS/2, if the NetBIOS protocol is in use, this value corresponds to the number of NetBIOS sessions that will be concurrently reserved for use by the application. The range of values for OS/2 NetBIOS sessions is **1** to **254**. If the value **0** (the default value for this attribute) is specified, 5 OS/2 NetBIOS sessions will be reserved. Reserved NetBIOS sessions cannot be used by other applications. The number of NetBIOS sessions (connections) specified by this attribute will be applied to any adapter number that DB2 NetBIOS protocol uses to connect to the remote data source.
		Note: The adapter number is specified in the node directory when a NetBIOS node is cataloged.
		The value that is in effect when the first connection to a data source is established is the value that will be used throughout the life of the application; once the first connection has been established, all attempts to change this value will be rejected.
		This attribute can also be changed by calling the **SQLSetConnectAttr()** function. However, it is recommended that an application set this attribute at the environment level (with the **SQLSetEnvAttr()** function) rather than on a per connection basis (with the **SQLSetConnectAttr()** function). ODBC applications must set this attribute at the connection level for each connection, using the **SQLSetConnectAttr()** function, since this attribute is not supported by ODBC's **SQLSetEnvAttr()** function.
		This is an IBM defined attribute.

Table 8-5 Environment Attributes (Continued)

Attribute	Data Type	Description
SQL_ATTR_ODBC_VERSION	32-bit INTEGER	Determines whether certain functionality exhibits ODBC 2.0 (DB2 CLI 2.0) behavior or ODBC 3.x behavior (DB2 CLI 5.2). Valid values for this attribute are: SQL_OV_ODBC3: The ODBC Driver Manager and the CLI Library exhibit the following ODBC 3.x behavior: • DB2 CLI returns and expects ODBC 3.x codes for date, time, and timestamp. • DB2 CLI returns ODBC 3.x SQLSTATE codes when SQLError(), SQLGetDiagField(), or SQLGetDiagRec() are called. • The *CatalogName* parameter in the SQLTables() function accepts a search pattern. SQL_OV_ODBC2: The ODBC Driver Manager and the CLI Library exhibit the following ODBC 2.0 (and earlier) behavior: • DB2 CLI returns and expects ODBC 2.0 codes for date, time, and timestamp. • DB2 CLI returns ODBC 2.0 SQLSTATE codes when SQLError(), SQLGetDiagField(), or SQLGetDiagRec() are called. • The *CatalogName* parameter in the SQLTables() function does not accept a search pattern. An application must set this environment attribute before calling any function requiring a valid environment handle as an input parameter, or the call returns SQLSTATE **HY**010 (Function sequence error).
SQL_ATTR_OUTPUT_NTS	32-bit INTEGER	Determines how the DB2 CLI returns string data. Valid values for this attribute are: SQL_TRUE: DB2 CLI appends a NULL-terminator character to string data before it is returned. This is the default value for this attribute.

Table 8–5   *Environment Attributes (Continued)*

Attribute	Data Type	Description
		SQL_FALSE: DB2 CLI does not append a NULL-terminator character to string data before it is returned.
SQL_ATTR_SYNC_POINT	32-bit **INTEGER**	Allows an application to choose between one-phase coordinated (commit) transactions and two-phase coordinated (commit) transactions. Valid values for this attribute are:
		SQL_ONEPHASE: One-phase commit is used to commit the work done by each data source in a multiple data source transaction. To ensure data integrity, each transaction must ensure that only one data source, if any, gets updated. The first data source that has updates performed on it within a transaction becomes the only updateable data source in that transaction; all other data sources accessed are treated as read-only. All attempts to update a read-only data source within this transaction are rejected.
		SQL_TWOPHASE: Two-phase commit is used to commit the work done by each data source in a multiple data source transaction. This value requires the use of a Transaction Manager to coordinate two phase commits amongst the connected data sources that support this protocol. Multiple read-writeable and multiple updateable data sources are allowed within a single transaction.
		All data source connections within an application must have the same **SQL_ATTR_CONNECTTYPE** and **SQL_ATTR_SYNC_POINT** values. This attribute can also be changed by calling the **SQLSetConnectAttr()** function. However, it is recommended that an application set this attribute at the environment level (with the **SQLSetEnvAttr()** function) rather than on a per connection basis (with the

Table 8–5 Environment Attributes (Continued)

Attribute	Data Type	Description
		SQLSetConnectAttr() function). ODBC applications that are designed to take advantage of coordinated DB2 transaction processing must set this attribute at the connection level for each connection, using the **SQLSetConnectAttr()** function, since this attribute is not supported by ODBC's **SQLSetEnvAttr()** function.
		This is an IBM defined attribute.
		Note: In embedded SQL, there is an additional sync point value (**SYNCPOINT_ NONE**) that is more restrictive than the **SQL_CONCURRENT_TRANS** value (**SQL_ATTR_CONNECTTYPE** attribute). Because the **SYNCPOINT_NONE** value does not allow multiple connections to the same data source, DB2 CLI does not support it.

(The preceding information was adapted from the table on pages 945–947 of *Microsoft ODBC 3.0 Software Development Kit & Programmer's Reference*.)

All environment attributes successfully set by an application for a specified environment persist until the environment handle is freed with the **SQLFreeHandle()** function. Because more than one environment handle can be allocated simultaneously, environment attribute settings on one environment are not affected when another environment is allocated.

Return Codes SQL_SUCCESS, SQL_INVALID_HANDLE, or SQL_ERROR

SQLSTATEs If this function returns SQL_ERROR, one of the following SQLSTATE values may be obtained by calling the **SQLGetDiagRec()** function:

HY001, or **HY**092

Refer to Appendix B for detailed information about each SQLSTATE value that can be returned.

Comments
- If the *Value* parameter contains a NULL pointer, no length is returned in the *StringLength* parameter.
- If an attribute that returns a string value is specified in the *Attribute* parameter, the *Value* parameter must contain a pointer to a buffer in which this function can return the string.
- If an attribute that returns a string value is specified in the *Attribute* parameter, and if that string value's actual length is greater than or equal to the maximum

string size value specified in the *ValueMaxSize* parameter, the value is truncated to *ValueMaxSize*–1 (the length of a NULL-termination character) characters.

■ The `SQL_ATTR_OUTPUT_NTS` environment attribute is supported by all standards-compliant applications.

Prerequisites   An environment handle must be allocated before this function is called.

Restrictions   There are no restrictions associated with this function call.

See Also   `SQLSetEnvAttr()`, `SQLGetConnectAttr()`, `SQLSetConnectAttr()`, `SQLGetStmtAttr()`, `SQLSetStmtAttr()`

Example   The following Visual C++ program illustrates how to retrieve and change the current value of an environment attribute.

```
/*------------------------------------------------------------*/
/* NAME:    CH8EX5.CPP                                        */
/* PURPOSE: Illustrate How To Use The Following CLI API Functions */
/*          In A C++ Program:                                 */
/*                                                            */
/*                  SQLGetEnvAttr()                           */
/*                  SQLSetEnvAttr()                           */
/*                                                            */
/* OTHER CLI APIs SHOWN:                                      */
/*          SQLAllocHandle()              SQLFreeHandle()     */
/*                                                            */
/*------------------------------------------------------------*/

// Include The Appropriate Header Files
#include <windows.h>
#include <sqlcli1.h>
#include <iostream.h>

// Define The CLI_Class Class
class CLI_Class
{
    // Attributes
    public:
        SQLHANDLE    EnvHandle;
        SQLRETURN    rc;

    // Operations
    public:
        CLI_Class();                              // Constructor
        ~CLI_Class();                             // Destructor
        SQLRETURN  GetMaxConnectionValue();
        SQLRETURN  SetMaxConnectionValue(SQLINTEGER MCValue);
};

// Define The Class Constructor
CLI_Class::CLI_Class()
{
    // Initialize The Return Code Variable
    rc = SQL_SUCCESS;
```

```
    // Allocate An Environment Handle
    rc = SQLAllocHandle(SQL_HANDLE_ENV, SQL_NULL_HANDLE, &EnvHandle);

    // Set The ODBC Application Version To 3.x
    if (rc == SQL_SUCCESS)
        rc = SQLSetEnvAttr(EnvHandle, SQL_ATTR_ODBC_VERSION,
                      (SQLPOINTER) SQL_OV_ODBC3, SQL_IS_UINTEGER);
}

// Define The Class Destructor
CLI_Class::~CLI_Class()
{
    // Free The Environment Handle
    if (EnvHandle != NULL)
        SQLFreeHandle(SQL_HANDLE_ENV, EnvHandle);
}

// Define The GetMaxConnectionValue() Member Function
SQLRETURN CLI_Class::GetMaxConnectionValue(void)
{
    // Declare The Local Memory Variables
    SQLINTEGER  MCValue;
    SQLINTEGER  ValueLength;

    // Retrieve The Maximum Number Of Connections Allowed
    rc = SQLGetEnvAttr(EnvHandle, SQL_ATTR_MAXCONN,
              (SQLPOINTER) &MCValue, SQL_IS_UINTEGER, &ValueLength);

    // Display The Information Retrieved
    if (rc == SQL_SUCCESS)
    {
        cout << "Maximum Number Of Connections Allowed : ";
          if (MCValue == 0)
                cout << "No Limit";
        else
             cout << MCValue;
        cout << endl;
    }

    // Return The CLI API Return Code To The Calling Function
    return(rc);
}

// Define The SetMaxConnectionValue() Member Function
SQLRETURN CLI_Class::SetMaxConnectionValue(SQLINTEGER MCValue)
{
    // Set The Maximum Connections Environment Attribute
    rc = SQLSetEnvAttr(EnvHandle, SQL_ATTR_MAXCONN,
              (SQLPOINTER) MCValue, SQL_IS_UINTEGER);

    // Return The CLI API Return Code To The Calling Function
    return(rc);
}
```

```
/*————————————————————————————————————————*/
/* The Main Function                                              */
/*————————————————————————————————————————*/
int main()
{
    // Declare The Local Memory Variables
    SQLRETURN  rc = SQL_SUCCESS;

    // Create An Instance Of The CLI_Class Class
    CLI_Class  Example;

    // Determine The Maximum Number Of Connections Allowed
    rc = Example.GetMaxConnectionValue();

    // Tell The Driver To Allow Only 5 Concurrent Connections
    rc = Example.SetMaxConnectionValue(5);

    // See If The Maximum Number Of Connections Allowed Has Been
    // Set To 5
    rc = Example.GetMaxConnectionValue();

    // Return To The Operating System
    return(rc);
}
```

SQLSetEnvAttr

COMPATIBILITY

X/OPEN 95 CLI	ISO/IEC 92 CLI	DB2 CLI 5.2	DB2 CLI 2.0	ODBC 3.x
☑	☑	☑	☑	☑

ODBC API CONFORMANCE LEVEL   CORE

Purpose   The SQLSetEnvAttr() function is used to modify the current value of a specified environment attribute.

Syntax
```
SQLRETURN SQLSetEnvAttr    (SQLHENV      EnvironmentHandle,
                            SQLINTEGER   Attribute,
                            SQLPOINTER   Value,
                            SQLINTEGER   StringLength);
```

Parameters   *EnvironmentHandle*   An environment handle that refers to a previously allocated environment information storage buffer (data structure).

Attribute   The environment attribute whose value is to be modified. This parameter must be set to one of the following values:

■ **SQL_ATTR_CONNECTION_POOLING**

■ **SQL_ATTR_CONNECTTYPE**

■ **SQL_ATTR_CP_MATCH**

■ **SQL_ATTR_MAXCONN**

■ **SQL_ATTR_ODBC_VERSION**

■ **SQL_ATTR_OUTPUT_NTS**

■ **SQL_ATTR_SYNC_POINT**

Value	A pointer to a location in memory where the new value for the environment attribute is stored. Depending on the environment attribute being set, this pointer can reference either a 32-bit integer value, or a NULL-terminated character string.
StringLength	The length of the environment attribute value stored in the *Value* parameter. If the attribute value is a 32-bit integer value, this parameter is ignored.

Description The **SQLSetEnvAttr()** function is used to modify the current value of a specified environment attribute. Refer to the **SQLGetEnvAttr()** function for more information about each environment attribute available.

All environment attributes successfully set by an application for the specified environment persist until the environment handle is freed with the **SQLFreeHandle()** function. Because more than one environment handle can be allocated simultaneously, environment attribute settings on one environment are not affected when another environment is allocated. Once an environment attribute is set, that attribute's value affects all data source connections that exist or become allocated under the specified environment.

Return Codes **SQL_SUCCESS**, **SQL_SUCCESS_WITH_INFO**, **SQL_INVALID_HANDLE**, or **SQL_ERROR**

SQLSTATEs If this function returns **SQL_SUCCESS_WITH_INFO** or **SQL_ERROR**, one of the following SQLSTATE values may be obtained by calling the **SQLGetDiagRec()** function:

HY009, HY011, HY024, HY090, HY092, or **HYC00**

Refer to Appendix B for detailed information about each SQLSTATE value that can be returned.

Comments ■ This function can be called more than once to set any environment attribute; if this function is called more than once with the same attribute specified, the value for that attribute is overridden.

■ An application using pooled connections should always evaluate, and if necessary, set the **SQL_ATTR_CP_MATCH** attribute. This attribute determines how a requested connection is matched to a pooled connection when pooled connections are used. If the **SQL_ATTR_CP_MATCH** environment attribute is set to **SQL_CP_STRICT_MATCH**, the match must be exact for a connection in the pool to be used. If the **SQL_ATTR_CP_MATCH** environment attribute is set to **SQL_CP_RELAXED_MATCH**, the connection options specified in the call to **SQLConnect()** must match, but not all the connection attributes must match.

Prerequisites An environment handle must be allocated before this function is called.

Restrictions An application can only call this function if no connection handle has been allocated on the environment.

See Also SQLGetEnvAttr(), SQLGetConnectAttr(), SQLSetConnectAttr(), SQLGetStmtAttr(), SQLSetStmtAttr()

Example See the example provided for the **SQLGetEnvAttr()** function, on page 204

SQLGetConnectAttr

COMPATIBILITY

X/OPEN 95 CLI	ISO/IEC 92 CLI	DB2 CLI 5.2	DB2 CLI 2.0	ODBC 3.x
✓	✓	✓	☐	✓

ODBC API CONFORMANCE LEVEL   **CORE**

Purpose The **SQLGetConnectAttr()** function is used to retrieve the current setting of a specified connection attribute.

Syntax
```
SQLRETURN SQLGetConnectAttr (SQLHDBC      ConnectionHandle,
                             SQLINTEGER   Attribute,
                             SQLPOINTER   Value,
                             SQLINTEGER   ValueMaxSize,
                             SQLINTEGER   *StringLength);
```

Parameters *ConnectionHandle*   A data source connection handle that refers to a previously allocated connection information storage buffer (data structure).

Attribute   The connection attribute whose value is to be retrieved. This parameter must be set to one of the following values:

- **SQL_ATTR_ACCESS_MODE**
- **SQL_ATTR_ASYNC_ENABLE**
- **SQL_ATTR_AUTO_IPD**
- **SQL_ATTR_AUTOCOMMIT**
- **SQL_ATTR_CONN_CONTEXT**
- **SQL_ATTR_CONNECTTYPE**

■ **SQL_ATTR_CURRENT_SCHEMA**

■ **SQL_ATTR_DB2ESTIMATE**

■ **SQL_ATTR_DB2EXPLAIN**

■ **SQL_ATTR_LONGDATA_COMPAT**

■ **SQL_ATTR_MAXCONN**

■ **SQL_ATTR_QUIET_MODE**

■ **SQL_ATTR_SYNC_POINT**

■ **SQL_ATTR_TRANSLATE_LIB**

■ **SQL_ATTR_TRANSLATE_OPTION**

■ **SQL_ATTR_TXN_ISOLATION**

■ **SQL_ATTR_WCHARTYPE**

Value
A pointer to a location in memory where this function is to store the current value of the specified connection attribute.

ValueMaxSize
The size of the memory storage buffer where this function is to store the current value of the specified connection attribute. If an ODBC-defined attribute is to be retrieved and if the attribute value is a 32-bit integer value, this parameter is ignored. If a DB2 CLI attribute is to be retrieved, this parameter may be set as follows:

■ If the value of the specified connection attribute is a character string, this parameter may be set to the actual length of the string or to **SQL_NTS**.

■ If the value of the specified connection attribute is a binary string, this parameter may be set to the result of the **SQL_LEN_BINARY_ATTR**(length) macro. Usually, this macro places a negative value in this parameter.

■ If the value of the specified connection attribute is anything other than a character string or binary string, this parameter may be set to **SQL_IS_POINTER**.

■ If the value of the specified connection attribute is a fixed-length data type, this parameter may be set to **SQL_IS_INTEGER** or **SQL_IS_UINTEGER**, as appropriate.

StringLength
A pointer to a location in memory where this function is to store the actual number of bytes written to the attribute value memory storage buffer (*Value*). If the attribute value retrieved is not a character string value, this parameter is ignored.

Description   The **SQLGetConnectAttr()** function is used to retrieve the current setting of a specified connection attribute. This function can be called at any time after a connection handle is allocated, as long as that connection handle has not been freed. Table 8–6 lists alphabetically each value that can be specified for the *Attribute* parameter, along with a description of the information returned for that value when this function is executed.

 NOTE: *This function replaces the DB2 CLI 2.0 function* **SQLGetConnectOption()**.

Return Codes   SQL_SUCCESS, SQL_SUCCESS_WITH_INFO, SQL_NO_DATA, SQL_INVALID_HANDLE, or SQL_ERROR

Table 8-6   *Connection Attributes*

Attribute	Data Type	Description
SQL_ATTR_ACCESS_MODE	SQLUINTEGER	Specifies the type of SQL requests that can be made to the connected data source. Valid values for this attribute are: **SQL_MODE_READ_ONLY:** Indicates that the connection is not required to support SQL statements causing updates to occur. This mode can be used to optimize locking strategies, transaction management, or other areas as appropriate to the driver or data source. **SQL_MODE_READ_WRITE:** Indicates that the connection is required to support SQL statements causing updates to occur. This is the default value for this attribute. Note: When this attribute is set to **SQL_MODE_READ_ONLY**, DB2 CLI does not prevent the submission of SQL statements that cause updates to occur from reaching the data source.
SQL_ATTR_ASYNC_ENABLE	SQLUINTEGER	Specifies whether a CLI function called by an SQL statement on the specified connection is executed asynchronously. Valid values for this attribute are: **SQL_ASYNC_ENABLE_OFF:** All future statement handles allocated on this connection cannot be executed asynchronously. This is the default value for this attribute. **SQL_ASYNC_ENABLE_ON:** All future statement handles allocated on this connection can be executed asynchronously. This setting also enables asynchronous execution for existing statement handles associated with the connection. An error is returned if asynchronous execution is enabled while there is an active statement on the connection.

Table 8-6 Connection Attributes (Continued)

Attribute	Data Type	Description
		This attribute can be set as long as the **SQLGetInfo()** function returns **SQL_AM_CONNECTION** or **SQL_AM_STATEMENT** when it is called with the **SQL_ASYNC_MODE** option specified.
		After a function has been called asynchronously, only the original function, **SQLAllocHandle()**, **SQLCancel()**, **SQLGetDiagField()**, or **SQLGetDiagRec()** can be called on the statement handle or the connection handle associated with the statement handle, until the original function returns a code other than **SQL_STILL_EXECUTING**. Any other function called on the statement handle or the connection handle associated with the statement handle returns **SQL_ERROR** with an SQLSTATE of **HY**010 (Function sequence error). Functions can be called on other statement handles.
		In general, applications should only execute CLI functions asynchronously on single-thread operating systems. On multithread operating systems, applications should execute CLI functions on separate threads, rather than executing them asynchronously on the same thread.
		The following functions can be executed asynchronously:
		SQLColAttribute(), **SQLColumnPrivileges()**, **SQLColumns()**, **SQLCopyDesc()**, **SQLDescribeCol()**, **SQLDescribeParam()**, **SQLExecDirect()**, **SQLExecute()**, **SQLFetch()**, **SQLFetchScroll()**, **SQLForeignKeys()**, **SQLGetData()**, **SQLGetDescField()**,[1] **SQLGetDescRec()**,[1] **SQLGetDiagField()**, **SQLGetDiagRec()**, **SQLGetTypeInfo()**, **SQLMoreResults()**, **SQLNumParams()**, **SQLNumResultCols()**, **SQLParamData()**, **SQLPrepare()**, **SQLPrimaryKeys()**, **SQLProcedureColumns()**, **SQLProcedures()**, **SQLPutData()**, **SQLSetPos()**, **SQLSpecialColumns()**, **SQLStatistics()**, **SQLTablePrivileges()**, **SQLTables()**
		[1]These functions can only be called if the descriptor used is an implementation descriptor.
SQL_ATTR_AUTO_IPD	**SQLUINTEGER**	Specifies whether automatic population of the implementation parameter descriptor (IPD) after a **SQLPrepare()** function call is supported. Valid values for this attribute are:
		SQL_TRUE: Automatic population of the IPD after a call to **SQLPrepare()** is supported by the driver.
		SQL_FALSE: Automatic population of the IPD after a call to **SQLPrepare()** is not supported by the driver.

Table 8-6 Connection Attributes (Continued)

Attribute	Data Type	Description
		This connection attribute is a read-only attribute; its value can be retrtieved by the **SQLGetConnectAttr()** function, but it cannot be set by the **SQLSetConnectAttr()** function.
		If the **SQL_ATTR_AUTO_IPD** connection attribute is set to **SQL_TRUE**, the statement attribute **SQL_ATTR_ENABLE_ AUTO_IPD** can be set to **SQL_TRUE** or **SQL_FALSE** (to turn automatic population of the IPD on or off).
		If the **SQL_ATTR_AUTO_IPD** connection attribute is set to **SQL_FALSE**, the statement attribute **SQL_ATTR_ENABLE_ AUTO_IPD** can only be set to **SQL_FALSE**.
		The default value of the **SQL_ATTR_AUTO_IPD** connection attribute is the same as the value of the **SQL_ATTR_ AUTO_IPD** statement attribute.
		Servers that don't support prepared statements cannot populate the IPD automatically.
SQL_ATTR_AUTOCOMMIT	**SQLUINTEGER**	Specifies whether to use auto-commit or manual-commit mode. Valid values for this attribute are:
		SQL_AUTOCOMMIT_OFF: DB2 CLI uses manual-commit mode, and the application must explicitly commit or roll back transactions with the **SQLEndTran()** function.
		SQL_AUTOCOMMIT_ON: DB2 CLI uses auto-commit mode, therefore each SQL statement is committed immediately after it is executed. This is the default value for this attribute.
		Any open transactions on the connection are automatically committed when the **SQL_ATTR_AUTOCOMMIT** connection attribute is set to **SQL_AUTOCOMMIT_ON** (to change from manual-commit mode to auto-commit mode).
		Note: Some data sources delete the access plans and close the cursors for all SQL statements on a connection each time an SQL statement is committed; auto-commit mode can cause this to happen after each non-query statement is executed, or when the cursor associated with a query is closed.
		When a batch of statements are executed in auto-commit mode, two things are possible:
		1. The entire batch can be treated as an auto-commitable unit, or
		2. Each statement in the batch is treated as an autocommitable unit.

Table 8-6 Connection Attributes (Continued)

Attribute	Data Type	Description
		It is driver-defined whether a batch is treated as an auto-commitable unit, or whether each individual statement within the batch is auto-commitable. Some data sources may support both these behaviors and may provide a way of choosing one or the other.
SQL_ATTR_CONN_CONTEXT	SQLPOINTER	Specifies the context the connection should use. Valid values for this attribute are: • a valid context (i.e. a context that was allocated by the SQLBeginCtx() API) • a NULL pointer (to reset the context) This attribute can only be used when an application is using the DB2 context APIs to manage multi-threaded applications. By default, DB2 CLI manages contexts by allocating one context for each connection handle and ensuring that executing threads are attached to the correct context. This is an IBM defined attribute.
SQL_ATTR_CONNECTTYPE	32-bit INTEGER	Specifies whether this application is to operate in a coordinated or uncoordinated distributed environment. If processing needs to be coordinated, then this attribute must be taken into consideration, along with the SQL_SYNC_POINT environment attribute. Valid values for this attribute are: SQL_CONCURRENT_TRANS: The application can have concurrent multiple connections to any one data source or to multiple data sources at any given time. Each data source connection has its own commit scope. No effort is made to enforce coordination of transactions. If an application issues a commit using the environment handle with the SQLEndTrans() function and not all of the connections get committed successfully, the application is responsible for handling recovery. This value corresponds to the specification of the Type 1 CONNECT SQL statement. When this value is specified, the current setting of the SQL_ATTR_SYNC_POINT attribute is ignored. This is the default value for this attribute. SQL_COORDINATED_TRANS: The application wishes to have commits and rollbacks coordinated among multiple data source connections. This value corresponds to the specification of the Type 2 CONNECT SQL statement and must be considered in conjunction with the SQL_ATTR_SYNC_POINT environment attribute. In contrast to the SQL_CONCURRENT_TRANS value described above, the application is permitted only one open connection per data source.

Table 8-6   Connection Attributes (Continued)

Attribute	Data Type	Description
		This attribute can only be changed when there are no connection handles allocated under this environment. All data source connections within an application must have the same **SQL_ATTR_CONNECTTYPE** and **SQL_ATTR_SYNC_POINT** values. This attribute can also be changed by calling the **SQLSetConnectAttr()** function. However, it is recommended that an application set this attribute at the environment level (with the **SQLSetEnvAttr()** function) rather than on a per connection basis (with the **SQLSetConnectAttr()** function). ODBC applications that are designed to take advantage of coordinated DB2 transaction processing must set this attribute at the connection level for each connection, using the **SQLSetConnectAttr()** function, because this attribute is not supported by ODBC's **SQLSetEnvAttr()** function.
		This is an IBM defined attribute.
SQL_ATTR_CURRENT_SCHEMA	character string	Specifies the name of the schema to be used by DB2 CLI for the **SQLColumns()** function call whenever the *SchemaName* parameter is set to NULL. This option is useful when an application developer has coded a generic call to the **SQLColumns()** function that normally does not restrict the result set by schema name, but needs to constrain the result data set at isolated places in the code.
		This option can be set at any time and will become effective on the next call to the **SQLColumns()** function where the *SchemaName* parameter is set to NULL. To disable this option, assign it a 0 length string or a NULL pointer.
		This is an IBM defined attribute.
SQL_ATTR_DB2ESTIMATE	**SQLUINTEGER**	Specifies whether DB2 CLI will display a dialog box to report estimates returned by the optimizer at the end of SQL query preparation. Valid values for this attribute are:
		0: DB2 CLI will not report estimates. This is the default value for this attribute.
		A large positive number: If the number specified (recommended value is 60000), is larger than the value stored in the SQLERRD(4) field of the SQLCA data structure associated with the **PREPARE** operation, the estimates dialog box will be displayed. This graphical dialog box displays optimizer estimates and prompts the user to either continue with the execution of the query or cancel processing.
		This attribute can be set at any time and will become effective the next time an SQL statement is prepared for the specified connection.

Table 8-6 Connection Attributes (Continued)

Attribute	Data Type	Description
		This attribute is used in conjunction with the **SQL_ATTR_QUIET_MODE** attribute and is only applicable for applications that use graphical interfaces. An application can implement this feature directly, without using this attribute, by calling the **SQLGetSQLCA()** function immediately after calling the **SQLPrepare()** function and then displaying the appropriate information in a dialog box, thus allowing a more integrated overall interface.
		This is an IBM defined attribute.
SQL_ATTR_DB2EXPLAIN	SQLUINTEGER	Specifies whether Explain snapshot and/or Explain table information should be generated by the server. Valid values for this attribute are:
		SQL_DB2EXPLAIN_OFF: Neither Explain snapshot nor Explain table information is to be generated (i.e., **SET CURRENT EXPLAIN SNAPSHOT = NO** and **SET CURRENT EXPLAIN MODE = NO** SQL statements are sent to the server). This is the default value for this attribute.
		SQL_DB2EXPLAIN_SNAPSHOT_ON: Explain snapshot information is to be generated, Explain table information is not (i.e., **SET CURRENT EXPLAIN SNAPSHOT = YES** and **SET CURRENT EXPLAIN MODE = NO** SQL statements are sent to the server).
		SQL_DB2EXPLAIN_MODE_ON: Explain table information is to be generated, Explain snapshot information is not (i.e., **SET CURRENT EXPLAIN SNAPSHOT = NO** and **SET CURRENT EXPLAIN MODE = YES** SQL statements are sent to the server).
		SQL_DB2EXPLAIN_SNAPSHOT_MODE_ON: Both Explain snapshot information and Explain table information is to be generated (i.e., **SET CURRENT EXPLAIN SNAPSHOT = YES** and **SET CURRENT EXPLAIN MODE = YES** SQL statements are sent to the server).
		Before Explain information can be generated, the Explain tables must be created and the current user authorization ID must have **INSERT** privileges for these tables.
		This option can be set at any time and will become effective the next time an SQL statement is prepared for the specified connection.
		This is an IBM defined attribute.
SQL_ATTR_LONGDATA_COMPAT	SQLUINTEGER	Specifies whether or not binary, character, and double byte character large object data types (**BLOB**, **CLOB**, and **DBCLOB**) should be reported as **SQL_LONGBINARY**, **SQL_LONGVARCHAR**, and **SQL_LONGVARGRAPHIC** respectively, thereby enabling existing applications to access

Table 8-6   Connection Attributes (Continued)

Attribute	Data Type	Description
		large object data types seamlessly. Valid values for this attribute are: **SQL_LD_COMPAT_NO:** Large object data types (**BLOB**, **CLOB**, and **DBCLOB**) are reported as themselves (i.e., as **SQL_BLOB**, **SQL_CLOB**, and **SQL_DBCLOB**). This is the default value for this attribute. **SQL_LD_COMPAT_YES:** Large object data types (**BLOB**, **CLOB** and **DBCLOB**) are reported as **SQL_LONGVARBINARY**, **SQL_LONGVARCHAR** and **SQL_LONVARGRAPHIC** data types. This is an IBM defined attribute.
SQL_ATTR_MAXCONN	32-bit **INTEGER**	Specifies the maximum number of concurrent data source connections that an application can have open at one time. This attribute can be used to control the maximum number of connections allowed on a per application basis. The value specified for this attribute must be **0** or a positive number. The default value for this attribute is **0**, which means that an application can establish as many data source connections as system resources permit. On OS/2, if the NetBIOS protocol is in use, this value corresponds to the number of NetBIOS sessions that will be concurrently reserved for use by the application. The range of values for OS/2 NetBIOS sessions is **1** to **254**. If the value **0** (the default value for this attribute) is specified, 5 OS/2 NetBIOS sessions will be reserved. Reserved NetBIOS sessions cannot be used by other applications. The number of NetBIOS sessions (connections) specified by this attribute will be applied to any adapter number that DB2 NetBIOS protocol uses to connect to the remote data source. Note: The adapter number is specified in the node directory when a NetBIOS node is cataloged. The value that is in effect when the first connection to a data source is established is the value that will be used throughout the life of the application; once the first connection has been established, all attempts to change this value will be rejected. This attribute can also be changed by calling the **SQLSetConnectAttr()** function. However, it is recommended that an application set this attribute at the environment level (with the **SQLSetEnvAttr()** function) rather than on a per connection basis (with the **SQLSetConnectAttr()** function). ODBC applications must set this attribute at the connection level for each connection, using the **SQLSetConnectAttr()** function, because this attribute is not supported by ODBC's **SQLSetEnvAttr()** function. This is an IBM defined attribute.

Table 8-6 Connection Attributes (Continued)

Attribute	Data Type	Description
SQL_ATTR_QUIET_MODE	32-bit window handle (HWND)	Specifies the platform-specific parent window handlle to use when displaying child dialogs. If the window handle is a NULL pointer, DB2 CLI does not display any dialogs. If the window handle is not a NULL pointer, it should be the parent window handle of the application—this is the default value for this attribute.
		Note: The SQL_ATTR_QUIET_MODE connection attribute does not apply to the dialog displayed by the SQLDriverConnect() function.
SQL_ATTR_SYNC_POINT	32-bit INTEGER	Allows an application to choose between one-phase coordinated (commit) transactions and two-phase coordinated (commit) transactions. Valid values for this attribute are:
		SQL_ONEPHASE: One-phase commit is used to commit the work done by each data source in a multiple data source transaction. To ensure data integrity, each transaction must ensure that only one data source, if any, gets updated. The first data source that has updates performed on it within a transaction becomes the only updateable data source in that transaction; all other data sources accessed are treated as read-only. All attempts to update a read-only data source within this transaction are rejected.
		SQL_TWOPHASE: Two-phase commit is used to commit the work done by each data source in a multiple data source transaction. This value requires the use of a Transaction Manager to coordinate two phase commits amongst the connected data sources that support this protocol. Multiple read-writeable and multiple updateable data sources are allowed within a single transaction.
		All data source connections within an application must have the same SQL_ATTR_CONNECTTYPE and SQL_ATTR_SYNC_POINT values. This attribute can also be changed by calling the SQLSetConnectAttr() function. However, it is recommended that an application set this attribute at the environment level (with the SQLSetEnvAttr() function) rather than on a per connection basis (with the SQLSetConnectAttr() function). ODBC applications that are designed to take advantage of coordinated DB2 transaction processing must set this attribute at the connection level for each connection, using the SQLSetConnectAttr() function, since this attribute is not supported by ODBC's SQLSetEnvAttr() function.
		This is an IBM defined attribute.
		Note: In embedded SQL, there is an additional sync point value (SYNCPOINT_NONE) that is more restrictive than the SQL_CONCURRENT_TRANS value (SQL_ATTR_CONNECTTYPE attribute). Because the SYNCPOINT_NONE

Table 8-6   Connection Attributes (Continued)

Attribute	Data Type	Description
		value does not allow multiple connections to the same data source, DB2 CLI does not support it.
SQL_ATTR_TRANSLATE_LIB	Null-terminated character string	Specifies the name of a library that contains the functions **SQLDriverToDataSource()** and **SQLDataSourceToDriver()** that DB2 CLI uses to perform tasks such as character set translation (i.e. the directory where the DB2 Client Application Enabler for Windows or the Software Developers Kit for Windows has been installed—DB2TRANS.DLL is the library that performs character set translations).
		This connection attribute is defined by ODBC, but is only supported by DB2 CLI on Windows 3.1.
SQL_ATTR_TRANSLATE_OPTION	32-bit **INTEGER**	Specifies a codepage value that is to be passed to the DB2 CLI translation library (DB2TRANS.DLL).
		Defines the codepage number (it can be obtained by querying the database configuration parameters). Specifying a codepage value enables the translation of characters from the codepage number of a DB2 Version 1 database (**437 or 850**) to the Windows codepage **1004**.
		This connection attribute is defined by ODBC, but is only supported by DB2 CLI on Windows 3.1.
SQL_ATTR_TXN_ISOLATION	32-bit bitmask	Specifies the transaction isolation level to use for the current connection. The following terms are used to define transaction isolation levels:
		Dirty Read: Transaction 1 changes a row. Transaction 2 reads the changed row before Transaction 1 commits the change. If Transaction 1 rolls back the change, Transaction 2 will have read a row that is considered to have never existed.
		Nonrepeatable Read: Transaction 1 reads a row. Transaction 2 updates or deletes that row and commits this change. If Transaction 1 attempts to reread the row, it will receive different row values or discover that the row has been deleted.
		Phantom: Transaction 1 reads a set of rows that satisfy some search criteria. Transaction 2 generates one or more rows (either through inserts or updates) that match the search criteria. If Transaction 1 reexecutes the statement that reads the rows, it receives a different set of rows.
		If the data source supports transactions, the driver returns one of the following bitmasks:
		SQL_TXN_READ_UNCOMMITTED: Dirty reads, nonrepeatable reads, and phantoms are possible.

Table 8-6 Connection Attributes (Continued)

Attribute	Data Type	Description
		SQL_TXN_READ_COMMITTED: Dirty reads are not possible. Nonrepeatable reads and phantoms are possible. This is the default value for this attribute.
		SQL_TXN_REPEATABLE_READ: Dirty reads and nonrepeatable reads are not possible. Phantoms are possible.
		SQL_TXN_SERIALIZABLE: Transactions are serializable. Serializable transactions do not allow dirty reads, nonrepeatable reads, or phantoms.
		SQL_TXN_NOCOMMIT: Changes are effectively committed at the end of a successful operation; no explicit commit or rollback is allowed (this is analogous to autocommit). This is not an SQL92 isolation level, but an IBM defined extension, that is only supported by DB2 for AS/400.
		In IBM terminology, **SQL_TXN_READ_UNCOMMITTED** is Uncommitted Read; **SQL_TXN_READ_COMMITTED** is Cursor Stability; **SQL_TXN_REPEATABLE_READ** is Read Stability; and **SQL_TXN_SERIALIZABLE** is Repeatable Read.
		An application must call **SQLEndTran()** to commit or roll back all open transactions on a connection, before calling the **SQLSetConnectAttr()** function with this attribute specified.
SQL_ATTR_WCHARTYPE	32-bit **INTEGER**	Specifies, which **wchar_t** (**SQLDBCHAR**) character format to use in an application running in a double-byte character system environment. This option provides the ability to choose between having **wchar_t** data in multi-byte format or in wide-character format. Valid values for this attribute are:
		SQL_WCHARTYPE_CONVERT: Character codes are converted between graphic SQL data in the database and the data types of application variables. This allows an application to fully exploit the ANSI C mechanisms for dealing with wide character strings (L-literals, 'wc' string functions, etc.) without having to explicitly convert the data to multi-byte format before communicating with the database. The disadvantage is that the implicit conversions may have an impact on the runtime performance and memory requirements of the application.
		SQL_WCHARTYPE_NOCONVERT: No implicit character code conversion occurs between the application and the database. Data in the application variable is sent to and received from the database as unaltered DBCS characters. The application must either refrain from using wide-character data in **wchar_t**

Table 8-6   Connection Attributes (Continued)

Attribute	Data Type	Description
		(**SQLDBCHAR**) application variables, or it must explicitly call the wcstombs( ) and mbstowcs( ) ANSI C functions to convert to and from multi-byte format when exchanging data with the database. This is the default value for this attribute.
		This is an IBM defined attribute.

(The information above was adapted from the table on pages 945–947 *of Microsoft ODBC 3.0 Software Development Kit & Programmer's Reference.*)

SQLSTATEs   If this function returns **SQL_SUCCESS_WITH_INFO** or **SQL_ERROR**, one of the following SQLSTATE values may be obtained by calling the **SQLGetDiagRec()** function:

01000, **01**004, **08**003, **HY**000, **HY**001, **HY**010, **HY**090, **HY**092, or **HYC**00

Refer to Appendix B for detailed information about each SQLSTATE value that can be returned.

Comments   ▪ If the *Value* parameter contains a NULL pointer, no length is returned in the *StringLength* parameter.
▪ If an attribute that returns a string value is specified in the *Attribute* parameter, and if that string value's actual length is greater than or equal to the maximum string size value specified in the *ValueMaxSize* parameter, the value is truncated to *ValueMaxSize*-1 (the length of a NULL-termination character) characters.
▪ If an attribute that returns a string value is specified in the *Attribute* parameter, the *Value* parameter must contain a pointer to a buffer in which this function can return the string.
▪ If the value returned for the attribute specified in the *Attribute* parameter is a Unicode string, the *ValueMaxSize* parameter must contain an even number.
▪ An application may or may not have to establish a connection to a data source before calling this function, depending on the attribute value being retrieved.
▪ If this function is called and an attribute that does not have a value is specified, **SQL_NO_DATA** is returned. An attributes value can be either a default value or a value that was set by a prior call to **SQLSetConnectAttr()**.
▪ While an application can set SQL statement attributes with the **SQLSetConnectAttr()** function, an application cannot use this function to retrieve SQL statement attribute values; the **SQLGetStmtAttr()** function must be used instead.

■ The value of the `SQL_ATTR_AUTO_IPD` connection attribute can be returned by this function, but it cannot be set by the `SQLSetConnectAttr()` function.

Prerequisites   A connection handle must be allocated before this function is called.

Restrictions   There are no restrictions associated with this function call.

See Also   `SQLSetConnectAttr()`, `SQLGetEnvAttr()`, `SQLSetEnvAttr()`, `SQLGetStmtAttr()`, `SQLSetStmtAttr()`

Example   The following Visual C++ program illustrates how to retrieve and change the current value of a connection attribute.

```
/*─────────────────────────────────────────────────────────*/
/* NAME:     CH8EX6.CPP                                      */
/* PURPOSE: Illustrate How To Use The Following CLI API Functions  */
/*          In A C++ Program:                                */
/*                                                           */
/*                SQLGetConnectAttr()                        */
/*                SQLSetConnectAttr()                        */
/*                                                           */
/* OTHER CLI APIs SHOWN:                                     */
/*          SQLAllocHandle()            SQLSetEnvAttr()      */
/*          SQLConnect()                SQLDisconnect()      */
/*          SQLFreeHandle()                                  */
/*                                                           */
/*─────────────────────────────────────────────────────────*/

// Include The Appropriate Header Files
#include <windows.h>
#include <sqlcli1.h>
#include <iostream.h>

// Define The CLI_Class Class
class CLI_Class
{
    // Attributes
    public:
        SQLHANDLE    EnvHandle;
        SQLHANDLE    ConHandle;
        SQLRETURN    rc;
        SQLUINTEGER  ACValue;

    // Operations
    public:
        CLI_Class();                              // Constructor
        ~CLI_Class();                             // Destructor
        SQLRETURN  GetAutoCommitValue();
        SQLRETURN  SetAutoCommitValue(SQLUINTEGER ACValue);
};

// Define The Class Constructor
CLI_Class::CLI_Class()
```

```
{
    // Initialize The Return Code Variable
    rc = SQL_SUCCESS;

    // Allocate An Environment Handle
    rc = SQLAllocHandle(SQL_HANDLE_ENV, SQL_NULL_HANDLE, &EnvHandle);

    // Set The ODBC Application Version To 3.x
    if (rc == SQL_SUCCESS)
        rc = SQLSetEnvAttr(EnvHandle, SQL_ATTR_ODBC_VERSION,
                (SQLPOINTER) SQL_OV_ODBC3, SQL_IS_UINTEGER);

    // Allocate A Connection Handle
    if (rc == SQL_SUCCESS)
        rc = SQLAllocHandle(SQL_HANDLE_DBC, EnvHandle, &ConHandle);
}

// Define The Class Destructor
CLI_Class::~CLI_Class()
{
    // Free The Connection Handle
    if (ConHandle != NULL)
        SQLFreeHandle(SQL_HANDLE_DBC, ConHandle);

    // Free The Environment Handle
    if (EnvHandle != NULL)
        SQLFreeHandle(SQL_HANDLE_ENV, EnvHandle);
}

// Define The GetAutoCommitValue() Member Function
SQLRETURN CLI_Class::GetAutoCommitValue(void)
{
    // Declare The Local Memory Variables
    SQLINTEGER  ValueLength;

    // Determine Whether Or Not The Driver Is In Auto-Commit Mode
    rc = SQLGetConnectAttr(ConHandle, SQL_ATTR_AUTOCOMMIT,
            (SQLPOINTER) &ACValue, SQL_IS_UINTEGER, &ValueLength);

    // Display The Information Retrieved
    if (rc == SQL_SUCCESS)
    {
        if (ACValue == SQL_AUTOCOMMIT_ON)
            cout << "The driver is in auto-commit mode.";
        else
            cout << "The driver is in manual-commit node.";
        cout << endl;
    }

    // Return The CLI API Return Code To The Calling Function
    return(rc);
}
```

```
// Define The SetAutoCommitValue() Member Function
SQLRETURN CLI_Class::SetAutoCommitValue(SQLUINTEGER ACValue)
{
    // Set The Auto-Commit Connection Attribute
    rc = SQLSetConnectAttr(ConHandle, SQL_ATTR_AUTOCOMMIT,
            (SQLPOINTER) ACValue, SQL_IS_UINTEGER);

    // Return The CLI API Return Code To The Calling Function
    return(rc);
}

/*──────────────────────────────────────────────────────*/
/* The Main Function                                     */
/*──────────────────────────────────────────────────────*/
int main()
{
    // Declare The Local Memory Variables
    SQLRETURN   rc = SQL_SUCCESS;

    // Create An Instance Of The CLI_Class Class
    CLI_Class   Example;

    // Connect To The DB2 Sample Database
    if (Example.ConHandle != NULL)
    {
        rc = SQLConnect(Example.ConHandle, (SQLCHAR *) "SAMPLE",
                SQL_NTS, (SQLCHAR *) "userid", SQL_NTS,
                (SQLCHAR *) "password", SQL_NTS);

        // Determine Whether Or Not The Driver Is In Auto-Commit Mode
        rc = Example.GetAutoCommitValue();

        // Tell The Driver To Use Manual-Commit Mode
        rc = Example.SetAutoCommitValue(SQL_AUTOCOMMIT_OFF);

        // Determine Whether Or Not The Driver Is Now Using
        // Manual-Commit Mode
        rc = Example.GetAutoCommitValue();

        // Disconnect From The DB2 Sample Database
        rc = SQLDisconnect(Example.ConHandle);
    }

    // Return To The Operating System
    return(rc);
}
```

SQLSetConnectAttr

COMPATIBILITY

X/OPEN 95 CLI	ISO/IEC 92 CLI	DB2 CLI 5.2	DB2 CLI 2.0	ODBC 3.x
☑	☑	☑	☐	☑

ODBC API CONFORMANCE LEVEL   CORE

Purpose   The `SQLSetConnectAttr()` function is used to modify the current value of a specified connection attribute.

Syntax
```
SQLRETURN SQLGetConnectAttr    (SQLHDBC      ConnectionHandle,
                                SQLINTEGER   Attribute,
                                SQLPOINTER   Value,
                                SQLINTEGER   StringLength);
```

Parameters   *ConnectionHandle*   A data source connection handle that refers to a previously allocated connection information storage buffer (data structure).

Attribute   The connection attribute whose value is to be modified. This parameter must be set to one of the following values:

- `SQL_ATTR_ACCESS_MODE`
- `SQL_ATTR_ASYNC_ENABLE`
- `SQL_ATTR_AUTO_IPD`
- `SQL_ATTR_AUTOCOMMIT`
- `SQL_ATTR_CONN_CONTEXT`
- `SQL_ATTR_CONNECTTYPE`
- `SQL_ATTR_CURRENT_SCHEMA`
- `SQL_ATTR_DB2ESTIMATE`
- `SQL_ATTR_DB2EXPLAIN`
- `SQL_ATTR_LONGDATA_COMPAT`
- `SQL_ATTR_MAXCONN`
- `SQL_ATTR_QUIET_MODE`
- `SQL_ATTR_SYNC_POINT`
- `SQL_ATTR_TRANSLATE_LIB`
- `SQL_ATTR_TRANSLATE_OPTION`
- `SQL_ATTR_TXN_ISOLATION`
- `SQL_ATTR_WCHARTYPE`

<table>
<tr><td>Value</td><td>A pointer to a location in memory where the new value for the connection attribute is stored. Depending on the connection attribute being set, this pointer can reference either a 32-bit integer value, or a NULL-terminated character string.</td></tr>
<tr><td>StringLength</td><td>The length of the connection attribute value stored in the Value parameter. If an ODBC-defined attribute value is to be set and if the attribute value is a 32-bit integer value, this parameter is ignored. If a DB2 CLI attribute value is to be set, this parameter must be set as follows:</td></tr>
</table>

- If the value of the specified connection attribute is a character string, this parameter should be set to the actual length of the string or to **SQL_NTS**.

- If the value of the specified connection attribute is a binary string, this parameter should be set to the result of the **SQL_LEN_BINARY_ATTR(length)** macro. Usually, this macro places a negative value in this parameter.

- If the value of the specified connection attribute is anything other than a character string or binary string, this parameter should be set to **SQL_IS_POINTER**.

- If the value of the specified connection attribute is a fixed-length data type, this parameter should be set to **SQL_IS_INTEGER** or **SQL_IS_UINTEGER**, as appropriate.

Description The **SQLSetConnectAttr()** function is used to modify the current value of a specified connection attribute. Refer to the **SQLGetConnectAttr()** function for more information about each connection attribute available.

All connection and statement attributes successfully set by an application for a specified connection handle persist until the connection handle is freed with the **SQLFreeHandle()** function.

An application can call this function at any time between the time the connection handle is allocated and freed, however, some connection attributes can only be set before a connection has been made, while others can only be set after a connection has been made. Table 8–7 identifies when each connection attribute can be set.

NOTE: *This function replaces the DB2 CLI 2.0 function* **SQLSetConnectOption()**.

Return Codes **SQL_SUCCESS**, **SQL_SUCCESS_WITH_INFO**, **SQL_INVALID_HANDLE**, or **SQL_ERROR**

SQLSTATEs If this function returns **SQL_SUCCESS_WITH_INFO** or **SQL_ERROR**, one of the following SQLSTATE values may be obtained by calling the **SQLGetDiagRec()** function:

Table 8-7 When connection attributes can be set

Attribute	Set Before Connection	Set After Connection
SQL_ATTR_ACCESS_MODE	Yes	Yes
SQL_ATTR_ASYNC_ENABLE	Yes	Yes
SQL_ATTR_AUTO_IPD	No	Yes
SQL_ATTR_AUTOCOMMIT	Yes	Yes
SQL_ATTR_CONNECT_TYPE	Yes	No
SQL_ATTR_CURRENT_SCHEMIA	Yes	Yes
SQL_ATTR_DB2ESTIMATE	No	Yes
SQL_ATTR_DB2EXPLAIN	No	Yes
SQL_ATTR_LOGIN_TIMEOUT	Yes	No
SQL_ATTR_LONGDATA_COMPAT	Yes	Yes
SQL_ATTR_MAXCONN	Yes	No
SQL_ATTR_QUIET_MODE	Yes	Yes
SQL_ATTR_SYNC_POINT	Yes	No
SQL_ATTR_TRANSLATE_LIB	Yes	Yes
SQL_ATTR_TRANSLATE_OPTION	Yes	Yes
SQL_ATTR_TXN_ISOLATION	No	Yes[1]
SQL_ATTR_WCHARTYPE	Yes	Yes[1]

(Adapted from table 147 on pages 520-521 of *IBM Universal Database Call Level Interface Guide and Reference*.)

[1]**SQL_ATTR_TXN_ISOLATION** can only be set if there are no open transactions on the connection.

01000, **01**S02, **08**002, **08**003, **08**S01, **24**000, **HY**000, **HY**001, **HY**009, **HY**010, **HY**011, **HY**024, **HY**090, **HY**092, or **HY**C00

Refer to Appendix B for detailed information about each SQLSTATE value that can be returned.

Comments
- If a driver-specific value is specified in the *Attribute* parameter, a signed integer value may be stored in the memory location referred to by the *Value* parameter.
- In DB2 CLI 5.2, statement attributes cannot be set at the connection level. This does not include the **SQL_ATTR_METADATA_ID** and **SQL_ATTR_ASYNC_ENABLE** attributes, because both are connection and statement attributes and can be set at either the connection level or the statement level.
- DB2 CLI 5.2 applications should never use the **SQLSetConnectAttr()** function to set SQL statement attributes at the connection level.
- Some connection attributes support substitution of a similar value if the data source does not support the value specified in the *Value* parameter. In such cases, DB2 CLI returns **SQL_SUCCESS_WITH_INFO** and SQLSTATE **01**S02 (Option value

changed). For example, if *Attribute* is **SQL_ATTR_DB2ESTIMATE** and if the value specified in *Value* parameter exceeds the maximum estimate size, the driver substitutes the maximum size. An application can call the **SQLGetConnectAttr()** function after setting a connection attribute to determine whether a substitution occurred, and if so, to obtain the substituted value.

■ The *StringLength* parameter is ignored if the length is defined by the attribute itself, which is the case for all attributes introduced in DB2 CLI 2.0 or earlier.

Prerequisites   A connection handle must be allocated before this function is called.

Restrictions   There are no restrictions associated with this function call.

See Also   **SQLGetConnectAttr(), SQLGetEnvAttr(), SQLSetEnvAttr(), SQLGetStmtAttr(), SQLSetStmtAttr()**

Example   See the example provided for the **SQLGetConnectAttr()** function, on page 221.

SQLGetStmtAttr

COMPATIBILITY

X/OPEN 95 CLI	ISO/IEC 92 CLI	DB2 CLI 5.2	DB2 CLI 2.0	ODBC 3.X
☑	☑	☑	☐	☑

ODBC API CONFORMANCE LEVEL   **CORE**

Purpose   The **SQLGetStmtAttr()** function is used to retrieve the current setting of a specified SQL statement attribute.

Syntax

```
SQLRETURN SQLGetStmtAttr    (SQLHSTMT      StatementHandle,
                             SQLINTEGER    Attribute,
                             SQLPOINTER    Value,
                             SQLINTEGER    ValueMaxSize,
                             SQLINTEGER    *StringLength);
```

Parameters   *StatementHandle*   An SQL statement handle that refers to a previously allocated SQL statement information storage buffer (data structure).

Attribute   The SQL statement attribute whose value is to be retrieved. This parameter must be set to one of the following values:

     ■ **SQL_ATTR_APP_PARAM_DESC**

     ■ **SQL_ATTR_APP_ROW_DESC**

     ■ **SQL_ATTR_ASYNC_ENABLE**

- SQL_ATTR_BIND_TYPE
- SQL_ATTR_CONCURRENCY
- SQL_ATTR_CURSOR_HOLD
- SQL_ATTR_CURSOR_TYPE
- SQL_ATTR_DEFERRED_PREPARE
- SQL_ATTR_EARLYCLOSE
- SQL_ATTR_ENABLE_AUTO_IPD
- SQL_ATTR_FETCH_BOOKMARK_PTR
- SQL_ATTR_IMP_PARAM_DESC
- SQL_ATTR_IMP_ROW_DESC
- SQL_ATTR_KEYSET_SIZE
- SQL_ATTR_MAX_LENGTH
- SQL_ATTR_MAX_ROWS
- SQL_ATTR_METADATA_ID
- SQL_ATTR_NOSCAN
- SQL_ATTR_PARAM_BIND_OFFSET_PTR
- SQL_ATTR_PARAM_BIND_TYPE
- SQL_ATTR_PARAM_OPERATION_PTR
- SQL_ATTR_PARAM_STATUS_PTR
- SQL_ATTR_PARAMOPT_ATOMIC
- SQL_ATTR_PARAMS_PROCESSED_PTR
- SQL_ATTR_PARAMSET_SIZE
- SQL_ATTR_QUERY_TIMEOUT
- SQL_ATTR_RETRIEVE_DATA
- SQL_ATTR_ROW_ARRAY_SIZE
- SQL_ATTR_ATTR_ROW_BIND_OFFSET_PTR
- SQL_ATTR_ROW_BIND_TYPE
- SQL_ATTR_ROW_NUMBER
- SQL_ATTR_ROW_OPERATION_PTR
- SQL_ATTR_ROW_STATUS_PTR
- SQL_ATTR_ROWS_FETCHED_PTR
- SQL_ATTR_STMTTXN_ISOLATION
- SQL_ATTR_TXN_ISOLATION
- SQL_ATTR_USE_BOOKMARKS

Value   A pointer to a location in memory where this function is to store the current value of the specified SQL statement attribute.

ValueMaxSize		The size of the memory storage buffer where this function is to store the current value of the specified SQL statement attribute. If an ODBC-defined attribute is to be retrieved and if the attribute value is a 32-bit integer value, this parameter is ignored. If a DB2 CLI attribute is to be retrieved, this parameter may be set as follows:

■ If the value of the specified SQL statement attribute is a character string, this parameter may be set to the actual length of the string or to **SQL_NTS**.

■ If the value of the specified SQL statement attribute is a binary string, this parameter may be set to the result of the **SQL_LEN_BINARY_ATTR** *(length)* macro. Usually, this macro places a negative value in this parameter.

■ If the value of the specified SQL statement attribute is anything other than a character string or binary string, this parameter may be set to **SQL_IS_POINTER**.

■ If the value of the specified SQL statement attribute is a fixed-length data type, this parameter may be set to **SQL_IS_INTEGER** or **SQL_IS_UINTEGER**, as appropriate.

StringLength		A pointer to a location in memory where this function is to store the actual number of bytes written to the attribute value memory storage buffer *(Value)*. If the attribute value retrieved is not a character string value, this parameter ignored.

Description The **SQLGetStmtAttr()** function is used to retrieve the current setting of a specified SQL statement attribute. Table 8–8 lists alphabetically each value that can be specified for the *Attribute* parameter, along with a description of the information returned for that value when this function is executed.

Table 8–8 SQL Statement Attributes

Attribute	Data Type	Description
SQL_ATTR_APP_PARAM_ DESC	Descriptor handle	Specifies the application parameter descriptor (APD) that is to be used with the specified SQL statement handle by subsequent calls to **SQLExecute()** and **SQLExecDirect()**. Initially, this attribute contains the handle of the APD descriptor that was implicitly allocated when the statement handle was allocated. If this attribute is set to **SQL_NULL_DESC**, any explicitly allocated APD descriptor handle associated with the statement handle is dissociated from it, and this attribute is reset to its initial value (that is, it will contain the handle of the APD descriptor that was implicitly allocated and assigned to the statement handle).

Table 8–8 *SQL Statement Attributes (Continued)*

Attribute	Data Type	Description
		This attribute cannot contain a handle to a descriptor that was implicitly allocated for another statement handle or the handle of another descriptor that was implicitly set on the same statement; implicitly allocated descriptor handles cannot be associated with more than one statement at a time.
`SQL_ATTR_APP_ROW_DESC`	Descriptor handle	Specifies the application row descriptor (ARD) that is to be used with the specified SQL statement handle by subsequent calls to **SQLFetch()**, **SQLFetchScroll()**, or **SQLSetPos()**. Initially, this attribute contains the handle of the ARD descriptor that was implicitly allocated when the statement handle was allocated. If this attribute is set to **SQL_NULL_DESC**, any explicitly allocated ARD descriptor handle associated with the statement handle is dissociated from it, and this attribute is reset to its initial value (that is, it will contain the handle of the ARD descriptor that was implicitly allocated ARD and assigned to the statement handle.)
		This attribute cannot contain a handle to a descriptor that was implicitly allocated for another statement handle or the handle of another descriptor that was implicitly set on the same statement; implicitly allocated descriptor handles cannot be associated with more than one statement at a time.
`SQL_ATTR_ASYNC_ENABLE`	`SQLUINTEGER`	Specifies whether a CLI function called with the specified SQL statement handle is executed asynchronously. Valid values for this attribute are:
		SQL_ASYNC_ENABLE_OFF: A function called with the specified SQL statement handle is not executed asynchronously. This is the default value for this attribute.
		SQL_ASYNC_ENABLE_ON: A function called with the specified SQL statement handle is executed asynchronously.
		After a function has been called asynchronously, only the original function, **SQLCancel()**, **SQLGetDiagRec()**, or **SQLGetDiagField()**, can be called on the statement handle, and only the original function, **SQLAllocHandle()**, **SQLAllocStmt()**, **SQLGetDiagRec()**, **SQLGetDiagField()**, or **SQLGetFunctions()** can be called on the connection handle associated with the statement handle until the original function returns a code other than **SQL_STILL_EXECUTING**. Any other function called on the statement handle or the connection handle associated with the statement handle returns **SQL_ERROR** and SQLSTATE **HY**010 (Function sequence error). Functions can be called on other statement handles.

Table 8–8 *SQL Statement Attributes (Continued)*

Attribute	Data Type	Description
		In general, applications should only execute CLI functions asynchronously on single-thread operating systems. On multithread operating systems, applications should execute CLI functions on separate threads, rather than executing them asynchronously on the same thread.

The following functions can be executed asynchronously:

SQLColAttribute()	SQLColumnPrivileges()
SQLColumns()	SQLCopyDesc()
SQLDescribeCol()	SQLDescribeParam()
SQLExecDirect()	SQLExecute()
SQLFetch()	SQLFetchScroll()
SQLForeignKeys()	SQLGetData()
SQLGetDescField()[1]	SQLGetDescRec()[1]
SQLGetDiagField()	SQLGetDiagRec()
SQLGetTypeInfo()	SQLMoreResults()
SQLNumParams()	SQLNumResultCols()
SQLParamData()	SQLPrepare()
SQLPrimaryKeys()	SQLProcedureColumns()
SQLProcedures()	SQLPutData()
SQLSetPos(),	SQLSpecialColumns()
SQLStatistics()	SQLTablePrivileges()
SQLTables()	

[1]These functions can only be called if the descriptor used is an implementation deescriptor.

This attribute is a read-only attribute for drivers with connection-level, asynchronous execution support and its initial value is the same as the value of the connection level **SQL_ATTR_ASYNC_ENABLE** attribute at the time the statement handle was allocated.

Attribute	Data Type	Description
SQL_ATTR_BIND_TYPE	32-bit **INTEGER**	Specifies the binding orientation to be used when the SQLExtendedFetch( ) function is called with the specified statement handle. Valid values for this attribute are:

SQL_BIND_BY_COLUMN:
Column-wise binding is to be used. This is the default value for this attribute.

The length of the structure or buffer into which result data set columns will be bound:
Row-wise binding is to be used.

For row-wise binding, the length value specified must include space for all bound columns and any padding of the structure or buffer that is necessary to ensure that when the address of a bound column is incremented with the specified length, it will point to the beginning of the same column in the next row (By using the **sizeof()** operator with structures or unions in ANSI C, this behavior is guaranteed).

Table 8–8 SQL Statement Attributes (Continued)

Attribute	Data Type	Description
SQL_ATTR_CONCURRENCY	SQLUINTEGER	Specifies the cursor concurrency level to use. Valid values for this attribute are: **SQL_CONCUR_READ_ONLY:** Cursors are read-only. No updates are allowed. This is the default value for this attribute. **SQL_CONCUR_LOCK:** Cursors use the lowest level of locking sufficient to ensure that the row can be updated. **SQL_CONCUR_ROWVER:** Cursors use optimistic concurrency control, comparing row versions. **SQL_CONCUR_VALUES:** Cursors use optimistic concurrency control, comparing values. This attribute cannot be specified for a cursor that is already open. If the **SQL_ATTR_CURSOR_TYPE** attribute is changed to a cursor type value that doesn't support the current value of the **SQL_ATTR_CONCURRENCY** attribute, the **SQL_ATTR_CONCURRENCY** attribute is changed and a warning is issued the next time the **SQLExecDirect()** or the **SQLPrepare()** function is called. If the driver supports the **SELECT FOR UPDATE** SQL statement, and if such a statement is executed while the **SQL_ATTR_CONCURRENCY** attribute is set to **SQL_CONCUR_READ_ONLY**, **SQL_ERROR** is returned. If the **SQL_ATTR_CONCURRENCY** attribute is changed to a value the driver supports for some values of the **SQL_ATTR_CURSOR_TYPE** attribute, but not for the current value of the **SQL_ATTR_CURSOR_TYPE** attribute, the value of the **SQL_ATTR_CURSOR_TYPE** attribute is changed and SQLSTATE **01S02** (Option value changed) is returned the next time the **SQLExecDirect()** or the **SQLPrepare()** function is called. If the specified concurrency value is not supported by the data source, the driver substitutes a different concurrency value and SQLSTATE **01S02** (Option value changed) is returned. The driver substitutes **SQL_CONCUR_ROWVER** for **SQL_CONCUR_VALUES**, and vice versa. The driver substitutes, in order, **SQL_CONCUR_ROWVER** or **SQL_CONCUR_VALUES** for **SQL_CONCUR_LOCK**. The validity of the substituted value is not checked until execution time.

Table 8-8 *SQL Statement Attributes (Continued)*

Attribute	Data Type	Description
SQL_ATTR_CURSOR_HOLD	32-bit INTEGER	Specifies whether the cursor associated with the specified SQL statement handle is preserved (with the cursor pointer positioned in the same position) after a COMMIT operation, and whether the application that opened the cursor can continue retrieving data from it without having to open the cursor again. Valid values for this attribute are: SQL_CURSOR_HOLD_ON: The cursor is preserved. This is the default value for this attribute. SQL_CURSOR_HOLD_OFF: The cursor is not preserved. This attribute cannot be changed if an open cursor is already associated with the statement handle specified. This is an IBM defined attribute.
SQL_ATTR_CURSOR_TYPE	SQLUINTEGER	Specifies the cursor type. Valid values for this attribute are: SQL_CURSOR_FORWARD_ONLY: The cursor can only scroll forward. This is the default value for this attribute. SQL_CURSOR_STATIC: The data in the result set is static, therefore the cursor is static. SQL_CURSOR_KEYSET_DRIVEN: The cursor is a keyset cursor; the driver saves and uses the keys for the number of rows specified in the SQL_ATTR_KEYSET_SIZE statement attribute. SQL_CURSOR_DYNAMIC: The cursor is a dynamic (block) cursor; the driver only saves and uses the keys for the rows in the rowset. This attribute cannot be specified after the SQL statement associated with the statement handle specified has been prepared. If the specified cursor type is not supported by the data source, the driver substitutes the SQL_CURSOR_FORWARD_ONLY cursor type and SQLSTATE 01S02 (Option value changed) is returned.
SQL_ATTR_DEFERRED_PREPARE	SQLUINTEGER	Specifies whether a PREPARE request is deferred until the corresponding EXECUTE request is issued. Valid values for this attribute are: SQL_DEFERRED_PREPARE_OFF: PREPARE requests will be executed the moment they are issued.

Table 8–8 *SQL Statement Attributes (Continued)*

Attribute	Data Type	Description
		SQL_DEFERRED_PREPARE_ON: Defer execution of **PREPARE** requests until the corresponding **EXECUTE** request is issued (combine the two requests into one command/reply flow to minimize network traffic and to improve performance). This is the default value for this attribute.
		If the target DB2 database or DB2 Connect/DDCS gateway does not support deferred prepare, deferred prepare is disabled for that connection.
		Note: When deferred prepare is enabled, the row and cost estimates normally returned in SQLERRD[3] and SQLERRD[4] of the SQLCA data structure associated with a **PREPARE** SQL statement may be set to zero. This may be of concern to users who want to use these values to decide whether or not to continue the SQL statement processing.
		This attribute is turned off if the **SQL_ATTR_ DB2ESTIMATE** connection attribute is set to a value other than zero.
		This is an IBM defined attribute.
SQL_ATTR_EARLYCLOSE	**SQLUINTEGER**	Specifies whether or not the temporary cursor used on the server workstation can be automatically closed (without closing the cursor on the client workstation) when the last record is sent to the client workstation. Valid values for this attribute are:
		SQL_EARLYCLOSE_OFF: Do not close the temporary cursor on the server early.
		SQL_EARLYCLOSE_ON: Close the temporary cursor on the server early. This value eliminates network requests to explicitly close cursors. This is the default value for this attribute.
		If the **SQL_ATTR_EARLYCLOSE** attribute is turned on, performance will be improved for client/server applications that use several small result data sets.
		The **SQL_ATTR_EARLYCLOSE** attribute is ignored if the SQL statement that generated the result data set does not use blocking or if the **SQL_ATTR_CURSOR_TYPE** attribute is set to anything other than **SQL_CURSOR_FORWARD_ONLY**.
		This is an IBM defined attribute.
SQL_ATTR_ENABLE_ AUTO_IPD	**SQLUINTEGER**	Specifies whether automatic population of implementation parameter descriptors (IPD) is to be performed after **SQLPrepare()** executes. Valid values for this attribute are:

Table 8–8 SQL Statement Attributes (Continued)

Attribute	Data Type	Description
		SQL_TRUE: The IPD descriptor is to be populated automatically after **SQLPrepare()** is called.
		SQL_FALSE: The IPD descriptor is not to be populated automatically after **SQLPrepare()** is called.
		The default value of this attribute is the same as the value of the **SQL_ATTR_AUTO_IPD** connection attribute.
		If the **SQL_ATTR_AUTO_IPD** connection attribute is set to **SQL_FALSE**, this attribute can only be set to **SQL_FALSE**.
SQL_ATTR_FETCH_ BOOKMARK_PTR	Pointer	Retrieves/stores a pointer to a binary bookmark value. When the **SQLFetchScroll()** function is called with the *FetchOrientation* parameter set to **SQL_FETCH_ BOOKMARK**, DB2 CLI retrieves the bookmark value from this attribute. The default value for this attribute is a NULL pointer.
SQL_ATTR_IMP_PARAM_ DESC	Descriptor handle	Identifies the implementation parameter descriptor (IPD) that was implicitly allocated when the statement handle was initially allocated. This attribute can be retrieved by the **SQLGetStmtAttr()** function, but it can not be set by the **SQLSetStmtAttr()** function.
SQL_ATTR_IMP_ROW_ DESC	Descriptor handle	Identifies the implementation row descriptor (IRD) that was implicitly allocated when the statement handle was initially allocated. This attribute can be retrieved by the **SQLGetStmtAttr()** function, but it can not be set by the **SQLSetStmtAttr()** function.
SQL_ATTR_KEYSET_SIZE	**SQLUINTEGER**	Specifies the number of rows to be in the keyset of a keyset-driven cursor. If the keyset size is **0** (the default value for this attribute), the cursor is fully keyset-driven. If the keyset size is greater than **0**, the cursor is a mixed cursor (keyset-driven within the keyset and dynamic outside of the keyset).
		If the specified keyset size exceeds the maximum keyset size allowed, DB2 CLI substitutes that size and returns SQLSTATE **01S02** (Option value changed).
		SQLFetch() or **SQLFetchScroll()** returns an error if the keyset size is greater than **0** and less than the rowset size.
SQL_ATTR_MAX_LENGTH	**SQLUINTEGER**	Specifies the maximum amount of data that DB2 CLI will return from a character or binary column.
		If this attribute is set to **0** (which is the default value for this attribute), DB2 CLI attempts to return all available data.

Table 8–8 SQL Statement Attributes (Continued)

Attribute	Data Type	Description
		If the maximum length specified is smaller than the length of the data available, the data is truncated by the **SQLFetch()** or **SQLGetData()** function and **SQL_SUCCESS** is returned.
		This attribute can be set while a cursor is open; however, the setting may not take effect immediately, in which case DB2 CLI returns SQLSTATE **01S02** (Option value changed), and the attribute is reset to its original value.
		This attribute is intended to reduce network traffic and should not be used by applications to truncate data.
SQL_ATTR_MAX_ROWS	**SQLUINTEGER**	Specifies the maximum number of rows to return to the application for a **SELECT** SQL statement. Conceptually, this attribute's value is applied when a result data set is created and limits the result data set to the specified number of rows. If the number of rows in the result data set is larger that the number of rows specified, the result data set is truncated.
		If this attribute is set to **0** (which is the default value for this attribute), DB2 CLI returns all rows available.
		The value of this attribute applies to all result data sets associated with the statement handle, including the result data sets returned by the catalog functions.
		This attribute can be set while a cursor is open; however, the setting may not take effect immediately, in which case DB2 CLI returns SQLSTATE **01S02** (Option value changed), and the attribute is reset to its original value.
SQL_ATTR_METADATA_ID	**SQLUINTEGER**	Specifies how the string parameters (arguments) of catalog functions are to be treated. Valid values for this attribute are:
		SQL_TRUE: The string parameters of catalog functions are treated as identifiers. For non-delimited strings, the driver removes any trailing spaces, and the string is folded to upper case. For delimited strings, the driver removes any leading or trailing spaces, and takes literally whatever is between the delimiters. Case is insignificant. If one of these arguments is set to a NULL pointer, the catalog function returns **SQL_ERROR** and SQLSTATE **HY**009 (Invalid use of NULL pointer).
		SQL_FALSE: The string parameters of catalog functions are not treated as identifiers (that is, string parameters can contain either a simple string or a string search pattern, depending on the parameter. Case is significant. This is the default value for this attribute.

Table 8–8 SQL Statement Attributes (Continued)

Attribute	Data Type	Description
		The *TableType* parameter of the **SQLTables()** function, which takes a list of values, is not affected by this attribute.
		This attribute can also be set at the connection level. (This attribute and the **SQL_ATTR_ASYNC_ENABLE** attribute are the only statement attributes that are also connection attributes.)
SQL_ATTR_NOSCAN	**SQLUINTEGER**	Specifies whether DB2 CLI is to scan SQL statements for escape sequences. Valid values for this attribute are:
		SQL_NOSCAN_OFF: DB2 CLI is to scan SQL statements for escape sequences. This is the default value for this attribute.
		SQL_NOSCAN_ON: DB2 CLI is to send the SQL statement directly to the data source without scanning for escape sequences.
SQL_ATTR_PARAM_BIND_ OFFSET_PTR	**SQLUINTEGER** pointer	Specifies an offset to be added to pointers to change the binding of dynamic parameters. If this attribute contains a vaild pointer, the driver dereferences the pointer, adds the dereferenced value to each of the deferred fields in the descriptor record (**SQL_DESC_DATA_PTR**, **SQL_DESC_INDICATOR_PTR**, and **SQL_DESC_OCTET_ LENGTH_PTR**), and uses the new pointer values when binding. By default, this attribute contains a NULL pointer.
		The bind offset is always added directly to the **SQL_ DESC_DATA_PTR**, **SQL_DESC_INDICATOR_PTR**, and **SQL_DESC_OCTET_LENGTH_PTR** descriptor record fields. If the offset is changed to a different value, the new value is added directly to the value in the descriptor field (earlier offset values are ignored). This statement attribute corresponds to the **SQL_DESC_BIND_OFFSET_ PTR** field of the application parameter descriptor header record.
SQL_ATTR_PARAM_ BIND_TYPE	**SQLUINTEGER**	Specifies the binding orientation to be used for dynamic parameters. By default, this attribute is set to **SQL_ PARAM_BIND_BY_COLUMN** to specify column-wise binding. To select row-wise binding, this attribute is set to the length of the structure (or the instance of a buffer) that is bound to a set of dynamic parameters. This length must include space for all the bound parameters and any padding of the structure or buffer to ensure that when the address of a bound parameter is incremented with the specified length, the result points to the beginning of the same parameter in the next set of parameter values. By using the **sizeof()** operator in ANSI C, this behavior is guaranteed.

Table 8–8   SQL Statement Attributes (Continued)

Attribute	Data Type	Description
		This statement attribute corresponds to the **SQL_DESC_BIND_TYPE** field of the application parameter descriptor header record.
SQL_ATTR_PARAM_ OPERATION_PTR	SQLUSMALLINT pointer	Contains a pointer to an array of parameter operation values that can be set by the application to indicate whether a set of parameter values are to be used or ignored when **SQLExecute()** or **SQLExecDirect()** is called. Each element in this array can contain the following values:
		SQL_PARAM_PROCEED: The set of parameter values are to be used by the **SQLExecute()** or **SQLExecDirect()** function call.
		SQL_PARAM_IGNORE: The set of parameter values are not to be used by the **SQLExecute()** or **SQLExecDirect()** function call.
		If no elements in the array are set, all sets of parameter values are used by **SQLExecute()** or **SQLExecDirect()** function calls.
		If this statement attribute contains a NULL pointer, all sets of parameter values are used by **SQLExecute()** or **SQLExecDirect()** function calls, however, no parameter status values are returned by the driver.
		This attribute can be set at any time, but the new value is not used until the next time **SQLExecute()** or **SQLExecDirect()** is called.
		This statement attribute corresponds to the **SQL_DESC_ARRAY_STATUS_PTR** field of the application parameter descriptor header record.
SQL_ATTR_PARAM_ STATUS_PTR	SQLUSMALLINT pointer	Contains a pointer to an array of parameter status values that will contain status information about each set of parameter values used after **SQLExecute()** or **SQLExecDirect()** has been executed. This statement attribute is only required if the **SQL_ATTR_PARAMSET_ SIZE** attribute contains a value greater than **1**.
		An application must allocate an array of **SQLUSMALLINT** values with as many elements as there are parameter values, and store a pointer to the array in this attribute. When **SQLExecute()** or **SQLExecDirect()** is called, the driver populates the specified array; If this attribute contains a NULL pointer (the default), no status values are generated and the array is not populated.
		Each element in the array can contain one of the following values:
		SQL_PARAM_SUCCESS: The SQL statement was successfully executed using the set of parameter values.

Table 8-8 SQL Statement Attributes (Continued)

Attribute	Data Type	Description
		SQL_PARAM_SUCCESS_WITH_INFO: The SQL statement was successfully executed using the set of parameter values; however, warning information was generated and is available in one or more diagnostic records.
		SQL_PARAM_ERROR: An error occurred while processing the SQL statement using the set of parameter values. Additional error information is available in one or more diagnostic records.
		SQL_PARAM_UNUSED: The set of parameter values was not used, possibly because some previous set of parameter values caused an error that aborted further processing, or because **SQL_PARAM_IGNORE** was set for the set of parameter values in the specified array.
		SQL_PARAM_DIAG_UNAVAILABLE: Diagnostic information is not available. For example, when the driver treats arrays of parameter values as a monolithic unit, error information is not generated.
		If a call to **SQLExecute()** or **SQLExecDirect()** did not return **SQL_SUCCESS** or **SQL_SUCCESS_WITH_INFO**, the contents of the array pointed to by this attribute are undefined.
		This attribute can be set at any time, but the new value is not used until the next time **SQLFetch()**, **SQLFetchScroll()**, or **SQLSetPos()** is called.
		This statement attribute corresponds to the **SQL_DESC_ ARRAY_STATUS_PTR** field of the implementation parameter descriptor header record.
SQL_ATTR_PARAMS_ PROCESSED_PTR	SQLUINTEGER pointer	Contains a pointer to a buffer that contains the number of sets of parameter values that have already been processed (including parameter value sets that caused an error to occur).
		If this attribute contains a NULL pointer, no number is returned by a call to **SQLExecute()** or **SQLExecDirect()**.
		If the call to **SQLExecute()** or **SQLExecDirect()** that fills in the buffer pointed to by this attribute does not return **SQL_SUCCESS** or **SQL_SUCCESS_WITH_INFO**, the contents of the buffer are undefined.
		This statement attribute corresponds to the **SQL_DESC_ROWS_PROCESSED_PTR** field of the implementation parameter descriptor header record.
SQL_ATTR_PARAMSET_ SIZE	SQLUINTEGER	Specifies the number of values available for each parameter marker.

Table 8–8   SQL Statement Attributes (Continued)

Attribute	Data Type	Description
		By default, the value for this attribute is **1**. If this attribute contains a value greater than **1**, the **SQL_DESC_DATA_PTR**, **SQL_DESC_INDICATOR_PTR**, and **SQL_DESC_OCTET_LENGTH_PTR** fields of each parameter/column descriptor record contain pointers to arrays (APD or ARD descriptors only). The cardinality of each array is equal to the value of this attribute.
		This statement attribute corresponds to the **SQL_DESC_ARRAY_SIZE** field of the application parameter descriptor header record.
SQL_ATTR_QUERY_ TIMEOUT	SQLUINTEGER	Specifies the number of seconds to wait for an SQL statement to execute before returning control to the application. If this attribute is equal to **0** (the default value for this attribute), there is no time out period. If the specified timeout exceeds the maximum timeout supported by the data source or is smaller than the minimum timeout supported by the data source, DB2 CLI substitutes the timeout value and returns SQLSTATE **01**S02 (Option value changed). The query timeout specified in this statement attribute is valid in both synchronous and asynchronous modes.
		This attribute is not valid on platforms other than Windows 3.1.
SQL_ATTR_RETRIEVE_DATA	SQLUINTEGER	Specifies whether the **SQLFetchScroll()** and the **SQLFetch()** functions are to retrieve data after they position the cursor. Valid values for this attribute are:
		SQL_RD_ON: **SQLFetchScroll()** and **SQLFetch()** retrieve data after they position the cursor to the specified location. This is the default value for this attribute.
		SQL_RD_OFF: **SQLFetchScroll()** and **SQLFetch()** do not retrieve data after they position the cursor.
		By setting this attribute to **SQL_RD_OFF**, an application can either verify whether a row exists or retrieve a bookmark for a row without incurring the overhead of retrieving data.
		This attribute can be set while a cursor is open; however, the setting may not take effect immediately, in which case DB2 CLI will return SQLSTATE **01**S02 (Option value changed), and the attribute is reset to its original value.
SQL_ATTR_ROW_ARRAY_ SIZE	SQLUINTEGER	Specifies the number of rows to be returned by each call to **SQLFetch()** or **SQLFetchScroll()** (number of rows in the rowset). By default, the value for this attribute is

Table 8–8 *SQL Statement Attributes (Continued)*

Attribute	Data Type	Description
		1. If the specified rowset size exceeds the maximum rowset size supported by the data source, DB2 CLI substitutes that value and returns SQLSTATE **01S02** (Option value changed).
		This statement attribute corresponds to the **SQL_ DESC_ARRAY_SIZE** field of the application row descriptor header record.
SQL_ATTR_ROW_BIND_ OFFSET_PTR	**SQLUINTEGER** pointer	Contains a pointer to an offset that is to be added to pointers to change the binding of column data. By default, this attribute contains a NULL pointer. If this attribute contains a pointer to a binding offset, instead of a NULL pointer, DB2 CLI dereferences the pointer and adds the dereferenced value to each deferred field that has a non-NULL value in the **SQL_DESC_DATA_ PTR**, **SQL_DESC_INDICATOR_PTR**, and **SQL_DESC_ OCTET_LENGTH_PTR** fields of the application row descriptor and uses the new pointer values when binding.
		This statement attribute corresponds to the **SQL_DESC_BIND_OFFSET_PTR** field of the application row descriptor header record.
SQL_ATTR_ROW_BIND_ TYPE	**SQLUINTEGER**	Specifies the binding orientation to use when the **SQLFetch()** or **SQLFetchScroll()** function is called.
		By default, this attribute is set to **SQL_BIND_BY_ COLUMN** and column-wise binding is used. Row-wise binding is specified by setting this attribute to the length of a structure or an instance of a buffer into which all result data set columns are bound. If a length is specified, it must include space for all the bound columns and any padding of the structure or buffer to ensure that when the address of a bound column is incremented with the specified length, the result points to the beginning of the same column in the next row. By using the **sizeof()** operator in ANSI C, this behavior is guaranteed.
		This statement attribute corresponds to the **SQL_DESC_BIND_TYPE** field of the application row descriptor header record.
SQL_ATTR_ROW_NUMBER	**SQLUINTEGER**	Identifies the number of the current row in the entire result data set. If the number of the current row cannot be determined or if there is no current row, this attribute contains the number **0**.
		This attribute can be retrieved by the **SQLGetStmtAttr()** function, but it can not be set by the **SQLSetStmtAttr()** function.

Table 8–8 *SQL Statement Attributes (Continued)*

Attribute	Data Type	Description
SQL_ATTR_ROW_ OPERATION_PTR	SQLUSMALLINT pointer	Contains a pointer to an array of row operation values that can be set by the application to indicate whether or not the row is to be ignored by the **SQLSetPos()** function. Each element in the array can contain the following values:
		SQL_ROW_PROCEED: The row is included in the bulk operation performed by the **SQLSetPos()** function. (This setting does not guarantee the operation will occur on the row. If the row has the status **SQL_ROW_ERROR** in the IRD row status array, the driver may not be able to perform the operation on the row.)
		SQL_ROW_IGNORE: The row is excluded from the bulk operation performed by the **SQLSetPos()** function.
		If no elements in the array are set, or if this attribute contains a NULL pointer, all rows are included in the bulk operation performed by the **SQLSetPos()** function.
		If an element in the array is set to **SQL_ROW_IGNORE**, the value in the row status array for the ignored row is not changed
		This attribute can be set at any time, but the new value is not used until the next time **SQLSetPos()** is called.
		This statement attribute corresponds to the **SQL_ DESC_ARRAY_STATUS_PTR** field of the application row descriptor header record.
SQL_ATTR_ROW_STATUS_PTR	SQLUSMALLINT pointer	Contains a pointer to an array of row status values that will contain status information after the **SQLFetch()**, **SQLFetchScroll()**, or **SQLSetPos()** function has been executed.
		An application must allocate an array of **SQLUSMALLINT** values with as many elements as there are rows in the rowset and store a pointer to the array in this attribute. When the **SQLFetch()**, **SQLFetchScroll()**, or **SQLSetPos()** function is called, the driver populates the specified array; If this attribute contains a NULL pointer (the default), no status values are generated and the array is not populated. Each element in the array can contain the following values:
		SQL_ROW_SUCCESS: The row was successfully fetched and has not been changed since it was last fetched.
		SQL_ROW_SUCCESS_WITH_INFO: The row was successfully fetched and has not been changed since it was last fetched. However, a warning was returned about the row.

Table 8–8 SQL Statement Attributes (Continued)

Attribute	Data Type	Description
		SQL_ROW_ERROR: An error occurred while fetching the row. **SQL_ROW_UPDATED**: The row was successfully fetched and has been changed since it was last fetched. If the row is fetched again, its status is **SQL_ROW_SUCCESS**. **SQL_ROW_DELETED**: The row has been deleted since it was last fetched. **SQL_ROW_NOROW**: The rowset overlapped the end of the result data set and no row was returned that corresponded to an element of the row status array. If a call to **SQLFetch()**, **SQLFetchScroll()**, or **SQLSetPos()** did not return **SQL_SUCCESS** or **SQL_SUCCESS_WITH_INFO**, the contents of the array referenced by this attribute are undefined. This attribute can be set at any time, but the new value is not used until the next time **SQLFetch()**, **SQLFetchScroll()**, or **SQLSetPos()** is called. This statement attribute corresponds to the **SQL_DESC_ARRAY_STATUS_PTR** field of the implementation row descriptor header record.
SQL_ATTR_ROWS_FETCHED_PTR	**SQLUINTEGER** pointer	Contains a pointer to a buffer containing the number of rows fetched by **SQLFetch()** or **SQLFetchScroll()** or the number of rows affected (including rows that returned errors) by a bulk operation performed by **SQLSetPos()**. If this attribute contains a NULL pointer, no value is returned. The value stored in this attribute is only valid if a call to **SQLFetch()**, **SQLFetchScroll()**, or **SQLSetPos()** returned **SQL_SUCCESS** or **SQL_SUCCESS_WITH_INFO**. If **SQL_SUCCESS** or **SQL_SUCCESS_WITH_INFO** was not returned, the contents of the buffer pointed to by this attribute are undefined unless **SQL_NO_DATA** was returned, in which case the number **0** was also returned. This statement attribute corresponds to the **SQL_DESC_ROWS_PROCESSED_PTR** field of the implementation row descriptor header record.
SQL_ATTR_ROWSET_SIZE	32-bit **INTEGER**	Specifies the number of rows that can be retrieved into a single rowset. A rowset is the array of rows that is returned by each call to the **SQLExtendedFetch()** function. The value specified for this attribute must be 1

Table 8–8   *SQL Statement Attributes (Continued)*

Attribute	Data Type	Description
		or a positive number. The default value for this option is 1, which means that 1 row will be retrieved—thereby making **SQLExtendedFetch()** equivalent to **SQLFetch()**.
		This option can be changed even if there is an open cursor on the associated SQL statement handle. The change becomes effective the next time the **SQLExtendedFetch()** function is called.
		Note: Because **SQLExtendedFetch()** has been replaced by **SQLFetchScroll()**, this attribute should only be used if working with DB2 CLI 2.0 or earlier.
SQL_ATTR_STMTTXN_ISOLATION or **SQL_ATTR_TXN_ISOLATION**	32-bit **INTEGER**	Specifies the transaction isolation level to use for the current connection. The following terms are used to define transaction isolation levels:
		Dirty Read: Transaction 1 changes a row. Transaction 2 reads the changed row before Transaction 1 commits the change. If Transaction 1 rolls back the change, Transaction 2 will have read a row that is considered to have never existed.
		Nonrepeatable Read: Transaction 1 reads a row. Transaction 2 updates or deletes that row and commits this change. If Transaction 1 attempts to reread the row, it will receive different row values or discover that the row has been deleted.
		Phantom: Transaction 1 reads a set of rows that satisfy some search criteria. Transaction 2 generates one or more rows (either through inserts or updates) that match the search criteria. If Transaction 1 reexecutes the statement that reads the rows, it receives a different set of rows.
		If the data source supports transactions, the driver returns one of the following bitmasks:
		SQL_TXN_READ_UNCOMMITTED: Dirty reads, nonrepeatable reads, and phantoms are possible.
		SQL_TXN_READ_COMMITTED: Dirty reads are not possible. Nonrepeatable reads and phantoms are possible. This is the default value for this attribute.

Table 8–8 SQL Statement Attributes (Continued)

Attribute	Data Type	Description
		SQL_TXN_REPEATABLE_READ: Dirty reads and nonrepeatable reads are not possible. Phantoms are possible.
		SQL_TXN_SERIALIZABLE: Transactions are serializable. Serializable transactions do not allow dirty reads, nonrepeatable reads, or phantoms.
		SQL_TXN_NOCOMMIT: Changes are effectively committed at the end of a successful operation; no explicit commit or rollback is allowed (this is analogous to autocommit). This is not an SQL92 isolation level, but an IBM defined extension, that is only supported by DB2 for AS/400.
		In IBM terminology, **SQL_TXN_READ_UNCOMMITTED** is Uncommitted Read; **SQL_TXN_READ_COMMITTED** is Cursor Stability; **SQL_TXN_REPEATABLE_READ** is Read Stability; and **SQL_TXN_SERIALIZABLE** is Repeatable Read.
		This attribute cannot be changed if there is an open cursor on the associated SQL statement handle.
		If this attribute is set, the default value set at the connection level is overridden.
		Note: The value **SQL_ATTR_STMTTXN_ISOLATION** is synonymous with the value **SQL_ATTR_TXN_ISOLATION**. However, since the ODBC Driver Manager does not recognize **SQL_ATTR_TXN_ISOLATION** as a statement attribute, ODBC applications that need to set translation isolation levels at the statement level must use the **SQL_ATTR_STMTTXN_ISOLATION** attribute.
		This is an IBM defined statement level attribute.
SQL_ATTR_USE_BOOKMARKS (ODBC 2.0)	**SQLUINTEGER**	Specifies whether an application uses bookmarks with a cursor. Valid values for this attribute are:
		SQL_UB_OFF: An application does not use bookmarks with a cursor. This is the default value for this attribute.
		SQL_UB_VARIABLE : An application uses bookmarks with a cursor, and DB2 CLI provides variable-length bookmarks if they are supported.
		To use bookmarks with a cursor, the application must specify this attribute with the **SQL_UB_VARIABLE** value before opening the cursor.

NOTE: *This function replaces the DB2 CLI 2.0 function* `SQLGetStmtOption()`.

Return Codes   `SQL_SUCCESS`, `SQL_SUCCESS_WITH_INFO`, `SQL_INVALID_HANDLE`, or `SQL_ERROR`

SQLSTATEs   If this function returns `SQL_SUCCESS_WITH_INFO` or `SQL_ERROR`, one of the following SQLSTATE values may be obtained by calling the `SQLGetDiagRec()` function:

01000, **01**004, **24**000, **HY**000, **HY**001, **HY**010, **HY**013, **HY**090, **HY**092, **HY**109, or **HYC**00

Comments
- If the *Value* parameter contains a NULL pointer, no length is returned in the *StringLength* parameter.
- If an attribute that returns a string value is specified in the *Attribute* parameter, and if that string value's actual length is greater than or equal to the maximum string size value specified in the *ValueMaxSize* parameter, the value is truncated to *ValueMaxSize*-1 (the length of a NULL-termination character) characters and NULL terminated by the driver.
- If an attribute that returns a string value is specified in the *Attribute* parameter, the *Value* parameter must contain a pointer to a buffer in which this function can return the string.
- If the value returned for the attribute specified in the *Attribute* parameter is a Unicode string, the *ValueMaxSize* parameter must contain an even number.
- The `SQL_ATTR_IMP_PARAM_DESC`, `SQL_ATTR_IMP_ROW_DESC`, and `SQL_ATTR_ROW_NUMBER` statement attributes are read-only; therefore, they can be retrieved by this function, but they can not be set by the `SQLSetStmtAttr()` function.

Prerequisites   An SQL statement handle must be allocated before this function is called.

Restrictions   There are no restrictions associated with this function call.

See Also   `SQLSetStmtAttr()`, `SQLGetEnvAttr()`, `SQLSetEnvAttr()`, `SQLGetConnectAttr()`, `SQLSetConnectAttr()`

Example   The following Visual C++ program illustrates how to retrieve and change the current value of an SQL statement attribute.

```
/*-------------------------------------------------------------*/
/* NAME:     CH8EX7.CPP                                        */
/* PURPOSE: Illustrate How To Use The Following CLI API Functions */
/*          In A C++ Program:                                  */
/*                                                             */
/*                  SQLGetStmtAttr()                           */
/*                  SQLSetStmtAttr()                           */
/*                                                             */
/* OTHER CLI APIs SHOWN:                                       */
```

```
/*            SQLAllocHandle()            SQLSetEnvAttr()          */
/*            SQLConnect()                SQLDisconnect()          */
/*            SQLFreeHandle()                                      */
/*                                                                */
/*──────────────────────────────────────────────────────────────*/

// Include The Appropriate Header Files
#include <windows.h>
#include <sqlcli1.h>
#include <iostream.h>

// Define The CLI_Class Class
class CLI_Class
{
    // Attributes
    public:
        SQLHANDLE     EnvHandle;
        SQLHANDLE     ConHandle;
        SQLHANDLE     StmtHandle;
        SQLRETURN     rc;
        SQLUINTEGER   MaxRows;

    // Operations
    public:
        CLI_Class();                            // Constructor
        ~CLI_Class();                           // Destructor
        SQLRETURN   GetMaxRowsValue();
        SQLRETURN   SetMaxRowsValue(SQLUINTEGER MaxRows);
};

// Define The Class Constructor
CLI_Class::CLI_Class()
{
    // Initialize The Return Code Variable
    rc = SQL_SUCCESS;

    // Allocate An Environment Handle
    rc = SQLAllocHandle(SQL_HANDLE_ENV, SQL_NULL_HANDLE, &EnvHandle);

    // Set The ODBC Application Version To 3.x
    if (rc == SQL_SUCCESS)
        rc = SQLSetEnvAttr(EnvHandle, SQL_ATTR_ODBC_VERSION,
                (SQLPOINTER) SQL_OV_ODBC3, SQL_IS_UINTEGER);

    // Allocate A Connection Handle
    if (rc == SQL_SUCCESS)
        rc = SQLAllocHandle(SQL_HANDLE_DBC, EnvHandle, &ConHandle);
}

// Define The Class Destructor
CLI_Class::~CLI_Class()
{
    // Free The Connection Handle
    if (ConHandle != NULL)
```

```
                    SQLFreeHandle(SQL_HANDLE_DBC, ConHandle);

        // Free The Environment Handle
        if (EnvHandle != NULL)
            SQLFreeHandle(SQL_HANDLE_ENV, EnvHandle);
    }

// Define The GetMaxRowsValue() Member Function
SQLRETURN CLI_Class::GetMaxRowsValue(void)
{
    // Declare The Local Memory Variables
    SQLINTEGER  ValueLength;

    // Determine The Number Of Rows The Driver Will Return For A
    // SELECT SQL Statement
    rc = SQLGetStmtAttr(StmtHandle, SQL_ATTR_MAX_ROWS,
            (SQLPOINTER) &MaxRows, SQL_IS_UINTEGER, &ValueLength);

    // Display The Information Retrieved
    if (rc == SQL_SUCCESS)
    {
        cout << "Maximum number of rows to return : ";
        cout << MaxRows << endl;
    }

    // Return The CLI API Return Code To The Calling Function
    return(rc);
}

// Define The SetMaxRowsValue() Member Function
SQLRETURN CLI_Class::SetMaxRowsValue(SQLUINTEGER MaxRows)
{
    // Specify The Number Of Rows That The Driver Is To Return For A
    // SELECT SQL Statement
    rc = SQLSetStmtAttr(StmtHandle, SQL_ATTR_MAX_ROWS,
            (SQLPOINTER) MaxRows, SQL_IS_UINTEGER);

    // Return The CLI API Return Code To The Calling Function
    return(rc);
}

/*-------------------------------------------------------------------*/
/* The Main Function                                                 */
/*-------------------------------------------------------------------*/
int main()
{
    // Declare The Local Memory Variables
    SQLRETURN  rc = SQL_SUCCESS;

    // Create An Instance Of The CLI_Class Class
    CLI_Class  Example;

    // Connect To The IBM Sample Database
    if (Example.ConHandle != NULL)
    {
```

```
        rc = SQLConnect(Example.ConHandle, (SQLCHAR *) "SAMPLE",
                SQL_NTS, (SQLCHAR *) "userid", SQL_NTS,
                (SQLCHAR *) "password", SQL_NTS);

        // Allocate An SQL Statement Handle
        rc = SQLAllocHandle(SQL_HANDLE_STMT, Example.ConHandle,
                &Example.StmtHandle);

        if (rc == SQL_SUCCESS)
        {
            // Determine The Number Of Rows The Driver Will Return
            // For A SELECT SQL Statement
            rc = Example.GetMaxRowsValue();

            // Tell The Driver To Return Up To 25 Rows For A
            // SELECT SQL Statement
            rc = Example.SetMaxRowsValue(25);

            // Determine Whether Or Not The Driver Will Now Return
            // Up To 25 Rows For A SELECT SQL Statement
            rc = Example.GetMaxRowsValue();

            // Free The SQL Statement Handle
            if (Example.StmtHandle != NULL)
                SQLFreeHandle(SQL_HANDLE_STMT, Example.StmtHandle);
        }

        // Disconnect From The IBM Sample Database
        rc = SQLDisconnect(Example.ConHandle);
    }

    // Return To The Operating System
    return(rc);
}
```

SQLSetStmtAttr

COMPATIBILITY

X/OPEN 95 CLI	ISO/IEC 92 CLI	DB2 CLI 5.2	DB2 CLI 2.0	ODBC 3.x
☑	☑	☑	☐	☑

ODBC API CONFORMANCE LEVEL   CORE

Purpose The SQLSetStmtAttr() function is used to modify the current value of a specified SQL statement attribute.

Syntax	`SQLRETURN SQLSetStmtAttr`	`(SQLHSTMT`	`StatementHandle,`
		`SQLINTEGER`	`Attribute,`
		`SQLPOINTER`	`Value,`
		`SQLINTEGER`	`StringLength);`

Parameters   *StatementHandle*   An SQL statement handle that refers to a previously allocated SQL statement information storage buffer (data structure).

Attribute   The SQL statement attribute whose value is to be modified. This parameter must be set to one of the following values:

- `SQL_ATTR_APP_PARAM_DESC`
- `SQL_ATTR_APP_ROW_DESC`
- `SQL_ATTR_ASYNC_ENABLE`
- `SQL_ATTR_BIND_TYPE`
- `SQL_ATTR_CONCURRENCY`
- `SQL_ATTR_CURSOR_HOLD`
- `SQL_ATTR_CURSOR_TYPE`
- `SQL_ATTR_DEFERRED_PREPARE`
- `SQL_ATTR_EARLYCLOSE`
- `SQL_ATTR_ENABLE_AUTO_IPD`
- `SQL_ATTR_FETCH_BOOKMARK_PTR`
- `SQL_ATTR_IMP_PARAM_DESC`
- `SQL_ATTR_IMP_ROW_DESC`
- `SQL_ATTR_KEYSET_SIZE`
- `SQL_ATTR_MAX_LENGTH`
- `SQL_ATTR_MAX_ROWS`
- `SQL_ATTR_METADATA_ID`
- `SQL_ATTR_NOSCAN`
- `SQL_ATTR_PARAM_BIND_OFFSET_PTR`
- `SQL_ATTR_PARAM_BIND_TYPE`
- `SQL_ATTR_PARAM_OPERATION_PTR`
- `SQL_ATTR_PARAM_STATUS_PTR`
- `SQL_ATTR_PARAMOPT_ATOMIC`
- `SQL_ATTR_PARAMS_PROCESSED_PTR`
- `SQL_ATTR_PARAMSET_SIZE`
- `SQL_ATTR_QUERY_TIMEOUT`
- `SQL_ATTR_RETRIEVE_DATA`
- `SQL_ATTR_ROW_ARRAY_SIZE`
- `SQL_ATTR_ATTR_ROW_BIND_OFFSET_PTR`

- SQL_ATTR_ROW_BIND_TYPE
- SQL_ATTR_ROW_NUMBER
- SQL_ATTR_ROW_OPERATION_PTR
- SQL_ATTR_ROW_STATUS_PTR
- SQL_ATTR_ROWS_FETCHED_PTR
- SQL_ATTR_STMTTXN_ISOLATION
- SQL_ATTR_TXN_ISOLATION
- SQL_ATTR_USE_BOOKMARKS

Value

A pointer to a location in memory where the new value for the SQL statement attribute is stored. Depending upon the SQL statement attribute being set, this pointer can reference either a 32-bit integer value or a NULL-terminated character string.

StringLength

The length of the SQL statement attribute value stored in the *Value* parameter. If an ODBC-defined attribute value is to be set and if the attribute value is a 32-bit integer value, this parameter is ignored. If a DB2 CLI attribute value is to be set, this parameter must be set as follows:

- If the value of the specified SQL statement attribute is a character string, this parameter should be set to the actual length of the string or to **SQL_NTS**.

- If the value of the specified SQL statement attribute is a binary string, this parameter should be set to the result of the **SQL_LEN_BINARY_ATTR**(*length*) macro. Usually, this macro will place a negative value in this parameter.

- If the value of the specified SQL statement attribute is anything other than a character string or binary string, this parameter should be set to **SQL_IS_POINTER**.

- If the value of the specified SQL statement attribute is a fixed-length data type, this parameter should be set to **SQL_IS_INTEGER** or **SQL_IS_UINTEGER**, as appropriate.

Description

The **SQLSetStmtAttr()** function is used to modify the current value of a specified SQL statement attribute. Refer to the **SQLGetStmtAttr()** function for more information about each statement attribute available.

Each statement handle's statement attributes for a statement remain in effect until they are changed by another call to **SQLSetStmtAttr()** or until the statement handle is freed with the **SQLFreeHandle()** function.

Many statement attributes correspond to a descriptor's header field—setting these attributes actually results in the setting of the descriptor fields. Setting fields by calling **SQLSetStmtAttr()**, rather than **SQLSetDescField()**, has the advantage of not having to obtain a descriptor handle before a field can be set.

Setting attributes for one SQL statement can affect other SQL statements. Especially when the Application Parameter Descriptor (APD) or the Application Row Descriptor (ARD) associated with the statement handle is explicitly allocated and associated with other statement handles. Because **SQLSetStmtAttr()** modifies the APD or ARD, the modifications apply to all statements with which these descriptors are associated. If this is not the desired behavior, the application should disassociate this descriptor from the other statements (by calling **SQLSetStmtAttr()** to set the **SQL_ATTR_APP_ROW_DESC** or **SQL_ATTR_APP_PARAM_DESC** field to a different descriptor handle) before calling **SQLSetStmtAttr()** again.

When a descriptor field is set as a result of the corresponding statement attribute being set, the field is set only for the applicable descriptors that are currently associated with the statement handle specified in the *StatementHandle* parameter, and the attribute setting does not affect any descriptors that may be associated with that statement handle in the future. Likewise, when a descriptor field that is also a statement attribute is set by a calling **the SQLSetDescField()** function, the corresponding statement attribute is also set.

Table 8–9 shows the statement attributes that correspond to descriptor header fields.

NOTE: *This function replaces the DB2 CLI 2.0 function* **SQLSetStmtOption()**.

Return Codes   SQL_SUCCESS, SQL_SUCCESS_WITH_INFO, SQL_INVALID_HANDLE, or SQL_ERROR

Table 8–9   *Statement Attributes that Correspond to Descriptor Header Record Fields*

Statement Attribute	Descriptor Header Record Field	Descriptor Type
SQL_ATTR_PARAM_BIND_OFFSET_PTR	SQL_DESC_BIND_OFFSET_PTR	APD
SQL_ATTR_PARAM_BIND_TYPE	SQL_DESC_BIND_TYPE	APD
SQL_ATTR_PARAM_STATUS_PTR	SQL_DESC_ARRAY_STATUS_PTR	IPD
SQL_ATTR_PARAMS_PROCESSED_PTR	SQL_DESC_ROWS_PROCESSED_PTR	IPD
SQL_ATTR_PARAMSET_SIZE	SQL_DESC_ARRAY_SIZE	APD
SQL_ATTR_ROW_BIND_OFFSET_PTR	SQL_DESC_BIND_OFFSET_PTR	ARD
SQL_ATTR_ROW_BIND_TYPE	SQL_DESC_BIND_TYPE	ARD
SQL_ATTR_ROW_STATUS_PTR	SQL_DESC_ARRAY_STATUS_PTR	IRD
SQL_ATTR_ROWS_FETCHED_PTR	SQL_DESC_ROWS_PROCESSED_PTR	IRD
SQL_ATTR_ROWSET_SIZE	SQL_DESC_ARRAY_SIZE	ARD

(Adapted from table 169 on page 590 of *IBM DB2 Universal Database Call Level Interface Guide and Reference.*)

SQLSTATEs   If this function returns **SQL_SUCCESS_WITH_INFO** or **SQL_ERROR**, one of the following SQLSTATE values may be obtained by calling the **SQLGetDiagRec()** function:

01000, **01**S02, **08**S01, **24**000, **HY**000, **HY**001, **HY**009, **HY**010, **HY**011, **HY**017, **HY**024, **HY**090, **HY**092, or **HY**C00

Refer to Appendix B for detailed information about each SQLSTATE value that can be returned.

Comments
- If a driver-specific value is specified in the *Attribute* parameter, an assigned integer value may be stored in the memory location referred to by the *Value* parameter.

- In DB2 CLI 5.2, connection attributes cannot be set at the statement level. This does not include the **SQL_ATTR_METADATA_ID** and **SQL_ATTR_ASYNC_ENABLE** attributes, because both are connection and statement attributes and can be set at either the connection level or the statement level.

- Some statement attributes support substitution of a similar value if the data source does not support the value specified in the *Value* parameter. In such cases, DB2 CLI returns **SQL_SUCCESS_WITH_INFO** and SQLSTATE **01**S02 (Option value changed). For example, if *Attribute* is **SQL_ATTR_CONCURRENCY**, *Value* is **SQL_CONCUR_ROWVER**, and the data source does not support this, the driver substitutes **SQL_CONCUR_VALUES** and returns **SQL_SUCCESS_WITH_INFO**. An application can call the **SQLGetStmtAttr()** function after setting a statement attribute to determine whether a substitution occurred, and if so, to obtain the substituted value.

Prerequisites   An SQL statement handle must be allocated before this function is called.

Restrictions   There are no restrictions associated with this function call.

See Also   **SQLGetStmtAttr()**, **SQLGetEnvAttr()**, **SQLSetEnvAttr()**, **SQLGetConnectAttr()**, **SQLSetConnectAttr()**

Examples   See the example provided for the **SQLGetStmtAttr()** function, on page 246.

CHAPTER 9

Preparing and Executing SQL Statements

CLI applications perform most of their data retrieval and data manipulation operations by submitting SQL statements to a data source for processing. This chapter is designed to introduce you to the set of API functions that are used to prepare and execute SQL statements. The first part of this chapter introduces the functions used to prepare an SQL statement for execution. This is followed by a discussion about the functions used to associate application variables and buffers to parameter markers that may be coded in an SQL statement. Next, the functions used to submit SQL statements to the data source for processing are described. Then, the functions used to send large data values to the data source and to terminate transactions are discussed. Finally, a detailed reference section covering each CLI function that can be used to prepare, associate application variables to, and submit SQL statements for execution is provided.

Allocating an SQL Statement Handle

Just as a handle is used to access and modify an application's environment, a handle is used to submit an SQL statement to a data source for processing and to access any results generated. Thus, before an SQL statement can be prepared and executed, a statement handle must first be allocated. To do this, an application:

1. Creates (declares) an SQL statement handle variable.

and

2. Calls the **SQLAllocHandle()** function with the statement handle variable address specified.

When this function is called, the CLI Library or the ODBC Driver Manager allocates a structure in the connection handle specified to store information about the SQL statement, and stores the handle to this structure in the SQL statement handle variable specified.

Allocating statement handles is an expensive task. Therefore, it is usually more efficient for an application to use an existing SQL statement handle repeatedly than to free existing statement handles when they are no longer needed and allocate new ones. However, when result data sets are created on statement handles, applications must be careful to close the cursor and destroy the result data set associated with the statement handle before it is reused.

Using SQL Statement Parameter Markers

Literal values can be, and often are, hard-coded directly into SQL statements. For example, suppose you want to add a record to a table named Parts that has columns named PartID, Description, and Price. You could do this by preparing and executing the following SQL statement:

```
INSERT INTO Parts (PartID, Description, Price) VALUES (2100, 'Drive
     shaft', 50.00)
```

Although this SQL statement correctly inserts a new record in the Parts table, its use is limited because it can only insert one specific record into the table. Therefore, this approach would not be a good solution for a data entry application that might need to insert several different records into the Parts table. An alternative approach is to construct one or more SQL statements at application run time using the specific values that need to be inserted into the table. Although this approach provides more flexibility, it is not the best solution because of the complexity required to construct and execute multiple SQL statements at run time. The best approach to this type of problem is to construct a single SQL statement that contains parameter markers in place of literal values. For example, our previous SQL statement could be constructed like this:

```
INSERT INTO Parts (PartID, Description, Price) VALUES (?, ?, ?)
```

When SQL statements are coded in this manner, each parameter marker used must be associated with, or *bound* to an application variable. Once all parameter markers have been bound, an application can simply set/change the values of each bound variable and prepare/execute the SQL statement. If the SQL statement is to be executed multiple times, the process can be made even more efficient by preparing and executing the statement in separate steps.

Parameter markers provide the flexibility gained by constructing SQL statements at run time while eliminating most of the added complexity (particularly the additional coding needed to convert numerical data values to and from text). For example, suppose the PartID column of the Parts table described in the previous examples was defined to hold integer data. If an SQL statement designed to insert new records is constructed at application run time (without parameter markers), the application must convert the Part ID to text (to build the SQL statement) and the data source must convert it back to an integer (to store it in the column). By using a parameter marker, the application could send the Part ID to the data source as an integer, thereby saving one or more data conversions. For long data values this becomes critical because the text forms of such values often exceed the maximum length allowed for an SQL statement.

Parameter markers are only allowed in certain places in SQL statements. For example, they cannot be used in the list of columns to be returned by a **SELECT** SQL statement, nor can they be used as the operand of a binary operator such as the equal sign (=). In general, parameter markers are legal if they are used in Data Manipulation Language (DML) statements; parameter markers are not legal when used in DDL statements.

Binding Parameters to Application Variables

As mentioned earlier, each parameter marker in an SQL statement must be associated with, or bound to, an application variable before the statement is executed. When an application binds a variable to a parameter marker in an SQL statement, it describes the variable (that is, memory address, C data type, and so on) to DB2 CLI. It also describes the parameter itself (that is, the SQL data type, precision, etc.). DB2 CLI stores this information in the structure it maintains for the SQL statement (referred to by the statement handle) and uses the information to retrieve the value from the variable and send it to the data source when the SQL statement is executed.

The **SQLBindParameter()** function is used to bind parameter markers in an SQL statement to application variables, one parameter at a time. Each time this function is called the application specifies:

■ The parameter marker number. Parameters are numbered in increasing order as they appear from left to right in the SQL statement, beginning with the number 1. While it is legal to specify a parameter marker number higher than the actual number of parameter markers used in the SQL statement, additional parameter marker values are ignored when the SQL statement is executed.

■ The parameter type (that is, input, output, or input/output). Except for parameter markers used in stored procedure calls, all parameters are treated as input parameters.

■ The C data type, memory address, and size (length), in bytes, of the application variable being bound to the parameter marker. The driver used must be able to convert the data from the C data type specified to the SQL data type used by the data source or an error will occur.

■ The SQL data type, precision, and scale of the parameter itself.

■ Optionally, the memory address of a length/indicator variable. This variable is used to provide the byte length of binary or character data, specify that the data is a NULL value, or specify that the data is long and will be sent with the `SQLPutData()` function.

Parameter markers can be bound to application variables in any order.

Application variables can be bound to parameter markers in an SQL statement any time before the statement is sent to the data source for execution. Once an application variable is bound to a parameter marker, it remains bound until one of the following occurs:

■ A different application variable is bound to the same parameter marker.

■ All parameter markers are unbound. This is done by calling the `SQLFreeStmt()` function with the `SQL_RESET_PARAMS` option specified.

■ The statement handle associated with the SQL statement containing the parameter marker is released (freed).

To bind a parameter marker to a different variable, an application simply rebinds the parameter marker with the new variable; the previous binding is automatically released. However, if a parameter marker is rebound after an SQL statement has been executed, the new binding does not take effect until the SQL statement is re-executed. Applications must ensure that variables are not freed until after they are unbound.

BINDING PARAMETERS TO ARRAYS   CLI applications can extend the flexibility that parameters provide by specifying multiple values (stored in arrays) for each parameter marker used in an SQL statement. For example, by using an array of values with a parameterized **INSERT** SQL statement, an application can insert several rows of data into a data source *with a single function call* (provided the data source supports the use of parameter value arrays).

There are several advantages to using arrays of parameter values. First, network traffic is reduced because the data for many SQL statements can be sent in a single packet. Second, some data sources can execute SQL statements using arrays faster than they can execute an equivalent amount of separate SQL statements. Finally, when data is stored in an array, as is often the case for screen data, all the rows in a particular column can be bound to a parameter with a single function call and multiple rows can be updated by executing a single SQL statement.

An application binds parameters to arrays in the same manner that it binds parameters to other application variables—by calling the `SQLBindParameter()` function. The only difference is that the addresses specified in the `SQLBindParameter()` call reference arrays instead of variables. However, before binding parameters to arrays, an application must decide which of the following binding styles it will use:

■ *Column-wise binding*   An array is bound to each parameter in the SQL statement This is called column-wise binding because a column of values is bound to one parameter in the statement.

■ *Row-wise binding*   A data structure that holds a single data value for each parameter in the SQL statement is defined and each element of the first structure in an array of these structures is bound to each parameter in the SQL statement. This is called row-wise binding because a row of values is bound to all parameters in the statement.

Whether to use column-wise binding or row-wise binding is largely a matter of preference. Column-wise binding is the default binding style used; applications can change from column-wise binding to row-wise binding by setting the `SQL_ATTR_PARAM_BIND_TYPE` statement attribute. Depending on how the processor being used accesses memory, row-wise binding might execute faster. However, any performance difference is likely to be negligible except in cases where very large numbers of rows of parameter values are used.

COLUMN-WISE BINDING   When column-wise binding is used, two arrays are bound to each parameter in an SQL statement for which data values are to be provided. The first array holds the data values used by the statement and the second array holds length/indicator values that correspond to the data values stored in the first array. Both arrays contain as many elements as are needed to store the values for the parameter. If several parameters in an SQL statement are to be bound to arrays, all the arrays must contain the same number of elements. Figure 9–1 illustrates how column-wise binding works.

ROW-WISE BINDING   When row-wise binding is used, a data structure that holds a single data value and a corresponding length/indicator value for each parameter in an SQL statement for which data values are to be provided is defined by the application (elements can be placed in this structure in any order). Then, the application sets the `SQL_ATTR_PARAM_BIND_TYPE` statement attribute to the size of this data structure to notify the driver that row-wise binding is being used. The application then allocates an array of these data structures that contains as many elements as are needed to store the values for the parameter. Finally, the address of each element in the first structure of this array is bound to each parameter in the SQL statement.

Figure 9–2 illustrates how row-wise binding works.

INSERT INTO PARTS (PART_ID, PRICE) VALUES(? , ?)

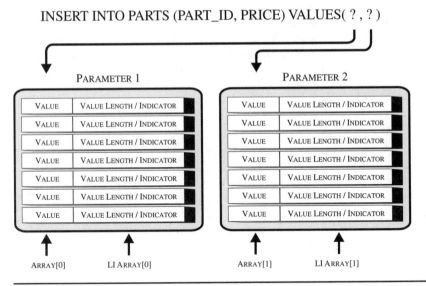

Figure 9–1   Column-wise parameter binding

INSERT INTO PARTS (PART_ID, PRICE) VALUES(? , ?)

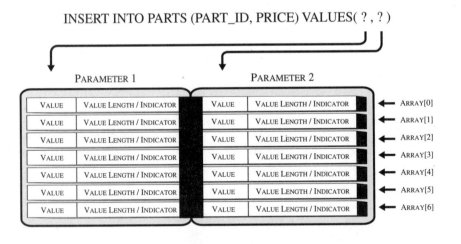

Figure 9–2   Row-wise parameter binding

During execution, the driver calculates the address of the data for a particular row and column by solving the equation:

```
Address = Bound Address + ((Row Number - 1) * Structure Size) + Offset
```

where rows are numbered from 1 to the size of the array, and the offset, if any, is the value stored in the **SQL_ATTR_PARAM_BIND_OFFSET_PTR** statement attribute.

Setting Parameter Values

To set the value of a parameter that has been (or that will be) bound to an application variable, an application simply assigns a value to the variable. When application variables are set is not important, as long they are set sometime before the SQL statement to which they are bound is executed. Thus, an application can set the value of a variable before or after it is bound to a parameter and it can change the value as many times as it wants. Each time the SQL statement is executed, the driver simply retrieves the current value of each variable bound to the statement and sends it to the data source.

If a length/indicator variable was bound to a parameter (when the application variable was bound), it must be set to one of the following values before the SQL statement is executed:

■ The actual length, in bytes, of the data value stored in the bound application variable. The driver only checks this length if the application variable contains character or binary data.

■ **SQL_NTS** (A NULL-terminated string is stored in the bound application variable).

■ **SQL_NULL_DATA** (A NULL value is stored in the bound application variable. In this case, the driver ignores the value of the bound variable).

■ **SQL_DATA_AT_EXEC** or the result of the **SQL_LEN_DATA_AT_EXEC**(*length*) macro (The value stored in the bound application variable is to be sent to the data source by the **SQLPutData()** function).

Setting Arrays of Parameter Values

When using arrays of values, the setup is a bit more involved. If column-wise binding was used, the application assigns a value to each element of the array containing parameter values, just as it would set a single application variable. Then, the application sets each element of the corresponding length/indicator array using the same rules that apply for setting a single bound length/indicator variable. If row-wise binding is used, the application assigns a value to each parameter value element of each structure in the array. Then, it sets each length/indicator element of each structure in the array.

Once the appropriate values have been stored in all bound arrays, the application must then tell DB2 CLI how many elements are in the arrays. The application must also provide DB2 CLI with the address of a variable in which it can return information about the number of elements (sets of parameter values) it processes. Finally, the application must also provide DB2 CLI with the address of a variable in which it can return status information about each element (sets of parameter values) it processes. This is done by setting the **SQL_ATTR_PARAMSET_SIZE**, **SQL_ATTR_PARAMS_PROCESSED_PTR**, and the **SQL_ATTR_PARAM_STATUS_PTR** statement attributes with the **SQLSetStmtAttr()** function.

CLI applications can also use the **SQL_ATTR_PARAM_OPERATION_PTR** statement attribute to ignore one or more rows of parameter values—if an element of the array stored in this attribute is set to **SQL_PARAM_IGNORE**, the set of parameter values corresponding to that element is excluded from processing when the **SQLExecute()** or

`SQLExecDirect()` functions are called. The array stored in the `SQL_ATTR_PARAM_OPERATION_PTR` attribute is allocated and set by the application and read by the driver.

Changing Parameter Bindings (and Values) with Offsets

CLI applications can specify that an offset be added to a bound parameter's address and to the corresponding length/indicator buffer address when `SQLExecute()` or `SQLExecDirect()` is called. This feature allows an application to change parameter bindings (and values) without calling the `SQLBindParameter()` function to rebind previously bound parameters. When offsets are used, the original bindings represent a *template* of how the application buffers are laid out–the application can move this template to different areas of memory simply by changing the offset. New offsets can be specified at any time; each time an offset is specified, it is added to the originally bound buffer address. This means that offset additions are not cumulative–each offset cancels the previous offset used. It goes without saying that the sum of the address and the offset must always be a valid address (either or both the offset and the address to which the offset is added, can be invalid, as long as the sum of the two is a valid address).

Executing SQL Statements

With DB2 CLI, there are four ways to execute SQL statements. Each depends on when the SQL statement is prepared by the data source and who defined it. The four methods available are:

- *Direct execution* — The SQL statement is prepared and executed in a single step at application run time. The SQL statement is defined by the application.

- *Prepared execution* — The SQL statement is prepared and executed in two separate steps at application run time. With this approach, the SQL statement can be prepared once and executed multiple times. The SQL statement is defined by the application.

- *Stored procedures* — One or more SQL statements are compiled at development time and stored in the data source as a procedure that can be executed later. A stored procedure can be executed one or more times at application run time. The application can obtain information about available stored procedures by using the CLI catalog function `SQLProcedures()`. The SQL statements used in a stored procedure are usually defined by a separate application.

- *Catalog functions* — The application can call a CLI function that returns a predefined result data set that contains information about a data source's system catalog. Catalog functions usually submit a predefined SQL statement or call a stored procedure created specifically for this purpose. A catalog function can be executed one or more times at application run time.

Direct Execution

The direct execution method is the simplest method to use to execute an SQL statement. When an SQL statement is executed using this method, the data source compiles it into an access plan and immediately executes that plan. The major drawback of using this method is that the SQL statement must be parsed and compiled each time it is executed. In addition, an application cannot retrieve information about the result data set created by the statement (if any) until after the statement is executed (this restriction is removed if the statement is prepared and executed in two separate steps). For these reasons, the direct execution method works best for SQL statements that are only going to be executed once.

EXECUTING SQL STATEMENTS WITH THE DIRECT EXECUTION METHOD   To execute an SQL statement using the direct execution method, an application:

1. Binds any parameter markers that were coded in the SQL statement to application variables.
2. Sets the values of all bound variables.
3. Calls the **SQLExecDirect()** function with the SQL statement specified.

   When the **SQLExecDirect()** function is called, DB2 CLI:

1. Modifies the SQL statement to use the data source's SQL grammar (this includes replacing any escape sequences that may have been used with the appropriate SQL grammar unless the **SQL_ATTR_NOSCAN** statement attribute has been set).
2. Retrieves the current values of the variables bound to parameter markers in the statement and converts them as necessary.
3. Sends the statement, along with the converted parameter values, to the data source for processing.
4. Returns any errors detected (including sequencing or state errors, syntactic errors, and semantic errors) to the application that called the **SQLExecDirect()** function.

Prepared Execution

If an SQL statement is to be executed more than once, prepared execution is a much more efficient method to use. With prepared execution, an SQL statement is compiled (prepared) to produce an access plan in one step and executed in another. Because the access plan is created in a separate step it can be executed one or more times—either immediately after the statement is prepared, or sometime later in the program.

Prepared execution is faster than direct execution for statements that are to be executed more than once, primarily because the statement only has to be parsed and compiled once; whereas statements executed directly must be parsed and compiled each time they are executed. Prepared execution can also provide a reduction in network traffic because DB2 CLI can send an access plan identifier to the data source each time the statement is executed (provided the data source supports access plan identifiers) as opposed to sending an entire SQL statement. Another advantage of prepared execution is that it provides an application with the ability to retrieve information about the result data set that will be generated (if any) any time after the statement has been prepared.

Direct execution should be used instead of prepared execution when an SQL statement is only going to be executed once; in this case prepared execution is slightly slower than direct execution because an additional CLI function call is required. Prepared execution is commonly used to repeatedly execute the same, parameterized SQL statement.

NOTE: *Some data sources automatically delete access plans that have been created for prepared execution each time a transaction is terminated (either by explicitly calling the* **SQLEndTran()** *function or by running in autocommit mode). Applications working with these data sources should either run in manual commit mode or use direct execution.*

EXECUTING SQL STATEMENTS WITH THE PREPARED EXECUTION METHOD   To execute an SQL statement using the prepared execution method, an application:

1. Binds application variables to any parameter markers that were coded in the statement.

2. Calls the **SQLPrepare()** function with the SQL statement specified.

3. Sets the values of all bound variables. (This step can also be performed before the SQL statement is prepared.)

4. Calls the **SQLExecute()** function with the prepared SQL statement specified.

5. Repeats steps 2 and 3 as necessary.

When the **SQLPrepare()** function is called, DB2 CLI:

1. Modifies the SQL statement to use the data source's SQL grammar (this includes replacing any escape sequences that may have been used with the appropriate SQL grammar unless the **SQL_ATTR_NOSCAN** statement attribute has been set).

2. Sends the statement to the data source for preparation.

3. Stores the returned access plan identifier for later execution (if the preparation succeeded) or returns any errors detected (if the preparation failed) to the application that called the **SQLPrepare()** function.

When the **SQLExecute()** function is called, DB2 CLI:

1. Retrieves the current values of the variables bound to parameter markers in the statement and converts them as necessary.

2. Sends the access plan identifier along with the converted parameter values to the data source for execution.

3. Returns any errors detected to the application that called the `SQLExecute()` function. These are generally run-time errors such as SQLSTATE 24000 (Invalid cursor state). However, some drivers also return syntactic and semantic errors at this point.

Stored Procedures

A stored procedure is an executable object that is stored in the data source. It generally consists of one or more precompiled SQL statements. There are a number of advantages to using stored procedures—all are based on the fact that using stored procedures moves SQL statement processing from the application to the data source. These advantages include:

- Increased performance. Stored procedures are usually the fastest way to execute SQL statements. Like prepared execution, the SQL statement(s) used are compiled and executed in two separate steps. However, with stored procedures, SQL statements are parsed and compiled when the procedure is developed and executed at application run time.

- Adherence to business rules. A business rule is simply a rule about the way in which a company does business. For example, only someone with the title *Sales Person* might be allowed to add new sales orders. Incorporating business rules in stored procedures allows individual companies to customize vertical applications simply by rewriting one or more procedures called by an application.

- Replaceability. Because business rules can be incorporated into stored procedures, procedures can be replaced without affecting the application(s) that use them.

- Interoperable applications can use DBMS-specific SQL. Stored procedures provide a way for applications to exploit DBMS-specific SQL and still remain interoperable.

- Stored procedures survive transactions. The access plans for all prepared statements on a connection are deleted when a transaction is committed or rolled back by some data sources. SQL statements in stored procedures survive all transactions because they are permanently stored in the data source (whether the procedures survive in a prepared, partially prepared, or unprepared state is data source-specific).

- Separate development. Stored procedures can be developed separately from the rest of the application. In large corporations, this might provide a way to further exploit the skills of highly specialized programmers; application programmers can write user interface code and database programmers can write stored procedures.

Unfortunately, there are also a few disadvantages to using stored procedures:

- Procedures must be written and compiled for each DBMS with which the application expects to work. While this is not a problem for DB2 applications, it can significantly increase development and maintenance time for applications designed to work with several different DBMSs.

■ Many DBMSs do not provide support for stored procedures. Again, this is most likely to be a problem for applications designed to work with a number of DBMSs.

■ DB2 CLI does not define a standard grammar for creating procedures. This means that although applications can call procedures interoperably, they cannot create them interoperably.

EXECUTING STORED PROCEDURES To execute a stored procedure, an application:

1. Binds any parameter markers that were coded in the SQL statement to application variables.

2. Sets the values of all bound variables.

3. Calls the `SQLExecDirect()` function with the SQL statement specified. This statement can use the escape sequence defined by ODBC or DBMS-specific syntax to call a stored procedure.

When the `SQLExecDirect()` function is called, DB2 CLI:

1. Retrieves the current values of the variables that were bound to parameter markers in the statement and converts them as necessary.

2. Calls the procedure stored in the data source and sends it the converted parameter values for processing.

3. Returns the values of output and input/output parameters, and/or the procedure return code value to the application that called the stored procedure (if the procedure executed successfully). Note that these values might not be available until after all other results (row counts and result data sets) generated by the procedure have been processed.

Catalog Functions

Because the CLI catalog functions create result data sets, they are similar to other result data set-generating SQL statements. Almost anything that applies to SQL statements that create result data sets also applies to the CLI catalog functions. For example, the `SQL_ATTR_MAX_ROWS` statement attribute limits the number of rows returned by a catalog function, just as it limits the number of rows returned by a `SELECT` SQL statement.

To execute any of the catalog functions, an application simply calls the appropriate function. Refer to Chapter 14, "Querying the Data Source System Catalog," for more information about the CLI catalog functions.

Working with Batches of SQL Statements

Although SQL statements are typically processed one at a time, occasionally two or more SQL statements need to be handled as a single unit, otherwise referred to as a *batch*. This is often more efficient than submitting statements separately, because network traffic can often be reduced and the data source can sometimes optimize the execution of a batch of SQL statements in ways that it can't optimize the execution of individual statements. In most batch implementations, the entire set of SQL statements are executed before any results are returned to the calling application. In other implementations, a CLI API function (**SQLMoreResults()**) must be called to trigger the execution of the next statement in the batch.

CLI supports the following types of batches:

- Explicit batches. An explicit batch contains two or more SQL statements separated by semicolons (;). Note that no semicolon follows the last statement in the list.

- Stored Procedures. If a stored procedure contains more than one SQL statement, it is considered to contain a batch of SQL statements.

- Arrays of parameter values. Arrays of parameter values can be used with a parameterized SQL statement as an effective way to perform batch operations. For example, arrays of parameter values can be used with an **INSERT** SQL statement to insert multiple rows of data into a table while executing only a single SQL statement.

We saw in Chapter 6 that SQL statements can be loosely divided into the following five categories:

- Result data set-generating statements. These are SQL statements that generate a result data set. For example, the **SELECT** SQL statement is a result data set-generating statement.

- Row count-generating statements. These are SQL statements that generate a count of affected rows. For example, **INSERT**, **UPDATE**, and **DELETE** are row-count-generating statements.

- Data Definition Language (DDL) statements. These are SQL statements that modify the structure of the database. For example, **CREATE TABLE** and **DROP INDEX** are DDL statements.

- Context-changing statements. These are SQL statements that change the context of a database.

- Administrative statements. These are SQL statements that are used to perform administrative tasks for a database. For example, **GRANT** and **REVOKE** are administrative statements.

SQL statements in the first two categories are collectively known as result-generating statements. SQL statements in the latter three categories are collectively known as result-free statements. DB2 CLI only supports batches that contain result-generating statements because the semantics of result-free statements can vary greatly from data source to data source.

When an error occurs while a batch of SQL statements is being executed, one of four things can happen; which one happens is data source-specific and may depend on the statements included in the batch:

■ No statements in the batch are executed.

■ No statements in the batch are executed and the current transaction is rolled back.

■ All the statements in the batch that were processed before the error was generated are executed.

■ All of the statements in the batch except the statement that caused the error are executed.

In the first two cases, **SQLExecute()** and **SQLExecDirect()** return **SQL_ERROR**. In the latter two cases, **SQLExecute()** and **SQLExecDirect()** may return **SQL_SUCCESS_WITH_INFO** or **SQL_SUCCESS**, depending on the driver's implementation. In all cases, diagnostic information can be retrieved by calling **SQLGetDiagRec()** or **SQLGetDiagField()**. However, it is unlikely that the information returned will identify the statement that generated the error.

Sending Long (Large) Data Values to the Data Source

When an application variable is bound to a parameter marker in an SQL statement, the driver automatically retrieves the data value from the variable and sends it to the data source when the statement is executed. This handles most situations provided the value to be sent to the data source does not exceed a predefined size (usually 254 characters or bytes). However, in some cases, larger data values need to be sent. For example, an application may want to store a long text document or a large graphic image in a DB2 database that is capable of storing this kind of data. Because such data would typically be stored in a file, rather than in a single buffer, the data would have to be sent to the data source in several small pieces, rather than as a whole.

The process of breaking large data values into smaller parts and sending them to a data source is known as a *data-at-execution sequence*, and parameter markers that serve as placeholders for large data values are known as *data-at-execution parameters*.

To initiate a data-at-execution sequence, an application:

1. Binds any data-at-execution parameter markers coded in the SQL statement to both application variables and corresponding length/indicator variables.

2. Stores in each bound variable a meaningful value that will be used later to identify the data value to be sent to the data source in parts. For example, this value might be the name or handle of a file containing the data (the value stored in the bound variable is not used by the driver).

3. Stores **SQL_DATA_AT_EXEC**, or the result of the **SQL_LEN_DATA_AT_EXEC(*length*)**, macro in each bound length/indicator buffer. The **SQL_LEN_DATA_AT_EXEC(*length*)** is used when the data source that is to receive the data needs to know how many bytes of data will be sent so it can pre-allocate space. Both of these values indicate to DB2 CLI that the data for the parameter will be sent with the **SQLPutData()** function.

4. Calls the **SQLExecute()** or the **SQLExecDirect()** function with the SQL statement specified.

When the **SQLExecute()** or the **SQLExecDirect()** function is called, DB2 CLI:

1. Discovers that a length/indicator buffer contains the value **SQL_DATA_AT_EXEC** or the result of the **SQL_LEN_DATA_AT_EXEC(*length*)** macro.

2. Returns **SQL_NEED_DATA** to the application that called the **SQLExecute()** or the **SQLExecDirect()** function.

When the application receives the **SQL_NEED_DATA** return code, it then:

1. Calls **SQLParamData()** to retrieve the address of the application variable bound to the data-at-execution parameter and to start the data-at-execution sequence.

2. Calls the **SQLPutData()** function to send the parameter data to the data source. If the data is too large to fit into a single buffer, as is usually the case with long data, the **SQLPutData()** function is called repeatedly (to send the data in parts) until all the data has been sent to the data source; it is up to DB2 CLI and the data source to reassemble the data as it is received.

3. Calls the **SQLParamData()** function again to indicate that all data has been sent for the parameter.

When the **SQLParamData()** function is called to indicate that all data has been sent for the parameter, DB2 CLI:

1. Returns **SQL_NEED_DATA** and the value identifying the next parameter to the application that called the **SQLParamData()** function (if another data-at-execution parameter exists). Each time **SQL_NEED_DATA** is returned to the application, the same steps are repeated to send the appropriate parameter data to the data source.

or

2. Returns **SQL_SUCCESS** or **SQL_SUCCESS_WITH_INFO** along with any return value or diagnostic value that **SQLExecute()** or **SQLExecDirect()** can return to the function that called the **SQLParamData()** function (provided no other data-at-execution parameter exists).

After the **SQLExecute()** or **SQLExecDirect()** function returns **SQL_NEED_DATA** and before all data has been sent for the last data-at-execution parameter in the SQL statement, the statement is in the "Need Data" state and only the **SQLPutData()**, **SQLParamData()**, **SQLCancel()**, **SQLGetDiagRec()**, **SQLError()**, and **SQLGetDiagField()** functions can be called. If the **SQLCancel()** function is called while the SQL statement is in the "Need Data" state, all statement processing is terminated and the statement is returned to its previous state.

NOTE: *An application can send any type of data value to the data source at SQL statement execution time with the* **SQLPutData()** *function. However, if the data is small enough to fit in a single buffer, there is generally no reason to use the* **SQLPutData()**

function—it is much easier to bind an application variable to the SQL statement and let the driver retrieve the data from the variable when the statement is executed.

When arrays of parameter values and data-at-execution parameters are used in the same SQL statement, you need to be aware of a couple of problems that can occur. First, if an array of parameter values is bound to a data-at-execution parameter, the **SQLParamData()** function does not automatically extract and return an element of this array to the application. Instead, it returns the scalar value the application supplied. This means that the value returned by the **SQLParamData()** is insufficient for specifying the parameter for which the application needs to send data; the current row number must also be taken into consideration.

When only some of the elements of a parameter array are data-at-execution parameters, the application must provide the address of an array containing elements for all the parameters when the **SQLBindParameter()** function is called. This array is interpreted normally for the parameters that are not data-at-execution parameters. However, for the data-at-execution parameters, the value the **SQLParamData()** function provides to the application, which usually would be used to identify the data being requested, is always the address of the array—not the address of an element in the array.

Asynchronous Execution

By default, all CLI functions execute synchronously; that is, an application calls a function and DB2 CLI does not return control to the application until that function has finished executing. However, some functions can be executed asynchronously; that is, an application calls a function and DB2 CLI, after performing some minimal processing, returns control to the application. The application can then call other functions while the first function is still executing.

Asynchronous execution is primarily supported for functions that, for the most part, are executed on the data source, such as the functions that prepare and execute SQL statements and retrieve (fetch) data. Refer to the **SQL_ATTR_ASYNC_ENABLE** attribute in Table 8–9 for a list of CLI functions that can be executed asynchronously. Asynchronous execution is most useful when the function being executed takes a considerable amount of time to complete (for example, when a complex SQL query statement is executed against a large database).

Asynchronous execution is controlled on either a per-statement basis or on a per-connection basis, depending on the data source being used. In other words, an application does not specify that a particular function is to be executed asynchronously; instead, it specifies that all functions executed on a particular statement or connection handle are to be executed asynchronously.

When an application executes a function after asynchronous processing has been enabled, DB2 CLI performs a minimal amount of processing (such as checking arguments for errors), hands the rest of the processing off to the data source, and returns **SQL_STILL_EXECUTING** along with control, to the application. The application is then free to perform other tasks. However, the application must poll DB2 CLI at regular intervals to determine whether or not the function has finished executing (by calling the function again with the same arguments that were originally used). As long as the function is executing, **SQL_STILL_EXECUTING** is returned. When the function completes execution, the return code that would have been returned if the function had been executed synchronously (such as **SQL_SUCCESS**, **SQL_ERROR**, or **SQL_NEED_DATA**) is returned.

When the application polls DB2 CLI to determine whether a function is still executing, it must use the same statement handle that was used when the function was first called. That's because asynchronous execution is tracked on a per-statement handle basis. The application must also supply valid values for the other function parameters to get past error checking. However, after DB2 CLI checks the statement handle and determines that the statement is executing asynchronously, it ignores all other parameters.

While a function is being executed asynchronously, the application can call functions on other statement handles, and it can call functions on any connection handle other than the one with which the asynchronous function's statement handle is associated. The application can only call the same function (to poll the driver), **SQLCancel()**, **SQLGetDiagRec()**, **SQLError()**, and **SQLGetDiagField()**, on the statement handle on which the asynchronous function is running—**SQLGetDiagRec()** and **SQLGetDiagField()** can be called to return diagnostic header information, but not diagnostic record information. The application can only call the **SQLAllocHandle()** (to allocate a statement handle), **SQLGetDiagRec()**, **SQLGetDiagField()**, or **SQLGetFunctions()** function on the connection handle associated with the statement handle on which the asynchronous function is running.

After the driver returns **SQL_STILL_EXECUTING** and before it returns a return code indicating the function has completed execution, the **SQLCancel()** function can be called to try to terminate the function's execution. Unfortunately, when **SQLCancel()** is called, there is no guarantee that function execution was actually canceled (for example, if the function finished execution before **SQLCancel()** was called execution would not be canceled). In this case, the return code returned by **SQLCancel()** doesn't help—it indicates whether **SQLCancel()** successfully attempted to cancel the function, not whether the function was actually canceled. The only way an application can determine whether the asynchronous function's processing was canceled is by polling the driver (that is, calling the function again). If the function was canceled, the driver returns **SQL_ERROR** and SQLSTATE **HY**008 (Operation canceled). Otherwise, the driver returns a different code (for example, **SQL_STILL_EXECUTING**, **SQL_SUCCESS**, or **SQL_ERROR** with a different SQLSTATE) to indicate that the function was not canceled.

NOTE: *In general, applications should only execute functions asynchronously on single-threaded operating systems. On multithread operating systems, functions should be executed synchronously on separate threads, rather than asynchronously on the same thread.*

Committing and Rolling Back Transactions

DB2 CLI applications can execute in two different modes: auto-commit and manual-commit mode. In auto-commit mode, each SQL statement is treated as a complete transaction that is automatically committed when the SQL statement is processed. In manual-commit mode, when an application submits an SQL statement to the data source for processing and no transaction is open, DB2 CLI implicitly starts a transaction and it is up to the application to terminate it (either by committing it or by rolling it back). To commit or roll back a transaction while operating in manual-commit mode, an application must call the **SQLEndTran()** function.

Freeing SQL Statement Handles

When an application has finished working with a particular SQL statement, it can call either the **SQLFreeHandle()** function or the **SQLFreeStmt()** function to free the statement handle associated with the SQL statement. When a statement handle is freed, the memory used to store the structure containing information about the SQL statement is released and the handle can no longer be used.

NOTE: *When the* **SQLDisconnect()** *function is called, all statement handles associated with the specified connection are automatically freed.*

Often, it is more efficient to reuse statement handles, rather than free them and allocate new ones. However, before executing a new SQL statement on an existing statement handle, an application should ensure that the current statement settings (that is, statement attributes, parameter bindings, and result data set bindings) are appropriate. Generally, all parameter and result data set bindings associated with the old SQL statement need to be unbound before new parameter and result data set bindings are established for the new SQL statement.

It is an application programming error to use any freed handle in a CLI function call; doing so has undefined but probably fatal consequences.

The SQL Statement Processing Functions

Table 9–1 lists the CLI functions that are used to prepare and submit SQL statements to a data source for processing.

Each of these functions are described in detail in the remainder of this chapter.

Table 9–1 *The ODBC Statement Processing Functions*

Function Name	Description
SQLPrepare()	Prepares an SQL statement for execution.
SQLBindParameter()	Assigns data storage for a parameter marker in an SQL statement.
SQLNumParams()	Retrieves the number of parameter markers used in an SQL statement.
SQLDescribeParam()	Retrieves information about a specific parameter marker in an SQL statement.
SQLExecute()	Executes a prepared SQL statement.
SQLExecDirect()	Prepares and executes an SQL statement immediately.
SQLNativeSql()	Retrieves the text of an SQL statement after it has been translated by the data source driver.
SQLParamData()	Used in conjunction with the **SQLPutData()** function to process data-at-execution parameters (that is, to support long data processing).
SQLPutData()	Used in conjunction with the **SQLParamData()** function to send part or all of a data value associated with a parameter marker from the application to the data source (that is, to process long data values).
SQLCancel()	Cancels SQL statement processing.
SQLEndTran()	Rolls back or commits the current transaction.
SQLFreeStmt()	Ends SQL statement processing, closes the associated cursor, discards pending result data, and, optionally, frees all resources associated with a statement handle.

SQLPrepare

X/OPEN 95 CLI	ISO/IEC 92 CLI	DB2 CLI 5.2	DB2 CLI 2.0	ODBC 3.x
☑	☑	☑	☑	☑

ODBC API CONFORMANCE LEVEL   **CORE**

Purpose   The **SQLPrepare()** function is used to send an SQL statement to a data source so it can be prepared (compiled) for execution.

Syntax
```
SQLRETURN  SQLPrepare  (SQLHSTMT      StatementHandle,
                        SQLCHAR       *SQLString,
                        SQLINTEGER    SQLStringSize);
```

Parameters *StatementHandle*   An SQL statement handle that refers to a previously allocated SQL statement information storage buffer (data structure).

SQLString   A pointer to a location in memory where the SQL statement string to be prepared is stored.

SQLStringSize   The length of the SQL statement string stored in the *SQLString* parameter.

Description   The **SQLPrepare()** function is used to send an SQL statement (associated with an SQL statement handle) to a data source so it can be prepared (compiled) for execution. Once an SQL statement has been prepared, it can be submitted to the data source for execution or the statement handle associated with the prepared statement can be used to obtain information about the format of the result data set that will be produced (if any) when the prepared statement is executed.

SQL statements that have been prepared can be executed multiple times by the **SQLExecute()** function without having to be re-prepared; provided the statement handle associated with the prepared SQL statement is not freed by the **SQLFreeHandle()** function or the **SQLFreeStmt()** function or modified by an **SQLPrepare()**, **SQLExecDirect()**, or catalog function (**SQLColumns()**, **SQLTables()**, etc.) function call.

Return Codes   SQL_SUCCESS, SQL_SUCCESS_WITH_INFO, SQL_STILL_EXECUTING, SQL_INVALID_HANDLE, or SQL_ERROR

SQLSTATEs   If this function returns **SQL_SUCCESS_WITH_INFO** or **SQL_ERROR**, one of the following SQLSTATE values may be obtained by calling the **SQLGetDiagRec()** function:

01504, **01**508, **08**S01, **21**S01, **21**S02, **22**018, **22**019, **22**025, **24**000, **34**000, **37**xxx, **40**001, **40**003, **42**xxx, **58**004, **S0**001, **S0**002, **S0**011, **S0**012, **S0**021, **S0**022, **HY**001, **HY**008, **HY**009, **HY**010, **HY**013, **HY**014, **HY**090, or **HYT**00

Refer to Appendix B for detailed information about each SQLSTATE value that can be returned.

Comments

◼ The driver may modify the SQL statement specified to match the SQL grammar used by the data source before it submits the statement to the data source for preparation. The driver also replaces most ODBC escape sequences used with the appropriate SQL syntax.

◼ Some drivers cannot return syntax errors or access violations when this function is called; instead, syntax errors or access violations are only returned when subsequent related functions (such as **SQLNumResultCols()**, **SQLDescribeCol()**, **SQLColAttribute()**, and **SQLExecute()**) are called. Therefore, applications must be designed in such a way that delayed error reporting by the **SQLPrepare()** function does not create problems.

◼ Depending on the capabilities of the driver and its underlying data source, parameter information (such as data types) is checked either when the SQL statement is prepared (if all parameters have been bound), or when the statement is executed (if all parameters have not been bound).

◼ For maximum interoperability, an application should unbind all parameters that applied to an old SQL statement before preparing a new SQL statement on the same statement handle. This prevents errors caused by old parameter information being applied to the new SQL statement from occurring.

◼ For some implementations, it may be more efficient to call the **SQLDescribeCol()** or the **SQLDescribeParam()** function after an SQL statement has been executed (with the **SQLExecute()** or **SQLExecDirect()** function) rather than after the SQL statement has been prepared (with this function).

◼ Some data sources automatically delete access plans that have been created for prepared execution each time a transaction is terminated (either by explicitly calling the **SQLEndTran()** function or by running in autocommit mode).

◼ If an open cursor exists on the statement handle specified when this function is called, **SQL_ERROR** and SQLSTATE **24**000 (Invalid cursor state) will be returned.

◼ If the SQL statement being prepared is a positioned UPDATE or a positioned DELETE statement, the cursor referenced by the statement must be defined on a separate statement handle, under the same connection handle, using the same isolation level.

Prerequisites There are no prerequisites for using this function call.

Restrictions If an application uses this function to prepare and the **SQLExecute()** function to submit a **COMMIT** or **ROLLBACK** SQL statement, the application will no longer be interoperable. Because the **COMMIT** and/or **ROLLBACK** SQL statement is not supported by all DBMSs, use of these statements should be avoided.

See Also SQLAllocHandle(), SQLBindParameter(), SQLExecute(), SQLExecDirect(), SQLCancel(), SQLEndTran()

Example   The following Visual C++ program illustrates how to use the **SQLPrepare()** function to send an SQL statement to the data source so it can be prepared for processing.

```
/*-----------------------------------------------------------------*/
/* NAME:     CH9EX1.CPP                                            */
/* PURPOSE: Illustrate How To Use The Following CLI API Functions  */
/*          In A C++ Program:                                      */
/*                                                                 */
/*               SQLPrepare()                                      */
/*               SQLExecute()                                      */
/*                                                                 */
/* OTHER CLI APIs SHOWN:                                           */
/*          SQLAllocHandle()            SQLSetEnvAttr()            */
/*          SQLConnect()                SQLDisconnect()            */
/*          SQLBindCol()                SQLFetch()                 */
/*          SQLFreeHandle()                                        */
/*                                                                 */
/*-----------------------------------------------------------------*/

// Include The Appropriate Header Files
#include <windows.h>
#include <sqlcli1.h>
#include <iostream.h>

// Define The CLI_Class Class
class CLI_Class
{
    // Attributes
    public:
        SQLHANDLE    EnvHandle;
        SQLHANDLE    ConHandle;
        SQLHANDLE    StmtHandle;
        SQLRETURN    rc;

    // Operations
    public:
        CLI_Class();                            // Constructor
        ~CLI_Class();                           // Destructor
        SQLRETURN ShowResults();
};

// Define The Class Constructor
CLI_Class::CLI_Class()
{
    // Initialize The Return Code Variable
    rc = SQL_SUCCESS;

    // Allocate An Environment Handle
    rc = SQLAllocHandle(SQL_HANDLE_ENV, SQL_NULL_HANDLE, &EnvHandle);

    // Set The ODBC Application Version To 3.x
    if (rc == SQL_SUCCESS)
```

```
        rc = SQLSetEnvAttr(EnvHandle, SQL_ATTR_ODBC_VERSION,
                (SQLPOINTER) SQL_OV_ODBC3, SQL_IS_UINTEGER);

    // Allocate A Connection Handle
    if (rc == SQL_SUCCESS)
        rc = SQLAllocHandle(SQL_HANDLE_DBC, EnvHandle, &ConHandle);
}


// Define The Class Destructor
CLI_Class::~CLI_Class()
{
    // Free The Connection Handle
    if (ConHandle != NULL)
        SQLFreeHandle(SQL_HANDLE_DBC, ConHandle);

    // Free The Environment Handle
    if (EnvHandle != NULL)
        SQLFreeHandle(SQL_HANDLE_ENV, EnvHandle);
}


// Define The ShowResults() Member Function
SQLRETURN CLI_Class::ShowResults(void)
{
    // Declare The Local Memory Variables
    SQLCHAR    LastName[50];
    SQLCHAR    FirstName[50];

    // Bind The Columns In The Result Data Set Returned To
    // Application Variables
    rc = SQLBindCol(StmtHandle, 1, SQL_C_CHAR, (SQLPOINTER)
            LastName, sizeof(LastName), NULL);

    rc = SQLBindCol(StmtHandle, 2, SQL_C_CHAR, (SQLPOINTER)
            FirstName, sizeof(FirstName), NULL);

    // Display A Header
    cout << "Employees :" << endl << endl;

    // While There Are Records In The Result Data Set Generated,
    // Retrieve And Display Them
    while (rc != SQL_NO_DATA)
    {
        rc = SQLFetch(StmtHandle);
        if (rc != SQL_NO_DATA)
            cout << FirstName << " " << LastName << endl;
    }

    // Return The CLI API Return Code To The Calling Function
    return(rc);
}

/*-----------------------------------------------------------*/
/* The Main Function                                         */
/*-----------------------------------------------------------*/
int main()
```

```
{
    // Declare The Local Memory Variables
    SQLRETURN   rc = SQL_SUCCESS;
    SQLCHAR     SQLStmt[255];

    // Create An Instance Of The CLI_Class Class
    CLI_Class   Example;

    // Connect To The DB2 Sample Database
    if (Example.ConHandle != NULL)
    {
        rc = SQLConnect(Example.ConHandle, (SQLCHAR *) "SAMPLE",
                SQL_NTS, (SQLCHAR *) "userid", SQL_NTS,
                (SQLCHAR *) "password", SQL_NTS);

        // Allocate An SQL Statement Handle
        rc = SQLAllocHandle(SQL_HANDLE_STMT, Example.ConHandle,
                &Example.StmtHandle);
        if (rc == SQL_SUCCESS)
        {
            // Define A SELECT SQL Statement
            strcpy((char *) SQLStmt, "SELECT LASTNAME, FIRSTNME ");
            strcat((char *) SQLStmt, "FROM EMPLOYEE");

            // Prepare The SQL Statement
            rc = SQLPrepare(Example.StmtHandle, SQLStmt, SQL_NTS);

            // Execute The SQL Statement
            rc = SQLExecute(Example.StmtHandle);

            // Display The Results Of The SQL Query
            if (rc == SQL_SUCCESS)
                Example.ShowResults();

            // Free The SQL Statement Handle
            if (Example.StmtHandle != NULL)
                SQLFreeHandle(SQL_HANDLE_STMT, Example.StmtHandle);
        }

        // Disconnect From The DB2 Sample Database
        rc = SQLDisconnect(Example.ConHandle);
    }

    // Return To The Operating System
    return(rc);
}
```

SQLBindParameter

COMPATIBILITY

X/OPEN 95* CLI	ISO/IEC 92* CLI	DB2 CLI 5.2	DB2 CLI 2.0	ODBC 3.x
☑	☑	☐	☑	☑

ODBC API CONFORMANCE LEVEL   CORE**

*IN X/OPEN 95 AND ISO/IEC 92, THIS FUNCTION IS CALLED BINDPARAM

**IN ODBC 2.0, THIS FUNCTION WAS A LEVEL 1 API CONFORMANCE LEVEL FUNCTION

Pupose   The **SQLBindParameter()** function is used to associate (bind) parameter markers in an SQL statement with application variables or LOB locators.

Syntax
```
SQLRETURN  SQLBindParameter    (SQLHSTMT        StatementHandle,
                                SQLUSMALLINT    ParamMarkerNum,
                                SQLSMALLINT     ParameterType,
                                SQLSMALLINT     CDataType,
                                SQLSMALLINT     SQLDataType,
                                SQLUINTEGER     ValueSize,
                                SQLSMALLINT     Decimals,
                                SQLPOINTER      Value,
                                SQLINTEGER      ValueBufferSize,
                                SQLINTEGER      *ValueSize_Indicator);
```

Parameters

StatementHandle   An SQL statement handle that refers to a previously allocated SQL statement information storage buffer (data structure).

ParamMarkerNum   Specifies the parameter marker's location in the SQL statement text. Parameter markers are numbered sequentially from left to right, starting with 1, as they appear in the SQL statement.

ParameterType   Specifies the type of parameter marker being bound. This parameter must be set to one of the following values:

■ **SQL_PARAM_INPUT**
Specifies that the parameter marker is associated with an SQL statement other than a stored procedure call or that the parameter marker is associated with an input parameter of a called stored procedure.

■ **SQL_PARAM_OUTPUT**
Specifies that the parameter marker is associated with an output parameter of a called stored procedure or with the return value of a called stored procedure.

■ **SQL_PARAM_INPUT_OUTPUT**
Specifies that the parameter marker is associated with an input/output parameter of a called stored procedure.

CDataType   The C language data type of the parameter being bound. This parameter must be set to one of the following values:

■ **SQL_C_CHAR**

■ **SQL_C_DBCHAR**

■ **SQL_C_SHORT**

■ **SQL_C_LONG**

■ **SQL_C_FLOAT**

■ **SQL_C_DOUBLE**

■ **SQL_C_BIT**

■ **SQL_C_TINYINT**

■ **SQL_C_BINARY**

■ **SQL_C_TYPE_DATE**

■ **SQL_C_TYPE_TIME**

■ **SQL_C_TYPE_TIMESTAMP**

■ **SQL_C_BLOB_LOCATOR**

■ **SQL_C_CLOB_LOCATOR**

■ **SQL_C_DBCLOB_LOCATOR**

■ **SQL_C_NUMERIC**

■ **SQL_C_DEFAULT**

NOTE: *The* **SQL_C_DEFAULT** *value causes data to be transferred from its default C data type to the SQL data type specified.*

SQLDataType   The SQL data type of the parameter being bound. This parameter must be set to one of the following values:

■ **SQL_CHAR**

■ **SQL_VARCHAR**

■ **SQL_LONGVARCHAR**

■ **SQL_DECIMAL**

■ **SQL_NUMERIC**

■ **SQL_SMALLINT**

■ **SQL_INTEGER**

■ **SQL_REAL**

■ **SQL_FLOAT**

■ **SQL_DOUBLE**

- SQL_GRAPHIC
- SQL_VARGRAPHIC
- SQL_LONGVARGRAPHIC
- SQL_BINARY
- SQL_VARBINARY
- SQL_LONGVARBINARY
- SQL_BLOB
- SQL_BLOB_LOCATOR
- SQL_CLOB
- SQL_CLOB_LOCATOR
- SQL_DBCLOB
- SQL_DBCLOB_LOCATOR
- SQL_TYPE_DATE
- SQL_TYPE_TIME
- SQL_TYPE_TIMESTAMP

NOTE: SQL_BLOB_LOCATOR, SQL_CLOB_LOCATOR, *and* SQL_DBCLOB_LOCATOR *are application-related concepts, so they do not map to a specific data type.*

ValueSize	The total number of bytes of data to be sent to the data source for the specified parameter marker OR the size of the maximum number of digits used by the data type (precision) of the column or parameter (if the *SQLDataType* parameter is set to SQL_DECIMAL, SQL_NUMERIC, SQL_FLOAT, SQL_REAL, or SQL_DOUBLE).
Decimals	The number of digits to the right of the decimal point if the *SQLDataType* parameter is set to SQL_DECIMAL, SQL_NUMERIC, SQL_TYPE_TIME, or SQL_TYPE_TIMESTAMP.
Value	A pointer to a location in memory where the value associated with the parameter marker is stored.
ValueBufferSize	The size of the memory storage buffer used to store the value associated with the parameter marker.
ValueSize_Indicator	A pointer to a location in memory where either the size of the data value associated with the parameter marker or a special indicator value associated with the parameter marker is stored. This parameter can be set to one of the following indicator values:

- SQL_NTS
  The data value associated with the parameter marker is a NULL-terminated string.

■ **SQL_NULL_DATA**

The data value associated with the parameter marker is a NULL value.

■ **SQL_DATA_AT_EXEC**

The data value associated with the parameter marker will be sent to the data source with the **SQLPutData()** function.

■ The result of the **SQL_LEN_DATA_AT_EXEC(*length*)** macro. The data value associated with the parameter marker will be sent to the data source with the **SQLPutData()** function.

Description   The **SQLBindParameter()** function is used to associate (bind) parameter markers in an SQL statement to application variables and/or large object (LOB) locators. A parameter marker is represented by a question mark character (?) in an SQL statement and is used to indicate a position in the statement where an application supplied value is to be substituted when that statement is executed. When parameter markers are bound to application variables and/or LOB locators, data is transferred from the application to the appropriate data source when either the **SQLExecute()** or the **SQLExecDirect()** function is called. If necessary, data conversion occurs as the data is transferred.

Return Codes   **SQL_SUCCESS**, **SQL_SUCCESS_WITH_INFO**, **SQL_INVALID_HANDLE**, or **SQL_ERROR**

SQLSTATEs   If this function returns **SQL_SUCCESS_WITH_INFO** or **SQL_ERROR**, one of the following SQLSTATE values may be obtained by calling the **SQLGetDiagRec()** function:

07006, **08**S01, **40**003, **58**004, **HY**001, **HY**003, **HY**004, **HY**009, **HY**010, **HY**013, **HY**021, **HY**090, **HY**093, **HY**094, **HY**104, **HY**105, or **HYC00**

Refer to Appendix B for detailed information about each SQLSTATE value that can be returned.

Comments   ■ An application calls this function repeatedly to bind application variables to each parameter marker used in an SQL statement. All bindings remain in effect until the parameter markers are rebound, the **SQLFreeStmt()** function is called with the **SQL_RESET_PARAMS** option specified, or the **SQLSetDescField()** function is used to set the **SQL_DESC_COUNT** field of the application parameter descriptor (APD) header record to **0**.

■ An application variable must be bound to each parameter marker specified in an SQL statement before that statement can be executed. When this function is executed, the variables specified in both the *Value* and the *ValueSize_Indicator* parameters are treated as deferred arguments. However, their storage locations must be valid and they must contain data values when the SQL statement they are bound to is executed.

■ If the value specified in the *ParameterNumber* parameter is greater than the value of the **SQL_DESC_COUNT** field of the application parameter descriptor (APD) header record associated with the statement handle being used, the value of the **SQL_DESC_COUNT** field is changed to the value specified.

- Parameter markers in SQL statements that do not call stored procedures (for example **SELECT** and **INSERT** statements) are treated as input parameters; therefore, the *ParameterType* parameter should be set to **SQL_PARAM_INPUT** when binding to parameter markers in these types of statements.

- The **SQLProcedureColumns()** function can be used to determine the parameter type (input, output, input/output) of a stored procedure parameter; if an application cannot determine the parameter type for a stored procedure parameter, the *ParameterType* parameter should be set to **SQL_PARAM_INPUT**.

- If the *ParameterType* parameter is set to **SQL_PARAM_INPUT** and the stored procedure's parameter is an output or an input/output parameter, the value that would have been returned for the parameter is discarded by the driver.

- When an SQL statement that has been bound to application variables is executed, each bound application variable must contain a valid value or the corresponding length/indicator variable must contain **SQL_NULL_DATA**, **SQL_DATA_AT_EXEC**, or the result of the **SQL_LEN_DATA_AT_EXEC(length)** macro.

- If the *CDataType* parameter contains one of the datetime data types, the **SQL_DESC_TYPE** field of the parameter's APD descriptor record is set to **SQL_DATETIME**, and the **SQL_DESC_CONCISE_TYPE** field is set to the concise datetime C data type.

- If the *CDataType* parameter contains a numeric data type, the **SQL_DESC_PRECISION** field of the parameter's APD descriptor record is set to the driver-defined precision and the **SQL_DESC_SCALE** field is set to **0**. If either default value is inappropriate, the application should explicitly set the descriptor fields to the appropriate value (by calling either the **SQLSetDescField()** or the **SQLSetDescRec()** function).

- If the *SQLDataType* parameter contains a datetime data type, the **SQL_DESC_TYPE** field of the parameter's IPD descriptor record is set to **SQL_DATETIME**, and the **SQL_DESC_CONCISE_TYPE** field is set to the concise datetime SQL data type.

- If the *SQLDataType* parameter contains a numeric data type, the **SQL_DESC_PRECISION** field of the parameter's IPD descriptor record is set to the driver-defined precision and the **SQL_DESC_SCALE** field is set to **0**. If either default value is not appropriate, the application should explicitly set the descriptor fields to the appropriate value (by calling either the **SQLSetDescField()** or the **SQLSetDescRec()** function).

- If the *SQLDataType* parameter is set to **SQL_CHAR**, **SQL_VARCHAR**, **SQL_LONGVARCHAR**, **SQL_BINARY**, **SQL_VARBINARY**, **SQL_LONGVARBINARY**, or one of the concise SQL datetime or interval data types, the **SQL_DESC_LENGTH** field of the parameter's IPD descriptor record is set to the value stored in the *ValueSize* parameter.

- If the *SQLDataType* parameter is set to **SQL_DECIMAL**, **SQL_NUMERIC**, **SQL_FLOAT**, **SQL_REAL**, or **SQL_DOUBLE**, the **SQL_DESC_PRECISION** field of the parameter's IPD descriptor record is set to the value stored in the *ValueSize* parameter.

- If the *SQLDataType* parameter is set to **SQL_TYPE_TIME**, **SQL_TYPE_TIMESTAMP**, **SQL_NUMERIC**, or **SQL_DECIMAL**, the **SQL_DESC_PRECISION** field of the parameter's

IPD descriptor record is set to the value stored in the *Decimals* parameter. For all other data types, the value stored in the *Decimals* parameter is ignored.

■ The C data type specified in the *CDataType* parameter must be compatible with the SQL data type specified in the *SQLDataType* parameter, or an error will occur.

■ A NULL pointer can be stored in the *Value* parameter, provided the corresponding *ValueSize_Indicator* parameter is set to `SQL_NULL_DATA` or `SQL_DATA_AT_EXEC`. (This applies only to input or input/output parameters.)

■ If a NULL pointer is not stored in the *Value* parameter, and if the corresponding *ValueSize_Indicator* parameter does not contain `SQL_NTS`, `SQL_NULL_DATA`, `SQL_DATA_AT_EXEC`, a value greater than or equal to `0`, or a value less than or equal to the result of the `SQL_LEN_DATA_AT_EXEC(length)` macro), `SQL_ERROR` and SQLSTATE **HY**090 (Invalid string or buffer length) is returned.

■ An application can pass a parameter's value to the data source by either placing the value in the buffer referenced by the *Value* parameter or by making one or more calls to the `SQLPutData()` function. If the second option is used, the associated parameter is treated as a data-at-execution parameter. If a data-at-execution parameter is specified (by setting the *ValueSize_Indicator* parameter to `SQL_DATA_AT_EXEC` or to the result of the `SQL_LEN_DATA_AT_EXEC(length)` macro), an application-defined, 32-bit value associated with the parameter can be stored in the *Value* parameter. For example, the value might be a token such as a parameter number, a pointer to data, or a pointer to a structure the application used to bind input parameter values. This value is returned to the application by a subsequent `SQLParamData()` function call (which initiates a data-at-execution sequence) and can be used to identify the data-at-execution parameter.

■ A parameter can be bound to a Unicode C data type, even if the underlying driver does not support Unicode data.

■ If the *ParameterType* parameter is set to `SQL_PARAM_INPUT_OUTPUT` or `SQL_PARAM_OUTPUT`, the *Value* parameter must contain a pointer to a buffer where the output value can be stored.

■ If a stored procedure returns one or more result data sets/row counts, the buffer in which the output value is to be stored (referenced by the *Value* parameter) is not guaranteed to be populated until all result data sets/row counts have been processed. This means that the values of a stored procedure's output parameters and return values are unavailable until the `SQLMoreResults()` function returns `SQL_NO_DATA`. If the cursor for the statement handle associated with a stored procedure is closed, these values are discarded.

■ If a stored procedure returns one or more result data sets/row counts, the buffer in which the length/indicator value is to be stored (referenced by the *ValueSize_Indicator* parameter) is not guaranteed to be populated until all result data sets/row counts have been processed. This means that the values of a stored procedure's output parameters and return values are unavailable until the `SQLMoreResults()` function returns `SQL_NO_DATA`. If the cursor for the statement handle associated with the stored procedure is closed, these values are discarded.

- If the value of the **SQL_ATTR_PARAMSET_SIZE** statement attribute is greater than **1**, the *Value* parameter must point to an array.

- If the value of the **SQL_ATTR_PARAMSET_SIZE** statement attribute is greater than **1**, the *ValueSize_Indicator* parameter must point to an array of **SQLINTEGER**s.

- If the *Value* parameter points to an array, the *ValueBufferSize* parameter should be set to the length of a single element in the array. This value is used to determine the location of values in the array, both with input and with output parameters.

- If the *ParameterType* parameter is set to **SQL_PARAM_INPUT_OUTPUT**, and if a character data type is specified in the *CDataType* parameter, and if the size of the data to be returned to the application is greater than or equal to the memory storage buffer size value specified in the *ValueBufferSize* parameter, the data is truncated to *ValueBufferSize*-1 (the length of a NULL-termination character) and NULL-terminated by the driver.

- If the *ParameterType* parameter is set to **SQL_PARAM_INPUT_OUTPUT**, and if a binary data type is specified in the *CDataType* parameter, and if the size of the data to be returned to the application is greater than or equal to the memory storage buffer size value specified in the *ValueBufferSize* parameter, the data will be truncated to *ValueBufferSize* bytes.

- If the *ParameterType* parameter is set to **SQL_PARAM_INPUT_OUTPUT** and if a data type other than a character or binary data type is specified in the *CDataType* parameter, the value stored in the *ValueBufferSize* parameter is ignored.

- If the *ParameterType* parameter is set to **SQL_PARAM_INPUT** and if a NULL pointer is stored in the *ValueSize_Indicator* parameter, the driver assumes that all parameter values are non-NULL and that all character and binary data is NULL-terminated.

- If the *ParameterType* parameter is set to **SQL_PARAM_OUTPUT** and if a NULL pointer is stored in both the *Value* and the *ValueSize_Indicator* parameters, the driver discards the output value.

- A NULL pointer should never be stored in the *ValueSize_Indicator* parameter when the data type of the parameter is **SQL_C_BINARY**. To ensure that a driver does not accidentally truncate **SQL_C_BINARY** data, the *ValueSize_Indicator* parameter should always contain a pointer to a valid length value.

- If the *ParameterType* parameter is set to **SQL_PARAM_OUTPUT** or **SQL_PARAM_INPUT_OUTPUT**, the *ValueSize_Indicator* parameter should point to a buffer in which the driver can return **SQL_NULL_DATA**, the number of bytes of data available in the *Value* parameter (excluding the NULL-termination byte of character data), or **SQL_NO_TOTAL** (if the number of bytes of data available in the *Value* parameter cannot be determined).

- The value specified in the *ParameterType* parameter is stored in the **SQL_DESC_PARAMETER_TYPE** field of the corresponding IPD descriptor record.

- The **SQL_DESC_DATA_PTR** field of the APD descriptor record for the parameter is set to the value stored in the *Value* parameter.

▪ The `SQL_DESC_OCTET_LENGTH` field of the parameter's APD descriptor record is set to the value stored in the *ValueBufferSize* parameter.

▪ The `SQL_DESC_OCTET_LENGTH` field and the `SQL_DESC_INDICATOR_PTR` field of the parameter's APD descriptor record is set to the value stored in the *ValueSize_Indicator* parameter.

▪ Because the values stored in the variables referenced by the *Value* and *ValueSize_Indicator* parameters are not verified until the SQL statement is executed, data content or format errors are not detected or reported until either the `SQLExecute()` or the `SQLExecDirect()` function is called.

▪ If the SQL data type is a binary or a single-byte character string, the value in the *ValueSize* parameter must specify the length, in bytes, of the string. If the SQL data type is a double-byte (graphic) character string, the value in the *ValueSize* parameter must specify the length, in double-byte characters, of the string.

▪ The value specified in the `ValueBufferSize` parameter is used by DB2 CLI to determine whether to truncate character or binary output data for stored procedure output parameters. This data truncation is performed as follows:

  • For character data, if the number of bytes to be returned is greater than or equal to the *ValueBufferSize* parameter value, the data will be truncated to *ValueBufferSize*-1 byte and is null-terminated (unless null-termination has been turned off).

  • For binary data, if the number of bytes to be returned is greater than or equal to the *ValueBufferSize* parameter value, the data will be truncated to *ValueBufferSize* bytes.

▪ If the value specified in the `CDataType` parameter is `SQL_C_CHAR`, the value stored in the *ValueSize_Indicator* parameter must be the exact length of the data string to be passed to the data source if the data string is not NULL-terminated (the length is determined by the number of characters in the string).

▪ If the value specified in the *CDataType* parameter is `SQL_C_CHAR` and the value specified in the *SQLDataType* parameter is `SQL_GRAPHIC`, the value stored in the *ValueSize_Indicator* parameter must never be `SQL_NTS` and the data passed to the data source must never be a NULL string.

▪ The value specified in the *ValueSize_Indicator* parameter for `SQL_GRAPHIC` data types should identify the number of octets occupied by the double-byte data; therefore, this value should always be a multiple of 2.

▪ When parameter markers are bound to LOB locator variables, the LOB locator values themselves are supplied by the connected data source; therefore, only the LOB locator, not the LOB data itself, is transferred from the application to the data source when the SQL statement is executed.

▪ LOB parameter markers can be bound directly to a file by using the `SQLBindFileToParam()` function. In this case, when the SQL statement is executed, DB2 CLI transfers the contents of the specified file directly to the connected data source.

■ All LOB locators bound by this function remain in effect until the transaction in which they were created is ended or until they are freed by the **FREE LOCATOR** SQL statement.

■ When this function is used to bind an application variable to an output parameter for a stored procedure, DB2 CLI can provide some performance enhancement if the *Value* buffer is placed consecutively in memory after the *ValueSize_Indicator* buffer, for example:

```
struct {    SQLINTEGER      ValueSizeIndicator;
            SQLCHAR         Value[MAX_BUFFER];
       } column;
```

■ A parameter marker can be bound to either a file or a storage location, but not to both. The most recent bind parameter function call used determines which type of binding is in effect when the SQL statement is executed.

Prerequisites   The **SQLPrepare()** function should be called to prepare the SQL statement for execution before this function is called whenever attributes for the result data set columns that may be produced when the SQL statement is executed are not already known.

Restrictions   The value **SQL_DEFAULT_PARAM** (a *ValueSize_Indicator* parameter value) was introduced in ODBC 2.0 to indicate that a stored procedure uses the default value of a parameter rather than a data value sent from the calling application. Because DB2 stored-procedure arguments do not have default values, specifying **SQL_DEFAULT_PARAM** for a **Value** parameter value will result in an error when the **CALL** SQL statement is executed.

ODBC 2.0 also introduced the **SQL_LEN_DATA_AT_EXEC**(*length*) macro to calculate data lengths in the *Value* argument. This macro specifies the sum total length of all the data sent to the data source or stored procedure for character or binary C data via the subsequent **SQLPutData()** calls. Since the DB2 ODBC driver does not need this information, this macro is not needed. An ODBC application can determine whether or not another data source or driver needs this information by calling the **SQLGetInfo()** function with the **SQL_NEED_LONG_DATA_LEN** option specified. (The DB2 ODBC driver will return the value "N" to indicate that this information is not needed by the **SQLPutData()** function.)

See Also   SQLPrepare(), SQLExecute(), SQLExecDirect(), SQLParamData(), SQLParamOptions(), SQLPutData()

Example   The following Visual C++ program illustrates how to use the **SQLBindParameter()** function to associate (bind) a local memory variable to a parameter marker in an SQL statement.

```
/*—————————————————————————————————————————————*/
/* NAME:     CH9EX2.CPP                                     */
/* PURPOSE: Illustrate How To Use The Following CLI API Function */
/*          In A C++ Program:                               */
/*                                                          */
/*               SQLBindParameter()                         */
/*                                                          */
/* OTHER CLI APIs SHOWN:                                    */
/*               SQLAllocHandle()          SQLSetEnvAttr()  */
/*               SQLConnect()              SQLDisconnect()  */
```

```
/*           SQLPrepare()              SQLExecute()            */
/*           SQLBindCol()              SQLFetch()              */
/*           SQLFreeHandle()                                   */
/*                                                             */
/*-----------------------------------------------------------*/

// Include The Appropriate Header Files
#include <windows.h>
#include <sqlcli1.h>
#include <iostream.h>

// Define The CLI_Class Class
class CLI_Class
{
    // Attributes
    public:
        SQLHANDLE   EnvHandle;
        SQLHANDLE   ConHandle;
        SQLHANDLE   StmtHandle;
        SQLRETURN   rc;

    // Operations
    public:
        CLI_Class();                            // Constructor
        ~CLI_Class();                           // Destructor
        SQLRETURN ShowResults();
};

// Define The Class Constructor
CLI_Class::CLI_Class()
{
    // Initialize The Return Code Variable
    rc = SQL_SUCCESS;

    // Allocate An Environment Handle
    rc = SQLAllocHandle(SQL_HANDLE_ENV, SQL_NULL_HANDLE, &EnvHandle);

    // Set The ODBC Application Version To 3.x
    if (rc == SQL_SUCCESS)
        rc = SQLSetEnvAttr(EnvHandle, SQL_ATTR_ODBC_VERSION,
                (SQLPOINTER) SQL_OV_ODBC3, SQL_IS_UINTEGER);

    // Allocate A Connection Handle
    if (rc == SQL_SUCCESS)
        rc = SQLAllocHandle(SQL_HANDLE_DBC, EnvHandle, &ConHandle);
}

// Define The Class Destructor
CLI_Class::~CLI_Class()
{
    // Free The Connection Handle
    if (ConHandle != NULL)
        SQLFreeHandle(SQL_HANDLE_DBC, ConHandle);

    // Free The Environment Handle
```

```
        if (EnvHandle != NULL)
            SQLFreeHandle(SQL_HANDLE_ENV, EnvHandle);
}


// Define The ShowResults() Member Function
SQLRETURN CLI_Class::ShowResults(void)
{
    // Declare The Local Memory Variables
    SQLCHAR  ProjectName[50];

    // Bind The Column In The Result Data Set Returned To An
    // Application Variable
    rc = SQLBindCol(StmtHandle, 1, SQL_C_CHAR, (SQLPOINTER)
             ProjectName, sizeof(ProjectName), NULL);

    // Display A Header
    cout << "Project Name :" << endl << endl;

    // While There Are Records In The Result Data Set Generated,
    // Retrieve And Display Them
    while (rc != SQL_NO_DATA)
    {
        rc = SQLFetch(StmtHandle);
        if (rc != SQL_NO_DATA)
            cout << ProjectName << endl;
    }

    // Return The CLI API Return Code To The Calling Function
    return(rc);
}

/*—————————————————————————————————————————————————*/
/* The Main Function                                 */
/*—————————————————————————————————————————————————*/
int main()
{
    // Declare The Local Memory Variables
    SQLRETURN    rc = SQL_SUCCESS;
    SQLCHAR      SQLStmt[255];
    SQLSMALLINT  PRStaff;

    // Create An Instance Of The CLI_Class Class
    CLI_Class    Example;

    // Connect To The DB2 Sample Database
    if (Example.ConHandle != NULL)
    {
        rc = SQLConnect(Example.ConHandle, (SQLCHAR *) "SAMPLE",
                SQL_NTS, (SQLCHAR *) "userid", SQL_NTS,
                (SQLCHAR *) "password", SQL_NTS);

        // Allocate An SQL Statement Handle
        rc = SQLAllocHandle(SQL_HANDLE_STMT, Example.ConHandle,
                &Example.StmtHandle);
```

```
    if (rc == SQL_SUCCESS)
    {
        // Define A SELECT SQL Statement That Uses A Parameter
        // Marker
        strcpy((char *) SQLStmt, "SELECT PROJNAME FROM PROJECT ");
        strcat((char *) SQLStmt, "WHERE PRSTAFF > ?");

        // Prepare The SQL Statement
        rc = SQLPrepare(Example.StmtHandle, SQLStmt, SQL_NTS);

        // Bind The Parameter Marker In The SQL Statement To A
        // Local Application Variable
        rc = SQLBindParameter(Example.StmtHandle, 1,
                SQL_PARAM_INPUT, SQL_C_SHORT, SQL_SMALLINT, 0,
                0, (SQLPOINTER) &PRStaff, 0, NULL);

        // Populate The "Bound" Application Variable
        PRStaff = 5;

        /*----------------------------------------------------------*/
        /* Note: Normally, A Bound Application Variable Would       */
        /* Be Populated By The User, Via A User Interface           */
        /*----------------------------------------------------------*/

        // Execute The SQL Statement
        rc = SQLExecute(Example.StmtHandle);

        // Display The Results Of The SQL Query
        if (rc == SQL_SUCCESS)
            Example.ShowResults();

        // Free The SQL Statement Handle
        if (Example.StmtHandle != NULL)
            SQLFreeHandle(SQL_HANDLE_STMT, Example.StmtHandle);
    }

    // Disconnect From The DB2 Sample Database
    rc = SQLDisconnect(Example.ConHandle);
}

// Return To The Operating System
return(rc);
}
```

COLUMN-WISE BINDING The following Visual C++ program illustrates how to use the `SQLBindParameter()` function to bind parameter markers in an SQL statement to arrays—using column-wise binding:

```
/*----------------------------------------------------------------*/
/* NAME:     CH9EX2A.CPP                                          */
/* PURPOSE: Illustrate How To Use The SQLBindParameter() CLI API  */
/*          Function To Bind Parameters In An SQL Statement To    */
/*          Application Arrays Using Column-Wise Binding.         */
```

```
/*                                                                    */
/* OTHER CLI APIs SHOWN:                                              */
/*          SQLAllocHandle()          SQLSetEnvAttr()                 */
/*          SQLDriverConnect()        SQLSetStmtAttr()                */
/*          SQLPrepare()              SQLExecute()                    */
/*          SQLDisconnect()           SQLFreeHandle()                 */
/*                                                                    */
/*------------------------------------------------------------------- */

// Include The Appropriate Header Files
#include <windows.h>
#include <sqlcli1.h>
#include <iostream.h>

// Define The CLI_Class Class
class CLI_Class
{
    // Attributes
    public:
        SQLHANDLE    EnvHandle;
        SQLHANDLE    ConHandle;
        SQLHANDLE    StmtHandle;
        SQLRETURN    rc;

    // Operations
    public:
        CLI_Class();                            // Constructor
        ~CLI_Class();                           // Destructor
        SQLRETURN InsertRows();
};

// Define The Class Constructor
CLI_Class::CLI_Class()
{
    // Initialize The Return Code Variable
    rc = SQL_SUCCESS;

    // Allocate An Environment Handle
    rc = SQLAllocHandle(SQL_HANDLE_ENV, SQL_NULL_HANDLE, &EnvHandle);

    // Set The ODBC Application Version To 3.x
    if (rc == SQL_SUCCESS)
        rc = SQLSetEnvAttr(EnvHandle, SQL_ATTR_ODBC_VERSION,
                    (SQLPOINTER) SQL_OV_ODBC3, SQL_IS_UINTEGER);

    // Allocate A Connection Handle
    if (rc == SQL_SUCCESS)
        rc = SQLAllocHandle(SQL_HANDLE_DBC, EnvHandle, &ConHandle);
}

// Define The Class Destructor
CLI_Class::~CLI_Class()
{
    // Free The Connection Handle
```

```
    if (ConHandle != NULL)
        SQLFreeHandle(SQL_HANDLE_DBC, ConHandle);

    // Free The Environment Handle
    if (EnvHandle != NULL)
        SQLFreeHandle(SQL_HANDLE_ENV, EnvHandle);
}

// Define The InsertRows() Member Function
SQLRETURN CLI_Class::InsertRows(void)
{
    // Declare The Local Memory Variables
    SQLRETURN     rc;
    SQLCHAR       SQLStmt[255];
    SQLUINTEGER   ArraySize = 3;

    SQLINTEGER    DeptNumArray[3];
    SQLCHAR       DeptNameArray[3][6];
    SQLINTEGER    DeptNameLI_Array[3];
    SQLSMALLINT   ManagerIDArray[3];

    // Initialize The Input Array Variables
    DeptNumArray[0] = 97;
    DeptNumArray[1] = 98;
    DeptNumArray[2] = 99;

    strcpy((char *) DeptNameArray[0], "TEST1");
    strcpy((char *) DeptNameArray[1], "TEST2");
    strcpy((char *) DeptNameArray[2], "TEST3");

    DeptNameLI_Array[0] = SQL_NTS;
    DeptNameLI_Array[1] = SQL_NTS;
    DeptNameLI_Array[2] = SQL_NTS;

    ManagerIDArray[0] = 80;
    ManagerIDArray[1] = 90;
    ManagerIDArray[2] = 100;

    // Allocate An SQL Statement Handle
    rc = SQLAllocHandle(SQL_HANDLE_STMT, ConHandle, &StmtHandle);
    if (rc == SQL_SUCCESS)
    {
        // Set The SQL_ATTR_ROW_BIND_TYPE Statement Attribute To Tell
        // The Driver To Use Column-Wise Binding.
        rc = SQLSetStmtAttr(StmtHandle, SQL_ATTR_PARAM_BIND_TYPE,
                SQL_PARAM_BIND_BY_COLUMN, 0);

        // Tell The Driver That There Are 3 Values For Each Parameter
        // (By Setting The SQL_ATTR_PARAMSET_SIZE Statement
        // Attribute)
        rc = SQLSetStmtAttr(StmtHandle, SQL_ATTR_PARAMSET_SIZE,
                (SQLPOINTER) ArraySize, 0);

        // Define An INSERT SQL Statement That Uses Parameter
        // Markers
```

```
            strcpy((char *) SQLStmt, "INSERT INTO ORG ");
            strcat((char *) SQLStmt, "(DEPTNUMB, DEPTNAME, MANAGER) ");
            strcat((char *) SQLStmt, "VALUES (?, ?, ?)");

            // Prepare The SQL Statement
            rc = SQLPrepare(StmtHandle, SQLStmt, SQL_NTS);

            // Bind The Parameter Markers To Local Arrays
            rc = SQLBindParameter(StmtHandle, 1, SQL_PARAM_INPUT,
                    SQL_C_DEFAULT, SQL_INTEGER, 0, 0, DeptNumArray, 0,
                    NULL);

            rc = SQLBindParameter(StmtHandle, 2, SQL_PARAM_INPUT,
                    SQL_C_CHAR, SQL_CHAR, 6, 0, DeptNameArray, 6,
                    DeptNameLI_Array);

            rc = SQLBindParameter(StmtHandle, 3, SQL_PARAM_INPUT,
                    SQL_C_SHORT, SQL_SMALLINT, 0, 0, ManagerIDArray, 0,
                    NULL);

            // Execute The SQL Statement
            rc = SQLExecute(StmtHandle);

            // Free The SQL Statement Handle
            if (StmtHandle != NULL)
                SQLFreeHandle(SQL_HANDLE_STMT, StmtHandle);
        }

        // Return The CLI API Return Code To The Calling Function
        return(rc);
}

/*------------------------------------------------------------------*/
/* The Main Function                                                */
/*------------------------------------------------------------------*/
int main()
{
    // Declare The Local Memory Variables
    SQLRETURN  rc = SQL_SUCCESS;

    // Create An Instance Of The CLI_Class Class
    CLI_Class  Example;

    // Connect To The DB2 Sample Database
    if (Example.ConHandle != NULL)
    {
        rc = SQLConnect(Example.ConHandle, (SQLCHAR *) "SAMPLE",
                SQL_NTS, (SQLCHAR *) "userid", SQL_NTS,
                (SQLCHAR *) "password", SQL_NTS);

        // Insert 3 Rows Of Data Into The ORG Table In The DB2
        // Sample Database
        rc = Example.InsertRows();

        // If The Rows Were Added, Print A Message Saying So
```

```
        if (rc == SQL_SUCCESS)
        {
            cout << "3 rows have been added to the ORG table.";
            cout << endl;
        }

        // Disconnect From The DB2 Sample Database
        rc = SQLDisconnect(Example.ConHandle);
    }

    // Return To The Operating System
    return(rc);
}
```

ROW-WISE BINDING   The following Visual C++ program illustrates how to use the `SQLBindParameter()` function to bind parameter markers in an SQL statement to arrays—using row-wise binding.

```
/*------------------------------------------------------------*/
/* NAME:     CH9EX2B.CPP                                       */
/* PURPOSE: Illustrate How To Use The SQLBindParameter() CLI API */
/*          Function To Bind Parameters In An SQL Statement To */
/*          Application Arrays Using Row-Wise Binding.         */
/*                                                             */
/* OTHER CLI APIs SHOWN:                                       */
/*             SQLAllocHandle()          SQLSetEnvAttr()       */
/*             SQLDriverConnect()        SQLSetStmtAttr()      */
/*             SQLPrepare()              SQLExecute()          */
/*             SQLDisconnect()           SQLFreeHandle()       */
/*                                                             */
/*------------------------------------------------------------*/

// Include The Appropriate Header Files
#include <windows.h>
#include <sqlcli1.h>
#include <iostream.h>

// Define The CLI_Class Class
class CLI_Class
{
    // Attributes
    public:
        SQLHANDLE   EnvHandle;
        SQLHANDLE   ConHandle;
        SQLHANDLE   StmtHandle;
        SQLRETURN   rc;

    // Operations
    public:
        CLI_Class();                        // Constructor
        ~CLI_Class();                       // Destructor
        SQLRETURN InsertRows();
};

// Define The Class Constructor
```

```
CLI_Class::CLI_Class()
{
    // Initialize The Return Code Variable
    rc = SQL_SUCCESS;

    // Allocate An Environment Handle
    rc = SQLAllocHandle(SQL_HANDLE_ENV, SQL_NULL_HANDLE, &EnvHandle);

    // Set The ODBC Application Version To 3.x
    if (rc == SQL_SUCCESS)
        rc = SQLSetEnvAttr(EnvHandle, SQL_ATTR_ODBC_VERSION,
                    (SQLPOINTER) SQL_OV_ODBC3, SQL_IS_UINTEGER);

    // Allocate A Connection Handle
    if (rc == SQL_SUCCESS)
        rc = SQLAllocHandle(SQL_HANDLE_DBC, EnvHandle, &ConHandle);
}

// Define The Class Destructor
CLI_Class::~CLI_Class()
{
    // Free The Connection Handle
    if (ConHandle != NULL)
        SQLFreeHandle(SQL_HANDLE_DBC, ConHandle);

    // Free The Environment Handle
    if (EnvHandle != NULL)
        SQLFreeHandle(SQL_HANDLE_ENV, EnvHandle);
}

// Define The InsertRows() Member Function
SQLRETURN CLI_Class::InsertRows(void)
{
    // Declare The Local Memory Variables
    SQLRETURN    rc;
    SQLCHAR      SQLStmt[255];
    SQLUINTEGER  ArraySize = 3;

    // Define The ORG_INFO Structure And Allocate An Array
    // Of 3 Structures
    typedef struct {
        SQLUINTEGER  DeptNum;
        SQLINTEGER   DeptNum_LI;
        SQLCHAR      DeptName[6];
        SQLINTEGER   DeptName_LI;
        SQLUINTEGER  ManagerID;
        SQLINTEGER   ManagerID_LI;
    } ORG_INFO;

    ORG_INFO   OrgInfoArray[3];

    // Initialize The Input Structure Array
    OrgInfoArray[0].DeptNum = 97;
    OrgInfoArray[0].DeptNum_LI = 0;
    strcpy((char *) OrgInfoArray[0].DeptName, "TEST1");
```

```
OrgInfoArray[0].DeptName_LI = SQL_NTS;
OrgInfoArray[0].ManagerID = 80;
OrgInfoArray[0].ManagerID_LI = 0;

OrgInfoArray[1].DeptNum = 98;
OrgInfoArray[1].DeptNum_LI = 0;
strcpy((char *) OrgInfoArray[1].DeptName, "TEST2");
OrgInfoArray[1].DeptName_LI = SQL_NTS;
OrgInfoArray[1].ManagerID = 90;
OrgInfoArray[1].ManagerID_LI = 0;

OrgInfoArray[2].DeptNum = 99;
OrgInfoArray[2].DeptNum_LI = 0;
strcpy((char *) OrgInfoArray[2].DeptName, "TEST3");
OrgInfoArray[2].DeptName_LI = SQL_NTS;
OrgInfoArray[2].ManagerID = 100;
OrgInfoArray[2].ManagerID_LI = 0;

// Allocate An SQL Statement Handle
rc = SQLAllocHandle(SQL_HANDLE_STMT, ConHandle, &StmtHandle);
if (rc == SQL_SUCCESS)
{
    // Store The Size Of The ORG_INFO Structure In The
    // SQL_ATTR_PARAM_BIND_TYPE Statement Attribute -- This Tells
    // The Driver To Use Row-Wise Binding.
    rc = SQLSetStmtAttr(StmtHandle, SQL_ATTR_PARAM_BIND_TYPE,
            (SQLPOINTER) sizeof(ORG_INFO), 0);

    // Tell The Driver That There Are 3 Values For Each Parameter
    // (By Setting The SQL_ATTR_PARAMSET_SIZE Statement
    // Attribute)
    rc = SQLSetStmtAttr(StmtHandle, SQL_ATTR_PARAMSET_SIZE,
            (SQLPOINTER) ArraySize, 0);

    // Define An INSERT SQL Statement That Uses Parameter
    // Markers
    strcpy((char *) SQLStmt, "INSERT INTO ORG ");
    strcat((char *) SQLStmt, "(DEPTNUMB, DEPTNAME, MANAGER) ");
    strcat((char *) SQLStmt, "VALUES (?, ?, ?)");

    // Prepare The SQL Statement
    rc = SQLPrepare(StmtHandle, SQLStmt, SQL_NTS);

    // Bind The Parameter Markers To Local Variables
    rc = SQLBindParameter(StmtHandle, 1, SQL_PARAM_INPUT,
            SQL_C_ULONG, SQL_INTEGER, 0, 0,
            &OrgInfoArray[0].DeptNum, 0,
            &OrgInfoArray[0].DeptNum_LI);

    rc = SQLBindParameter(StmtHandle, 2, SQL_PARAM_INPUT,
            SQL_C_CHAR, SQL_CHAR, 6, 0,
            OrgInfoArray[0].DeptName, 6,
            &OrgInfoArray[0].DeptName_LI);

    rc = SQLBindParameter(StmtHandle, 3, SQL_PARAM_INPUT,
```

```cpp
                        SQL_C_SHORT, SQL_SMALLINT, 0, 0,
                        &OrgInfoArray[0].ManagerID, 0,
                        &OrgInfoArray[0].ManagerID_LI);

        // Execute The SQL Statement
        rc = SQLExecDirect(StmtHandle, SQLStmt, SQL_NTS);

        // Free The SQL Statement Handle
        if (StmtHandle != NULL)
            SQLFreeHandle(SQL_HANDLE_STMT, StmtHandle);
    }

    // Return The CLI API Return Code To The Calling Function
    return(rc);
}


/*-----------------------------------------------------------*/
/* The Main Function                                         */
/*-----------------------------------------------------------*/
int main()
{
    // Declare The Local Memory Variables
    SQLRETURN  rc = SQL_SUCCESS;

    // Create An Instance Of The CLI_Class Class
    CLI_Class  Example;

    // Connect To The DB2 Sample Database
    if (Example.ConHandle != NULL)
    {
        rc = SQLConnect(Example.ConHandle, (SQLCHAR *) "SAMPLE",
                  SQL_NTS, (SQLCHAR *) "userid", SQL_NTS,
                  (SQLCHAR *) "password", SQL_NTS);

        // Insert 3 Rows Of Data Into The ORG Table In The DB2
        // Sample Database
        rc = Example.InsertRows();

        // If The Rows Were Added, Print A Message Saying So
        if (rc == SQL_SUCCESS)
        {
            cout << "3 rows have been added to the ORG table.";
            cout << endl;
        }

        // Disconnect From The DB2 Sample Database
        rc = SQLDisconnect(Example.ConHandle);
    }

    // Return To The Operating System
    return(rc);
}
```

SQLNumParams

COMPATIBILITY

X/OPEN 95 CLI	ISO/IEC 92 CLI	DB2 CLI 5.2	DB2 CLI 2.0	ODBC 3.x
☐	☐	✓	✓	✓

ODBC API CONFORMANCE LEVEL   CORE*

*IN ODBC 2.0, THIS FUNCTION WAS A LEVEL 2 API CONFORMANCE LEVEL FUNCTION

Purpose   The SQLNumParams() function is used to retrieve the number of parameter markers used in a specified SQL statement.

Syntax

```
SQLRETURN  SQLNumParams       (SQLHSTMT       StatementHandle,
                               SQLSMALLINT    *PMarkerNumber);
```

Parameters *StatementHandle*   An SQL statement handle that refers to a previously allocated SQL statement information storage buffer (data structure).

PMarkerNumber   A pointer to a location in memory where this function is to store the number of parameter markers found in the SQL statement associated with the statement handle specified.

Description   The SQLNumParams() function is used to retrieve the number of parameter markers used in a specified SQL statement. This function is typically used to determine how many SQLBindParameter() function calls are needed to associate (bind) application variables and/or LOB locators to the SQL statement associated with an SQL statement handle.

Return Codes SQL_SUCCESS, SQL_SUCCESS_WITH_INFO, SQL_STILL_EXECUTING, SQL_INVALID_HANDLE, or SQL_ERROR

SQLSTATEs   If this function returns SQL_SUCCESS_WITH_INFO or SQL_ERROR, one of the following SQLSTATE values may be obtained by calling the SQLGetDiagRec() function:

40003, **08**S01, **HY**001, **HY**008, **HY**009, **HY**010, **HY**013, or **HYT**00

Refer to Appendix B for detailed information about each SQLSTATE value that can be returned.

Comments   ■ If the SQL statement associated with the statement handle specified in the *StatementHandle* parameter does not contain parameter markers, this function returns **0** to the *PMarkerNumber* parameter.

■ The SQL_DESC_COUNT field of the SQL statement handle's IPD descriptor header record contains the value that this function returns to the *PMarkerNumber* parameter.

Prerequisites The sqlPrepare() function must be called to prepare the SQL statement for executing before this function is called.

Restrictions There are no restrictions associated with this function call.

See Also SQLPrepare(), SQLDescribeParam(), SQLBindParameter()

Example The following Visual C++ program illustrates how to use the sqlNumParams() function to determine how many parameter markers were coded in an SQL statement:

```
/*————————————————————————————————————*/
/* NAME:     CH9EX3.CPP                                          */
/* PURPOSE: Illustrate How To Use The Following CLI API Function */
/*          In A C++ Program:                                    */
/*                                                               */
/*                SQLNumParams()                                 */
/*                                                               */
/* OTHER CLI APIs SHOWN:                                         */
/*          SQLAllocHandle()            SQLSetEnvAttr()          */
/*          SQLConnect()                SQLPrepare()             */
/*          SQLDisconnect()             SQLFreeHandle()          */
/*                                                               */
/*————————————————————————————————————*/

// Include The Appropriate Header Files
#include <windows.h>
#include <sqlcli1.h>
#include <iostream.h>

// Define The CLI_Class Class
class CLI_Class
{
    // Attributes
    public:
        SQLHANDLE   EnvHandle;
        SQLHANDLE   ConHandle;
        SQLHANDLE   StmtHandle;
        SQLRETURN   rc;

    // Operations
    public:
        CLI_Class();                        // Constructor
        ~CLI_Class();                       // Destructor
};

// Define The Class Constructor
CLI_Class::CLI_Class()
{
    // Initialize The Return Code Variable
    rc = SQL_SUCCESS;

    // Allocate An Environment Handle
    rc = SQLAllocHandle(SQL_HANDLE_ENV, SQL_NULL_HANDLE, &EnvHandle);
```

```
        // Set The ODBC Application Version To 3.x
        if (rc == SQL_SUCCESS)
            rc = SQLSetEnvAttr(EnvHandle, SQL_ATTR_ODBC_VERSION,
                    (SQLPOINTER) SQL_OV_ODBC3, SQL_IS_UINTEGER);

        // Allocate A Connection Handle
        if (rc == SQL_SUCCESS)
            rc = SQLAllocHandle(SQL_HANDLE_DBC, EnvHandle, &ConHandle);
}

// Define The Class Destructor
CLI_Class::~CLI_Class()
{
    // Free The Connection Handle
    if (ConHandle != NULL)
        SQLFreeHandle(SQL_HANDLE_DBC, ConHandle);

    // Free The Environment Handle
    if (EnvHandle != NULL)
        SQLFreeHandle(SQL_HANDLE_ENV, EnvHandle);
}

/*-----------------------------------------------------------------*/
/* The Main Function                                               */
/*-----------------------------------------------------------------*/
int main()
{
    // Declare The Local Memory Variables
    SQLRETURN       rc = SQL_SUCCESS;
    SQLCHAR         SQLStmt[255];
    SQLSMALLINT     NumParams;

    // Create An Instance Of The CLI_Class Class
    CLI_Class       Example;

    // Connect To The DB2 Sample Database
    if (Example.ConHandle != NULL)
    {
        rc = SQLConnect(Example.ConHandle, (SQLCHAR *) "SAMPLE",
                SQL_NTS, (SQLCHAR *) "userid", SQL_NTS,
                (SQLCHAR *) "password", SQL_NTS);

        // Allocate An SQL Statement Handle
        rc = SQLAllocHandle(SQL_HANDLE_STMT, Example.ConHandle,
                &Example.StmtHandle);
        if (rc == SQL_SUCCESS)
        {
            // Define An INSERT SQL Statement That Uses Parameter
            // Markers
            strcpy((char *) SQLStmt, "INSERT INTO ORG ");
            strcat((char *) SQLStmt, "(DEPTNUMB,DEPTNAME,MANAGER)");
            strcat((char *) SQLStmt, "VALUES (?, ?, ?)");

            // Prepare The SQL Statement
```

```
                    rc = SQLPrepare(Example.StmtHandle, SQLStmt, SQL_NTS);

                    // Obtain And Display The Number Of Parameter Markers
                    // Found In The SQL Statement
                    rc = SQLNumParams(Example.StmtHandle, &NumParams);
                    if (rc == SQL_SUCCESS)
                    {
                        cout << "Number of parameter markers found : ";
                        cout << NumParams << endl;
                    }

                    // Free The SQL Statement Handle
                    if (Example.StmtHandle != NULL)
                        SQLFreeHandle(SQL_HANDLE_STMT, Example.StmtHandle);
                }

                // Disconnect From The DB2 Sample Database
                rc = SQLDisconnect(Example.ConHandle);
            }

            // Return To The Operating System
            return(rc);
        }
```

SQLDescribeParam

COMPATIBILITY

X/OPEN 95 CLI	ISO/IEC 92 CLI	DB2 CLI 5.2	DB2 CLI 2.0	ODBC 3.x
☐	☐	☑	☑	☑

ODBC API CONFORMANCE LEVEL   LEVEL 2

Purpose   The SQLDescribeParam() function is used to retrieve information about a column or expression that a specified parameter marker in a prepared SQL statement is associated with.

Syntax

```
SQLRETURN   SQLDescribeParam   (SQLHSTMT       StatementHandle,
                                SQLUSMALLINT   ParamMarkerNum,
                                SQLSMALLINT    *SQLDataType,
                                SQLUINTEGER    *ValueSize,
                                SQLSMALLINT    *Decimals,
                                SQLSMALLINT    *Nullable);
```

Parameters   *StatementHandle*   An SQL statement handle that refers to a previously allocated SQL statement information storage buffer (data structure).

ParamMarkerNum	Specifies the parameter marker's location in the SQL statement text. Parameter markers are as numbered sequentially from left to right, starting with 1, as they appear in the SQL statement.
SQLDataType	A pointer to a location in memory where this function is to store the SQL data type associated with the specified parameter.
ValueSize	A pointer to a location in memory where this function is to store either the number of bytes of data expected by the data source for the specified parameter OR the size of the maximum number of digits used by the data type (precision) of the column or expression that the specified parameter marker is associated with.
Decimals	A pointer to a location in memory where this function is to store the number of digits expected to be to the right of the decimal point in the column or expression that the specified parameter marker is associated with.
Nullable	A pointer to a location in memory where this function is to store information about whether the column or expression that the specified parameter marker is associated with can accept NULL values. After this function executes, the memory location this parameter points to will contain one of the following values:

▇ **SQL_NO_NULLS**
The column or expression with which the specified parameter marker is associated does not allow NULL values.

▇ **SQL_NULLABLE**
The column or expression with which the specified parameter marker is associated allows NULL values.

▇ **SQL_NULLABLE_UNKNOWN**
Whether the column or expression with which the specified parameter marker is associated allows NULL values cannot be determined.

Description   The **SQLDescribeParam()** function is used to retrieve information about a column or expression that a specified parameter marker in a prepared SQL statement is associated with.

Return Codes   **SQL_SUCCESS, SQL_SUCCESS_WITH_INFO, SQL_STILL_EXECUTING, SQL_INVALID_HANDLE**, or **SQL_ERROR**

SQLSTATE   If this function returns **SQL_SUCCESS_WITH_INFO** or **SQL_ERROR**, one of the following SQLSTATE values may be obtained by calling the **SQLGetDiagRec()** function:

01000, **07**009, **08**S01, **21**S01, **HY**000, **HY**001, **HY**008, **HY**010, or **HY**013

Refer to Appendix B for detailed information about each SQLSTATE value that can be returned.

Comments
■ The information returned by this function is also available in the IPD descriptor associated with the statement handle specified.

■ The **SQL_DESC_CONCISE_TYPE** field of the SQL statement handle's IPD descriptor parameter record contains the value this function returns to the *SQLDataType* parameter. If the data type cannot be determined, **SQL_UNKNOWN_TYPE** is returned.

■ The **SQL_DESC_NULLABLE** field of the SQL statement handle's IPD descriptor parameter record contains the value this function returns to the *Nullable* parameter.

■ The *ParamMarkerNum* parameter can be set to **0** to describe the bookmark column.

■ When the *ParamMarkerNum* parameter is equal to **0** (for a bookmark column), **SQL_BINARY** is returned in the *SQLDataType* parameter for variable-length bookmarks.

■ This function does not return parameter type (i.e., input, input/output, or output) information for parameters used in SQL statements that call stored procedures. That's because parameters used in SQL statements other than those that call stored procedures are treated as input parameters. An application must call the **SQLProcedureColumns()** function to determine the parameter type of each parameter used in an SQL statement that calls a stored procedure.

Prerequisites There are no prerequisites for using this function call.

Restrictions There are no restrictions associated with this function call.

See Also SQLAllocHandle(), SQLFreeHandle(), SQLGetEnvAttr(), SQLSetEnvAttr()

Example The following Visual C++ program illustrates how to use the **SQLDescribeParam()** function to obtain information about a bound parameter:

```
/*────────────────────────────────────────────────────────────────*/
/* NAME:    CH9EX4.CPP                                              */
/* PURPOSE: Illustrate How To Use The Following CLI API Function    */
/*          In A C++ Program:                                       */
/*                                                                  */
/*              SQLDescribeParam()                                  */
/*                                                                  */
/* OTHER CLI APIs SHOWN:                                            */
/*              SQLAllocHandle()          SQLSetEnvAttr()           */
/*              SQLConnect()              SQLPrepare()              */
/*              SQLDisconnect()           SQLFreeHandle()           */
/*                                                                  */
/*────────────────────────────────────────────────────────────────*/

// Include The Appropriate Header Files
#include <windows.h>
#include <sqlcli1.h>
#include <iostream.h>
```

```cpp
// Define The CLI_Class Class
class CLI_Class
{
    // Attributes
    public:
        SQLHANDLE   EnvHandle;
        SQLHANDLE   ConHandle;
        SQLHANDLE   StmtHandle;
        SQLRETURN   rc;

    // Operations
    public:
        CLI_Class();                              // Constructor
        ~CLI_Class();                             // Destructor
};

// Define The Class Constructor
CLI_Class::CLI_Class()
{
    // Initialize The Return Code Variable
    rc = SQL_SUCCESS;

    // Allocate An Environment Handle
    rc = SQLAllocHandle(SQL_HANDLE_ENV, SQL_NULL_HANDLE, &EnvHandle);

    // Set The ODBC Application Version To 3.x
    if (rc == SQL_SUCCESS)
        rc = SQLSetEnvAttr(EnvHandle, SQL_ATTR_ODBC_VERSION,
                    (SQLPOINTER) SQL_OV_ODBC3, SQL_IS_UINTEGER);

    // Allocate A Connection Handle
    if (rc == SQL_SUCCESS)
        rc = SQLAllocHandle(SQL_HANDLE_DBC, EnvHandle, &ConHandle);
}

// Define The Class Destructor
CLI_Class::~CLI_Class()
{
    // Free The Connection Handle
    if (ConHandle != NULL)
        SQLFreeHandle(SQL_HANDLE_DBC, ConHandle);

    // Free The Environment Handle
    if (EnvHandle != NULL)
        SQLFreeHandle(SQL_HANDLE_ENV, EnvHandle);
}

/*-----------------------------------------------------------------*/
/* The Main Function                                               */
/*-----------------------------------------------------------------*/
int main()
{
    // Declare The Local Memory Variables
    SQLRETURN    rc = SQL_SUCCESS;
    SQLCHAR      SQLStmt[255];
```

```
SQLSMALLINT   DataType;
SQLUINTEGER   ColSize;
SQLSMALLINT   Decimals;
SQLSMALLINT   Nullable;

// Create An Instance Of The CLI_Class Class
CLI_Class    Example;

// Connect To The DB2 Sample Database
if (Example.ConHandle != NULL)
{
    rc = SQLConnect(Example.ConHandle, (SQLCHAR *) "SAMPLE",
            SQL_NTS, (SQLCHAR *) "userid", SQL_NTS,
            (SQLCHAR *) "password", SQL_NTS);

    // Allocate An SQL Statement Handle
    rc = SQLAllocHandle(SQL_HANDLE_STMT, Example.ConHandle,
            &Example.StmtHandle);
    if (rc == SQL_SUCCESS)
    {
        // Define An INSERT SQL Statement That Uses Parameter
        // Markers
        strcpy((char *) SQLStmt, "INSERT INTO ORG ");
        strcat((char *) SQLStmt, "(DEPTNUMB,DEPTNAME,MANAGER)");
        strcat((char *) SQLStmt, "VALUES (?, ?, ?)");

        // Prepare The SQL Statement
        rc = SQLPrepare(Example.StmtHandle, SQLStmt, SQL_NTS);

        // Obtain And Display Information About The Second
        // Parameter Marker Found In The SQL Statement
        rc = SQLDescribeParam(Example.StmtHandle, 2, &DataType,
                &ColSize, &Decimals, &Nullable);

        if (rc == SQL_SUCCESS)
        {
            cout << "Parameter 2 : " << endl << endl;
            cout << "Data Type   : " << DataType << endl;
            cout << "Column Size : " << ColSize << endl;
            cout << "Decimals    : " << Decimals << endl;
            cout << "Nullable    : " << Nullable << endl;
        }

        // Free The SQL Statement Handle
        if (Example.StmtHandle != NULL)
            SQLFreeHandle(SQL_HANDLE_STMT, Example.StmtHandle);
    }

    // Disconnect From The DB2 Sample Database
    rc = SQLDisconnect(Example.ConHandle);
}

// Return To The Operating System
return(rc);
}
```

SQLExecute

COMPATIBILITY

X/OPEN 95 CLI	ISO/IEC 92 CLI	DB2 CLI 5.2	DB2 CLI 2.0	ODBC 3.x
☑	☑	☑	☑	☑

ODBC API CONFORMANCE LEVEL   CORE

Purpose   The **SQLExecute()** function is used to execute an SQL statement that has been successfully prepared (by the **SQLPrepare()** function) using the current values of any parameter marker variables that have been bound to the SQL statement.

Syntax   SQLRETURN   SQLExecute   (SQLHSTMT   *StatementHandle*);

Parameters   *StatementHandle*   An SQL statement handle that refers to a previously allocated SQL statement information storage buffer (data structure).

Description   The **SQLExecute()** function is used to execute a specified SQL statement that has been successfully prepared by the **SQLPrepare()** function. The prepared SQL statement string may contain one or more parameter markers—a parameter marker is represented by a question mark character (?) in an SQL statement and is used to indicate a position in the statement where an application supplied value is to be substituted when this function is called. When the prepared SQL statement is executed, the current values of the application variables that have been bound to the parameter markers coded in the SQL statement are used to replace the parameter markers themselves.

Once the results from an **SQLExecute()** function call have been processed, the prepared SQL statement can be executed again, with new (or with the same) parameter marker values specified.

Return Codes   SQL_SUCCESS, SQL_SUCCESS_WITH_INFO, SQL_NEED_DATA, SQL_STILL_EXECUTING, SQL_NO_DATA, SQL_INVALID_HANDLE, or SQL_ERROR

SQLSTATEs   If this function returns SQL_SUCCESS_WITH_INFO or SQL_ERROR, one of the following SQLSTATE values may be obtained by calling the SQLGetDiagRec() function:

01504, 01508, 07001, 07006, 08S01, 21S01, 21S02, 22001, 22003, 22005, 22007, 22008, 22012, 23000, 24000, 24504, 34000, 37*xxx*, 40001, 40003, 42*xxx*, 428A1, 42895, 44000, 56084, 58004, S0001, S0002, S0011, S0012, S0021, S0022, HY001, HY010, HY013, HY014, HY092, HY503, or HYT00

Refer to Appendix B for detailed information about each SQLSTATE value that can be returned.

SQLExecute() can also return any SQLSTATE that can be returned by SQLPrepare() depending upon when the data source evaluates the SQL statement associated with the statement handle.

Comments
- An application must call the SQLCloseCursor() function before re-executing a SELECT SQL statement.

- If an application is running in manual-commit mode, and if a transaction has not already been initiated when this function is called, DB2 CLI initiates a transaction before it sends the SQL statement to the data source for processing.

- If an application uses this function to execute a prepared COMMIT or ROLLBACK SQL statement, the application is no longer interoperable. Because the COMMIT and/or the ROLLBACK SQL statement is not supported by all DBMSs, use of these SQL statements should be avoided.

- If the SQL statement being executed contains one or more data-at-execution parameters, SQL_NEED_DATA is returned to the calling application and the application is responsible for sending the appropriate data value to the data source (using the SQLParamData() and SQLPutData() functions).

- If the SQL statement being executed is a searched UPDATE statement or a searched DELETE statement that does not affect rows in the data source, SQL_NO_DATA is returned to the calling application.

- If the SQL statement being executed contains at least one parameter marker and if the value of the SQL_ATTR_PARAMSET_SIZE statement attribute is greater than 1, the parameter marker points to an array of parameter values and the SQL statement is executed once using each value in the array.

- If the SQL statement being executed is a query that cannot support bookmarks and if bookmarks are enabled, DB2 CL1 attempts, by changing an attribute value, to change the environment to one that supports bookmarks. If this occurs, SQLSTATE 01S02 (Option value changed) is returned to the calling application.

- When connection pooling is enabled, an application must not execute SQL statements that change the database or the context of the database.

Prerequisites The SQLPrepare() function must be called to prepare the SQL statement for execution and all parameter markers coded in the SQL statement must be bound to application variables before this function is called.

Restrictions There are no restrictions associated with this function call.

See Also SQLBindParameter(), SQLPrepare(), SQLExecDirect(), SQLParamData(), SQLPutData()

Example See the example provided for the SQLPrepare() function on page 276.

SQLExecDirect

COMPATIBILITY

X/OPEN 95 CLI	ISO/IEC 92 CLI	DB2 CLI 5.2	DB2 CLI 2.0	ODBC 3.x
☑	☑	☑	☑	☑

ODBC API CONFORMANCE LEVEL   CORE

Purpose   The `SQLExecDirect()` function is used to prepare and execute a preparable SQL statement, using the current values of any parameter marker variables that have been bound to the SQL statement.

Syntax

```
SQLRETURN    SQLExecDirect    (SQLHSTMT      StatementHandle,
                               SQLCHAR       *SQLString,
                               SQLINTEGER    SQLStringSize);
```

Parameters   *StatementHandle*   An SQL statement handle that refers to a previously allocated SQL statement information storage buffer (data structure).

SQLString   A pointer to a location in memory where the SQL statement to be prepared and executed is stored.

SQLStringSize   The length of the SQL statement stored in the *SQLString* parameter.

Description   The `SQLExecDirect()` function is used to prepare and execute a preparable SQL statement using the current values of any parameter marker variables that have been bound to the SQL statement. `SQLExecDirect()` is the fastest way to submit an SQL statement that is to be executed only once to the data source for processing. Because the SQL statement is both prepared and executed in the same step, the SQL statement specified must be reprepared each time it is executed.

The SQL statement string to be prepared and executed may contain one or more parameter markers—a parameter marker is represented by a question mark character (?) in an SQL statement and is used to indicate a position in the statement where an application supplied value is to be substituted when this function is called. When the SQL statement is executed, the current values of the application variables bound to the parameter markers coded in the SQL statement are used to replace the parameter markers themselves.

Return Codes   `SQL_SUCCESS`, `SQL_SUCCESS_WITH_INFO`, `SQL_NEED_DATA`, `SQL_STILL_EXECUTING`, `SQL_NO_DATA`, `SQL_INVALID_HANDLE`, or `SQL_ERROR`

SQLSTATEs   If this function returns `SQL_SUCCESS_WITH_INFO` or `SQL_ERROR`, one of the following SQLSTATE values may be obtained by calling the `SQLGetDiagRec()` function:

01504, 01508, 07001, 07006, 08S01, 21S01, 21S02, 22001, 22003, 22005, 22007, 22008, 22012, 23000, 24000, 24504, 34000, 37*xxx*, 40001, 40003, 42*xxx*, 428A1, 42895, 44000, 56084, 58004, S0001, S0002, S0011, S0012, S0021, S0022, HY001, HY009, HY013, HY014, HY090, HY092, HY503, or HYT00

Refer to Appendix B for detailed information about each SQLSTATE value that can be returned.

Comments
- The data source the SQL statement is passed to for processing must be able to dynamically prepare and execute SQL statements.

- If an application is running in manual-commit mode, and if a transaction has not already been initiated when this function is called, DB2 CLI initiates a transaction before it sends the SQL statement to the data source for processing.

- If an application uses this function to execute a prepared **COMMIT** or **ROLLBACK** SQL statement, the application is no longer interoperable. Because the **COMMIT** and/or **ROLLBACK** SQL statement is not supported by all DBMSs, use of these SQL statements should be avoided.

- If the SQL statement being executed contains one or more data-at-execution parameters, **SQL_NEED_DATA** is returned to the calling application and the application is responsible for sending the appropriate data value to the data source (using the **SQLParamData()** and **SQLPutData()** functions).

- If the SQL statement being executed is a searched **UPDATE** statement or a searched **DELETE** statement that does not affect rows in the data source, **SQL_NO_DATA** is returned to the calling application.

- If the SQL statement being executed contains at least one parameter marker and if the value of the **SQL_ATTR_PARAMSET_SIZE** statement attribute is greater than **1**, the parameter marker points to an array of parameter values and the SQL statement is executed once using each value in the array.

- If the SQL statement being executed is a query that cannot support bookmarks, and if bookmarks are enabled, the driver attempts, by changing an attribute value, to change the environment to one that supports bookmarks. If this occurs, SQLSTATE **01S02** (Option value changed) is returned to the calling application.

- When connection pooling is enabled, an application must not execute SQL statements that change the database or the context of the database.

Prerequisites There are no prerequisites for using this function call.

Restrictions There are no restrictions associated with this function call.

See Also SQLBindParameter(), SQLPrepare(), SQLExecute(), SQLParamData(), SQLPutData()

Example The following Visual C++ program illustrates how to use the **SQLExecDirect()** function to prepare and execute an SQL statement in a single step:

```
/*------------------------------------------------------------*/
/* NAME:     CH9EX5.CPP                                       */
/* PURPOSE: Illustrate How To Use The Following CLI API Function  */
/*             In A C++ Program:                              */
```

```
/*                                                              */
/*                  SQLExecDirect()                             */
/*                                                              */
/* OTHER CLI APIs SHOWN:                                        */
/*          SQLAllocHandle()              SQLSetEnvAttr()        */
/*          SQLConnect()                  SQLBindCol()           */
/*          SQLFetch()                    SQLDisconnect()        */
/*          SQLFreeHandle()                                      */
/*                                                              */
/*------------------------------------------------------------*/

// Include The Appropriate Header Files
#include <windows.h>
#include <sqlcli1.h>
#include <iostream.h>

// Define The CLI_Class Class
class CLI_Class
{
    // Attributes
    public:
        SQLHANDLE   EnvHandle;
        SQLHANDLE   ConHandle;
        SQLHANDLE   StmtHandle;
        SQLRETURN   rc;

    // Operations
    public:
        CLI_Class();                        // Constructor
        ~CLI_Class();                       // Destructor
        SQLRETURN ShowResults();
};

// Define The Class Constructor
CLI_Class::CLI_Class()
{
    // Initialize The Return Code Variable
    rc = SQL_SUCCESS;

    // Allocate An Environment Handle
    rc = SQLAllocHandle(SQL_HANDLE_ENV, SQL_NULL_HANDLE, &EnvHandle);

    // Set The ODBC Application Version To 3.x
    if (rc == SQL_SUCCESS)
        rc = SQLSetEnvAttr(EnvHandle, SQL_ATTR_ODBC_VERSION,
                (SQLPOINTER) SQL_OV_ODBC3, SQL_IS_UINTEGER);

    // Allocate A Connection Handle
    if (rc == SQL_SUCCESS)
        rc = SQLAllocHandle(SQL_HANDLE_DBC, EnvHandle, &ConHandle);
}

// Define The Class Destructor
CLI_Class::~CLI_Class()
```

```
    {
        // Free The Connection Handle
        if (ConHandle != NULL)
            SQLFreeHandle(SQL_HANDLE_DBC, ConHandle);

        // Free The Environment Handle
        if (EnvHandle != NULL)
            SQLFreeHandle(SQL_HANDLE_ENV, EnvHandle);
    }

    // Define The ShowResults() Member Function
    SQLRETURN CLI_Class::ShowResults(void)
    {
        // Declare The Local Memory Variables
        SQLCHAR   LastName[50];
        SQLCHAR   FirstName[50];

        // Bind The Columns In The Result Data Set Returned To
        // Application Variables
        rc = SQLBindCol(StmtHandle, 1, SQL_C_CHAR, (SQLPOINTER)
                LastName, sizeof(LastName), NULL);

        rc = SQLBindCol(StmtHandle, 2, SQL_C_CHAR, (SQLPOINTER)
                FirstName, sizeof(FirstName), NULL);

        // Display A Header
        cout << "Employees :" << endl << endl;

        // While There Are Records In The Result Data Set Generated,
        // Retrieve And Display Them
        while (rc != SQL_NO_DATA)
        {
            rc = SQLFetch(StmtHandle);
            if (rc != SQL_NO_DATA)
                cout << FirstName << " " << LastName << endl;
        }

        // Return The CLI API Return Code To The Calling Function
        return(rc);
    }

    /*-----------------------------------------------------------*/
    /* The Main Function                                         */
    /*-----------------------------------------------------------*/
    int main()
    {
        // Declare The Local Memory Variables
        SQLRETURN  rc = SQL_SUCCESS;
        SQLCHAR    SQLStmt[255];

        // Create An Instance Of The CLI_Class Class
        CLI_Class  Example;

        // Connect To The DB2 Sample Database
        if (Example.ConHandle != NULL)
```

```
    {
        rc = SQLConnect(Example.ConHandle, (SQLCHAR *) "SAMPLE",
                SQL_NTS, (SQLCHAR *) "userid", SQL_NTS,
                (SQLCHAR *) "password", SQL_NTS);

        // Allocate An SQL Statement Handle
        rc = SQLAllocHandle(SQL_HANDLE_STMT, Example.ConHandle,
                &Example.StmtHandle);
        if (rc == SQL_SUCCESS)
        {
            // Define A SELECT SQL Statement
            strcpy((char *) SQLStmt, "SELECT LASTNAME, FIRSTNME ");
            strcat((char *) SQLStmt, "FROM EMPLOYEE");

            // Prepare And Execute The SQL Statement
            rc = SQLExecDirect(Example.StmtHandle, SQLStmt, SQL_NTS);

            // Display The Results Of The SQL Query
            if (rc == SQL_SUCCESS)
                Example.ShowResults();

            // Free The SQL Statement Handle
            if (Example.StmtHandle != NULL)
                SQLFreeHandle(SQL_HANDLE_STMT, Example.StmtHandle);
        }

        // Disconnect From The DB2 Sample Database
        rc = SQLDisconnect(Example.ConHandle);
    }

    // Return To The Operating System
    return(rc);
}
```

SQLNativeSql

COMPATIBILITY

X/OPEN 95 CLI	ISO/IEC 92 CLI	DB2 CLI 5.2	DB2 CLI 2.0	ODBC 3.x
☐	☐	☑	☑	☑

ODBC API CONFORMANCE LEVEL   **CORE***

*IN ODBC 2.0, THIS FUNCTION WAS A LEVEL 2 API CONFORMANCE LEVEL FUNCTION

Purpose   The SQLNativeSql() function is used to display an SQL statement string as it will be seen by the data source (after it is modified by DB2 CLI).

Syntax	SQLRETURN	SQLNativeSql	(SQLHDBC	*ConnectionHandle*,
			SQLCHAR	**SQLStringIn*,
			SQLINTEGER	*SQLStringInSize*,
			SQLCHAR	**SQLStringOut*,
			SQLINTEGER	*SQLStringOutMaxSize*,
			SQLINTEGER	**SQLStringOutSize*);

Parameters

ConnectionHandle   A data source connection handle that refers to a previously allocated connection information storage buffer (data structure).

SQLStringIn   A pointer to a location in memory where the SQL statement string to be translated is stored.

SQLStringInSize   The length of the SQL statement string stored in the *SQLStringIn* parameter.

SQLStringOut   A pointer to a location in memory where this function is to store the translated SQL statement string (the SQL statement string as it will be seen by the data source).

SQLStringOutMaxSize   The maximum size of the memory storage buffer where this function is to store the translated SQL statement string.

SQLStringOutSize   A pointer to a location in memory where this function is to store the actual number of bytes written to the translated SQL statement string memory storage buffer (*SQLStringOut*).

Description   The **SQLNativeSql()** function displays a specified SQL statement string as it will be seen (transformed) by the data source. This function is used primarily to show how DB2 CLI interprets vendor escape clauses. The X/Open SQL CAE specification defines an escape clause as "a syntactic mechanism for vendor-specific SQL extensions to be implemented within the framework of standardized SQL." Both DB2 CLI and ODBC support vendor escape clauses, and escape clauses are currently used extensively by ODBC to define various SQL extensions. DB2 CLI translates these ODBC extensions into the correct SQL syntax.

If an application accesses only DB2 data sources, there is no reason to use escape clauses. However, if an application accesses other data sources that offer the same SQL support but use different syntax, then using escape clauses will increase the portability of that application.

The following are examples of what **SQLNativeSql()** might return for an input SQL string containing the ODBC scalar function **CONVERT()**. Assume that the column EmpID is of type **INTEGER** in the data source:

```
SELECT { fn CONVERT (EmpID, SQL_SMALLINT) } FROM Employee
```

A driver for Microsoft SQL Server might return the following translated SQL string:

```
SELECT convert (smallint, EmpID) FROM Employee
```

A driver for ORACLE Server might return the following translated SQL string:

```
SELECT to_number (EmpID) FROM Employee
```

A driver for Ingress might return the following translated SQL string:

```
SELECT int2 (EmpID) FROM Employee
```

Return Codes SQL_SUCCESS, SQL_SUCCESS_WITH_INFO, SQL_INVALID_HANDLE, or SQL_ERROR

SQLSTATEs If this function returns SQL_SUCCESS_WITH_INFO or SQL_ERROR, one of the following SQLSTATE values may be obtained by calling the SQLGetDiagRec() function:

01004, **08**003, **37**000, **HY**001, **HY**009, or **HY**090

Refer to Appendix B for detailed information about each SQLSTATE value that can be returned.

Comments ■ This function does not execute the SQL statement stored in the *SQLStringIn* parameter.

■ If the translated SQL statement string's actual length is greater than or equal to the maximum string size value specified in the *StringOutMaxSize* parameter, it is truncated to *StringOutMaxSize—1* (the length of a NULL-termination character) characters.

■ If the translated SQL statement string to be returned in the *SQLStringOut* parameter is a Unicode string, the *SQLStringOutMaxSize* parameter must contain an even number.

■ DB2 CLI can detect only vendor escape clause syntax errors; since the transformed SQL string is not passed to the data source for preparation, syntax errors that might be detected by the data source are not displayed. (The statement is not passed to the data source for preparation because the preparation might inadvertently initiate a transaction.)

■ Translation (mapping) only occurs if the input SQL statement string (*SQLStringIn*) contains one or more vendor escape clause sequences.

Prerequisites There are no prerequisites for using this function call.

Restrictions There are no restrictions associated with this function call.

Example The following Visual C++ program illustrates how to use the SQLNativeSql() function to show how an SQL statement will be converted before it is sent to the underlying data source for processing.

```
/*-----------------------------------------------------------*/
/* NAME:    CH9EX6.CPP                                       */
/* PURPOSE: Illustrate How To Use The Following CLI API Function  */
/*          In A C++ Program:                                */
/*                                                           */
/*              SQLNativeSql()                               */
/*                                                           */
```

```
/* OTHER CLI APIs SHOWN:                                               */
/*              SQLAllocHandle()         SQLSetEnvAttr()               */
/*              SQLConnect()             SQLDisconnect()               */
/*              SQLFreeHandle()                                        */
/*                                                                     */
/*---------------------------------------------------------------------*/

// Include The Appropriate Header Files
#include <windows.h>
#include <sqlcli1.h>
#include <iostream.h>

// Define The CLI_Class Class
class CLI_Class
{
    // Attributes
    public:
        SQLHANDLE    EnvHandle;
        SQLHANDLE    ConHandle;
        SQLHANDLE    StmtHandle;
        SQLRETURN    rc;

    // Operations
    public:
        CLI_Class();                           // Constructor
        ~CLI_Class();                          // Destructor
};

// Define The Class Constructor
CLI_Class::CLI_Class()
{
    // Initialize The Return Code Variable
    rc = SQL_SUCCESS;

    // Allocate An Environment Handle
    rc = SQLAllocHandle(SQL_HANDLE_ENV, SQL_NULL_HANDLE, &EnvHandle);

    // Set The ODBC Application Version To 3.x
    if (rc == SQL_SUCCESS)
        rc = SQLSetEnvAttr(EnvHandle, SQL_ATTR_ODBC_VERSION,
                (SQLPOINTER) SQL_OV_ODBC3, SQL_IS_UINTEGER);

    // Allocate A Connection Handle
    if (rc == SQL_SUCCESS)
        rc = SQLAllocHandle(SQL_HANDLE_DBC, EnvHandle, &ConHandle);
}

// Define The Class Destructor
CLI_Class::~CLI_Class()
{
    // Free The Connection Handle
    if (ConHandle != NULL)
        SQLFreeHandle(SQL_HANDLE_DBC, ConHandle);

    // Free The Environment Handle
```

```
        if (EnvHandle != NULL)
            SQLFreeHandle(SQL_HANDLE_ENV, EnvHandle);
}


/*————————————————————————————————————————————*/
/* The Main Function                                            */
/*————————————————————————————————————————————*/
int main()
{
    // Declare The Local Memory Variables
    SQLRETURN    rc = SQL_SUCCESS;
    SQLCHAR      SQLStmt[255];
    SQLCHAR      TranslatedStmt[255];
    SQLINTEGER   StmtLen;

    // Create An Instance Of The CLI_Class Class
    CLI_Class    Example;

    // Connect To The DB2 Sample Database
    if (Example.ConHandle != NULL)
    {
        rc = SQLConnect(Example.ConHandle, (SQLCHAR *) "SAMPLE",
                SQL_NTS, (SQLCHAR *) "userid", SQL_NTS,
                (SQLCHAR *) "password", SQL_NTS);

        // Define A SELECT SQL Statement That Contains A CLI
        // Scalar Function And An Escape Sequence
        strcpy((char *) SQLStmt, "SELECT {fn UCASE (LASTNAME) } ");
        strcat((char *) SQLStmt, "FROM EMPLOYEE");

        // Obtain And Display The Translated SQL Statement
        rc = SQLNativeSql(Example.ConHandle, SQLStmt, SQL_NTS,
                TranslatedStmt, sizeof(TranslatedStmt), &StmtLen);
        if (rc == SQL_SUCCESS)
        {
            cout << "Original Statement :" << endl << endl;
            cout << "    " << SQLStmt << endl << endl;
            cout << "Translated Statement :" <<endl << endl;
            cout << "    " << TranslatedStmt << endl;
        }

        // Disconnect From The DB2 Sample Database
        rc = SQLDisconnect(Example.ConHandle);
    }

    // Return To The Operating System
    return(rc);
}
```

SQLParamData

COMPATIBILITY

X/OPEN 95 CLI	ISO/IEC 92 CLI	DB2 CLI 5.2	DB2 CLI 2.0	ODBC 3.x
☑	☑	☑	☑	☑

ODBC API CONFORMANCE LEVEL   **CORE***

*IN ODBC 2.0, THIS FUNCTION WAS A LEVEL 1 API CONFORMANCE LEVEL FUNCTION

Purpose   The **SQLParamData()** function is used in conjunction with the **SQLPutData()** function to send data for data-at-execution parameters to the appropriate data source when an SQL statement is executed.

Syntax
```
SQLRETURN    SQLParamData        (SQLHSTMT      StatementHandle,
                                  SQLPOINTER    *Value);
```

Parameters   *StatementHandle*   An SQL statement handle that refers to a previously allocated SQL statement information storage buffer (data structure).

         Value   A pointer to a location in memory where the actual value associated with a bound parameter or column is stored. This will be the same location in memory that was specified with the **SQLBindParameter()** function.

Description   The **SQLParamData()** function is used in conjunction with the **SQLPutData()** function to send data for data-at-execution parameters to the appropriate data source when an SQL statement is executed.

Data-at-execution parameters are bound to application variables at the same time other parameters are bound to application variables; however, with data-at-execution parameters the value **SQL_DATA_AT_EXEC**, instead of the data value size, is specified (via length/indicator variables) during the binding process. When an application calls **SQLExecute()** or **SQLExecDirect()** (to execute the SQL statement), DB2 CLI returns **SQL_NEED_DATA** when it encounters a data-at-execution parameter. The application then calls this function to determine which data it should send. The value placed in the rowset buffer when the parameter was bound is returned. The application then uses this information to retrieve the data that is to be sent to the data source.

Once the application knows what data to send, it calls the **SQLPutData()** function repeatedly until all the data-at-execution data for the parameter has been sent. After all data has been sent, the application calls this function again to inform DB2 CLI that all the requested data has been sent and to advance to the next (if any) data-at-execution parameter. If no more data-at-execution parameters exist, the DB2 CLI returns **SQL_SUCCESS** or **SQL_SUCCESS_WITH_INFO** to the application and the SQL statement is executed.

Return Codes   `SQL_SUCCESS`, `SQL_SUCCESS_WITH_INFO`, `SQL_NEED_DATA`, `SQL_NO_DATA`, `SQL_STILL_EXECUTING`, `SQL_INVALID_HANDLE`, or `SQL_ERROR`

SQLSTATEs   If this function returns `SQL_SUCCESS_WITH_INFO` or `SQL_ERROR`, one of the following SQLSTATE values may be obtained by calling the `SQLGetDiagRec()` function:

07006, **08**S01, **22**026, **40**001, **40**003, **HY**000, **HY**001, **HY**008, **HY**010, **HY**013, **HY**092, **HY**506, **HY**509, or **HYT**00

Refer to Appendix B for detailed information about each SQLSTATE value that can be returned.

Since this function is called to send data for a data-at-execution parameter in an SQL statement, it can return any SQLSTATE that can be returned by the function called to execute the statement (`SQLExecute()` or `SQLExecDirect()`).

Comments   ▪ If the SQL statement being executed is a searched **UPDATE** statement or a searched **DELETE** statement that does not affect rows in the data source, `SQL_NO_DATA` is returned to the calling application when this function is called.

▪ The information returned by this function is also available in the `SQL_DESC_DATA_PTR` field of the IPD descriptor parameter record associated with the statement handle specified.

Prerequisites   There are no prerequisites for using this function call.

Restrictions   If this function returns `SQL_NEED_DATA` to an application, only `SQLPutData()` or `SQLCancel()` can be called.

See Also   `SQLPutData()`, `SQLCancel()`, `SQLBindParameter()`, `SQLExecute()`, `SQLExecDirect()`

Example   The following Visual C++ program illustrates how to use the `SQLParamData()` and `SQLPutData()` functions to send long data values to a data source.

```
/*------------------------------------------------------------------*/
/* NAME:    CH17EX7.CPP                                             */
/* PURPOSE: Illustrate How To Use The Following CLI API Functions   */
/*          In A C++ Program:                                       */
/*                                                                  */
/*              SQLParamData()                                      */
/*              SQLPutData()                                        */
/*              SQLCancel()                                         */
/*                                                                  */
/* OTHER CLI APIs SHOWN:                                            */
/*              SQLAllocHandle()              SQLSetEnvAttr()       */
/*              SQLConnect()                  SQLPrepare()          */
/*              SQLBindParameter()            SQLExecute()          */
/*              SQLDisconnect()               SQLFreeHandle()       */
/*                                                                  */
/*------------------------------------------------------------------*/

// Include The Appropriate Header Files
#include <windows.h>
#include <sqlcli1.h>
#include <iostream.h>
```

```
#include <fstream.h>

// Define The CLI_Class Class
class CLI_Class
{
    // Attributes
    public:
        SQLHANDLE    EnvHandle;
        SQLHANDLE    ConHandle;
        SQLHANDLE    StmtHandle;
        SQLRETURN    rc;

    // Operations
    public:
        CLI_Class();                            // Constructor
        ~CLI_Class();                           // Destructor
        SQLRETURN SendLongData();
};

// Define The Class Constructor
CLI_Class::CLI_Class()
{
    // Initialize The Return Code Variable
    rc = SQL_SUCCESS;

    // Allocate An Environment Handle
    rc = SQLAllocHandle(SQL_HANDLE_ENV, SQL_NULL_HANDLE, &EnvHandle);

    // Set The ODBC Application Version To 3.x
    if (rc == SQL_SUCCESS)
        rc = SQLSetEnvAttr(EnvHandle, SQL_ATTR_ODBC_VERSION,
                    (SQLPOINTER) SQL_OV_ODBC3, SQL_IS_UINTEGER);

    // Allocate A Connection Handle
    if (rc == SQL_SUCCESS)
        rc = SQLAllocHandle(SQL_HANDLE_DBC, EnvHandle, &ConHandle);
}

// Define The Class Destructor
CLI_Class::~CLI_Class()
{
    // Free The Connection Handle
    if (ConHandle != NULL)
        SQLFreeHandle(SQL_HANDLE_DBC, ConHandle);

    // Free The Environment Handle
    if (EnvHandle != NULL)
        SQLFreeHandle(SQL_HANDLE_ENV, EnvHandle);
}

// Define The SendLongData() Member Function
SQLRETURN CLI_Class::SendLongData(void)
{
    // Declare The Local Memory Variables
    ifstream     InFile;
```

```cpp
SQLPOINTER   Value;
SQLCHAR      Buffer[250];
SQLCHAR      InputParam[] = "Resume";
size_t       DataSize = 0;

// Open An External Data File - If An Error Occurs, Call
// The SQLCancel() Function To Terminate The Data-At-Execution
// Sequence And Exit
InFile.open("RESUME.TXT", ios::in | ios::nocreate | ios::binary);
if (InFile.fail())
{
    rc = SQLCancel(StmtHandle);
    return(SQL_ERROR);
}


// Start The Data-At-Execution Sequence By Calling
// SQLParamData()
rc = SQLParamData(StmtHandle, (SQLPOINTER *) &Value);

// Examine The Contents Of Value (Returned By SQLParamData())
// To Determine Which Data-At-Execution Parameter Currently
// Needs Data
if (strcmp((const char *) Value, (const char *) InputParam) == 0
    && rc ==  SQL_NEED_DATA)
{
    // As Long As Data Is Available For The Parameter, Retrieve
    // Part Of It From The External Data File And Send It To The
    // Data Source
    while (InFile.read(Buffer, sizeof(Buffer)))
    {
        rc = SQLPutData(StmtHandle, (SQLPOINTER) Buffer,
                sizeof(Buffer));
        DataSize = DataSize + sizeof(Buffer);

        // If The Amount Of Data Retrieved Exceeds The Size Of
        // The Column (Which Is 5120 Bytes), Call The
            // SQLCancel() Function To Terminate The Data-At-
            // Execution Sequence And Exit
        if (DataSize > 5120)
        {
            rc = SQLCancel(StmtHandle);
            return(SQL_ERROR);
        }
    }

    // Call SQLParamData() Again To Terminate The
    // Data-At-Execution Sequence
    rc = SQLParamData(StmtHandle, (SQLPOINTER *) &Value);

    // Display A Message Telling How Many Bytes Of Data Were Sent
    if (rc == SQL_SUCCESS || rc == SQL_SUCCESS_WITH_INFO)
    {
        cout << "Successfully inserted " << DataSize ;
        cout << " bytes of data into the database." << endl;
    }
```

```
    }

    // Close The External Data File
    InFile.close();

    // Return The CLI API Return Code To The Calling Function
    return(rc);
}


/*———————————————————————————————————————————————————————————*/
/* The Main Function                                          */
/*———————————————————————————————————————————————————————————*/
int main()
{
    // Declare The Local Memory Variables
    SQLRETURN      rc = SQL_SUCCESS;
    SQLCHAR        SQLStmt[255];
    SQLCHAR        InputParam[7] = "Resume";
    SQLINTEGER     Indicator = SQL_DATA_AT_EXEC;

    // Create An Instance Of The CLI_Class Class
    CLI_Class      Example;

    // Connect To The DB2 Sample Database
    if (Example.ConHandle != NULL)
    {
        rc = SQLConnect(Example.ConHandle, (SQLCHAR *) "SAMPLE",
                SQL_NTS, (SQLCHAR *) "userid", SQL_NTS,
                (SQLCHAR *) "password", SQL_NTS);

        // Allocate An SQL Statement Handle
        rc = SQLAllocHandle(SQL_HANDLE_STMT, Example.ConHandle,
                &Example.StmtHandle);
        if (rc == SQL_SUCCESS)
        {
            // Define An INSERT SQL Statement That Contains A
            // Data-At-Execution Parameter
            strcpy((char *) SQLStmt, "INSERT INTO EMP_RESUME ");
            strcat((char *) SQLStmt, "(EMPNO, RESUME_FORMAT,");
            strcat((char *) SQLStmt, " RESUME) VALUES ");
            strcat((char *) SQLStmt, "('000100', 'ASCII', ?)");

            // Prepare The SQL Statement
            rc = SQLPrepare(Example.StmtHandle, SQLStmt, SQL_NTS);

            // Bind The Parameter Marker In The SQL Statement To A
            // Local Application Variable - This Parameter Will Use
            // SQLParamData() And SQLPutData() To Send Data In Pieces
            // (Note: The Column Size Is 5120 Characters)
            rc = SQLBindParameter(Example.StmtHandle, 1,
                    SQL_PARAM_INPUT, SQL_C_DEFAULT, SQL_CHAR, 5120,
                    0, (SQLPOINTER) InputParam, 7, &Indicator);

            // Execute The SQL Statement
```

```
        rc = SQLExecute(Example.StmtHandle);

        // The Return Code SQL_NEED_DATA Should Be Returned,
        // Indicating That SQLParamData() And SQLPutData() Need
        // To Be Called
        if (rc == SQL_NEED_DATA)
            rc = Example.SendLongData();

        // Free The SQL Statement Handle
        if (Example.StmtHandle != NULL)
            SQLFreeHandle(SQL_HANDLE_STMT, Example.StmtHandle);
    }

    // Disconnect From The DB2 Sample Database
    rc = SQLDisconnect(Example.ConHandle);
}

    // Return To The Operating System
    return(rc);
}
```

SQLPutData

COMPATIBILITY

X/OPEN 95 CLI	ISO/IEC 92 CLI	DB2 CLI 5.2	DB2 CLI 2.0	ODBC 3.x
☑	☑	☑	☑	☑

ODBC API CONFORMANCE LEVEL   CORE*

*IN ODBC 2.0, THIS FUNCTION WAS A LEVEL 1 API CONFORMANCE LEVEL FUNCTION

Purpose   The **SQLPutData()** function is used in conjunction with the **SQLParamData()** function to send data for data-at-execution parameters to the appropriate data source when an SQL statement is executed.

Syntax
```
SQLRETURN    SQLPutData    (SQLHSTMT      StatementHandle,
                            SQLPOINTER    Value,
                            SQLINTEGER    ValueSize_Indicator);
```

Parameters   *StatementHandle*   An SQL statement handle that refers to a previously allocated SQL statement information storage buffer (data structure).

Value   A pointer to a location in memory where the data value (or a portion of the data value) for the parameter marker that was specified in the **SQLBindParameter()** function is stored.

ValueSize_Indicator	Either the number of bytes of data to be sent to the data source when this function is executed OR one of the following special indicator values:

> ▪ **SQL_NTS**
> The data value is a NULL-terminated string.

> ▪ **SQL_NULL_DATA**
> The data value is a NULL value.

Description   The **SQLPutData()** function is used in conjunction with the **SQLParamData()** function to send data for data-at-execution parameters to the appropriate data source when an SQL statement is executed.

Data-at-execution parameters are bound to application variables at the same time other parameters are bound to application variables; however, with data-at-execution parameters, the value **SQL_DATA_AT_EXEC**, instead of the data value size, is specified during the binding process. When an application calls **SQLExecute()** or **SQLExecDirect()** (to execute the SQL statement), DB2 CLI returns **SQL_NEED_DATA** when it encounters a data-at-execution parameter. The application then calls the **SQLParamData()** function to determine which data it should send; the value placed in the rowset buffer when the parameter was bound is returned. The application then uses this information to retrieve the data that is to be sent to the data source.

Once the application knows what data to send, it calls this function repeatedly until all the data-at-execution data for the parameter has been sent to the data source. After all data has been sent, the application calls the **SQLParamData()** function again to inform DB2 CLI that all the requested data has been sent and to advance to the next (if any) data-at-execution parameter. If no more data-at-execution parameters exist, DB2 CLI returns **SQL_SUCCESS** or **SQL_SUCCESS_WITH_INFO** to the application and the SQL statement is executed.

Return Codes   SQL_SUCCESS, SQL_SUCCESS_WITH_INFO, SQL_STILL_EXECUTING, SQL_INVALID_HANDLE, or SQL_ERROR

SQLSTATEs   If this function returns **SQL_SUCCESS_WITH_INFO** or **SQL_ERROR**, one of the following SQLSTATE values may be obtained by calling the **SQLGetDiagRec()** function:

01004, 08S01, **22**001, **22**003, **22**005, **22**007, **40**003, **HY**001, **HY**008, **HY**009, **HY**010, or **HYT**00

Refer to Appendix B for detailed information about each SQLSTATE value that can be returned.

NOTE: *Some of these SQLSTATEs may be reported on the final* **SQLParamData()** *function call rather than when the* **SQLPutData()** *function is called.*

Since this function is called to send data for a data-at-execution parameter in an SQL statement, it can return any SQLSTATE that can be returned by the function called to execute the statement (**SQLExecute()** or **SQLExecDirect()**).

Comments
- The value stored in the *ValueSize_Indicator* parameter is ignored unless:
  - The C data type of the parameter or column is **SQL_C_CHAR** or **SQL_C_BINARY**.
  - The C data type of the parameter or column is **SQL_C_DEFAULT** and the default C data type for the specified SQL data type is **SQL_C_CHAR** or **SQL_C_BINARY**.
  - The value is **SQL_NTS** or **SQL_NULL_DATA**.
- The amount of data sent to the data source by this function can vary for a given parameter.

Prerequisites The **SQLParamData()** function must be executed before this function is called.

Restrictions This function can be called multiple times to send large data values to the data source in several small pieces—but only when sending character or binary data to a column with a character, binary, or data source-specific data type. If this function is called multiple times under any other conditions, **SQL_ERROR** and SQLSTATE **HY**019 (Non-character and non-binary data sent in pieces) are returned.

See Also SQLParamData(), SQLCancel(), SQLBindParameter(), SQLExecute(), SQLExecDirect()

Example See the example provided for the **SQLParamData()** function on page 318.

SQLCancel

COMPATIBILITY

X/OPEN 95 CLI	ISO/IEC 92 CLI	DB2 CLI 5.2	DB2 CLI 2.0	ODBC 3.x
☑	☑	☑	☑	☑

ODBC API CONFORMANCE LEVEL   **CORE**

Purpose The **SQLCancel()** function is used to terminate SQL statement processing.

Syntax SQLRETURN SQLCancel   (SQLHSTMT   *StatementHandle*);

Parameters *StatementHandle*   An SQL statement handle that refers to a previously allocated SQL statement information storage buffer (data structure).

Description The **SQLCancel()** function is used to terminate SQL statement pro-cessing. Specifically, this function is used to end the following:
- A CLI function (processing an SQL statement) running asynchronously.
- A data-at-execution sequence.
- A function running on another thread.

CANCELING ASYNCHRONOUS PROCESSING When an application executes a function asynchronously, DB2 CLI performs a minimal amount of processing (such as checking arguments for errors), hands the rest of the processing to the data source, and returns control to the application, along with the **SQL_STILL_EXECUTING** return code. The application is then free to perform other tasks; however it must poll DB2 CLI at regular intervals, by calling the function with the same arguments that were originally used, to determine when the asynchronous function is finished.

After DB2 CLI returns **SQL_STILL_EXECUTING** and before it returns a return code indicating the function has completed execution, the **SQLCancel()** function can be called to try to terminate the function's execution. Unfortunately, when **SQLCancel()** is called, there is no guarantee that function execution was actually canceled; the return code returned by **SQLCancel()** only indicates whether **SQLCancel()** successfully attempted to cancel the function. The only way an application can determine whether the asynchronous function's processing was canceled is by polling DB2 CLI after **SQLCancel()** is called. If the function was canceled, DB2 CLI returns **SQL_ERROR** and SQLSTATE **HY**008 (Operation canceled).

CANCELING A DATA-AT-EXECUTION SEQUENCE Data-at-execution parameters are bound to application variables at the same time other parameters are bound to application variables; however, with data-at-execution parameter the value **SQL_DATA_AT_EXEC**, instead of the data value size, is specified (via a length/indicator variable) during the binding process. When an application calls **SQLExecute()** or **SQLExecDirect()** (to execute the SQL statement), DB2 CLI returns **SQL_NEED_DATA** when it encounters a data-at-execution parameter. The application then calls the **SQLParamData()** function to determine which data it should send.

Once the application knows what data to send, it calls the **SQLPutData()** function repeatedly until all the data-at-execution data for the parameter has been sent to the data source. After all data has been sent, the application calls the **SQLParamData()** function again to inform DB2 CLI that all the requested data has been sent and to advance to the next (if any) data-at-execution parameter. If no more data-at-execution parameters exist, DB2 CLI returns **SQL_SUCCESS** or **SQL_SUCCESS_WITH_INFO** to the application and the SQL statement is executed.

After the driver returns **SQL_NEED_DATA**, and before data has been sent for all data-at-execution parameters, the **SQLCancel()** function can be called to terminate the data-at-execution sequence. After the data-at-execution sequence has been canceled, the **SQLExecute()** or **SQLExecDirect()** function can be called again; canceling a data-at-execution sequence has no effect on the SQL statement, the cursor state, or the current cursor position.

CANCELING FUNCTIONS IN MULTITHREAD APPLICATIONS In a multithread application, an application can call a CLI function synchronously on another thread. An application can terminate a function running on a separate thread by calling **SQLCancel()** with the same statement handle that was used to invoke the target function. As with asynchronous functions, the **SQLCancel()** function's return code only indicates whether DB2 CLI processed the request successfully. If the function is indeed canceled, it returns **SQL_ERROR** and SQLSTATE **HY**008 (Operation canceled).

If an SQL statement is being executed by the function that **SQLCancel()** is attempting to terminate, it's possible for both the SQL statement and the cancel operation to execute successfully and return **SQL_SUCCESS**. In this case, DB2 CLI assumes that any cursor opened by the SQL statement during execution was closed by the cancel operation. The result of this is that the application is no longer able to use the cursor.

Return Codes   SQL_SUCCESS, SQL_SUCCESS_WITH_INFO, SQL_INVALID_HANDLE, or SQL_ERROR

SQLSTATEs   If this function returns **SQL_SUCCESS_WITH_INFO** or **SQL_ERROR**, one of the following SQLSTATE values may be obtained by calling the **SQLGetDiagRec()** function:

HY001, **HY**013, **HY**018, 08S01, or **HY**506

Refer to Appendix B for detailed information about each SQLSTATE value that can be returned.

Comments   ■ When this function is called, diagnostic records are returned for a function running asynchronously on the statement handle specified OR for a function on the statement handle specified that needs data; diagnostic records are not returned, however, for a function running on a statement handle on another thread.

Prerequisites   There are no prerequisites for using this function call.

Restrictions   There are no restrictions associated with this function call.

See Also   SQLPutData(), SQLParamData(), SQLExecute(), SQLExecDirect()

Example   See the example provided for the **SQLParamData()** function on page 318.

SQLEndTran

COMPATIBILITY

X/OPEN 95 CLI	ISO/IEC 92 CLI	DB2 CLI 5.2	DB2 CLI 2.0	ODBC 3.x
✓	✓	✓	☐	✓

ODBC API CONFORMANCE LEVEL   **CORE**

Purpose   The **SQLEndTran()** function is used to request a commit or a rollback operation for all active transactions associated with a specific environment or connection handle.

Syntax   SQLRETURN   SQLEndTran   (SQLSMALLINT   *HandleType,*
                                      SQLHANDLE   *Handle,*
                                      SQLSMALLINT   *Action);*

Parameters   *HandleType*   Specifies which type of handle to request a commit or rollback operation for. This parameter must be set to one of the following values:

SQL_HANDLE_ENV
Request a commit or rollback operation for an environment handle.

SQL_HANDLE_DBC
Request a commit or rollback operation for a connection handle.

Handle   The environment or connection handle whose transaction(s) are to be terminated.

Action   The action to use to terminate the current transaction. This parameter must be set to one of the following values:

SQL_COMMIT
Terminate the current transaction and make all changes made to the data source by that transaction permanent.

SQL_ROLLBACK
Terminate the current transaction and back out (remove) all changes made to the data source by that transaction.

Description   The `SQLEndTran()` function is used to request a commit or a rollback operation for all active transactions associated with a specific connection handle. This function can also request that a commit or rollback operation be performed for all active transactions found on all connections associated with a specific environment handle. When this function is called, all changes made to the data source (via the specified connection or environment handle) since the connection was established or since the last call to the `SQLEndTran()` function was made (whichever is the most recent) are either committed or rolled back.

A transaction ends when the application calls this function—all active transactions associated with a data source connection must be ended before the connection to the data source can be terminated.

NOTE: *This function replaces the DB2 CLI 2.0 function* `SQLTransact()`.

Return Codes   SQL_SUCCESS, SQL_SUCCESS_WITH_INFO, SQL_INVALID_HANDLE, or SQL_ERROR

SQLSTATEs   If this function returns `SQL_SUCCESS_WITH_INFO` or `SQL_ERROR`, one of the following SQLSTATE values may be obtained by calling the `SQLGetDiagRec()` function:

01000, **08**003, **08**007, **40**001, **HY**000, **HY**001, **HY**010, **HY**012, or **HY**092

Refer to Appendix B for detailed information about each SQLSTATE value that can be returned.

Comments   ▪ This function cannot be used to commit or roll back transactions on a shared environment. If this function is called with either a shared environment handle or a shared environment's connection handle specified in the *Handle* parameter, **SQL_ERROR** and SQLSTATE **HY**092 (Invalid attribute/option identifier) will be returned.

■ If a valid environment handle is specified in the *Handle* parameter, DB2 CLI attempts to commit or roll back each active transaction found on all connection handles that are in the "Connected" state. DB2 CLI only returns **SQL_SUCCESS** if it receives **SQL_SUCCESS** from the data source associated with each connection handle found. If DB2 CLI receives **SQL_ERROR** from one or more connection handles, it returns **SQL_ERROR** to the application. The **SQLGetDiagRec()** function can then be called on each connection handle to determine which connection(s) failed during the commit or rollback operation.

■ If the *Action* parameter is set to **SQL_COMMIT**, this function issues a commit request for all active operations on all statement handles associated with each affected connection handle.

■ If the *Action* parameter is set to **SQL_ROLLBACK**, this function issues a rollback request for all active operations on all statement handles associated with each affected connection handle.

■ If no transactions are active when this function is called, **SQL_SUCCESS** is returned (indicating that there is no work to be committed or rolled back) and the data sources being used are not affected.

■ An application can call the **SQLGetInfo()** function with the **SQL_CURSOR_COMMIT_BEHAVIOR** and **SQL_CURSOR_ROLLBACK_BEHAVIOR** information type values specified to determine how transaction operations affect cursor behavior. If either of these information types return **SQL_CB_DELETE**, all open cursors on all statement handles associated with the connection handle are closed and deleted (and pending results are discarded) when this function is executed— SQL statement handles are left in the "Allocated" (unprepared) state and the application can either reuse them or free them.

If the **SQL_CURSOR_COMMIT_BEHAVIOR** or **SQL_CURSOR_ROLLBACK_BEHAVIOR** information types return **SQL_CB_CLOSE**, all open cursors on all statement handles associated with the connection handle are closed and SQL statement handles are left in the "Prepared" state; the application can execute the SQL statement associated with the statement handle by calling the **SQLExecute()** function without calling the **SQLPrepare()** function first.

If the **SQL_CURSOR_COMMIT_BEHAVIOR** or **SQL_CURSOR_ROLLBACK_BEHAVIOR** information types return **SQL_CB_PRESERVE**, open cursors associated with the connection handle are not affected by this function—cursors remain where they were before this function was called.

■ Data sources that do not support transactions are effectively always in autocommit mode. In this case, if this function is called with the *Action* parameter set to **SQL_COMMIT**, **SQL_SUCCESS** is returned; if this function is called with the *Action* parameter set to **SQL_ROLLBACK**, **SQL_ERROR** and SQLSTATE **HYC00** (Driver not capable) is returned, indicating that a rollback operation can not be performed.

■ When a DB2 CLI application is running in autocommit mode, the DB2 CLI driver does not pass this function to the server.

Prerequisites   There are no prerequisites for using this function call.

Restrictions   There are no restrictions associated with this function call.

See Also   `SQLGetInfo()`, `SQLFreeHandle()`, `SQLFreeStmt()`

Example   The following Visual C++ program illustrates how to use the `SQLEndTran()` function to terminate a transaction.

```
/*-----------------------------------------------------------------*/
/* NAME:      CH9EX8.CPP                                           */
/* PURPOSE: Illustrate How To Use The Following CLI API Function   */
/*          In A C++ Program:                                      */
/*                                                                 */
/*              SQLEndTran()                                       */
/*                                                                 */
/* OTHER CLI APIs SHOWN:                                           */
/*          SQLAllocHandle()            SQLSetEnvAttr()            */
/*          SQLConnect()                SQLSetConnectAttr()        */
/*          SQLExecDirect()             SQLBindCol()               */
/*          SQLFetch()                  SQLDisconnect()            */
/*          SQLFreeHandle()                                        */
/*                                                                 */
/*-----------------------------------------------------------------*/

// Include The Appropriate Header Files
#include <windows.h>
#include <sqlcli1.h>
#include <iostream.h>

// Define The CLI_Class Class
class CLI_Class
{
    // Attributes
    public:
        SQLHANDLE    EnvHandle;
        SQLHANDLE    ConHandle;
        SQLHANDLE    StmtHandle;
        SQLRETURN    rc;

    // Operations
    public:
        CLI_Class();                           // Constructor
        ~CLI_Class();                          // Destructor
        SQLRETURN ShowResults();
};

// Define The Class Constructor
CLI_Class::CLI_Class()
{
    // Initialize The Return Code Variable
    rc = SQL_SUCCESS;

    // Allocate An Environment Handle
    rc = SQLAllocHandle(SQL_HANDLE_ENV, SQL_NULL_HANDLE, &EnvHandle);

    // Set The ODBC Application Version To 3.x
```

```
        if (rc == SQL_SUCCESS)
            rc = SQLSetEnvAttr(EnvHandle, SQL_ATTR_ODBC_VERSION,
                        (SQLPOINTER) SQL_OV_ODBC3, SQL_IS_UINTEGER);

    // Allocate A Connection Handle
    if (rc == SQL_SUCCESS)
        rc = SQLAllocHandle(SQL_HANDLE_DBC, EnvHandle, &ConHandle);
}

// Define The Class Destructor
CLI_Class::~CLI_Class()
{
    // Free The Connection Handle
    if (ConHandle != NULL)
        SQLFreeHandle(SQL_HANDLE_DBC, ConHandle);

    // Free The Environment Handle
    if (EnvHandle != NULL)
        SQLFreeHandle(SQL_HANDLE_ENV, EnvHandle);
}

// Define The ShowResults() Member Function
SQLRETURN CLI_Class::ShowResults(void)
{
    // Declare The Local Memory Variables
    SQLCHAR   LastName[50];
    SQLCHAR   FirstName[50];

    // Bind The Columns In The Result Data Set Returned To
    // Application Variables
    rc = SQLBindCol(StmtHandle, 1, SQL_C_CHAR, (SQLPOINTER)
            LastName, sizeof(LastName), NULL);

    rc = SQLBindCol(StmtHandle, 2, SQL_C_CHAR, (SQLPOINTER)
            FirstName, sizeof(FirstName), NULL);

    // Display A Header
    cout << "Employees :" << endl << endl;

    // While There Are Records In The Result Data Set Generated,
    // Retrieve And Display Them
    while (rc != SQL_NO_DATA)
    {
        rc = SQLFetch(StmtHandle);
        if (rc != SQL_NO_DATA)
            cout << FirstName << " " << LastName << endl;
    }

    // Return The CLI API Return Code To The Calling Function
    return(rc);
}

/*----------------------------------------------------------------*/
/* The Main Function                                              */
/*----------------------------------------------------------------*/
```

```cpp
int main()
{
    // Declare The Local Memory Variables
    SQLRETURN   rc = SQL_SUCCESS;
    SQLCHAR     SQLStmt[255];

    // Create An Instance Of The CLI_Class Class
    CLI_Class   Example;

    // Connect To The DB2 Sample Database
    if (Example.ConHandle != NULL)
    {
        rc = SQLConnect(Example.ConHandle, (SQLCHAR *) "SAMPLE",
                 SQL_NTS, (SQLCHAR *) "userid", SQL_NTS,
                 (SQLCHAR *) "password", SQL_NTS);

        // Allocate An SQL Statement Handle
        rc = SQLAllocHandle(SQL_HANDLE_STMT, Example.ConHandle,
                 &Example.StmtHandle);
        if (rc == SQL_SUCCESS)
        {
            // Turn Manual-Commit Mode On
            rc = SQLSetConnectAttr(Example.ConHandle,
                     SQL_ATTR_AUTOCOMMIT,
                     (SQLPOINTER) SQL_AUTOCOMMIT_OFF,
                     SQL_IS_UINTEGER);

            // Define A SELECT SQL Statement
            strcpy((char *) SQLStmt, "SELECT LASTNAME, FIRSTNME ");
            strcat((char *) SQLStmt, "FROM EMPLOYEE");

            // Prepare And Execute The SQL Statement
            rc = SQLExecDirect(Example.StmtHandle, SQLStmt, SQL_NTS);

            // Display The Results Of The SQL Query
            if (rc == SQL_SUCCESS)
                Example.ShowResults();

            // Commit The Transaction
            rc = SQLEndTran(SQL_HANDLE_DBC, Example.ConHandle,
                     SQL_COMMIT);
              if (rc == SQL_SUCCESS)
              {
                  cout << endl;
                  cout << "Transaction Ended Successfully" << endl;
              }

            // Free The SQL Statement Handle
            if (Example.StmtHandle != NULL)
                SQLFreeHandle(SQL_HANDLE_STMT, Example.StmtHandle);
        }

        // Disconnect From The DB2 Sample Database
        rc = SQLDisconnect(Example.ConHandle);
```

```
      }

      // Return To The Operating System
      return(rc);
}
```

SQLFreeStmt

COMPATIBILITY

X/OPEN 95 CLI	ISO/IEC 92 CLI	DB2 CLI 5.2	DB2 CLI 2.0	ODBC 3.x
☒	☑	☑	☑	☐

ODBC API CONFORMANCE LEVEL   **CORE**

Purpose   The `SQLFreeStmt()` function is used to stop all processing associated with a specific SQL statement handle, discard all pending results, close any open cursors, and/or free all memory associated with a statement handle.

Syntax
```
SQLRETURN    SQLFreeStmt      (SQLHSTMT        StatementHandle,
                               SQLUSMALLINT    Option);
```

Parameters *StatementHandle*   An SQL statement handle that refers to a previously allocated SQL statement information storage buffer (data structure).

Option   The method to use when freeing the SQL statement handle. This parameter must be set to one of the following values:

■ **SQL_CLOSE**
Close all cursors associated with the SQL statement handle and discard any pending results. In this case, the SQL statement handle itself is not destroyed.

■ **SQL_DROP**
Close all cursors associated with the SQL statement handle, discard any pending results, and free all resources associated with the SQL statement handle. In this case, the SQL statement handle is destroyed and must be reallocated before it can be used again.

■ **SQL_UNBIND**
Unbind (release) all column buffers currently bound to the SQL statement handle.

■ **SQL_RESET_PARAMS**
Release all parameter marker buffers bound to the SQL statement handle.

Description   The **SQLFreeStmt()** function invalidates and frees or re-initializes an SQL statement handle. When this function is invoked one or more of the following take place:

- All processing being done by the SQL statement associated with the SQL statement handle is stopped.
- All open cursors associated with the SQL statement handle are closed.
- All parameter bindings are reset.
- All result data set columns that have been bound to application variables and LOB locators are unbound.
- All DB2 CLI resources associated with the SQL statement handle are freed and the SQL statement handle is deleted (dropped).

This function can be called for each SQL statement handle created with the **SQLAllocHandle()** function when all processing associated with that SQL statement handle has been completed.

NOTE: *The* **SQLFreeHandle()** *function can be used in place of this function to free a statement handle.*

Return Codes   SQL_SUCCESS, SQL_SUCCESS_WITH_INFO, SQL_INVALID_HANDLE, or SQL_ERROR

SQLSTATEs   If this function returns **SQL_SUCCESS_WITH_INFO** or **SQL_ERROR**, one of the following SQLSTATE values may be obtained by calling the **SQLError()** function:

40003, **08**S01, **58**004, **HY**001, **HY**010, **HY**092, or **HY**506

Refer to Appendix B for detailed information about each SQLSTATE value that can be returned.

Comments
- An application can call this function to terminate processing of a **SELECT** SQL statement without freeing the statement handle.
- The **SQL_DROP** option frees all resources allocated by the **SQLAllocHandle()** function.
- If this function is called with the **SQL_CLOSE** option specified, all cursors associated with the SQL statement handle will be closed and all pending results will be discarded. You can reopen cursors by calling the **SQLExecute()** function (the same or different values can be supplied in application variables that were bound to the SQL statement handle before this function was called).
- The cursor name associated with an SQL statement handle is retained until the handle is dropped or until the next successful **SQLSetCursorName()** function call is executed.
- If this function is called with the **SQL_UNBIND** option specified, all associations between application variables and/or file references and the columns of the result data set are destroyed. Likewise, all associations between application variables and/or file references and the parameter markers in the SQL statement referenced by the SQL statement handle are destroyed.

■ This statement has no effect on LOB locators; the **SQLExecute()** or the **SQLExecDirect()** function must be called to execute a **FREE LOCATOR** SQL statement in order to free a LOB locator.

■ If an SQL statement handle is associated with a result data set that has columns bound to application variables and/or file references, and if the number or data type of the bound variables and/or file references changes, all bound columns must be unbound before the SQL statement handle can be reused.

■ The **SQL_SUCCESS_WITH_INFO** return code cannot be returned if this function is called with the **SQL_DROP** option specified, since there would no longer be a valid statement handle to pass to the **SQLGetDiagRec()** or **SQLGetDiagField()** functions.

Prerequisites   There are no prerequisites for using this function call.

Restrictions   There are no restrictions associated with this function call.

See Also   SQLEndTran(), SQLAllocHandle(), SQLCancel()

Example   The following Visual C++ program illustrates how to use the **SQLFreeStmt()** function to close an open cursor and release all column bindings associated with a statement handle.

```
/*─────────────────────────────────────────────────────────────────────*/
/* NAME:     CH9EX9.CPP                                                  */
/* PURPOSE: Illustrate How To Use The Following CLI API Function         */
/*          In A C++ Program:                                            */
/*                                                                       */
/*                  SQLFreeStmt()                                        */
/*                                                                       */
/* OTHER CLI APIs SHOWN:                                                 */
/*              SQLAllocHandle()              SQLSetEnvAttr()            */
/*              SQLConnect()                  SQLExecDirect()           */
/*              SQLBindCol()                  SQLFetch()                */
/*              SQLDisconnect()               SQLFreeHandle()           */
/*                                                                       */
/*─────────────────────────────────────────────────────────────────────*/

// Include The Appropriate Header Files
#include <windows.h>
#include <sqlclil.h>
#include <iostream.h>

// Define The CLI_Class Class
class CLI_Class
{
    // Attributes
    public:
        SQLHANDLE    EnvHandle;
        SQLHANDLE    ConHandle;
        SQLHANDLE    StmtHandle;
        SQLRETURN    rc;

    // Operations
    public:
```

```
            CLI_Class();                              // Constructor
            ~CLI_Class();                             // Destructor
            SQLRETURN ShowResults();
};

// Define The Class Constructor
CLI_Class::CLI_Class()
{
    // Initialize The Return Code Variable
    rc = SQL_SUCCESS;

    // Allocate An Environment Handle
    rc = SQLAllocHandle(SQL_HANDLE_ENV, SQL_NULL_HANDLE, &EnvHandle);

    // Set The ODBC Application Version To 3.x
    if (rc == SQL_SUCCESS)
        rc = SQLSetEnvAttr(EnvHandle, SQL_ATTR_ODBC_VERSION,
                    (SQLPOINTER) SQL_OV_ODBC3, SQL_IS_UINTEGER);

    // Allocate A Connection Handle
    if (rc == SQL_SUCCESS)
        rc = SQLAllocHandle(SQL_HANDLE_DBC, EnvHandle, &ConHandle);
}


// Define The Class Destructor
CLI_Class::~CLI_Class()
{
    // Free The Connection Handle
    if (ConHandle != NULL)
        SQLFreeHandle(SQL_HANDLE_DBC, ConHandle);

    // Free The Environment Handle
    if (EnvHandle != NULL)
        SQLFreeHandle(SQL_HANDLE_ENV, EnvHandle);
}

// Define The ShowResults() Member Function
SQLRETURN CLI_Class::ShowResults(void)
{
    // Declare The Local Memory Variables
    SQLCHAR    LastName[50];
    SQLCHAR    FirstName[50];
    int        Counter = 0;

    // Bind The Columns In The Result Data Set Returned To
    // Application Variables
    rc = SQLBindCol(StmtHandle, 1, SQL_C_CHAR, (SQLPOINTER)
            LastName, sizeof(LastName), NULL);

    rc = SQLBindCol(StmtHandle, 2, SQL_C_CHAR, (SQLPOINTER)
            FirstName, sizeof(FirstName), NULL);

    // Display A Header
    cout << "Employees :" << endl << endl;
```

```
    // While There Are Records In The Result Data Set Generated,
    // Retrieve And Display Them
    while (rc != SQL_NO_DATA)
    {
        rc = SQLFetch(StmtHandle);
        if (rc != SQL_NO_DATA)
            cout << FirstName << " " << LastName << endl;

        // Increment The Loop Counter - Stop When The First
        // 15 Records Have Been Displayed, Close The Cursor,
        // And Release All Column Bindings
        Counter++;
        if (Counter == 15)
        {
            rc = SQLFreeStmt(StmtHandle, SQL_CLOSE);
            rc = SQLFreeStmt(StmtHandle, SQL_UNBIND);
            break;
        }
    }

    // Return The CLI API Return Code To The Calling Function
    return(rc);
}

/*----------------------------------------------------------*/
/* The Main Function                                        */
/*----------------------------------------------------------*/
int main()
{
    // Declare The Local Memory Variables
    SQLRETURN  rc = SQL_SUCCESS;
    SQLCHAR    SQLStmt[255];

    // Create An Instance Of The CLI_Class Class
    CLI_Class  Example;

    // Connect To The DB2 Sample Database
    if (Example.ConHandle != NULL)
    {
        rc = SQLConnect(Example.ConHandle, (SQLCHAR *) "SAMPLE",
                SQL_NTS, (SQLCHAR *) "userid", SQL_NTS,
                (SQLCHAR *) "password", SQL_NTS);

        // Allocate An SQL Statement Handle
        rc = SQLAllocHandle(SQL_HANDLE_STMT, Example.ConHandle,
                &Example.StmtHandle);
        if (rc == SQL_SUCCESS)
        {
            // Define A SELECT SQL Statement
            strcpy((char *) SQLStmt, "SELECT LASTNAME, FIRSTNME ");
            strcat((char *) SQLStmt, "FROM EMPLOYEE");

            // Prepare And Execute The SQL Statement
            SQLExecDirect(Example.StmtHandle, SQLStmt, SQL_NTS);
```

```
                    // Display The Results Of The SQL Query
                    if (rc == SQL_SUCCESS)
                        Example.ShowResults();

                    // Free The SQL Statement Handle
                    if (Example.StmtHandle != NULL)
                        SQLFreeHandle(SQL_HANDLE_STMT, Example.StmtHandle);
                }

                // Disconnect From The DB2 Sample Database
                rc = SQLDisconnect(Example.ConHandle);
            }

            // Return To The Operating System
            return(rc);
        }
```

Retrieving Results (Basic)

When **SELECT** SQL statements, stored procedures containing **SELECT** SQL statements, or CLI catalog functions are submitted to a data source for execution, a conceptual table known as a *result data set* is created and populated with all data from the data source that matches the selection criteria specified. The process of retrieving rows of data from a result data set and returning them to an application, in tabular form, is called *fetching*. This chapter is designed to introduce you to the basic set of API functions used to fetch data from a result data set.

This chapter begins by examining the *metadata* that is used to describe a result data set. This is followed by an introduction to the functions used to retrieve metadata information and return that information to an application. Next, the process of associating (binding) application variables and buffers to columns in a result data set is described. Then, the basic *cursor* is introduced, along with the functions used to retrieve and set the name of the cursor associated with a result data set. This is followed by an introduction to the function used to fetch a row of data from a result data set and return results to all *bound* variables. Next, the function used to obtain data values from *unbound* columns in a result data set is discussed. Finally, a detailed reference section covering each CLI function that can be used to obtain result data set metadata and perform basic data retrieval is provided.

Was A Result Data Set Created?

When an application contains hard-coded SQL statements, the application developer usually knows whether one or more of the SQL statements used will generate a result data set. However, when an application constructs SQL statements at run time, the developer does not always know when a result data set will be created. This is particularly true if the application provides a way for users to enter and execute customized SQL statements. It is also true when an application constructs an SQL statement at run time that calls a stored procedure.

In both cases, an application can call the **SQLNumResultCols()** function to determine whether a result data set was produced when an SQL statement was executed. If the **SQLNumResultCols()** function returns **0**, no result data set was produced. If a result data set was produced, the **SQLNumResultCols()** function returns the number of columns that exist in the result data set created to the calling application.

Result Data Set Metadata

Before data in a result data set can be returned to an application, the characteristics of that result data set must be known. These characteristics are stored as *metadata*, which is simply data that describes other data. Result data set metadata contains detailed information about the result data set, including the number of columns in the result data set, the data types of each of those columns, their names, precision, nullability, and so on. Interoperable applications should always check the metadata of result data set columns. That is because the metadata for a column in a result data set might differ from the metadata returned for the same column by a catalog function. Even data types can be different because the data source might alter the data type when it creates the result data set.

Applications need the information stored in metadata to perform most result data set operations. For example, an application needs to know the data type of a column in order to bind a variable of the appropriate data type to that column.

Obtaining Metadata Information

Two functions, **SQLDescribeCol()** and **SQLColAttribute()**, can be used to obtain metadata for a result data set. The **SQLDescribeCol()** function returns five commonly used pieces of information about a column in a result data set (the column's name, data type, precision, scale, and nullability); the **SQLColAttribute()** function only returns a specific metadata value. However, when called multiple times, **SQLColAttribute()** can return a much richer selection of metadata values, including the column's case sensitivity, display size, updatability, and the ability to be used in an SQL statement **WHERE** clause. In addition, **SQLColAttribute()** can obtain driver-specific metadata; that is, a column's driver-specific C and SQL data types, descriptor types, information types, diagnostic types, and attributes.

Many applications, especially ones that only display data, only need the metadata returned by the **SQLDescribeCol()** function. Other applications, particularly applications that update data, need the additional metadata that can be returned by the **SQLColAttribute()** function. Often, applications call the **SQLDescribeCol()** function to obtain basic metadata information and follow it with one or more **SQLColAttribute()** function calls to retrieve additional specific metadata information.

An application can retrieve result set metadata at any time after an SQL statement has been prepared or executed and before the cursor referencing the result data set is closed. However, very few applications actually need to acquire result data set metadata before an SQL statement is executed. In fact, it is good programming practice to wait until an SQL statement has been executed before trying to retrieve result data set metadata. The main reason for this is that some data sources cannot return metadata for prepared statements, and emulation of this operation by the driver is often a slow process.

Retrieving metadata from the data source is often an expensive process. Because of this, applications should only request the metadata they absolutely need.

Binding Result Data Set Columns

Just as application variables and/or large object (LOB) locators can be bound to parameter markers used in SQL statements, application variables and/or LOB locators can be bound to the columns of a result data set. Conceptually, the process is the same. When an application binds a variable or a LOB locator to a column in the result data set, it describes that variable/LOB locator (its address, data type, etc.) to DB2 CLI. DB2 CLI stores this information in the structure it maintains for the statement handle and uses the information to retrieve the value from the column when a row of data is fetched.

An application can bind variables/LOB locators to as many or as few result data set columns as it wants (in fact, data can be retrieved from a result data set with no binding at all). Which result data set columns are bound and which columns are not is application-dependent.

Because column bindings are just records that contain information about an application buffer that has been associated with a result data set, and because they are independent of the result data set, they can be created in any order. For example, suppose an application binds application variables to the columns of the result data set generated by the following SQL statement:

```
SELECT * FROM Orders
```

If the application then executes the SQL statement:

```
SELECT * FROM Customers
```

using the same SQL statement handle, the column bindings for the first result data set remain in effect, because those are the bindings that were stored in the data structure associated with the statement handle.

NOTE: *In most cases, this is poor programming practice and should be avoided. Applications should call the* SQLFreeStmt() *function with the* SQL_UNBIND *option specified to remove all column bindings associated with a statement handle before reusing that statement handle with a new SQL statement.*

Using SQLBindCol()

The SQLBindCol() function is used to bind application variables and/or LOB locators to columns in a result data set, one column at a time. Each time this function is called, the application specifies:

- The column number. Columns are numbered in increasing order in the result data set as they appear from left to right, beginning with the number 1. If a bookmark column is included in the result data set, column number 0 is the bookmark column. If a column number higher than the actual number of columns in the result data set is specified, an error occurs; however, this kind of error will not be detected until the result data set is created, so it is returned by SQLFetch(), not SQLBindCol().

- The C data type, memory address, and size (length), in bytes, of the application variable or LOB locator being bound to the result data set column. DB2 CLI must be able to convert the data from the SQL data type used by the data source to the C data type specified (fetch operations) or from the C data type specified to the SQL data type used by the data source (positioned INSERT, UPDATE, and DELETE operations); otherwise, an error will occur. Again, this kind of error might not be detected until the result data set is created, so it is returned by SQLFetch(), not SQLBindCol().

- Optionally, the memory address of a length/indicator variable. This optional variable is used to obtain/set the byte length of binary or character data, or to determine/specify whether the data is NULL.

Once an application variable or a LOB locator is bound to a column in a result data set, it remains bound until one of the following occurs:

■ A different application variable is bound to the same column.

■ The column is unbound. This is done by calling the **SQLBindCol()** function with a NULL pointer specified as the variable's address.

■ All columns are unbound. This is done by calling the **SQLFreeStmt()** function with the **SQL_UNBIND** option specified.

■ The statement handle associated with the SQL statement containing the parameter marker is released (freed).

The actual use of bound application variables is deferred; that is, they are bound to result data set columns with the **SQLBindCol()** function, but DB2 CLI accesses them from other functions—namely **SQLFetch()**, **SQLFetchScroll()**, or **SQLSetPos()**. Therefore, applications must ensure that bound variables remain valid (are not freed) as long as the binding remains in effect.

To bind a column to a different variable, an application simply rebinds the column with the new variable. The previous binding is automatically released. However, the new binding does not take effect until the next row of data is fetched. New bindings are not applied to rows that have already been fetched.

Changing Column Bindings (and Values) with Offsets

CLI applications can specify that an offset be added to a bound variable's address and to the corresponding length/indicator buffer address when **SQLFetch()**, **SQLFetchScroll()**, or **SQLSetPos()** is called. This feature allows an application to change column bindings (and values) without calling the **SQLBindCol()** function to rebind previously bound result data set columns. When offsets are used, the original bindings represent a *template* of how the application buffers are laid out. The application can move this "template" to different areas of memory simply by changing the offset. New offsets can be specified at any time. Each time an offset is specified, it is added to the originally bound buffer address. This means that offset additions are not cumulative—each offset specified cancels the previous offset used. It goes without saying that the sum of the address and the offset must always be a valid address (either or both the offset and the address to which the offset is added can be invalid, as long as the sum of the two is a valid address).

 NOTE: *Binding offsets are not supported by DB2 CLI 2.0 and earlier versions.*

Binding Columns to Arrays

In addition to using offsets to change column bindings, columns can also be bound to arrays. Because this type of binding is typically used in more advanced data retrieval operations, it is not discussed here. Instead, this information is presented in Chapter 11, "Retrieving Results (Advanced)".

Fetching Data

An application fetches (retrieves) rows from a result data set by using a *cursor*. The name cursor, as it applies to databases, probably originated from the blinking cursor found on a computer screen. Just as that cursor indicates the current position on the screen and identifies where typed words will appear next, a database cursor indicates the current position in a result data set and identifies what row of data will be returned to an application next.

The cursor model used in CLI is based on the cursor model used in embedded SQL. However, one notable difference between these two models exists in how cursors are declared and opened. In embedded SQL, a cursor must be explicitly declared and opened before it can be used. In CLI, a cursor is implicitly defined and opened whenever an SQL statement that creates a result data set is executed. In both cases, when a cursor is opened, it is positioned just before the first row of data in the result data set. Likewise, a cursor must be closed after an application has finished using it.

The type of cursor used by DB2 CLI, known as a forward-only cursor, can only move forward through a result data set. Forward-only cursors provide a fast mechanism for making a single pass through a result data set. However, if an application using a forward-only cursor needs to return to a row that was fetched earlier, it must close and reopen the cursor, then re-fetch rows starting from the beginning of the result data set until it reaches the required row. Applications can get around this limitation by reading the result data set once and storing the fetched data locally (usually in an array or a linked list).

Naming Cursors

Whenever a cursor is implicitly created by CLI, the data source generates and assigns it a unique name. Applications can retrieve this name by calling the **SQLGetCursorName()** function, or they can assign a unique name to the cursor by calling the **SQLSetCursorName()** function before executing an SQL statement that creates a result data set (cursors are created and named when an SQL statement is prepared). For most fetch operations, the name of the cursor associated with a result data set is unimportant. Cursor names are typically used in conjunction with positioned **UPDATE** and **DELETE** operations.

Using SQLFetch()

The **SQLFetch()** function is used to retrieve (fetch) a row of data from a result data set. When called, **SQLFetch()** advances the cursor to the next row in the result data set and returns the data for all columns that were bound to application variables and/or LOB locators by the **SQLBindCol()** function. If no columns were bound, **SQLFetch()** advances the cursor without returning any data.

Generally, when **SQLFetch()** is called, the driver performs the following tasks for each bound column in a row:

1. Sets the length/indicator variable to **SQL_NULL_DATA** and proceeds to the next column if the data is NULL. If the data is NULL and no length/indicator buffer was bound, SQLSTATE **22**002 (Indicator variable required but not supplied) is returned, and DB2 CLI proceeds to the next row. If the data for the column is not NULL, the driver proceeds to step 2.

2. If the **SQL_ATTR_MAX_LENGTH** statement attribute is set to a nonzero value and the column contains character or binary data, it truncates the data to **SQL_ATTR_MAX_LENGTH** bytes.

NOTE: *The* **SQL_ATTR_MAX_LENGTH** *statement attribute is intended to reduce network traffic. It is generally implemented by the data source, which truncates the data before returning it across the network.*

3. Converts the data to the C data type specified for the bound application variable.

4. If the data was converted to a variable-length data type, such as a character or binary data type, DB2 CLI determines whether the length of the data exceeds the size of the bound variable/LOB locator. If the length of character data (including the NULL-termination character) exceeds the size of the bound variable, DB2 CLI truncates the data to the size of the bound variable-1 and NULL-terminates the data. If the length of binary data exceeds the size of the bound variable, DB2 CLI truncates it to the size of the bound variable. (The size of the bound variable is specified with the **SQLBindCol()** function).

Data truncation tends to be rare, because the size a buffer needs to be to hold the entire data value can be obtained from the result data set metadata before the buffer is bound to a column.

DB2 CLI never truncates data converted to fixed-length data types. It always assumes that the length of the data buffer is the size of the C data type specified.

5. Stores the converted (and possibly truncated) data in the bound application variable/LOB locator.

6. Stores the length of the data in the bound length/indicator variable. For character or binary data, this is the length of the data after conversion and before truncation. If DB2 CLI cannot determine the length of the data after conversion, as is sometimes the case with long data, it sets the length to **SQL_NO_TOTAL**. If data was truncated due to the value of the **SQL_ATTR_MAX_LENGTH** statement attribute, the value of this attribute (as opposed to the actual length) is stored in the bound length/indicator variable. For all other data types, this is the length of the data after conversion; that is, it is the size of the C data type to which the data was converted. If no length/indicator variable was bound to the column, DB2 CLI discards the data length value.

7. Returns **SQL_SUCCESS** to the calling application if the data was successfully transferred to the bound application variable/LOB locator.

Returns **SQL_SUCCESS_WITH_INFO** and SQLSTATE **01**S07 (Fractional truncation) if the data was truncated during conversion without a loss of significant digits (for example, if the real number 1.234 is truncated to 1 when converted to an integer).

Returns **SQL_SUCCESS_WITH_INFO** and SQLSTATE **01**004 (Data truncated) if the data was truncated because the length of the bound variable/buffer was too small (for example, if the string "abcdef" were to be returned to a 4-byte buffer).

Returns **SQL_SUCCESS** if data was truncated to the length specified in the **SQL_ATTR_MAX_LENGTH** statement attribute.

Returns **SQL_ERROR** (if the rowset size is 1) or **SQL_SUCCESS_WITH_INFO** (if the rowset size is greater than 1) and SQLSTATE **22**003 (Numeric value out of range) if data was truncated during conversion with a loss of significant digits. In this case, the application can continue fetching rows, but all data for the current row will be lost.

Returns **SQL_NO_DATA** if the cursor has reached the end of the result data set.

Keeping Track of the Number of Rows Fetched

A *rows fetched* buffer can be used to keep track of the number of rows fetched, including those rows for which no data was returned because an error occurred during the fetch operation. This buffer must be allocated by the application, and when its address is stored in the **SQL_ATTR_ROWS_FETCHED_PTR** statement attribute, its contents are updated each time **SQLFetch()** (and **SQLFetchScroll()**) is called. If the **SQL_ATTR_ROWS_FETCHED_PTR** statement attribute contains a NULL pointer, neither of these functions return the number of rows fetched. The contents of the rows fetched buffer is undefined if **SQLFetch()** or **SQLFetchScroll()** does not return **SQL_SUCCESS** or **SQL_SUCCESS_WITH_INFO**, except when **SQL_NO_DATA** is returned—in which case the value in the rows fetched buffer is set to **0**.

If a rows fetched buffer is specified, an application can often examine its contents to determine the row number for the current row in the result data set. If a rows fetched buffer is not used, an application can obtain the same information by examining the contents of the **SQL_ATTR_ROW_NUMBER** statement attribute.

Closing the Cursor

Often, developers assume that when the **SQLFetch()** function returns **SQL_NO_DATA**, the associated cursor is automatically closed. However, this is not the case. Although cursors are implicitly created and opened when SQL statements that create a result data set are executed, they must be explicitly closed. Even cursors for empty result data sets (result data sets created when an SQL statement that returned no rows was executed successfully) must be explicitly closed. The **SQLCloseCursor()** function is used to explicitly close an open cursor.

NOTE: *As long as a cursor remains open, the statement handle the cursor is associated with cannot be used for most other operations (for example, executing other SQL statements).*

Getting Long Data

Each time a row is fetched from a result data set, the driver automatically stores the data for bound columns in the appropriate application variables/LOB locators. What happens to the data stored in unbound columns is driver specific; most drivers either retrieve the data and discard it or never retrieve it at all.

Applications can retrieve data from unbound columns by calling the **SQLGetData()** function. The **SQLGetData()** function is commonly used to retrieve large data values, which often exceed a predefined size (usually 254 characters or bytes). Because such data often cannot be stored in a single buffer, it is retrieved in parts from the data source by the **SQLGetData()** function after all other data in the row has been fetched. With respect to a single column, **SQLGetData()** behaves in the same manner as **SQLFetch()**. It retrieves the data for a column, converts it to the application variable's data type (if appropriate), and stores the converted value in that variable. It also returns the byte length of the data in the length/indicator buffer provided.

NOTE: *An application can retrieve any type of data value from a result data set with the* **SQLGetData()** *function. However, if the data is small enough to fit in a single buffer, there is generally no reason to use the* **SQLGetData()** *function. It is much easier to bind an application variable to the result data set column and let the driver store the data in the variable when the* **SQLFetch()** *function is called.*

To retrieve large data from an unbound column, an application:

1. Calls **SQLFetch()** or **SQLFetchScroll()** to position the cursor on a row of data in the result data set. Either of these functions automatically retrieves data for all bound columns and stores it in the appropriate application variables/LOB locators.

2. Calls the **SQLGetData()** function. **SQLGetData()** has the same arguments as **SQLBindCol()**—a statement handle, a column number, the C data type, address, and byte length of an application variable/LOB locator, and the address of a length/indicator buffer. Both **SQLGetData()** and **SQLBindCol()** perform essentially the same task. Each describes an application variable/LOB locator to the driver and specifies that the data for a particular column should be returned in that variable/LOB locator. The major differences are that the **SQLGetData()** function is called after a row is fetched (and is sometimes called late binding for this reason), and that the binding specified by the **SQLGetData()** function only lasts for the duration of the function call.

When the **SQLGetData()** function is called, DB2 CLI:

1. Returns **SQL_NO_DATA** if it has already returned all the data for the column.

2. Sets the length/indicator variable to **SQL_NULL_DATA** if the data is NULL. If the data is NULL and no length/indicator buffer was bound, SQLSTATE **22**002 (indicator variable required but not supplied) is returned, and DB2 CLI proceeds to the next row. If the data for the column is not NULL, DB2 CLI proceeds to step 3.

3. If the **SQL_ATTR_MAX_LENGTH** statement attribute is set to a nonzero value, and the column contains character or binary data and **SQLGetData()** has not been called previously for the column, it truncates the data to **SQL_ATTR_MAX_LENGTH** bytes.

NOTE: The **SQL_ATTR_MAX_LENGTH** *statement attribute is intended to reduce network traffic. It is generally implemented by the data source, which truncates the data before returning it across the network.*

4. Converts the data to the C data type specified for the application variable. The data is given the default precision and scale for that data type.

5. If the data was converted to a variable-length data type, such as a character or binary data type, DB2 CLI determines whether the length of the data exceeds the size of the application variable. If the length of character data (including the NULL-termination character) exceeds the size of the variable, DB2 CLI truncates the data to the size of the variable-1 and NULL-terminates the data. If the length of binary data exceeds the size of the variable, DB2 CLI truncates it to the size of the variable.

   Data truncation tends to be rare, because the size a buffer needs to be in order to hold the entire data value can be obtained from the result data set metadata before the buffer is used.

   DB2 CLI never truncates data converted to fixed-length data types; rather, it always assumes that the length of the data buffer is the size of the C data type specified.

6. Stores the converted (and possibly truncated) data in the application variable/LOB locator.

7. Stores the length of the data in the length/indicator variable. For character or binary data, this is the length of the data after conversion and before truncation. If DB2 CLI cannot determine the length of the data after conversion, as is sometimes the case with long data, it sets the length to **SQL_NO_TOTAL**. (The last call to **SQLGetData()** for a particular column must always return the length of the data, not **0** or **SQL_NO_TOTAL**.) If data was truncated due to the value of the **SQL_ATTR_MAX_LENGTH** statement attribute, the value of this attribute (as opposed to the actual length) is stored in the length/indicator variable. For all other data types, this is the length of the data after conversion; that is, it is the size of the C data type to which the data was converted.

When **SQLGetData()** is called multiple times in succession for the same column, this is the length of the data available at the start of each call; that is, the value returned in the length/indicator buffer decreases with each **SQLGetData()** call by the number of bytes returned in the previous call.

8. Returns **SQL_SUCCESS** if all the data in the column has been retrieved.

   Returns **SQL_SUCCESS_WITH_INFO** and SQLSTATE **01**S07 (Fractional truncation) if the data was truncated during conversion without a loss of significant digits (for example, if the real number 1.234 is truncated to 1 when converted to an integer).

   Returns **SQL_SUCCESS_WITH_INFO** and SQLSTATE **01**004 (Data truncated) if the data was truncated because the length of the variable was too small (for example, if the string "abcdef" were to be returned to a 4-byte buffer).

   Returns **SQL_SUCCESS** if data was truncated to the length specified in the **SQL_ATTR_MAX_LENGTH** statement attribute.

   Returns **SQL_NO_DATA** if there is no more data to return.

Each time **SQL_SUCCESS_WITH_INFO** is returned to the application, **SQLGetData()** is called again (with the same column specified) to retrieve another part of or the remainder of the data stored in the column.

When large data values are retrieved in parts, the application is responsible for putting the parts together. Often, this is done by a simple concatenation of the parts of the data. However, because each part is NULL-terminated, the application must remove all but the last NULL-termination character when concatenating the parts.

Variable-length bookmarks can also be returned, in parts, by **SQLGetData()**. As with other data, a call to **SQLGetData()** to return variable-length bookmarks in parts returns **SQL_SUCCESS_WITH_INFO** and SQLSTATE **01**004 (String data, right truncated) when there is more data to be returned. This is different from the case where a variable-length bookmark is truncated by a call to **SQLFetch()** or **SQLFetchScroll()**, which returns **SQL_ERROR** and SQLSTATE **22**001 (String data, right truncated).

There are a number of restrictions that must be taken into consideration when using the **SQLGetData()** function. In general, columns accessed with **SQLGetData()**:

- Must be accessed in order of increasing column number (because of how the columns of a result data set are read from the data source).

- Cannot be bound to application variables.

- Must have a higher column number than the last bound column. For example, if the last bound column is column 3, it is an error to call **SQLGetData()** for column 2. For this reason, applications should always place long data columns at the end of select lists.

- Cannot be used if **SQLFetch()** or **SQLFetchScroll()** was called to retrieve more than one row.

Controlling Result Data Set Size

An application can reduce network traffic by limiting the number of rows returned in a result data set. This is done by setting the SQL_ATTR_MAX_ROWS statement attribute before executing an SQL statement that creates a result data set. If an application does not need all the data usually returned in a character or binary column, network traffic can be further reduced by setting the SQL_ATTR_MAX_LENGTH statement attribute before executing the statement. This restricts the number of bytes of data returned for any character or binary column. For example, suppose a column contains long text documents. If an application that browses the table containing this column only needs to display the first page of each document, the SQL_ATTR_MAX_LENGTH statement attribute can be used to limit the amount of data returned for a column to a single page. An application can also let DB2 CLI truncate character or binary data, by binding a small buffer to the column.

The Basic SQL Results Retrieval Functions

Table 10–1 lists the CLI functions that are used to perform the basic process of retrieving rows of data from a result data set.

Each of these functions are described, in detail, in the remaining portion of this chapter.

Table 10–1　The CLI Basic Results Retrieval Functions

Function Name	Description
SQLDescribeCol()	Describes a column found in a result data set.
SQLNumResultCols()	Retrieves and returns the number of columns in a result data set.
SQLColAttribute()	Retrieves information about a specific column in a result data set.
SQLBindCol()	Assigns (binds) data storage for a specific column in a result data set.
SQLGetCursorName()	Retrieves the cursor name for a cursor associated with an SQL statement handle.
SQLSetCursorName()	Specifies a cursor name for a cursor associated with an SQL statement handle.
SQLFetch()	Retrieves a single row of data from a result data set and returns it to bound application variables/LOB locators.
SQLCloseCursor()	Closes a cursor that has been opened on an SQL statement handle.
SQLGetData()	Retrieves data from a single column (in the current row) of a result data set.

SQLNumResultCols

COMPATIBILITY				
X/OPEN 95 CLI	ISO/IEC 92 CLI	DB2 CLI 5.2	DB2 CLI 2.0	ODBC 3.x
☑	☑	☑	☑	☑

ODBC API CONFORMANCE LEVEL **CORE**

Purpose The `SQLNumResultCols()` function is used to determine the number of columns that exist in a result data set.

Syntax
```
SQLRETURN   SQLNumResultCols (SQLHSTMT      StatementHandle,
                              SQLSMALLINT   *NumColumns);
```

Parameters *StatementHandle* An SQL statement handle that refers to a previously allocated SQL statement information storage buffer (data structure).

NumColumns A pointer to a location in memory where this function is to store the number of columns found in the result data set associated with the specified SQL statement handle.

Description The `SQLNumResultCols()` function is used to determine the number of columns that exist in a result data set. If the last SQL statement or CLI function executed (using the specified SQL statement handle) did not produce a result data set, the value 0 is returned in the *NumColumns* parameter (to indicate there is no result data set) when this function is executed.

An application can call this function any time after an SQL statement is prepared or executed. However, because some data sources cannot easily describe result data sets that will be created by examining prepared SQL statements, performance can suffer if this function is called after a statement is prepared—but before it is actually executed.

NOTE: *A result data set can be empty. This is different from a result data set not being created at all. Other than the fact that it has no rows of data in it, an empty result data set is like any other result data set. Thus, an application can retrieve metadata for, attempt to fetch rows from, and must close the cursor associated with an empty result data set.*

Return Codes `SQL_SUCCESS`, `SQL_SUCCESS_WITH_INFO`, `SQL_STILL_EXECUTING`, `SQL_INVALID_HANDLE`, or `SQL_ERROR`

SQLSTATEs If this function returns `SQL_SUCCESS_WITH_INFO` or `SQL_ERROR`, one of the following SQLSTATE values may be obtained by calling the `SQLGetDiagRec()` function:

40003, **08**S01, **58**004, **HY**001, **HY**008, **HY**009, **HY**010, **HY**013, or **HYT**00

Refer to Appendix B for detailed information about each SQLSTATE value that can be returned.

SQLNumResultCols() can return any SQLSTATE that can be returned by **SQLPrepare()** or **SQLExecute()** when called after **SQLPrepare()** and before **SQLExecute()**, depending upon when the data source evaluates the SQL statement associated with the statement handle specified.

Comments
- The value returned to the *NumColumns* parameter does not include the bookmark column (if the result data set contains a bound bookmark column).
- If the SQL statement associated with *StatementHandle* does not produce a result data set, 0 is returned in the *NumColumns* parameter.
- The **SQL_DESC_COUNT** field of the IRD descriptor header record associated with the SQL statement handle specified contains the value that this function returns to the *NumColumns* parameter.

Prerequisites   The **SQLPrepare()** function or the **SQLExecDirect()** function must be called before this function is called.

Restrictions   This function can only be called successfully if the SQL statement is in the "Prepared," "Executed," or "Positioned" state.

See Also   **SQLBindCol()**, **SQLDescribeCol()**, **SQLColAttribute()**, **SQLPrepare()**, **SQLExecute()**, **SQLExecDirect()**, **SQLGetData()**

Example   The following Visual C++ program illustrates how to use the **SQLNumResultCols()** function to determine how many columns exist in a result data set.

```
/*————————————————————————————————————————————  */
/* NAME:     CH10EX1.CPP                          */
/* PURPOSE: Illustrate How To Use The Following CLI API Function  */
/*          In A C++ Program:                     */
/*                                                */
/*              SQLNumResultCols()                */
/*                                                */
/* OTHER CLI APIs SHOWN:                          */
/*          SQLAllocHandle()        SQLSetEnvAttr()   */
/*          SQLConnect()            SQLExecDirect()   */
/*          SQLDisconnect()         SQLFreeHandle()   */
/*                                                */
/*————————————————————————————————————————————  */

// Include The Appropriate Header Files
#include <windows.h>
#include <sqlcli1.h>
#include <iostream.h>

// Define The CLI_Class Class
class CLI_Class
{
    // Attributes
    public:
        SQLHANDLE   EnvHandle;
```

```
            SQLHANDLE   ConHandle;
            SQLHANDLE   StmtHandle;
            SQLRETURN   rc;

    // Operations
    public:
        CLI_Class();                            // Constructor
        ~CLI_Class();                           // Destructor
};

// Define The Class Constructor
CLI_Class::CLI_Class()
{
    // Initialize The Return Code Variable
    rc = SQL_SUCCESS;

    // Allocate An Environment Handle
    rc = SQLAllocHandle(SQL_HANDLE_ENV, SQL_NULL_HANDLE, &EnvHandle);

    // Set The ODBC Application Version To 3.x
    if (rc == SQL_SUCCESS)
        rc = SQLSetEnvAttr(EnvHandle, SQL_ATTR_ODBC_VERSION,
                (SQLPOINTER) SQL_OV_ODBC3, SQL_IS_UINTEGER);

    // Allocate A Connection Handle
    if (rc == SQL_SUCCESS)
        rc = SQLAllocHandle(SQL_HANDLE_DBC, EnvHandle, &ConHandle);
}


// Define The Class Destructor
CLI_Class::~CLI_Class()
{
    // Free The Connection Handle
    if (ConHandle != NULL)
        SQLFreeHandle(SQL_HANDLE_DBC, ConHandle);

    // Free The Environment Handle
    if (EnvHandle != NULL)
        SQLFreeHandle(SQL_HANDLE_ENV, EnvHandle);
}


/*------------------------------------------------------------------ */
/* The Main Function                                                 */
/*------------------------------------------------------------------ */
int main()
{
    // Declare The Local Memory Variables
    SQLRETURN    rc = SQL_SUCCESS;
    SQLCHAR      SQLStmt[255];
    SQLSMALLINT  NumCols;

    // Create An Instance Of The CLI_Class Class
    CLI_Class  Example;

    // Connect To The DB2 Sample Database
```

```
        if (Example.ConHandle != NULL)
        {
            rc = SQLConnect(Example.ConHandle, (SQLCHAR *) "SAMPLE",
                    SQL_NTS, (SQLCHAR *) "userid", SQL_NTS,
                    (SQLCHAR *) "password", SQL_NTS);

            // Allocate An SQL Statement Handle
            rc = SQLAllocHandle(SQL_HANDLE_STMT, Example.ConHandle,
                    &Example.StmtHandle);
            if (rc == SQL_SUCCESS)
            {
                // Define A SELECT SQL Statement
                strcpy((char *) SQLStmt, "SELECT * FROM PROJECT");

                // Prepare And Execute The SQL Statement
                rc = SQLExecDirect(Example.StmtHandle, SQLStmt, SQL_NTS);

                // Find Out How Many Columns Exist In The Result Data Set
                // Produced By The SQL Query (Display The Result)
                if (rc == SQL_SUCCESS)
                {
                    rc = SQLNumResultCols(Example.StmtHandle, &NumCols);
                    cout << "Number Of Columns In The Result Data Set: ";
                    cout << NumCols << endl;
                }

                // Free The SQL Statement Handle
                if (Example.StmtHandle != NULL)
                    SQLFreeHandle(SQL_HANDLE_STMT, Example.StmtHandle);
            }

            // Disconnect From The DB2 Sample Database
            rc = SQLDisconnect(Example.ConHandle);
        }

        // Return To The Operating System
        return(rc);
    }
```

SQLDescribeCol

COMPATIBILITY

X/OPEN 95 CLI	ISO/IEC 92 CLI	DB2 CLI 5.2	DB2 CLI 2.0	ODBC 3.x
☑	☑	☑	☑	☑

ODBC API CONFORMANCE LEVEL   **CORE**

Purpose   The `SQLDescribeCol()` function is used to retrieve basic result data set metadata information (specifically, column name, SQL data type, column size, decimal precision, and nullability) for a specified column in a result data set.

Syntax

```
SQLRETURN   SQLDescribeCol   (SQLHSTMT        StatementHandle,
                              SQLUSMALLINT    ColumnNumber,
                              SQLCHAR         *ColumnName,
                              SQLSMALLINT     ColNameMaxSize,
                              SQLSMALLINT     *ColNameSize,
                              SQLSMALLINT     *SQLDataType,
                              SQLUINTEGER     *ColumnSize,
                              SQLSMALLINT     *Decimals,
                              SQLSMALLINT     *Nullable);
```

Parameters

StatementHandle	An SQL statement handle that refers to a previously allocated SQL statement information storage buffer (data structure).
ColumnNumber	Specifies the column's location in the result data set. Columns are numbered sequentially from left to right, starting with 1, as they appear in the result data set.
ColumnName	A pointer to a location in memory where this function is to store the name of the specified column.
ColNameMaxSize	The maximum size of the memory storage buffer where this function is to store the column name retrieved.
ColNameSize	A pointer to a location in memory where this function is to store the actual number of bytes written to the column name memory storage buffer (*ColumnName*).
SQLDataType	A pointer to a location in memory where this function is to store the SQL data type of the specified column. The following SQL data types are supported:

■ SQL_CHAR

■ SQL_VARCHAR

■ SQL_LONGVARCHAR

■ SQL_DECIMAL

■ SQL_NUMERIC

■ SQL_SMALLINT

■ SQL_INTEGER

■ SQL_REAL

■ SQL_FLOAT

■ SQL_DOUBLE

■ SQL_BINARY

■ SQL_VARBINARY

■ SQL_LONGVARBINARY

- SQL_GRAPHIC
- SQL_VARGRAPHIC
- SQL_LONGVARGRAPHIC
- SQL_TYPE_DATE
- SQL_TYPE_TIME
- SQL_TYPE_TIMESTAMP
- SQL_BLOB
- SQL_CLOB
- SQL_DBCLOB

ColumnSize   A pointer to a location in memory where this function is to store the maximum length, in bytes, of the column as it is defined in the data source.

Decimals   A pointer to a location in memory where this function is to store the number of digits to the right of the decimal point for columns that have one of the following SQL data types (*SQLDataType*):

- SQL_DECIMAL
- SQL_NUMERIC
- SQL_TYPE_TIMESTAMP

Nullable   A pointer to a location in memory where this function is to store information about whether the column accepts/allows NULL values. The following values are supported:

- SQL_NO_NULLS
  The specified column does not allow NULL values.

- SQL_NULLABLE
  The specified column allows NULL values.

- SQL_NULLABLE_UNKNOWN
  Whether the specified column allows NULL values cannot be determined.

Description   The sqlDescribeCol() function is used to retrieve basic metadata information (specifically, column name, SQL data type, column size, decimal precision, and nullability) for a specified column in a result data set. If the basic metadata for a column in a result data set is not known in advance, this function or the sqlColAttribute() function can be called to obtain the metadata so that an appropriate application variable or LOB locator can be bound to it.

An application can call this function any time after an SQL statement is prepared or executed. However, because some data sources cannot easily describe result data sets that will be created by examining prepared SQL statements, performance can suffer if this function is called after a statement is prepared—but before it is actually executed.

Return Codes   SQL_SUCCESS, SQL_SUCCESS_WITH_INFO, SQL_STILL_EXECUTING, SQL_INVALID_HANDLE, or SQL_ERROR

SQLSTATEs   If this function returns **SQL_SUCCESS_WITH_INFO** or **SQL_ERROR**, one of the following SQLSTATE values may be obtained by calling the **SQLGetDiagRec()** function:

01004, **07**005, **07**009, **08**S01, **40**003, **58**004, **HY**001, **HY**002, **HY**008, **HY**010, **HY**013, **HY**090, **HYC**00, or **HYT**00

Refer to Appendix B for detailed information about each SQLSTATE value that can be returned.

SQLDescribeCol() can return any SQLSTATE that can be returned by **SQLPrepare()** or **SQLExecute()** when called after **SQLPrepare()** and before **SQLExecute()**, depending on when the data source evaluates the SQL statement associated with the statement handle specified.

Comments   ▨ If the *ColumnNumber* parameter is set to **0**, metadata for the bookmark column is returned.

▨ If the column name string's actual length is greater than or equal to the maximum string size value specified in the *ColNameMaxSize* parameter, the column name string is truncated to *ColNameMaxSize*-1 (the length of a NULL-termination character) characters.

▨ If the column name string is a Unicode string, the *ColNameMaxSize* parameter must contain an even number.

▨ If the data type for a column cannot be determined, DB2 CLI returns **SQL_UNKNOWN_TYPE** to the *SQLDataType* parameter.

▨ If the data type returned for a column is **SQL_GRAPHIC** or **SQL_DBCLOB** (*SQLDataType* parameter), the value returned in the *ColumnSize* parameter identifies the maximum number of double-byte characters that the column can hold.

▨ If this function is called with a NULL pointer specified for any of the following parameters: *ColumnName, ColNameSize, SQLDataType, ColumnSize, Decimals,* and *Nullable,* DB2 CLI assumes that the corresponding information is not needed and no information is returned.

▨ If the number of decimal digits for a column cannot be determined or is not applicable, DB2 CLI returns **0** to the *Decimals* parameter.

▨ The **SQL_DESC_NAME** field of the IRD descriptor column record for the SQL statement handle contains the value that this function returns to the *ColumnName* parameter.

▨ The **SQL_DESC_CONCISE_TYPE** field of the IRD descriptor column record for the SQL statement handle contains the value that this function returns to the *SQLDataType* parameter.

▨ The **SQL_DESC_NULLABLE** field of the IRD descriptor column record for the SQL statement handle contains the value that this function returns to the *Nullable* parameter.

Prerequisites The **SQLPrepare()** function or the **SQLExecDirect()** function must be executed before this function is called.

Restrictions   This function can only be called successfully if the SQL statement is in the "Prepared," "Executed," or "Positioned" state.

See Also   `SQLColAttribute(), SQLPrepare(), SQLExecute(), SQLExecDirect(),`
`SQLNumResultCols()`

Example   The following Visual C++ program illustrates how to use the **SQLDescribeCol()** function
to obtain general information about a column in a result data set.

```
/*--------------------------------------------------------------------*/
/* NAME:    CH10EX2.CPP                                               */
/* PURPOSE: Illustrate How To Use The Following CLI API Function      */
/*          In A C++ Program:                                         */
/*                                                                    */
/*               SQLDescribeCol()                                     */
/*                                                                    */
/* OTHER CLI APIs SHOWN:                                              */
/*          SQLAllocHandle()              SQLSetEnvAttr()             */
/*          SQLConnect()                  SQLExecDirect()             */
/*          SQLNumResultCols()            SQLDisconnect()             */
/*          SQLFreeHandle()                                           */
/*                                                                    */
/*--------------------------------------------------------------------*/

// Include The Appropriate Header Files
#include <windows.h>
#include <sqlcli1.h>
#include <iostream.h>

// Define The CLI_Class Class
class CLI_Class
{
    // Attributes
    public:
        SQLHANDLE    EnvHandle;
        SQLHANDLE    ConHandle;
        SQLHANDLE    StmtHandle;
        SQLRETURN    rc;

    // Operations
    public:
        CLI_Class();                            // Constructor
        ~CLI_Class();                           // Destructor
        SQLRETURN ShowColInfo();
};

// Define The Class Constructor
CLI_Class::CLI_Class()
{
    // Initialize The Return Code Variable
    rc = SQL_SUCCESS;

    // Allocate An Environment Handle
    rc = SQLAllocHandle(SQL_HANDLE_ENV, SQL_NULL_HANDLE, &EnvHandle);

    // Set The ODBC Application Version To 3.x
    if (rc == SQL_SUCCESS)
```

```
        rc = SQLSetEnvAttr(EnvHandle, SQL_ATTR_ODBC_VERSION,
                (SQLPOINTER) SQL_OV_ODBC3, SQL_IS_UINTEGER);

    // Allocate A Connection Handle
    if (rc == SQL_SUCCESS)
        rc = SQLAllocHandle(SQL_HANDLE_DBC, EnvHandle, &ConHandle);
}

// Define The Class Destructor
CLI_Class::~CLI_Class()
{
    // Free The Connection Handle
    if (ConHandle != NULL)
        SQLFreeHandle(SQL_HANDLE_DBC, ConHandle);

    // Free The Environment Handle
    if (EnvHandle != NULL)
        SQLFreeHandle(SQL_HANDLE_ENV, EnvHandle);
}

// Define The ShowColInfo() Member Function
SQLRETURN CLI_Class::ShowColInfo(void)
{
    // Declare The Local Memory Variables
    SQLSMALLINT    NumCols;
    SQLCHAR        ColName[50];
    SQLSMALLINT    ColNameLen;
    SQLSMALLINT    ColType;
    SQLUINTEGER    ColSize;
    SQLSMALLINT    Scale;
    SQLSMALLINT    Nullable;

    // Find Out How Many Columns Exist In The Result Data Set
    rc = SQLNumResultCols(StmtHandle, &NumCols);
    if (rc == SQL_SUCCESS)
    {
        // Display A Header
        cout << "Column Names :" << endl << endl;

        // Obtain And Display The Name Of Each Column
        for (int i = 1; i <= (int) NumCols; i++)
        {
            rc = SQLDescribeCol(StmtHandle, i, ColName,
                    sizeof(ColName), &ColNameLen, &ColType,
                    &ColSize, &Scale, &Nullable);

            if (rc == SQL_SUCCESS)
                cout << ColName << endl;
        }
    }

    // Return The CLI API Return Code To The Calling Function
    return(rc);
}
```

```
/*——————————————————————————————————————————————————— */
/* The Main Function                                    */
/*——————————————————————————————————————————————————— */
int main()
{
    // Declare The Local Memory Variables
    SQLRETURN   rc = SQL_SUCCESS;
    SQLCHAR     SQLStmt[255];

    // Create An Instance Of The CLI_Class Class
    CLI_Class  Example;

    // Connect To The DB2 Sample Database
    if (Example.ConHandle != NULL)
    {
        rc = SQLConnect(Example.ConHandle, (SQLCHAR *) "SAMPLE",
                    SQL_NTS, (SQLCHAR *) "userid", SQL_NTS,
                    (SQLCHAR *) "password", SQL_NTS);

        // Allocate An SQL Statement Handle
        rc = SQLAllocHandle(SQL_HANDLE_STMT, Example.ConHandle,
                    &Example.StmtHandle);
        if (rc == SQL_SUCCESS)
        {
            // Define A SELECT SQL Statement
            strcpy((char *) SQLStmt, "SELECT * FROM PROJECT");

            // Prepare And Execute The SQL Statement
            rc = SQLExecDirect(Example.StmtHandle, SQLStmt, SQL_NTS);

            // Display Information About The Columns In The Result
            // Data Set Produced By The SQL Query
            if (rc == SQL_SUCCESS)
                Example.ShowColInfo();

            // Free The SQL Statement Handle
            if (Example.StmtHandle != NULL)
                SQLFreeHandle(SQL_HANDLE_STMT, Example.StmtHandle);
        }

        // Disconnect From The DB2 Sample Database
        rc = SQLDisconnect(Example.ConHandle);
    }

    // Return To The Operating System
    return(rc);
}
```

SQLColAttribute

COMPATIBILITY

X/OPEN 95 CLI	ISO/IEC 92 CLI	DB2 CLI 5.2	DB2 CLI 2.0	ODBC 3.x
☑	☑	☑	☐	☑

ODBC API CONFORMANCE LEVEL   CORE

Purpose   The **SQLColAttribute()** function is used to retrieve descriptor information (for example, column name, data type, column size, decimal precision, and nullability) for a specified column in a result data set.

Syntax
```
SQLRETURN   SQLColAttribute (SQLHSTMT        StatementHandle,
                             SQLUSMALLINT    ColumnNumber,
                             SQLUSMALLINT    Attribute,
                             SQLPOINTER      CharacterValue,
                             SQLSMALLINT     CharValueMaxSize,
                             SQLSMALLINT     *CharValueSize,
                             SQLPOINTER      NumericValue);
```

Parameters

StatementHandle   An SQL statement handle that refers to a previously allocated SQL statement information storage buffer (data structure).

ColumnNumber   Specifies the column's location in the result data set. Columns are numbered sequentially from left to right, starting with 1, as they appear in the result data set.

Attribute   Specifies the column attribute for which information is to be retrieved. This parameter must be set to one of the following values:

- SQL_DESC_AUTO_UNIQUE_VALUE
- SQL_DESC_BASE_COLUMN_NAME
- SQL_DESC_BASE_TABLE_NAME
- SQL_DESC_CASE_SENSITIVE
- SQL_DESC_CATALOG_NAME
- SQL_DESC_CONCISE_TYPE
- SQL_DESC_COUNT
- SQL_DESC_DISPLAY_SIZE
- SQL_DESC_DISTINCT_TYPE
- SQL_DESC_FIXED_PREC_SCALE
- SQL_DESC_LABEL
- SQL_DESC_LENGTH

- SQL_DESC_LITERAL_PREFIX
- SQL_DESC_LITERAL_SUFFIX
- SQL_DESC_LOCAL_TYPE_NAME
- SQL_DESC_NAME
- SQL_DESC_NULLABLE
- SQL_DESC_NUM_PREX_RADIX
- SQL_DESC_OCTET_LENGTH
- SQL_DESC_PRECISION
- SQL_DESC_SCALE
- SQL_DESC_SCHEMA_NAME
- SQL_DESC_SEARCHABLE
- SQL_DESC_TABLE_NAME
- SQL_DESC_TYPE
- SQL_DESC_TYPE_NAME
- SQL_DESC_UNNAMED
- SQL_DESC_UNSIGNED
- SQL_DESC_UPDATABLE

CharacterValue   A pointer to a location in memory where this function is to store the current value of the specified attribute (if the attribute value is a character value).

CharValueMaxSize   The size of the memory storage buffer where this function is to store the current value of the specified attribute (descriptor field). If an ODBC-defined attribute is to be retrieved, and if the attribute value is a 32-bit integer value, this parameter is ignored. If a DB2 CLI attribute is to be retrieved, this parameter may be set as follows:

- If the value of the specified attribute (descriptor field) is a character string, this parameter may be set to the actual length of the string or to **SQL_NTS**.

- If the value of the specified attribute (descriptor field) is a binary string, this parameter may be set to the result of the **SQL_LEN_BINARY_ATTR(length)** macro. Usually, this macro places a negative value in this parameter.

- If the value of the specified attribute (descriptor field) is anything other than a character string or binary string, this parameter may be set to **SQL_IS_POINTER**.

- If the value of the specified attribute (descriptor field) is a fixed-length data type, this parameter may be set to **SQL_IS_INTEGER, SQL_IS_UINTEGER, SQL_SMALLINT**, or **SQLUSMALLINT**, as appropriate.

CharValueSize	A pointer to a location in memory where this function is to store the actual number of bytes written to the attribute (descriptor field) character value memory storage buffer (*CharacterValue*). If the attribute (descriptor field) value retrieved is not a character string value, this parameter ignored.
NumberValue	A pointer to a location in memory where this function is to store the current value of the specified attribute (if the attribute value is a numeric value).

Description The **SQLColAttribute()** function is used to retrieve descriptor information (for example, column name, data type, column size, decimal precision, and nullability) for a specified column in a result data set. Table 10–2 lists alphabetically each value that can be specified for the *Attribute* parameter, along with a description of the information returned for that value when this function is executed.

If the various attributes about a result data set column are not known, this function (or the **SQLDescribeCol()** function) can be called after an SQL query statement has been prepared or executed, to determine the attributes of a column before binding it to an application variable or LOB locator.

NOTE: *This function replaces the DB2 CLI 2.0 function* **SQLColAttributes()**.

Return Codes **SQL_SUCCESS, SQL_SUCCESS_WITH_INFO, SQL_STILL_EXECUTING, SQL_INVALID_HANDLE,** or **SQL_ERROR**

SQLSTATEs If this function returns **SQL_SUCCESS_WITH_INFO** or **SQL_ERROR**, one of the following SQLSTATE values may be obtained by calling the **SQLGetDiagRec()** function:

01000, **01**004, **07**005, **07**009, **HY**000, **HY**001, **HY**008, **HY**010, **HY**090, **HY**091, or **HY**C00

Refer to Appendix B for detailed information about each SQLSTATE value that can be returned.

SQLColAttribute() can return any SQLSTATE that can be returned by **SQLPrepare()** or **SQLExecute()** when called after **SQLPrepare()** and before **SQLExecute()**, depending on when the data source evaluates the SQL statement associated with the statement handle specified.

Comments ▨ Attributes for columns can be retrieved in any order.

▨ When the *ColumnNumber* parameter is set to **0** (for a bookmark column), all attributes except **SQL_DESC_TYPE** and **SQL_DESC_OCTET_LENGTH** return undefined values.

▨ For character data, if the number of bytes of data available for the specified attribute is greater than or equal to the maximum string size value specified in the *CharValueMaxSize* parameter, the attribute string value is truncated to

CharValueMaxSize-1 (the length of a NULL-termination character) characters and is NULL-terminated by the driver. The *CharValueMaxSize* parameter is ignored for all other types of data. DB2 CLI assumes that the size of the data is 32 bits.

■ If the value returned for the attribute specified in the *Attribute* parameter is a Unicode string, the *CharValueMaxSize* must contain an even number.

■ This function returns either a character string value in the *CharacterValue* parameter or a 32-bit signed integer value in the *NumericValue* parameter. When information is returned in the *NumericValue* parameter, the *CharacterValue, CharValueMaxSize,* and *CharValueSize* parameters are ignored. When information is returned in the *CharacterValue* parameter, the *NumericValue* parameter is ignored.

■ This function is a more extensible alternative to the **SQLDescribeCol()** function. **SQLDescribeCol()** returns a fixed set of column metadata information based on the ANSI-89 SQL standards. **SQLColAttribute()** allows access to the more extensive set of column metadata (IRD descriptor information) defined in the ANSI SQL-92 standard and/or in DBMS vendor extensions.

■ Because the information returned by this function is stored in the IRD descriptor record associated with the column specified, this information can also be obtained by calling the **SQLGetDescField()** function with the appropriate IRD descriptor handle specified.

■ DB2 CLI will always return a value for each column attribute that corresponds to a descriptor record field. If a descriptor record field is not populated/supported by the data source being used, DB2 CLI will return 0 for non-supported attributes that would normally return a numerical value and an empty string (" ") for non-supported attributes that would normally return a character string value.

Table 10–2   Column Attribute (Descriptor) Information Returned By **SQLColAttribute()**

Attribute	Data Type	Description
SQL_DESC_AUTO_ UNIQUE_VALUE	32-bit **INTEGER**	Indicates whether the column's data type is an auto increment data type. Valid values for this attribute are:
		SQL_TRUE: The column's data type is an auto increment data type.
		SQL_FALSE: The column's data type is not an auto increment data type or the column does not contain numeric data.
		This attribute is only valid for columns containing numeric data types.
		Values can be inserted into auto increment data type columns; however, existing auto increment data type column values cannot be updated.
		When data is inserted into an auto-increment data type column, a unique value (determined by adding a predefined increment value to the last value used) is inserted into the column. The actual increment value used to construct the new unique value is not defined; instead it is data-source-specific. Thus, an application

Table 10–2 Column Attribute (Descriptor) Information Returned By `SQLColAttribute()` (Continued)

Attribute	Data Type	Description
		should not assume that an auto-increment column starts at any particular point or increments by any particular value.
		This attribute is set to **SQL_FALSE** for all DB2 SQL data types.
SQL_DESC_BASE_ COLUMN_NAME	Character string	Identifies the name assigned to the base column corresponding to the column in the result data set. If the base column is unnamed (as in the case when a column in a result data set corresponds to an expression), an empty string (" ") is returned for this attribute.
		This information is obtained from the **SQL_DESC_BASE_COLUMN_ NAME** field (a read-only field) of the IRD descriptor record.
SQL_DESC_BASE_ TABLE_NAME	Character string	Identifies the name of the base table containing the column. If the base table name cannot be determined, an empty string (" ") is returned for this attribute.
		This information is obtained from the **SQL_DESC_BASE_TABLE_ NAME** field (a read-only field) of the IRD descriptor record.
SQL_DESC_CASE_ SENSITIVE	32-bit **INTEGER**	Indicates whether the column's data type is treated as case sensitive for collations and comparisons. Valid values for this attribute are:
		SQL_TRUE: The column's data type is treated as case sensitive for collations and comparisons.
		SQL_FALSE: The column's data type is either not a character data type or is not treated as case sensitive for collations and comparisons.
SQL_DESC_ CATALOG_NAME	Character string	Identifies the catalog (qualifier) of the table containing the column. Because DB2 does not support catalogs (qualifiers), an empty string (" ") is returned for this attribute.
SQL_DESC_ CONCISE_TYPE	32-bit **INTEGER**	Identifies the concise data type (such as **SQL_TYPE_TIME** for datetime and interval data types.
		This information is obtained from the **SQL_DESC_CONCISE_TYPE** field of the IRD descriptor record.
SQL_DESC_COUNT	32-bit **INTEGER**	Identifies the number of columns that are available in the result data set. If there are no columns in the result data set, **0** is returned by this attribute.
		This information is obtained from the **SQL_DESC_COUNT** field or the IRD descriptor header record.
SQL_DESC_ DISPLAY_SIZE	32-bit **INTEGER**	Identifies the maximum number of characters needed to display data from the column.
SQL_DESC_ DISTINCT_TYPE	Character string	Identifies the user-defined distinct data type of the column. If the column has a built-in SQL data type instead of a user-defined data type, an empty string (" ") is returned for this attribute.
		This is an IBM defined attribute.
SQL_DESC_FIXED_ PREC_SCALE	32-bit **INTEGER**	Indicates whether the column has a fixed precision scale. Valid values for this attribute are:

Table 10–2   Column Attribute (Descriptor) Information Returned By **SQLColAttribute()** (Continued)

Attribute	Data Type	Description
		SQL_TRUE: The column has a fixed precision and non-zero scale that are data-source specific.
		SQL_FALSE: The column does not have a fixed precision and non-zero scale that are data-source specific.
SQL_DESC_LABEL	Character string	Identifies the label assigned to the column. If a column does not have a label, the column name is stored in this attribute. If the column is unlabeled and unnamed, an empty string (" ") is returned for this attribute.
SQL_DESC_LENGTH	32-bit **INTEGER**	Identifies the total number of bytes of data associated with the column. This is the length, in bytes, of the data that will be transferred when the **SQLFetch()** or **SQLGetData()** function is called for this column (provided **SQL_C_DEFAULT** is specified as the column's C data type).
		If the column contains fixed length character or binary string data, the actual length of the column (minus the size of the NULL termination character) is returned. If the column contains variable length character or binary string data, the maximum column length is returned. If the column contains numeric data, the length returned may be different from the size of the data stored in the data source.
		This information is obtained from the IRD record's **SQL_DESC_LENGTH** field of the IRD descriptor record.
SQL_DESC_LITERAL_PREFIX	Character string	Identifies one or more characters that are used as a prefix for a literal representation of the SQL data type used by the column. For example, a single quotation mark (') might be used for character data types, or '0x' might be used for binary data types. If a literal prefix is not applicable for the data type used, an empty string (" ") is returned for this attribute.
SQL_DESC_LITERAL_SUFFIX	Character string	Identifies one or more characters that are used as a suffix for a literal representation of the SQL data type used by the column. For example, a single quotation mark (') might be used for character data types. If a literal suffix is not applicable for the data type used, an empty string (" ") is returned for this attribute.
SQL_DESC_LOCAL_TYPE_NAME	Character string	Contains a character representation of any localized (native language) name for the data type used by the column that is different from the regular data type name used. If there is no localized name for the data type used, an empty string (" ") is returned for this attribute.
		This column is intended to be used for display purposes only. The string's character set is locale-dependent and usually defaults to the character set used by the data source.
SQL_DESC_NAME	Character string	Identifies the name or alias assigned to the column—if a column alias does not apply, the column name is returned for this attribute. If the column is unnamed, an empty string (" ") is returned for this attribute.

Table 10–2 Column Attribute (Descriptor) Information Returned By `SQLColAttribute()` (Continued)

Attribute	Data Type	Description
		DB2 CLI sets the `SQL_DESC_UNNAMED` attribute to `SQL_NAMED` if it populates this attribute; it sets the `SQL_DESC_UNNAMED` attribute to `SQL_UNNAMED` if it stores an empty string (" ") in this attribute.
		This information is obtained from the `SQL_DESC_NAME` field of the IRD descriptor header record.
`SQL_DESC_NULLABLE`	32-bit `INTEGER`	Indicates whether the column can contain NULL values. Valid values for this attribute are:
		`SQL_NULLABLE`: The column can contain NULL values.
		`SQL_NO_NULLS`: The column cannot contain NULL values.
		`SQL_NULLABLE_UNKNOWN`: Whether the column can contain NULL values is not known.
		This information is obtained from the `SQL_DESC_NULLABLE` field of the IRD descriptor record.
`SQL_DESC_NUM_PREX_RADIX`	32-bit `INTEGER`	Identifies the radix value of the data type used by the column.
		For approximate numeric data types, this attribute contains the value **2**, and the `SQL_DESC_PRECISION` attribute contains the number of bits allowed.
		For exact numeric data types, this attribute contains the value **10**, and the `SQL_DESC_PRECISION` attribute contains the number of decimal digits allowed.
		For numeric data types, this attribute can contain either **10** or **2**.
		For data types where radix is not applicable, this attribute is set to **0**.
`SQL_DESC_OCTET_LENGTH`	32-bit `INTEGER`	Identifies the length, in octets (bytes), of character string or binary data types. For fixed-length character types, this is the actual length in bytes. For variable-length character or binary types, this is the maximum length, in bytes. In either case, length values returned for character strings always include the NULL-termination character.
		This information is obtained from the `SQL_DESC_OCTECT_LENGTH` field of the IRD descriptor record.
`SQL_DESC_PRECISION`	32-bit `INTEGER`	Identifies the maximum number of bytes needed to display the column data in character form.
		For exact numeric data types, this attribute contains the precision in number of digits.
		For approximate numeric data types, this attribute contains the number of bits in the mantissa (binary precision).
		For `SQL_TYPE_TIME`, or `SQL_TYPE_TIMESTAMP` data types, this attribute contains the numbers of digits in the fractional seconds component of the value.

Table 10–2 Column Attribute (Descriptor) Information Returned By `SQLColAttribute()` (Continued)

Attribute	Data Type	Description
		For character data types, this attribute contains the maximum number of characters the column can hold.
		For graphic data types, this attribute contains the maximum number of double-byte characters the column can hold.
		This information is obtained from the `SQL_DESC_PRECISION` field of the IRD descriptor record.
`SQL_DESC_SCALE`	32-bit `INTEGER`	Identifies the scale defined for `DECIMAL` and `NUMERIC` data types.
		This field is undefined for all other data types.
		This information is obtained from the `SQL_DESC_SCALE` field of the IRD descriptor record.
`SQL_DESC_SCHEMA_NAME`	Character string	Identifies the schema (owner) of the table containing the column. Since DB2 does not support schemas (owners), an empty string (" ") is returned for this attribute.
`SQL_DESC_SEARCHABLE`	32-bit `INTEGER`	Indicates how the column data type is used in a `WHERE` clause. Valid values for this attribute are:
		`SQL_PRED_NONE`: The column cannot be used in a `WHERE` clause.
		`SQL_PRED_CHAR`: The column can be used in a `WHERE` clause, but only with the `LIKE` predicate.
		`SQL_PRED_BASIC`: The column can be used in a `WHERE` clause with all the comparison operators except `LIKE`.
		`SQL_PRED_SEARCHABLE`: The column can be used in a `WHERE` clause with any comparison operator.
		Columns with `SQL_LONGVARCHAR` and `SQL_LONGVARBINARY` data types usually have an `SQL_DESC_SEARCHABLE` attribute of `SQL_PRED_CHAR`.
`SQL_DESC_TABLE_NAME`	Character string	Identifies the name of the table containing the column. Because DB2 CLI cannot determine the value for this attribute, an empty string (" ") is always returned. If the column is an expression or part of a view, the value stored in this attribute is implementation defined.
`SQL_DESC_TYPE`	32-bit `INTEGER`	Identifies the concise SQL data type for the data type (other than datetime data types) used by the column. For datetime data types, this field specifies the verbose data type, which is `SQL_DATETIME`.
		If the column is a bookmark column (column number 0), this attribute contains `SQL_BINARY` if the bookmark is a variable-length bookmark, and `SQL_INTEGER` if the bookmark is a fixed-length bookmark.
		This information is obtained from the `SQL_DESC_TYPE` field of the IRD descriptor record.

Table 10–2 *Column Attribute (Descriptor) Information Returned By* **SQLColAttribute()** *(Continued)*

Attribute	Data Type	Description
SQL_DESC_ TYPE_NAME	Character string	Identifies the data source-specific character representation of the SQL data type used by the column. Valid values for this column include:

"CHAR"	**"VARCHAR"**
"LONG VARCHAR"	**"DECIMAL"**
"NUMERIC"	**"SMALLINT"**
"INTEGER"	**"REAL"**
"FLOAT"	**"DOUBLE PRECISION"**
"GRAPHIC"	**"VARGRAPHIC"**
"LONGVARGRAPHIC"	**"BINARY"**
"VARBINARY"	**"LONG VARBINARY"**
"DATE"	**"TIME"**
"TIMESTAMP"	**"BLOB"**
"BLOB LOCATOR"	**"CLOB"**
"CLOB LOCATOR"	**"DBCLOB"**
"DBCLOB LOCATOR"	

		If the data source-specific SQL data type name cannot be determined, an empty string is returned for this attribute.
SQL_DESC_ UNNAMED	32-bit **INTEGER**	Indicates whether a column in a result data set has an alias or a name. Valid values for this attribute are:

SQL_NAMED:
The **SQL_DESC_NAME** attribute contains a column alias, or if a column alias does not apply, a column name.

SQL_UNNAMED:
The **SQL_DESC_NAME** attribute does not contain a column alias or a column name.

This attribute is set by DB2 CLI when the **SQL_DESC_NAME** attribute is set.

This information is obtained from the **SQL_DESC_UNNAMED** field of the IRD descriptor record.

SQL_DESC_ UNSIGNED	32-bit **INTEGER**	Indicates whether the column data type is a signed or an unsigned data type. Valid values for this attribute are:

SQL_TRUE:
The column's data type is an unsigned data type.

SQL_FALSE:
The column's data type is a signed data type.

With DB2 CLI, **SQL_TRUE** is returned for all no-numeric data types; **SQL_FALSE** is returned for all numeric data types.

SQL_DESC_ UPDATABLE	32-bit **INTEGER**	Indicates whether the column data type is an updateable data type. Valid values for this attribute are:

SQL_ATTR_READONLY:
The column data type is read-only (this value is returned if the column was generated by a catalog function call).

Table 10–2   Column Attribute (Descriptor) Information Returned By `SQLColAttribute()` (Continued)

Attribute	Data Type	Description
		SQL_ATTR_WRITE: The column data type is updatable.
		SQL_ATTR_READWRITE_UNKNOWN: Whether the column data type is updateable is not known.
		This attribute describes the ability to update the column in the result data set, not the column in the base table. The ability to update the base column on which the result data set column is based may be different from the value of this attribute. Whether a column is updatable can be based on the data type, user privileges, and the definition of the result data set itself.

(Adapted from table 31 on pages 239–245 of *IBM DB2 Universal Database Call Level Interface Guide and Reference*.)

Prerequisites   The `SQLPrepare()` function or the `SQLExecDirect()` function must be called before this function is called. For performance reasons, an application should wait until an SQL statement has been executed before calling this function.

Restrictions   There are no restrictions associated with this function call.

See Also   `SQLDescribeCol()`, `SQLGetDescField()`, `SQLGetDescRec()`

Example   The following Visual C++ program illustrates how to use the `SQLColAttribute()` function to obtain specific information about a column in a result data set.

```
/*─────────────────────────────────────────────── */
/* NAME:      CH10EX3.CPP                           */
/* PURPOSE: Illustrate How To Use The Following CLI API Function */
/*           In A C++ Program:                      */
/*                                                  */
/*                SQLColAttribute()                 */
/*                                                  */
/* OTHER CLI APIs SHOWN:                            */
/*           SQLAllocHandle()         SQLSetEnvAttr()   */
/*           SQLConnect()             SQLExecDirect()   */
/*           SQLNumResultCols()       SQLDisconnect()   */
/*           SQLFreeHandle()                        */
/*                                                  */
/*─────────────────────────────────────────────── */

// Include The Appropriate Header Files
#include <windows.h>
#include <sqlcli1.h>
#include <iostream.h>

// Define The CLI_Class Class
class CLI_Class
{
    // Attributes
```

```
    public:
        SQLHANDLE   EnvHandle;
        SQLHANDLE   ConHandle;
        SQLHANDLE   StmtHandle;
        SQLRETURN   rc;

    // Operations
    public:
        CLI_Class();                            // Constructor
        ~CLI_Class();                           // Destructor
        SQLRETURN ShowColInfo();
};

// Define The Class Constructor
CLI_Class::CLI_Class()
{
    // Initialize The Return Code Variable
    rc = SQL_SUCCESS;

    // Allocate An Environment Handle
    rc = SQLAllocHandle(SQL_HANDLE_ENV, SQL_NULL_HANDLE, &EnvHandle);

    // Set The ODBC Application Version To 3.x
    if (rc == SQL_SUCCESS)
        rc = SQLSetEnvAttr(EnvHandle, SQL_ATTR_ODBC_VERSION,
                (SQLPOINTER) SQL_OV_ODBC3, SQL_IS_UINTEGER);

    // Allocate A Connection Handle
    if (rc == SQL_SUCCESS)
        rc = SQLAllocHandle(SQL_HANDLE_DBC, EnvHandle, &ConHandle);
}

// Define The Class Destructor
CLI_Class::~CLI_Class()
{
    // Free The Connection Handle
    if (ConHandle != NULL)
        SQLFreeHandle(SQL_HANDLE_DBC, ConHandle);

    // Free The Environment Handle
    if (EnvHandle != NULL)
        SQLFreeHandle(SQL_HANDLE_ENV, EnvHandle);
}

// Define The ShowColInfo() Member Function
SQLRETURN CLI_Class::ShowColInfo(void)
{
    // Declare The Local Memory Variables
    SQLSMALLINT  NumCols;
    SQLCHAR      TypeName[50];
    SQLSMALLINT  TypeNameLen;

    // Find Out How Many Columns Exist In The Result Data Set
    rc = SQLNumResultCols(StmtHandle, &NumCols);
    if (rc == SQL_SUCCESS)
```

```cpp
    {
        // Display A Header
        cout << "Column Data Types :" << endl << endl;

        // Obtain And Display The Name Of Each Column
        for (int i = 1; i <= (int) NumCols; i++)
        {
            rc = SQLColAttribute(StmtHandle, i, SQL_DESC_TYPE_NAME,
                    TypeName, sizeof(TypeName), &TypeNameLen, NULL);

            if (rc == SQL_SUCCESS)
                cout << "Column " << i << " : " << TypeName << endl;
        }
    }

    // Return The CLI API Return Code To The Calling Function
    return(rc);
}


/*————————————————————————————————————————————————— */
/* The Main Function                                 */
/*————————————————————————————————————————————————— */
int main()
{
    // Declare The Local Memory Variables
    SQLRETURN   rc = SQL_SUCCESS;
    SQLCHAR     SQLStmt[255];

    // Create An Instance Of The CLI_Class Class
    CLI_Class   Example;

    // Connect To The DB2 Sample Database
    if (Example.ConHandle != NULL)
    {
        rc = SQLConnect(Example.ConHandle, (SQLCHAR *) "SAMPLE",
                SQL_NTS, (SQLCHAR *) "userid", SQL_NTS,
                (SQLCHAR *) "password", SQL_NTS);

        // Allocate An SQL Statement Handle
        rc = SQLAllocHandle(SQL_HANDLE_STMT, Example.ConHandle,
                &Example.StmtHandle);
        if (rc == SQL_SUCCESS)
        {
            // Define A SELECT SQL Statement
            strcpy((char *) SQLStmt, "SELECT * FROM PROJECT");

            // Prepare And Execute The SQL Statement
            rc = SQLExecDirect(Example.StmtHandle, SQLStmt, SQL_NTS);

            // Display Information About The Columns In The Result
            // Data Set Produced By The SQL Query
            if (rc == SQL_SUCCESS)
                Example.ShowColInfo();

            // Free The SQL Statement Handle
```

```
                    if (Example.StmtHandle != NULL)
                        SQLFreeHandle(SQL_HANDLE_STMT, Example.StmtHandle);
                }

                // Disconnect From The DB2 Sample Database
                rc = SQLDisconnect(Example.ConHandle);
            }

            // Return To The Operating System
            return(rc);
        }
```

SQLBindCol

COMPATIBILITY

X/OPEN 95 CLI	ISO/IEC 92 CLI	DB2 CLI 5.2	DB2 CLI 2.0	ODBC 3.x
☑	☑	☑	☑	☑

ODBC API CONFORMANCE LEVEL   **CORE**

Purpose   The SQLBindCol() function is used to associate (bind) columns in a result data set with application variables and/or large object (LOB) locators.

Syntax

```
SQLRETURN   SQLBindCol   (SQLHSTMT      StatementHandle,
                          SQLUSMALLINT  ColumnNumber,
                          SQLSMALLINT   CDataType,
                          SQLPOINTER    Value,
                          SQLINTEGER    ValueMaxSize,
                          SQLINTEGER    *ValueSize_Indicator);
```

Parameters   *StatementHandle*   An SQL statement handle that refers to a previously allocated SQL statement information storage buffer (data structure).

ColumnNumber   Specifies the column's location in the result data set. Columns are numbered sequentially from left to right, starting with 1, as they appear in the result data set.

CDataType   The C language data type of the value memory storage buffer (*Value*) being bound. This parameter must be set to one of the following values:

- SQL_C_CHAR

- SQL_C_DBCHAR

- SQL_C_SHORT

- `SQL_C_LONG`
- `SQL_C_FLOAT`
- `SQL_C_DOUBLE`
- `SQL_C_NUMERIC`
- `SQL_C_BIT`
- `SQL_C_TINYINT`
- `SQL_C_BLOB_LOCATOR`
- `SQL_C_CLOB_LOCATOR`
- `SQL_C_DBCLOB_LOCATOR`
- `SQL_C_BINARY`
- `SQL_C_TYPE_DATE`
- `SQL_C_TYPE_TIME`
- `SQL_C_TYPE_TIMESTAMP`

Value

A pointer to a location in memory where DB2 CLI is to store column data (or an array of column data) when it is retrieved (fetched) from the result data set OR where the application is to store column data that is to be written to a data source with a positioned **UPDATE** or **DELETE** operation.

ValueMaxSize

The maximum size of the memory storage buffer where DB2 CLI is to store the column data retrieved.

ValueSize_Indicator

A pointer to a location in memory where DB2 CLI is to store (or retrieve) either the size of the data value associated with the column or a special indicator value associated with the column data.

Any of the following indicator values can be returned to this memory location by the driver (for fetch operations):

- `SQL_NO_TOTAL`
  The size of the column data value is unknown.

- `SQL_NULL_DATA`
  The data value associated with the column is NULL.

The application can store any of the following indicator values in this memory location (for positioned **INSERT**, **UPDATE**, and **DELETE** operations):

- `SQL_NTS`
  The data value associated with the column is a NULL-terminated string.

- `SQL_NULL_DATA`
  The data value associated with the column is NULL.

- `SQL_COLUMN_IGNORE`
  The data value associated with the column is to be ignored.

■ **SQL_DATA_AT_EXEC**

The data value associated with the column is to be sent to the application with the **SQLGetData()** function.

■ The result of the **SQL_LEN_DATA_AT_EXEC(*length*)** macro
The data value associated with the column is to be sent to the application with the **SQLGetData()** function.

Description   The **SQLBindCol()** function is used to associate (bind) columns in a result data set to application variables and/or LOB locators—and, optionally, to length/indicator variables. When columns in a result data set are bound to application variables, data is transferred from the data source to the appropriate application variable/buffer when the **SQLFetch()**, **SQLFetchScroll()**, or **SQLSetPos()** function is called. Conversely, data is transferred from bound application variable/buffers to the data source when a positioned **UPDATE** or **DELETE** operation is performed. If necessary, data conversion occurs as the data is transferred.

Return Codes   SQL_SUCCESS, SQL_SUCCESS_WITH_INFO, SQL_INVALID_HANDLE, SQL_ERROR

SQLSTATEs   If this function returns **SQL_SUCCESS_WITH_INFO** or **SQL_ERROR**, one of the following SQLSTATE values may be obtained by calling the **SQLGetDiagRec()** function:

07009, **08**S01, **40**003, **58**004, **HY**001, **HY**002, **HY**003, **HY**010, **HY**013, **HY**090, or **HY**C00

Refer to Appendix B for detailed information about each SQLSTATE value that can be returned.

Comments   ■ Columns are numbered in increasing column order as they appear in the result data set, starting at 0, where column 0 is the bookmark column. If bookmarks are not used (that is, if the **SQL_ATTR_USE_BOOKMARKS** SQL statement attribute is set to **SQL_UB_OFF**), column numbers start at 1.

■ When data is retrieved from a result data set by **SQLFetch()**, **SQLFetchScroll()**, or **SQLSetPos()**, DB2 CLI converts the data to the C data type specified in the *CDataType* parameter. When data is sent to the data source by a positioned **UPDATE** or **DELETE** operation, DB2 CLI converts the data from this C data type.

■ If a numeric data type (**SQL_C_NUMERIC**) is stored in the *CDataType* parameter, the default precision (driver-defined) and default scale (**0**), as set in the ARD descriptor's **SQL_DESC_PRECISION** and **SQL_DESC_SCALE** fields, are used for data conversion. If the default precision or scale is not appropriate, an application should explicitly set the appropriate descriptor field by calling **SQLSetDescField()** or **SQLSetDescRec()**.

■ If a NULL pointer is stored in the *Value* parameter, DB2 CLI unbinds any application variable currently bound to the column specified. An application can unbind the application variable currently bound to a column without unbinding the corresponding length/indicator buffer (if a NULL pointer is stored in the *Value* parameter and a valid value is stored in the *ValueSize_Indicator* parameter).

■ An application can unbind all bound columns by calling **SQLFreeStmt()** with the **SQL_UNBIND** option specified.

■ When DB2 CLI returns fixed-length data such as integer or date structure data to an application variable, it assumes the buffer is large enough to hold the data. Therefore, it is important for the application to use a variable or allocate a buffer that is large enough to hold the fixed-length data stored in the column; otherwise, DB2 CLI will write past the end of the buffer.

■ When a value less than 0 is stored in the *ValueMaxSize* parameter, SQLSTATE **HY**090 (Invalid string or buffer length) is returned. This is not the case when 0 is stored in the *ValueMaxSize* parameter; however, if a character data type is specified in the *CDataType* parameter, an application should not store 0 in the *ValueMaxSize* parameter because ISO CLI-compliant drivers return SQLSTATE **HY**090 (Invalid string or buffer length) when this condition is encountered.

■ If the indicator buffer and the length buffer are separate buffers, the indicator buffer can only return `SQL_NULL_DATA`, while the length buffer can return all other values specified.

■ If a NULL pointer is stored in the *ValueSize_Indicator* parameter, no length or indicator value is used.

■ If no length/indicator variable is bound to a column, `SQL_ERROR` is returned if a NULL value is found in the column when data is fetched.

■ Although it is not required, it is strongly recommended that an application set the `SQL_ATTR_USE_BOOKMARKS` statement attribute before binding an application variable to column 0.

Prerequisites There are no prerequisites for using this function call.

Restrictions There are no restrictions associated with this function call.

See Also `SQLFetch()`, `SQLFetchScroll()`, `SQLGetData()`, `SQLSetPos()`

Example The following Visual C++ program illustrates how to use the `SQLBindCol()` function to associate (bind) a local memory variable to a column in a result data set.

```
/*———————————————————————————————————————————————— */
/* NAME:      CH10EX4.CPP                                  */
/* PURPOSE: Illustrate How To Use The Following CLI API Functions */
/*          In A C++ Program:                              */
/*                                                         */
/*               SQLBindCol()                              */
/*               SQLFetch()                                */
/*                                                         */
/* OTHER CLI APIs SHOWN:                                   */
/*               SQLAllocHandle()          SQLSetEnvAttr() */
/*               SQLConnect()              SQLExecDirect()  */
/*               SQLDisconnect()           SQLFreeHandle()  */
/*                                                         */
/*———————————————————————————————————————————————— */

// Include The Appropriate Header Files
#include <windows.h>
```

```cpp
#include <sqlcli1.h>
#include <iostream.h>

// Define The CLI_Class Class
class CLI_Class
{
    // Attributes
    public:
        SQLHANDLE   EnvHandle;
        SQLHANDLE   ConHandle;
        SQLHANDLE   StmtHandle;
        SQLRETURN   rc;

    // Operations
    public:
        CLI_Class();                            // Constructor
        ~CLI_Class();                           // Destructor
        SQLRETURN ShowResults();
};

// Define The Class Constructor
CLI_Class::CLI_Class()
{
    // Initialize The Return Code Variable
    rc = SQL_SUCCESS;

    // Allocate An Environment Handle
    rc = SQLAllocHandle(SQL_HANDLE_ENV, SQL_NULL_HANDLE, &EnvHandle);

    // Set The ODBC Application Version To 3.x
    if (rc == SQL_SUCCESS)
        rc = SQLSetEnvAttr(EnvHandle, SQL_ATTR_ODBC_VERSION,
                (SQLPOINTER) SQL_OV_ODBC3, SQL_IS_UINTEGER);

    // Allocate A Connection Handle
    if (rc == SQL_SUCCESS)
        rc = SQLAllocHandle(SQL_HANDLE_DBC, EnvHandle, &ConHandle);
}

// Define The Class Destructor
CLI_Class::~CLI_Class()
{
    // Free The Connection Handle
    if (ConHandle != NULL)
        SQLFreeHandle(SQL_HANDLE_DBC, ConHandle);

    // Free The Environment Handle
    if (EnvHandle != NULL)
        SQLFreeHandle(SQL_HANDLE_ENV, EnvHandle);
}

// Define The ShowResults() Member Function
SQLRETURN CLI_Class::ShowResults(void)
{
```

```cpp
    // Declare The Local Memory Variables
    SQLCHAR   LastName[50];
    SQLCHAR   FirstName[50];

    // Bind The Columns In The Result Data Set Returned To
    // Application Variables
    rc = SQLBindCol(StmtHandle, 1, SQL_C_CHAR, (SQLPOINTER) LastName,
            sizeof(LastName), NULL);

    rc = SQLBindCol(StmtHandle, 2, SQL_C_CHAR, (SQLPOINTER) FirstName,
            sizeof(FirstName), NULL);

    // Display A Header
    cout << "Employees :" << endl << endl;

    // While There Are Records In The Result Data Set Generated,
    // Retrieve And Display Them
    while (rc != SQL_NO_DATA)
    {
        rc = SQLFetch(StmtHandle);
        if (rc != SQL_NO_DATA)
            cout << FirstName << " " << LastName << endl;
    }

    // Return The CLI API Return Code To The Calling Function
    return(rc);
}

/*-------------------------------------------------------------- */
/* The Main Function                                             */
/*-------------------------------------------------------------- */
int main()
{
    // Declare The Local Memory Variables
    SQLRETURN  rc = SQL_SUCCESS;
    SQLCHAR    SQLStmt[255];

    // Create An Instance Of The CLI_Class Class
    CLI_Class  Example;

    // Connect To The DB2 Sample Database
    if (Example.ConHandle != NULL)
    {
        rc = SQLConnect(Example.ConHandle, (SQLCHAR *) "SAMPLE",
                SQL_NTS, (SQLCHAR *) "userid", SQL_NTS,
                (SQLCHAR *) "password", SQL_NTS);

        // Allocate An SQL Statement Handle
        rc = SQLAllocHandle(SQL_HANDLE_STMT, Example.ConHandle,
                &Example.StmtHandle);
        if (rc == SQL_SUCCESS)
        {
            // Define A SELECT SQL Statement
            strcpy((char *) SQLStmt, "SELECT LASTNAME, FIRSTNME ");
```

```
                    strcat((char *) SQLStmt, "FROM EMPLOYEE");

                    // Prepare And Execute The SQL Statement
                    rc = SQLExecDirect(Example.StmtHandle, SQLStmt, SQL_NTS);

                    // Display The Results Of The SQL Query
                    if (rc == SQL_SUCCESS)
                        Example.ShowResults();

                    // Free The SQL Statement Handle
                    if (Example.StmtHandle != NULL)
                        SQLFreeHandle(SQL_HANDLE_STMT, Example.StmtHandle);
                }

                // Disconnect From The DB2 Sample Database
                rc = SQLDisconnect(Example.ConHandle);
            }

            // Return To The Operating System
            return(rc);
        }
```

SQLGetCursorName

COMPATIBILITY

X/OPEN 95 CLI	ISO/IEC 92 CLI	DB2 CLI 5.2	DB2 CLI 2.0	ODBC 3.x
☑	☑	☑	☑	☑

ODBC API CONFORMANCE LEVEL   CORE

Purpose   The SQLGetCursorName() function is used to retrieve the name of the cursor associated with a specific SQL statement handle.

Syntax

```
SQLRETURN   SQLGetCursorName   (SQLHSTMT      StatementHandle,
                                SQLCHAR       *CursorName,
                                SQLSMALLINT   CursorNameMaxSize,
                                SQLSMALLINT   *CursorNameSize);
```

Parameters   *StatementHandle*   An SQL statement handle that refers to a previously allocated SQL statement information storage buffer (data structure).

CursorName   A pointer to a location in memory where this function is to store the cursor name retrieved.

CursorNameMaxSize   The maximum size of the memory storage buffer where this function is to store the cursor name retrieved.

CursorNameSize	A pointer to a location in memory where this function is to store the actual number of bytes written to the cursor name memory storage buffer (*CursorName*).

Description

The `SQLGetCursorName()` function is used to retrieve the name of the cursor associated with a specific SQL statement handle. When this function is executed, the cursor name internally generated by DB2 CLI is returned unless that cursor name was explicitly renamed by the `SQLSetCursorName()` function—in which case, the new cursor name is returned.

Cursor names are only used in positioned **UPDATE** and **DELETE** statements (for example, **UPDATE [table-name]...WHERE CURRENT OF [cursor-name]**).

Return Codes

SQL_SUCCESS, SQL_SUCCESS_WITH_INFO, SQL_INVALID_HANDLE, or SQL_ERROR

SQLSTATEs

If this function returns `SQL_SUCCESS_WITH_INFO` or `SQL_ERROR`, one of the following SQLSTATE values may be obtained by calling the `SQLGetDiagRec()` function:

01004, **08**S01, **40**003, **58**004, **HY**001, **HY**010, **HY**013, or **HY**090

Refer to Appendix B for detailed information about each SQLSTATE value that can be returned.

Comments

■ If the cursor name string's actual length is greater than or equal to the maximum string size value specified in the *CursorNameMaxSize* parameter, it is truncated to *CursorNameMaxSize*-1 (the length of a NULL-termination character) characters.

■ If the name assigned to the cursor is a Unicode string, the *CursorNameMaxSize* parameter must contain an even number.

■ If the application does not call `SQLSetCursorName()` to define a cursor name, DB2 automatically generates a name. This name begins with the letters "SQLCUR" if DB2 CLI or an X/Open 95-ISO/IEC 92 compliant driver is being used (or the letters "SQL_CUR" if an ODBC driver is being used) and does not exceed `SQL_MAX_ID_LENGTH` (**18**) characters in length.

■ The `SQLSetCursorName()` function can be used to rename a cursor associated with an SQL statement handle, provided the cursor is in the "Allocated" or "Prepared" state.

■ Once a cursor name has been set, either explicitly or implicitly, it remains set until the SQL statement handle that the cursor is associated with is freed.

Prerequisites

There are no prerequisites for using this function call.

Restrictions

There are no restrictions associated with this function call.

See Also

`SQLSetCursorName()`, `SQLPrepare()`, `SQLExecute()`, `SQLExecDirect()`, `SQLFetch()`, `SQLCloseCursor()`

Example

The following Visual C++ program illustrates how to use the `SQLGetCursorName()` function to obtain the system-generated name of a cursor.

```
/*-------------------------------------------------------------- */
/* NAME:    CH10EX5.CPP                                          */
/* PURPOSE: Illustrate How To Use The Following CLI API Function */
/*          In A C++ Program:                                    */
/*                                                               */
/*                  SQLGetCursorName()                           */
/*                                                               */
/* OTHER CLI APIs SHOWN:                                         */
/*              SQLAllocHandle()            SQLSetEnvAttr()      */
/*              SQLConnect()                SQLExecDirect()      */
/*              SQLDisconnect()             SQLFreeHandle()      */
/*                                                               */
/*-------------------------------------------------------------- */

// Include The Appropriate Header Files
#include <windows.h>
#include <sqlcli1.h>
#include <iostream.h>

// Define The CLI_Class Class
class CLI_Class
{
    // Attributes
    public:
        SQLHANDLE   EnvHandle;
        SQLHANDLE   ConHandle;
        SQLHANDLE   StmtHandle;
        SQLRETURN   rc;

    // Operations
    public:
        CLI_Class();                        // Constructor
        ~CLI_Class();                       // Destructor
};

// Define The Class Constructor
CLI_Class::CLI_Class()
{
    // Initialize The Return Code Variable
    rc = SQL_SUCCESS;

    // Allocate An Environment Handle
    rc = SQLAllocHandle(SQL_HANDLE_ENV, SQL_NULL_HANDLE, &EnvHandle);

    // Set The ODBC Application Version To 3.x
    if (rc == SQL_SUCCESS)
        rc = SQLSetEnvAttr(EnvHandle, SQL_ATTR_ODBC_VERSION,
                (SQLPOINTER) SQL_OV_ODBC3, SQL_IS_UINTEGER);

    // Allocate A Connection Handle
    if (rc == SQL_SUCCESS)
        rc = SQLAllocHandle(SQL_HANDLE_DBC, EnvHandle, &ConHandle);
}

// Define The Class Destructor
```

```cpp
CLI_Class::~CLI_Class()
{
    // Free The Connection Handle
    if (ConHandle != NULL)
        SQLFreeHandle(SQL_HANDLE_DBC, ConHandle);

    // Free The Environment Handle
    if (EnvHandle != NULL)
        SQLFreeHandle(SQL_HANDLE_ENV, EnvHandle);
}

/*——————————————————————————————————————— */
/* The Main Function                                        */
/*——————————————————————————————————————— */
int main()
{
    // Declare The Local Memory Variables
    SQLRETURN     rc = SQL_SUCCESS;
    SQLCHAR       SQLStmt[255];
    SQLCHAR       CursorName[80];
    SQLSMALLINT   CNameSize;

    // Create An Instance Of The CLI_Class Class
    CLI_Class     Example;

    // Connect To The DB2 Sample Database
    if (Example.ConHandle != NULL)
    {
        rc = SQLConnect(Example.ConHandle, (SQLCHAR *) "SAMPLE",
                SQL_NTS, (SQLCHAR *) "userid", SQL_NTS,
                (SQLCHAR *) "password", SQL_NTS);

        // Allocate An SQL Statement Handle
        rc = SQLAllocHandle(SQL_HANDLE_STMT, Example.ConHandle,
                &Example.StmtHandle);
        if (rc == SQL_SUCCESS)
        {
            // Define A SELECT SQL Statement
            strcpy((char *) SQLStmt, "SELECT LASTNAME, FIRSTNME ");
            strcat((char *) SQLStmt, "FROM EMPLOYEE");

            // Prepare And Execute The SQL Statement
            rc = SQLExecDirect(Example.StmtHandle, SQLStmt, SQL_NTS);

            // Retrieve And Display The CLI-Generated Cursor Name
            if (rc == SQL_SUCCESS)
            {
                rc = SQLGetCursorName(Example.StmtHandle, CursorName,
                        sizeof(CursorName), &CNameSize);

                cout << "CLI-Generated Cursor Name : ";
                cout << CursorName << endl << endl;
            }

            // Free The SQL Statement Handle
```

```
                        if (Example.StmtHandle != NULL)
                            SQLFreeHandle(SQL_HANDLE_STMT, Example.StmtHandle);
                    }

                    // Disconnect From The DB2 Sample Database
                    rc = SQLDisconnect(Example.ConHandle);
                }

                // Return To The Operating System
                return(rc);
            }
```

SQLSetCursorName

COMPATIBILITY

X/OPEN 95 CLI	ISO/IEC 92 CLI	DB2 CLI 5.2	DB2 CLI 2.0	ODBC 3.x
☑	☑	☑	☑	☑

ODBC API CONFORMANCE LEVEL   CORE

Purpose   The **SQLSetCursorName()** function is used to assign a user-defined name to a cursor that is associated with an active SQL statement handle.

Syntax
```
SQLRETURN   SQLSetCursorName   (SQLHSTMT       StatementHandle,
                                SQLCHAR        *CursorName,
                                SQLSMALLINT    CursorNameSize);
```

Parameters   *StatementHandle*   An SQL statement handle that refers to a previously allocated SQL statement information storage buffer (data structure).

CursorName   A pointer to a location in memory where the user-defined cursor name is stored.

CursorNameSize   The length of the cursor name specified in the *CursorName* parameter.

Description   The **SQLSetCursorName()** function is used to assign a user-defined name to a cursor that is associated with an active SQL statement handle. Usually, DB2 CLI generates and uses an internally generated cursor name whenever a SQL query statement is either prepared or executed directly. This function allows an application to replace this internally generated cursor name with a user-defined name. This user-defined cursor name can then be used in place of the internally generated cursor name in positioned **UPDATE** and positioned **DELETE** SQL statements. Once assigned, a user-defined cursor name remains associated with the SQL statement handle specified until the SQL statement handle is deleted or until the cursor is renamed by another **SQLSetCursorName()** function call.

Return Codes   SQL_SUCCESS, SQL_SUCCESS_WITH_INFO, SQL_INVALID_HANDLE, or SQL_ERROR

SQLSTATEs   If this function returns SQL_SUCCESS_WITH_INFO or SQL_ERROR, one of the following SQLSTATE values may be obtained by calling the SQLGetDiagRec() function:

34000, **08**S01, **40**003, **58**004, **HY**001, **HY**009, **HY**010, **HY**013, or **HY**090

Refer to Appendix B for detailed information about each SQLSTATE value that can be returned.

Comments   ■ For efficient processing, the cursor name specified should not include any leading or trailing spaces. Also, if the cursor name includes a delimited identifier, the delimiter should be positioned as the first character in the cursor name.

■ All cursor names within a connection must be unique.

■ This function is optional since DB2 CLI automatically generates a cursor name whenever an SQL statement handle is allocated.

■ Although the SQLGetCursorName() function returns the user-defined cursor name if one has been set, error messages associated with positioned UPDATE and DELETE SQL statements will reference only internally generated cursor names. For this reason, it is recommended that you not use user-defined cursor names in place of internal names.

■ You must adhere to the following rules when creating user-defined cursor names:

■ Each cursor name must be less than or equal to 18 characters (bytes) in length. Any attempt to set a cursor name longer than 18 bytes will result in truncation of that cursor name to 18 bytes. No error or warning message is generated when a cursor name is truncated.

■ Since internally generated names begin with the characters "SQLCUR" or "SQL_CUR," user-defined cursor names cannot begin with either of these strings. This avoids conflicts with internal names.

■ Since a cursor name is considered an identifier in SQL, cursor names must begin with an English letter (a to z, A to Z) followed by any combination of digits (0 to 9), English letters, or the underscore character. If a cursor name needs to contain characters other than those listed (such as National Language Set or Double-Byte Character Set characters), it must be enclosed in double quotation marks.

■ Unless the cursor name is enclosed in double quotes, all leading and trailing blanks from the user-defined cursor name string will be removed. Therefore, for efficient processing, user-defined cursor names should not include leading or trailing spaces.

■ If the cursor name is enclosed in double quotes, the first and last character in the *CursorName* string must be a double quotation mark.

Prerequisites   There are no prerequisites for using this function call.

Restrictions   This function can only rename a cursor associated with an SQL statement handle that is in the "Allocated" or "Prepared" state.

See Also   SQLGetCursorName(), SQLPrepare(), SQLExecute(), SQLExecDirect(), SQLFetch(), SQLCloseCursor()

Example   The following Visual C++ program illustrates how to use the SQLSetCursorName() function to assign a user-defined name to a cursor.

```
/*----------------------------------------------------------------- */
/* NAME:     CH10EX6.CPP                                            */
/* PURPOSE: Illustrate How To Use The Following CLI API Function    */
/*          In A C++ Program:                                       */
/*                                                                  */
/*              SQLSetCursorName                                    */
/*                                                                  */
/* OTHER CLI APIs SHOWN:                                            */
/*              SQLAllocHandle()             SQLSetEnvAttr()         */
/*              SQLConnect()                 SQLPrepare()            */
/*              SQLExecute()                 SQLGetCursorName()      */
/*              SQLDisconnect()              SQLFreeHandle()         */
/*                                                                  */
/*----------------------------------------------------------------- */

// Include The Appropriate Header Files
#include <windows.h>
#include <sqlcli1.h>
#include <iostream.h>

// Define The CLI_Class Class
class CLI_Class
{
    // Attributes
    public:
        SQLHANDLE    EnvHandle;
        SQLHANDLE    ConHandle;
        SQLHANDLE    StmtHandle;
        SQLRETURN    rc;

    // Operations
    public:
        CLI_Class();                          // Constructor
        ~CLI_Class();                         // Destructor
};

// Define The Class Constructor
CLI_Class::CLI_Class()
{
    // Initialize The Return Code Variable
    rc = SQL_SUCCESS;

    // Allocate An Environment Handle
    rc = SQLAllocHandle(SQL_HANDLE_ENV, SQL_NULL_HANDLE, &EnvHandle);

    // Set The ODBC Application Version To 3.x
    if (rc == SQL_SUCCESS)
        rc = SQLSetEnvAttr(EnvHandle, SQL_ATTR_ODBC_VERSION,
```

```
                        (SQLPOINTER) SQL_OV_ODBC3, SQL_IS_UINTEGER);

    // Allocate A Connection Handle
    if (rc == SQL_SUCCESS)
        rc = SQLAllocHandle(SQL_HANDLE_DBC, EnvHandle, &ConHandle);
}

// Define The Class Destructor
CLI_Class::~CLI_Class()
{
    // Free The Connection Handle
    if (ConHandle != NULL)
        SQLFreeHandle(SQL_HANDLE_DBC, ConHandle);

    // Free The Environment Handle
    if (EnvHandle != NULL)
        SQLFreeHandle(SQL_HANDLE_ENV, EnvHandle);
}

/*———————————————————————————————————————— */
/* The Main Function                        */
/*———————————————————————————————————————— */
int main()
{
    // Declare The Local Memory Variables
    SQLRETURN      rc = SQL_SUCCESS;
    SQLCHAR        SQLStmt[255];
    SQLCHAR        CursorName[80];
    SQLSMALLINT    CNameSize;

    // Create An Instance Of The CLI_Class Class
    CLI_Class      Example;

    // Connect To The DB2 Sample Database
    if (Example.ConHandle != NULL)
    {
        rc = SQLConnect(Example.ConHandle, (SQLCHAR *) "SAMPLE",
                SQL_NTS, (SQLCHAR *) "userid", SQL_NTS,
                (SQLCHAR *) "password", SQL_NTS);

        // Allocate An SQL Statement Handle
        rc = SQLAllocHandle(SQL_HANDLE_STMT, Example.ConHandle,
                &Example.StmtHandle);
        if (rc == SQL_SUCCESS)
        {
            // Define A SELECT SQL Statement
            strcpy((char *) SQLStmt, "SELECT LASTNAME, FIRSTNME ");
            strcat((char *) SQLStmt, "FROM EMPLOYEE");

            // Prepare The SQL Statement
            rc = SQLPrepare(Example.StmtHandle, SQLStmt, SQL_NTS);

            // Set The Cursor Name
            rc = SQLSetCursorName(Example.StmtHandle, (SQLCHAR *)
                    "EMP_CURSOR", SQL_NTS);
```

```
                // Execute The SQL Statement
                rc = SQLExecute(Example.StmtHandle);

                // Retrieve And Display The New Cursor Name
                if (rc == SQL_SUCCESS)
                {
                    rc = SQLGetCursorName(Example.StmtHandle, CursorName,
                            sizeof(CursorName), &CNameSize);

                    cout << "User-Defined Cursor Name : ";
                    cout << CursorName << endl;
                }

                // Free The SQL Statement Handle
                if (Example.StmtHandle != NULL)
                    SQLFreeHandle(SQL_HANDLE_STMT, Example.StmtHandle);
            }

            // Disconnect From The DB2 Sample Database
            rc = SQLDisconnect(Example.ConHandle);
        }

        // Return To The Operating System
        return(rc);
    }
```

SQLFetch

COMPATIBILITY

X/OPEN 95 CLI	ISO/IEC 92 CLI	DB2 CLI 5.2	DB2 CLI 2.0	ODBC 3.x
☑	☑	☑	☑	☑

ODBC API CONFORMANCE LEVEL   CORE

Purpose   The SQLFetch() function is used to advance a cursor to the next row of data in a result data set and to retrieve data from any bound columns that exist for that row into their associated application variables/LOB locators.

Syntax   SQLRETURN   SQLFetch   (SQLHSTMT   *StatementHandle);

Parameters   *StatementHandle*   An SQL statement handle that refers to a previously allocated SQL statement information storage buffer (data structure).

Description   The SQLFetch() function is used to advance a cursor to the next row of data in a result data set and to retrieve data from any bound columns that exist for that row into their associated application variables/LOB locators. This function can only be called while a result data set exists (that is, after an SQL statement that creates a result set is executed and before the cursor associated with that result data set is closed). If the application has specified a pointer to a row status array or an application variable/buffer in which to return the number of rows fetched, **SQLFetch()** returns this information as well.

When the **SQLFetch()** function is called, the appropriate data transfer is performed along with any data conversion that was specified when the columns were bound. Data in unbound columns can also be retrieved individually after the **SQLFetch()** function executes by calling the **SQLGetData()** function.

Return Codes SQL_SUCCESS, SQL_SUCCESS_WITH_INFO, SQL_NO_DATA, SQL_STILL_EXECUTING, SQL_INVALID_HANDLE, SQL_ERROR

For all those SQLSTATEs that can return **SQL_SUCCESS_WITH_INFO** or **SQL_ERROR** (except **01**xxx SQLSTATEs), **SQL_SUCCESS_WITH_INFO** is returned if an error occurs on one or more, but not all, rows of a multi-row operation, and **SQL_ERROR** is returned if an error occurs on a single-row operation.

SQLSTATEs If this function returns **SQL_SUCCESS_WITH_INFO** or **SQL_ERROR**, one of the following SQLSTATE values may be obtained by calling the **SQLGetDiagRec()** function:

01004, **07**002, **07**006, **07**009, **08**501, **22**002, **22**003, **22**005, **22**007, **22**008, **22**012, **24**000, **40**003, **428A1**, **54**028, **56**084, **58**004, **HY**001, **HY**008, **HY**010, **HY**013, **HY**092, **HYC**00, or **HYT**00

Refer to Appendix B for detailed information about each SQLSTATE value that can be returned.

Comments
- Calls to **SQLFetch()** can be mixed with calls to **SQLFetchScroll()**.
- When a result data set is first created, the cursor is positioned before the start of the first row in the result data set.
- In DB2 CLI 5.2, **SQLFetch()** fetches the next rowset. This is equivalent to calling **SQLFetchScroll()** with the **SQL_FETCH_NEXT** orientation specified.
- The contents of all bound application variables/LOB locators and their corresponding length/indicator variables are undefined if this function does not return **SQL_SUCCESS** or **SQL_SUCCESS_WITH_INFO**.
- If the number of columns that have been bound to application variables/LOB locators exceed the actual number of columns found in the result data set, this function will return **SQL_ERROR** when it is called.
- This function will advance the cursor to the next row without returning data to the calling application if no columns in the result dat set have been bound to application variables/LOB locators.
- Data stored in unbound columns is discarded when the cursor is advanced to the next row.
- If data for numeric data types is truncated to the right of the decimal point, when this function is called, **SQL_SUCCESS_WITH_INFO** is returned and a warning is generated. If truncation occurs to the left of the decimal point, **SQL_ERROR** is returned.

Prerequisites This function can only be called after a result data set has been generated for the SQL statement handle specified. A result data set can be generated either by executing an SQL query, by calling the **SQLGetTypeInfo()** function, or by calling any CLI catalog function described in Chapter 15.

Restrictions There are no restrictions associated with this function call.

See Also **SQLFetchScroll()**, **SQLBindCol()**, **SQLExecute()**, **SQLExecDirect()**, **SQLGetData()**

Example See the example provided for the **SQLBindCol()** function on page 375.

SQLCloseCursor

COMPATIBILITY

X/OPEN 95 CLI	ISO/IEC 92 CLI	DB2 CLI 5.2	DB2 CLI 2.0	ODBC 3.x
☑	☑	☑	☐	☑

ODBC API CONFORMANCE LEVEL   CORE

Purpose The **SQLCloseCursor()** function is used to close a cursor that has been opened on an SQL statement handle.

Syntax `SQLRETURN   SQLCloseCursor   (SQLHSTMT        StatementHandle);`

Parameters *StatementHandle* An SQL statement handle that refers to a previously allocated SQL statement information storage buffer (data structure).

Description The **SQLCloseCursor()** function is used to close a cursor that has been opened on an SQL statement handle. If a cursor is closed while it contains results that are pending, those results are discarded.

Return Codes SQL_SUCCESS, SQL_SUCCESS_WITH_INFO, SQL_INVALID_HANDLE, SQL_ERROR

SQLSTATEs If this function returns **SQL_SUCCESS_WITH_INFO** or **SQL_ERROR**, one of the following SQLSTATE values may be obtained by calling the **SQLGetDiagRec()** function:

01000, **24**000, **HY**000, **HY**001, **HY**010, or **HY**013

Refer to Appendix B for detailed information about each SQLSTATE value that can be returned.

Comments ■ If this function is called when no cursor is open, **SQL_ERROR** is returned along with SQLSTATE **24**000 (Invalid cursor state).

■ Calling this function is equivalent to calling the **SQLFreeStmt()** function with the **SQL_CLOSE** option specified with one exception. The **SQLFreeStmt()** function does not return an error if it is called when no cursor is open.

Prerequisites   There are no prerequisites for using this function call.

Restrictions   There are no restrictions associated with this function call.

See Also   `SQLGetCursorName()`, `SQLSetCursorName()`, `SQLFetch()`

Example   The following Visual C++ program illustrates how to use the `SQLCloseCursor()` function to close a cursor and discard remaining results.

```
/*———————————————————————————————————*/
/* NAME:      CH10EX7.CPP                                      */
/* PURPOSE: Illustrate How To Use The Following CLI API Function  */
/*          In A C++ Program:                                 */
/*                                                            */
/*              SQLCloseCursor()                              */
/*                                                            */
/* OTHER CLI APIs SHOWN:                                      */
/*          SQLAllocHandle()              SQLSetEnvAttr()     */
/*          SQLConnect()                  SQLExecDirect()     */
/*          SQLBindCol()                  SQLFetch()          */
/*          SQLDisconnect()               SQLFreeHandle()     */
/*                                                            */
/*———————————————————————————————————*/

// Include The Appropriate Header Files
#include <windows.h>
#include <sqlcli1.h>
#include <iostream.h>

// Define The CLI_Class Class
class CLI_Class
{
    // Attributes
    public:
        SQLHANDLE  EnvHandle;
        SQLHANDLE  ConHandle;
        SQLHANDLE  StmtHandle;
        SQLRETURN  rc;

    // Operations
    public:
        CLI_Class();                          // Constructor
        ~CLI_Class();                         // Destructor
        SQLRETURN ShowResults();
};

// Define The Class Constructor
CLI_Class::CLI_Class()
{
    // Initialize The Return Code Variable
    rc = SQL_SUCCESS;

    // Allocate An Environment Handle
    rc = SQLAllocHandle(SQL_HANDLE_ENV, SQL_NULL_HANDLE, &EnvHandle);
```

```cpp
    // Set The ODBC Application Version To 3.x
    if (rc == SQL_SUCCESS)
        rc = SQLSetEnvAttr(EnvHandle, SQL_ATTR_ODBC_VERSION,
                    (SQLPOINTER) SQL_OV_ODBC3, SQL_IS_UINTEGER);

    // Allocate A Connection Handle
    if (rc == SQL_SUCCESS)
        rc = SQLAllocHandle(SQL_HANDLE_DBC, EnvHandle, &ConHandle);
}

// Define The Class Destructor
CLI_Class::~CLI_Class()
{
    // Free The Connection Handle
    if (ConHandle != NULL)
        SQLFreeHandle(SQL_HANDLE_DBC, ConHandle);

    // Free The Environment Handle
    if (EnvHandle != NULL)
        SQLFreeHandle(SQL_HANDLE_ENV, EnvHandle);
}

// Define The ShowResults() Member Function
SQLRETURN CLI_Class::ShowResults(void)
{
    // Declare The Local Memory Variables
    SQLCHAR   LastName[50];
    SQLCHAR   FirstName[50];
    int       Counter = 0;

    // Bind The Columns In The Result Data Set Returned To
    // Application Variables
    rc = SQLBindCol(StmtHandle, 1, SQL_C_CHAR, (SQLPOINTER)
            LastName, sizeof(LastName), NULL);

    rc = SQLBindCol(StmtHandle, 2, SQL_C_CHAR, (SQLPOINTER)
            FirstName, sizeof(FirstName), NULL);

    // Display A Header
    cout << "Employees :" << endl << endl;

    // While There Are Records In The Result Data Set Generated,
    // Retrieve And Display Them
    while (rc != SQL_NO_DATA)
    {
        rc = SQLFetch(StmtHandle);
        if (rc != SQL_NO_DATA)
            cout << FirstName << " " << LastName << endl;

        // Increment The Loop Counter - Stop When The First
        // 15 Records Have Been Displayed
        Counter++;
        if (Counter == 15)
        {
            rc = SQLCloseCursor(StmtHandle);
```

```c
                break;
        }
    }

    // Return The CLI API Return Code To The Calling Function
    return(rc);
}

/*---------------------------------------------------------------------------*/
/* The Main Function                                                         */
/*---------------------------------------------------------------------------*/
int main()
{
    // Declare The Local Memory Variables
    SQLRETURN   rc = SQL_SUCCESS;
    SQLCHAR     SQLStmt[255];

    // Create An Instance Of The CLI_Class Class
    CLI_Class   Example;

    // Connect To The DB2 Sample Database
    if (Example.ConHandle != NULL)
    {
        rc = SQLConnect(Example.ConHandle, (SQLCHAR *) "SAMPLE",
                SQL_NTS, (SQLCHAR *) "userid", SQL_NTS,
                (SQLCHAR *) "password", SQL_NTS);

        // Allocate An SQL Statement Handle
        rc = SQLAllocHandle(SQL_HANDLE_STMT, Example.ConHandle,
                &Example.StmtHandle);
        if (rc == SQL_SUCCESS)
        {
            // Define A SELECT SQL Statement
            strcpy((char *) SQLStmt, "SELECT LASTNAME, FIRSTNME ");
            strcat((char *) SQLStmt, "FROM EMPLOYEE");

            // Prepare And Execute The SQL Statement
            SQLExecDirect(Example.StmtHandle, SQLStmt, SQL_NTS);

            // Display The Results Of The SQL Query
            if (rc == SQL_SUCCESS)
                Example.ShowResults();

            // Free The SQL Statement Handle
            if (Example.StmtHandle != NULL)
                SQLFreeHandle(SQL_HANDLE_STMT, Example.StmtHandle);
        }

        // Disconnect From The DB2 Sample Database
        rc = SQLDisconnect(Example.ConHandle);
    }

    // Return To The Operating System
    return(rc);
}
```

SQLGetData

COMPATIBILITY

X/OPEN 95 CLI	ISO/IEC 92 CLI	DB2 CLI 5.2	DB2 CLI 2.0	ODBC 3.x
☑	☑	☑	☑	☑

ODBC API CONFORMANCE LEVEL   CORE*

*IN ODBC 2.0, THIS FUNCTION WAS A LEVEL 1 API CONFORMANCE LEVEL FUNCTION

Purpose   The SQLGetData() function is used to retrieve data for a single unbound column in the current row of a result data set.

Syntax

```
SQLRETURN    SQLGetData    (SQLHSTMT        StatementHandle,
                            SQLUSMALLINT    ColumnNumber,
                            SQLSMALLINT     CDataType,
                            SQLPOINTER      Value,
                            SQLINTEGER      ValueMaxSize,
                            SQLINTEGER      *ValueSize_Indicator);
```

Parameters

StatementHandle   An SQL statement handle that refers to a previously allocated SQL statement information storage buffer (data structure).

ColumnNumber   Specifies the column's location in the result data set. Columns are numbered sequentially from left to right, starting with 1, as they appear in the result data set.

CDataType   The C language data type of the value memory storage buffer (*Value*) that the column data being retrieved is to be stored in. This parameter must be set to one of the following values:

- SQL_C_CHAR
- SQL_C_DBCHAR
- SQL_C_SHORT
- SQL_C_LONG
- SQL_C_FLOAT
- SQL_C_DOUBLE
- SQL_C_NUMERIC
- SQL_C_BIT
- SQL_C_TINYINT
- SQL_C_BINARY
- SQL_C_BLOB_LOCATOR
- SQL_C_CLOB_LOCATOR

- SQL_C_DBCLOB_LOCATOR
- SQL_C_TYPE_DATE
- SQL_C_TYPE_TIME
- SQL_C_TYPE_TIMESTAMP
- SQL_C_DEFAULT

NOTE: *If this field contains the value* SQL_C_DEFAULT, *DB2 CLI selects the appropriate C data type to use based on the SQL data type of the column in the data source.*

Value	A pointer to a location in memory where this function is to store column data when it is retrieved from the result data set.
ValueMaxSize	The maximum size of the memory storage buffer where this function is to store the column data retrieved.
ValueSize_Indicator	A pointer to a location in memory where this function is to store either the size of the data value associated with the column or a special indicator value associated with the column data. Any of the following indicator values can be stored in this memory location:

SQL_NO_TOTAL:
The size of the column data value is unknown.

SQL_NULL_DATA:
The data value associated with the column is NULL.

Description   The SQLGetData() function is used to retrieve data for a single, unbound column in the current row of a result data set. This function is an alternative to the SQLBindCol() function and can be used to transfer data directly into application variables (either whole, or in parts) once the cursor has been positioned on a row of data. The SQLGetData() function is commonly used to retrieve large data values which often exceed a predefined size (usually 254 characters or bytes). Because such data often cannot be stored in a single buffer, it is retrieved from the data source in parts with the SQLGetData() function after all other data in the row has been fetched. With respect to a single column, SQLGetData() behaves in the same manner as SQLFetch(). It retrieves the data for a column, converts it to the data type of the application variable (if appropriate), and stores the converted value in that variable. It also returns the byte length of the data in the length/indicator buffer.

Return Codes   SQL_SUCCESS, SQL_SUCCESS_WITH_INFO, SQL_NO_DATA, SQL_STILL_EXECUTING, SQL_INVALID_HANDLE, SQL_ERROR

SQLSTATEs   If this function returns SQL_SUCCESS_WITH_INFO or SQL_ERROR, one of the following SQLSTATE values may be obtained by calling the SQLGetDiagRec() function:

01004, 07006, 08S01, 22002, 22003, 22005, 22007, 22008, 24000, 40003, 58004, HY001, HY002, HY003, HY009, HY010, HY013, HY090, HYC00, or HYT00

Refer to Appendix B for detailed information about each SQLSTATE value that can be returned.

Comments

- Columns are numbered in increasing column order as they appear in the result data set, starting at 0, where column 0 is the bookmark column. If bookmarks are not used (that is, if the **SQL_ATTR_USE_BOOKMARKS** SQL statement attribute is set to **SQL_UB_OFF**), column numbers start at 1.

- This function can only be called after one or more rows have been fetched from the result data set by **SQLFetch()** or **SQLFetchScroll()**.

- It is possible to bind some columns in a row and call **SQLGetData()** for others, although this is subject to some restrictions.

- When DB2 CLI returns fixed-length data such as integer or date structure data to an application variable, it assumes the buffer is large enough to hold the data. Therefore, it is important for the application to use a variable or allocate a buffer large enough to hold the fixed-length data stored in the column; otherwise, DB2 CLI will write past the end of the buffer.

- When a value less than **0** is stored in the *ValueMaxSize* parameter, SQLSTATE **HY**090 (Invalid string or buffer length) is returned. This is not the case when **0** is stored in the *ValueMaxSize* parameter; however, if a character data type is specified in the *CDataType* parameter, an application should not store **0** in the *ValueMaxSize* parameter because ISO CLI-compliant drivers return SQLSTATE **HY**090 (Invalid string or buffer length) when this condition is encountered.

- If a NULL pointer is stored in the *Value* parameter, the value stored in the *ValueMaxSize* parameter is ignored by DB2 CLI.

- If a NULL pointer is stored in the *ValueSize_Indicator* parameter, no length or indicator value is used.

- If no length/indicator variable is used, **SQL_ERROR** is returned if a NULL value is found in a column when data is retrieved.

- If a numeric data type (**SQL_C_NUMERIC**) is stored in the *CDataType* parameter, the default precision (driver-defined) and default scale (**0**), as set in the ARD descriptor's **SQL_DESC_PRECISION** and **SQL_DESC_SCALE** fields, are used for data conversion. If the default precision or scale is not appropriate, an application should explicitly set the appropriate descriptor field by calling **SQLSetDescField()** or **SQLSetDescRec()** to set the **SQL_DESC_CONCISE_TYPE** field to **SQL_C_NUMERIC** and call **SQLGetData()** with **SQL_ARD_TYPE** specified in the *CDataType* parameter, which causes the precision and scale values in the descriptor record fields to be used.

- If data for numeric data types is truncated to the right of the decimal point, when this function is called, **SQL_SUCCESS_WITH_INFO** is returned and a warning is generated. If truncation occurs to the left of the decimal point, **SQL_ERROR** is returned.

- If this function is called again after a preceding call to this function (for the same column) retrieved all of the data available for this column, **SQL_NO_DATA** will be returned.

- If a zero-length string is retrieved from a column when this function is called, a NULL terminator will be returned to the *Value* parameter and **0** will be returned to the *ValueSize_Indicator* parameter.

Prerequisites   The `SQLFetch()` function must be called before this function is called. If the `SQLFetch()` call fails, this function should not be called.

Restrictions   There are no restrictions associated with this function call.

See Also   `SQLBindCol()`, `SQLFetch()`, `SQLGetStmtAttr()`

Example   The following Visual C++ program illustrates how to use the `SQLGetData()` function to retrieve data from an unbound column of a result data set.

```
/*———————————————————————————————————— */
/* NAME:      CH10EX8.CPP                                    */
/* PURPOSE: Illustrate How To Use The Following CLI API Function */
/*          In A C++ Program:                                */
/*                                                           */
/*              SQLGetData()                                 */
/*                                                           */
/* OTHER CLI APIs SHOWN:                                     */
/*          SQLAllocHandle()          SQLSetEnvAttr()        */
/*          SQLConnect()              SQLExecDirect()        */
/*          SQLBindCol()              SQLFetch()             */
/*          SQLDisconnect()           SQLFreeHandle()        */
/*                                                           */
/*———————————————————————————————————— */

// Include The Appropriate Header Files
#include <windows.h>
#include <sqlcli1.h>
#include <iostream.h>

// Define The CLI_Class Class
class CLI_Class
{
    // Attributes
    public:
        SQLHANDLE   EnvHandle;
        SQLHANDLE   ConHandle;
        SQLHANDLE   StmtHandle;
        SQLRETURN   rc;

    // Operations
    public:
        CLI_Class();                        // Constructor
        ~CLI_Class();                       // Destructor
        SQLRETURN ShowResults();
};

// Define The Class Constructor
CLI_Class::CLI_Class()
{
    // Initialize The Return Code Variable
    rc = SQL_SUCCESS;

    // Allocate An Environment Handle
    rc = SQLAllocHandle(SQL_HANDLE_ENV, SQL_NULL_HANDLE, &EnvHandle);
```

```
     // Set The ODBC Application Version To 3.x
     if (rc == SQL_SUCCESS)
         rc = SQLSetEnvAttr(EnvHandle, SQL_ATTR_ODBC_VERSION,
                    (SQLPOINTER) SQL_OV_ODBC3, SQL_IS_UINTEGER);

     // Allocate A Connection Handle
     if (rc == SQL_SUCCESS)
         rc = SQLAllocHandle(SQL_HANDLE_DBC, EnvHandle, &ConHandle);
}

// Define The Class Destructor
CLI_Class::~CLI_Class()
{
    // Free The Connection Handle
    if (ConHandle != NULL)
        SQLFreeHandle(SQL_HANDLE_DBC, ConHandle);

    // Free The Environment Handle
    if (EnvHandle != NULL)
        SQLFreeHandle(SQL_HANDLE_ENV, EnvHandle);
}

// Define The ShowResults() Member Function
SQLRETURN CLI_Class::ShowResults(void)
{
    // Declare The Local Memory Variables
    SQLCHAR    LastName[50];
    SQLCHAR    FirstName[50];

    // Bind The First Column In The Result Data Set Returned To
    // An Application Variable
    rc = SQLBindCol(StmtHandle, 1, SQL_C_CHAR, (SQLPOINTER)
            LastName, sizeof(LastName), NULL);

    // Display A Header
    cout << "Employees :" << endl << endl;

    // While There Are Records In The Result Data Set Generated,
    // Retrieve And Display Them
    while (rc != SQL_NO_DATA)
    {
        rc = SQLFetch(StmtHandle);
        if (rc != SQL_NO_DATA)
        {
            // Retrieve The Value In The Second Column Of The Result
            // Data Set (Stored In The Current Row)
            rc = SQLGetData(StmtHandle, 2, SQL_C_CHAR, (SQLPOINTER)
                    FirstName, sizeof(FirstName), NULL);

            // Display The Record
            if (rc != SQL_NO_DATA)
                cout << FirstName << " " << LastName << endl;
        }
    }
```

```
    // Return The CLI API Return Code To The Calling Function
    return(rc);
}


/*————————————————————————————————————————— */
/* The Main Function                                             */
/*————————————————————————————————————————— */
int main()
{
    // Declare The Local Memory Variables
    SQLRETURN   rc = SQL_SUCCESS;
    SQLCHAR     SQLStmt[255];

    // Create An Instance Of The CLI_Class Class
    CLI_Class  Example;

    // Connect To The DB2 Sample Database
    if (Example.ConHandle != NULL)
    {
        rc = SQLConnect(Example.ConHandle, (SQLCHAR *) "SAMPLE",
                 SQL_NTS, (SQLCHAR *) "userid", SQL_NTS,
                 (SQLCHAR *) "password", SQL_NTS);

        // Allocate An SQL Statement Handle
        rc = SQLAllocHandle(SQL_HANDLE_STMT, Example.ConHandle,
                 &Example.StmtHandle);
        if (rc == SQL_SUCCESS)
        {
            // Define A SELECT SQL Statement
            strcpy((char *) SQLStmt, "SELECT LASTNAME, FIRSTNME ");
            strcat((char *) SQLStmt, "FROM EMPLOYEE");

            // Prepare And Execute The SQL Statement
            rc = SQLExecDirect(Example.StmtHandle, SQLStmt, SQL_NTS);

            // Display The Results Of The SQL Query
            if (rc == SQL_SUCCESS)
                Example.ShowResults();

            // Free The SQL Statement Handle
            if (Example.StmtHandle != NULL)
                SQLFreeHandle(SQL_HANDLE_STMT, Example.StmtHandle);
        }

        // Disconnect From The DB2 Sample Database
        rc = SQLDisconnect(Example.ConHandle);
    }

    // Return To The Operating System
    return(rc);
}
```

Retrieving Results (Advanced)

The last chapter introduced the basic set of CLI functions that are used to fetch (retrieve) data from a result data set. This chapter continues this discussion by introducing you to the advanced set of CLI functions that can be used to fetch data. The chapter begins by describing the two types of attributes used in CLI extended cursors. This is followed by a discussion about block cursors and how application variables can be bound to columns in a result data set when block cursors are used. Then, scrollable cursors are described, and the types of scrollable cursors available to CLI applications are introduced. Next, bookmarks are discussed—including how bookmark data can be stored and retrieved. This is followed by a brief discussion about multiple results. Finally, a detailed reference section covering each CLI function used to perform advanced data retrieval is provided.

CLI Extended Cursors

Most DBMSs provide a simple model for retrieving data from result data sets created in response to a query. In this model, rows of data are returned to an application, one at a time, in the order specified by the query, until the end of the result data set is reached. You saw in the last chapter that the mechanism used to implement this simple model is the forward-only cursor.

Early in the development of ODBC (in fact, before the term ODBC was invented), Rick Vicik of Microsoft took a collection of ideas and proposals for cursor management and pioneered the design of a more advanced cursor model for client/server architectures. This model, which became the foundation upon which cursors in ODBC, DB2 CLI, and several other products are based, contains several *extended* cursors that are designed to overcome many of the limitations imposed by the simple forward-only cursor found in most DBMSs.

The extended cursors used in CLI are defined in terms of two broad types of attributes (*block* and *scrollable*), and they can contain components of either or both.

Block Cursors

In the client/server environment, many applications spend a significant amount of time retrieving data from the database. Part of this time is spent actually bringing the data across the network, and part of it is spent on network overhead (for example, a call made by a driver to request a row of data). Often, the time spent on network overhead can be reduced by using block (otherwise referred to as "fat") cursors, which can return more than one row at a time.

The rows returned when data is fetched with a block cursor are known as a *rowset*. It is important not to confuse a rowset with a result data set. The result data set is maintained at the data source, while the rowset is maintained in application buffers. Also, while the result data set is fixed, the rowset is not—it changes position and contents each time a new set of rows are fetched.

Just as a traditional SQL forward-only cursor points to the current row, a block cursor points to the current rowset—when a block cursor first returns a rowset, the current row is the first row of that rowset. If an application wants to perform operations that operate on a single row (that is, make calls to **SQLGetData()**, perform positioned updates, and positioned deletes, etc.) it must indicate which row in the rowset is to be treated as the current row. Figure 11–1 shows the relationship of a block cursor, a result data set, a rowset, and a current row in a rowset.

Whether a cursor is a block cursor is independent of whether it is scrollable.

Binding Columns for use with Block Cursors

Because block cursors return multiple rows of data, applications that use them must bind an array of variables/LOB locators to each column in the result data set. Collectively, these arrays are sometimes referred to as *rowset buffers*. An application binds

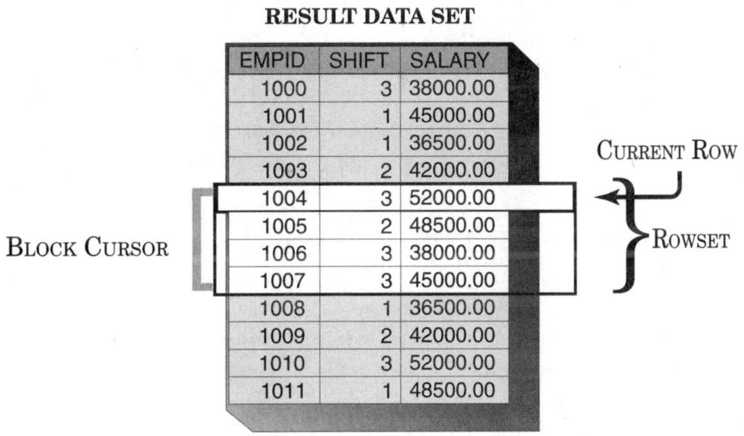

RESULT DATA SET

EMPID	SHIFT	SALARY
1000	3	38000.00
1001	1	45000.00
1002	1	36500.00
1003	2	42000.00
1004	3	52000.00
1005	2	48500.00
1006	3	38000.00
1007	3	45000.00
1008	1	36500.00
1009	2	42000.00
1010	3	52000.00
1011	1	48500.00

CURRENT ROW

ROWSET

BLOCK CURSOR

Figure 11–1   Components of a Block Cursor.

columns to arrays in the same manner that it binds columns to other application variables/LOB locators—by calling the **SQLBindCol()** function. The only difference is that the addresses specified in the **SQLBindCol()** function call reference arrays instead of individual variables/LOB locators. However, before binding columns to arrays, an application must decide which of the following binding styles it will use:

■ Column-wise binding   One or more arrays are bound to each column in the result data set for which data is to be returned. This is called column-wise binding, because each array (or set of arrays) is associated with a single column in the result data set.

■ Row-wise binding   A data structure that holds a single data value for each column in a row is defined, and each element of the first structure in an array of these structures is bound to each column in the result data set for which data is to be returned. This is called row-wise binding, because each data structure contains the data for a single row in the result data set.

Whether to use column-wise binding or row-wise binding is largely a matter of preference. Column-wise binding is the default binding style used. Applications can change from column-wise binding to row-wise binding by setting the **SQL_ATTR_ROW_BIND_TYPE** statement attribute. Row-wise binding might correspond more closely to the application's data layout, in which case it could provide better performance.

COLUMN-WISE BINDING   When column-wise binding is used, one, two, and in some cases, three arrays are bound to each column in a result data set for which data values are to be returned. The first array holds the data values that will be retrieved from the column, and the second array holds length/indicator values that correspond to the data values returned in the first array. Length values and indicator values are returned in separate arrays if the **SQL_DESC_INDICATOR_PTR** and **SQL_DESC_OCTET_LENGTH_PTR** descriptor fields contain different array address values. In this case, a third array is bound to the column. Each array contains as many elements as there are rows in the rowset.

An application informs DB2 CLI that it is using column-wise binding by setting the `SQL_ATTR_ROW_BIND_TYPE` statement attribute. DB2 CLI then returns the data for each row in the rowset in successive elements of each array. Figure 11–2 shows how column-wise binding works (in this illustration, length values and indicator values are returned in the same array).

ROW-WISE BINDING When row-wise binding is used, a data structure containing one, two, or in some cases, three elements for each column in a result data set for which data values are to be returned is defined by the application (elements can be placed in this structure in any order). The first element holds the data values to be retrieved from the column, and the second element holds length/indicator values that correspond to the data values returned in the first element. Again, length values and indicator values are returned in separate elements if the `SQL_DESC_INDICATOR_PTR` and `SQL_DESC_OCTET_LENGTH_PTR` descriptor fields contain different structure element address values. If this is the case, the structure must also contain a third element for each column. The application then allocates an array of these structures that contains as many elements as there are rows in the rowset. Next, the application informs the driver that it is using row-wise binding by storing the size

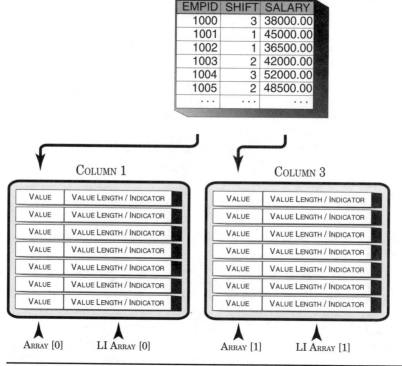

Figure 11–2 Column-Wise Result Data Set Column Binding.

of the data structure used in the `SQL_ATTR_ROW_BIND_TYPE` statement attribute. Finally, the address of each element in the first structure of the allocated array is bound to the appropriate column in the result data set. Figure 11–3 shows how row-wise binding works.

During execution, DB2 CLI calculates the data address for a particular row and column by solving the equation:

```
Address = Bound Address + ((Row Number - 1) * Structure Size)
```

where rows are numbered from 1 to the size of the rowset. (One is subtracted from the row number because array indexing in C/C++ is zero-based.)

Generally, the data structure definition only contains elements for each column that is to be bound. However, it can also contain elements that are not related to result data set columns.

Using Block Cursors

To use block cursors, an application simply sets the rowset size, binds the rowset buffers (as described in the previous section), optionally sets up a *rows fetched* and a *row status* array, and calls a CLI fetch function that provides block cursor support. In CLI 2.0 and earlier, block cursor support was provided by the `SQLExtendedFetch()` function call. In CLI 5.0

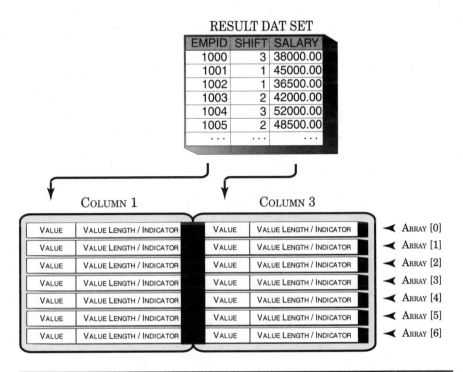

Figure 11–3   *Row-Wise Result Data Set Column Binding.*

and later, block cursor support is provided by the **SQLFetch()** and **SQLScrollFetch()** functions—**SQLExtendedFetch()** is no longer used.

Setting the Rowset Size

Screen-based applications often set the rowset size to match the number of rows that will be displayed on the screen. If the user resizes the screen, the application changes the rowset size accordingly. Other applications tend to set the rowset size to match the largest number of rows the application can reasonably handle. With larger rowsets, network overhead is sometimes reduced. Exactly how large such a rowset can be depends on the size of each row in the result data set and the amount of memory available.

Rowset size is controlled by the value stored in the **SQL_ATTR_ROW_ARRAY_SIZE** statement attribute. An application can change the rowset size or bind new rowset buffers (by calling **SQLBindCol()** or by specifying a binding offset) before or after rows have been fetched. However, the implications of changing the rowset size once rows have been fetched depends largely on the function being used:

■ **SQLFetch()** and **SQLFetchScroll()** use the rowset size that was in effect at the time they are called. Note, however, that when **SQLFetchScroll()** is called with the **SQL_FETCH_NEXT** fetch orientation specified, the cursor is incremented based on the rowset size of the previous fetch, then a new rowset is fetched, based on the current rowset size.

■ **SQLSetPos()** uses the rowset size that was in effect during the preceding call to **SQLFetch()** or **SQLFetchScroll()**. That is because **SQLSetPos()** operates on a rowset that has already been set.

Using a Rows Fetched Buffer

A *rows fetched* buffer is often used to tell an application how many rows were fetched (including those rows for which no data was returned because an error occurred while they were being fetched) when a block cursor is used. This buffer's address is specified by setting the **SQL_ATTR_ROWS_FETCHED_PTR** statement attribute. If a rows fetched buffer is used, it must be allocated by the application; it is automatically populated by DB2 CLI when a block cursor is used. In addition, when a rows fetched buffer is used, an application must make sure that its address remains valid as long as the block cursor associated with it remains open.

NOTE: *If a rows fetched buffer is used in a CLI application, the* **SQL_ATTR_ROW_NUMBER** *statement attribute contains the number of the current row in the result data set. DB2 CLI applications can call the* **SQLGetStmtAttr()** *function to retrieve this value.*

Using a Row Status Array

In addition to data, **SQLFetch()** and **SQLFetchScroll()** can return status information about each row in the rowset to a *row status* array. This array is allocated by the application and must have as many elements as there are rows in the rowset. The address of this buffer is then stored in the **SQL_ATTR_ROW_STATUS_PTR** statement attribute. Values that describe the status of each row in the rowset and indicate when that status has changed since it was last fetched are stored in this array whenever **SQLFetch()**, **SQLFetchScroll()**, and **SQLSetPos()** are executed. Table 11–1 lists the values that can be returned for each element in a row status array.

The contents of the row status array are undefined if **SQLFetch()** or **SQLFetch-Scroll()** does not return **SQL_SUCCESS** or **SQL_SUCCESS_WITH_INFO**.

SQLGetData() and Block Cursors

Because **SQLGetData()** is designed to retrieve data from a single column within a single row, it cannot be used to populate an array with data from multiple rows. The reason for this is that the primary use of **SQLGetData()** is to fetch long data in parts, and there is little or no reason to do this for more than one row at a time. Therefore, in order to use **SQLGetData()** with a block cursor, an application must first position the cursor on a single row within the rowset returned. This positioning can be done by calling **SQLSetPos()** with the **SQL_POSITION** operation specified.

Scrollable Cursors

Interactive applications, especially those written for personal computers, often need to provide a way for a user to scroll through data in a result data set by using the arrow keys, the PgUp or PgDn key, or the scroll bar and a mouse. For such applications, returning to a previously fetched row can be a problem. One possible solution is to close and reopen the cursor, then fetch rows until the cursor reaches the required row. Another possibility is to read the result data set once and store it locally in order to implement

Table 11–1   Row Status Values

Row Status	Description
SQL_ROW_SUCCESS	The row was successfully fetched and it has not been changed since it was last fetched.
SQL_ROW_SUCCESS_WITH_INFO	The row was successfully fetched and it has not been changed since it was last fetched. However, a warning was generated about the row.
SQL_ROW_ERROR	An error occurred while fetching the row.
SQL_ROW_NOROW	The rowset overlapped the end of the result set and no row was returned that corresponded to this element of the row status array.

scrolling in the application. Both methods only work well with small result data sets, and the latter method is difficult to implement. A better solution is to use a cursor that can move forward *and* backward in the result data set. A cursor that provides the ability to move forward and backward within a result data set is called a *scrollable cursor*.

The ability to move backward in a result data set raises an important question: Should the cursor detect changes made to rows previously fetched? In other words, should it detect updated, deleted, and newly inserted rows? This question arises because the definition of a result data set (that is, the set of rows matching certain criteria) does not state when rows are checked to see if they match that criteria, nor does it state whether rows must contain the same data each time they are fetched. The former omission makes it possible for scrollable cursors to detect whether rows have been inserted or deleted, while the latter makes it possible for them to detect updated data.

At this time, DB2 CLI only supports one type of scrollable cursor: a *Static cursor.*

Static Cursors

A *static cursor* is a cursor in which the result data set appears to be static. That is because static cursors do not usually detect changes made to the result data set after the cursor is opened. For example, suppose a static cursor fetches a row of data from a result data set. Now suppose another application then updates that row. If the static cursor refetches the row, it does not see the changes made by the other application. Static cursors never detect inserts, updates, and deletes made by other applications. This type of cursor is most useful for read-only applications that do not need the most up-to-date data available or for applications in which multiple users never need to modify data concurrently.

Static cursors are commonly implemented by locking the rows in the result data set or by making a copy, or snapshot, of the result data set. While locking rows is relatively easy to do, the drawback of this approach is that it significantly reduces transaction concurrency. Making a copy or a snapshot of a result data set allows greater concurrency; however, a copy is more expensive to make and can differ from the underlying data when that data is changed by other applications.

Scrolling and Fetching Rows

When using a scrollable cursor, applications can call **SQLFetchScroll()** to position the cursor and fetch rows. This function supports relative scrolling (next, prior, and relative *n* rows), absolute scrolling (first, last, and row *n*), and positioning by bookmark. The *FetchOrientation* and *RowNumber* parameters of this function specify which rowset to fetch. An example is shown in Figure 11–4.

SQLFetchScroll() positions the cursor on the specified row and returns the rows in the rowset starting with that row. If the specified rowset overlaps the end of the result data set, a partial rowset is returned. If the specified rowset overlaps the start of the result set, the first rowset in the result data set is usually returned. Once a rowset has been retrieved, an application can call **SQLSetPos()** to move to a particular row within the rowset or to refresh all rows in the rowset.

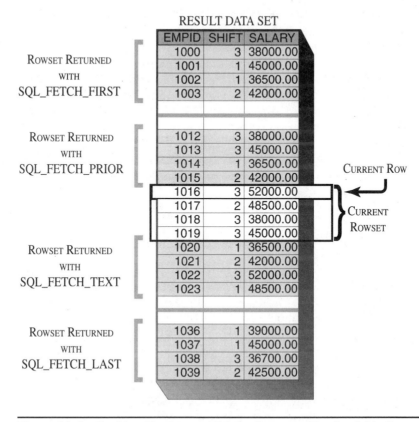

Figure 11–4   *Fetching Absolute and Relative Rowsets with a Scrollable Cursor.*

In some cases, an application may want to position the cursor without retrieving any data. For example, it might want to test whether a row exists or just get the bookmark for the row without bringing other data across the network. To do this, it sets the **SQL_ATTR_ RETRIEVE_DATA** statement attribute to **SQL_RD_OFF** before calling the **SQLFetchScroll()** function. Note that the variable bound to the bookmark column (if any) is always updated, regardless of the setting of this statement attribute (option).

The Effect of Added, Updated, and Deleted, Rows on Scrollable Cursor Movement

Static cursors can sometimes detect when rows are added to a result data set. However, whether a cursor provides this functionality is driver-dependent (an application can determine whether a driver provides this functionality by calling the **SQLGetInfo()** function and examining the values of the **SQL_CA2_SENSITIVITY_ADDITIONS**, **SQL_CA2_SENSITIVITY_**

DELETIONS, and **SQL_CA2_SENSITIVITY_UPDATES** bitmasks). If the cursors being used can detect deleted rows but cannot remove them, addition and deletion operations have no effect on cursor movements.

On the other hand, if the cursor being used can detect when rows are added to the result data set and/or remove deleted rows from the result data set, it appears as if the cursor detects these changes only when it fetches data. This means that when **SQLFetchScroll()** is used to refetch the same rowset, additions and deletions are seen, but when **SQLSetPos()** is called with the **SQL_REFRESH** option specified they are not. That is because in the latter case, data in the rowset buffers is refreshed but not refetched; therefore, deleted rows are not removed from the result data set. Thus, when a row is inserted into or deleted from the current rowset, the cursor does not modify the rowset buffers. Instead, the cursor only detects the changes when it fetches a rowset that previously included the deleted row(s) or that now includes the inserted row(s).

When **SQLFetchScroll()** returns a rowset with a position relative to the current rowset (that is, the next rowset, the previous rowset, or a relative rowset), it does not include changes to the current rowset when calculating the starting position of the new rowset. However, it does include changes outside the current rowset—if it is capable of detecting them. On the other hand, when **SQLFetchScroll()** returns a rowset with a position that is independent of the current rowset (that is, the first rowset, the last rowset, or an absolute rowset), it includes all changes it is capable of detecting even if they are in the current rowset.

A partial rowset considered to end at the last valid row (that is, the last row for which the row status is not **SQL_ROW_NOROW**) is used to determine whether newly added rows are inside or outside the current rowset. For example, suppose the cursor is capable of detecting newly added rows and that the current rowset is a partial rowset. When the application adds new rows to the rowset, the cursor adds them to the end of the result data set. If the application then calls **SQLFetchScroll()** with the **SQL_FETCH_NEXT** fetch orientation specified, **SQLFetchScroll()** returns the rowset starting with the first newly added row.

Determining the Number of Affected Rows

After an application inserts, updates, or deletes rows, it can call the **SQLRowCount()** function to find out how many rows were actually affected by the insert, update, or delete operation. The **SQLRowCount()** function returns this information regardless of whether the insert, update, or delete operation was performed by executing an **INSERT**, **UPDATE**, or **DELETE** SQL statement, by executing a positioned **UPDATE** or **DELETE** SQL statement, or by calling **SQLSetPos()**. If a batch of **INSERT**, **UPDATE**, or **DELETE** SQL statements was executed, the number of affected rows might be a total for all SQL statements in the batch, or it might be the number for an individual statement that gets updated after each statement in the batch is executed.

The number of affected rows is also returned in the **SQL_DIAG_ROW_COUNT** field of the diagnostic header record associated with the statement handle used. However, the value of this field is reset after each function call (on the statement handle), whereas the value returned by **SQLRowCount()** remains the same until **SQLPrepare()**, **SQLExecute()**, **SQLExecDirect()**, **SQLSetPos()**, or **SQLBulkOperations()** is called again.

Bookmarks

A *bookmark* is a value that is used to identify a row of data. The bookmark value itself is known only to DB2 CLI or the data source. It can be as simple as a row number or as complex as a disk address. Bookmarks in DB2 CLI are a bit different from bookmarks in real books. In an actual book, the reader places a bookmark at a specific page, then looks for that bookmark to return to the page. In CLI, the application requests a bookmark for a particular row, stores it, and passes it back to the cursor to return to the row. Thus, bookmarks in CLI are similar to a reader writing down a page number, remembering it, and then looking up the page at a later point in time. Bookmarks may or may not remain valid after the cursor using them is closed. Building and maintaining bookmarks can be an expensive operation, so bookmarks should be enabled only when an application can make good use of them.

Bookmark Data Types

In DB2 CLI, all bookmarks are variable length values; 32-bit fixed-length values are supported, but only for backward compatibility. This allows a primary key or a unique index associated with a table to be used as a bookmark. Before opening any cursor that is to use bookmarks, an application must set the **SQL_ATTR_USE_BOOKMARK** statement attribute to inform DB2 CLI that bookmarks will be used. Because a variable-length bookmark can be a long value, an application should not bind to the bookmark column (column 0) unless it will use the bookmark for many of the rows in the rowset.

Retrieving Bookmark Values

Bookmarks are always returned as column 0 of a result data set. An application can retrieve them in three different ways:

- Bind column 0 of the result data set containing bookmarks to an application variable/buffer. In this case, the bookmarks for each row in the rowset are returned, along with the data for other bound columns in the row, when **SQLFetch()** or **SQLFetchScroll()** is executed.
- Call **SQLSetPos()** to position the cursor on a row in the rowset, then call **SQLGetData()** for column 0.

Scrolling By Bookmark

When using **SQLFetchScroll()** to fetch rows, a CLI application can use a bookmark as a basis for selecting the starting row. This is a form of absolute addressing, because it is not dependent on the current cursor position. To scroll to a bookmarked row, an application calls **SQLFetchScroll()** with the **SQL_FETCH_BOOKMARK** fetch orientation specified. This causes the fetch operation to use the bookmark pointed to by the **SQL_ATTR_FETCH_BOOKMARK_PTR** statement attribute; the rowset starting with the row identified by that bookmark is returned.

Comparing Bookmarks

Because bookmarks are byte-comparable, they can be compared for equality or inequality. To do so, an application treats each bookmark as an array of bytes and compares two bookmarks byte by byte. However, because bookmarks are only guaranteed to be distinct within a result data set, it makes no sense to compare bookmarks obtained from different result data sets.

Multiple Results

Whenever two or more **SELECT** SQL statements are executed in a batch, multiple result data sets are produced. To process multiple result data sets, an application must call the **SQLMoreResults()** function. This function discards the contents of the current result data set and makes the next result data set available. For example, suppose the following statements are executed as a batch:

```
SELECT * FROM Parts WHERE Price <= 100.00;
SELECT * FROM Parts WHERE Price > 100
```

After these statements are executed, the application can begin fetching rows from the result data set created by the first **SELECT** SQL statement because it automatically has access to it. When it is done fetching rows, it must call **SQLMoreResults()** to make the result data set generated by the second **SELECT** SQL statement available. If necessary, **SQLMoreResults()** automatically discards any unfetched rows in the first result data set and closes the cursor. The application can then begin fetching rows from the second result data set.

The Advanced SQL Results Retrieval Functions

Table 11–2 lists the CLI functions that are used to perform advanced data retrieval operations on result data sets.

Each of these functions is described in detail in the remaining portion of this chapter.

Table 11-2 The CLI Advanced Results Retrieval Functions

Function Name	Description
SQLFetchScroll()	Retrieves multiple rows of data (a rowset) from a result data set and returns data for all bound columns.
SQLSetPos()	Positions a cursor within a fetched block of data and allows an application to refresh data in the rowset.
SQLMoreResults()	Determines whether there are more result data sets for processing available, and if there are, initializes them.
SQLRowCount()	Retrieves and returns the number of rows affected by the execution of an **INSERT**, **UPDATE**, or **DELETE SQL** operation.

SQLFetchScroll

COMPATIBILITY

X/OPEN 95 CLI	ISO/IEC 92 CLI	DB2 CLI 5.2	DB2 CLI 2.0	ODBC 3.x
☑	☑	☑	☐	☑

ODBC API CONFORMANCE LEVEL   **CORE**

Purpose   The **SQLFetchScroll()** function is used to retrieve a block containing multiple rows (a rowset) of data from a result data set.

Syntax
```
SQLRETURN   SQLFetchScroll   (SQLHSTMT      StatementHandle,
                              SQLUSMALLINT  FetchOrientation,
                              SQLINTEGER    RowNumber);
```

Parameters   *StatementHandle*   An SQL statement handle that refers to a previously allocated SQL statement information storage buffer (data structure).

FetchOrientation   Specifies the direction and type of fetch DB2 CLI is to perform. This parameter must be set to one of the following values:

■ **SQL_FETCH_FIRST**
Returns the first rowset in the result data set.

■ **SQL_FETCH_NEXT**
Returns the next rowset in the result data set. If the cursor is positioned before the start of the result data set, this is equivalent to **SQL_FETCH_FIRST**.

▨ **SQL_FETCH_PRIOR**

Returns the prior rowset in the result data set. If the cursor is positioned after the end of the result data set, this is equivalent to **SQL_FETCH_LAST**.

▨ **SQL_FETCH_LAST**

Returns the last complete rowset in the result data set.

▨ **SQL_FETCH_ABSOLUTE**

Returns the rowset starting at the row number specified in the *RowNumber* parameter. If the *RowNumber* parameter is set to **0**, **SQL_NO_DATA** is returned and the cursor is positioned before the start of the result data set.

▨ **SQL_FETCH_RELATIVE**

Returns the rowset *RowNumber* rows from the start of the current rowset. If the *RowNumber* parameter is set to **0**, the driver simply refreshes the current rowset. If the cursor is positioned before the start of the result data set and the *RowNumber* parameter contains a value greater than **0**, or if the cursor is positioned after the end of the result data set and the *RowNumber* parameter contains a value less than **0**, this is equivalent to **SQL_FETCH_ABSOLUTE**.

▨ **SQL_FETCH_BOOKMARK**

Returns the rowset *RowNumber* rows from the bookmark specified by the **SQL_ATTR_FETCH_BOOKMARK_PTR** SQL statement attribute.

RowNumber   Specifies the ordinal position of the first row in the rowset to fetch (provided the *FetchOrientation* parameter is set to **SQL_FETCH_ABSOLUTE, SQL_FETCH_RELATIVE,** or **SQL_FETCH_BOOKMARK**).

Description   **SQLFetchScroll()** extends the functionality of **SQLFetch()** by retrieving multiple rows of data (a rowset) for each bound column in a result data set. **SQLFetchScroll()** returns rowset data (one or more rows) in the form of an array. The size of the rowset (number of rows) returned is specified by the **SQL_ATTR_ROWSET_SIZE** statement attribute value. Rowsets can be specified by an absolute row position, a relative row position, or by a bookmark.

When the **SQLFetchScroll()** function is called, the appropriate data transfer is performed along with any data conversion specified when the columns were bound. If the application has specified a pointer to a row status array or buffer in which to return the number of rows fetched, **SQLFetchScroll()** returns this information as well. Refer to the section on "Block Cursors" in this chapter for more information.

NOTE: *This function replaces the DB2 CLI 2.0 function* **SQLExtendedFetch()**.

Return Codes   SQL_SUCCESS, SQL_SUCCESS_WITH_INFO, SQL_NO_DATA, SQL_STILL_EXECUTING, SQL_INVALID_HANDLE, SQL_ERROR

If an error occurs on one or more, but not all, rows of a multi-row operation, SQL_ERROR is returned.

SQLSTATEs   If this function returns SQL_SUCCESS_WITH_INFO or SQL_ERROR, one of the following SQLSTATE values may be obtained by calling the SQLGetDiagRec() function:

01000, 01004, 01S01, 01S06, 01S07, 07002, 07006, 07009, 08S01, 22001, 22002, 22003, 22007, 22012, 22018, 24000, 40001, HY000, HY001, HY008, HY010, HY106, HY107, HY111, or HYC00

Refer to Appendix B for detailed information about each SQLSTATE value that can be returned.

Comments
- SQLFetch() should be used instead of SQLFetchScroll() to fetch one row of data at a time, in a forward direction.

- An application can mix SQLFetchScroll() and SQLFetch() function calls for the same cursor. However, SQLFetchScroll() function calls cannot be mixed with SQLExtendedFetch() function calls for the same cursor.

- Before this function is called for the first time, the cursor is positioned before the start of the result data set. When called, this function positions the block cursor based on the values stored in the *FetchOrientation* and *RowNumber* parameters. After this function is executed, the current row is the first row in the rowset.

- The SQL_ATTR_ROW_ARRAY_SIZE statement attribute specifies the size (number of rows) of the rowset. If the rowset being fetched overlaps the end of the result data set, a partial rowset is returned. All remaining rows will be empty and will have a status of SQL_ROW_NOROW.

- SQLFetchScroll() and SQLFetch() store values in the appropriate row status array (if one exists) in a similar manner.

- SQLFetchScroll() and SQLFetch() store values in the rows fetched buffer (if one exists) in a similar manner.

- SQLFetchScroll() and SQLFetch() return error information in a similar manner.

- SQLFetchScroll() and SQLFetch() interact with descriptors in a similar manner.

- SQLFetchScroll() and SQLFetch() return data to bound columns in a similar manner. If no columns are bound, SQLFetchScroll() moves the cursor to the specified position without returning data.

- If the SQL_ATTR_CURSOR_TYPE statement attribute is set to SQL_CURSOR_FORWARD_ONLY, SQL_FETCH_NEXT must be specified in the *FetchOrientation* parameter; otherwise SQL_ERROR and SQLSTATE HY106 (Fetch type out of range) is returned.

- If the SQL_ATTR_CONCURRENCY statement attribute is set to SQL_CONCUR_VALUES or SQL_CONCUR_ROWVER, this function updates the optimistic concurrency values used by the data source to detect whether a row has changed. This happens each time this function fetches a new rowset, including when it refetches the current rowset (SQLFetchScroll() is called with the *FetchOrientation* parameter set to SQL_FETCH_RELATIVE and the *RowNumber* parameter set to 0).

Prerequisites   There are no prerequisites for using this function call.

Restrictions   This function must be called after an SQL statement that creates a result data set is executed and before the cursor for that result data set is closed.

See Also   SQLFetch()

Example   **COLUMN-WISE BINDING**   The following Visual C++ program illustrates how to use the SQLFetchScroll() function to retrieve multiple rows of data from a result data set (in a single function call), using column-wise binding.

```
/*────────────────────────────────────────────────────── */
/* NAME:     CH11EX1A.CPP                                  */
/* PURPOSE: Illustrate How To Use The SQLFetchScroll() CLI API   */
/*           Function To Retrieve Record Values And Return Them To  */
/*           Arrays That Were Bound To The Columns In The Result   */
/*           Data Set Using Column-Wise Binding.           */
/*                                                         */
/* OTHER CLI APIs SHOWN:                                   */
/*           SQLAllocHandle()          SQLSetEnvAttr()      */
/*           SQLConnect()              SQLExecDirect()      */
/*           SQLSetStmtAttr()          SQLBindCol()         */
/*           SQLCloseCursor()          SQLDisconnect()      */
/*           SQLFreeHandle()                               */
/*                                                         */
/*────────────────────────────────────────────────────── */

// Include The Appropriate Header Files
#include <windows.h>
#include <sqlcli1.h>
#include <iostream.h>

// Define The CLI_Class Class
class CLI_Class
{
    // Attributes
    public:
        SQLHANDLE   EnvHandle;
        SQLHANDLE   ConHandle;
        SQLHANDLE   StmtHandle;
        SQLRETURN   rc;

    // Operations
    public:
        CLI_Class();                          // Constructor
        ~CLI_Class();                         // Destructor
        SQLRETURN ShowResults();
};

// Define The Class Constructor
```

```
CLI_Class::CLI_Class()
{
    // Initialize The Return Code Variable
    rc = SQL_SUCCESS;

    // Allocate An Environment Handle
    rc = SQLAllocHandle(SQL_HANDLE_ENV, SQL_NULL_HANDLE, &EnvHandle);

    // Set The ODBC Application Version To 3.x
    if (rc == SQL_SUCCESS)
        rc = SQLSetEnvAttr(EnvHandle, SQL_ATTR_ODBC_VERSION,
                (SQLPOINTER) SQL_OV_ODBC3, SQL_IS_UINTEGER);

    // Allocate A Connection Handle
    if (rc == SQL_SUCCESS)
        rc = SQLAllocHandle(SQL_HANDLE_DBC, EnvHandle, &ConHandle);
}

// Define The Class Destructor
CLI_Class::~CLI_Class()
{
    // Free The Connection Handle
    if (ConHandle != NULL)
        SQLFreeHandle(SQL_HANDLE_DBC, ConHandle);

    // Free The Environment Handle
    if (EnvHandle != NULL)
        SQLFreeHandle(SQL_HANDLE_ENV, EnvHandle);
}

// Define The ShowResults() Member Function
SQLRETURN CLI_Class::ShowResults(void)
{
    // Declare The Local Memory Variables
    SQLRETURN    rc;
    SQLUINTEGER  ArraySize = 6;
    SQLCHAR      FirstNameArray[6][14];
    SQLINTEGER   FirstNameLI_Array[6];
    SQLCHAR      LastNameArray[6][16];
    SQLINTEGER   LastNameLI_Array[6];
    SQLUINTEGER  SalaryArray[6];
    SQLINTEGER   SalaryLI_Array[6];

    SQLUSMALLINT RowStatusArray[6];
    SQLUINTEGER  NumRowsFetched;

    // Set The SQL_ATTR_ROW_BIND_TYPE Statement Attribute To Tell The
    // Driver To Use Column-Wise Binding
    rc = SQLSetStmtAttr(StmtHandle, SQL_ATTR_ROW_BIND_TYPE,
            SQL_BIND_BY_COLUMN, 0);

    // Declare The Rowset Size (By Setting The
    // SQL_ATTR_ROW_ARRAY_SIZE Statement Attribute)
    rc = SQLSetStmtAttr(StmtHandle, SQL_ATTR_ROW_ARRAY_SIZE,
            (SQLPOINTER) ArraySize, 0);
```

```cpp
// Store The Address Of A Row Status Array In The
// SQL_ATTR_ROW_STATUS_PTR Statement Attribute
rc = SQLSetStmtAttr(StmtHandle, SQL_ATTR_ROW_STATUS_PTR,
        RowStatusArray, 0);

// Store The Address Of A Rows Fetched Buffer In The
// SQL_ATTR_ROWS_FETCHED_PTR Statement Attribute
rc = SQLSetStmtAttr(StmtHandle, SQL_ATTR_ROWS_FETCHED_PTR,
        &NumRowsFetched, 0);

// Bind The Columns In The Result Data Set Returned To
// Application Arrays
rc = SQLBindCol(StmtHandle, 1, SQL_C_CHAR, LastNameArray,
        sizeof(LastNameArray[0]), LastNameLI_Array);

rc = SQLBindCol(StmtHandle, 2, SQL_C_CHAR, FirstNameArray,
        sizeof(FirstNameArray[0]), FirstNameLI_Array);

rc = SQLBindCol(StmtHandle, 3, SQL_C_LONG, SalaryArray, 0,
        SalaryLI_Array);

// Display A Header
cout << "Employees :" << endl << endl;

// As Long As There Is Data, Retrieve Records From The Result
// Data Set And Display Them
while (rc != SQL_NO_DATA)
{
    // Fetch Up To The Rowset Size Number Of Rows
    rc = SQLFetchScroll(StmtHandle, SQL_FETCH_NEXT, 0);

    // Check The Row Status Array And Print Only Those Rows
    // That Were Successfully Fetched
    for (unsigned int i = 0; i < NumRowsFetched; i++)
    {
        if (RowStatusArray[i] == SQL_ROW_SUCCESS ||
            RowStatusArray[i] == SQL_ROW_SUCCESS_WITH_INFO)
        {
            // Print The First Name
            cout.setf(ios::left);
            cout.width(20);
            if (FirstNameLI_Array[i] == SQL_NULL_DATA)
                cout << "<NULL>";
            else
                cout << FirstNameArray[i];

            // Print The Last Name
            cout.setf(ios::left);
            cout.width(20);
            if (LastNameLI_Array[i] == SQL_NULL_DATA)
                cout << "<NULL>";
            else
                cout << LastNameArray[i];
```

```
                      // Print The Salary
                      cout.setf(ios::left);
                      cout.width(20);
                      if (SalaryLI_Array[i] == SQL_NULL_DATA)
                          cout << "<NULL>";
                      else
                          cout << SalaryArray[i];

                      cout << endl;
                  }
              }
          }

          // Close The Cursor
          rc = SQLCloseCursor(StmtHandle);

          // Return The CLI API Return Code To The Calling Function
          return(rc);
      }

/*—————————————————————————————————————————————————————————————————*/
/* The Main Function                                                */
/*—————————————————————————————————————————————————————————————————*/
int main()
{
      // Declare The Local Memory Variables
      SQLRETURN   rc = SQL_SUCCESS;
      SQLCHAR     SQLStmt[255];

      // Create An Instance Of The CLI_Class Class
      CLI_Class   Example;

      // Connect To The DB2 Sample Database
      if (Example.ConHandle != NULL)
      {
          rc = SQLConnect(Example.ConHandle, (SQLCHAR *) "SAMPLE",
                  SQL_NTS, (SQLCHAR *) "userid", SQL_NTS,
                  (SQLCHAR *) "password", SQL_NTS);

          // Allocate An SQL Statement Handle
          rc = SQLAllocHandle(SQL_HANDLE_STMT, Example.ConHandle,
                  &Example.StmtHandle);
          if (rc == SQL_SUCCESS)
          {
              // Define A SELECT SQL Statement
              strcpy((char *) SQLStmt, "SELECT FIRSTNME, LASTNAME, ");
              strcat((char *) SQLStmt, "SALARY FROM EMPLOYEE ");

              // Prepare And Execute The SQL Statement
              rc = SQLExecDirect(Example.StmtHandle, SQLStmt, SQL_NTS);

              // Display The Results Of The SQL Query
              if (rc == SQL_SUCCESS)
                  Example.ShowResults();
```

```
                    // Free The SQL Statement Handle
                    if (Example.StmtHandle != NULL)
                        SQLFreeHandle(SQL_HANDLE_STMT, Example.StmtHandle);
                }

                // Disconnect From The DB2 Sample Database
                rc = SQLDisconnect(Example.ConHandle);
            }

            // Return To The Operating System
            return(rc);
        }
```

ROW-WISE BINDING   The following Visual C++ program illustrates how to use the `SQLFetchScroll()` function to retrieve multiple rows of data from a result data set (in a single function call), using row-wise binding.

```
/*--------------------------------------------------------------- */
/* NAME:      CH11EX1B.CPP                                         */
/* PURPOSE: Illustrate How To Use The SQLFetchScroll() CLI API     */
/*          Function To Retrieve Record Values And  Return Them To */
/*          Arrays That Were Bound To The Columns In The Result    */
/*          Data Set Using Row-Wise Binding.                       */
/*                                                                 */
/* OTHER CLI APIs SHOWN:                                           */
/*          SQLAllocHandle()          SQLSetEnvAttr()              */
/*          SQLConnect()              SQLExecDirect()              */
/*          SQLSetStmtAttr()          SQLBindCol()                 */
/*          SQLCloseCursor()          SQLDisconnect()              */
/*          SQLFreeHandle()                                        */
/*                                                                 */
/*--------------------------------------------------------------- */

// Include The Appropriate Header Files
#include <windows.h>
#include <sqlcli1.h>
#include <iostream.h>

// Define The CLI_Class Class
class CLI_Class
{
    // Attributes
    public:
        SQLHANDLE   EnvHandle;
        SQLHANDLE   ConHandle;
        SQLHANDLE   StmtHandle;
        SQLRETURN   rc;

    // Operations
    public:
        CLI_Class();                          // Constructor
        ~CLI_Class();                         // Destructor
        SQLRETURN ShowResults();
};
```

```cpp
// Define The Class Constructor
CLI_Class::CLI_Class()
{
    // Initialize The Return Code Variable
    rc = SQL_SUCCESS;

    // Allocate An Environment Handle
    rc = SQLAllocHandle(SQL_HANDLE_ENV, SQL_NULL_HANDLE, &EnvHandle);

    // Set The ODBC Application Version To 3.x
    if (rc == SQL_SUCCESS)
        rc = SQLSetEnvAttr(EnvHandle, SQL_ATTR_ODBC_VERSION,
                    (SQLPOINTER) SQL_OV_ODBC3, SQL_IS_UINTEGER);

    // Allocate A Connection Handle
    if (rc == SQL_SUCCESS)
        rc = SQLAllocHandle(SQL_HANDLE_DBC, EnvHandle, &ConHandle);
}

// Define The Class Destructor
CLI_Class::~CLI_Class()
{
    // Free The Connection Handle
    if (ConHandle != NULL)
        SQLFreeHandle(SQL_HANDLE_DBC, ConHandle);

    // Free The Environment Handle
    if (EnvHandle != NULL)
        SQLFreeHandle(SQL_HANDLE_ENV, EnvHandle);
}

// Define The ShowResults() Member Function
SQLRETURN CLI_Class::ShowResults(void)
{
    // Declare The Local Memory Variables
    SQLRETURN    rc;
    SQLUINTEGER  ArraySize = 6;

    // Define The SALARY_INFO Structure And Allocate An Array
    // Of 6 Structures
    typedef struct {
        SQLCHAR      FirstName[14];
        SQLINTEGER   FirstName_LI;
        SQLCHAR      LastName[16];
        SQLINTEGER   LastName_LI;
        SQLUINTEGER  Salary;
        SQLINTEGER   Salary_LI;
    } SALARY_INFO;

    SALARY_INFO   SalaryInfoArray[6];

    SQLUSMALLINT RowStatusArray[6];
    SQLUINTEGER  NumRowsFetched;
```

```
// Store The Size Of The SALARY_INFO Structure In The
// SQL_ATTR_ROW_BIND_TYPE Statement Attribute - This Tells
// The Driver To Use Row-Wise Binding
rc = SQLSetStmtAttr(StmtHandle, SQL_ATTR_ROW_BIND_TYPE,
        (SQLPOINTER) sizeof(SALARY_INFO), 0);

// Declare The Rowset Size (By Setting The
// SQL_ATTR_ROW_ARRAY_SIZE Statement Attribute)
rc = SQLSetStmtAttr(StmtHandle, SQL_ATTR_ROW_ARRAY_SIZE,
        (SQLPOINTER) ArraySize, 0);

// Store The Address Of A Row Status Array In The
// SQL_ATTR_ROW_STATUS_PTR Statement Attribute
rc = SQLSetStmtAttr(StmtHandle, SQL_ATTR_ROW_STATUS_PTR,
        RowStatusArray, 0);

// Store The Address Of A Rows Fetched Buffer In The
// SQL_ATTR_ROWS_FETCHED_PTR Statement Attribute
rc = SQLSetStmtAttr(StmtHandle, SQL_ATTR_ROWS_FETCHED_PTR,
        &NumRowsFetched, 0);

// Bind The Columns In The Result Data Set Returned To
// The Elements Of The SALARY_INFO Structure
rc = SQLBindCol(StmtHandle, 1, SQL_C_CHAR,
        SalaryInfoArray[0].FirstName,
        sizeof(SalaryInfoArray[0].FirstName),
        &SalaryInfoArray[0].FirstName_LI);

rc = SQLBindCol(StmtHandle, 2, SQL_C_CHAR,
        SalaryInfoArray[0].LastName,
        sizeof(SalaryInfoArray[0].LastName),
        &SalaryInfoArray[0].LastName_LI);

rc = SQLBindCol(StmtHandle, 3, SQL_C_LONG,
        &SalaryInfoArray[0].Salary, 0,
        &SalaryInfoArray[0].Salary_LI);

// Display A Header
cout << "Employees :" << endl << endl;

// As Long As There Is Data, Retrieve Records From The Result
// Data Set And Display Them
while (rc != SQL_NO_DATA)
{
    // Fetch Up To The Rowset Size Number Of Rows
    rc = SQLFetchScroll(StmtHandle, SQL_FETCH_NEXT, 0);

    // Check The Row Status Array And Print Only Those Rows
    // That Were Successfully Fetched
    for (unsigned int i = 0; i < NumRowsFetched; i++)
    {
        if (RowStatusArray[i] == SQL_ROW_SUCCESS ||
            RowStatusArray[i] == SQL_ROW_SUCCESS_WITH_INFO)
        {
```

```
                            // Print The First Name
                            cout.setf(ios::left);
                            cout.width(20);
                            if (SalaryInfoArray[i].FirstName_LI ==
                                    SQL_NULL_DATA)
                                cout << "<NULL>";
                            else
                                cout << SalaryInfoArray[i].FirstName;

                            // Print The Last Name
                            cout.setf(ios::left);
                            cout.width(20);
                            if (SalaryInfoArray[i].LastName_LI ==
                                    SQL_NULL_DATA)
                                cout << "<NULL>";
                            else
                                cout << SalaryInfoArray[i].LastName;

                            // Print The Salary
                            cout.setf(ios::left);
                            cout.width(20);
                            if (SalaryInfoArray[i].Salary_LI ==
                                    SQL_NULL_DATA)
                                cout << "<NULL>";
                            else
                                cout << SalaryInfoArray[i].Salary;

                            cout << endl;
                    }
                }
        }

        // Close The Cursor
        rc = SQLCloseCursor(StmtHandle);

        // Return The CLI API Return Code To The Calling Function
        return(rc);
}


/*——————————————————————————————————————————— */
/* The Main Function                                            */
/*——————————————————————————————————————————— */
int main()
{
    // Declare The Local Memory Variables
    SQLRETURN   rc = SQL_SUCCESS;
    SQLCHAR     SQLStmt[255];

    // Create An Instance Of The CLI_Class Class
    CLI_Class   Example;

    // Connect To The DB2 Sample Database
    if (Example.ConHandle != NULL)
    {
```

```
rc = SQLConnect(Example.ConHandle, (SQLCHAR *) "SAMPLE",
        SQL_NTS, (SQLCHAR *) "userid", SQL_NTS,
        (SQLCHAR *) "password", SQL_NTS);

// Allocate An SQL Statement Handle
rc = SQLAllocHandle(SQL_HANDLE_STMT, Example.ConHandle,
        &Example.StmtHandle);
if (rc == SQL_SUCCESS)
{
    // Define A SELECT SQL Statement
    strcpy((char *) SQLStmt, "SELECT FIRSTNME, LASTNAME, ");
    strcat((char *) SQLStmt, "SALARY FROM EMPLOYEE ");

    // Prepare And Execute The SQL Statement
    rc = SQLExecDirect(Example.StmtHandle, SQLStmt, SQL_NTS);

    // Display The Results Of The SQL Query
    if (rc == SQL_SUCCESS)
        Example.ShowResults();

    // Free The SQL Statement Handle
    if (Example.StmtHandle != NULL)
        SQLFreeHandle(SQL_HANDLE_STMT, Example.StmtHandle);
}

// Disconnect From The DB2 Sample Database
rc = SQLDisconnect(Example.ConHandle);
}

// Return To The Operating System
return(rc);
}
```

SQLSetPos

COMPATIBILITY

X/OPEN 95 CLI	ISO/IEC 92 CLI	DB2 CLI 5.2	DB2 CLI 2.0	ODBC 3.x
☐	☐	☑	☑	☑

ODBC API CONFORMANCE LEVEL   LEVEL 1*

*IN ODBC 2.0, THIS FUNCTION WAS A LEVEL 2 API CONFORMANCE LEVEL FUNCTION

Purpose   The `SQLSetPos()` function is used to set the cursor position in a rowset or refresh data in a rowset.

Syntax	SQLRETURN	SQLSetPos	(SQLHSTMT	*StatementHandle,*
			SQLUSMALLINT	*RowNumber,*
			SQLUSMALLINT	*Operation,*
			SQLUSMALLINT	*LockType);*

Parameters   *StatementHandle*   An SQL statement handle that refers to a previously allocated SQL statement information storage buffer (data structure).

RowNumber   Specifies the ordinal position of the row in the rowset on which to perform the operation specified in the *Operation* parameter. If this parameter is set to 0, the operation specified is performed on every row in the rowset.

Operation   Specifies the operation to perform. This parameter must be set to one of the following values:

- **SQL_POSITION**
- **SQL_REFRESH**

LockType   Specifies how to lock the row after performing the operation specified in the *Operation* parameter. This parameter must be set to the following value:

- **SQL_LOCK_NO_CHANGE**
  DB2 CLI ensures that the row is in the same locked or unlocked state as it was before **SQLSetPos()** was called. This value allows data sources that do not support explicit row-level locking to use whatever locking is required by the data source to support the current concurrency and transaction isolation levels being used.

Description   The **SQLSetPos()** function is used to set the cursor position in a rowset or to allow an application to refresh data in a rowset. Which operation this function actually performs is dependent on the value specified in the *Operation* parameter. Table 11–3 lists each value that can be specified for the *Operation* parameter, along with a description of the operation performed when **SQLSetPos()** is executed.

Return Codes   SQL_SUCCESS, SQL_SUCCESS_WITH_INFO, SQL_NEED_DATA, SQL_STILL_EXECUTING, SQL_INVALID_HANDLE, SQL_ERROR

Table 11–3   **SQLSetPos()** Operations

Operation	Description
SQL_POSITION	DB2 CLI positions the cursor on the row specified. The contents of the row status array pointed to by the **SQL_ATTR_ROW_OPERATION_PTR** statement attribute are ignored for this operation.
SQL_REFRESH	DB2 CLI positions the cursor on the row specified and refreshes data in the rowset buffers for that row.

Table 11–3 SQLSetPos() Operations (Continued)

Operation	Description
	This operation updates the status and content of the rows within the current fetched rowset (this includes any bookmarks used). Because the data in the buffers is refreshed, but not *refetched*, the membership in the rowset is fixed. A successful refresh does not cause added rows to appear in a rowset. This is different from the refresh operation performed by the SQLFetchScroll() function (with the SQL_FETCH_RELATIVE orientation specified), which refetches the rowset from the result data set so it can show added data and remove deleted data.
	A successful refresh changes a row status value of SQL_ROW_ADDED to SQL_ROW_SUCCESS (if the row status array exists). A successful refresh changes a row status value of SQL_ROW_UPDATED to the row's new status (if the row status array exists).
	A successful refresh does not change rows with a row status value of SQL_ROW_DELETED— deleted rows within the rowset continue to be marked as deleted until the data is refetched.
	If an error occurs while a row is being refreshed, SQL_ROW_ERROR will be stored in the corresponding row status array element (if a row status arry exists).
	If a cursor is opened while the SQL_ATTR_CONCURRENCY statement attribute is set to SQL_CONCUR_ROWVER or SQL_CONCUR_VALUES, a successful refresh might update the optimistic concurrency values used by the data source to detect that the row has changed. If this occurs, the row versions or values used to ensure cursor concurrency are updated whenever the rowset buffers are refreshed from the server. This happens for each row that is refreshed. In this case, the contents of the row status array pointed to by the SQL_ATTR_ROW_OPERATION_PTR statement attribute are ignored for the SQL_REFRESH operation.

NOTE: SQL_SUCCESS_WITH_INFO *is returned for all SQLSTATEs that can return* SQL_SUCCESS_WITH_INFO *or* SQL_ERROR *(except* 01xxx *SQLSTATEs), if an error occurs on one or more, but not all, rows of a multirow operation.* SQL_ERROR *is returned if an error occurs on a single-row operation.*

SQLSTATEs   If this function returns SQL_SUCCESS_WITH_INFO or SQL_ERROR, one of the following SQLSTATE values may be obtained by calling the SQLGetDiagRec() function:

01000, 01004, 01S01, 01S07, 07006, 07009, 21S02, 22001, 22003, 22007, 22008, HY000, HY001, HY008, HY010, HY011, HY090, HY092, HY107, HY109, HYC00, or HYT00

Refer to Appendix B for detailed information about each SQLSTATE value that can be returned.

Comments   ■ In the C programming language, arrays are 0-based, while the *RowNumber* parameter is 1-based. This means that when a C/C++ application updates the fifth row of a rowset, it modifies the rowset buffers at array index **4** but specifies **5** in the *RowNumber* parameter.

■ All operations position the cursor on the row specified in the *RowNumber* parameter. For example, if this function is called with the *RowNumber* parameter set to **2**, the cursor is positioned on the second row of the rowset. The following operations require a cursor position:

■ Calls to the **SQLGetData()** function.

■ The *LockType* parameter is generally only used for file-based support. Usually, data sources that support concurrency levels and transaction processing only support the **SQL_LOCK_NO_CHANGE** locking option.

■ If the driver is unable to lock a row, either to perform the requested operation or to perform the locking operation specified in the *LockType* parameter, **SQL_ERROR** and SQLSTATE **42**000 (Syntax error or access violation) is returned.

■ Although the lock type specified in the *LockType* parameter is specified for a single statement handle, the selected lock provides the same privileges to all statement handles on the connection. In particular, a lock acquired by one statement handle on a connection can be unlocked by a different statement handle on the same connection.

■ A row locked by **SQLSetPos()** remains locked until the statement handle used to lock the row is freed, or until the application commits or rolls back a transaction on the connection handle associated with the statement handle used.

■ **SQLSetPos()** can be called before **SQLFetch()** or **SQLFetchScroll()** is called.

Prerequisites   There are no prerequisites for using this function call.

Restrictions   There are no restrictions associated with this function call.

See Also   SQLBindCol(),SQLFetch(), SQLFetchScroll()

Examples   The following Visual C++ program illustrates how to use the **SQLSetPos()** function to position the cursor on a specific row in a rowset.

```
/*────────────────────────────────────────── */
/* NAME:     CH11EX2.CPP                       */
/* PURPOSE: Illustrate How To Use The Following CLI API Function */
/*          In A C++ Program:                  */
/*                                             */
/*              SQLSetPos()                    */
/*                                             */
/* OTHER CLI APIs SHOWN:                       */
/*              SQLAllocHandle()      SQLSetEnvAttr()    */
/*              SQLConnect()          SQLSetStmtAttr()   */
/*              SQLExecDirect()       SQLBindCol()       */
/*              SQLFetchScroll()      SQLGetData()       */
/*              SQLCloseCursor()      SQLDisconnect()    */
/*              SQLFreeHandle()                */
/*                                             */
/*────────────────────────────────────────── */

// Include The Appropriate Header Files
#include <windows.h>
#include <sqlcli1.h>
#include <iostream.h>

// Define The CLI_Class Class
class CLI_Class
```

```cpp
{
    // Attributes
    public:
        SQLHANDLE    EnvHandle;
        SQLHANDLE    ConHandle;
        SQLHANDLE    StmtHandle;
        SQLRETURN    rc;

    // Operations
    public:
        CLI_Class();                        // Constructor
        ~CLI_Class();                       // Destructor
        SQLRETURN ShowRecords();
};

// Define The Class Constructor
CLI_Class::CLI_Class()
{
    // Initialize The Return Code Variable
    rc = SQL_SUCCESS;

    // Allocate An Environment Handle
    rc = SQLAllocHandle(SQL_HANDLE_ENV, SQL_NULL_HANDLE, &EnvHandle);

    // Set The ODBC Application Version To 3.x
    if (rc == SQL_SUCCESS)
        rc = SQLSetEnvAttr(EnvHandle, SQL_ATTR_ODBC_VERSION,
                (SQLPOINTER) SQL_OV_ODBC3, SQL_IS_UINTEGER);

    // Allocate A Connection Handle
    if (rc == SQL_SUCCESS)
        rc = SQLAllocHandle(SQL_HANDLE_DBC, EnvHandle, &ConHandle);
}

// Define The Class Destructor
CLI_Class::~CLI_Class()
{
    // Free The Connection Handle
    if (ConHandle != NULL)
        SQLFreeHandle(SQL_HANDLE_DBC, ConHandle);

    // Free The Environment Handle
    if (EnvHandle != NULL)
        SQLFreeHandle(SQL_HANDLE_ENV, EnvHandle);
}

// Define The ShowRecords() Member Function
SQLRETURN CLI_Class::ShowRecords(void)
{
    // Declare The Local Memory Variables
    SQLRETURN       rc;
    SQLCHAR         SQLStmt[255];

    SQLUINTEGER     ArraySize = 10;
    SQLCHAR         FirstNameArray[10][14];
```

```
SQLINTEGER      FirstNameLI_Array[10];
SQLCHAR         LastNameArray[10][16];
SQLINTEGER      LastNameLI_Array[10];

SQLUSMALLINT    RowStatusArray[10];
SQLUINTEGER     NumRowsFetched;

SQLUSMALLINT    Choice;
SQLUSMALLINT    RowNum;
SQLDOUBLE       Salary;
SQLINTEGER      SalaryLI;

// Declare The Rowset Size (By Setting The
// SQL_ATTR_ROW_ARRAY_SIZE Statement Attribute
rc = SQLSetStmtAttr(StmtHandle, SQL_ATTR_ROW_ARRAY_SIZE,
          (SQLPOINTER) ArraySize, 0);

// Tell The Driver To Use A Static Cursor (By Setting The
// SQL_ATTR_CURSOR_TYPE Statement Attribute)
rc = SQLSetStmtAttr(StmtHandle, SQL_ATTR_CURSOR_TYPE,
          (SQLPOINTER) SQL_CURSOR_STATIC, 0);

// Set The SQL_ATTR_ROW_STATUS_PTR Statement Attribute To Point
// To A Row Status Array
rc = SQLSetStmtAttr(StmtHandle, SQL_ATTR_ROW_STATUS_PTR,
          RowStatusArray, 0);

// Set The SQL_ATTR_ROWS_FETCHED_PTR Statement Attribute To Point
// To A Rows Fetched Buffer
rc = SQLSetStmtAttr(StmtHandle, SQL_ATTR_ROWS_FETCHED_PTR,
          &NumRowsFetched, 0);

// Define A SELECT SQL Statement
strcpy((char *) SQLStmt, "SELECT FIRSTNME, LASTNAME, ");
strcat((char *) SQLStmt, "SALARY FROM EMPLOYEE ");

// Prepare And Execute The SQL Statement
rc = SQLExecDirect(StmtHandle, SQLStmt, SQL_NTS);

// Bind The Columns In The Result Data Set Returned To
// Application Variables
rc = SQLBindCol(StmtHandle, 1, SQL_C_CHAR, LastNameArray,
          sizeof(LastNameArray[0]), LastNameLI_Array);

rc = SQLBindCol(StmtHandle, 2, SQL_C_CHAR, FirstNameArray,
          sizeof(FirstNameArray[0]), FirstNameLI_Array);

// Display A Header
cout.setf(ios::left);
cout.width(10);
cout << "Record";
cout.setf(ios::left);
cout.width(16);
cout << "Last Name";
cout.setf(ios::left);
```

```cpp
cout.width(16);
cout << "First Name" << endl << endl;

// As Long As There Is Data, Retrieve Records From The Result
// Data Set And Display Them
while (rc != SQL_NO_DATA)
{
    // Fetch Up To The Rowset Size Number Of Rows
    rc = SQLFetchScroll(StmtHandle, SQL_FETCH_NEXT, 0);

    // If No Data Was Found, Exit The Loop
    if (rc == SQL_NO_DATA)
       break;

       // Check The Row Status Array And Print Only Those Rows
       // That Were Successfully Fetched
       for (unsigned int i = 0; i < NumRowsFetched; i++)
       {
            if (RowStatusArray[i] != SQL_ROW_DELETED)
            {
                 // Print The Row Number
                 cout.setf(ios::left);
                 cout.width(10);
                 cout << (i + 1);

                 // Print The First Name
                 cout.setf(ios::left);
                 cout.width(16);
                 if (FirstNameLI_Array[i] == SQL_NULL_DATA)
                      cout << "<NULL>";
                 else
                      cout << FirstNameArray[i];

                 // Print The Last Name
                 cout.setf(ios::left);
                 cout.width(16);
                 if (LastNameLI_Array[i] == SQL_NULL_DATA)
                      cout << "<NULL>";
                 else
                      cout << LastNameArray[i];

                 cout << endl;
            }
       }

ASK:
       // Ask The User What To Do Next
       cout << endl << "Select An Option: (1) View an employee's ";
       cout << "salary, (2) Continue, or (3) Quit";
       cout << endl << "  Choice : ";
       cin >> Choice;

       // Process The User's Choice
       switch(Choice)
```

```
                   {
                   case 3:
                           rc = SQL_NO_DATA;
                   case 2:
                           break;
                   case 1:
                           // Get The Number Of The Record To Retrieve Salary
                           // Information For
                           cout << endl << "Employee record number to retrieve ";
                           cout << "salary information for ? ";
                           cin >> RowNum;

                           // If The Row Number Entered Is Valid ...
                           if (RowNum > 0 && RowNum <= NumRowsFetched)
                           {
                               // Move The Cursor To The Correct Position
                               rc = SQLSetPos(StmtHandle, RowNum, SQL_POSITION,
                                       SQL_LOCK_NO_CHANGE);

                               // Retrieve The Salary Value For The Specified
                               // Employee (Stored In The Second Column Of The
                               // Current Row Of The Result Data Set)
                               rc = SQLGetData(StmtHandle, 3, SQL_C_DOUBLE,
                                       &Salary, 0, &SalaryLI);

                               // Print The Salary
                               if (rc == SQL_SUCCESS)
                               {
                                   cout << "Salary : ";
                                   if (SalaryLI == SQL_NULL_DATA)
                                       cout << "Unknown" << endl;
                                   else
                                   {
                                       cout << "$ ";
                                       cout.setf(ios::fixed | ios::showpoint);
                                       cout.width(8);
                                       cout.precision(2);
                                       cout << Salary << endl;
                                   }
                               }
                           }

                           // Loop Back And Prompt User For A New Choice
                           goto ASK;
                   }
               }

           // Close The Cursor
           rc = SQLCloseCursor(StmtHandle);

           // Return The CLI API Return Code To The Calling Function
           return(rc);
       }
```

```
/*————————————————————————————————————————————*/
/* The Main Function                                            */
/*————————————————————————————————————————————*/
int main()
{
    // Declare The Local Memory Variables
    SQLRETURN  rc = SQL_SUCCESS;

    // Create An Instance Of The CLI_Class Class
    CLI_Class  Example;

    // If A Connection Handle Exists
    if (Example.ConHandle != NULL)
    {
        // Connect To The DB2 Sample Database
        rc = SQLConnect(Example.ConHandle, (SQLCHAR *) "SAMPLE",
                SQL_NTS, (SQLCHAR *) "userid", SQL_NTS,
                (SQLCHAR *) "password", SQL_NTS);

        // Allocate An SQL Statement Handle
        rc = SQLAllocHandle(SQL_HANDLE_STMT, Example.ConHandle,
                &Example.StmtHandle);
        if (rc == SQL_SUCCESS)
        {
            // Show The Records Records
            rc = Example.ShowRecords();

            // Free The SQL Statement Handle
            if (Example.StmtHandle != NULL)
                SQLFreeHandle(SQL_HANDLE_STMT, Example.StmtHandle);
        }

        // Disconnect From The DB2 Sample Database
        rc = SQLDisconnect(Example.ConHandle);
    }

    // Return To The Operating System
    return(rc);
}
```

SQLMoreResults

COMPATIBILITY

X/OPEN 95 CLI	ISO/IEC 92 CLI	DB2 CLI 5.2	DB2 CLI 2.0	ODBC 3.x
☐	☐	☑	☑	☑

ODBC API CONFORMANCE LEVEL   **LEVEL 1***

*IN ODBC 2.0, THIS FUNCTION WAS A LEVEL 2 API CONFORMANCE LEVEL FUNCTION

Purpose   The `SQLMoreResults()` function is used to determine whether more result data sets or row counts are available for an SQL statement handle, and if so, to initialize processing for the next result data set available.

Syntax   `SQLRETURN    SQLMoreResults    (SQLHSTMT          StatementHandle);`

Parameters   *StatementHandle*   An SQL statement handle that refers to a previously allocated SQL statement information storage buffer (data structure).

Description   The `SQLMoreResults()` function is used to access multiple result data sets in a sequential manner upon the successful execution of:

- An SQL query that was bound to one or more arrays of input parameter values.
- A stored procedure containing one or more **SELECT** SQL statements (whose cursor has been left open).

After executing any of these, the application automatically has access to the first result data set created. Once the first result data set has been processed, this function can be called to determine whether another result data set is available. If another result data set is available, this function initializes it and makes it available for additional processing.

Return Codes   SQL_SUCCESS, SQL_SUCCESS_WITH_INFO, SQL_NO_DATA, SQL_STILL_EXECUTING, SQL_INVALID_HANDLE, SQL_ERROR

SQLSTATEs   If this function returns **SQL_SUCCESS_WITH_INFO** or **SQL_ERROR**, one of the following SQLSTATE values may be obtained by calling the **SQLGetDiagRec()** function:

08S01, **40**003, **58**004, **HY**001, **HY**010, **HY**013, or **HYT**00

Refer to Appendix B for detailed information about each SQLSTATE value that can be returned.

Comments
- An application can call **SQLBindCol()**, **SQLFetch()**, **SQLFetchScroll()**, **SQLGetData()**, **SQLSetPos()**, and all the metadata functions on the first or any subsequent result data sets created, just as it would if only one result data set existed.
- If the current result data set contains unfetched rows when this function is called, the current result data set is discarded and the next result data set is made available.
- If all result data sets have been processed when this function is called, **SQL_NO_DATA** is returned.
- Column bindings that were established for the previous result data set remain valid after this function is called. If the columns are different in the new result data set, an error or data truncation may occur when **SQLFetch()** or **SQLFetchScroll()** is called. To prevent this, an application must explicitly rebind the columns in the new result data set as appropriate (or set the appropriate descriptor fields). Alternatively, an application can call **SQLFreeStmt()** with the **SQL_UNBIND** option specified to unbind all columns in the result data set.

■ The values of statement attributes such as cursor type, cursor concurrency, keyset size, or maximum length, may change as an application navigates through the result data sets returned by this function. If this happens, **SQL_SUCCESS_WITH_INFO** is returned.

■ Calling **SQLCloseCursor()** or **SQLFreeStmt()** with the **SQL_CLOSE** option specified causes all result data sets and row counts available as a result of the execution of a batch of SQL statements to be discarded (the statement handle is returned to either the "Allocated" or "Prepared" state).

■ Calling **SQLCancel()** to cancel an asynchronously executing function when a batch of SQL statements has been executed and when the statement handle is in the "Executed," "Cursor-Positioned," or "Asynchronous" state, causes all result data sets generated by the batch to be discarded—provided the cancel operation was successful (the statement handle is returned to the "Prepared" or "Allocated" state).

■ If a batch of SQL statements or a stored procedure contains a mixture of **SELECT** SQL statements along with other SQL statements, the other statements have no effect on this function.

■ If one of the SQL statements in a batch fails, this function returns either **SQL_ERROR** or **SQL_SUCCESS_WITH_INFO**. If the batch was aborted when the statement failed, or if the failed statement was the last statement in the batch, **SQL_ERROR** is returned. If the batch was not aborted when the statement failed, and the failed statement was not the last statement in the batch, **SQL_SUCCESS_WITH_INFO** is returned. **SQL_SUCCESS_WITH_INFO** indicates that at least one result data set or row count value was generated, and that the batch was not aborted.

Prerequisites　　There are no prerequisites for using this function call.

Restrictions　　The ODBC 3.x specification for **SQLMoreResults()** allows count information associated with the execution of parameterized **INSERT**, **UPDATE**, and **DELETE** SQL statements using arrays of parameter values to be returned to an application. However, DB2 CLI does not provide this capability.

See Also　　**SQLSetStmtAttr()**

Example　　The following Visual C++ program illustrates how to use the **SQLMoreResults()** function to move through multiple result data sets that were generated by executing a single SQL statement (using an array of parameter marker values).

```
/*-------------------------------------------------------------*/
/* NAME:     CH11EX3.CPP                                        */
/* PURPOSE: Illustrate How To Use The Following CLI API Function */
/*          In A C++ Program:                                   */
/*                                                              */
/*              SQLMoreResults()                                */
/*                                                              */
/* OTHER CLI APIs SHOWN:                                        */
```

```
/*              SQLAllocHandle()            SQLSetEnvAttr()              */
/*              SQLDriverConnect()          SQLSetStmtAttr()            */
/*              SQLPrepare()                SQLBindParameter()          */
/*              SQLExecute()                SQLBindCol()                */
/*              SQLFetch()                  SQLDisconnect()             */
/*              SQLFreeHandle()                                          */
/*                                                                       */
/*---------------------------------------------------------------------*/

// Include The Appropriate Header Files
#include <windows.h>
#include <sqlcli1.h>
#include <iostream.h>

// Define The CLI_Class Class
class CLI_Class
{
    // Attributes
    public:
        SQLHANDLE    EnvHandle;
        SQLHANDLE    ConHandle;
        SQLHANDLE    StmtHandle;
        SQLRETURN    rc;

    // Operations
    public:
        CLI_Class();                            // Constructor
        ~CLI_Class();                           // Destructor
        SQLRETURN ShowResults();
};

// Define The Class Constructor
CLI_Class::CLI_Class()
{
    // Initialize The Return Code Variable
    rc = SQL_SUCCESS;

    // Allocate An Environment Handle
    rc = SQLAllocHandle(SQL_HANDLE_ENV, SQL_NULL_HANDLE, &EnvHandle);

    // Set The ODBC Application Version To 3.x
    if (rc == SQL_SUCCESS)
        rc = SQLSetEnvAttr(EnvHandle, SQL_ATTR_ODBC_VERSION,
                (SQLPOINTER) SQL_OV_ODBC3, SQL_IS_UINTEGER);

    // Allocate A Connection Handle
    if (rc == SQL_SUCCESS)
        rc = SQLAllocHandle(SQL_HANDLE_DBC, EnvHandle, &ConHandle);
}

// Define The Class Destructor
CLI_Class::~CLI_Class()
{
    // Free The Connection Handle
```

```
    if (ConHandle != NULL)
        SQLFreeHandle(SQL_HANDLE_DBC, ConHandle);

    // Free The Environment Handle
    if (EnvHandle != NULL)
        SQLFreeHandle(SQL_HANDLE_ENV, EnvHandle);
}

// Define The ShowResults() Member Function
SQLRETURN CLI_Class::ShowResults(void)
{
    // Declare The Local Memory Variables
    SQLRETURN    rc2 = 0;
    SQLCHAR      SQLStmt[255];
    SQLUINTEGER  ArraySize = 3;
    SQLSMALLINT  Years[3] = {5, 7, 10};
    SQLCHAR      LastName[10];

    // Allocate An SQL Statement Handle
    rc = SQLAllocHandle(SQL_HANDLE_STMT, ConHandle, &StmtHandle);
    if (rc == SQL_SUCCESS)
    {
        // Set The SQL_ATTR_ROW_BIND_TYPE Statement Attribute To Tell
        // The Driver To Use Column-Wise Binding
        rc = SQLSetStmtAttr(StmtHandle, SQL_ATTR_PARAM_BIND_TYPE,
                SQL_PARAM_BIND_BY_COLUMN, 0);

        // Tell The Driver That There Are 3 Values For Each
        // Parameter (By Setting The SQL_ATTR_PARAMSET_SIZE
        // Statement Attribute)
        rc = SQLSetStmtAttr(StmtHandle, SQL_ATTR_PARAMSET_SIZE,
                (SQLPOINTER) ArraySize, 0);

        // Define A SELECT SQL Statement That Uses A Parameter Marker
        strcpy((char *) SQLStmt, "SELECT NAME FROM STAFF ");
        strcat((char *) SQLStmt, "WHERE YEARS = ?");

        // Prepare The SQL Statement
        rc = SQLPrepare(StmtHandle, SQLStmt, SQL_NTS);

        // Bind The Parameter Marker In The SQL Statement To A Local
        // Application Variable
        rc = SQLBindParameter(StmtHandle, 1, SQL_PARAM_INPUT,
                SQL_C_SHORT, SQL_SMALLINT, 0, 0, (SQLPOINTER)
                Years, 0, NULL);

        // Execute The SQL Statement
        rc = SQLExecute(StmtHandle);

        // Bind The Columns In The Result Data Set Returned To
        // Application Variables
        rc = SQLBindCol(StmtHandle, 1, SQL_C_CHAR, (SQLPOINTER)
                LastName, sizeof(LastName), NULL);
```

```
                // Retrieve Records From Each Result Data Set Generated
                for (int i = 1; rc2 != SQL_NO_DATA; i++)
                {
                    // Identify The Result Data Set
                    cout << "Staff Members With " << Years[i - 1];
                    cout << " Years Of Service :" << endl << endl;

                    // As Long As There Is Data, Retrieve Records And
                    // Display Them
                    while (rc != SQL_NO_DATA)
                    {
                        rc = SQLFetch(StmtHandle);
                        if (rc != SQL_NO_DATA)
                            cout << LastName << endl;
                    }

                    // Move To The Next Result Data Set
                    cout << endl;
                    rc = 0;
                    rc2 = SQLMoreResults(StmtHandle);
                }

            // Free The SQL Statement Handle
            if (StmtHandle != NULL)
                SQLFreeHandle(SQL_HANDLE_STMT, StmtHandle);
        }

    // Return The CLI API Return Code To The Calling Function
    return(rc);
}

/*————————————————————————————————————————————————————— */
/* The Main Function                                     */
/*————————————————————————————————————————————————————— */
int main()
{
    // Declare The Local Memory Variables
    SQLRETURN  rc = SQL_SUCCESS;

    // Create An Instance Of The CLI_Class Class
    CLI_Class  Example;

    // Connect To The DB2 Sample Database
    if (Example.ConHandle != NULL)
    {
        rc = SQLConnect(Example.ConHandle, (SQLCHAR *) "SAMPLE",
                SQL_NTS, (SQLCHAR *) "userid", SQL_NTS,
                (SQLCHAR *) "password", SQL_NTS);

        // Execute A Select SQL Statement And Show The Results
        Example.ShowResults();

        // Disconnect From The DB2 Sample Database
        rc = SQLDisconnect(Example.ConHandle);
    }
```

```
// Return To The Operating System
return(rc);
}
```

SQLRowCount

COMPATIBILITY

X/OPEN 95 CLI	ISO/IEC 92 CLI	DB2 CLI 5.2	DB2 CLI 2.0	ODBC 3.x
✓	✓	✓	✓	✓

ODBC API CONFORMANCE LEVEL   CORE

Purpose   The SQLRowCount() function is used to obtain a count of the number of rows in a table that were affected by the execution of an INSERT, UPDATE, or DELETE SQL statement.

Syntax
```
SQLRETURN    SQLRowCount    (SQLHSTMT      StatementHandle,
                             SQLINTEGER    *RowCount);
```

Parameters   *StatementHandle*   An SQL statement handle that refers to a previously allocated SQL statement information storage buffer (data structure).

RowCount   A pointer to a location in memory where this function is to store a count of the actual number of rows in a table that were affected by an INSERT, UPDATE, or DELETE operation.

Description   The SQLRowCount() function is used to obtain a count of the number of rows in a table that were affected by the execution of an INSERT, UPDATE, or DELETE SQL statement.

Rows in other tables that might have been affected by an INSERT, UPDATE, or DELETE operation (for example, if cascaded deletes occurred) are not included in the row count returned by this function.

Each time SQLExecute(), SQLExecDirect(), SQLSetPos(), or SQLMoreResults() is called, a count of the actual number of rows affected by an INSERT, UPDATE, or DELETE operation is stored in the SQL_DIAG_ROW_COUNT field of the diagnostic header record associated with the statement handle specified. This value is cached (stored) in memory in an implementation-dependent way. SQLRowCount() returns the cached row count value—not the value stored in the SQL_DIAG_ROW_COUNT diagnostic header record field. Cached row count values remain valid until the statement handle is returned to the "Prepared" or "Allocated" state, the SQL statement is re-executed, or the SQLCloseCursor() function is called.

NOTE: *If another CLI function is called after the SQL_DIAG_ROW_COUNT diagnostic header record field is set, the value returned by SQLRowCount() might be different from the actual value stored in the SQL_DIAG_ROW_COUNT field. That is because the SQL_DIAG_ROW_COUNT field is reset to 0 each time a DB2 CLI function is called.*

Return Codes SQL_SUCCESS, SQL_SUCCESS_WITH_INFO, SQL_INVALID_HANDLE, SQL_ERROR

SQLSTATEs If this function returns SQL_SUCCESS_WITH_INFO or SQL_ERROR, one of the following SQLSTATE values may be obtained by calling the SQLGetDiagRec() function:

08S01, 40003, 58004, HY001, HY010, or HY013

Refer to Appendix B for detailed information about each SQLSTATE value that can be returned.

Comments ■ If the number of rows affected by an INSERT, UPDATE, or DELETE SQL statement cannot be determined, or if the statement did not execute successfully, this function returns -1 in the *RowCount* parameter.

Prerequisites The SQLExecute() function or the SQLExecDirect() function should be used to execute an INSERT, UPDATE, or DELETE SQL statement before this function is called.

Restrictions There are no restrictions associated with this function call.

See Also SQLExecute(), SQLExecDirect(), SQLMoreResults(), SQLSetPos()

Example The following Visual C++ program illustrates how to use the SQLRowCount() function to determine how many rows were affected by an INSERT, UPDATE, or DELETE operation.

```
/*————————————————————————————————————————— */
/* NAME:      CH11EX4.CPP                                    */
/* PURPOSE: Illustrate How To Use The Following CLI API Function */
/*          In A C++ Program:                                */
/*                                                           */
/*                   SQLRowCount()                           */
/*                                                           */
/* OTHER CLI APIs SHOWN:                                     */
/*          SQLAllocHandle()            SQLSetEnvAttr()      */
/*          SQLDriverConnect()          SQLSetStmtAttr()     */
/*          SQLPrepare()                SQLExecute()         */
/*          SQLDisconnect()             SQLFreeHandle()      */
/*                                                           */
/*————————————————————————————————————————— */

// Include The Appropriate Header Files
#include <windows.h>
#include <sqlcli1.h>
#include <iostream.h>

// Define The CLI_Class Class
class CLI_Class
{
    // Attributes
    public:
        SQLHANDLE   EnvHandle;
        SQLHANDLE   ConHandle;
        SQLHANDLE   StmtHandle;
        SQLRETURN   rc;
```

```
    // Operations
    public:
        CLI_Class();                                  // Constructor
        ~CLI_Class();                                 // Destructor
        SQLRETURN InsertRows();
};

// Define The Class Constructor
CLI_Class::CLI_Class()
{
    // Initialize The Return Code Variable
    rc = SQL_SUCCESS;

    // Allocate An Environment Handle
    rc = SQLAllocHandle(SQL_HANDLE_ENV, SQL_NULL_HANDLE, &EnvHandle);

    // Set The ODBC Application Version To 3.x
    if (rc == SQL_SUCCESS)
        rc = SQLSetEnvAttr(EnvHandle, SQL_ATTR_ODBC_VERSION,
                (SQLPOINTER) SQL_OV_ODBC3, SQL_IS_UINTEGER);

    // Allocate A Connection Handle
    if (rc == SQL_SUCCESS)
        rc = SQLAllocHandle(SQL_HANDLE_DBC, EnvHandle, &ConHandle);
}

// Define The Class Destructor
CLI_Class::~CLI_Class()
{
    // Free The Connection Handle
    if (ConHandle != NULL)
        SQLFreeHandle(SQL_HANDLE_DBC, ConHandle);

    // Free The Environment Handle
    if (EnvHandle != NULL)
        SQLFreeHandle(SQL_HANDLE_ENV, EnvHandle);
}

// Define The InsertRows() Member Function
SQLRETURN CLI_Class::InsertRows(void)
{
    // Declare The Local Memory Variables
    SQLRETURN     rc;
    SQLCHAR       SQLStmt[255];
    SQLUINTEGER   ArraySize = 3;

    SQLINTEGER    DeptNumArray[3];
    SQLCHAR       DeptNameArray[3][6];
    SQLINTEGER    DeptNameLI_Array[3];
    SQLSMALLINT   ManagerIDArray[3];

    // Initialize The Input Array Variables
    DeptNumArray[0] = 97;
    DeptNumArray[1] = 98;
    DeptNumArray[2] = 99;
```

```
            strcpy((char *) DeptNameArray[0], "TEST1");
            strcpy((char *) DeptNameArray[1], "TEST2");
            strcpy((char *) DeptNameArray[2], "TEST3");

            DeptNameLI_Array[0] = SQL_NTS;
            DeptNameLI_Array[1] = SQL_NTS;
            DeptNameLI_Array[2] = SQL_NTS;

            ManagerIDArray[0] = 80;
            ManagerIDArray[1] = 90;
            ManagerIDArray[2] = 100;

            // Set The SQL_ATTR_ROW_BIND_TYPE Statement Attribute To Tell
            // The Driver To Use Column-Wise Binding.
            rc = SQLSetStmtAttr(StmtHandle, SQL_ATTR_PARAM_BIND_TYPE,
                    SQL_PARAM_BIND_BY_COLUMN, 0);

            // Tell The Driver That There Are 3 Values For Each Parameter
            // (By Setting The SQL_ATTR_PARAMSET_SIZE Statement
            // Attribute)
            rc = SQLSetStmtAttr(StmtHandle, SQL_ATTR_PARAMSET_SIZE,
                    (SQLPOINTER) ArraySize, 0);

            // Define An INSERT SQL Statement That Uses Parameter
            // Markers
            strcpy((char *) SQLStmt, "INSERT INTO ORG ");
            strcat((char *) SQLStmt, "(DEPTNUMB, DEPTNAME, MANAGER) ");
            strcat((char *) SQLStmt, "VALUES (?, ?, ?)");

            // Prepare The SQL Statement
            rc = SQLPrepare(StmtHandle, SQLStmt, SQL_NTS);

            // Bind The Parameter Markers To Local Arrays
            rc = SQLBindParameter(StmtHandle, 1, SQL_PARAM_INPUT,
                    SQL_C_DEFAULT, SQL_INTEGER, 0, 0, DeptNumArray, 0,
                    NULL);

            rc = SQLBindParameter(StmtHandle, 2, SQL_PARAM_INPUT,
                    SQL_C_CHAR, SQL_CHAR, 6, 0, DeptNameArray, 6,
                    DeptNameLI_Array);

            rc = SQLBindParameter(StmtHandle, 3, SQL_PARAM_INPUT,
                    SQL_C_SHORT, SQL_SMALLINT, 0, 0, ManagerIDArray, 0,
                    NULL);

            // Execute The SQL Statement
            rc = SQLExecute(StmtHandle);

            // Return The CLI API Return Code To The Calling Function
            return(rc);
        }

/*─────────────────────────────────────────────────────────────── */
/* The Main Function                                               */
/*─────────────────────────────────────────────────────────────── */
```

```
int main()
{
    // Declare The Local Memory Variables
    SQLRETURN    rc = SQL_SUCCESS;
    SQLINTEGER   RowCount;

    // Create An Instance Of The CLI_Class Class
    CLI_Class    Example;

    // Connect To The DB2 Sample Database
    if (Example.ConHandle != NULL)
    {
        rc = SQLConnect(Example.ConHandle, (SQLCHAR *) "SAMPLE",
                SQL_NTS, (SQLCHAR *) "userid", SQL_NTS,
                (SQLCHAR *) "password", SQL_NTS);

        // Allocate An SQL Statement Handle
        rc = SQLAllocHandle(SQL_HANDLE_STMT, Example.ConHandle,
                &Example.StmtHandle);
        if (rc == SQL_SUCCESS)
        {

            // Insert 3 Rows Of Data Into The ORG Table In The DB2
            // Sample Database
            rc = Example.InsertRows();

            // Obtain And Display Information About The Number Of
            // Rows That Were Affected When The INSERT SQL
            // Statement Was Executed
            rc = SQLRowCount(Example.StmtHandle, &RowCount);
            if (rc == SQL_SUCCESS)
            {
                cout << "Number of rows affected by the INSERT ";
                cout << "SQL statement : " << RowCount << endl;
            }

            // Free The SQL Statement Handle
            if (Example.StmtHandle != NULL)
                SQLFreeHandle(SQL_HANDLE_STMT, Example.StmtHandle);
        }

        // Disconnect From The DB2 Sample Database
        rc = SQLDisconnect(Example.ConHandle);
    }

    // Return To The Operating System
    return(rc);
}
```

Working with Descriptors

In the earlier versions of DB2, descriptors remained behind the scenes and applications had no way (or need) to access them. With version 5.0 of CLI, descriptors were brought out of hiding, and some applications developers found they could be used to help streamline several kinds of processing. This chapter is designed to introduce you to CLI descriptors and to the functions that are used to access them. The first part of this chapter defines descriptors and explains how they are used. This is followed by a discussion of the four main types of descriptors and the basic descriptor parts. Next, the different ways descriptors can be allocated, copied, and freed is discussed. Then, the concise functions that can be used to modify the fields of a descriptor record are introduced. Finally, a detailed reference section covering each CLI function that can be used to control explicitly allocated descriptors is provided.

What Are Descriptors?

Most applications that use embedded SQL to interact with a DBMS have access to a special data structure known as the *SQL Descriptor Area* (SQLDA) structure. This structure is typically used in conjunction with **PREPARE**, **DESCRIBE**, **EXECUTE**, **OPEN**, **FETCH**, and **CALL** SQL statements to pass detailed information (usually about column data) between an application and the database. In DB2 CLI, descriptors are comparable to the SQLDA structure used with embedded SQL.

CLI functions that work with parameter and column data (for example, the **SQLBindCol()** and **SQLFetch()** functions) implicitly set and retrieve descriptor field information as they execute. For instance, when the **SQLBindCol()** function is used to bind column data to an application variable, it sets one or more descriptor fields to describe the complete binding assignment.

Because CLI functions implicitly use descriptors as needed, applications usually do not concern themselves with how descriptors are managed. In fact, there are no database operations that require an application to gain direct access to a descriptor. However, for some applications, gaining direct access to one or more descriptors helps to streamline many operations.

Types of Descriptors

Whenever an SQL statement handle is allocated, DB2 CLI implicitly allocates the following four types of descriptors and assigns them to the statement handle:

- An *Application Parameter Descriptor* (APD)
- An *Application Row Descriptor* (ARD)
- An *Implementation Parameter Descriptor* (IPD)
- An *Implementation Row Descriptor* (IRD)

Each descriptor is used to describe one of the following items:

- A set of zero or more dynamic parameters (represented by parameter markers) in an SQL statement:

  The APD contains the input parameter values as set by the application (dynamic input parameters) or the parameter values returned by a stored procedure invoked by a **CALL** SQL statement (dynamic output parameters) execution.

  The IPD contains the same information as the APD after any specified data conversion is performed (dynamic input parameters), or the parameter values that are returned by a stored procedure invoked by a **CALL** SQL statement before any specified data conversion is performed (dynamic output parameters).

  For dynamic input parameters, an application must operate on the APD before executing any SQL statement that contains dynamic parameter markers. For both dynamic input and dynamic output parameters, an application may specify different data types from those stored in the IPD to achieve data conversion.

■ A single row of data source data:

The IRD contains the current row from the data source. (These buffers conceptually contain data as written to, or read from, the data source. However, the stored form of data source data is not specified. Therefore, the data in an IRD could have been converted from its original form.)

The ARD contains the current row of data as presented to the application after any specified data conversion has been applied.

An application operates on an ARD in any case where column data from the data source must appear in application variables. An application may specify different data types from those found in the IRD to perform data conversion of column data.

Although these four descriptors are usually used in a specific manner, each may perform a different role. For example, a row descriptor in one statement can serve as a parameter descriptor in another. For either parameter or row descriptors, if the application specifies different data types in corresponding records of the implementation and application descriptor, the driver automatically performs the necessary data conversion when it uses the descriptor.

Parts of a Descriptor

Each descriptor contains one header record and zero or more parameter or column records, depending on the descriptor type (parameter descriptor or row descriptor). The descriptor header record contains general information about the descriptor itself, and each parameter/column record contains information that describes a single parameter or column. Each time a new parameter or column is associated with (bound to) an application variable or LOB locator, a new parameter or column record is added to the descriptor. Each time a parameter or column is unbound, the corresponding parameter or column record field is removed from the descriptor. Changing a field value in the descriptor header record affects all parameters or columns associated with the descriptor; changing a field value in a parameter or column only affects the parameter or column associated with that record.

Implicitly Allocated Descriptors

It was mentioned earlier that when an SQL statement handle is allocated by an application, four descriptors are automatically allocated and assigned to the statement handle—an APD, an IPD, an ARD, and an IRD. An application can obtain handles to these implicitly allocated descriptors by calling the **SQLGetStmtAttr()** function with the appropriate attributes specified. DB2 CLI is responsible for allocating and maintaining whatever storage it needs to store the records that are or that will be assigned to these four descriptors. The application does not explicitly specify the size of any of these descriptors, nor does it allocate storage each time new records are added. When an SQL statement handle is freed, DB2 CLI automatically frees the four implicitly allocated descriptors that were assigned to the handle.

When an application variable or LOB locator is associated in some way with an SQL statement parameter marker or result data set column, several fields of the corresponding parameter/column record that are automatically added to the descriptor initially contain a NULL value. Because these field values, known as deferred fields, are not used when the record is created, DB2 CLI saves the addresses of the variables they are associated with for later use.

Once the application provides data for these deferred fields, the record is said to be bound. If the descriptor is an APD, this happens when the **SQLExecute()** or the **SQLExecDirect()** function is called. In this case, each bound record constitutes a bound parameter. For input parameters, the application must bind a parameter for each dynamic parameter marker in the SQL statement before executing the statement. For output parameters, the application is not required to bind the parameter. If the descriptor is an ARD, binding occurs when the **SQLFetch()** or the **SQLScrollFetch()** function is called. In this case, each bound record constitutes a bound column.

Whenever a parameter/column record in an APD, ARD, or IPD descriptor becomes bound, the driver performs a consistency check to ensure that the value of the variable and the values applicable to the deferred fields in the same record are valid and consistent. Consistency checks cannot be performed on IRD descriptors.

Explicitly Allocated Descriptors

Aside from the four implicitly allocated descriptors assigned to each SQL statement handle, an application can explicitly allocate one or more application descriptors (using the **SQLAllocHandle()** function) and assign them to a specific connection handle—but only after the application has connected to a data source. The application can then direct DB2 CLI to use that descriptor in place of the corresponding implicitly allocated application descriptor (APD and ARD descriptors) by calling the **SQLSetStmtAttr()** function with the new descriptor handle specified. Unlike implicitly allocated descriptors, explicitly allocated descriptors can be associated with more than one SQL statement handle; that is, different SQL statements can share the same explicitly allocated application descriptor. Implementation descriptors, however, cannot be explicitly allocated.

Obtaining and Setting Descriptor Information

Applications can call the **SQLGetDescRec()** or the **SQLGetDescField()** function to retrieve information from a descriptor record. By calling **SQLGetDescRec()**, applications can retrieve the contents of several parameter or column record fields (which identify the data type and storage of a parameter or column) in a single function call. However, this function cannot be used to retrieve information from a descriptor header record. Applications can retrieve information from a descriptor header record by calling the **SQLGetDiagField()** function. Because many statement attributes correspond to descriptor header fields, the **SQLGetStmtAttr()** function can also be used to examine descriptor header information.

By calling the **SQLSetDescRec()** function, applications can modify the descriptor record fields that affect the data type and storage of parameters and/or columns associated with explicitly allocated descriptors. Specific fields of any explicitly allocated descriptor record (including the header record) can be changed or set by calling the **SQLSetDescField()** function. Again, because many statement attributes correspond to descriptor header fields, the **SQLSetStmtAttr()** function can be called in place of the **SQLSetDescField()** function to change descriptor header record information. Setting an attribute through the **SQLSetStmtAttr()** function and setting the corresponding descriptor header field by calling the **SQLSetDescField()** have the same effect. Using the **SQLGetStmtAttr()** and **SQLSetStmtAttr()** functions, as opposed to using the **SQLGetDescField()** and **SQLSetDescField()** functions, provides one advantage—no descriptor handle is needed.

The **SQLSetDescField()** function can also be used to define the initial (default) values that are used to populate record fields when an application row descriptor is first allocated. To provide a standard method for presenting database data to an application, the initial value of an explicitly allocated descriptor's **SQL_DESC_TYPE** field is always **SQL_DEFAULT**. An application may change this at any time by setting one or more fields of the descriptor record.

The concept of a default value is not valid for IRD fields. In fact, the only time an application can gain access to IRD fields is when a prepared or executed SQL statement is associated with it.

Copying Descriptors

The **SQLCopyDesc()** function can be used to copy all the record fields of one descriptor to another. Record fields can be copied from any type of descriptor; however, they can only be copied to an APD, ARD, or IPD descriptor—not to an IRD descriptor. The **SQLCopyDesc()** function does not copy the **SQL_DESC_ALLOC_TYPE** field, because a descriptor's allocation type cannot be changed. Otherwise, all record fields copied automatically overwrite any existing record fields.

Because an ARD on one statement handle can serve as an APD on another statement handle, an application can copy rows between tables without copying data at the application level. To do this, a row descriptor describing a column in a fetched row of a table is reused as a parameter descriptor for a parameter in an **INSERT** SQL statement. However, the **SQL_MAX_CONCURRENT_ACTIVITIES** information type (returned by **SQLGetInfo()**) must be greater than **1** for this operation to succeed.

Copying Rows Between Tables

Using descriptors, an application can indirectly copy data from one data source table to another. To do this, an application simply binds the same data buffers and descriptor information to two different SQL statements. One SQL statement fetches the data from one data source table, while the other SQL statement inserts the data into a different data source table. The binding can be accomplished either by sharing an application descriptor (by binding an explicitly allocated descriptor as the ARD to one statement and as the APD to the other) or by using the **SQLCopyDesc()** function to copy the bindings between two different ARD and APD descriptors associated with the SQL statements. If the SQL statements reside on two different connections, the **SQLCopyDesc()** function must be used, because explicitly allocated descriptors can only be assigned to a single connection handle. The **SQLCopyDesc()** function also has to be called to copy the bindings between the IRD and the IPD descriptors of the two SQL statements.

> **NOTE:** *In order for two SQL statements to be associated with the same connection handle, the driver being used must support multiple active statements. The driver's ability to support multiple active statements can be determined by calling the* **SQLGetInfo()** *function with the* **SQL_ACTIVE_STATEMENTS** *information type specified. The value returned must be greater than* **1**.

Freeing Descriptors

Implicitly allocated descriptors can only be freed by calling either the **SQLDisconnect()** function, which drops any statements or descriptors open on the specified connection handle, or the **SQLFreeHandle()** function with the statement handle that the descriptors are associated with specified, which frees the statement handle and all implicitly allocated descriptors associated with it. Even when freed, implicitly allocated descriptors remain valid, and the **SQLGetDescRec()** and **SQLGetDescField()** functions can be used to examine their contents.

Explicitly allocated descriptors can be freed either by calling the **SQLFreeHandle()** function with the descriptor handle specified (explicitly), or by calling the **SQLFreeHandle()** function with the connection handle that the descriptor is associated with specified (which implicitly frees the descriptor when the connection handle is freed). When an explicitly allocated descriptor is freed, all statement handles attached to the freed descriptor automatically revert to the descriptors that were implicitly allocated for them.

Automatic Population of the IPD

Some drivers are capable of setting an IPD descriptor's fields after a parameterized query has been prepared. When that is the case, all parameter records associated with the descriptor are automatically populated with information about the parameter, including the data type, precision, scale, and other characteristics. This information can be particularly valuable to an application when it has no other way to discover it, such as when an ad-hoc query is performed with parameters that the application does not know about.

An application can determine whether a driver supports automatic IPD population by calling the **SQLGetConnectAttr()** function with the **SQL_ATTR_AUTO_IPD** option specified. If this attribute is set to **SQL_TRUE**, the driver supports automatic IPD population, and the application can enable it by setting the **SQL_ATTR_ENABLE_AUTO_IPD** statement attribute to **SQL_TRUE**.

When automatic population is supported and enabled, the driver populates the IPD fields after an SQL statement containing parameter markers has been prepared by the **SQLPrepare()** function. An application can retrieve then IPD information by calling the **SQLGetDescField()** function, the **SQLGetDescRec()** function, or the **SQLDescribeParam()** function. The information obtained by calling any of these functions can be used to ensure that the most appropriate application variables are bound to parameters, or if not, that the appropriate data conversion is specified.

Unfortunately, automatic population of the IPD may produce a decrease in performance. If performance becomes an issue, an application can turn off automatic IPD population by setting the **SQL_ATTR_ENABLE_AUTO_IPD** statement attribute back to **SQL_FALSE** (which is the default value).

Using Concise Functions to Modify Descriptors

Some DB2 CLI functions gain implicit access to descriptors, and sometimes an application developer may find these functions more convenient to use than the **SQLSetDescField()** and **SQLGetDescField()** functions. These functions are known as concise functions, because they perform a number of tasks including setting or getting descriptor field contents. In fact, some concise functions let an application set or retrieve several related descriptor fields in a single function call.

Concise functions can be called without first obtaining a descriptor handle. That is because these functions work with descriptor fields that are associated with the statement handle with which they are called. For example, the concise functions **SQLBindCol()** and **SQLBindParameter()** bind a parameter or column by setting the descriptor fields that correspond to the parameter/column values they receive. Both of these functions perform more tasks than simply setting descriptors—they provide a complete specification of a dynamic parameter's binding or of a specific result data set column's binding. An application can, however, change individual details of a binding specification by calling the **SQLSetDescField()** function or the **SQLSetDescRec()** function. In fact, a binding specification for a parameter or a column can be created by making a series of suitable calls to these two functions.

The concise functions **SQLColAttribute()**, **SQLDescribeCol()**, **SQLDescribeParam()**, **SQLNumParams()**, and **SQLNumResultCols()** retrieve descriptor field values. When the **SQLColAttribute()** function is called to describe column data, it returns data stored in descriptor column record fields. In some cases, the **SQLSetStmtAttr()** and **SQLGetStmtAttr()** functions also serve as concise functions. In a sense, the **SQLGetDescRec()** and **SQLSetDescRec()** functions are also concise functions that when called, retrieve or set the values of several descriptor fields that affect the data type and storage of parameter or column data. In fact, the **SQLSetDescRec()** function provides an effective way to change data associated with the binding information of a parameter or a column in one step.

Table 12–1   The CLI Descriptor Control Functions

Function Name	Description
SQLGetDescRec()	Retrieves the current values of multiple fields of a descriptor parameter/column record that describe the name, data type, and storage sizes used by the data associated with a particular parameter marker or column in a result data set.
SQLSetDescRec()	Modifies the current values of multiple fields of a descriptor parameter/column record.
SQLGetDescField()	Retrieves the current value of a field in a descriptor header or parameter/column record.
SQLSetDescField()	Changes or sets the value of a field in a descriptor header or parameter/column record
SQLCopyDesc()	Copies all records in one descriptor to another descriptor.

The Descriptor Control Functions

Table 12–1 lists the CLI functions that are used to obtain information about and modify (explicitly allocated only) descriptors.

Each of these functions are described in detail in the remaining portion of this chapter.

SQLGetDescRec

COMPATIBILITY

X/OPEN 95 CLI	ISO/IEC 92 CLI	DB2 CLI 5.2	DB2 CLI 2.0	ODBC 3.x
☑	☑	☑	☐	☑

ODBC API CONFORMANCE LEVEL   CORE

Purpose   The `SQLGetDescRec()` function is used to retrieve the current values of multiple fields of a descriptor parameter/column record.

Syntax

```
SQLRETURN    SQLGetDescRec    (SQLHDESC       DescriptorHandle,
                               SQLSMALLINT    RecNumber,
                               SQLCHAR        *Name,
                               SQLSMALLINT    NameMaxSize,
                               SQLSMALLINT    *NameSize,
                               SQLSMALLINT    *Type,
                               SQLSMALLINT    *SubType,
                               SQLINTEGER     *OctetLength,
                               SQLSMALLINT    *Precision,
                               SQLSMALLINT    *Scale,
                               SQLSMALLINT    *Nullable);
```

Parameters   *DescriptorHandle*   A descriptor handle that refers to a previously allocated descriptor information storage buffer (data structure).

RecNumber   Specifies the descriptor record that this function is to retrieve information from. Records are numbered sequentially, starting with 1 (record 0 is the bookmark record).

Name   A pointer to a location in memory where this function is to store the name of the parameter or column associated with the specified descriptor record.

NameMaxSize   The maximum size of the memory storage buffer where this function is to store the parameter or column name retrieved.

NameSize   A pointer to a location in memory where this function is to store the actual number of bytes written to the parameter/column name memory storage buffer (*DescName*).

Type   A pointer to a location in memory where this function is to store the concise SQL or C data type of the parameter or column associated with the specified descriptor record.

SubType	A pointer to a location in memory where this function is to store the interval leading precision value of the parameter or column associated with the specified descriptor record (for records whose *Type* is **SQL_DATETIME** or **SQL_INTERVAL**).
OctetLength	A pointer to a location in memory where this function is to store the length, in bytes, of the parameter or column data associated with the specified descriptor record.
Precision	A pointer to a location in memory where this function is to store the number of digits used by the data value of the parameter or column associated with the specified descriptor record (for records whose *Type* is an exact numeric data type).
Scale	A pointer to a location in memory where this function is to store the number of digits to the right of the decimal point that are used by the data value of the parameter or column associated with the specified descriptor record (for records whose *Type* is a decimal or a numeric data type).
Nullable	A pointer to a location in memory where this function is to store a value that indicates whether the parameter or column associated with the specified descriptor record can contain NULL values.

Description   **SQLGetDescRec()** is used to retrieve the current values of multiple fields of a descriptor parameter/column record that describe the name, data type, and storage sizes used by the data associated with a particular parameter marker in an SQL statement or a column in a result data set. Unlike the **SQLGetDescField()** function, which returns a single value from one field of a descriptor record per call, the **SQLGetDescRec()** function returns the values of several commonly used fields of a descriptor record, including the name of the parameter or column (**SQL_DESC_NAME** field), the concise SQL or C data type of the parameter or column (**SQL_DESC_TYPE** field), the interval leading precision value of the parameter or column (**SQL_DESC_DATETIME_INTERVAL_CODE** field), the length in bytes of the data (**SQL_DESC_OCTET_LENGTH** field), the number of digits used by the data value (**SQL_DESC_PRECISION** field), the number of digits to the right of the decimal point (**SQL_DESC_SCALE** field), and whether the parameter or column can contain NULL values (**SQL_DESC_NULLABLE** field). Refer to the **SQLGetDescField()** function for a complete description of each field found in a descriptor record.

Return Codes   **SQL_SUCCESS, SQL_SUCCESS_WITH_INFO, SQL_NO_DATA, SQL_INVALID_HANDLE, SQL_ERROR**

SQLSTATEs   If this function returns **SQL_SUCCESS_WITH_INFO** or **SQL_ERROR**, one of the following SQLSTATE values may be obtained by calling the **SQLGetDiagRec()** function:

01000, **01**004, **07**009, **08**S01, **HY**000, **HY**001, **HY**007, **HY**010, or **HY**013

Refer to Appendix B for detailed information about each SQLSTATE value that can be returned.

Comments

- If the parameter or column name string's actual length is greater than or equal to the maximum string size value specified in the *NameMaxSize* parameter, the parameter/column name string is truncated to *NameMaxSize*-1 (the length of a NULL-termination character) characters.

- An application can determine the total number of parameter/column descriptor records available in a descriptor by calling the `SQLGetDescField()` function to retrieve the value of the `SQL_DESC_COUNT` field.

- If the value specified in the *RecNumber* parameter is less than or equal to the total number of descriptor records available, but the corresponding descriptor record does not contain data for a parameter or a column, the default values of each field are returned.

- If the value specified in the *RecNumber* parameter is greater than the total number of descriptor records available, `SQL_NO_DATA` is returned.

- If this function is called with an IRD descriptor handle specified in the *DescriptorHandle* parameter, and if the SQL statement associated with the IRD is in the "Prepared" or "Executed" state but there is no open cursor associated with it, `SQL_NO_DATA` is returned.

- If this function is called with a NULL pointer specified for the *Name*, *Type*, *SubType*, *OctetLength*, *Precision*, *Scale*, or *Nullable* parameter, no value is returned for that parameter.

- When this function is used to retrieve descriptor record field values that are undefined for a particular descriptor type, `SQL_SUCCESS` is returned—but the actual values returned are undefined. For example, if this function is called using an APD or ARD descriptor, `SQL_SUCCESS` is returned—but the values returned to the *Name* and *Nullable* parameters are undefined.

- When this function is used to retrieve descriptor record field values that are defined for a particular descriptor type, but have no default value and have not been set by some other DB2 CLI function, `SQL_SUCCESS` is returned. However, the actual value returned for the field is undefined.

- The values of individual descriptor fields can be retrieved by calling the `SQLGetDescField()` function.

Prerequisites   A descriptor handle must be allocated before this function is called.

Restrictions   There are no restrictions associated with this function call.

See Also   `SQLSetDescRec()`, `SQLGetDescField()`, `SQLSetDescField()`, `SQLCopyDesc()`

Example   The following Visual C++ program illustrates how to use the `SQLGetDescRec()` function to retrieve general information from a descriptor record.

```
/*------------------------------------------------------------------ */
/* NAME:    CH12EX1.CPP                                              */
/* PURPOSE: Illustrate How To Use The Following CLI API Function     */
/*          In A C++ Program:                                        */
/*                                                                   */
```

```
/*                 SQLGetDescRec()                                      */
/*                                                                      */
/* OTHER CLI APIs SHOWN:                                                */
/*              SQLAllocHandle()           SQLSetEnvAttr()              */
/*              SQLConnect()               SQLExecDirect()             */
/*              SQLGetStmtAttr()           SQLDisconnect()             */
/*              SQLFreeHandle()                                         */
/*                                                                      */
/*————————————————————————————————————————————————————————————————     */

// Include The Appropriate Header Files
#include <windows.h>
#include <sqlcli1.h>
#include <iostream.h>

// Define The CLI_Class Class
class CLI_Class
{
    // Attributes
    public:
        SQLHANDLE    EnvHandle;
        SQLHANDLE    ConHandle;
        SQLHANDLE    DescHandle;
        SQLHANDLE    StmtHandle;
        SQLRETURN    rc;

    // Operations
    public:
        CLI_Class();                            // Constructor
        ~CLI_Class();                           // Destructor
        SQLRETURN GetDescriptorInfo();
};

// Define The Class Constructor
CLI_Class::CLI_Class()
{
    // Initialize The Return Code Variable
    rc = SQL_SUCCESS;

    // Allocate An Environment Handle
    rc = SQLAllocHandle(SQL_HANDLE_ENV, SQL_NULL_HANDLE, &EnvHandle);

    // Set The ODBC Application Version To 3.x
    if (rc == SQL_SUCCESS)
        rc = SQLSetEnvAttr(EnvHandle, SQL_ATTR_ODBC_VERSION,
                (SQLPOINTER) SQL_OV_ODBC3, SQL_IS_UINTEGER);

    // Allocate A Connection Handle
    if (rc == SQL_SUCCESS)
        rc = SQLAllocHandle(SQL_HANDLE_DBC, EnvHandle, &ConHandle);
}

// Define The Class Destructor
CLI_Class::~CLI_Class()
```

```
{
    // Free The Connection Handle
    if (ConHandle != NULL)
        SQLFreeHandle(SQL_HANDLE_DBC, ConHandle);

    // Free The Environment Handle
    if (EnvHandle != NULL)
        SQLFreeHandle(SQL_HANDLE_ENV, EnvHandle);
}


// Define The GetDescriptorInfo() Member Function
SQLRETURN CLI_Class::GetDescriptorInfo(void)
{
    // Declare The Local Memory Variables
    SQLINTEGER    ValueLen;
    SQLCHAR       Name[50];
    SQLSMALLINT   NameLen;
    SQLSMALLINT   Type;
    SQLSMALLINT   SubType;
    SQLINTEGER    Width;
    SQLSMALLINT   Precision;
    SQLSMALLINT   Scale;
    SQLSMALLINT   Nullable;

    // Retrieve A Handle To The Implementation Row Descriptor (IRD)
    // Associated With The SQL Statement
    rc = SQLGetStmtAttr(StmtHandle, SQL_ATTR_IMP_ROW_DESC,
            (SQLPOINTER) &DescHandle, 0, &ValueLen);

    // Obtain And Display Information About Each Column In The
    // Result Data Set
    for (int i = 1; i <= 2; i++)
    {
        rc = SQLGetDescRec(DescHandle, i, Name, sizeof(Name),
                &NameLen, &Type, &SubType, &Width, &Precision,
                &Scale, &Nullable);
        if (rc == SQL_SUCCESS)
        {
            cout << "Column " << i << endl << endl;
            cout << "Name       : " << Name << endl;
            cout << "Data Type  : " << Type << endl;
            cout << "Sub-Type   : " << SubType << endl;
            cout << "Width      : " << Width << endl;
            cout << "Precision  : " << Precision << endl;
            cout << "Scale      : " << Scale << endl;
            cout << "Nullable   : " << Nullable << endl << endl;
            cout << endl;
        }
    }

    // Return The CLI API Return Code To The Calling Function
    return(rc);
}
```

```c
/*------------------------------------------------------------------*/
/* The Main Function                                                */
/*------------------------------------------------------------------*/
int main()
{
    // Declare The Local Memory Variables
    SQLRETURN  rc = SQL_SUCCESS;
    SQLCHAR    SQLStmt[255];

    // Create An Instance Of The CLI_Class Class
    CLI_Class  Example;

    // Connect To The DB2 Sample Database
    if (Example.ConHandle != NULL)
    {
        rc = SQLConnect(Example.ConHandle, (SQLCHAR *) "SAMPLE",
                  SQL_NTS, (SQLCHAR *) "userid", SQL_NTS,
                  (SQLCHAR *) "password", SQL_NTS);

        // Allocate An SQL Statement Handle
        rc = SQLAllocHandle(SQL_HANDLE_STMT, Example.ConHandle,
                  &Example.StmtHandle);
        if (rc == SQL_SUCCESS)
        {
            // Define A SELECT SQL Statement
            strcpy((char *) SQLStmt, "SELECT LASTNAME, FIRSTNME ");
            strcat((char *) SQLStmt, "FROM EMPLOYEE");

            // Prepare And Execute The SQL Statement
            rc = SQLExecDirect(Example.StmtHandle, SQLStmt, SQL_NTS);

            // Display Information About The Implementation Row
            // Descriptor (IRD) That Is Associated With The SQL
            // Statement
            if (rc == SQL_SUCCESS)
                Example.GetDescriptorInfo();

            // Free The SQL Statement Handle
            if (Example.StmtHandle != NULL)
                SQLFreeHandle(SQL_HANDLE_STMT, Example.StmtHandle);
        }

        // Disconnect From The DB2 Sample Database
        rc = SQLDisconnect(Example.ConHandle);
    }

    // Return To The Operating System
    return(rc);
}
```

SQLSetDescRec

COMPATIBILITY

X/OPEN 95 CLI	ISO/IEC 92 CLI	DB2 CLI 5.2	DB2 CLI 2.0	ODBC 3.x
☑	☑	☑	☐	☑

ODBC API CONFORMANCE LEVEL   CORE

Purpose   The **SQLSetDescRec()** function is used to set the values of multiple fields of a descriptor parameter/column record.

Syntax

```
SQLRETURN    SQLSetDescRec    (SQLHDESC       DescriptorHandle,
                               SQLSMALLINT    RecNumber,
                               SQLSMALLINT    Type,
                               SQLSMALLINT    SubType,
                               SQLINTEGER     OctetLength,
                               SQLSMALLINT    Precision,
                               SQLSMALLINT    Scale,
                               SQLPOINTER     Data,
                               SQLINTEGER     *StringLength,
                               SQLINTEGER     *Indicator);
```

Parameters

DescriptorHandle	A descriptor handle that refers to a previously allocated descriptor information storage buffer (data structure).
RecNumber	Specifies the descriptor record that this function is to assign information to. Records are numbered sequentially, starting with 1 (record 0 is the bookmark record).
Type	The concise SQL or C data type of the parameter or column associated with the specified descriptor record.
SubType	The interval leading precision value of the parameter or column associated with the specified descriptor record (for records whose *Type* is **SQL_DATETIME** or **SQL_INTERVAL**).
OctetLength	The length in bytes of the parameter or column data associated with the specified descriptor record (for records whose *Type* is a character string or binary data type).
Precision	The number of digits used by the parameter or column data value associated with the specified descriptor record (for records whose *Type* is an exact numeric data type).
Scale	The number of digits to the right of the decimal point that are used by the data value of the parameter or column associated with the specified descriptor record (for records whose *Type* is a decimal or a numeric data type).

Data   A pointer to a location in memory where the parameter or
                      column value associated with the specified descriptor record
                      is stored.

StringLength   A pointer to a location in memory where the total length in
                      bytes of the parameter or column data value associated
                      with the specified descriptor record is stored.

Indicator   A pointer to a location in memory where an indicator value
                      that specifies whether or not a NULL data value is
                      assigned to the parameter or column associated with the
                      specified descriptor record is stored.

Description   The `SQLSetDescRec()` function is used to set multiple field values of a descriptor
                  parameter/column record. An application can call `SQLSetDescRec()` to set the following
                  fields of a single column or parameter descriptor record:

- `SQL_DESC_TYPE`
- `SQL_DESC_DATETIME_INTERVAL_CODE` (for records whose type is `SQL_DATETIME` or
  `SQL_INTERVAL`). Note: this field is supported by ODBC but not by DB2 CLI.
- `SQL_DESC_OCTET_LENGTH`
- `SQL_DESC_PRECISION`
- `SQL_DESC_SCALE`
- `SQL_DESC_DATA_PTR`
- `SQL_DESC_OCTET_LENGTH_PTR`
- `SQL_DESC_INDICATOR_PTR`

Refer to the `SQLGetDescField()` function for a complete description of each field
found in a descriptor record.

Once a parameter marker in an SQL statement or a column in a result data set has
been bound to an application variable, the `SQLSetDescRec()` function allows you to change
multiple fields affecting the binding without having to call the `SQLBindParameter()` function or the `SQLBindCol()` function again. This function can also be used to bind a parameter marker to an application variable; however, the `SQLBindParameter()` should be
used to perform the first bind operation, because it sets more descriptor record field values than the `SQLSetDescRec()` function. In addition, it can set both APD and IPD descriptor record field values in one call, and it does not require the allocation of a descriptor
handle.

Return Codes   `SQL_SUCCESS`, `SQL_SUCCESS_WITH_INFO`, `SQL_INVALID_HANDLE`, `SQL_ERROR`

SQLSTATEs   If this function returns `SQL_SUCCESS_WITH_INFO` or `SQL_ERROR`, one of the following
               SQLSTATE values may be obtained by calling the `SQLGetDiagRec()` function:

01000, **07**009, **08**S01, **HY**000, **HY**001, **HY**010, **HY**013, **HY**016, or **HY**021

Refer to Appendix B for detailed information about each SQLSTATE value that can
be returned.

Comments

- An application can determine the total number of parameter/column descriptor records available in a descriptor by calling the **SQLGetDescField()** function to retrieve the value of the **SQL_DESC_COUNT** field.

- If the value specified in the *RecNumber* parameter is greater than the total number of descriptor records available, the value of the **SQL_DESC_COUNT** descriptor header record field is changed to the value specified in the *RecNumber* parameter.

- If an ARD descriptor handle is specified in the *DescriptorHandle* parameter, and if a NULL pointer is specified in the *Data* parameter, the parameter or column associated with the descriptor record is unbound.

- If a NULL pointer is specified in the *Data* parameter, the **SQL_DESC_DATA_PTR** field of the corresponding parameter/column descriptor record is set to a NULL pointer.

- If a NULL pointer is specified in the *StringLength* parameter, the **SQL_DESC_OCTET_LENGTH_PTR** field of the corresponding parameter/column descriptor record is set to a NULL pointer.

- If a NULL pointer is specified in the *Indicator* parameter, the **SQL_DESC_INDICATOR_PTR** field of the specified parameter/column descriptor record is set to a NULL pointer.

- This function can be used to set the descriptor record field values of a descriptor that is not currently associated with an SQL statement.

- While it is not mandatory, it is strongly recommended that an application sets the **SQL_ATTR_USE_BOOKMARKS** statement attribute before this function is used to set the values of bookmark descriptor record fields (that is, before this function is called with 0 specified in the *RecNumber* parameter).

- When this function fails, **SQL_ERROR** is returned, and the contents of the fields of the descriptor record identified by the *RecNumber* parameter are undefined.

- A consistency check is automatically performed by DB2 CLI whenever an application sets (changes) the value of the **SQL_DESC_DATA_PTR** field of an APD, ARD, or IPD descriptor record. If the consistency check fails, **SQL_ERROR** and SQLSTATE **HY021** (Inconsistent descriptor information) is returned. Consistency checks cannot be performed on IRD descriptor records.

- The **SQL_DESC_DATA_PTR** field of an IPD descriptor is not normally set. However, an application can assign a value to this field to force a consistency check on all IPD descriptor fields. However, because the value that the **SQL_DESC_DATA_PTR** field of an IPD descriptor references is not actually stored in the descriptor, it cannot be retrieved by the **SQLGetDescRec()** or **SQLGetDescField()** function.

Prerequisites A descriptor handle must be allocated before this function is called.

Restrictions There are no restrictions associated with this function call.

See Also SQLSetDescRec(), SQLGetDescField(), SQLSetDescField(), SQLCopyDesc()

Example The following Visual C++ program illustrates how to use the **SQLSetDescRec()** function to specify general information for a descriptor record.

```
/*————————————————————————————————————————————————*/
/* NAME:      CH12EX2.CPP                                         */
/* PURPOSE: Illustrate How To Use The Following CLI API Function  */
/*          In A C++ Program:                                     */
/*                                                                */
/*                    SQLSetDescRec()                             */
/*                                                                */
/* OTHER CLI APIs SHOWN:                                          */
/*             SQLAllocHandle()          SQLSetEnvAttr()          */
/*             SQLConnect()              SQLSetStmtAttr()         */
/*             SQLPrepare()              SQLGetDescRec()          */
/*             SQLExecute()              SQLDisconnect()          */
/*             SQLFreeHandle()                                    */
/*                                                                */
/*————————————————————————————————————————————————*/

// Include The Appropriate Header Files
#include <windows.h>
#include <sqlcli1.h>
#include <iostream.h>

// Define The CLI_Class Class
class CLI_Class
{
    // Attributes
    public:
        SQLHANDLE   EnvHandle;
        SQLHANDLE   ConHandle;
        SQLHANDLE   DescHandle;
        SQLHANDLE   StmtHandle;
        SQLRETURN   rc;

    // Operations
    public:
        CLI_Class();                             // Constructor
        ~CLI_Class();                            // Destructor
        SQLRETURN GetDescriptorInfo();
        SQLRETURN ShowResults();
};

// Define The Class Constructor
CLI_Class::CLI_Class()
{
    // Initialize The Return Code Variable
    rc = SQL_SUCCESS;

    // Allocate An Environment Handle
    rc = SQLAllocHandle(SQL_HANDLE_ENV, SQL_NULL_HANDLE, &EnvHandle);

    // Set The ODBC Application Version To 3.x
    if (rc == SQL_SUCCESS)
        rc = SQLSetEnvAttr(EnvHandle, SQL_ATTR_ODBC_VERSION,
                (SQLPOINTER) SQL_OV_ODBC3, SQL_IS_UINTEGER);

    // Allocate A Connection Handle
```

```
        if (rc == SQL_SUCCESS)
            rc = SQLAllocHandle(SQL_HANDLE_DBC, EnvHandle, &ConHandle);
}

// Define The Class Destructor
CLI_Class::~CLI_Class()
{
    // Free The Connection Handle
    if (ConHandle != NULL)
        SQLFreeHandle(SQL_HANDLE_DBC, ConHandle);

    // Free The Environment Handle
    if (EnvHandle != NULL)
        SQLFreeHandle(SQL_HANDLE_ENV, EnvHandle);
}

// Define The GetDescriptorInfo() Member Function
SQLRETURN CLI_Class::GetDescriptorInfo(void)
{
    // Declare The Local Memory Variables
    SQLCHAR       Name[50];
    SQLSMALLINT   NameLen;
    SQLSMALLINT   Type;
    SQLSMALLINT   SubType;
    SQLINTEGER    Width;
    SQLSMALLINT   Precision;
    SQLSMALLINT   Scale;
    SQLSMALLINT   Nullable;

    // Obtain And Display Information About Each Column In The
    // Result Data Set
    for (int i = 1; i <= 2; i++)
    {
        rc = SQLGetDescRec(DescHandle, i, Name, sizeof(Name),
                 &NameLen, &Type, &SubType, &Width, &Precision,
                 &Scale, &Nullable);
        if (rc == SQL_SUCCESS)
        {
            cout << "Column " << i << endl << endl;
            cout << "Data Type : " << Type << endl;
            cout << "Width     : " << Width << endl << endl;
            cout << endl;
        }
    }

    // Return The CLI API Return Code To The Calling Function
    return(rc);
}

/*---------------------------------------------------------- */
/* The Main Function                                         */
/*---------------------------------------------------------- */
int main()
{
```

```
// Declare The Local Memory Variables
SQLRETURN     rc = SQL_SUCCESS;
SQLCHAR       SQLStmt[255];
SQLSMALLINT   Type;
SQLINTEGER    Length;
SQLCHAR       Data[50];
SQLINTEGER    DataLen;

// Create An Instance Of The CLI_Class Class
CLI_Class     Example;

// Connect To The DB2 Sample Database
if (Example.ConHandle != NULL)
{
    rc = SQLConnect(Example.ConHandle, (SQLCHAR *) "SAMPLE",
            SQL_NTS, (SQLCHAR *) "userid", SQL_NTS,
            (SQLCHAR *) "password", SQL_NTS);

    // Allocate An SQL Statement Handle
    rc = SQLAllocHandle(SQL_HANDLE_STMT, Example.ConHandle,
            &Example.StmtHandle);
    if (rc == SQL_SUCCESS)
    {
        // Define A SELECT SQL Statement
        strcpy((char *) SQLStmt, "SELECT LASTNAME, FIRSTNME ");
        strcat((char *) SQLStmt, "FROM EMPLOYEE");

        // Explicitly Allocate A Descriptor Handle
        rc = SQLAllocHandle(SQL_HANDLE_DESC, Example.ConHandle,
                &Example.DescHandle);

        // Assign The Descriptor Handle To The Statement Handle
        rc = SQLSetStmtAttr(Example.StmtHandle,
                SQL_ATTR_APP_ROW_DESC, (SQLPOINTER)
                Example.DescHandle, 0);

        // Prepare The SQL Statement
        rc = SQLPrepare(Example.StmtHandle, SQLStmt, SQL_NTS);

        // Modify The Information Stored In The Application Row
        // Descriptor (Which Was Populated When The SQL Statement
        // Was Prepared)
        Type = SQL_CHAR;
        Length = 50;
        rc = SQLSetDescRec(Example.DescHandle, 2, Type, 0,
                Length, 0, 0, Data, &DataLen, NULL);

        // Display The Modified Descriptor Information
        if (rc == SQL_SUCCESS)
            Example.GetDescriptorInfo();

        // Execute The SQL Statement
        rc = SQLExecute(Example.StmtHandle);
```

```
                        // Free The Descriptor Handle
                        if (Example.DescHandle != NULL)
                            SQLFreeHandle(SQL_HANDLE_DESC, Example.DescHandle);

                        // Free The SQL Statement Handle
                        if (Example.StmtHandle != NULL)
                            SQLFreeHandle(SQL_HANDLE_STMT, Example.StmtHandle);
                    }

                    // Disconnect From The DB2 Sample Database
                    rc = SQLDisconnect(Example.ConHandle);
                }

                // Return To The Operating System
                return(rc);
            }
```

SQLGetDescField

COMPATIBILITY

X/OPEN 95 CLI	ISO/IEC 92 CLI	DB2 CLI 5.2	DB2 CLI 2.0	ODBC 3.x
☑	☑	☑	☐	☑

ODBC API CONFORMANCE LEVEL   CORE

Purpose

The `SQLGetDescField()` function is used to retrieve the current value of a specified descriptor record field.

Syntax

```
SQLRETURN   SQLGetDescField   (SQLHDESC      DescriptorHandle,
                               SQLSMALLINT   RecNumber,
                               SQLSMALLINT   Identifier,
                               SQLPOINTER    Value,
                               SQLINTEGER    ValueMaxSize,
                               SQLINTEGER    *StringLength);
```

Parameters

DescriptorHandle   A descriptor handle that refers to a previously allocated descriptor information storage buffer (data structure).

RecNumber   Specifies the descriptor record that this function is to retrieve information from. If any field of the descriptor header record is specified in the *Identifier* parameter, this parameter is ignored. Otherwise, this parameter should contain a number greater than or equal to **0** (Descriptor records are numbered, starting at **0**, with record number **0** being the bookmark record).

Identifier

The field of the descriptor header record or a descriptor parameter/column record whose value is to be retrieved. This parameter must be set to one of the following values:

Header Record Fields

- `SQL_DESC_ALLOC_TYPE`
- `SQL_DESC_ARRAY_SIZE`
- `SQL_DESC_ARRAY_STATUS_PTR`
- `SQL_DESC_BIND_OFFSET_PTR`
- `SQL_DESC_BIND_TYPE`
- `SQL_DESC_COUNT`
- `SQL_DESC_ROWS_PROCESSED_PTR`

Parameter/Column Record Fields

- `SQL_DESC_AUTO_UNIQUE_VALUE`
- `SQL_DESC_BASE_COLUMN_NAME`
- `SQL_DESC_BASE_TABLE_NAME`
- `SQL_DESC_CASE_SENSITIVE`
- `SQL_DESC_CATALOG_NAME`
- `SQL_DESC_CONCISE_TYPE`
- `SQL_DESC_DATA_PTR`
- `SQL_DESC_DATETIME_INTERVAL_CODE`
- `SQL_DESC_DATETIME_INTERVAL_PRECISION`
- `SQL_DESC_DISPLAY_SIZE`
- `SQL_DESC_FIXED_PREC_SCALE`
- `SQL_DESC_INDICATOR_PTR`
- `SQL_DESC_LABEL`
- `SQL_DESC_LENGTH`
- `SQL_DESC_LITERAL_PREFIX`
- `SQL_DESC_LITERAL_SUFFIX`
- `SQL_DESC_LOCAL_TYPE_NAME`
- `SQL_DESC_NAME`
- `SQL_DESC_NULLABLE`
- `SQL_DESC_NUM_PREC_RADIX`
- `SQL_DESC_OCTET_LENGTH`
- `SQL_DESC_OCTET_LENGTH_PTR`
- `SQL_DESC_PARAMETER_TYPE`
- `SQL_DESC_PRECISION`

- SQL_DESC_ROWVER
- SQL_DESC_SCALE
- SQL_DESC_SCHEMA_NAME
- SQL_DESC_SEARCHABLE
- SQL_DESC_TABLE_NAME
- SQL_DESC_TYPE
- SQL_DESC_TYPE_NAME
- SQL_DESC_UNNAMED
- SQL_DESC_UNSIGNED
- SQL_DESC_UPDATABLE

Value	A pointer to a location in memory where this function is to store the current value of the specified descriptor record field.
ValueMaxSize	The size of the memory storage buffer where this function is to store the current value of the specified descriptor record field. If an ODBC-defined descriptor record field is to be retrieved, and if the field value is a 32-bit integer value, this parameter is ignored. If a DB2 CLI descriptor record field is to be retrieved, this parameter may be set as follows:

- If the value of the specified descriptor record field is a character string, this parameter may be set to the actual length of the string or to SQL_NTS.

- If the value of the specified descriptor record field is a binary string, this parameter may be set to the result of the SQL_LEN_BINARY_ATTR(*length*) macro. Usually, this macro places a negative value in this parameter.

- If the value of the specified descriptor record field is anything other than a character string or binary string, this parameter may be set to SQL_IS_POINTER.

- If the value of the specified descriptor record field is a fixed-length data type, this parameter may be set to SQL_IS_INTEGER or SQL_IS_UINTEGER, as appropriate.

StringLength	A pointer to a location in memory where this function is to store the actual number of bytes written to the descriptor record field value memory storage buffer (*Value*). If the descriptor record field value retrieved is not a character string value, this parameter is ignored.

Description   The SQLGetDescField() function is used to retrieve the current value of a specified descriptor record field. Table 12–2 lists alphabetically each value that can be specified for the *Identifier* parameter, along with a description of the information that will be returned for that value when this function is executed.

This function can be used to retrieve the value (setting) of any field in any descriptor record (regardless of the descriptor type), including header record fields, parameter/column record fields, and bookmark record fields.

Table 12–2 *Descriptor Record Fields*

Field Name	Data Type	Description
Header Record Fields		
SQL_DESC_ALLOC_TYPE	SQLSMALLINT	This field identifies how the descriptor was allocated. Valid values for this field are:
		SQL_DESC_ALLOC_AUTO: The descriptor was automatically allocated by the driver.
		SQL_DESC_ALLOC_USER: The descriptor was explicitly allocated by the application.
SQL_DESC_ARRAY_SIZE	SQLUINTEGER	For APD descriptors, this field contains a count of the number of values available for each parameter associated with the descriptor.
		For ARD descriptors, this field contains a count of the number of rowset rows associated with the descriptor.
		By default, the value for this field is **1**. If it contains a value greater than **1**, the **SQL_DESC_DATA_PTR, SQL_ DESC_INDICATOR_PTR**, and **SQL_DESC_OCTET_ LENGTH_PTR** fields of each parameter/column descriptor record contain pointers to arrays (APD or ARD descriptors only).
SQL_DESC_ARRAY_ STATUS_PTR	SQLUSMALLINT *	For APD descriptors, this field contains a pointer to an array of parameter operation values that can be set by the application to indicate whether a set of parameter values are to be used or ignored when **SQLExecute()** or **SQLExecDirect()** is called. Each element in this array can contain the following values:
		SQL_PARAM_PROCEED: The set of parameter values are to be used by the **SQLExecute()** or **SQLExecDirect()** function call.
		SQL_PARAM_IGNORE: The set of parameter values are not to be used by the **SQLExecute()** or **SQLExecDirect()** function call.
		If no elements in the array are set, or if this field contains a NULL pointer, all sets of parameters are used by **SQLExecute()** or **SQLExecDirect()** function calls.
		For IPD descriptors, this field contains a pointer to an array of parameter status values that contains status information about each set of parameter values (after **SQLExecute()** or **SQLExecDirect()** has been executed). An application must allocate an array of **SQLUSMALLINT**s with as many elements as there are

Table 12–2 Descriptor Record Fields (Continued)

Field Name	Data Type	Description
		parameter values, and store a pointer to the array in this field. When **SQLExecute()** or **SQLExecDirect()** is called, the driver populates the specified array, unless this field contains a NULL pointer (the default), in which case no status values are generated and the array is not populated. Each element in the array can contain the following values:

SQL_PARAM_SUCCESS:
The SQL statement was successfully executed using the set of parameter values specified.

SQL_PARAM_SUCCESS_WITH_INFO:
The SQL statement was successfully executed using the set of parameter values specified; however, warning information was generated and is available in one or more diagnostic records.

SQL_PARAM_ERROR:
An error occurred while processing the SQL statement using the set of parameter values specified. Additional error information is available in one or more diagnostic records.

SQL_PARAM_UNUSED:
The set of parameter values specified was not used, possibly because some previous set of parameter values caused an error that aborted further processing, or because **SQL_PARAM_IGNORE** was set for the set of parameter values in the specified array.

SQL_PARAM_DIAG_UNAVAILABLE:
Diagnostic information is not available. An example is when DB2 CLI treats arrays of parameter values as a monolithic unit, in which case error information is not generated.

If a call to **SQLExecute()** or **SQLExecDirect()** did not return **SQL_SUCCESS** or **SQL_SUCCESS_WITH_INFO**, the contents of the array pointed to by this field are undefined.

For ARD descriptors, this field contains a pointer to an array of row operation values that can be set by the application to indicate whether the row is to be ignored by the **SQLSetPos()** function. Each element in the array can contain the following values:

SQL_ROW_PROCEED:
The row is to be included in the bulk operation performed by the **SQLSetPos()** function. (This setting does not guarantee that the operation will occur on the row. If the row has the status **SQL_ROW_ERROR** in the IRD row status array, the driver may not be able to perform the operation in the row.)

Table 12–2 Descriptor Record Fields (Continued)

Field Name	Data Type	Description
		SQL_ROW_IGNORE: The row is to be excluded from the bulk operation performed by the **SQLSetPos()** function.
		If no elements in the array are set, or if this field contains a NULL pointer, all rows are included in the bulk operation performed by the **SQLSetPos()** function.
		If an element in the array is set to **SQL_ROW_IGNORE**, the value in the row status array for the ignored row is not changed.
		For IRD descriptors, this field contains a pointer to an array of row status values that contains status information after the **SQLFetch()**, **SQLFetchScroll()**, or **SQLSetPos()** function is called.
		An application must allocate an array of **SQLUSMALLINT**s with as many elements as there are rows in the rowset, and store a pointer to the array in this field. When the **SQLFetch()**, **SQLFetchScroll()**, or **SQLSetPos()** function is called, DB2 CLI populates the specified array, unless this field contains a NULL pointer (the default), in which case no status values are generated and the array is not populated. Each element in the array can contain the following values:
		SQL_ROW_SUCCESS: The row was successfully fetched and has not been changed since it was last fetched.
		SQL_ROW_SUCCESS_WITH_INFO: The row was successfully fetched and has not been changed since it was last fetched. However, a warning about the row was returned.
		SQL_ROW_ERROR: An error occurred while fetching the row.
		SQL_ROW_NOROW: The rowset overlapped the end of the result data set and no row was returned that corresponded to an element of the row status array.
		If a call to **SQLFetch()**, **SQLFetchScroll()**, or **SQLSetPos()** did not return **SQL_SUCCESS** or **SQL_SUCCESS_WITH_INFO**, the contents of the array referenced by this field are undefined.
		NOTE: If an application sets the elements of the row status array, the behavior of DB2 CLI is undefined.
SQL_DESC_BIND_OFFSET_PTR	**SQLINTEGER** *	For APD and ARD descriptors, this field contains a pointer to the binding offset used. By default, this field contains a NULL pointer. If this field contains a pointer to the binding offset used, instead of a NULL

Table 12–2 Descriptor Record Fields (Continued)

Field Name	Data Type	Description
		pointer, DB2 CLI dereferences the pointer and adds the dereferenced value to each deferred field that has a non-NULL value in the **SQL_DESC_DATA_PTR**, **SQL_DESC_INDICATOR_PTR**, and **SQL_DESC_OCTET_ LENGTH_PTR** fields and uses the new pointer values when binding.
		The binding offset is always added directly to the values in the **SQL_DESC_DATA_PTR**, **SQL_DESC_ INDICATOR_PTR**, and **SQL_DESC_OCTET_LENGTH_PTR** fields. If the offset is changed to a different value, the new value is still added directly to the value in each of these fields—earlier offset values are ignored.
		This field is a deferred field: It is not used at the time it is set, but is used later by DB2 CLI when it needs to determine addresses for data buffers.
SQL_DESC_BIND_TYPE	**SQLINTEGER**	In APD descriptors, this field specifies the binding orientation to use for binding dynamic parameters.
		In ARD descriptors, this field specifies the binding orientation to use when the **SQLFetch()** or **SQLFetchScroll()** function is called.
		By default, this field is set to **SQL_BIND_BY_ COLUMN** and column-wise binding is used for both parameters and columns.
SQL_DESC_COUNT	**SQLSMALLINT**	This field contains the 1-based index value of the highest-numbered descriptor parameter/column record that contains data. When DB2 CLI sets the header record for the descriptor, it must set this field to show how many parameter/column records are significant. When an application allocates a descriptor handle, it does not have to specify how many descriptor records to reserve room for. Instead, as the application specifies the contents of descriptor records, DB2 CLI takes any action necessary to ensure that the descriptor handle always refers to a descriptor (data structure) of adequate size.
		This field does not contain a count of all parameters (if the descriptor is an APD or IPD descriptor) or all data columns (if the descriptor is an ARD or IRD descriptor) that are bound. Instead it contains a count of the total number of parameter/column records in the descriptor itself.
		If the highest-numbered parameter or column is unbound, the value of this field is changed to the number of the next highest-numbered parameter/column record. However, if a parameter or column with a number less than the highest-numbered parameter/column record is unbound, the value of this field is not changed.

Table 12–2 *Descriptor Record Fields (Continued)*

Field Name	Data Type	Description
		On the other hand, if additional parameters or columns are bound with numbers greater than the highest-numbered parameter/column record containing data, DB2 CLI automatically increases the value stored in this field.
		If the **SQLFreeStmt()** function is called with the **SQL_RESET_PARAMS** option specified, the **SQL_DESC_COUNT** fields in APD and IPD descriptors are set to **0**. If the **SQLFreeStmt()** function is called with the **SQL_UNBIND** option specified, the **SQL_DESC_COUNT** fields in ARD and IRD descriptors are set to **0**.
		An application can explicitly set the value of this field by calling the **SQLSetDescField()** function with the **SQL_DESC_COUNT** field specified. If the value stored in the **SQL_DESC_COUNT** field is explicitly decreased with this approach, all records with numbers greater than the new value are effectively removed. If the value is explicitly set to **0**, and the descriptor is an ARD descriptor, all data buffers except those associated with a bound bookmark column are released.
		The record count in the **SQL_DESC_COUNT** field of an ARD descriptor does not include a bound bookmark column. The only way to unbind a bound bookmark column is to store a NULL pointer in the corresponding **SQL_DESC_DATA_PTR** field.
SQL_DESC_ROWS_ PROCESSED_PTR	SQLUINTEGER *	In an IPD descriptor, this field contains a pointer to a buffer that contains the number of parameter value sets that have already been processed (including parameter value sets that caused an error to occur).
		In an IRD descriptor, this field contains a pointer to a buffer that contains the number of rows fetched by **SQLFetch()** or **SQLFetchScroll()**, or the number of rows affected (including rows that returned errors) by a bulk operation performed by **SQLBulkOperations()** or **SQLSetPos()**.
		If this field contains a NULL pointer, no value is returned.
		The value stored in this field is only valid if a call to **SQLExecute()**, **SQLExecDirect()**, **SQLParamData()** (IPD descriptor), **SQLFetch()**, or **SQLFetchScroll()** (IRD descriptor), returned **SQL_SUCCESS** or **SQL_SUCCESS_WITH_INFO**.
		If **SQL_SUCCESS** or **SQL_SUCCESS_WITH_INFO** was not returned, the contents of the buffer pointed to by this field are undefined, unless **SQL_NO_DATA** was returned, in which case the number **0** was also returned.

Table 12–2 Descriptor Record Fields (Continued)

Field Name	Data Type	Description
Parameter/Column Record Fields		
SQL_DESC_AUTO_ UNIQUE_VALUE	SQLINTEGER	For IRD descriptors, this field indicates whether a column in a result data is an auto-incrementing column. Valid values for this field are: **SQL_TRUE**: The column is an auto-incrementing column. **SQL_FALSE**: The column is not an auto-incrementing column.
SQL_DESC_BASE_ COLUMN_NAME	SQLCHAR *	For IRD descriptors, this field contains the name of the base column in the data source that corresponds to a column in a result data set. This field contains an empty string (" ") if a base column name does not exist (as is the case for columns that are based on expressions).
SQL_DESC_BASE_ TABLE_NAME	SQLCHAR *	For IRD descriptors, this field contains the name of the base table in the data source that corresponds to a column in a result data set. This field contains an empty string (" ") if a base table name does not exist or is not applicable.
SQL_DESC_CASE_ SENSITIVE	SQLINTEGER	For IPD and IRD descriptors, this field indicates whether a parameter or column is treated as case-sensitive for collations and comparisons. Valid values for this field are: **SQL_TRUE**: The parameter or column is treated as case-sensitive for collations and comparisons. **SQL_FALSE**: The column is not treated as case-sensitive for collations and comparisons, or the parameter or column does not contain a character value.
SQL_DESC_CATALOG_NAME	SQLCHAR *	For IRD descriptors, this field contains the catalog name for the base table in the data source that corresponds to a column in a result data set. This field contains an empty string (" ") if the data source does not support catalogs or if the catalog name cannot be determined. It is driver-dependant what this field contains if the column is associated with an expression or if the column is part of a view.
SQL_DESC_CONCISE_TYPE	SQLSMALLINT	This field specifies the concise data type for all data types, including datetime and interval data types, stored in the descriptor record (that is, that are stored in the **SQL_DESC_CONCISE_TYPE**, **SQL_DESC_ TYPE**, and **SQL_DESC_DATETIME_INTERVAL_CODE** fields).

Table 12–2   Descriptor Record Fields (Continued)

Field Name	Data Type	Description
		The values in the **SQL_DESC_CONCISE_TYPE**, **SQL_DESC_TYPE**, and **SQL_DESC_DATETIME_ INTERVAL_CODE** fields are interdependent—each time one field is set, the remaining fields must also be set. The **SQL_DESC_CONCISE_TYPE** field can be set by the **SQLBindParameter()**, **SQLBindCol()**, or **SQLSetDescField()** function. The **SQL_DESC_ TYPE** can be set by the **SQLSetDescField()** or **SQLSetDescRec()** function.
		If this field is set to a concise datetime or interval data type, the **SQL_DESC_TYPE** field is set to the corresponding verbose type (**SQL_DATETIME** or **SQL_INTERVAL**), and the **SQL_DESC_DATETIME_ INTERVAL_CODE** field is set to the appropriate datetime or interval subcode.
		If this field is set to a concise data type other than an datatime or interval data type, the **SQL_DESC_TYPE** field is set to the same value, and the **SQL_DESC_ DATETIME_INTERVAL_CODE** field is set to **0**.
SQL_DESC_DATA_PTR	**SQLPOINTER**	For APD and IPD descriptors, this field contains a pointer to an application variable that contains a parameter value.
		For ARD descriptors, this field contains a pointer to an application variable that is to receive the value of a column in a result data set. If a call to **SQLFetch()** or **SQLFetchScroll()** does not return **SQL_ SUCCESS** or **SQL_SUCCESS_WITH_INFO**, the contents of the variable that is to receive the column value is undefined.
		Whenever this field is set for an APD, ARD, or IPD descriptor, DB2 CLI verifies that the **SQL_DESC_ TYPE** field contains a valid ODBC or driver-specific data type, and that all other descriptor fields containing data type information are consistent. Therefore, this field should only be set in an IPD descriptor to prompt DB2 CLI to perform a consistency check.
		If an application sets the **SQL_DESC_DATA_PTR** field of an IPD descriptor and later retrieves the value of the **SQL_DESC_DATA_PTR** field, it may not receive the same value that it set.
		The column referenced by the **SQL_DESC_DATA_PTR** field of an ARD descriptor is unbound if this field is set to a NULL pointer (by calling the **SQLBindCol()**, **SQLSetDescField()** or **SQLSetDescRec()** function) —all other fields are not affected.

Table 12–2 *Descriptor Record Fields (Continued)*

Field Name	Data Type	Description
		This field is a deferred field: It is not used at the time it is set, but is used later by DB2 CLI when it needs to determine addresses for data buffers.
SQL_DESC_DATETIME_ INTERVAL_CODE	SQLSMALLINT	This field contains the subtype code for datetime and interval data types (both SQL and C data types). Valid values for this field are:
		SQL_CODE_DATE SQL_CODE_TIME SQL_CODE_TIMESTAMP
		ODBC recognizes other values for this field that DB2 CLI does not support.
		The subcode consists of the data type name with CODE substituted for either TYPE, C_TYPE (for date-time data types), INTERVAL or C_INTERVAL (for interval data types).
		If the SQL_DESC_TYPE and SQL_DESC_CONCISE_TYPE fields of an APD or ARD descriptor are set to SQL_C_DEFAULT and if the descriptor is not associated with an SQL statement handle, the contents of this field are undefined.
SQL_DESC_DATETIME_ INTERVAL_PRECISION	SQLINTEGER	This field contains the leading interval precision value for datetime and interval data types.
		DB2 CLI does not support interval data types.
SQL_DESC_DISPLAY_SIZE	SQLINTEGER	For IRD descriptors, this field contains the maximum number of characters needed to display the data of a column in a result data set.
SQL_DESC_FIXED_ PREC_SCALE	SQLSMALLINT	For IPD and IRD descriptors, this field indicates whether a column in a result data set is an exact numeric column. Valid values for this field are:
		SQL_TRUE: The column is an exact numeric column and has a fixed precision and a non-zero scale.
		SQL_FALSE: The column is not an exact numeric column, therefore it does not have a fixed precision and scale.
SQL_DESC_INDICATOR_PTR	SQLINTEGER *	For APD and ARD descriptors, this field contains a pointer to an indicator variable.
		For APD descriptors, the indicator variable specified should be set to SQL_NULL_DATA if a dynamic parameter is set to NULL—if this field contains a NULL pointer, the application cannot use the descriptor record to specify NULL arguments.

Table 12–2 Descriptor Record Fields (Continued)

Field Name	Data Type	Description
		For ARD descriptors, the indicator variable specified contains **SQL_NULL_DATA** if the column in a result data set contains a NULL value—if this field contains a NULL pointer, DB2 CLI is prevented from returning information about whether the column is NULL and SQLSTATE **22**002 (Indicator variable required but not supplied) is returned by **SQLFetch()** or **SQLFetchScroll()** if the column is indeed NULL. If a call to **SQLFetch()** or **SQLFetchScroll()** does not return **SQL_SUCCESS** or **SQL_SUCCESS_WITH_INFO**, the contents of the indicator variable that this field references is undefined.
		The **SQL_DESC_INDICATOR_PTR** field determines whether the field pointed to by **SQL_DESC_OCTET_LENGTH_PTR** is set.
		If the data value for a column is NULL, the driver sets the indicator variable to **SQL_NULL_DATA** and the buffer pointed to by the **SQL_DESC_OCTET_LENGTH_PTR** field is not set. If the data value for a column is not NULL, the indicator variable this field references is set to **0**, (unless the same pointer is used in both the **SQL_DESC_INDICATOR_PTR** and **SQL_DESC_OCTET_LENGTH_PTR** fields) and the buffer pointed to by the **SQL_DESC_OCTET_LENGTH_PTR** is set to the length of the data.
		This field is a deferred field: It is not used at the time it is set, but is used later by DB2 CLI when it needs to indicate nullability (APD descriptors) or to determine nullability (ARD descriptors).
SQL_DESC_LABEL	**SQLCHAR ***	For IRD descriptors, this field contains the column label or title of a column in a result data set. If the column does not have a label, this field contains the column name. Otherwise, if the column is unlabeled and unnamed, this field contains an empty string (" ").
SQL_DESC_LENGTH	**SQLUINTEGER**	This field contains either the maximum character length for a fixed-length data type, or the actual character length of a character string (excluding the NULL-termination character) or a binary (variable-length) data type.
		For datetime and interval data types, this field contains the length, in characters, of the character string representation of the datetime or interval value. Note that this length is a count of characters, not a count of bytes.

Table 12–2 Descriptor Record Fields (Continued)

Field Name	Data Type	Description
SQL_DESC_LITERAL_PREFIX	SQLCHAR *	For IRD descriptors, this field contains one or more characters DB2 CLI recognizes as a prefix for a literal representation of the data type. For example, a single quotation mark (') might be used for character data types, or '0x' might be used for binary data types. This field contains an empty string (" ") if a literal prefix is not applicable.
SQL_DESC_LITERAL_SUFFIX	SQLCHAR *	For IRD descriptors, this field contains one or more characters DB2 CLI recognizes as a suffix for a literal representation of the data type. For example, a single quotation mark (') might be used for character data types. This field contains an empty string (" ") if a literal suffix is not applicable.
SQL_DESC_LOCAL_TYPE_NAME	SQLCHAR *	For IPD and IRD descriptors, this field contains any localized (native language) name for the data type that may be different from the regular name of the data type. This field contains an empty string (" ") if no localized name has been defined. This field is provided for display purposes only.
SQL_DESC_NAME	SQLCHAR *	For IPD descriptors, this field contains either the name or an alias of a parameter. If the version of DB2 CLI being used supports named parameters and is capable of describing parameters, the parameter name is returned in this field. If the version of DB2 CLI being used does not support named parameters, this field is undefined. For IRD descriptors, this field contains the alias of a column in a result data set. If the column does not have an alias or if a column alias does not apply, this field contains the column name. If the column does not have an alias or name, DB2 CLI returns an empty string (" ") to this field. DB2 CLI sets the SQL_DESC_UNNAMED field to SQL_NAMED if it populates this field; it sets the SQL_DESC_UNNAMED field to SQL_UNNAMED if it returns an empty string (" ") to this field.
SQL_DESC_NULLABLE	SQLSMALLINT	For IRD descriptors, this field contains a value that indicates whether a column in a result data set can contain NULL values. Valid values for this field are: SQL_NULLABLE: The column can contain NULL values. SQL_NO_NULLS: The column can not contain NULL values. SQL_NULLABLE_UNKNOWN: Whether the column can contain NULL values is not known.

Table 12–2   Descriptor Record Fields (Continued)

Field Name	Data Type	Description
		This field pertains to a column in a result data set—not to the underlying base column.
		In IPD descriptors, this field is always set to **SQL_NULLABLE** (and cannot be set by an application) because dynamic parameters are always nullable.
SQL_DESC_NUM_PREC_RADIX	**SQLINTEGER**	This field contains the radix value of the data type.
		For approximate numeric data types, this field contains the value **2** and the **SQL_DESC_PRECISION** field contains the number of bits allowed.
		For exact numeric data types, this field contains the value **10**, and the **SQL_DESC_PRECISION** field contains the number of decimal digits allowed.
		For numeric data types, this field can contain either **10** or **2**.
		For data types where radix is not applicable, this field will be set to **0**.
SQL_DESC_OCTET_LENGTH	**SQLINTEGER**	This field contains the length, in octets (bytes), of character string or binary data types. For fixed-length character types, this is the actual length in bytes. For variable-length character or binary types, this is the maximum length, in bytes.
		For APD and ARD descriptors, length values for character strings include the NULL-termination character.
		For IPD and IRD descriptors, length values for character strings do not include the NULL-termination character.
		In APD descriptors, this field is only defined for output or input/output parameters.
SQL_DESC_OCTET_LENGTH_PTR	**SQLINTEGER ***	For APD descriptors, this field contains a pointer to a variable that contains the total length, in bytes, of a dynamic argument. The value of the variable that this field references is ignored for all parameter values except character string and binary data values. If this field contains a NULL pointer, DB2 CLI assumes that character strings and binary values are NULL-terminated (binary data values should not be NULL-terminated, but should be given a length to avoid truncation); if the variable that this field references contains the value **SQL_NTS**, the dynamic parameter value must be NULL-terminated.
		To indicate that a bound parameter is a *data-at-execution* parameter, an application must set this field to a variable that, at execution time, will contain the value **SQL_DATA_AT_EXEC** or the result of the **SQL_LEN_DATA_AT_EXEC()** macro. If there is more

Table 12–2 Descriptor Record Fields (Continued)

Field Name	Data Type	Description
		than one such field, the **SQL_DESC_DATA_PTR** field can be set to a value that uniquely identifies the parameter to help the application determine which parameter data is being requested for.
		For ARD descriptors, this field contains a pointer to a variable that contains the total length, in bytes of a bound column value. If this field contains a NULL pointer, DB2 CLI does not return length information for the specified column in a result data set.
		If a call to **SQLFetch()** or **SQLFetchScroll()** does not return **SQL_SUCCESS** or **SQL_SUCCESS_WITH_INFO**, the contents of the variable that this field references is undefined.
		This field is a deferred field: It is not used at the time it is set, but is used later by DB2 CLI when it needs to determine addresses for data buffers.
SQL_DESC_PARAMETER_ TYPE	**SQLSMALLINT**	For IPD descriptors, this field indicates whether a parameter is an input, output, or input/output parameter. Valid values for this field are:
		SQL_PARAM_INPUT: The parameter is an input parameter. This is the default value for this field.
		SQL_PARAM_OUTPUT: The parameter is an output parameter.
		SQL_PARAM_INPUT_OUTPUT: The parameter is an input/output parameter.
		For IPD descriptors, this field is set to **SQL_PARAM_ INPUT**, by default, if the IPD descriptor is not automatically populated by DB2 CLI (the **SQL_ATTR_ ENABLE_AUTO_IPD** statement attribute is **SQL_ FALSE**). An application should set this field in an IPD descriptor, for parameters that are not input parameters.
SQL_DESC_PRECISION	**SQLSMALLINT**	This field contains the maximum number of bytes needed to display the column data in character format.
		For exact numeric data types, this field contains the number of digits in the value.
		For approximate numeric data types, this field contains the number of bits in the mantissa (binary precision).
		For **SQL_TYPE_TIME**, **SQL_TYPE_TIMESTAMP**, or **SQL_INTERVAL_SECOND** data types, this field contains the numbers of digits in the fractional seconds component of the value.

Table 12–2   Descriptor Record Fields (Continued)

Field Name	Data Type	Description
		For all other data types, this field is undefined.
SQL_DESC_ROWVER	SQLSMALLINT	For IPD and IRD descriptors, this field indicates whether a column is automatically modified by the DBMS when a row is updated. Valid values for this field are: **SQL_TRUE:** The column is a row versioning column. **SQL_FALSE:** The column is not a row versioning column. Setting this field is similar to calling **SQLSpecialColumns()** with the RowIdentifier parameter set to **SQL_ROWVER**.
SQL_DESC_SCALE	SQLSMALLINT	This field contains the scale defined for **DECIMAL** and **NUMERIC** data types. This field is undefined for all other data types. The value in this field may be different from the value for *scale* as defined in DB2 CLI 2.0.
SQL_DESC_SCHEMA_NAME	SQLCHAR *	For IRD descriptors, this field contains the schema name for the base table in the data source that corresponds to a column in a result data set. This field contains an empty string (" ") if the data source does not support schemas or if the schema name cannot be determined.
SQL_DESC_SEARCHABLE	SQLSMALLINT	For IRD descriptors, this field indicates how a column in a result data set can be used in an SQL **WHERE** clause. Valid values for this field are: **SQL_PRED_SEARCHABLE:** The column can be used with any comparison operator in a **WHERE** clause. **SQL_PRED_CHAR:** The column can only be used in a **WHERE** clause **LIKE** predicate. **SQL_PRED_BASIC:** The column can be used with all comparison operators in a **WHERE** clause except a **LIKE** predicate. **SQL_PRED_NONE:** The column cannot be used in a **WHERE** clause.
SQL_DESC_TABLE_NAME	SQLCHAR *	For IRD descriptors, this field contains the name of the base table in the data source that corresponds to a column in a result data set. This field contains an empty string (" ") if the table name cannot be determined.

Table 12–2 Descriptor Record Fields (Continued)

Field Name	Data Type	Description
SQL_DESC_TYPE	SQLSMALLINT	This field specifies the concise SQL or C data type for all data types except datetime and interval data types. For datetime and interval data types, this field specifies the verbose data type, which is **SQL_DATETIME** or **SQL_INTERVAL**, respectively.
		The values in the **SQL_DESC_CONCISE_TYPE**, **SQL_DESC_TYPE**, and **SQL_DESC_DATETIME_INTERVAL_CODE** fields are interdependent—each time one field is set, the remaining fields must also be set. Thus, if **SQL_DESC_TYPE** is set to the verbose datetime or interval data type (**SQL_DATETIME** or **SQL_INTERVAL**), the **SQL_DESC_DATETIME_INTERVAL_CODE** field is set to the appropriate sub-code for the concise datatime or interval data type, and the **SQL_DESC_CONCISE TYPE** field is set to the corresponding concise data type.
		If **SQL_DESC_TYPE** is set to a concise data type other than an interval or datetime data type, the **SQL_DESC_CONCISE_TYPE** field is set to the same value, and the **SQL_DESC_DATETIME_INTERVAL_CODE** field is set to **0**.
		The **SQL_DESC_CONCISE_TYPE** field can be set by the **SQLBindParameter()**, **SQLBindCol()**, or **SQLSetDescField()** function. The **SQL_DESC_TYPE** can be set by the **SQLSetDescField()** or **SQLSetDescRec()** function.
SQL_DESC_TYPE_NAME	SQLCHAR *	For IPD and IRD descriptors, this field contains the data source-dependent data type name (for example, **CHAR**, **VARCHAR**, etc.). This field contains an empty string (" ") if the data type name is unknown.
SQL_DESC_UNNAMED	SQLSMALLINT	For an IPD descriptor, this field indicates whether a parameter has an alias or a name. In this case, valid values for this field are:
		SQL_NAMED: The **SQL_DESC_NAME** field contains a parameter alias or a parameter name.
		SQL_UNNAMED: The **SQL_DESC_NAME** field does not contain a parameter alias or a parameter name.
		For an IRD descriptor, this field indicates whether a column in a result data set has an alias or a name. In this case, valid values for this field are:
		SQL_NAMED: The **SQL_DESC_NAME** field contains a column alias, or a column name if a column alias does not apply.

478 Part 3: Call Level Interface (CLI) Functions

Table 12–2 Descriptor Record Fields (Continued)

Field Name	Data Type	Description
		SQL_UNNAMED: The **SQL_DESC_NAME** field does not contain a column alias, or a column name. For both IPD and IRD descriptors, this field is set by DB2 CLI when the **SQL_DESC_NAME** field is set. An application can set the **SQL_DESC_UNNAMED** field of an IPD descriptor to **SQL_UNNAMED**, however SQLSTATE **HY**091 (Invalid descriptor field identifier) is returned if an application attempts to set the **SQL_DESC_UNNAMED** field to **SQL_NAMED**. The **SQL_DESC_UNNAMED** field of an IRD descriptor is read-only and cannot be set.
SQL_DESC_UNSIGNED	**SQLSMALLINT**	For IRD descriptors, this field indicates whether a column in a result data set's data type is signed or unsigned. Valid values for this field are: **SQL_TRUE**: The column's data type is unsigned or non-numeric. **SQL_FALSE**: The column's data type is signed.
SQL_DESC_UPDATABLE	**SQLSMALLINT**	For IRD descriptors, this field indicates whether a column in a result data set can be updated. Valid values for this field are: **SQL_ATTR_READ_ONLY**: The column can only be read (read-only). **SQL_ATTR_WRITE**: The column can be updated (read/write). **SQL_ATTR_READWRITE_UNKNOWN**: Whether the column can be updated is not known. This field describes the ability of a result data set column to be updated, not the ability of a base table column to be updated. The ability of the column to be updated in the base table on which a result data set column is based may be different from the value of this field. Whether a column in a result data set is updatable is based on the data type, user privileges, and the definition of the result data set itself.

Return Codes SQL_SUCCESS, SQL_SUCCESS_WITH_INFO, SQL_NO_DATA, SQL_INVALID_HANDLE, SQL_ERROR

SQLSTATEs If this function returns **SQL_SUCCESS_WITH_INFO** or **SQL_ERROR**, one of the following SQLSTATE values may be obtained by calling the **SQLGetDiagRec()** function:

01000, **01**004, **07**009, **08**S01, **HY**000, **HY**001, **HY**007, **HY**010, **HY**013, **HY**021, **HY**090, or **HY**091

Refer to Appendix B for detailed information about each SQLSTATE value that can be returned.

Comments

- An application can determine the total number of parameter/column descriptor records available in a descriptor by calling this function to retrieve the `SQL_DESC_COUNT` field value.

- If a descriptor header record field is specified in the *Identifier* parameter, the *RecNumber* parameter is ignored.

- If the value specified in the *RecNumber* parameter is less than or equal to the total number of descriptor records available, and if the corresponding descriptor record does not contain data for a parameter or column, this function returns the default value of the specified field.

- For performance reasons, an application should not call this function for an IRD descriptor until after the SQL statement associated with the descriptor has been executed.

- The `SQLGetStmtAttr()` function can be called to obtain the current value of any descriptor header record field that has a corresponding SQL statement attribute.

- The `SQLColAttribute()`, `SQLDescribeCol()`, and `SQLDescribeParam()` functions can be called to obtain the current value of descriptor parameter/column or bookmark record fields.

- If the value specified in the *RecNumber* parameter is greater than the total number of descriptor records available, `SQL_NO_DATA` is returned.

- If this function is called with an IRD handle specified in the *DescriptorHandle* parameter, and if the SQL statement associated with the IRD is in the "Prepared" or "Executed" state but there is no open cursor associated with it, `SQL_NO_DATA` is returned.

- When this function is used to retrieve the value of a descriptor record field that is undefined for a particular descriptor type, `SQL_SUCCESS` is returned, but the actual value returned for the field is undefined.

- If this function is used to retrieve the value of a field that is undefined for the descriptor type specified SQL_ERROR and SQLSTATE **HY**091 (Invalid descriptor field identifier).

- When this function is used to retrieve the value of a descriptor record field that is defined for a particular descriptor type, but has no default value and has not been set by some other CLI function, `SQL_SUCCESS` is returned—but the actual value returned for the field is undefined.

- The current values of descriptor record fields describing the name, data type, and storage of parameter or column data can be retrieved in a single call with the `SQLGetDescRec()` function.

- If the value returned for the descriptor field specified in the *Identifier* parameter is a Unicode string, the *ValueMaxSize* parameter must contain an even number.

Prerequisites   A descriptor handle must be allocated before this function is called.

Restrictions   There are no restrictions associated with this function call.

See Also   `SQLSetDescField()`, `SQLGetDescRec()`, `SQLSetDescRec()`, `SQLCopyDesc()`

Example   The following Visual C++ program illustrates how to use the `SQLGetDescField()` function to obtain specific information from a descriptor record.

```
/*─────────────────────────────────────────────────────────────*/
/* NAME:     CH12EX3.CPP                                         */
/* PURPOSE: Illustrate How To Use The Following CLI API Function */
/*          In A C++ Program:                                    */
/*                                                               */
/*              SQLGetDescField()                                */
/*                                                               */
/* OTHER CLI APIs SHOWN:                                         */
/*          SQLAllocHandle()            SQLSetEnvAttr()           */
/*          SQLConnect()                SQLExecDirect()           */
/*          SQLGetStmtAttr()            SQLDisconnect()           */
/*          SQLFreeHandle()                                      */
/*                                                               */
/*─────────────────────────────────────────────────────────────*/

// Include The Appropriate Header Files
#include <windows.h>
#include <sqlcli1.h>
#include <iostream.h>

// Define The CLI_Class Class
class CLI_Class
{
    // Attributes
    public:
        SQLHANDLE   EnvHandle;
        SQLHANDLE   ConHandle;
        SQLHANDLE   DescHandle;
        SQLHANDLE   StmtHandle;
        SQLRETURN   rc;

    // Operations
    public:
        CLI_Class();                            // Constructor
        ~CLI_Class();                           // Destructor
        SQLRETURN GetDescriptorInfo();
};

// Define The Class Constructor
CLI_Class::CLI_Class()
{
    // Initialize The Return Code Variable
    rc = SQL_SUCCESS;

    // Allocate An Environment Handle
    rc = SQLAllocHandle(SQL_HANDLE_ENV, SQL_NULL_HANDLE, &EnvHandle);
```

```
    // Set The ODBC Application Version To 3.x
    if (rc == SQL_SUCCESS)
        rc = SQLSetEnvAttr(EnvHandle, SQL_ATTR_ODBC_VERSION,
                    (SQLPOINTER) SQL_OV_ODBC3, SQL_IS_UINTEGER);

    // Allocate A Connection Handle
    if (rc == SQL_SUCCESS)
        rc = SQLAllocHandle(SQL_HANDLE_DBC, EnvHandle, &ConHandle);
}

// Define The Class Destructor
CLI_Class::~CLI_Class()
{
    // Free The Connection Handle
    if (ConHandle != NULL)
        SQLFreeHandle(SQL_HANDLE_DBC, ConHandle);

    // Free The Environment Handle
    if (EnvHandle != NULL)
        SQLFreeHandle(SQL_HANDLE_ENV, EnvHandle);
}

// Define The GetDescriptorInfo() Member Function
SQLRETURN CLI_Class::GetDescriptorInfo(void)
{
    // Declare The Local Memory Variables
    SQLINTEGER    ValueLen;
    SQLCHAR       ColName[50];
    SQLINTEGER    ColNameLen;
    SQLSMALLINT   DisplaySize;

    // Retrieve A Handle To The Implementation Row Descriptor (IRD)
    // Associated With The SQL Statement
    rc = SQLGetStmtAttr(StmtHandle, SQL_ATTR_IMP_ROW_DESC,
            (SQLPOINTER) &DescHandle, 0, &ValueLen);

    // Obtain And Display Information About The First Column In The
    // Result Data Set
    rc = SQLGetDescField(DescHandle, 1, SQL_DESC_BASE_COLUMN_NAME,
            ColName, sizeof(ColName), &ColNameLen);

    rc = SQLGetDescField(DescHandle, 1, SQL_DESC_DISPLAY_SIZE,
            &DisplaySize, 0, NULL);

    if (rc == SQL_SUCCESS)
    {
        cout << "Column 1 : " << endl << endl;
        cout << "Base Column Name : " << ColName << endl;
        cout << "Display Size     : " << DisplaySize << endl;
    }

    // Return The CLI API Return Code To The Calling Function
    return(rc);
}
```

```
/*---------------------------------------------------------------*/
/* The Main Function                                             */
/*---------------------------------------------------------------*/
int main()
{
    // Declare The Local Memory Variables
    SQLRETURN  rc = SQL_SUCCESS;
    SQLCHAR    SQLStmt[255];

    // Create An Instance Of The CLI_Class Class
    CLI_Class  Example;

    // Connect To The DB2 Sample Database
    if (Example.ConHandle != NULL)
    {
        rc = SQLConnect(Example.ConHandle, (SQLCHAR *) "SAMPLE",
                SQL_NTS, (SQLCHAR *) "userid", SQL_NTS,
                (SQLCHAR *) "password", SQL_NTS);

        // Allocate An SQL Statement Handle
        rc = SQLAllocHandle(SQL_HANDLE_STMT, Example.ConHandle,
                &Example.StmtHandle);
        if (rc == SQL_SUCCESS)
        {
            // Define A SELECT SQL Statement
            strcpy((char *) SQLStmt, "SELECT LASTNAME, FIRSTNME ");
            strcat((char *) SQLStmt, "FROM EMPLOYEE");

            // Prepare And Execute The SQL Statement
            rc = SQLExecDirect(Example.StmtHandle, SQLStmt, SQL_NTS);

            // Display Information About The Implementation Row
            // Descriptor (IRD) That Is Associated With The SQL
            // Statement
            if (rc == SQL_SUCCESS)
                Example.GetDescriptorInfo();

            // Free The SQL Statement Handle
            if (Example.StmtHandle != NULL)
                SQLFreeHandle(SQL_HANDLE_STMT, Example.StmtHandle);
        }

        // Disconnect From The DB2 Sample Database
        rc = SQLDisconnect(Example.ConHandle);
    }

    // Return To The Operating System
    return(rc);
}
```

SQLSetDescField

COMPATIBILITY

X/OPEN 95 CLI	ISO/IEC 92 CLI	DB2 CLI 5.2	DB2 CLI 2.0	ODBC 3.x
☑	☑	☑	☐	☑

ODBC API CONFORMANCE LEVEL   CORE

Purpose   The `SQLSetDescField()` function is used to modify the value of a specified descriptor record field.

Syntax
```
SQLRETURN   SQLSetDescField   (SQLHDESC      DescriptorHandle,
                               SQLSMALLINT   RecNumber,
                               SQLSMALLINT   Identifier,
                               SQLPOINTER    Value,
                               SQLINTEGER    ValueSize);
```

Parameters   *DescriptorHandle*   A descriptor handle that refers to a previously allocated descriptor information storage buffer (data structure).

RecNumber   Specifies the descriptor record that this function is to modify. If any field of the descriptor header record is specified in the *Identifier* parameter, this parameter is ignored. Otherwise, this parameter should contain a number greater than or equal to 0 (Descriptor records are numbered starting at 0, with record number 0 being the bookmark record).

Identifier   The field of the descriptor header record or descriptor parameter/column record whose value is to be modified. This parameter must be set to one of the following values:

Header Record Fields

▨ SQL_DESC_ALLOC_TYPE

▨ SQL_DESC_ARRAY_SIZE

▨ SQL_DESC_ARRAY_STATUS_PTR

▨ SQL_DESC_BIND_OFFSET_PTR

▨ SQL_DESC_BIND_TYPE

▨ SQL_DESC_COUNT

▨ SQL_DESC_ROWS_PROCESSED_PTR

Parameter/Column Record Fields

- SQL_DESC_AUTO_UNIQUE_VALUE
- SQL_DESC_BASE_COLUMN_NAME
- SQL_DESC_BASE_TABLE_NAME
- SQL_DESC_CASE_SENSITIVE
- SQL_DESC_CATALOG_NAME
- SQL_DESC_CONCISE_TYPE
- SQL_DESC_DATA_PTR
- SQL_DESC_DATETIME_INTERVAL_CODE
- SQL_DESC_DATETIME_INTERVAL_PRECISION
- SQL_DESC_DISPLAY_SIZE
- SQL_DESC_FIXED_PREC_SCALE
- SQL_DESC_INDICATOR_PTR
- SQL_DESC_LABEL
- SQL_DESC_LENGTH
- SQL_DESC_LITERAL_PREFIX
- SQL_DESC_LITERAL_SUFFIX
- SQL_DESC_LOCAL_TYPE_NAME
- SQL_DESC_NAME
- SQL_DESC_NULLABLE
- SQL_DESC_NUM_PREC_RADIX
- SQL_DESC_OCTET_LENGTH
- SQL_DESC_OCTET_LENGTH_PTR
- SQL_DESC_PARAMETER_TYPE
- SQL_DESC_PRECISION
- SQL_DESC_ROWVER
- SQL_DESC_SCALE
- SQL_DESC_SCHEMA_NAME
- SQL_DESC_SEARCHABLE
- SQL_DESC_TABLE_NAME
- SQL_DESC_TYPE
- SQL_DESC_TYPE_NAME
- SQL_DESC_UNNAMED
- SQL_DESC_UNSIGNED
- SQL_DESC_UPDATABLE

Value A pointer to a location in memory where the new value for the specified descriptor record field is stored.

ValueSize   The size of the new value to be stored in the specified descriptor record field (*Value*). If an ODBC-defined descriptor record field is to be modified, and if the field value is a 32-bit integer value, this parameter is ignored. If a DB2 CLI descriptor record field value is to be modified, this parameter must be set as follows:

- ▨ If the new value of the specified descriptor record field is a character string, this parameter should be set to the actual length of the string or to **SQL_NTS**.

- ▨ If the new value of the specified descriptor record field is a binary string, this parameter should be set to the result of the **SQL_LEN_BINARY_ATTR***(length)* macro. Usually, this macro places a negative value in this parameter.

- ▨ If the new value of the specified descriptor record field is anything other than a character string or binary string, this parameter should be set to **SQL_IS_POINTER**.

- ▨ If the new value of the specified descriptor record field is a fixed-length data type, this parameter should be set to **SQL_IS_INTEGER** or **SQL_IS_UINTEGER**, as appropriate.

Description   The **SQLSetDescField()** function is used to modify the value of a specified descriptor record field. Refer to the **SQLGetDescField()** function for a complete description of each field found in a descriptor record.

When descriptor record fields are set by an application, a specific sequence must be followed:

1. The **SQL_DESC_TYPE**, **SQL_DESC_CONCISE_TYPE**, or the **SQL_DESC_DATETIME_INTERVAL_CODE** field must be set.

2. After one of these fields has been set, the appropriate data type must be set. DB2 CLI sets all data type attribute fields to the appropriate default values for the data type specified. Automatic defaulting of type attribute fields ensures that the descriptor is always ready for use once a data type has been specified. Later, if an application explicitly sets a data type attribute, it is overriding the default attribute provided by DB2 CLI.

3. The **SQL_DESC_DATA_PTR** field must be set. This prompts a consistency check of all descriptor record fields. If the application changes the data type or attributes after setting the **SQL_DESC_DATA_PTR** field, DB2 CLI sets **SQL_DESC_DATA_PTR** to a NULL pointer, and the record is unbound. This forces the application to complete the proper steps in sequence, before the descriptor record is made usable.

When a descriptor record is allocated, its fields can be initialized with a specific default value, initialized without a default value, or undefined, depending on the descriptor type for which the descriptor record is allocated. Table 12–3 shows how each descriptor record field for each descriptor type (APD, IPD, ARD, and IRD) can be initialized. This table also indicates whether a field is *read/write* (R/W) or *read-only* (R).

Table 12–3 *Descriptor Record Field Initialization*

Field Name	Initialized With . . .	Field Characteristics
Header Record Fields		
SQL_DESC_ALLOC_TYPE	APD: **SQL_DESC_ALLOC_AUTO** (implicitly allocated descriptor) or **SQL_DESC_ALLOC_USER** (explicitly allocated descriptor)	APD: Read-Only
	IPD: **SQL_DESC_ALLOC_AUTO**	IPD: Read-Only
	ARD: **SQL_DESC_ALLOC_AUTO** (implicitly allocated descriptor) or **SQL_DESC_ALLOC_USER** (explicitly allocated descriptor)	ARD: Read-Only
	IRD: **SQL_DESC_ALLOC_AUTO**	IRD: Read-Only
SQL_DESC_ARRAY_SIZE	APD: Undefined unless the IPD is automatically populated by DB2 CLI	APD: Read/Write
	IPD: Unused	IPD: Unused
	ARD: Undefined unless the IPD is automatically populated by DB2 CLI	ARD: Read/Write
	IRD: Unused	IRD: Unused
SQL_DESC_ARRAY_STATUS_PTR	APD: A NULL pointer	APD: Read/Write
	IPD: A NULL pointer	IPD: Read/Write
	ARD: A NULL pointer	ARD: Read/Write
	IRD: A NULL pointer	IRD: Read/Write
SQL_DESC_BIND_OFFSET_PTR	APD: A NULL pointer	APD: Read/Write
	IPD: Unused	IPD: Unused
	ARD: A NULL pointer	ARD: Read/Write
	IRD: Unused	IRD: Unused
SQL_DESC_BIND_TYPE	APD: **SQL_BIND_BY_COLUMN**	APD: Read/Write
	IPD: Unused	IPD: Unused
	ARD: **SQL_BIND_BY_COLUMN**	ARD: Read/Write
	IRD: Unused	IRD: Unused
SQL_DESC_COUNT	APD: 0	APD: Read/Write
	IPD: 0	IPD: Read/Write
	ARD: 0	ARD: Read/Write
	IRD: A DB2 CLI-supplied default value	IRD: Read-Only
SQL_DESC_ROWS_PROCESSED_PTR	APD: Unused	APD: Unused
	IPD: A NULL pointer	IPD: Read/Write
	ARD: Unused	ARD: Unused
	IRD: A NULL pointer	IRD: Read/Write

Table 12–3 Descriptor Record Field Initialization (Continued)

Field Name	Initialized With ...	Field Characteristics
Parameter/Column Record Fields		
SQL_DESC_AUTO_UNIQUE_VALUE	APD: Unused	APD: Unused
	IPD: Unused	IPD: Unused
	ARD: Unused	ARD: Unused
	IRD: A DB2 CLI-supplied default value	IRD: Read-Only
SQL_DESC_BASE_COLUMN_NAME	APD: Unused	APD: Unused
	IPD: Unused	IPD: Unused
	ARD: Unused	ARD: Unused
	IRD: A DB2 CLI-supplied default value	IRD: Read-Only
SQL_DESC_BASE_TABLE_NAME	APD: Unused	APD: Unused
	IPD: Unused	IPD: Unused
	ARD: Unused	ARD: Unused
	IRD: A DB2 CLI-supplied default value	IRD: Read-Only
SQL_DESC_CASE_SENSITIVE	APD: Unused	APD: Unused
	IPD: A DB2 CLI-supplied default value	IPD: Read-Only
	ARD: Unused	ARD: Unused
	IRD: A DB2 CLI-supplied default value[1]	IRD: Read-Only
SQL_DESC_CATALOG_NAME	APD: Unused	APD: Unused
	IPD: Unused	IPD: Unused
	ARD: Unused	ARD: Unused
	IRD: A DB2 CLI-supplied default value	IRD: Read-Only
SQL_DESC_CONCISE_TYPE	APD: SQL_C_DEFAULT	APD: Read/Write
	IPD: Not initialized	IPD: Read/Write
	ARD: SQL_C_DEFAULT	ARD: Read/Write
	IRD: A DB2 CLI-supplied default value	IRD: Read-Only
SQL_DESC_DATA_PTR	APD: A NULL pointer	APD: Read/Write
	IPD: Unused [2]	IPD: Unused
	ARD: A NULL pointer	ARD: Read/Write
	IRD: Unused	IRD: Unused
SQL_DESC_DATETIME_ INTERVAL_CODE	APD: No default value	APD: Read/Write
	IPD: No default value	IPD: Read/Write
	ARD: No default value	ARD: Read/Write
	IRD: A DB2 CLI-supplied default value	IRD: Read-Only

Table 12–3 *Descriptor Record Field Initialization (Continued)*

Field Name	Initialized With . . .	Field Characteristics
SQL_DESC_DATETIME_ INTERVAL_PRECISION	APD: No default value	APD: Read/Write
	IPD: No default value	IPD: Read/Write
	ARD: No default value	ARD: Read/Write
	IRD: A DB2 CLI-supplied default value	IRD: Read-Only
SQL_DESC_DISPLAY_SIZE	APD: Unused	APD: Unused
	IPD: Unused	IPD: Unused
	ARD: Unused	ARD: Unused
	IRD: A DB2 CLI-supplied default value	IRD: Read-Only
SQL_DESC_FIXED_PREC_SCALE	APD: Unused	APD: Unused
	IPD: A DB2 CLI-supplied default value[1]	IPD: Read-Only
	ARD: Unused	ARD: Unused
	IRD: A DB2 CLI-supplied default value	IRD: Read-Only
SQL_DESC_INDICATOR_PTR	APD: A NULL pointer	APD: Read/Write
	IPD: Unused	IPD: Unused
	ARD: A NULL pointer	ARD: Read/Write
	IRD: Unused	IRD: Unused
SQL_DESC_LABEL	APD: Unused	APD: Unused
	IPD: Unused	IPD: Unused
	ARD: Unused	ARD: Unused
	IRD: A DB2 CLI-supplied default value	IRD: Read-Only
SQL_DESC_LENGTH	APD: No default value	APD: Read/Write
	IPD: No default value	IPD: Read/Write
	ARD: No default value	ARD: Read/Write
	IRD: A DB2 CLI-supplied default value	IRD: Read-Only
SQL_DESC_LITERAL_PREFIX	APD: Unused	APD: Unused
	IPD: Unused	IPD: Unused
	ARD: Unused	ARD: Unused
	IRD: A DB2 CLI-supplied default value	IRD: Read-Only
SQL_DESC_LITERAL_SUFFIX	APD: Unused	APD: Unused
	IPD: Unused	IPD: Unused
	ARD: Unused	ARD: Unused
	IRD: A DB2 CLI-supplied default value	IRD: Read-Only
SQL_DESC_LOCAL_TYPE_NAME	APD: Unused	APD: Unused
	IPD: A DB2 CLI-supplied default value[1]	IPD: Read-Only

Table 12–3   *Descriptor Record Field Initialization (Continued)*

Field Name	Initialized With . . .	Field Characteristics
	ARD: Unused	ARD: Unused
	IRD: A DB2 CLI-supplied default value	IRD: Read-Only
SQL_DESC_NAME	APD: No default value	APD: Unused
	IPD: No default value	IPD: Read/Write
	ARD: No default value	ARD: Unused
	IRD: A DB2 CLI-supplied default value	IRD: Read-Only
SQL_DESC_NULLABLE	APD: No default value	APD: Unused
	IPD: No default value	IPD: Read-Only
	ARD: No default value	ARD: Unused
	IRD: A DB2 CLI-supplied default value	IRD: Read-Only
SQL_DESC_NUM_PREC_RADIX	APD: No default value	APD: Read/Write
	IPD: No default value	IPD: Read/Write
	ARD: No default value	ARD: Read/Write
	IRD: A DB2 CLI-supplied default value	IRD: Read-Only
SQL_DESC_OCTET_LENGTH	APD: No default value	APD: Read/Write
	IPD: No default value	IPD: Read/Write
	ARD: No default value	ARD: Read/Write
	IRD: A DB2 CLI-supplied default value	IRD: Read-Only
SQL_DESC_OCTET_LENGTH_PTR	APD: A NULL pointer	APD: Read/Write
	IPD: Unused	IPD: Unused
	ARD: A NULL pointer	ARD: Read/Write
	IRD: Unused	IRD: Unused
SQL_DESC_PARAMETER_TYPE	APD: Unused	APD: Unused
	IPD: A DB2 CLI-supplied default value or **SQL_PARAM_INPUT**	IPD: Read/Write
	ARD: Unused	ARD: Unused
	IRD: Unused	IRD: Unused
SQL_DESC_PRECISION	APD: No default value	APD: Read/Write
	IPD: No default value	IPD: Read/Write
	ARD: No default value	ARD: Read/Write
	IRD: A DB2 CLI-supplied default value	IRD: Read-Only
SQL_DESC_ROWVER	APD: Unused	APD: Unused
	IPD: No default value	IPD: Read-Only
	ARD: Unused	ARD: Unused

Table 12–3   *Descriptor Record Field Initialization (Continued)*

Field Name	Initialized With . . .	Field Characteristics
SQL_DESC_SCALE	IRD: No default value	IRD: Read-Only
	ARD: No default value	ARD: Read/Write
	APD: No default value	APD: Read/Write
	IRD: A DB2 CLI-supplied default value	IRD: Read-Only
SQL_DESC_SCHEMA_NAME	IPD: No default value	IPD: Read/Write
	APD: Unused	APD: Unused
	IPD: Unused	IPD: Unused
	ARD: Unused	ARD: Unused
SQL_DESC_SEARCHABLE	IRD: A DB2 CLI-supplied default value	IRD: Read-Only
	APD: Unused	APD: Unused
	IPD: Unused	IPD: Unused
	ARD: Unused	ARD: Unused
SQL_DESC_TABLE_NAME	IRD: A DB2 CLI-supplied default value	IRD: Read-Only
	APD: Unused	APD: Unused
	IPD: Unused	IPD: Unused
	ARD: Unused	ARD: Unused
SQL_DESC_TYPE	IRD: A DB2 CLI-supplied default value	IRD: Read-Only
	APD: **SQL_C_DEFAULT**	APD: Read/Write
	IPD: No default value	IPD: Read/Write
	ARD: **SQL_C_DEFAULT**	ARD: Read/Write
SQL_DESC_TYPE_NAME	IRD: A DB2 CLI-supplied default value	IRD: Read-Only
	APD: Unused	APD: Unused
	IPD: A DB2 CLI-supplied default value	IPD: Read-Only
	ARD: Unused	ARD: Unused
SQL_DESC_UNNAMED	IRD: A DB2 CLI-supplied default value	IRD: Read-Only
	APD: No default value	APD: Unused
	IPD: No default value	IPD: Read/Write
	ARD: No default value	ARD: Unused
SQL_DESC_UNSIGNED	IRD: A DB2 CLI-supplied default value	IRD: Read-Only
	APD: Unused	APD: Unused
	IPD: A DB2 CLI-supplied default value[1]	IPD: Read-Only
	ARD: Unused	ARD: Unused
	IRD: A DB2 CLI-supplied default value	IRD: Read-Only

Table 12-3 Descriptor Record Field Initialization (Continued)

Field Name	Initialized With . . .	Field Characteristics
SQL_DESC_UPDATABLE	APD: Unused	APD: Unused
	IPD: Unused	IPD: Unused
	ARD: Unused	ARD: Unused
	IRD: A DB2 CLI-supplied default value	IRD: Read-Only

[1]These fields are defined only when the IPD is automatically populated by DB2 CLI. If not, they are undefined. If an application attempts to set these fields, SQLSTATE **HY091** (Invalid descriptor field identifier) is returned.

[2]The **SQL_DESC_DATA_PTR** field in the IPD can be set to force a consistency check. In a subsequent call to **SQLGetDescField()** or **SQLGetDescRec()**, DB2 CLI is not required to return the value that **SQL_DESC_DATA_PTR** was set to.

(Adapted from table 155 on pages 546–552 of *IBM DB2 Universal Database Call Level Interface Guide and Reference.*)

Return Codes SQL_SUCCESS, SQL_SUCCESS_WITH_INFO, SQL_INVALID_HANDLE, SQL_ERROR

SQLSTATEs If this function returns **SQL_SUCCESS_WITH_INFO** or **SQL_ERROR**, one of the following SQLSTATE values may be obtained by calling the **SQLGetDiagRec()** function:

01000, **01**S02, **07**009, **08**S01, **HY**000, **HY**001, **HY**009, **HY**010, **HY**016, **HY**021, **HY**091, **HY**092, or **HY**105

Refer to Appendix B for detailed information about each SQLSTATE value that can be returned.

Comments ■ An application can determine the total number of parameter/column descriptor records available in a descriptor by calling the **SQLGetDescField()** function to retrieve the value of the **SQL_DESC_COUNT** field.

■ If a descriptor header record field is specified in the *Identifier* parameter, the *RecNumber* parameter is ignored.

■ If the value specified in the *Value* parameter is a 4-byte value, either all four of the bytes are used or just two of the bytes are used, depending on the value specified in the *Identifier* parameter.

■ This function can be used to change the binding of a parameter or column by adding an offset to the buffer pointers stored in the **SQL_DESC_DATA_PTR**, **SQL_DESC_INDICATOR_PTR**, or **SQL_DESC_OCTET_LENGTH_PTR** descriptor record fields. Adding offsets to these pointer values changes the binding buffers without having to calling the **SQLBindParameter()** or **SQLBindCol()** functions, which in turn allows an application to change the **SQL_DESC_DATA_PTR** field without having to change other descriptor record fields (for example, **SQL_DESC_DATA_TYPE**).

■ The **SQLSetStmtAttr()** function can be called to change the value of any descriptor header record field that has a corresponding SQL statement attribute.

■ The `SQLBindParameter()`, `SQLBindCol()`, and `SQLSetDescRec()` function can be used to make a complete specification for the binding of a parameter or column by setting a specific group of descriptor record fields with a single function call.

■ When this function fails, `SQL_ERROR` is returned, and the contents of the field of the descriptor record identified by the *RecNumber* and *Identifier* parameters are undefined.

■ While it is not mandatory, it is strongly recommended that an application set the `SQL_ATTR_USE_BOOKMARKS` statement attribute before this function is used to set the values of bookmark descriptor record fields (that is, before this function is called with **0** specified in the *RecNumber* parameter).

■ The fields of an IRD descriptor will contain default values only after the SQL statement associated with the descriptor has been prepared or executed and the IRD has been populated, not when the statement handle or descriptor has been allocated. Any attempt to gain access to an unpopulated field of an IRD descriptor will cause `SQL_ERROR` to be returned.

■ Some descriptor fields are defined for one or more, but not all, of the descriptor types (ARD, IRD, APD, or IPD). When a field is undefined for a descriptor type, it is not needed by any of the functions that use that descriptor.

■ The descriptor record fields that can be accessed by the `SQLGetDescField()` function cannot necessarily be set by this function. Refer to Table 12–3 to determine which fields are read/write fields and which fields are read-only.

■ A consistency check is automatically performed by DB2 CLI whenever an application sets (changes) the value of the `SQL_DESC_DATA_PTR` field of an APD, ARD, or IPD descriptor record. If the consistency check fails, `SQL_ERROR` and SQLSTATE **HY**021 (inconsistent descriptor information) is returned. Consistency checks cannot be performed on IRD descriptor records.

■ The `SQL_DESC_DATA_PTR` field of an IPD descriptor is not normally set. However, an application can assign a value to this field to force a consistency check on all IPD descriptor record fields. However, because the value that the `SQL_DESC_DATA_PTR` field of an IPD descriptor references is not actually stored in the descriptor, it cannot be retrieved by the `SQLGetDescRec()` or `SQLGetDescField()` function.

Prerequisites A descriptor handle must be allocated before this function is called.

Restrictions There are no restrictions associated with this function call.

See Also `SQLGetDescField()`, `SQLGetDescRec()`, `SQLSetDescRec()`, `SQLCopyDesc()`

Example The following Visual C++ program illustrates how to use the `SQLSetDescField()` function to specify specific information for a descriptor record.

```
/*————————————————————————————————————————————*/
/* NAME:    CH12EX4.CPP                                      */
/* PURPOSE: Illustrate How To Use The Following CLI API Function  */
/*          In A C++ Program:                                */
```

```
/*                                                                    */
/*                  SQLSetDescField()                                 */
/*                                                                    */
/* OTHER CLI APIs SHOWN:                                              */
/*          SQLAllocHandle()            SQLSetEnvAttr()               */
/*          SQLConnect()                SQLSetStmtAttr()              */
/*          SQLPrepare()                SQLGetDescField()             */
/*          SQLExecute()                SQLDisconnect()               */
/*          SQLFreeHandle()                                           */
/*                                                                    */
/*——————————————————————————————————————————————————————————————————*/

// Include The Appropriate Header Files
#include <windows.h>
#include <sqlcli1.h>
#include <iostream.h>

// Define The CLI_Class Class
class CLI_Class
{
    // Attributes
    public:
        SQLHANDLE    EnvHandle;
        SQLHANDLE    ConHandle;
        SQLHANDLE    DescHandle;
        SQLHANDLE    StmtHandle;
        SQLRETURN    rc;

    // Operations
    public:
        CLI_Class();                              // Constructor
        ~CLI_Class();                             // Destructor
        SQLRETURN GetDescriptorInfo();
};

// Define The Class Constructor
CLI_Class::CLI_Class()
{
    // Initialize The Return Code Variable
    rc = SQL_SUCCESS;

    // Allocate An Environment Handle
    rc = SQLAllocHandle(SQL_HANDLE_ENV, SQL_NULL_HANDLE, &EnvHandle);

    // Set The ODBC Application Version To 3.x
    if (rc == SQL_SUCCESS)
        rc = SQLSetEnvAttr(EnvHandle, SQL_ATTR_ODBC_VERSION,
                (SQLPOINTER) SQL_OV_ODBC3, SQL_IS_UINTEGER);

    // Allocate A Connection Handle
    if (rc == SQL_SUCCESS)
        rc = SQLAllocHandle(SQL_HANDLE_DBC, EnvHandle, &ConHandle);
}

// Define The Class Destructor
```

```
CLI_Class::~CLI_Class()
{
    // Free The Connection Handle
    if (ConHandle != NULL)
        SQLFreeHandle(SQL_HANDLE_DBC, ConHandle);

    // Free The Environment Handle
    if (EnvHandle != NULL)
        SQLFreeHandle(SQL_HANDLE_ENV, EnvHandle);
}

// Define The GetDescriptorInfo() Member Function
SQLRETURN CLI_Class::GetDescriptorInfo(void)
{
    // Declare The Local Memory Variables
    SQLUINTEGER   OLength;

    // Obtain And Display Information About The First Column In The
    // Result Data Set
    rc = SQLGetDescField(DescHandle, 1, SQL_DESC_OCTET_LENGTH,
            (SQLPOINTER) &OLength, SQL_IS_POINTER, NULL);

    if (rc == SQL_SUCCESS)
    {
        cout << "Column 1 : " << endl << endl;
        cout << "Octet Length : " << OLength << endl;
    }

    // Return The CLI API Return Code To The Calling Function
    return(rc);
}

/*-------------------------------------------------------------- */
/* The Main Function                                             */
/*-------------------------------------------------------------- */
int main()
{
    // Declare The Local Memory Variables
    SQLRETURN     rc = SQL_SUCCESS;
    SQLCHAR       SQLStmt[255];
    SQLCHAR       ProjName[3] = "A%";

    // Create An Instance Of The CLI_Class Class
    CLI_Class   Example;

    // Connect To The DB2 Sample Database
    if (Example.ConHandle != NULL)
    {
        rc = SQLConnect(Example.ConHandle, (SQLCHAR *) "SAMPLE",
                SQL_NTS, (SQLCHAR *) "userid", SQL_NTS,
                (SQLCHAR *) "password", SQL_NTS);

        // Allocate An SQL Statement Handle
        rc = SQLAllocHandle(SQL_HANDLE_STMT, Example.ConHandle,
                &Example.StmtHandle);
```

```
if (rc == SQL_SUCCESS)
{
    // Define A SELECT SQL Statement That Uses A Parameter
    // Marker
    strcpy((char *) SQLStmt, "SELECT PROJNAME FROM PROJECT ");
    strcat((char *) SQLStmt, "WHERE PROJNAME LIKE ?");

    // Explicitly Allocate A Descriptor Handle
    rc = SQLAllocHandle(SQL_HANDLE_DESC, Example.ConHandle,
            &Example.DescHandle);

    // Assign The Descriptor Handle To The Statement Handle
    rc = SQLSetStmtAttr(Example.StmtHandle,
            SQL_ATTR_APP_PARAM_DESC, (SQLPOINTER)
            Example.DescHandle, 0);

    // Prepare The SQL Statement
    rc = SQLPrepare(Example.StmtHandle, SQLStmt, SQL_NTS);

    // Bind The Parameter Marker In The SQL Statement To A
    // Local Application Variable
    rc = SQLBindParameter(Example.StmtHandle, 1,
            SQL_PARAM_INPUT, SQL_C_CHAR, SQL_VARCHAR, 3,
            0, (SQLPOINTER) ProjName, 3, NULL);

    // Modify The Information Stored In The Application Row
    // Descriptor (Which Was Populated When The SQL Statement
    // Was Prepared)
    rc = SQLSetDescField(Example.DescHandle, 1,
            SQL_DESC_OCTET_LENGTH, (SQLPOINTER) 12,
            SQL_IS_UINTEGER);

    // Display The Modified Descriptor Information
    if (rc == SQL_SUCCESS)
        Example.GetDescriptorInfo();

    // Free The Descriptor Handle
    if (Example.DescHandle != NULL)
        SQLFreeHandle(SQL_HANDLE_DESC, Example.DescHandle);

    // Free The SQL Statement Handle
    if (Example.StmtHandle != NULL)
        SQLFreeHandle(SQL_HANDLE_STMT, Example.StmtHandle);
}

// Disconnect From The DB2 Sample Database
rc = SQLDisconnect(Example.ConHandle);
}

// Return To The Operating System
return(rc);
}
```

SQLCopyDesc

COMPATIBILITY

X/OPEN 95 CLI	ISO/IEC 92 CLI	DB2 CLI 5.2	DB2 CLI 2.0	ODBC 3.x
✓	✓	✓	☐	✓

ODBC API CONFORMANCE LEVEL   CORE

Purpose
The SQLCopyDesc() function is used to copy information from one descriptor to another.

Syntax
```
SQLRETURN    SQLCopyDesc    (SQLHDESC      SourceDescHandle,
                            SQLHDESC      TargetDescHandle);
```

Parameters

SourceDescHandle   The descriptor handle that refers to a previously allocated descriptor information storage buffer (data structure) that is to be copied.

TargetDescHandle   A descriptor handle that refers to a previously allocated descriptor information storage buffer (data structure) to which the source descriptor is to be copied.

Description
The SQLCopyDesc() function is used to copy information from one descriptor to another. When this function executes, all descriptor record fields of the source (*SourceDescHandle*) descriptor, except for the SQL_DESC_ALLOC_TYPE field (which specifies whether the descriptor handle was implicitly or explicitly allocated), are copied to the destination (*TargetDescHandle*) descriptor—regardless of whether a specific field is defined for the destination descriptor type.

Return Codes
SQL_SUCCESS, SQL_SUCCESS_WITH_INFO, SQL_INVALID_HANDLE, SQL_ERROR

SQLSTATEs
If this function returns SQL_SUCCESS_WITH_INFO or SQL_ERROR, one of the following SQLSTATE values may be obtained by calling the SQLGetDiagRec() function:

01000, **08**S01, **HY**000, **HY**001, **HY**007, **HY**010, **HY**016, **HY**021, or **HY**092

Refer to Appendix B for detailed information about each SQLSTATE value that can be returned.

Comments
■ Descriptor record fields can be copied from any type of descriptor, however they can only be copied to an APD, ARD, or an IPD descriptor (not to an IRD descriptor).

■ If an IRD descriptor handle is specified in the *TargetDescHandle* parameter, SQL_ERROR and SQLSTATE **HY**016 (Cannot modify an implementation row descriptor) are returned.

■ Fields can only be copied from an IRD descriptor if the SQL statement associated with the descriptor is in the "Prepared" or "Executed" state; otherwise, **SQL_ERROR** and SQLSTATE **HY**007 (Associated statement is not prepared) are returned.

■ If an SQL statement containing dynamic parameters has been prepared, and if automatic population of IPD descriptors is supported and has been enabled, this function copies IPD descriptor field contents as they were populated by the driver (if the IPD is specified in the *SourceDescHandle* parameter). Otherwise, if the IPD is not populated by the driver, the original contents of the IPD descriptor fields are copied.

■ When this function fails, **SQL_ERROR** is returned, and the contents of the fields of the descriptor specified in the *TargetDescHandle* parameter are undefined.

■ All existing data in the descriptor specified in the *TargetDescHandle* parameter is overwritten when this function is executed.

■ The driver copies all descriptor fields if the *SourceDescHandle* and *TargetDescHandle* arguments are associated with the same driver, even if the drivers are on two different connections or environments.

■ When the **SQL_DESC_DATA_PTR** descriptor record field is copied, a consistency check is performed on the target descriptor. If the consistency check fails, **SQL_ERROR** and SQLSTATE **HY**021 (Inconsistent descriptor information) is returned, and the call to **SQLCopyDesc()** is immediately aborted.

■ An application may be able to associate an explicitly allocated descriptor handle with a SQL statement handle, rather than calling this function to copy fields from one descriptor to another. An explicitly allocated descriptor can be associated with another SQL statement handle on the same connection by setting the **SQL_ATTR_APP_ROW_DESC** or **SQL_ATTR_APP_PARAM_DESC** statement attribute to the handle of the explicitly allocated descriptor. In this case, this function does not have to be used to copy descriptor record field values from one descriptor to another.

Prerequisites Two descriptor handles must be allocated before this function is called.

Restrictions There are no restrictions associated with this function call.

See Also SQLGetDescField(), SQLSetDescField(), SQLGetDescRec(), SQLSetDescRec()

Examples The following Visual C++ program illustrates how to use the **SQLCopyDescRec()** function to copy the information stored in an implicitly allocated descriptor to an explicitly allocated descriptor.

```
/*————————————————————————————————————— */
/* NAME:     CH12EX5.CPP                                    */
/* PURPOSE: Illustrate How To Use The Following CLI API Function   */
/*          In A C++ Program:                               */
/*                                                          */
/*               SQLCopyDesc()                              */
/*                                                          */
/* OTHER CLI APIs SHOWN:                                    */
```

```
/*              SQLAllocHandle()        SQLSetEnvAttr()             */
/*              SQLConnect()            SQLSetStmtAttr()            */
/*              SQLPrepare()            SQLGetStmtAttr()            */
/*              SQLGetDescRec()         SQLSetDescRec()             */
/*              SQLExecute()            SQLDisconnect()             */
/*              SQLFreeHandle()                                     */
/*                                                                  */
/*————————————————————————————————————————————————————————————————— */

// Include The Appropriate Header Files
#include <windows.h>
#include <sqlcli1.h>
#include <iostream.h>

// Define The CLI_Class Class
class CLI_Class
{
    // Attributes
    public:
        SQLHANDLE   EnvHandle;
        SQLHANDLE   ConHandle;
        SQLHANDLE   StmtHandle;
        SQLHANDLE   DescHandle;
        SQLHANDLE   IRDDescHandle;
        SQLRETURN   rc;

    // Operations
    public:
        CLI_Class();                            // Constructor
        ~CLI_Class();                           // Destructor
        SQLRETURN GetDescriptorInfo(SQLHANDLE Descriptor);
};

// Define The Class Constructor
CLI_Class::CLI_Class()
{
    // Initialize The Return Code Variable
    rc = SQL_SUCCESS;

    // Allocate An Environment Handle
    rc = SQLAllocHandle(SQL_HANDLE_ENV, SQL_NULL_HANDLE, &EnvHandle);

    // Set The ODBC Application Version To 3.x
    if (rc == SQL_SUCCESS)
        rc = SQLSetEnvAttr(EnvHandle, SQL_ATTR_ODBC_VERSION,
                (SQLPOINTER) SQL_OV_ODBC3, SQL_IS_UINTEGER);

    // Allocate A Connection Handle
    if (rc == SQL_SUCCESS)
        rc = SQLAllocHandle(SQL_HANDLE_DBC, EnvHandle, &ConHandle);
}

// Define The Class Destructor
CLI_Class::~CLI_Class()
{
```

```
    // Free The Connection Handle
    if (ConHandle != NULL)
        SQLFreeHandle(SQL_HANDLE_DBC, ConHandle);

    // Free The Environment Handle
    if (EnvHandle != NULL)
        SQLFreeHandle(SQL_HANDLE_ENV, EnvHandle);
}

// Define The GetDescriptorInfo() Member Function
SQLRETURN CLI_Class::GetDescriptorInfo(SQLHANDLE Descriptor)
{
    // Declare The Local Memory Variables
    SQLCHAR        Name[25] = "";
    SQLSMALLINT    NameLen;
    SQLSMALLINT    Type;
    SQLSMALLINT    SubType;
    SQLINTEGER     Width;
    SQLSMALLINT    Precision;
    SQLSMALLINT    Scale;
    SQLSMALLINT    Nullable;

    // Obtain And Display Information About The Second Column In The
    // Result Data Set
    rc = SQLGetDescRec(Descriptor, 2, Name, 25,
            &NameLen, &Type, &SubType, &Width, &Precision,
            &Scale, &Nullable);
    if (rc == SQL_SUCCESS)
    {
        cout << "Column 2 : " << endl << endl;
        cout << "Name      : " << Name << endl;
        cout << "Data Type : " << Type << endl;
        cout << "Sub-Type  : " << SubType << endl;
        cout << "Width     : " << Width << endl;
        cout << "Precision : " << Precision << endl;
        cout << "Scale     : " << Scale << endl << endl;
        cout << endl;
    }

    // Return The CLI API Return Code To The Calling Function
    return(rc);
}

/*---------------------------------------------------------------- */
/* The Main Function                                               */
/*---------------------------------------------------------------- */
int main()
{
    // Declare The Local Memory Variables
    SQLRETURN    rc = SQL_SUCCESS;
    SQLCHAR      SQLStmt[255];
    SQLINTEGER   ValueLength;

    // Create An Instance Of The CLI_Class Class
```

```
CLI_Class    Example;

// Connect To The DB2 Sample Database
if (Example.ConHandle != NULL)
{
    rc = SQLConnect(Example.ConHandle, (SQLCHAR *) "SAMPLE",
            SQL_NTS, (SQLCHAR *) "userid", SQL_NTS,
            (SQLCHAR *) "password", SQL_NTS);

    // Allocate An SQL Statement Handle
    rc = SQLAllocHandle(SQL_HANDLE_STMT, Example.ConHandle,
            &Example.StmtHandle);
    if (rc == SQL_SUCCESS)
    {
        // Define A SELECT SQL Statement
        strcpy((char *) SQLStmt, "SELECT LASTNAME, SALARY ");
        strcat((char *) SQLStmt, "FROM EMPLOYEE");

        // Prepare The SQL Statement
        rc = SQLPrepare(Example.StmtHandle, SQLStmt, SQL_NTS);

        // Retrieve A Handle To The Implementation Row
        // Descriptor (IRD) Associated With The SQL Statement
        rc = SQLGetStmtAttr(Example.StmtHandle,
                SQL_ATTR_IMP_ROW_DESC, (SQLPOINTER)
                &Example.IRDDescHandle, 0,
                &ValueLength);

        // Display Descriptor Information For The Second Column
        if (rc == SQL_SUCCESS)
            Example.GetDescriptorInfo(Example.IRDDescHandle);

        // Explicitly Allocate A Descriptor Handle
        rc = SQLAllocHandle(SQL_HANDLE_DESC, Example.ConHandle,
                &Example.DescHandle);

        // Copy The Implicitly Allocated IRD Descriptor To The
        // Explicitly Allocated ARD Descriptor
        rc = SQLCopyDesc(Example.IRDDescHandle,
                Example.DescHandle);

        // Assign The Explicitly Allocated Descriptor Handle To
        // The Statement Handle
        rc = SQLSetStmtAttr(Example.StmtHandle,
                SQL_ATTR_APP_ROW_DESC, (SQLPOINTER)
                Example.DescHandle, 0);

        // Modify The Descriptor Information Associated With The
        // Second Column
        rc = SQLSetDescField(Example.DescHandle, 2,
                SQL_DESC_SCALE, (SQLPOINTER) 4,
                SQL_IS_UINTEGER);

        // Display The Modified Descriptor Information
        if (rc == SQL_SUCCESS)
```

```
                    Example.GetDescriptorInfo(Example.DescHandle);

            // Execute The SQL Statement, Using The Modified
            // Descriptor
            rc = SQLExecute(Example.StmtHandle);

            // Free The SQL Statement Handle
            if (Example.StmtHandle != NULL)
                SQLFreeHandle(SQL_HANDLE_STMT, Example.StmtHandle);
        }

        // Disconnect From The DB2 Sample Database
        rc = SQLDisconnect(Example.ConHandle);
    }

    // Return To The Operating System
    return(rc);
}
```

13

Retrieving Status and Error Information

When an application calls a CLI function, it needs to know if the function call was completed successfully or if it failed. If the function was successful, the application can continue to the next step; if the function failed, the application can take corrective measures and, if necessary, call the function again. This chapter is designed to introduce you to the mechanisms used by DB2 CLI to report the success or failure of a CLI function to the calling application. This chapter begins by examining the primary component DB2 CLI uses to inform an application that a warning or error has occurred: the function return code.

This is followed by a discussion about the components used to provide specific error/warning information to an application: the diagnostic record and the *SQL Communications Area* (SQLCA) data structure. Next, the functions used to obtain diagnostic record and SQLCA information after a CLI function is executed are described. Finally, a detailed reference section covering each CLI function that can be used to obtain SQLCA/diagnostic record information is provided.

CLI Return Codes

Each time a CLI function call is executed, a special value known as a *return code* is returned to the calling application. Unlike some functions, which are designed to return many different values and data types, the CLI functions are designed to return a limited number of return code values. Table 13–1 lists all possible return codes that can be generated by a DB2 CLI function.

The return code **SQL_INVALID_HANDLE** always indicates a programming error and should never be encountered at run time. All other return codes provide run-time information about the overall success or failure of the function (although the **SQL_ERROR** return code can sometimes indicate a programming error).

Table 13–1   Return Codes Generated by CLI API Functions

Return Code	Meaning
SQL_SUCCESS	The CLI function completed successfully. The application can call the **SQLGetDiagField()** function to obtain additional information from the diagnostic header record.
SQL_SUCCESS_WITH_INFO	The CLI function completed successfully, however a warning or a non-fatal error was generated. The application can call the **SQLGetDiagRec()** function or the **SQLGetDiagField()** function to obtain additional information.
SQL_NO_DATA	The CLI function completed successfully, but no relevant data was found. The application can call the **SQLGetDiagRec()** function or the **SQLGetDiagField()** function to obtain additional information.
SQL_INVALID_HANDLE	The CLI function failed to execute because an invalid environment, connection, statement, or descriptor handle was specified. This code is only returned when the specified handle is either a NULL pointer or the wrong handle type (for example, when a statement handle is specified for a connection handle parameter). Because this is a programming error, no additional information is available.
SQL_NEED_DATA	The application tried to execute an SQL statement, but the CLI function failed because data the application had indicated would be available at execution time was missing—such as when parameter data is sent at execution time or when additional connection information is needed. The application can call the **SQLGetDiagRec()** function or the **SQLGetDiagField()** function to obtain additional information.
SQL_STILL_EXECUTING	A CLI function that was started asynchronously is still executing. The application can call the **SQLGetDiagRec()** function or the **SQLGetDiagField()** function to obtain additional information.
SQL_ERROR	The CLI function failed to complete. The application can call the **SQLGetDiagRec()** function or the **SQLGetDiagField()** function to obtain additional information.

(Adapted from table 2 on page 25 of *IBM DB2 Universal Database Call Level Interface Guide and Reference.*)

The return code value should always be checked after a CLI function is called to determine whether or not the function executed successfully. If by examining the return code the application discovers that an error or warning was generated, it should then examine the diagnostic record(s) generated and process the error accordingly.

Diagnostic Records

Although the return code informs an application that an error or warning condition occurred that prevented the CLI function call from executing properly, it does not provide the application (or the developer, or the user) with specific information about what caused the error or warning condition to occur. Because this information is also needed, each CLI function generates one or more diagnostic records that provide detailed information about the success or failure of the function, along with the return code.

Diagnostic records can be used during application development to catch programming errors such as the use of invalid handles and the use of incorrect syntax in hard-coded SQL statements. Diagnostic records can be used at application run time to catch and process run-time errors and warnings such as data truncation warnings, access violations, and incorrect syntax in user-supplied SQL statements.

Two types of diagnostic records are available: one header record (record 0) and zero or more status records (records 1 and above). Both types of diagnostic records are composed of several different predefined fields. The fields in the diagnostic header record contain general information about a function's execution, including the return code, row count, number of status records, and the type of statement executed. The fields in each diagnostic status record contain information about specific errors or warnings returned by the CLI Library, the ODBC Driver Manager, or the data source. Both types of diagnostic records can be thought of as data structures, however, there is no requirement for them to actually be stored as structures.

One diagnostic header record is always created each time a CLI function is executed (unless the return code **SQL_INVALID_HANDLE** is returned). Additionally, one or more diagnostic status records are created whenever the return code **SQL_ERROR, SQL_SUCCESS_WITH_ INFO, SQL_NO_DATA, SQL_NEED_DATA,** or **SQL_STILL_EXECUTING** is returned—there is no limit to the number of diagnostic status records that can be stored at any one time. Of all the information returned in a diagnostic status record, the SQLSTATE value, the native error number, and the diagnostic message text are used most often to determine exactly why a function did not perform as expected.

SQLSTATEs

Because each database product usually has its own set of product-specific diagnostic messages, the X/Open CLI and ISO/IEC 92 standards specifications (upon which DB2 CLI is based) define a standardized set of diagnostic message codes that are known as SQLSTATEs. By using SQLSTATEs, an application developer can use consistent error and warning message handling routines across different relational database product platforms.

SQLSTATEs are alphanumeric strings, five characters (bytes) in length, with the format *ccsss*, where *cc* indicates the error message class, and *sss* indicates the error message subclass. An SQLSTATE with a class of **01** is a warning; an SQLSTATE with a class of **HY** is an error generated by either a data source or a driver, and an SQLSTATE with a class of **IM** is an error generated by the ODBC Driver Manager.

Unlike return codes, SQLSTATEs are often treated as guidelines, and drivers are not required to return them. Thus, while drivers should return the proper SQLSTATE for any error or warning they are capable of detecting, applications should not count on this always happening.

Because SQLSTATEs are not returned reliably, most applications just display them to the user along with their associated diagnostic message (which is often tailored to the specific error or warning that occurred) and native error code. There is rarely any loss of functionality in doing this because applications cannot base programming logic on most SQLSTATEs anyway. For example, suppose `SQLExecDirect()` returns SQLSTATE **42000** (Syntax error or access violation). If the SQL statement that caused this error to occur is hard-coded or built by the application, this is a programming error and the code needs to be fixed before the application is delivered. However, if the SQL statement that caused this error to occur was entered by the user, this is a user error, and the application has already done all that it can do by informing the user of the problem.

When applications do base programming logic on SQLSTATE values, they need to be able to handle situations in which the SQLSTATE value they are looking for is not returned.

Native Error Codes

Each diagnostic status record contains a native error code if the SQLSTATE value was generated by the data source. Native error codes are data source-specific codes, therefore the information they provide is data source specific. Native error codes are provided so that the maximum amount of diagnostic information will be available to an application; they should never be used as a basis for programming logic.

Diagnostic Messages

A diagnostic message designed to clarify the meaning of an SQLSTATE value is often stored in a diagnostic status record, along with the SQLSTATE value. The content of this message can vary and often, a number of different diagnostic messages can be returned for the same SQLSTATE value. For example, SQLSTATE **42000** (Syntax error or access violation) is returned for most cases in which an error exists in SQL syntax. However, each syntax error found can also have its own diagnostic message.

Diagnostic Status Record Sequence

If two or more diagnostic status records are generated, they are ranked (by the DB2 CLI Library or by the ODBC Driver Manager) according to the following rules:

- Status records describing errors have the highest rank. Among error records, records indicating a transaction failure or possible transaction failure outrank all other records. If two or more records describe the same error condition, SQLSTATEs defined by the X/Open CLI specification (classes **03** through **HZ**) outrank SQLSTATES defined by DB2 CLI.

- Status records describing driver-defined "No Data" values (class **02**) have the second highest rank.

- Status records describing warnings (class **01**) have the lowest rank. If two or more records describe the same warning condition, SQLSTATEs defined by the X/Open CLI specification outrank SQLSTATES defined by DB2 CLI.

The diagnostic status record with the highest rank is always the first record in the list. If there are two or more records ranking highest, it is undefined as to which record will be first. The order of all other records is also undefined. Therefore, because warnings may appear after the first error and before other errors, all status records should be checked whenever a CLI function returns any code other than **SQL_SUCCESS**.

Obtaining Diagnostic Information

Applications can call the **SQLGetDiagRec()** or the **SQLGetDiagField()** function to retrieve diagnostic information. These functions accept an environment, connection, statement, or descriptor handle as an input parameter and return diagnostic information about the CLI function that was last executed using the handle specified. If multiple diagnostic records were generated, the application must call one or more of these functions several times. The total number of records available can be determined by calling the **SQLGetDiagField()** function with record number **0** (the header record number) and the **SQL_DIAG_NUMBER** option specified.

Applications can retrieve the SQLSTATE, native error code, and diagnostic message in a single step by calling **SQLGetDiagRec()**. However, this function cannot be used to retrieve information from the diagnostic header record. Applications can retrieve information from the diagnostic header record by calling the **SQLGetDiagField()** function. The **SQLGetDiagField()** function can also be used to obtain the values of individual diagnostic record fields. When **SQLGetDiagField()** is used in this manner, it is important to recognize that certain diagnostic fields do not have any meaning for certain types of handles.

The diagnostics logged on a particular handle are automatically discarded when a new function (other than **SQLGetDiagRec()** or **SQLGetDiagField()**) is executed using that handle or when the handle is freed.

Obtaining SQLCA Information

Embedded SQL applications rely solely on the *SQL Communications Area* (SQLCA) data structure for all diagnostic information. Although DB2 CLI applications can obtain much of the same information by calling the **SQLGetDiacRec()** and **SQLGetDiagField()** functions, occasionally there may be a need to access SQLCA information related to the last SQL statement processed. When these situations arise, an application can call the **SQLGetSQLCA()** function. However, in order for the SQLCA data structure to have meaningful information, the last SQL statement executed must have had some type of interaction with the data source.

Guidelines for Error Handling

At a minimum, an application should notify the user when an error or warning occurs and provide enough information so that the problem can be corrected. The following is a set of guidelines that an application should follow to correctly process warnings and errors:

■ Always check the CLI function return code before calling the **SQLGetDiagRec()** or **SQLGetDiagField()** function to determine whether diagnostic information is available.

■ Use the standard set of SQLSTATEs, rather than the native error codes to increase application portability.

■ Only build dependencies on the subset of SQLSTATE values defined by the X/Open CLI and the ISO/IEC 92 standards specifications—return any additional SQLSTATE values as information only. (Dependencies refer to the application making logic flow decisions based on specific SQLSTATES.)

■ For maximum diagnostic information, retrieve and display the diagnostic text message, the SQLSTATE value, and the native error code. If possible, include the name of the CLI function that returned the error in the diagnostic information displayed.

The Error/Diagnostic Message Retrieval Functions

Table 13–2 lists the CLI functions that are used to obtain diagnostic information when an CLI function returns a return code other than **SQL_SUCCESS**.

Each of these functions are described, in detail, in the remaining portion of this chapter.

Table 13–2   The CLI Error/Diagnostic Message Retrieval Functions

Function Name	Description
SQLGetDiagRec()	Retrieves error, warning, and/or status information from a diagnostic status record that was generated by the last CLI function executed.
SQLGetDiagField()	Retrieves the current value of a field of a diagnostic header or status record that was generated by the last CLI function executed.
SQLGetSQLCA()	Retrieves SQLCA data structure values associated with the most recently executed SQL statement.

SQLGetDiagRec

COMPATIBILITY

X/OPEN 95 CLI	ISO/IEC 92 CLI	DB2 CLI 5.2	DB2 CLI 2.0	ODBC 3.x
☑	☑	☑	☐	☑

ODBC API CONFORMANCE LEVEL   **CORE**

Purpose   The `SQLGetDiagRec()` function is used to retrieve the current values of several commonly used fields of a diagnostic status record. A diagnostic status record contains error, warning, and/or status information that was generated by the last CLI function executed.

Syntax

```
SQLRETURN    SQLGetDiagRec    (SQLSMALLINT    HandleType,
                               SQLHANDLE      Handle,
                               SQLSMALLINT    RecNumber,
                               SQLCHAR        *SQLSTATE,
                               SQLINTEGER     *NativeError,
                               SQLCHAR        *ErrorMsg,
                               SQLSMALLINT    ErrorMsgMaxSize,
                               SQLSMALLINT    *ErrorMsgSize);
```

Parameters   *HandleType*   Specifies the type of handle for which to retrieve diagnostic information for. This parameter must be set to one of the following values:

■ `SQL_HANDLE_ENV`
Retrieve diagnostic information for an environment handle.

■ `SQL_HANDLE_DBC`
Retrieve diagnostic information for a connection handle.

■ `SQL_HANDLE_STMT`
Retrieve diagnostic information for an SQL statement handle.

■ `SQL_HANDLES_DESC`
Retrieve diagnostic information for a descriptor handle.

         Handle   An environment, connection, SQL statement, or descriptor handle that refers to a previously allocated environment, connection, statement, or descriptor information storage buffer (data structure).

         RecNumber   Specifies the diagnostic status record that this function is to retrieve information from. This parameter should contain a number greater than 0 (diagnostic status records are numbered, starting at 1).

SQLSTATE	A pointer to a location in memory where this function is to store the SQLSTATE value retrieved. This value is stored as a NULL-terminated 5 character string. The first two characters of this string indicate the error class, and the last three characters indicate the error subclass.
NativeError	A pointer to a location in memory where this function is to store the data source-specific error code retrieved.
ErrorMsg	A pointer to a location in memory where this function is to store the error message text retrieved.
ErrorMsgMaxSize	The maximum size of the memory storage buffer where this function is to store the error message text retrieved.
ErrorMsgSize	A pointer to a location in memory where this function is to store the actual number of bytes written to the error message text memory storage buffer (*ErrorMsg*).

Description   The `SQLGetDiagRec()` function is used to retrieve the current values of several commonly used fields of a diagnostic status record. A diagnostic status record contains error, warning, and/or status information that was generated by the last CLI function executed. Unlike the `SQLGetDiagField()` function, which returns a single value from one field of a diagnostic record per call, the `SQLGetDiagRec()` function returns several commonly used fields of a diagnostic status record, including the SQLSTATE (`SQL_DIAG_SQLSTATE` field), the native error code (`SQL_DIAG_NATIVE` field), and the diagnostic error, warning, or status message text (`SQL_DIAG_MESSAGE_TEXT` field). Refer to the `SQLGetDiagField()` function for a complete description of each field found in a diagnostic information record.

An application typically calls this function when a previous call to a CLI function has returned something other than `SQL_SUCCESS` or `SQL_INVALID_HANDLE`. However, because any CLI function can post zero or more diagnostic records when it is called, an application can call this function immediately after making any CLI function call.

Return Codes   SQL_SUCCESS, SQL_SUCCESS_WITH_INFO, SQL_INVALID_HANDLE, SQL_ERROR

SQLSTATEs   No SQLSTATE values are returned for this function because it does not generate diagnostic information for itself. Instead, this function uses the following return codes to report the outcome of its own execution:

▪ **SQL_SUCCESS**
The function successfully returned diagnostic information.

▪ **SQL_SUCCESS_WITH_INFO**
The error message buffer (*ErrorMsg*) was not large enough to hold the requested diagnostic message. No diagnostic records were generated.

▪ **SQL_NO_DATA**
The record number specified in the *RecNumber* parameter was greater than the number of diagnostic records that existed for the handle specified. This function also returns **SQL_NO_DATA** if a positive number is specified in the *RecNumber* parameter and there are no diagnostic records for the specified handle.

■ **SQL_INVALID_HANDLE**
The handle specified in the *HandleType* and *Handle* parameters was not a valid handle.

■ **SQL_ERROR**
One of the following occurred:

■ The value specified in the *RecNumber* parameter was less than or equal to **0**.

■ The value specified in the *ErrorMsgMaxSize* parameter was less than **0**.

Comments

■ An application can call this function multiple times to return information from some or all of the records stored in the diagnostic information data structure. DB2 CLI imposes no limit on the number of diagnostic records that can be stored in this structure at any one time.

■ This function cannot be used to retrieve information from the fields of a diagnostic header record (that is, the *RecNumber* parameter must contain a number greater than **0**). An application should call the **SQLGetDiagField()** function if it needs to obtain information from the diagnostic header record.

■ If the diagnostic information generated by a DB2 CLI function call is not retrieved before a CLI function other than **SQLGetDiagRec()**, **SQLGetDiagField()**, or **SQLGetSQLCA()** is called using the same environment, connection, statement, or descriptor handle, that information is lost. Diagnostic information stored on a given handle is not removed if a CLI function call is made using an associated handle of a different type.

■ If the error message text to be returned to the *ErrorMsg* parameter is a Unicode string, the *ErrorMsgValueMaxSize* parameter must contain an even number.

■ An application can compare the maximum size of the memory storage buffer where this function is to store the error message text retrieved (the *ErrorMsgMaxSize* parameter) to the actual number of bytes written to the error message text memory storage buffer (the *ErrorMsgSize* parameter) to determine whether an error message was truncated.

■ Multiple diagnostic messages may be generated by a CLI function call. When this is the case, each diagnostic message can be retrieved one at a time by repeatedly incrementing the value of the *RecNumber* parameter and calling this function. Calls to this function are non-destructive to the diagnostic header and diagnostic status records of the diagnostic information data structure.

■ An application can determine the total number of diagnostic records available in the diagnostic information data structure by calling the **SQLGetDiagField()** function to retrieve the value of the **SQL_DIAG_NUMBER** field.

■ Each type of handle (environment, connection, statement, and descriptor) can have diagnostic information associated with it. However, some diagnostic header and status record fields do not contain values for all types of handles. The **SQLGetDiagField()** function can be used to determine which diagnostic header and status record fields are applicable for each type of handle.

■ If this function is called with the *HandleType* parameter set to `SQL_HANDLE_ENV`, either a shared or an unshared environment handle can be specified in the *Handle* parameter.

Prerequisites   There are no prerequisites for using this function call.

Restrictions   There are no restrictions associated with this function call.

See Also   `SQLGetDiagField()`, `SQLGetSQLCA()`

Example   The following Visual C++ program illustrates how to use the `SQLGetDiagRec()` function to obtain general diagnostic information when a CLI function fails to execute properly.

```
/*─────────────────────────────────────────────────────────────*/
/* NAME:     CH13EX1.CPP                                          */
/* PURPOSE: Illustrate How To Use The Following CLI API Function  */
/*          In A C++ Program:                                     */
/*                                                                */
/*               SQLGetDiagRec()                                  */
/*                                                                */
/* OTHER CLI APIs SHOWN:                                          */
/*               SQLAllocHandle()              SQLSetEnvAttr()     */
/*               SQLDriverConnect()            Disconnect()        */
/*               SQLFreeHandle()                                  */
/*                                                                */
/*─────────────────────────────────────────────────────────────*/

// Include The Appropriate Header Files
#include <windows.h>
#include <sqlcli1.h>
#include <iostream.h>

// Define The CLI_Class Class
class CLI_Class
{
    // Attributes
    public:
        SQLHANDLE     EnvHandle;
        SQLHANDLE     ConHandle;
        SQLRETURN     rc;

    // Operations
    public:
        CLI_Class();                            // Constructor
        ~CLI_Class();                           // Destructor
};

// Define The Class Constructor
CLI_Class::CLI_Class()
{
    // Initialize The Return Code Variable
    rc = SQL_SUCCESS;

    // Allocate An Environment Handle
```

```
    rc = SQLAllocHandle(SQL_HANDLE_ENV, SQL_NULL_HANDLE, &EnvHandle);

    // Set The ODBC Application Version To 3.x
    if (rc == SQL_SUCCESS)
        rc = SQLSetEnvAttr(EnvHandle, SQL_ATTR_ODBC_VERSION,
                (SQLPOINTER) SQL_OV_ODBC3, SQL_IS_UINTEGER);

    // Allocate A Connection Handle
    if (rc == SQL_SUCCESS)
        rc = SQLAllocHandle(SQL_HANDLE_DBC, EnvHandle, &ConHandle);
}

// Define The Class Destructor
CLI_Class::~CLI_Class()
{
    // Free The Connection Handle
    if (ConHandle != NULL)
        SQLFreeHandle(SQL_HANDLE_DBC, ConHandle);

    // Free The Environment Handle
    if (EnvHandle != NULL)
        SQLFreeHandle(SQL_HANDLE_ENV, EnvHandle);
}


/*————————————————————————————————————————————— */
/* The Main Function                             */
/*————————————————————————————————————————————— */
int main()
{
    // Declare The Local Memory Variables
    SQLRETURN    rc = SQL_SUCCESS;
    SQLINTEGER   NativeErr;
    SQLCHAR      SQLState[6];
    SQLCHAR      ErrMsg[255];
    SQLSMALLINT  ErrMsgLen;

    // Create An Instance Of The CLI_Class Class
    CLI_Class    Example;

    // Attempt To Connect To The DB2 Sample Database Without
    // Providing A User ID And Password (An Error Should Be
    // Generated)
    if (Example.ConHandle != NULL)
    {
        rc = SQLConnect(Example.ConHandle, (SQLCHAR *) "SAMPLE",
                SQL_NTS, NULL, 0, NULL, 0);

        // If The Specified Connection Was Not Established, Retrieve
        // And Display The Diagnostic Information Generated
        if (rc != SQL_SUCCESS && rc != SQL_SUCCESS_WITH_INFO)
        {
            rc = SQLGetDiagRec(SQL_HANDLE_DBC, Example.ConHandle,
                    1, SQLState, &NativeErr, ErrMsg, 255,
                    &ErrMsgLen);
            cout << "SQLSTATE : " << SQLState << endl << endl;
```

```
            cout << ErrMsg << endl;
        }

        // If The Specified Connection Was Established, Display
        // A Success Message And Disconnect
        else
        {
            cout << "Connected to DB2 Sample database." << endl;
            rc = SQLDisconnect(Example.ConHandle);
        }
    }

    // Return To The Operating System
    return(rc);
}
```

SQLGetDiagField

COMPATIBILITY

X/OPEN 95 CLI	ISO/IEC 92 CLI	DB2 CLI 5.2	DB2 CLI 2.0	ODBC 3.x
✓	✓	✓	☐	✓

ODBC API CONFORMANCE LEVEL   **CORE**

Purpose The SQLGetDiagField() function is used to retrieve the current value of a field in a diagnostic header or status record (that is associated with a specific environment, connection, statement, or descriptor handle).

Syntax
```
SQLRETURN   SQLGetDiagField (SQLSMALLINT   HandleType,
                             SQLHANDLE     Handle,
                             SQLSMALLINT   RecNumber,
                             SQLSMALLINT   Identifier,
                             SQLPOINTER    Value,
                             SQLSMALLINT   ValueMaxSize,
                             SQLSMALLINT   *ValueSize);
```

Parameters *HandleType* Specifies the type of handle to retrieve diagnostic information for. This parameter must be set to one of the following values:

■ **SQL_HANDLE_ENV**
Retrieve diagnostic information for an environment handle.

■ **SQL_HANDLE_DBC**
Retrieve diagnostic information for a connection handle.

■ **SQL_HANDLE_STMT**
Retrieve diagnostic information for an SQL statement handle.

■ **SQL_HANDLES_DESC**
Retrieve diagnostic information for a descriptor handle.

Handle An environment, connection, SQL statement, or descriptor handle that refers to a previously allocated environment, connection, statement, or descriptor information storage buffer (data structure).

RecNumber Specifies the diagnostic status record that this function is to retrieve information for. If any field of the diagnostic header record is specified in the *Identifier* parameter, this parameter is ignored. Otherwise, this parameter should contain a number greater than 0 (status records are numbered, starting at 1).

Identifier The field of the diagnostic header record or status record whose value is to be retrieved. This parameter must be set to one of the following values:

Header Record Fields

■ **SQL_DIAG_CURSOR_ROW_COUNT**

■ **SQL_DIAG_DYNAMIC_FUNCTION**

■ **SQL_DIAG_DYNAMIC_FUNCTION_CODE**

■ **SQL_DIAG_NUMBER**

■ **SQL_DIAG_RETURNCODE**

■ **SQL_DIAG_ROW_COUNT**

Status Record Fields

■ **SQL_DIAG_CLASS_ORIGIN**

■ **SQL_DIAG_COLUMN_NUMBER**

■ **SQL_DIAG_CONNECTION_NAME**

■ **SQL_DIAG_MESSAGE_TEXT**

■ **SQL_DIAG_NATIVE**

■ **SQL_DIAG_ROW_NUMBER**

■ **SQL_DIAG_SERVER_NAME**

■ **SQL_DIAG_SQLSTATE**

■ **SQL_DIAG_SUBCLASS_ORIGIN**

Value A pointer to a location in memory where this function is to store the current value of the diagnostic record field specified.

ValueMaxSize The size of the memory storage buffer that this function is to store the current value of the specified diagnostic record field in. If an ODBC-defined diagnostic record field is to be retrieved, and if the field value is a 32-bit integer value, this parameter is ignored. If a DB2 CLI diagnostic record field is to be retrieved, this parameter may be set as follows:

- If the value of the specified diagnostic record field is a character string, this parameter may be set to the actual length of the string or to **SQL_NTS**.

- If the value of the specified diagnostic record field is a binary string, this parameter may be set to the result of the **SQL_LEN_BINARY_ATTR(length)** macro. Usually, this macro places a negative value in this parameter.

- If the value of the specified diagnostic record field is anything other than a character string or binary string, this parameter may be set to **SQL_IS_POINTER**.

- If the value of the specified diagnostic record field is a fixed-length data type, this parameter may be set to **SQL_IS_INTEGER** or **SQL_IS_UINTEGER**, as appropriate.

ValueSize   A pointer to a location in memory where this function is to store the actual number of bytes written to the diagnostic record field value memory storage buffer (*Value*). If the value retrieved is not a character string value, this parameter ignored.

Description   The **SQLGetDiagField()** function is used to retrieve the current value of a field in a diagnostic header or status record that is associated with a specific environment, connection, statement, or descriptor handle. A diagnostic record contains error, warning, and/or status information that was generated by the last CLI function executed. Table 13–3 alphabetically lists each diagnostic header and status record field available, along with a description of the information returned for each field when this function is executed.

Table 13–3   Diagnostic Record Fields

Field Name	Data Type	Description
Header Record Fields		
SQL_DIAG_CURSOR_ROW_COUNT	SQLINTEGER	This field contains a count of the number of rows in the current cursor. The contents of this field are only valid for SQL statement handles and then only after the **SQLExecute()**, **SQLExecDirect()**, or **SQLMoreResults()** function has been called.
SQL_DIAG_DYNAMIC_FUNCTION	SQLCHAR *	This field contains a string that describes the SQL statement the underlying function executed (refer to Table 13–4 for a list of valid values for this field). The contents of this field are only valid for SQL statement handles, and then only after the **SQLExecute()**, **SQLExecDirect()**, or **SQLMoreResults()** function has been called. The contents of this field is undefined before the **SQLExecute()** or the **SQLExecDirect()** function is called.

Table 13–3 *Diagnostic Record Fields (Continued)*

Field Name	Data Type	Description
SQL_DIAG_DYNAMIC_FUNCTION_CODE	SQLINTEGER	This field contains a numeric code that describes the SQL statement that was executed by the underlying function (refer to Table 13–4 for a list of valid values for this field). The contents of this field are only defined for statement handles and only after the **SQLExecute()**, **SQLExecDirect()**, or **SQLMoreResults()** function has been called.
		The value of this field is undefined before a the **SQLExecute()** or **SQLExecDirect()** function is called.
SQL_DIAG_NUMBER	SQLINTEGER	The number of status records available for the specified handle.
SQL_DIAG_RETURNCODE	SQLRETURN	The return code returned by the CLI function. Refer to Table 13–1 for a list of valid return codes. If no function has yet been called on the handle specified, **SQL_SUCCESS** is returned for **SQL_DIAG_RETURNCODE**.
SQL_DIAG_ROW_COUNT	SQLINTEGER	The number of rows affected by an **INSERT**, **UPDATE**, or **DELETE** operation performed by **SQLExecute()**, **SQLExecDirect()**, or **SQLSetPos()**. The contents of this field are only defined for statement handles. The data in this field is also returned by **SQLRowCount()**. The data in this field is reset after every non-diagnostic function call, whereas the row count returned by **SQLRowCount()** remains the same until the statement is set back to the "Prepared" or "Allocated" state.
Status Record Fields		
SQL_DIAG_CLASS_ORIGIN	SQLCHAR *	A string indicating the document that defines the class portion of the SQLSTATE value in this record. Its value is "**ISO 9075**" for all SQLSTATEs defined by X/Open and ISO call-level interface. For ODBC-specific SQLSTATEs (all those whose SQLSTATE class is **IM**), its value is "**ODBC 3.0**."
SQL_DIAG_COLUMN_NUMBER	SQLINTEGER	If the **SQL_DIAG_ROW_NUMBER** field is a valid row number in a rowset or a set of parameters, this field contains the value representing the column number in the result data set or the parameter number in the set of parameters. Result data set

Table 13–3 *Diagnostic Record Fields (Continued)*

Field Name	Data Type	Description
		column numbers always start at **1**; if this status record pertains to a bookmark column, the field can be **0**. Parameter numbers start at **1**. It has the value **SQL_NO_COLUMN_NUMBER** if the status record is not associated with a column number or parameter number. If DB2 CLI cannot determine the column number or parameter number this record is associated with, this field has the value **SQL_COLUMN_NUMBER_UNKNOWN**. The contents of this field are defined only for statement handles.
SQL_DIAG_CONNECTION_NAME	**SQLCHAR ***	A string indicating the name of the connection the diagnostic record relates to. This field is driver-defined. For diagnostic data structures associated with the environment handle and for diagnostics that do not relate to any connection, this field is a zero-length string.
SQL_DIAG_MESSAGE_TEXT	**SQLCHAR ***	An informational message about the error or warning. This field is formatted as described in the *Diagnostic Messages* section of this chapter. There is no maximum length to the diagnostic message text.
SQL_DIAG_NATIVE	**SQLINTEGER**	A driver/data source-specific native error code. If there is no native error code, the driver returns **0**.
SQL_DIAG_ROW_NUMBER	**SQLINTEGER**	This field contains the row number in the rowset, or the parameter number in the set of parameters, with which the status record is associated. Row numbers and parameter numbers start with **1**. This field has the value **SQL_NO_ROW_NUMBER** if this status record is not associated with a row number or parameter number. If the driver cannot determine the row number or parameter number this record is associated with, this field has the value **SQL_ROW_NUMBER_UNKNOWN**. The contents of this field are defined only for statement handles.
SQL_DIAG_SERVER_NAME	**SQLCHAR ***	A string indicating the server name to which the diagnostic record relates. It is the same as the value returned for a call to **SQLGetInfo()** with the **SQL_DATA_SOURCE_NAME** *InfoType* specified. For diagnostic data structures associated with the

Table 13–3 *Diagnostic Record Fields (Continued)*

Field Name	Data Type	Description
		environment handle and for diagnostics that do not relate to any server, this field is a zero-length string.
`SQL_DIAG_SQLSTATE`	SQLCHAR *	A five-character SQLSTATE diagnostic code.
`SQL_DIAG_SUBCLASS_ORIGIN`	SQLCHAR *	A string with the same format and valid values as `SQL_DIAG_CLASS_ORIGIN` that identifies the defining portion of the sub-class portion of the SQLSTATE code. DB2 CLI always returns an empty string for `SQL_DIAG_CLASS_ORIGIN`.

(Adapted from table 97 on pages 387–388 of *IBM DB2 Universal Database Call Level Interface Guide and Reference*.)

Table 13–4 describes the values of the `SQL_DYNAMIC_FUNCTION` and `SQL_DYNAMIC_FUNCTION_CODE` fields of a diagnostic header record that apply to each type of SQL statement that can be executed with the `SQLExecute()` or `SQLExecDirect()` function.

An application typically calls this function to accomplish one of three goals:

- To obtain specific error or warning information when a CLI function call has returned `SQL_SUCCESS_WITH_INFO`, `SQL_ERROR` or, in some cases, `SQL_NEED_DATA`.

- To find out how many rows in a data source were affected when an `INSERT`, `UPDATE`, or `DELETE` operation was performed by calling the `SQLExecute()`, `SQLExecDirect()`, or `SQLSetPos()` function (stored in the `SQL_DIAG_ROW_COUNT` header field), or to find out the number of rows that exist in the current open cursor, if the driver is able to provide this information (stored in the `SQL_DIAG_CURSOR_ROW_COUNT` header field).

- To determine which SQL operation was executed when the `SQLExecute()` or the `SQLExecDirect()` function was called (stored in the `SQL_DIAG_DYNAMIC_FUNCTION` and `SQL_DIAG_DYNAMIC_FUNCTION_CODE` header fields).

An application typically calls this function when a previous call to a CLI function has returned something other than `SQL_SUCCESS` or `SQL_INVALID_HANDLE`. However, because any CLI function can post zero or more diagnostic records when it is called, an application can call this function immediately after making any CLI function call.

Status records are placed in a sequence that is based on row number and the type of diagnostic information they contain. If two or more status records exist, the sequence of the records is determined first by row number. The following rules apply to determining the sequence of diagnostic record by row:

- Records that do not correspond to any row appear in front of records that correspond to a particular row, because `SQL_NO_ROW_NUMBER` is defined to be -1.

- Records for which the row number is unknown appear in front of all other records, because `SQL_ROW_NUMBER_UNKNOWN` is defined to be -2.

Table 13–4   Values Returned in the **SQL_DYNAMIC_FUNCTION** and **SQL_DYNAMIC_FUNCTION_CODE** Fields of a Diagnostic Header Record for Specific Types of SQL Statements

Type Of SQL Statement	Value Of SQL_DIAG_DYNAMIC_FUNCTION	Value Of SQL_DIAG_DYNAMIC_FUNCTION_CODE
Alter Table	"ALTER TABLE"	SQL_DIAG_ALTER_TABLE
Call	"CALL"	SQL_DIAG_PROCEDURE_CALL
Create Index	"CREATE INDEX"	SQL_DIAG_CREATE_INDEX
Create Table	"CREATE TABLE"	SQL_DIAG_CREATE_TABLE
Create View	"CREATE VIEW"	SQL_DIAG_CREATE_VIEW
Cursor Specification	"SELECT CURSOR"	SQL_DIAG_SELECT_CURSOR
Drop Index	"DROP INDEX"	SQL_DIAG_DROP_INDEX
Drop Table	"DROP TABLE"	SQL_DIAG_DROP_TABLE
Drop View	"DROP VIEW"	SQL_DIAG_DROP_VIEW
Grant Authorizations	"GRANT"	SQL_DIAG_GRANT
Insert	"INSERT"	SQL_DIAG_INSERT
Positioned Delete	"DYNAMIC DELETE CURSOR"	SQL_DIAG_DYNAMIC_DELETE_CURSOR
Positioned Update	"DYNAMIC UPDATE CURSOR"	SQL_DIAG_DYNAMIC_UPDATE_CURSOR
Revoke Authorizations	"REVOKE"	SQL_DIAG_REVOKE
Schema Definition	"CREATE SCHEMA"	SQL_DIAG_CREATE_SCHEMA
Searched Delete	"DELETE WHERE"	SQL_DIAG_DELETE_WHERE
Searched Update	"UPDATE WHERE"	SQL_DIAG_UPDATE_WHERE
Unknown	empty string	SQL_DIAG_UNKNOWN_STATEMENT

(Adapted from table 98 on page 388 of *IBM DB2 Universal Database Call Level Interface Guide and Reference.*)

- All records pertaining to specific rows are sorted by the value in the SQL_DIAG_ROW_NUMBER field. All errors and warnings of the first row affected are listed, then all errors and warnings of the next row affected, and so on.

Return Codes   SQL_SUCCESS, SQL_SUCCESS_WITH_INFO, SQL_NO_DATA, SQL_INVALID_HANDLE, SQL_ERROR

SQLSTATEs   No SQLSTATE values are returned for this function because it does not generate diagnostic information for itself. Instead, this function uses the following return codes to report the outcome of its own execution:

- **SQL_SUCCESS**
  The function successfully returned diagnostic information.

- **SQL_SUCCESS_WITH_INFO**
  The diagnostic field value buffer (*Value*) was not large enough to hold the requested diagnostic field value.

■ **SQL_NO_DATA**

The record number specified in the *RecNumber* parameter was greater than the number of diagnostic records that existed for the handle specified. This function also returns **SQL_NO_DATA** if a positive number is specified in the *RecNumber* parameter and there are no diagnostic records for the specified handle.

■ **SQL_INVALID_HANDLE**

The handle specified in the *HandleType* and *Handle* parameters was not a valid handle.

■ **SQL_ERROR**

One of the following occurred:

■ The value specified in the *Identifier* parameter was not valid.

■ The value specified in the *Identifier* parameter was **SQL_DIAG_CURSOR_ROW_COUNT**, **SQL_DIAG_DYNAMIC_FUNCTION**, **SQL_DIAG_DYNAMIC_FUNCTION_CODE**, or **SQL_DIAG_ROW_COUNT** and an environment, connection, or descriptor handle was specified in the *Handle* parameter.

■ The value specified in the *RecNumber* parameter was less than or equal to **0** and a record field was specified in the *Identifier* parameter. The *RecNumber* parameter is ignored when a header field is specified.

■ A character string value was requested and the value specified in the *ValueMaxSize* parameter was less than **0**.

Comments

■ An application can call this function multiple times to return information from some or all of the records stored in the diagnostic information data structure. DB2 CLI imposes no limit on the number of diagnostic records that can be stored in this structure at any one time.

■ If the value returned for the diagnostic record field specified in the *Identifier* parameter is a Unicode string, the *ValueMaxSize* parameter must contain an even number.

■ If the diagnostic information generated by a DB2 CLI function call is not retrieved before a CLI function other than **SQLGetDiagRec()**, **SQLGetDiagField()**, or **SQLGetSQLCA()** is called using the same environment, connection, statement, or descriptor handle, that information is lost. Diagnostic information stored on a given handle is not removed if a CLI function call is made using an associated handle of a different type.

■ Multiple diagnostic messages may be generated by a CLI function call. When this is the case, each diagnostic message can be retrieved, one at a time, by repeatedly incrementing the value of the *RecNumber* parameter and calling the **SQLGetDiagRec()** function. Calls to this function are non-destructive to diagnostic header and status record fields.

■ An application can determine the total number of diagnostic records available in the diagnostic information data structure by calling this function to retrieve the value of the **SQL_DIAG_NUMBER** field.

■ Each type of handle (environment, connection, statement, and descriptor) can have diagnostic information associated with it. However, some diagnostic header and status record fields do not contain values for all types of handles. This function can be used to determine which diagnostic header and status record fields are applicable for each type of handle.

■ If this function is called with the *HandleType* parameter set to SQL_HANDLE_ENV, either a shared or an unshared environment handle can be specified in the *Handle* parameter.

■ An application can call this function to return any diagnostic header or status record field value at any time, with the exception of the SQL_DIAG_CURSOR_ROW_ COUNT or SQL_DIAG_ROW_COUNT field, which returns SQL_ERROR if a statement handle is not specified. If any other diagnostic record field is undefined, this function returns SQL_SUCCESS (provided no other diagnostic is encountered), and an undefined value is returned for the field.

■ If the value specified for the *RecNumber* parameter is greater than or equal to 1, the data in the specified field describes the diagnostic information returned by a function. If the value specified for the *RecNumber* parameter is equal to 0, the field is in the diagnostic header record and contains data pertaining to the function call that returned the diagnostic information instead of more specific information.

Prerequisites   There are no prerequisites for using this function call.

Restrictions   There are no restrictions associated with this function call.

See Also   SQLGetDiagRec(), SQLGetSQLCA()

Example   The following Visual C++ program illustrates how to use the SQLGetDiagField() to obtain specific diagnostic information when a CLI function fails to execute properly.

```
/*------------------------------------------------------------*/
/* NAME:      CH13EX2.CPP                                      */
/* PURPOSE: Illustrate How To Use The Following CLI API Function */
/*          In A C++ Program:                                 */
/*                                                            */
/*               SQLGetDiagField()                            */
/*                                                            */
/* OTHER CLI APIs SHOWN:                                      */
/*          SQLAllocHandle()            SQLSetEnvAttr()        */
/*          SQLDriverConnect()          Disconnect()          */
/*          SQLFreeHandle()                                   */
/*                                                            */
/*------------------------------------------------------------*/

// Include The Appropriate Header Files
#include <windows.h>
#include <sqlcli1.h>
#include <iostream.h>

// Define The CLI_Class Class
class CLI_Class
```

```
            {
                // Attributes
                public:
                    SQLHANDLE      EnvHandle;
                    SQLHANDLE      ConHandle;
                    SQLRETURN      rc;

                // Operations
                public:
                    CLI_Class();                              // Constructor
                    ~CLI_Class();                             // Destructor
            };

            // Define The Class Constructor
            CLI_Class::CLI_Class()
            {
                // Initialize The Return Code Variable
                rc = SQL_SUCCESS;

                // Allocate An Environment Handle
                rc = SQLAllocHandle(SQL_HANDLE_ENV, SQL_NULL_HANDLE, &EnvHandle);

                // Set The ODBC Application Version To 3.x
                if (rc == SQL_SUCCESS)
                    rc = SQLSetEnvAttr(EnvHandle, SQL_ATTR_ODBC_VERSION,
                            (SQLPOINTER) SQL_OV_ODBC3, SQL_IS_UINTEGER);

                // Allocate A Connection Handle
                if (rc == SQL_SUCCESS)
                    rc = SQLAllocHandle(SQL_HANDLE_DBC, EnvHandle, &ConHandle);
            }

            // Define The Class Destructor
            CLI_Class::~CLI_Class()
            {
                // Free The Connection Handle
                if (ConHandle != NULL)
                    SQLFreeHandle(SQL_HANDLE_DBC, ConHandle);

                // Free The Environment Handle
                if (EnvHandle != NULL)
                    SQLFreeHandle(SQL_HANDLE_ENV, EnvHandle);
            }

            /*------------------------------------------------------------- */
            /* The Main Function                                            */
            /*------------------------------------------------------------- */
            int main()
            {
                // Declare The Local Memory Variables
                SQLRETURN    rc = SQL_SUCCESS;
                SQLCHAR      ErrMsg[255];
                SQLSMALLINT  ErrMsgLen;
```

```
// Create An Instance Of The CLI_Class Class
CLI_Class     Example;

// Attempt To Connect To The DB2 Sample Database Without
 // Providing A User ID And Password (An Error Should Be
 // Generated)
if (Example.ConHandle != NULL)
{
    rc = SQLConnect(Example.ConHandle, (SQLCHAR *) "SAMPLE",
            SQL_NTS, NULL, 0, NULL, 0);

    // If The Specified Connection Was Not Established, Retrieve
    // And Display The Error Message Generated
    if (rc != SQL_SUCCESS && rc != SQL_SUCCESS_WITH_INFO)
    {
        rc = SQLGetDiagField(SQL_HANDLE_DBC, Example.ConHandle,
                1, SQL_DIAG_MESSAGE_TEXT, ErrMsg, 255,
                &ErrMsgLen);
        cout << ErrMsg << endl;
    }

    // If The Specified Connection Was Established, Display
    // A Success Message And Disconnect
    else
    {
        cout << "Connected to DB2 Sample database." << endl;
        rc = SQLDisconnect(Example.ConHandle);
    }
}

// Return To The Operating System
return(rc);
}
```

SQLGetSQLCA

COMPATIBILITY

X/OPEN 95 CLI	ISO/IEC 92 CLI	DB2 CLI 5.2	DB2 CLI 2.0	ODBC 3.x
☐	☐	☑	☑	☐

ODBC API CONFORMANCE LEVEL   **NONE**

Purpose   The sqlGetsQLCA() function is used to retrieve the SQLCA data structure values that are associated with preparing and executing a SQL statement, retrieving data from a cursor (fetching), or closing a cursor.

Syntax

```
SQLRETURN      SQLGetSQLCA      (SQLHENV          EnvironmentHandle,
                                SQLHDBC           ConnectionHandle,
                                SQLHSTMT          StatementHandle,
                                struct sqlca FAR  *sqlca);
```

Parameters

EnvironmentHandle   An environment handle that refers to a previously allocated environment information storage buffer (data structure).

ConnectionHandle   A data source connection handle that refers to a previously allocated connection information storage buffer (data structure).

StatementHandle   An SQL statement handle that refers to a previously allocated SQL statement information storage buffer (data structure).

sqlca   A pointer to a location in memory where this function is to store the contents of an *SQL Communication Area* (SQLCA) data structure that is used to associate with the handle specified.

Description   The **SQLGetSQLCA()** function is used to retrieve SQLCA data structure values that are associated with preparing and executing a SQL statement, retrieving data from a cursor (fetching), or closing a cursor. In some cases, the SQLCA data structure can provide diagnostic information that cannot be obtained with the **SQLGetDiagRec()** or the **SQLGetDiagField()** function.

The *SQL Communications Area* (SQLCA) data structure is a collection of application variables that are updated each time an executable SQL statement is processed. The SQLCA data structure is defined in *sqlca.h* as follows:

```
struct sqlca
{
char   sqlcaid[8];    /* An "eye catcher" for storage dumps. This  */
                      /* field contains the value "SQLCA   ".      */
long   sqlcabc;       /* The size of the SQLCA structure (136 bytes) */
long   sqlcode;       /* The SQL return code value. A value of 0   */
                      /* means "successful execution," a positive  */
                      /* value means "successful execution with    */
                      /* warnings," and a negative value means     */
                      /* "error." Refer to the IBMDB2 Universal    */
                      /* Database Messages Reference for specific  */
                      /* meanings of SQL return code values.       */
short  sqlerrml;      /* The size, in bytes, of the data stored in */
                      /* the sqlerrmc field of this structure. This */
                      /* value can be any number between 0 and 70. A */
                      /* value of 0 indicates that no data is stored */
                      /* in the sqlerrmc field.                    */
char   sqlerrmc[70];  /* One or more error message tokens, separated */
                      /* by 0xFF, that are substituted for variables */
                      /* in the descriptions of error conditions.  */
                      /* This field is also used when a successful */
                      /* connection is established. Refer to the IBM */
                      /* DB2 Universal Database Messages Reference for */
                      /* specific meanings of SQL return code values. */
```

```
char    sqlerrp[8];     /* A diagnostic value that begins with a three-  */
                        /* letter code identifying the product followed  */
                        /* by five digits that identify the version,     */
                        /* release, and modification level of the        */
                        /* product. For example, "SQL05020" means DB2    */
                        /* Universal Database, version 5, release 2,      */
                        /* modification level 0. If the sqlcode field     */
                        /* contains a negative value, this field          */
                        /* identifies the module that returned an error.  */
long    sqlerrd[6];     /* An array of six integer values that provide   */
                        /* additional diagnostic information             */
char    sqlwarn[11];    /* An array of warning indicators, each          */
                        /* containing a blank or the letter 'W'. If       */
                        /* compound SQL was used, this field will         */
                        /* contain an accumulation of the warning         */
                        /* indicators set for all SQL sub-statements     */
char    sqlstate[5];    /* The SQLSTATE value that indicates the outcome */
                        /* of the most recently executed SQL statement    */
};
```

Table 13–5 describes the types of diagnostic information that can be returned in the *sqlerrd* array, and Table 13–6 describes the types of warning information that can be returned in the *sqlwarn* array.

Table 13–5   Elements of the sqlca.sqlerrd Array

Array Element	Diagnostic Information
sqlerrd[0]	If a **CONNECT** statement was successfully invoked, this element will contain the maximum expected difference in length of mixed character data (**CHAR** data types) when converted from the application code page to the database code page. A value of **0** or **1** indicates no expansion; a value greater than **1** indicates a possible expansion in length; a negative value indicates a possible contraction in length.
sqlerrd[1]	If the SQLCA data reflects a **NOT ATOMIC** compound SQL statement that encountered one or more errors, this element will contain a count of the number of SQL statements that failed.
sqlerrd[2]	If the SQLCA data reflects a **PREPARE** statement that was successfully invoked, this element will contain an estimate of the number of rows that will be returned.
	If the SQLCA data reflects an **INSERT**, **UPDATE**, or **DELETE** statement that was successfully invoked, this element will contain a count of the number of rows that were affected by the operation.
	If the SQLCA data reflects a compound SQL statement that was successfully invoked, this element will contain a count of the number of rows that were affected by all sub-statements.
	If the SQLCA data reflects a **CONNECT** statement that was successfully invoked, this element will contain **1** if the database can be updated; **2** if the database is read only.
sqlerrd[3]	If the SQLCA data reflects a **PREPARE** statement that was successfully invoked, this element will contain a relative cost estimate of the resources required to process the statement.

Table 13–5   Elements of the sqlca.sqlerrd Array (Continued)

Array Element	Diagnostic Information
	If the SQLCA data reflects a compound SQL statement that was successfully invoked, this element will contain a count of the number of sub-statements that were successful.
	If the SQLCA data reflects a **CONNECT** statement that was successfully invoked, this element will contain **0** if a one-phase commit from a down-level client is being used; **1** if a one-phase commit is being used; **2** if a one-phase, read-only commit is being used; and **3** if a two-phase commit is being used.
sqlerrd[4]	This element contains the total number of rows that were inserted, updated, or deleted as a result of: ■ The enforcement of constraints after a successful delete operation. ■ The processing of triggered SQL statements from activated triggers. If the SQLCA data reflects a compound SQL statement was successfully invoked, this element will contain a count of all such rows for all SQL sub-statements processed. If the SQLCA data reflects a **CONNECT** statement that was successfully invoked, this element will contain **0** if server authentication is used; **1** if client authentication is used; **2** if authentication is handled by DB2 Connect; **3** if authentication is handled by DCE Security Services; **255** if authentication is not specified. In some cases, when an error is encountered this field contains a negative value that is used as an internal error pointer.
sqlerrd[5]	For a partitioned database, this element contains the partition number of the partition that encountered the error or warning. If no errors or warnings were encountered, this element contains the partition number of the coordinator node (the number stored in this element is the same as that specified for the partition in the *db2nodes.cfg* file).

Table 13–6   Elements of the sqlca.sqlwarn Array

Array Element	Warning Information
SQLWARN0	This element is blank if all other indicators are blank; it contains a 'W' if at least one other indicator is not blank.
SQLWARN1	This element contains a 'W' if the value of a string column was truncated when assigned to a host variable. It contains a 'N' if the null terminator was truncated.
SQLWARN2	This element contains a 'W' if NULL values were eliminated from the argument of a function.
SQLWARN3	This element contains a 'W' if the number of columns is not equal to the number of host variables provided.
SQLWARN4	This element contains a 'W' if a prepared **UPDATE** or **DELETE** statement does not include a **WHERE** clause.
SQLWARN5	Reserved for future use.
SOLWARN6	This element contains a 'W' if the result of a date calculation was adjusted to avoid an invalid date.
SQLWARN7	Reserved for future use.

Table 13–6 *Elements of the sqlca.sqlwarn Array (Continued)*

Array Element	Warning Information
SQLWARN8	This element contains a 'W' if a character that could not be converted was replaced with a substitution character.
SQLWARN9	This element contains a 'W' if arithmetic expressions containing errors were ignored during column function processing.
SQLWARNA	This element contains a 'W' if there was a conversion error while converting a character data value in one of the fields in the SQLCA data structure.

Return Codes SQL_SUCCESS, SQL_INVALID_HANDLE, SQL_ERROR

SQLSTATEs No SQLSTATE values are returned for this function because it does not generate diagnostic informatin for itself.

Comments
- To obtain SQLCA information for an environment handle, specify a valid environment handle in the *EnvironmentHandle* parameter, set the connection handle (*ConnectionHandle*) parameter to SQL_NULL_HDBC, and set the statement handle (*StatementHandle*) parameter to SQL_NULL_HSTMT.

- To obtain SQLCA information for a connection handle, specify a valid data source connection handle in the *ConnectionHandle* parameter and set the statement handle (*StatementHandle*) parameter to SQL_NULL_HSTMT. The environment handle (*EnvironmentHandle*) will be ignored.

- To obtain SQLCA information for an SQL statement handle, specify a valid statement handle in the *StatementHandle* parameter. The environment handle (*EnvironmentHandle*) and connection handle (*ConnectionHandle*) will be ignored.

- If the diagnostic information generated by a DB2 CLI function call is not retrieved before a CLI function other than SQLGetDiagRec(), SQLGetDiagField(), or SQLGetSQLCA() is called using the same environment, connection, statement, or descriptor handle, that information is lost. Diagnostic information stored on a given handle is not removed if a CLI function call is made using an associated handle of a different type.

- Meaningful SQLCA information is only returned for the following DB2 CLI functions:
  - SQLBrowseConnect()
  - SQLConnect()
  - SQLSetConnectAttr() (for SQL_ATTR_AUTOCOMMIT and SQL_ATTR_DB2EXPLAIN attributes)
  - SQLColAttribute()
  - SQLDisconnect()
  - SQLDataSources()
  - SQLDescribeCol()

- `SQLDescribeParam()`
- `SQLCopyDesc()`
- `SQLFreeHandle()`
- `SQLRowCount()`
- `SQLPrepare()`
- `SQLExecute()`
- `SQLExecDirect()`
- `SQLFetch()`
- `SQLFetchScroll()`
- `SQLCloseCursor()`
- `SQLMoreResults()`
- `SQLGetData()` (if one or more LOB columns are involved)
- `SQLCancel()`
- `SQLEndTran()`
- `SQLTables()`
- `SQLTablePrivileges()`
- `SQLColumns()`
- `SQLColumnPrivileges()`
- `SQLStatistics()`
- `SQLPrimaryKeys()`
- `SQLForeignKeys()`
- `SQLProcedures()`
- `SQLProcedureColumns()`

- If an application is connected to a DB2 Universal Database data source, two fields in the SQLCA data structure variable may be of particular interest:

  - The SQLERRD(3) field (sqlca.errd[2])

    After an SQL statement is prepared, this field contains an estimate of the number of rows that will be returned when the SQL statement is executed. An application can inform the user of this information to help assess whether or not the appropriate query has been issued. After an **INSERT**, **UPDATE**, or **DELETE** SQL statement is executed, this field contains the actual number of affected rows. After processing compound SQL statements, this field contains an accumulation of all substatement rows affected by **INSERT**, **UPDATE**, or **DELETE** statements.

- The SQLERRD(4) field (sqlca.errd[3])

After an SQL statement is prepared, this field contains a relative cost estimate of the resources required to process the statement. This is the number that is compared to either the **DB2ESTIMATE** configuration keyword or the **SQL_DB2ESTIMATE** connection attribute. After processing compound SQL statements, this field contains an accumulation of all successfully executed SQL substatements.

The accuracy of the information returned in the SQLERRD(3) and SQLERRD(4) fields of a SQLCA data structure depends on many factors, such as the use of parameter markers and expressions within the SQL statement. The main factor, which can be easily controlled, is the accuracy of the data source statistics (when the statistical information about the data source was last updated), i.e., the last time the **RUNSTATS** command was executed.

SQLCA data structure information is not available for CLI functions that are processed strictly on the application side (for example, allocating a statement handle). In this case, an empty SQLCA data structure is produced, and all field values are set to zero.

Restrictions There are no restrictions associated with this function call.

See Also SQLGetDiagRec(), SQLGetDiagField()

Examples The following C++ program illustrates how to use the SQLGetSQLCA() function to obtain statistical information for a SQL statement before it is executed:

```
/*———————————————————————————————— */
/* NAME:     CH13EX3.CPP                                      */
/* PURPOSE: Illustrate How To Use The Following CLI API Function */
/*          In A C++ Program:                                 */
/*                                                            */
/*              SQLGetSQLCA()                                 */
/*                                                            */
/* OTHER CLI APIs SHOWN:                                      */
/*              SQLAllocHandle()         SQLSetEnvAttr()      */
/*              SQLDriverConnect()       Disconnect()         */
/*              SQLFreeHandle()                               */
/*                                                            */
/*———————————————————————————————— */

// Include The Appropriate Header Files
#include <windows.h>
#include <sqlcli1.h>
#include <sqlenv.h>
#include <iostream.h>

// Define The CLI_Class Class
class CLI_Class
```

```
{
    // Attributes
    public:
        SQLHANDLE      EnvHandle;
        SQLHANDLE      ConHandle;
        SQLRETURN      rc;

    // Operations
    public:
        CLI_Class();                          // Constructor
        ~CLI_Class();                         // Destructor
};

// Define The Class Constructor
CLI_Class::CLI_Class()
{
    // Initialize The Return Code Variable
    rc = SQL_SUCCESS;

    // Allocate An Environment Handle
    rc = SQLAllocHandle(SQL_HANDLE_ENV, SQL_NULL_HANDLE, &EnvHandle);

    // Set The ODBC Application Version To 3.x
    if (rc == SQL_SUCCESS)
        rc = SQLSetEnvAttr(EnvHandle, SQL_ATTR_ODBC_VERSION,
                 (SQLPOINTER) SQL_OV_ODBC3, SQL_IS_UINTEGER);

    // Allocate A Connection Handle
    if (rc == SQL_SUCCESS)
        rc = SQLAllocHandle(SQL_HANDLE_DBC, EnvHandle, &ConHandle);
}

// Define The Class Destructor
CLI_Class::~CLI_Class()
{
    // Free The Connection Handle
    if (ConHandle != NULL)
        SQLFreeHandle(SQL_HANDLE_DBC, ConHandle);

    // Free The Environment Handle
    if (EnvHandle != NULL)
        SQLFreeHandle(SQL_HANDLE_ENV, EnvHandle);
}

/*----------------------------------------------------------------*/
/* The Main Function                                              */
/*----------------------------------------------------------------*/
int main()
{
    // Declare The Local Memory Variables
    SQLRETURN     rc = SQL_SUCCESS;
    struct sqlca sqlca;
    char          ErrMsg[1024];
```

```cpp
// Create An Instance Of The CLI_Class Class
CLI_Class      Example;

// Attempt To Connect To The DB2 Sample Database Without
// Providing A User ID And Password (An Error Should Be
// Generated)
if (Example.ConHandle != NULL)
{
    rc = SQLConnect(Example.ConHandle, (SQLCHAR *) "SAMPLE",
            SQL_NTS, NULL, 0, NULL, 0);

    // If The Specified Connection Was Not Established, Retrieve
    // And Display The Error Message Generated
    if (rc != SQL_SUCCESS && rc != SQL_SUCCESS_WITH_INFO)
    {
        // Retrieve The SQLCA Data Structure Values Associated
        // With The Function
        rc = SQLGetSQLCA(NULL, Example.ConHandle,
                SQL_NULL_HSTMT, &sqlca);

        // Pass The SQLCA Structure Values To The GET ERROR
        // MESSAGE API
        rc = sqlaintp(ErrMsg, 1024, 70, &sqlca);
        cout << ErrMsg << endl;
    }

    // If The Specified Connection Was Established, Display
    // A Success Message And Disconnect
    else
    {
        cout << "Connected to DB2 Sample database." << endl;
        rc = SQLDisconnect(Example.ConHandle);
    }
}

// Return To The Operating System
return(rc);
}
```

14

Querying the Data Source System Catalog

DB2 CLI provides several functions that are used to retrieve information from the system catalog of a specified data source. This chapter is designed to introduce you to the system catalog and to these CLI functions. The first part of this chapter describes the system catalog and explains how it is used. This is followed by a detailed discussion about the kinds of information returned by the CLI catalog functions. Next, the different types of parameters used by the catalog functions are described. Then, the information available for stored procedures and the catalog functions used to obtain it is discussed. Finally, a detailed reference section covering each CLI catalog function is provided.

The System Catalog and Catalog Functions

All databases have an internal structure that outlines how data is to be stored. This structure, along with information about access privileges, referential integrity, functions, and procedures is stored in a special set of system tables known as the *system catalog* (sometimes referred to as the *data dictionary*). Occasionally, it becomes necessary for a CLI application to retrieve information from this set of system tables. Although queries can be issued directly against the tables that comprise the system catalog, CLI provides a set of functions, known as *catalog functions*, that are specifically designed to interact directly with a database's system catalog. By using these generic interface functions instead of custom queries, an application can avoid having to develop database product-specific or database product release-specific system catalog queries.

Data Returned by the Catalog Functions

The catalog functions are essentially a set of predefined, parameterized **SELECT** SQL statements. When called, each catalog function returns a result data set to the application via an SQL statement handle. An application can retrieve (fetch) individual rows of data from this result data set in the same manner that it would retrieve data from any other result data set.

The columns in the result data set returned by a catalog function are defined in a specific order, so that in future releases of DB2 CLI, additional columns can be added without creating a problem for existing applications.

Identifiers returned in the result data set produced by a catalog function are not quoted, even if they contain special characters. For example, suppose the identifier quote character for a database is a double quotation mark ("), and suppose a table in the database named **Accounts_Payable** contains a column named **Customer_Name**. When the **SQLColumns()** catalog function is called using this scenario, the value returned in the **TABLE_NAME** column for this particular column is **Accounts_Payable**, not "Accounts_ Payable", and the value returned in the **COLUMN_NAME** column is **Customer_Name**, not "Customer_Name". However, a **SELECT** SQL statement designed to retrieve the names of customers in the **Accounts_Payable** table must quote both of these names. For example:

```
SELECT "Customer_Name" FROM "Accounts_Payable"
```

The catalog functions are based on an SQL-like authorization model in which a connection is made based on a valid user ID (authorization name) and password, and only data for which the user has an authorization to retrieve is returned. The result data sets returned by the catalog functions are almost never updateable and applications should not expect to be able to change the structure of a database by changing the data in these result data sets.

The execution of some catalog functions can result in the subsequent execution of fairly complex queries. Because of this, the catalog functions should only be called when needed. If the data produced by a catalog function will be used several times, an application can improve its overall performance by calling the catalog function once and saving the information returned, as opposed to making repeated function calls to obtain the same information.

Parameters (Arguments) Used in Catalog Functions

Each catalog function accepts input parameters (argument) values that are used to either identify or constrain the amount of information returned when the catalog function is executed. Catalog function input parameters fall into one of four different categories:

- Ordinary
- Pattern Value
- Identifier
- Value List

Most string parameters can be of one of two different types, depending upon the value of the **SQL_ATTR_METADATA_ID** SQL statement attribute. Table 14–1 lists each catalog function, along with the input parameters used and the category of each parameter according to the value of the **SQL_ATTR_METADATA_ID** statement attribute (**SQL_TRUE** or **SQL_FALSE**).

Table 14–1 The Category of Each Catalog Query Function Input Parameter as Determined by the Value of the **SQL_ATTR_METADATA_ID** Statement Attribute.

Function	Argument	Type when SQL_ATTR_ METADATA_ID= SQL_FALSE	Type when SQL_ATTR_ METADATA_ID= SQL_TRUE
SQLTables()	CatalogName	Pattern Value	Identifier
	SchemaName	Pattern Value	Identifier
	TableName	Pattern Value	Identifier
	TableType	Value List	Value List
SQLTablePrivileges()	CatalogName	Ordinary	Identifier
	SchemaName	Pattern Value	Identifier
	TableName	Pattern Value	Identifier
SQLColumns()	CatalogName	Ordinary	Identifier
	SchemaName	Pattern Value	Identifier
	TableName	Pattern Value	Identifier
	ColumnName	Pattern Value	Identifier

Table 14–1   The Category of Each Catalog Query Function Input Parameter as Determined by the Value of the **SQL_ATTR_METADATA_ID** Statement Attribute (Continued)

Function	Argument	Type when SQL_ATTR_ METADATA_ID= SQL_FALSE	Type when SQL_ATTR_ METADATA_ID= SQL_TRUE
SQLColumnPrivileges()	*CatalogName*	Ordinary	Identifier
	SchemaName	Ordinary	Identifier
	TableName	Ordinary	Identifier
	ColumnName	Pattern Value	Identifier
SQLSpecialColumns()	*CatalogName*	Ordinary	Identifier
	SchemaName	Ordinary	Identifier
	TableName	Ordinary	Identifier
SQLStatistics()	*CatalogName*	Ordinary	Identifier
	SchemaName	Ordinary	Identifier
	TableName	Ordinary	Identifier
SQLPrimaryKeys()	*CatalogName*	Ordinary	Identifier
	SchemaName	Ordinary	Identifier
	TableName	Ordinary	Identifier
SQLForeignKeys()	*PKCatalogName*	Ordinary	Identifier
	PKSchemaName	Ordinary	Identifier
	PKTableName	Ordinary	Identifier
	FKCatalogName	Ordinary	Identifier
	FKSchemaName	Ordinary	Identifier
	FKTableName	Ordinary	Identifier
SQLProcedures()	*ProcCatalogName*	Ordinary	Identifier
	ProcSchemaName	Pattern Value	Identifier
	ProcedureName	Pattern Value	Identifier
SQLProcedureColumns	*ProcCatalogName*	Ordinary	Identifier
	ProcSchemaName	Pattern Value	Identifier
	ProcedureName	Pattern Value	Identifier
	ColumnName	Pattern Value	Identifier

Ordinary Parameters

When a catalog function input parameter (argument) is treated as an *Ordinary* parameter, it can only accept ordinary strings. If the **SQL_ATTR_METADATA_ID** statement attribute is set to **SQL_FALSE**, Ordinary parameters are treated as literal string parameters. If this attribute is set to **SQL_TRUE**, they are treated as Identifier parameters. Ordinary parameters do not accept a string search pattern or a list of values. Ordinary parameters are case-sensitive (the case of the letters in the string is significant), and quote characters in strings are taken literally. Furthermore, if an Ordinary parameter contains a NULL pointer and the parameter is a required parameter, the catalog function returns **SQL_ERROR** and SQLSTATE **HY**009 (Invalid use of NULL pointer).

Pattern Value Parameters

When a catalog function input parameter (argument) is treated as a *Pattern Value* para-meter, it can accept both ordinary strings and strings containing one or more predefined search pattern characters. If the **SQL_ATTR_METADATA_ID** statement attribute is set to **SQL_FALSE**, Pattern Value parameters are treated as string parameters that accept search patterns. If this attribute is set to **SQL_TRUE**, they are treated as Identifier para-meters that do not accept search patterns. The following search pattern values can be used in any Pattern Value parameter:

■ The underscore character (_). Any single character can be used in place of the underscore character.

■ The percent character (%). Any sequence of 0 or more characters can be used in place of the percent character.

■ An escape character. A driver-specific character that is used to treat an underscore character, a percent character, and/or the escape character itself as a literal value instead of as a "wild card" value (for example, % = "%"). The driver-specific escape character can be retrieved by calling the **SQLGetInfo()** function with the **SQL_SEARCH_PATTERN_ESCAPE** information type specified. The escape character must precede any underscore, percent sign, or escape character in a Pattern Value parameter in order for that character to be treated as a literal character.

When using Pattern Value parameters, special care must be taken to escape appro-priate search pattern characters. This is particularly true for the underscore character (_), which is commonly used in identifiers such as table names and column names. In fact, one mistake that is often made is to retrieve a value from one catalog function's result data set and pass it, unaltered, to a Pattern Value parameter of another catalog function. For example, suppose an application retrieves the table name **MY_TABLE** from the result data set produced by the **SQLTables()** function and passes this name to the **SQLColumns()** function to generate a list of the columns in **MY_TABLE**. Instead of getting a list of the columns defined for **MY_TABLE**, the application would get a list of the columns defined for all the tables matching the search pattern **MY_TABLE,** such as **MY_TABLE**, **MY1TABLE**, **MY2TABLE**, etc.

Another thing to keep in mind is that specifying a NULL pointer for a Pattern Value parameter does not constrain the search for that particular parameter. That is because a NULL pointer and the search pattern "%" (any characters) are treated the same. How-ever, an empty string search pattern (that is, a valid pointer to a blank string, zero char-acters in length) constrains the search to match only the empty string (" ").

Identifier Parameters

When a catalog function input parameter (argument) is treated as an *Identifier* para-meter, it can accept both ordinary strings and strings containing one or more predefined search pattern characters. If the **SQL_ATTR_METADATA_ID** statement attribute is set to **SQL_TRUE**, Identifier parameters are treated as Identifier parameters. In this case, the underscore character (_) and the percent sign (%) are treated as literal characters, not as search pattern characters. If the **SQL_ATTR_METADATA_ID** statement attribute is set to **SQL_FALSE**, Identifier parameters are treated either as Ordinary parameters or as Pattern Value parameters, depending upon the parameter value.

If an Identifier parameter contains a quoted string, DB2 CLI removes all leading and trailing blanks and treats the string within the quotation marks literally. If the string is not quoted, DB2 CLI removes trailing blanks and converts the string to uppercase. Specifying a NULL pointer for an Identifier parameter causes all catalog functions to return **SQL_ERROR** and SQLSTATE **HY**009 (Invalid use of NULL pointer), unless the parameter specifies a catalog name for a database that does not support catalog names. Although identifiers containing special characters must be quoted in SQL statements, they must not be quoted when passed as catalog function parameters. Quote characters passed to catalog functions are interpreted literally.

Keep in mind that quoted Identifier values are often used to distinguish a true column name from a pseudo-column with the same name. For example, if "**ROWID**" is specified in a catalog function, the function will work with the **ROWID** pseudo-column if it exists. If the pseudo-column does not exist, the function will work with the **ROWID** column. However, if **ROWID** is specified (unquoted), the function will only work with the **ROWID** column.

Value List Parameters

When a catalog function input parameter (argument) is treated as a *Value List* parameter, the parameter value consists of a list of comma-separated values that are to be used for value matching. Currently, there is only one Value List parameter used in the CLI catalog functions—the *TableType* parameter of the **SQLTables()** function. Specifying a NULL pointer for this parameter is the same as specifying **SQL_ALL_TABLE_TYPES**, which enumerates all possible members of the value list. Value List parameters are not affected by the **SQL_ATTR_METADATA_ID** statement attribute.

Obtaining Information About Stored Procedures

Stored procedures are usually invoked from a CLI application by passing the appropriate **CALL** SQL statement to the data source with either the **SQLExecDirect()** function or with the **SQLPrepare()** function, followed by the **SQLExecute()** function. To obtain a list of stored procedures that are available for execution, an application can call the **SQLProcedures()** catalog function.

If a stored procedure requires information from the calling application, input parameter markers corresponding to the stored procedure's arguments must be coded in the **CALL** SQL statement. The parameter markers in the **CALL** statement must then be bound to application variables or LOB locators with the **SQLBindParameter()** function. Before application variable binding takes place, an application can call the **SQLProcedureColumns()** catalog function to find out what kind of information a stored procedure call is expecting.

Although most stored procedure arguments can be used both for input and for output, an application should specify one type or the other when the **SQLBindParameter()** function is called. This helps avoid sending unnecessary data between the client and the server.

The CLI Data Source Catalog Query Functions

Table 14–2 lists the CLI functions that are used to retrieve information from the system catalog of a specified data source.

Each of these functions are described in detail in the remaining portion of this chapter.

Table 14–2   The ODBC Error/Diagnostic Message Retrieval Functions

Function Name	Description
SQLTables()	Retrieves a list of catalog names, schema names, table names, or table types that have been defined for a data source.
SQLTablePrivileges()	Retrieves a list of table names, along with the authorization information associated with those tables, that have been defined for a data source.
SQLColumns()	Retrieves a list of column names that have been defined for one or more tables.
SQLColumnPrivileges()	Retrieves a list of column names, along with the authorization information associated with those columns, that have been defined for a specified table.
SQLSpecialColumns()	Retrieves a list of the optimal set of columns that uniquely identify a row of data in a specified table.
SQLStatistics()	Retrieves statistical information about a specified table along with a list of associated indexes for that table.
SQLPrimaryKeys()	Retrieves a list of column names that comprise the primary key of a specified table.
SQLForeignKeys()	Retrieves a list of foreign keys in a specified table or a list of foreign keys that refer to a specified table.
SQLProcedures()	Retrieves a list of stored procedure names that are stored in and that are available for a data source.
SQLProcedureColumns()	Retrieves a list of input and output parameters, the return value, and the columns in the result data set produced (if any) by a specified stored procedure.

SQLTables

COMPATIBILITY

X/OPEN 95 CLI	ISO/IEC 92 CLI	DB2 CLI 5.2	DB2 CLI 2.0	ODBC 3.x
☑	☑	☑	☑	☑

ODBC API CONFORMANCE LEVEL   CORE*

*IN ODBC 2.0, THIS FUNCTION WAS A LEVEL 2 API CONFORMANCE LEVEL FUNCTION

Purpose The SQLTables() function is used to retrieve a list of table names (and all associated information) stored in a specified data source's system catalog.

Syntax

```
SQLRETURN    SQLTables    (SQLHSTMT      StatementHandle,
                           SQLCHAR       *CatalogName,
                           SQLSMALLINT   CatalogNameSize,
                           SQLCHAR       *SchemaName,
                           SQLSMALLINT   SchemaNameSize,
                           SQLCHAR       *TableName,
                           SQLSMALLINT   TableNameSize,
                           SQLCHAR       *TableType,
                           SQLSMALLINT   TableTypeSize);
```

Parameters

StatementHandle   An SQL statement handle that refers to a previously allocated SQL statement information storage buffer (data structure).

CatalogName   A pointer to a location in memory where either the catalog qualifier portion of a three-part table name is stored or a catalog name search pattern is stored. Since DB2 CLI does not support three-part names, this parameter must contain either a NULL pointer or a zero length string.

CatalogNameSize   The length of the catalog qualifier name or search pattern value stored in the *CatalogName* parameter. Since DB2 CLI does not support three-part names, this parameter must be set to 0.

SchemaName   A pointer to a location in memory where a schema name search pattern is stored.

SchemaNameSize   The length of the schema name search pattern stored in the *SchemaName* parameter.

TableName   A pointer to a location in memory where a table name search pattern is stored.

TableNameSize   The length of the table name search pattern value stored in the *TableName* parameter.

TableType	A pointer to a location in memory where information about the types of tables to retrieve data for is stored. Examples of table types that might be specified include:

- "**TABLE**"
- "**VIEW**"
- "**ALIAS**"
- "**SYNONYM**"
- "**SYSTEM TABLE**"
- "**LOCAL TEMPORARY**"
- "**GLOBAL TEMPORARY**"
- "**INOPERATIVE VIEW**"

	If a NULL pointer is specified for this parameter, all table types found will be returned.
TableTypeSize	The length of the table type value stored in the *TableType* parameter.

Description   The **SQLTables()** function is used to retrieve a list of table names (and all associated information) stored in a specified data source's system catalog. The information returned by this function is placed in a result data set, which can be processed by using the same CLI functions that are used to process result data sets generated by SQL queries. Table 14–3 lists the columns in this result data set.

Return Codes   SQL_SUCCESS, SQL_SUCCESS_WITH_INFO, SQL_STILL_EXECUTING, SQL_INVALID_HANDLE, SQL_ERROR

SQLSTATEs   If this function returns **SQL_SUCCESS_WITH_INFO** or **SQL_ERROR**, one of the following SQLSTATE values may be obtained by calling the **SQLGetDiagRec()** function:

08S01, **24**000, **40003**, **HY**001, **HY**008, **HY**009, **HY**010, **HY**014, **HY**090, **HY**C00, or **HY**T00

Refer to Appendix B for detailed information about each SQLSTATE value that can be returned.

Comments   ■ Because this function, in many cases, maps to a complex—and therefore, expensive query against a data source's system catalog tables, it should be used sparingly. If the result data set produced is to be used more than once, it should be saved, rather than be regenerated each time it is needed.

■ An empty string (" ") can be stored in the memory location the *SchemaName* parameter refers to for schemas without names.

■ If the **SQL_ATTR_METADATA_ID** attribute for the statement handle specified is set to **SQL_TRUE**, the values specified for the *CatalogName*, *SchemaName*, and *TableName* parameters are treated as identifier values, and their case is insignificant. However, if the **SQL_ATTR_METADATA_ID** attribute is set to **SQL_FALSE**, the values specified for the *CatalogName*, *SchemaName*, and *TableName* parameters are

Table 14–3   Result Data Set Returned By `SQLTables()`

Column Number	Column Name	Data Type	Description
1	TABLE_CAT	VARCHAR(128)	The name of the catalog (qualifier) containing the TABLE_SCHEM value. Since DB2 CLI does not support three-part table names, this column is always set to NULL.
2	TABLE_SCHEM	VARCHAR(128)	The name of the schema containing the TABLE_NAME value.
3	TABLE_NAME	VARCHAR(128)	The name of the table, view, alias, synonym, system table, local temporary table, global temporary table, or inoperative view.
4	TABLE_TYPE	VARCHAR(128)	The type of object the name in the TABLE_NAME column represents. Valid values for this column are: "TABLE" "SYSTEM TABLE" "VIEW" "LOCAL TEMPORARY" "ALIAS" "GLOBAL TEMPORARY" "SYNONYM" "INOPERATIVE VIEW"
5	REMARKS	VARCHAR(254)	Descriptive information about the table, view, alias, synonym, system table, local temporary table, global temporary table, inoperative view, or data source-specific object.

(Adapted from table 181 on page 626 of *IBM DB2 Universal Database Call Level Interface Guide and Reference*.)

treated literally, and their case is significant. Refer to the "Parameters (Arguments) Used in Catalog Functions" section earlier in this chapter and to the `SQLGetStmtAttr()` function for more information.

■ The values specified for the *SchemaName*, *TableName*, and *ColumnName* parameters can contain the following search pattern values:

  ■ The underscore character (_)
    Any single character can be used in place of the underscore character.

  ■ The percent character (%)
    Any sequence of 0 or more characters can be used in place of the percent character.

  ■ An escape character
    A driver-specific character used to treat an underscore character, a percent character, and/or the escape character itself as a literal value instead of as a wild card value (that is, % = "%").

■ If the `SQL_ODBC_VERSION` environment attribute is set to `SQL_OV_ODBC3`, the value specified for the *CatalogName* parameter can contain the same search patterns that values specified for the *SchemaName*, *TableName*, and *ColumnName* parameters can contain.

- To support enumeration of catalog names, schema names, and table types, the following special semantics are defined:

  - If the value specified for the *CatalogName* parameter is a single percent character (%), and if the values specified for the *SchemaName* and *TableName* parameters are empty strings, then the result data set produced contains a list of valid catalogs for the current data source. (All columns in the result data set except the **TABLE_CAT** column contain NULLs.)

  - If the value specified for the *SchemaName* parameter is a single percent character (%), and if the values specified for the *CatalogName* and *TableName* parameters are empty strings, then the result data set produced contains a list of valid schemas for the current data source. (All columns in the result data set except the **TABLE_SCHEM** column contain NULLs.)

  - If the value specified for the *TableType* parameter is a single percent character (%), and if the values specified for the *CatalogName*, *SchemaName*, and *TableName* parameters are empty strings, the result data set produced contains a list of valid table types for the data source. (All columns in the result data set except the **TABLE_TYPE** column contain NULLs.)

- The result data set returned by this function is ordered by **TABLE_TYPE**, **TABLE_CAT**, **TABLE_SCHEM**, and **TABLE_NAME**.

- The **SQLTablePrivileges()** function or the **SQLGetInfo()** function with the **SQL_ACCESSIBLE_TABLES** information type specified can be used to determine the type of access allowed on any given table in the result data set produced by this function. If neither of these functions are used to obtain table authorization information, an application must be coded so that it can handle situations in which a user selects a table for which they have not been granted **SELECT** authorization privileges.

- If the value specified for the *TableType* parameter is not an empty string, it must contain a list of upper-case, comma-separated values specifying the table types to retrieve information for. Each value in this list can either be enclosed in single quotes, or left unquoted. For example, either "'**TABLE**', '**VIEW**'" or "**TABLE**, **VIEW**" are valid.

- If the current data source does not recognize or support a specified table type, no information is returned for that particular type of table.

- The actual amount of memory needed to store the value found in each **VARCHAR** column in the result data set produced by this function is dependent on the data source. An application can choose to set aside 128 characters (plus the NULL-terminator) for **VARCHAR** columns (to be consistent with the SQL92 standard limits), or alternatively, to allocate the actual amount of memory required by first calling the **SQLGetInfo()** function with the *InfoType* parameter set to **SQL_MAX_CATALOG_NAME_LEN**, **SQL_MAX_SCHEMA_NAME_LEN**, **SQL_MAX_TABLE_NAME_LEN**, and/or **SQL_MAX_COLUMN_NAME_LEN** to determine respectively the actual lengths of the **TABLE_CAT**, **TABLE_SCHEM**, **TABLE_NAME**, and **COLUMN_NAME** columns that are supported by the current data source.

Prerequisites　There are no prerequisites for using this function call.

Restrictions　There are no restrictions associated with this function call.

See Also　`SQLTablePrivileges()`, `SQLColumns()`

Example　The following Visual C++ program illustrates how to use the `SQLTables()` function to obtain information about the tables that are available in a data source.

```
/*————————————————————————————————*/
/* NAME:     CH14EX1.CPP                                          */
/* PURPOSE: Illustrate How To Use The Following CLI API Function  */
/*          In A C++ Program:                                     */
/*                                                                */
/*              SQLTables()                                       */
/*                                                                */
/* OTHER CLI APIs SHOWN:                                          */
/*          SQLAllocHandle()              SQLSetEnvAttr()         */
/*          SQLConnect()                  SQLBindCol()            */
/*          SQLFetch()                    SQLDisconnect()         */
/*          SQLFreeHandle()                                       */
/*                                                                */
/*————————————————————————————————*/

// Include The Appropriate Header Files
#include <windows.h>
#include <sqlcli1.h>
#include <iostream.h>

// Define The CLI_Class Class
class CLI_Class
{
    // Attributes
    public:
        SQLHANDLE   EnvHandle;
        SQLHANDLE   ConHandle;
        SQLHANDLE   StmtHandle;
        SQLRETURN   rc;

    // Operations
    public:
        CLI_Class();                            // Constructor
        ~CLI_Class();                           // Destructor
        SQLRETURN   ShowTableInfo();
};

// Define The Class Constructor
CLI_Class::CLI_Class()
{
    // Initialize The Return Code Variable
    rc = SQL_SUCCESS;

    // Allocate An Environment Handle
    rc = SQLAllocHandle(SQL_HANDLE_ENV, SQL_NULL_HANDLE, &EnvHandle);
```

```cpp
    // Set The ODBC Application Version To 3.x
    if (rc == SQL_SUCCESS)
        rc = SQLSetEnvAttr(EnvHandle, SQL_ATTR_ODBC_VERSION,
                (SQLPOINTER) SQL_OV_ODBC3, SQL_IS_UINTEGER);

    // Allocate A Connection Handle
    if (rc == SQL_SUCCESS)
        rc = SQLAllocHandle(SQL_HANDLE_DBC, EnvHandle, &ConHandle);
}

// Define The Class Destructor
CLI_Class::~CLI_Class()
{
    // Free The Connection Handle
    if (ConHandle != NULL)
        SQLFreeHandle(SQL_HANDLE_DBC, ConHandle);

    // Free The Environment Handle
    if (EnvHandle != NULL)
        SQLFreeHandle(SQL_HANDLE_ENV, EnvHandle);
}

// Define The ShowTableInfo() Member Function
SQLRETURN CLI_Class::ShowTableInfo(void)
{
    // Declare The Local Memory Variables
    SQLCHAR   TableName[129];

    // Allocate An SQL Statement Handle
    rc = SQLAllocHandle(SQL_HANDLE_STMT, ConHandle, &StmtHandle);
    if (rc == SQL_SUCCESS)
    {
        // Retrieve Information About The Tables In The Data Source
        rc = SQLTables(StmtHandle, NULL, 0, NULL, 0,
                (SQLCHAR *) "%", SQL_NTS, (SQLCHAR *) "TABLE", 5);
        if (rc == SQL_SUCCESS)
        {
            // Bind A Column In The Result Data Set Returned To
            // An Application Variable
            rc = SQLBindCol(StmtHandle, 3, SQL_C_CHAR, (SQLPOINTER)
                    &TableName, sizeof(TableName), NULL);

            // Display A Header
            cout << "Tables :" << endl << endl;

            // While There Are Records In The Result Data Set
            // Generated, Retrieve And Display Them
            while (rc != SQL_NO_DATA)
            {
                rc = SQLFetch(StmtHandle);
                if (rc != SQL_NO_DATA && rc != SQL_ERROR)
                    cout << TableName << endl;
            }
        }
    }
```

```
        // Free The SQL Statement Handle
        if (StmtHandle != NULL)
            SQLFreeHandle(SQL_HANDLE_STMT, StmtHandle);
    }

    // Return The CLI API Return Code To The Calling Function
    return(rc);
}

/*————————————————————————————————*/
/* The Main Function                                              */
/*————————————————————————————————*/
int main()
{
    // Declare The Local Memory Variables
    SQLRETURN  rc = SQL_SUCCESS;

    // Create An Instance Of The CLI_Class Class
    CLI_Class  Example;

    // Connect To The DB2 Sample Database
    if (Example.ConHandle != NULL)
    {
        rc = SQLConnect(Example.ConHandle, (SQLCHAR *) "SAMPLE",
                 SQL_NTS, (SQLCHAR *) "userid", SQL_NTS,
                 (SQLCHAR *) "password", SQL_NTS);

        // Call The ShowTableInfo() Member Function
        if (rc == SQL_SUCCESS || rc == SQL_SUCCESS_WITH_INFO)
            Example.ShowTableInfo();

        // Disconnect From The DB2 Sample Database
        rc = SQLDisconnect(Example.ConHandle);
    }

    // Return To The Operating System
    return(rc);
}
```

SQLTablePrivileges

COMPATIBILITY

X/OPEN 95 CLI	ISO/IEC 92 CLI	DB2 CLI 5.2	DB2 CLI 2.0	ODBC 3.x
☐	☐	☑	☑	☑

ODBC API CONFORMANCE LEVEL   LEVEL 2

Purpose   The **SQLTablePrivileges()** function is used to retrieve a list of table names stored in a specified data source's system catalog, along with and the privileges associated with them.

Syntax

```
SQLRETURN    SQLTablePrivileges  (SQLHSTMT       StatementHandle,
                                  SQLCHAR        *CatalogName,
                                  SQLSMALLINT    CatalogNameSize,
                                  SQLCHAR        *SchemaName,
                                  SQLSMALLINT    SchemaNameSize,
                                  SQLCHAR        *TableName,
                                  SQLSMALLINT    TableNameSize);
```

Parameters   *StatementHandle*   An SQL statement handle that refers to a previously allocated SQL statement information storage buffer (data structure).

CatalogName   A pointer to a location in memory where the catalog qualifier portion of a three-part table name is stored. Since DB2 CLI does not support three-part names, this parameter must contain either a NULL pointer or a zero length string.

CatalogNameSize   The length of the catalog qualifier name value stored in the *CatalogName* parameter. Since DB2 CLI does not support three-part names, this parameter must be set to **0**.

SchemaName   A pointer to a location in memory where a schema name search pattern is stored.

SchemaNameSize   The length of the schema name search pattern value stored in the *SchemaName* parameter.

TableName   A pointer to a location in memory where a table name search pattern is stored.

TableNameSize   The length of the table name search pattern value stored in the *TableName* parameter.

Description   The **SQLTablePrivileges()** function is used to retrieve a list of table names stored in the system catalog of a specified data source, along with the privileges associated with them. The information returned by this function is placed in a result data set that can be processed by using the same CLI functions that are used to process result data sets generated by SQL queries. Table 14–4 lists the columns in this result data set.

Return Codes   SQL_SUCCESS, SQL_SUCCESS_WITH_INFO, SQL_STILL_EXECUTING, SQL_INVALID_HANDLE, SQL_ERROR

SQLSTATEs   If this function returns SQL_SUCCESS_WITH_INFO or SQL_ERROR, one of the following SQLSTATE values may be obtained by calling the SQLGetDiagRec() function:

08S01, **24**000, **40**003, **HY**001, **HY**008, **HY**009, **HY**010, **HY**014, **HY**090, **HY**C00, or **HY**T00

Refer to Appendix B for detailed information about each SQLSTATE value that can be returned.

Table 14–4 Result Data Set Returned by **SQLTablePrivileges()**

Column Number	Column Name	Data Type	Description
1	TABLE_CAT	VARCHAR(128)	The name of the catalog (qualifier) containing the **TABLE_SCHEM** value. Since DB2 CLI does not support three-part table names, this column is always set to NULL.
2	TABLE_SCHEM	VARCHAR(128)	The name of the schema containing the **TABLE_NAME** value.
3	TABLE_NAME	VARCHAR(128) NOT NULL	The name of the table.
4	GRANTOR	VARCHAR(128)	The name or authorization ID of the user granting the table privilege.
5	GRANTEE	VARCHAR(128) NOT NULL	The name or authorization ID of the user to whom the privilege was granted.
6	PRIVILEGE	VARCHAR(128) NOT NULL	The table privilege that was granted. Valid values for this column are:

"**SELECT**":
The **GRANTEE** is permitted to retrieve data from one or more columns of the table.

"**INSERT**":
The **GRANTEE** is permitted to insert new rows of data into one or more columns of the table.

"**UPDATE**":
The **GRANTEE** is permitted to modify the data in one or more columns of the table.

"**DELETE**":
The **GRANTEE** is permitted to remove rows of data from the table.

"**REFERENCES**":
The **GRANTEE** is permitted to reference one or more columns of the table in a constraint (for example, a unique, referential, or table check constraint).

"**ALTER**"
The **GRANTEE** is permitted to add columns to, create or drop primary and foreign keys on, and create or drop check constraints on the table.

"**INDEX**"
The **GRANTEE** is permitted to create indexes on the table.

"**CONTROL**"
The **GRANTEE** is permitted to drop, grant and revoke authorizations for, and update statistics for the table.

Table 14-4 Result Data Set Returned by **SQLTablePrivileges()** (Continued)

Column Number	Column Name	Data Type	Description
7	IS_GRANTABLE	VARCHAR(3)	Indicates whether the **GRANTEE** is permitted to grant the privilege to other users. Valid values for this column are: **"YES"** **"NO"** **NULL**: Unknown or not applicable to the data source. A **PRIVILEGE** can be either grantable or not grantable, but not both.

(Adapted from table 178 on page 621 of *IBM DB2 Universal Database Call Level Interface Guide and Reference*.)

Comments

■ Because this function, in many cases, maps to a complex—and therefore, expensive query against a data source's system catalog tables, it should be used sparingly. If the result data set produced is to be used more than once, it should be saved, rather than be regenerated each time it is needed.

■ An empty string (" ") can be stored in the memory location the *SchemaName* parameter refers to for schemas without names.

■ If the **SQL_ATTR_METADATA_ID** attribute for the statement handle specified is set to **SQL_TRUE**, the values specified for the *CatalogName*, *SchemaName*, and *TableName* parameters are treated as identifier values, and their case is insignificant. However, if the **SQL_ATTR_METADATA_ID** attribute is set to **SQL_FALSE**, the values specified for the *CatalogName*, *SchemaName*, and *TableName* parameters are treated literally, and their case is significant. Refer to the "Parameters (Arguments) Used in Catalog Functions" section at the beginning of this chapter and to the **SQLGetStmtAttr()** function for more information.

■ The values specified for the *SchemaName* and *TableName* parameters can contain the following search pattern values:

   ■ The underscore character (_)
   Any single character can be used in place of the underscore character.

   ■ The percent character (%)
   Any sequence of 0 or more characters can be used in place of the percent character.

   ■ An escape character
   A driver-specific character used to treat an underscore character, a percent character, and/or the escape character itself as a literal value instead of as a wild card value (i.e., % = "%").

■ The result data set returned by this function is ordered by **TABLE_CAT**, **TABLE_SCHEM**, **TABLE_NAME**, and **PRIVILEGE**.

■ If multiple privileges are associated with a given table, each privilege is returned as a separate row in the result data set.

■ The actual amount of memory needed to store the value found in each **VARCHAR** column in the result data set produced by this function is dependent on the data source. An application can choose to set aside 128 characters (plus the NULL-terminator) for **VARCHAR** columns (to be consistent with the SQL92 standard limits), or alternatively, to allocate the actual amount of memory required by first calling the **SQLGetInfo()** function with the *InfoType* parameter set to **SQL_MAX_CATALOG_NAME_LEN**, **SQL_MAX_SCHEMA_NAME_LEN**, **SQL_MAX_TABLE_NAME_LEN**, and/or **SQL_MAX_COLUMN_NAME_LEN** to determine respectively the actual lengths of the **TABLE_CAT**, **TABLE_SCHEM**, **TABLE_NAME**, and **COLUMN_NAME** columns that are supported by the current data source.

Prerequisites   There are no prerequisites for using this function call.

Restrictions   There are no restrictions associated with this function call.

See Also   **SQLTables()**, **SQLColumnPrivileges()**

Example   The following Visual C++ program illustrates how to use the **SQLTablePrivileges()** function to obtain information about the privileges associated with the tables that are available in a data source.

```
/*────────────────────────────────────────────────────────────*/
/* NAME:     CH14EX2.CPP                                        */
/* PURPOSE: Illustrate How To Use The Following CLI API Function */
/*          In A C++ Program:                                   */
/*                                                              */
/*              SQLTablePrivileges()                            */
/*                                                              */
/* OTHER CLI APIs SHOWN:                                        */
/*          SQLAllocHandle()          SQLSetEnvAttr()           */
/*          SQLConnect()              SQLBindCol()              */
/*          SQLFetch()                SQLDisconnect()           */
/*          SQLFreeHandle()                                     */
/*                                                              */
/*────────────────────────────────────────────────────────────*/

// Include The Appropriate Header Files
#include <windows.h>
#include <sqlcli1.h>
#include <iostream.h>

// Define The CLI_Class Class
class CLI_Class
{
    // Attributes
    public:
        SQLHANDLE    EnvHandle;
        SQLHANDLE    ConHandle;
        SQLHANDLE    StmtHandle;
        SQLRETURN    rc;
```

```
    // Operations
    public:
        CLI_Class();                              // Constructor
        ~CLI_Class();                             // Destructor
        SQLRETURN  ShowTablePrivilegeInfo();
};


// Define The Class Constructor
CLI_Class::CLI_Class()
{
    // Initialize The Return Code Variable
    rc = SQL_SUCCESS;

    // Allocate An Environment Handle
    rc = SQLAllocHandle(SQL_HANDLE_ENV, SQL_NULL_HANDLE, &EnvHandle);

    // Set The ODBC Application Version To 3.x
    if (rc == SQL_SUCCESS)
        rc = SQLSetEnvAttr(EnvHandle, SQL_ATTR_ODBC_VERSION,
                (SQLPOINTER) SQL_OV_ODBC3, SQL_IS_UINTEGER);

    // Allocate A Connection Handle
    if (rc == SQL_SUCCESS)
        rc = SQLAllocHandle(SQL_HANDLE_DBC, EnvHandle, &ConHandle);
}


// Define The Class Destructor
CLI_Class::~CLI_Class()
{
    // Free The Connection Handle
    if (ConHandle != NULL)
        SQLFreeHandle(SQL_HANDLE_DBC, ConHandle);

    // Free The Environment Handle
    if (EnvHandle != NULL)
        SQLFreeHandle(SQL_HANDLE_ENV, EnvHandle);
}


// Define The ShowTablePrivilegeInfo() Member Function
SQLRETURN CLI_Class::ShowTablePrivilegeInfo(void)
{
    // Declare The Local Memory Variables
    SQLCHAR   GrantorName[129];

    // Allocate An SQL Statement Handle
    rc = SQLAllocHandle(SQL_HANDLE_STMT, ConHandle, &StmtHandle);
    if (rc == SQL_SUCCESS)
    {
        // Retrieve Information About The Privileges Associated With
        // The EMPLOYEE Table In The Data Source
        rc = SQLTablePrivileges(StmtHandle, NULL, 0, NULL, 0,
                (SQLCHAR *) "EMPLOYEE", SQL_NTS);
        if (rc == SQL_SUCCESS)
        {
            // Bind A Column In The Result Data Set Returned To
```

```
        // An Application Variable
        rc = SQLBindCol(StmtHandle, 4, SQL_C_CHAR, (SQLPOINTER)
                 &GrantorName, sizeof(GrantorName), NULL);

        // Display A Header
        cout << "Table Privilege Grantor :" << endl << endl;

        // While There Are Records In The Result Data Set
        // Generated, Retrieve And Display Them
        while (rc != SQL_NO_DATA)
        {
            rc = SQLFetch(StmtHandle);
            if (rc != SQL_NO_DATA && rc != SQL_ERROR)
                cout << GrantorName << endl;
        }
    }

    // Free The SQL Statement Handle
    if (StmtHandle != NULL)
        SQLFreeHandle(SQL_HANDLE_STMT, StmtHandle);
    }

    // Return The CLI API Return Code To The Calling Function
    return(rc);
}


/*————————————————————————————————————————————*/
/* The Main Function                                            */
/*————————————————————————————————————————————*/
int main()
{
    // Declare The Local Memory Variables
    SQLRETURN  rc = SQL_SUCCESS;

    // Create An Instance Of The CLI_Class Class
    CLI_Class  Example;

    // Connect To The DB2 Sample Database
    if (Example.ConHandle != NULL)
    {
        rc = SQLConnect(Example.ConHandle, (SQLCHAR *) "SAMPLE",
                 SQL_NTS, (SQLCHAR *) "userid", SQL_NTS,
                 (SQLCHAR *) "password", SQL_NTS);

        // Call The ShowTablePrivilegeInfo() Member Function
        if (rc == SQL_SUCCESS || rc == SQL_SUCCESS_WITH_INFO)
            Example.ShowTablePrivilegeInfo();

        // Disconnect From The DB2 Sample Database
        rc = SQLDisconnect(Example.ConHandle);
    }

    // Return To The Operating System
    return(rc);
}
```

SQLColumns

COMPATIBILITY

X/OPEN 95 CLI	ISO/IEC 92 CLI	DB2 CLI 5.2	DB2 CLI 2.0	ODBC 3.x
☑	☑	☑	☑	☑

ODBC API CONFORMANCE LEVEL   CORE*

*IN ODBC 2.0, THIS FUNCTION WAS A LEVEL 2 API CONFORMANCE LEVEL FUNCTION

Purpose   The **SQLColumns()** function is used to retrieve a list of column names associated with a specified table.

Syntax
```
SQLRETURN    SQLColumns    (SQLHSTMT        StatementHandle,
                            SQLCHAR         *CatalogName,
                            SQLSMALLINT     CatalogNameSize,
                            SQLCHAR         *SchemaName,
                            SQLSMALLINT     SchemaNameSize,
                            SQLCHAR         *TableName,
                            SQLSMALLINT     TableNameSize,
                            SQLCHAR         *ColumnName,
                            SQLSMALLINT     ColumnNameSize);
```

Parameters

StatementHandle An SQL statement handle that refers to a previously allocated SQL statement information storage buffer (data structure).

CatalogName A pointer to a location in memory where the catalog qualifier portion of a three-part table name is stored. Since DB2 CLI does not support three-part names, this parameter must contain either a NULL pointer or a zero length string.

CatalogNameSize The length of the catalog qualifier name value stored in the *CatalogName* parameter. Since DB2 CLI does not support three-part names, this parameter must be set to 0.

SchemaName A pointer to a location in memory where the schema portion of a three-part table name is stored.

SchemaNameSize The length of the schema name value stored in the *SchemaName* parameter.

TableName A pointer to a location in memory where a table name search pattern is stored.

TableNameSize The length of the table name search pattern value stored in the *TableName* parameter.

ColumnName	A pointer to a location in memory where a column name search pattern is stored.
ColumnNameSize	The length of the column name search pattern value stored in the *ColumnName* parameter.

Description   The `SQLColumns()` function is used to retrieve a list of columns names for a specified base table, view, system table, alias (synonym), etc. The information returned by this function is placed in a result data set that can be processed by using the same CLI functions that are used to process result data sets generated by SQL queries. Table 14–5 lists the columns in this result data set.

Table 14–5   Result Data Set Returned by `SQLColumns()`

Column Number	Column Name	Data Type	Description
1	`TABLE_CAT`	`VARCHAR(128)`	The name of the catalog (qualifier) containing the `TABLE_SCHEM` value. Since DB2 CLI does not support three-part table names, this column is always set to NULL.
2	`TABLE_SCHEM`	`VARCHAR(128)`	The name of the schema containing the `TABLE_NAME` value.
3	`TABLE_NAME`	`VARCHAR(128)` `NOT NULL`	The name of the table, view, alias, or synonym.
4	`COLUMN_NAME`	`VARCHAR(128)` `NOT NULL`	The name of a column in the table identified in the `TABLE_NAME` column. This column contains an empty string (" ") for columns without a name.
5	`DATA_TYPE`	`SMALLINT` `NOT NULL`	The SQL data type of the column identified in the `COLUMN_NAME` column. Valid values for this column include:

`SQL_CHAR`	`SQL_VARCHAR`
`SQL_LONGVARCHAR`	`SQL_DECIMAL`
`SQL_NUMERIC`	`SQL_SMALLINT`
`SQL_INTEGER`	`SQL_REAL`
`SQL_FLOAT`	`SQL_DOUBLE`
`SQL_BIT`	`SQL_TINYINT`
`SQL_BIGINT`	`SQL_BINARY`
`SQL_VARBINARY`	`SQL_LONGVARBINARY`
`SQL_TYPE_DATE`	`SQL_TYPE_TIME`
`SQL_TYPE_TIMESTAMP`	`SQL_GRAPHIC`
`SQL_VARGRAPHIC`	`SQL_LONGVARGRAPHIC`
`SQL_BLOB`	`SQL_CLOB`
`SQL_DBCLOB`	

For datetime and interval data types, this column contains the concise data type (such as `SQL_TYPE_DATE` or `SQL_INTERVAL_YEAR_TO_MONTH`, rather than the non-concise data type such as `SQL_DATETIME` or `SQL_INTERVAL`).

Table 14–5   Result Data Set Returned by **SQLColumns()**   (Continued)

Column Number	Column Name	Data Type	Description
6	TYPE_NAME	VARCHAR(128) NOT NULL	The data source-specific character representation of the SQL data type name identified in the **DATA_TYPE** column. Valid values for this column include:
7	COLUMN_SIZE	INTEGER	The maximum number of bytes needed to display the column data in character format.
8	BUFFER_LENGTH	INTEGER	The maximum number of bytes needed for the associated C application variable (buffer) to store data from this column if the value **SQL_C_DEFAULT** is specified for the *CDataType* parameter of the **SQLBindParameter() SQLBindCol()**, or **SQLGetData()** function. This length does not include the NULL-terminator character used by NULL terminated strings.
9	DECIMAL_ DIGITS	SMALLINT	The total number of significant digits to the right of the decimal point.

For column 6 (TYPE_NAME), valid values include:

"CHAR"	"VARCHAR"
"LONG VARCHAR"	"DECIMAL"
"NUMERIC"	"SMALLINT"
"INTEGER"	"REAL"
"FLOAT"	"DOUBLE PRECISION"
"BIT"	"TINYINT"
"BIGINT"	"BINARY"
"VARBINARY"	"LONG VARBINARY"
"DATE"	"TIME"
"TIMESTAMP"	"GRAPHIC"
"VARGRAPHIC"	"LONG VARGRAPHIC"
"BLOB"	"CLOB"
"DBCLOB"	

For column 7 (COLUMN_SIZE):

For numeric data types, this is either the total number of digits, or the total number of bits allowed in the column, depending on the value in the **NUM_PREC_RADIX** column.

For character or binary string data types, this is the size of the string (length), in bytes.

For date, time, and timestamp data types, this is the total number of characters required to display the value when it is converted to a character string.

For graphic data types, this is the total number of double byte characters used.

For column 9 (DECIMAL_DIGITS):

If the **DATA_TYPE** column contains **SQL_TYPE_TIME** or **SQL_TYPE_TIMESTAMP**, this column contains the number of digits in the fractional seconds component of the time value.

For interval data types that do not contain a time component, this column contains the value zero (**0**).

Table 14–5   Result Data Set Returned by **SQLColumns()** (Continued)

Column Number	Column Name	Data Type	Description
			For data types where decimal digits are not applicable, this column is set to NULL.
			For all other data types, this column contains the decimal digits of the column on the data source.
10	NUM_PREC_ RADIX	SMALLINT	The radix value of the column.
			For approximate numeric data types, this column contains the value **2** and the **COLUMN_SIZE** column contains the number of bits allowed in the column.
			For exact numeric data types, this column contains the value **10** and the **COLUMN_SIZE** column contains the number of decimal digits allowed for the column.
			For numeric data types, this column can contain either **10** or **2**.
			For data types where radix is not applicable, this column is set to NULL.
11	NULLABLE	SMALLINT NOT NULL	Indicates whether the column accepts a NULL value. Valid values for this column are:
			SQL_NO_NULLS: The column does not accept NULL values.
			SQL_NULLABLE: The column accepts NULL values.
			SQL_NULLABLE_UNKNOWN: Whether the column accepts NULL values is not known.
			The value in this column is different from the value in the **IS_NULLABLE** column. The **NULLABLE** column indicates with certainty that a column can accept NULLs, but it cannot indicate with certainty that a column does not accept NULLs. The **IS_NULLABLE** column indicates with certainty that a column cannot accept NULLs, but it cannot indicate with certainty that a column accepts NULLs.
12	REMARKS	VARCHAR(254)	Descriptive information about the column (if any exists).
13	COLUMN_DEF	VARCHAR(254)	The column's default value.
			If the default value is a numeric literal, this column contains the character representation of the numeric literal with no enclosing single quotes.
			If the default value is a character string, this column contains that string enclosed in single quotes.

Table 14–5 Result Data Set Returned by **SQLColumns()** (Continued)

Column Number	Column Name	Data Type	Description
			If the default value is a pseudo-literal, (as is the case for **DATE**, **TIME**, and **TIMESTAMP** columns), this column contains the keyword of the pseudo-literal (for example: "**CURRENT DATE**") with no enclosing single quotes.
			If the default value is NULL or if no default value was specified, this column contains the word "**NULL**" with no enclosing single quotes.
			If the default value cannot be represented without truncation, this column contains the word "**TRUNCATED**" with no enclosing single quotes.
			The value of this column can be used in generating a new column definition, except when it contains the value "**TRUNCATED**".
14	SQL_DATA_TYPE	SMALLINT NOT NULL	The SQL data type of the column identified in the **COLUMN_NAME** column, as it would appear in the **SQL_DESC_TYPE** field of an implementation row descriptor record.
			This column usually contains the same value as the **DATA_TYPE** column, with the following exception:
			For datetime and interval data types, this column contains the non-concise data type (such as **SQL_DATETIME**), rather than the concise data type (such as **SQL_TYPE_DATE**). If this column contains **SQL_DATETIME**, the specific data type can be obtained from the **SQL_DATETIME_SUB** column.
15	DATETIME_SUB	SMALLINT	The subtype code for datetime and interval data types. For all other data types, this column is set to NULL.
			Valid values for this column are:
			SQL_CODE_DATE SQL_CODE_TIME SQL_CODE_TIMESTAMP
16	CHAR_OCTET_LENGTH	INTEGER	Contains the maximum length, in octets (bytes), for a character data type column. For single byte character sets, this column contains the same value as the **COLUMN_SIZE** column. For all other character sets, this column is set to NULL.
17	ORDINAL_POSITION	INTEGER NOT NULL	The column's sequence number in the table. The first column in the table is number 1, the second column is number 2, and so on.

Table 14–5   Result Data Set Returned by **SQLColumns()**   (Continued)

Column Number	Column Name	Data Type	Description
18	IS_NULLABLE	VARCHAR(254)	Indicates whether the column is known to be nullable (can contain NULL values), according to the rules in the ISO SQL92 standard. Valid values for this column are: **"YES"** The column can contain NULL values. **"NO"** The column cannot contain NULL values. The value returned for this column is different from the value returned for the **NULLABLE** column. (See the description of the **NULLABLE** column for details.)

(Adapted from table 37 on pages 257-258 of *IBM DB2 Universal Database Call Level Interface Guide and Reference*.)

Return Codes   SQL_SUCCESS, SQL_SUCCESS_WITH_INFO, SQL_STILL_EXECUTING, SQL_INVALID_HANDLE, SQL_ERROR

SQLSTATEs   If this function returns SQL_SUCCESS_WITH_INFO or SQL_ERROR, one of the following SQLSTATE values may be obtained by calling the SQLGetDiagRec() function:

08S01, **24**000, **40**003, **HY**001, **HY**008, **HY**010, **HY**014, **HY**090, **HY**C00, or **HY**T00

Refer to Appendix B for detailed information about each SQLSTATE value that can be returned.

Comments
- Because this function, in many cases, maps to a complex—and therefore, expensive query against a data source's system catalog tables, it should be used sparingly. If the result data set produced is to be used more than once, it should be saved, rather than be regenerated each time it is needed.

- An empty string (" ") can be stored in the memory location the *SchemaName* parameter refers to for schemas without names.

- If the SQL_ATTR_METADATA_ID attribute for the statement handle specified is set to SQL_TRUE, the values specified for the *CatalogName*, *SchemaName*, *TableName*, and *ColumnName* parameters are treated as identifier values and their case is insignificant. However, if the SQL_ATTR_METADATA_ID attribute is set to SQL_FALSE, the values specified for the *CatalogName*, *SchemaName*, *TableName*, and *ColumnName* parameters are treated literally, and their case is significant. Refer to the "Parameters (Arguments) Used In Catalog Functions" section at the beginning of this chapter and to the SQLGetStmtAttr() function for more information.

- The values specified for the *TableName* and *ColumnName* parameters can contain the following search pattern values:

■ The underscore character (_).
Any single character can be used in place of the underscore character.

■ The percent character (%).
Any sequence of 0 or more characters can be used in place of the percent character.

■ An escape character.
A driver-specific character used to treat an underscore character, a percent character, and/or the escape character itself as a literal value instead of as a wild card value (that is, % = "%").

■ The result data set returned by this function is ordered by **TABLE_CAT**, **TABLE_SCHEM**, **TABLE_NAME**, and **ORDINAL_POSITION**.

■ The actual amount of memory needed to store the value found in each **VARCHAR** column in the result data set produced by this function is dependent on the data source. An application can choose to set aside 128 characters (plus the NULL-terminator) for **VARCHAR** columns (to be consistent with the SQL92 standard limits), or alternatively, to allocate the actual amount of memory required by first calling the **SQLGetInfo()** function with the *InfoType* parameter set to **SQL_MAX_CATALOG_NAME_LEN**, **SQL_MAX_SCHEMA_NAME_LEN**, **SQL_MAX_TABLE_NAME_LEN**, and/or **SQL_MAX_COLUMN_NAME_LEN** to determine respectively the actual lengths of the **TABLE_CAT**, **TABLE_SCHEM**, **TABLE_NAME**, and **COLUMN_NAME** columns that are supported by the current data source.

■ If the **SQL_LONGDATA_COMPAT** connection attribute has been set to **SQL_LD_COMPAT_YES** (either by calling the **SQLSetConnectAttr()** or by setting the **LONGDATACOMPAT** option in the DB2 CLI initialization file), large object (LOB) data types will be reported as **SQL_LONGVARCHAR**, **SQL_LONGVARBINARY**, or **SQL_LONGVARGRAPHIC**.

■ Some columns that may be returned by the **SQLStatistics()** function are not returned by this function. For example, this function does not return columns in an index that was created from an expression or filter (for example, **SALARY + BENEFITS** or **DEPT = 0012**).

Prerequisites   There are no prerequisites for using this function call.

Restrictions   There are no restrictions associated with this function call.

See Also   SQLTables(), SQLColumnPrivileges(), SQLSpecialColumns()

Example   The following Visual C++ program illustrates how to use the **SQLColumns()** function to obtain information about the columns that are available in a data source.

```
/*-----------------------------------------------------------------*/
/* NAME:     CH14EX3.CPP                                           */
/* PURPOSE: Illustrate How To Use The Following CLI API Function   */
/*          In A C++ Program:                                      */
/*                                                                 */
/*               SQLColumns()                                      */
/*                                                                 */
/* OTHER CLI APIs SHOWN:                                           */
```

```
/*          SQLAllocHandle()          SQLSetEnvAttr()              */
/*          SQLConnect()              SQLBindCol()                 */
/*          SQLFetch()                SQLDisconnect()              */
/*          SQLFreeHandle()                                        */
/*                                                                 */
/*----------------------------------------------------------------*/

// Include The Appropriate Header Files
#include <windows.h>
#include <sqlcli1.h>
#include <iostream.h>

// Define The CLI_Class Class
class CLI_Class
{
    // Attributes
    public:
        SQLHANDLE   EnvHandle;
        SQLHANDLE   ConHandle;
        SQLHANDLE   StmtHandle;
        SQLRETURN   rc;

    // Operations
    public:
        CLI_Class();                           // Constructor
        ~CLI_Class();                          // Destructor
        SQLRETURN   ShowColumnInfo();
};

// Define The Class Constructor
CLI_Class::CLI_Class()
{
    // Initialize The Return Code Variable
    rc = SQL_SUCCESS;

    // Allocate An Environment Handle
    rc = SQLAllocHandle(SQL_HANDLE_ENV, SQL_NULL_HANDLE, &EnvHandle);

    // Set The ODBC Application Version To 3.x
    if (rc == SQL_SUCCESS)
        rc = SQLSetEnvAttr(EnvHandle, SQL_ATTR_ODBC_VERSION,
                (SQLPOINTER) SQL_OV_ODBC3, SQL_IS_UINTEGER);

    // Allocate A Connection Handle
    if (rc == SQL_SUCCESS)
        rc = SQLAllocHandle(SQL_HANDLE_DBC, EnvHandle, &ConHandle);
}

// Define The Class Destructor
CLI_Class::~CLI_Class()
{
    // Free The Connection Handle
    if (ConHandle != NULL)
        SQLFreeHandle(SQL_HANDLE_DBC, ConHandle);
```

```
                // Free The Environment Handle
                if (EnvHandle != NULL)
                    SQLFreeHandle(SQL_HANDLE_ENV, EnvHandle);
        }

        // Define The ShowColumnInfo() Member Function
        SQLRETURN CLI_Class::ShowColumnInfo(void)
        {
            // Declare The Local Memory Variables
            SQLCHAR   ColumnName[129];

            // Allocate An SQL Statement Handle
            rc = SQLAllocHandle(SQL_HANDLE_STMT, ConHandle, &StmtHandle);
            if (rc == SQL_SUCCESS)
            {
                // Retrieve Information About The Columns Defined For The
                // STAFF Table In The Data Source
                rc = SQLColumns(StmtHandle, NULL, 0, NULL, 0,
                        (SQLCHAR *) "STAFF", SQL_NTS, NULL, 0);
                if (rc == SQL_SUCCESS)
                {
                    // Bind A Column In The Result Data Set Returned To
                    // An Application Variable
                    rc = SQLBindCol(StmtHandle, 4, SQL_C_CHAR, (SQLPOINTER)
                            &ColumnName, sizeof(ColumnName), NULL);

                    // Display A Header
                    cout << "Columns :" << endl << endl;

                    // While There Are Records In The Result Data Set
                    // Generated, Retrieve And Display Them
                    while (rc != SQL_NO_DATA)
                    {
                        rc = SQLFetch(StmtHandle);
                        if (rc != SQL_NO_DATA && rc != SQL_ERROR)
                            cout << ColumnName << endl;
                    }
                }

                // Free The SQL Statement Handle
                if (StmtHandle != NULL)
                    SQLFreeHandle(SQL_HANDLE_STMT, StmtHandle);
            }

            // Return The CLI API Return Code To The Calling Function
            return(rc);
        }

/*-----------------------------------------------------------*/
/* The Main Function                                         */
/*-----------------------------------------------------------*/
int main()
{
    // Declare The Local Memory Variables
    SQLRETURN   rc = SQL_SUCCESS;
```

```
// Create An Instance Of The CLI_Class Class
CLI_Class  Example;

// Connect To The DB2 Sample Database
if (Example.ConHandle != NULL)
{
    rc = SQLConnect(Example.ConHandle, (SQLCHAR *) "SAMPLE",
            SQL_NTS, (SQLCHAR *) "userid", SQL_NTS,
            (SQLCHAR *) "password", SQL_NTS);

        // Call The ShowColumnInfo() Member Function
        if (rc == SQL_SUCCESS || rc == SQL_SUCCESS_WITH_INFO)
            Example.ShowColumnInfo();

        // Disconnect From The DB2 Sample Database
        rc = SQLDisconnect(Example.ConHandle);
}

// Return To The Operating System
return(rc);
}
```

SQLColumnPrivileges

COMPATIBILITY

X/OPEN 95 CLI	ISO/IEC 92 CLI	DB2 CLI 5.2	DB2 CLI 2.0	ODBC 3.x
☐	☐	✓	✓	✓

ODBC API CONFORMANCE LEVEL   LEVEL 2

Purpose   The `SQLColumnPrivileges()` function is used to retrieve, for a specified table, a list of column names and their associated privileges.

Syntax

```
SQLRETURN   SQLColumnPrivileges    (SQLHSTMT        StatementHandle,
                                    SQLCHAR         *CatalogName,
                                    SQLSMALLINT     CatalogNameSize,
                                    SQLCHAR         *SchemaName,
                                    SQLSMALLINT     SchemaNameSize,
                                    SQLCHAR         *TableName,
                                    SQLSMALLINT     TableNameSize,
                                    SQLCHAR         *ColumnName,
                                    SQLSMALLINT     ColumnNameSize);
```

Parameters   *StatementHandle*   An SQL statement handle that refers to a previously allocated SQL statement information storage buffer (data structure).

CatalogName	A pointer to a location in memory where the catalog qualifier portion of a three-part table name is stored. Since DB2 CLI does not support three-part names, this parameter must contain either a NULL pointer or a zero length string.
CatalogNameSize	The length of the catalog qualifier name value stored in the *CatalogName* parameter. Since DB2 CLI does not support three-part names, this parameter must be set to 0.
SchemaName	A pointer to a location in memory where the schema portion of a three-part table name is stored.
SchemaNameSize	The length of the schema name value stored in the *SchemaName* parameter.
TableName	A pointer to a location in memory where the table name portion of a three-part table name is stored.
TableNameSize	The length of the table name value stored in the *TableName* parameter.
ColumnName	A pointer to a location in memory where a column name search pattern is stored.
ColumnNameSize	The length of the column name search pattern value stored in the *ColumnName* parameter.

Description   The `SQLColumnPrivileges()` function is used to retrieve a list of column names and the privileges associated with them for a specified table. The information returned by this function is placed in a result data set, which can be processed by using the same CLI functions that are used to process result data sets generated by SQL queries. Table 14–6 lists the columns in this result data set.

Table 14–6   Result Data Set Returned by `SQLColumnPrivileges()`

Column Number	Column Name	Data Type	Description
1	TABLE_CAT	VARCHAR(128)	The name of the catalog (qualifier) containing the TABLE_SCHEM value. Since DB2 CLI does not support three-part table names, this column is always set to NULL.
2	TABLE_SCHEM	VARCHAR(128)	The name of the schema containing the TABLE_NAME value.
3	TABLE_NAME	VARCHAR(128) NOT NULL	The name of the table or view.
4	COLUMN_NAME	VARCHAR(128) NOT NULL	The name of a column in the table or view identified in the TABLE_NAME column. This column contains an empty string (" ") for columns without a name.

Table 14–6   Result Data Set Returned by **SQLColumnPrivileges()**   (Continued)

Column Number	Column Name	Data Type	Description
5	GRANTOR	VARCHAR(128)	The name or authorization ID of the user granting the privilege.
6	GRANTEE	VARCHAR(128) NOT NULL	The name or authorization ID of the user to whom the privilege was granted.
7	PRIVILEGE	VARCHAR(128) NOT NULL	The column privilege that was granted. Valid values for this column are: "SELECT" The GRANTEE is permitted to retrieve data from the column. "INSERT" The GRANTEE is permitted to provide data for the column when inserting new rows of data into the associated table. "UPDATE:" The GRANTEE is permitted to modify the data in the column. "REFERENCES:" The GRANTEE is permitted to reference the column in a constraint (for example, a unique, referential, or table check constraint).
8	IS_GRANTABLE	VARCHAR(3)	Indicates whether the GRANTEE is permitted to grant the PRIVILEGE to other users. Valid values for this column are: "YES" "NO" NULL: Unknown or not applicable to the data source. A PRIVILEGE can be either grantable or not grantable, but not both.

(Adapted from table 34 on pages 250-251 of *IBM DB2 Universal Database Call Level Interface Guide and Reference*.)

Return Codes   SQL_SUCCESS, SQL_SUCCESS_WITH_INFO, SQL_STILL_EXECUTING, SQL_INVALID_HANDLE, SQL_ERROR

SQLSTATEs   If this function returns SQL_SUCCESS_WITH_INFO or SQL_ERROR, one of the following SQLSTATE values may be obtained by calling the SQLGetDiagRec() function:

08S01, 24000, 40001, 40003, HY001, HY008, HY009, HY010, HY014, HY090, HYC00, or HYT00

Refer to Appendix B for detailed information about each SQLSTATE value that can be returned.

Comments

■ Because this function, in many cases, maps to a complex—and therefore, expensive query against a data source's system catalog tables, it should be used sparingly. If the result data set produced is to be used more than once, it should be saved, rather than be regenerated each time it is needed.

■ An empty string (" ") can be stored in the memory location the *SchemaName* parameter refers to for schemas without names.

■ The *TableName* parameter can not contain to a NULL pointer.

■ If the **SQL_ATTR_METADATA_ID** attribute for the SQL statement is set to **SQL_TRUE**, the values specified for the *CatalogName*, *SchemaName*, *TableName*, and *ColumnName* parameters are treated as identifier values and their case is insignificant. However, if the **SQL_ATTR_METADATA_ID** attribute is set to **SQL_FALSE**, the values specified for the *CatalogName*, *SchemaName*, *TableName*, and *ColumnName* parameters are treated literally, and their case is significant. Refer to the "Parameters (Arguments) Used In Catalog Functions" section earlier in this chapter and to the **SQLGetStmtAttr()** function for more information.

■ The value specified for the *ColumnName* parameter can contain the following search pattern values:

    ■ The underscore character (_)
    Any single character can be used in place of the underscore character.

    ■ The percent character (%)
    Any sequence of 0 or more characters can be used in place of the percent character.

    ■ An escape character.
    A driver-specific character used to treat an underscore character, a percent character, and/or the escape character itself as a literal value instead of as a wild card value (that is, % = "%").

■ The result data set returned by this function is ordered by **TABLE_CAT**, **TABLE_SCHEM**, **TABLE_NAME**, **COLUMN_NAME**, and **PRIVILEGE**.

■ The actual amount of memory needed to store the value found in each **VARCHAR** column in the result data set that is produced by this function is dependent on the data source. An application can choose to set aside 128 characters (plus the NULL-terminator) for **VARCHAR** columns (to be consistent with the SQL92 standard limits), or alternatively, to allocate the actual amount of memory required by first calling the **SQLGetInfo()** function with the *InfoType* parameter set to **SQL_MAX_CATALOG_NAME_LEN**, **SQL_MAX_SCHEMA_NAME_LEN**, **SQL_MAX_TABLE_NAME_LEN**, and/or **SQL_MAX_COLUMN_NAME_LEN** to determine respectively the actual lengths of the **TABLE_CAT**, **TABLE_SCHEM**, **TABLE_NAME**, and **COLUMN_NAME** columns that are supported by the current data source.

Prerequisites   There are no prerequisites for using this function call.

Restrictions   There are no restrictions associated with this function call.

See Also   SQLColumns(), SQLTables()

Example   The following Visual C++ program illustrates how to use the SQLColumnPrivileges()
function to obtain information about the privileges associated with the columns that are
available in a data source.

```
/*————————————————————————————————————————————————————*/
/* NAME:    CH14EX4.CPP                                          */
/* PURPOSE: Illustrate How To Use The Following CLI API Function */
/*          In A C++ Program:                                    */
/*                                                               */
/*              SQLColumnPrivileges()                            */
/*                                                               */
/* OTHER CLI APIs SHOWN:                                         */
/*          SQLAllocHandle()            SQLSetEnvAttr()          */
/*          SQLConnect()                SQLBindCol()             */
/*          SQLFetch()                  SQLDisconnect()          */
/*          SQLFreeHandle()                                      */
/*                                                               */
/*————————————————————————————————————————————————————*/

// Include The Appropriate Header Files
#include <windows.h>
#include <sqlcli1.h>
#include <iostream.h>

// Define The CLI_Class Class
class CLI_Class
{
    // Attributes
    public:
        SQLHANDLE    EnvHandle;
        SQLHANDLE    ConHandle;
        SQLHANDLE    StmtHandle;
        SQLRETURN    rc;

    // Operations
    public:
        CLI_Class();                            // Constructor
        ~CLI_Class();                           // Destructor
        SQLRETURN    ShowColumnPrivilegeInfo();
};

// Define The Class Constructor
CLI_Class::CLI_Class()
{
    // Initialize The Return Code Variable
    rc = SQL_SUCCESS;

    // Allocate An Environment Handle
    rc = SQLAllocHandle(SQL_HANDLE_ENV, SQL_NULL_HANDLE, &EnvHandle);

    // Set The ODBC Application Version To 3.x
    if (rc == SQL_SUCCESS)
        rc = SQLSetEnvAttr(EnvHandle, SQL_ATTR_ODBC_VERSION,
                (SQLPOINTER) SQL_OV_ODBC3, SQL_IS_UINTEGER);
```

```
        // Allocate A Connection Handle
        if (rc == SQL_SUCCESS)
            rc = SQLAllocHandle(SQL_HANDLE_DBC, EnvHandle, &ConHandle);
}

// Define The Class Destructor
CLI_Class::~CLI_Class()
{
    // Free The Connection Handle
    if (ConHandle != NULL)
        SQLFreeHandle(SQL_HANDLE_DBC, ConHandle);

    // Free The Environment Handle
    if (EnvHandle != NULL)
        SQLFreeHandle(SQL_HANDLE_ENV, EnvHandle);
}

// Define The ShowColumnPrivilegeInfo() Member Function
SQLRETURN CLI_Class::ShowColumnPrivilegeInfo(void)
{
    // Declare The Local Memory Variables
    SQLCHAR   GrantorName[129];

    // Allocate An SQL Statement Handle
    rc = SQLAllocHandle(SQL_HANDLE_STMT, ConHandle, &StmtHandle);
    if (rc == SQL_SUCCESS)
    {
        // Retrieve Information About The Privileges Associated With
        // The Columns Defined For The STAFF Table In The Data
        // Source
        rc = SQLColumnPrivileges(StmtHandle, NULL, 0, NULL, 0,
                    (SQLCHAR *) "STAFF", SQL_NTS,
                    (SQLCHAR *) "%", SQL_NTS);
        if (rc == SQL_SUCCESS)
        {
            // Bind A Column In The Result Data Set Returned To
            // An Application Variable
            rc = SQLBindCol(StmtHandle, 5, SQL_C_CHAR, (SQLPOINTER)
                    &GrantorName, sizeof(GrantorName), NULL);

            // Display A Header
            cout << "Column Privilege Grantor :" << endl << endl;

            // While There Are Records In The Result Data Set
            // Generated, Retrieve And Display Them
            while (rc != SQL_NO_DATA)
            {
                rc = SQLFetch(StmtHandle);
                if (rc != SQL_NO_DATA && rc != SQL_ERROR)
                    cout << GrantorName << endl;
            }
        }

        // Free The SQL Statement Handle
        if (StmtHandle != NULL)
```

```
                    SQLFreeHandle(SQL_HANDLE_STMT, StmtHandle);
    }

    // Return The CLI API Return Code To The Calling Function
    return(rc);
}

/*---------------------------------------------------------------------*/
/* The Main Function                                                   */
/*---------------------------------------------------------------------*/
int main()
{
    // Declare The Local Memory Variables
    SQLRETURN  rc = SQL_SUCCESS;

    // Create An Instance Of The CLI_Class Class
    CLI_Class  Example;

    // Connect To The DB2 Sample Database
    if (Example.ConHandle != NULL)
    {
        rc = SQLConnect(Example.ConHandle, (SQLCHAR *) "SAMPLE",
                SQL_NTS, (SQLCHAR *) "userid", SQL_NTS,
                (SQLCHAR *) "password", SQL_NTS);

        // Call The ShowColumnPrivilegeInfo() Member Function
        if (rc == SQL_SUCCESS || rc == SQL_SUCCESS_WITH_INFO)
            Example.ShowColumnPrivilegeInfo();

        // Disconnect From The DB2 Sample Database
        rc = SQLDisconnect(Example.ConHandle);
    }

    // Return To The Operating System
    return(rc);
}
```

SQLSpecialColumns

COMPATIBILITY

X/OPEN 95 CLI	ISO/IEC 92 CLI	DB2 CLI 5.2	DB2 CLI 2.0	ODBC 3.x
☑	☑	☑	☑	☑

ODBC API CONFORMANCE LEVEL	CORE*

*IN ODBC 2.0, THIS FUNCTION WAS A LEVEL 2 API CONFORMANCE LEVEL FUNCTION

Purpose   The `SQLSpecialColumns()` function is used to retrieve unique row identifier information (that is, primary key or unique index information) for a specified table.

Syntax
```
SQLRETURN    SQLSpecialColumns   (SQLHSTMT          StatementHandle,
                                  SQLUSMALLINT      RowIdentifier,
                                  SQLCHAR           *CatalogName,
                                  SQLSMALLINT       CatalogNameSize,
                                  SQLCHAR           *SchemaName,
                                  SQLSMALLINT       SchemaNameSize,
                                  SQLCHAR           *TableName,
                                  SQLSMALLINT       TableNameSize,
                                  SQLUSMALLINT      Scope,
                                  SQLUSMALLINT      Nullable);
```

Parameters   *StatementHandle*

An SQL statement handle that refers to a previously allocated SQL statement information storage buffer (data structure).

RowIdentifier

Specifies the type of column information to return. This parameter must be set to the following value:

■ **SQL_BEST_ROWID**
Indicates that the optimal column or set of columns that can uniquely identify any row in the specified table is to be placed in the result data set produced by this function.

CatalogName

A pointer to a location in memory where the catalog qualifier portion of a three-part table name is stored. Since DB2 CLI does not support three-part names, this parameter must contain either a NULL pointer or a zero length string.

CatalogNameSize

The length of the catalog qualifier name value stored in the *CatalogName* parameter. Since DB2 CLI does not support three-part names, this parameter must be set to **0**.

SchemaName

A pointer to a location in memory where the schema portion of a three-part table name is stored.

SchemaNameSize

The length of the schema name value stored in the *SchemaName* parameter.

TableName

A pointer to a location in memory where the table name portion of a three-part table name is stored.

TableNameSize

The length of the table name value stored in the *TableName* parameter.

Scope

Specifies the minimum duration for which the unique row identifier will be valid. This parameter must be set to one of the following values:

■ **SQL_SCOPE_CURROW**
The unique row identifier is only guaranteed to be valid while positioned on that row.

■ **SQL_SCOPE_TRANSACTION**
The unique row identifier is guaranteed to be valid for the duration of the current transaction.

■ **SQL_SCOPE_SESSION**
The unique row identifier is guaranteed to be valid for the duration of the current connection (valid across transaction boundaries).

Nullable   Specifies whether special columns that can contain NULL values are returned by this function. This parameter must be set to one of the following values:

■ **SQL_NO_NULLS**
Special columns that can contain NULL values should be excluded from the result data set produced by this function.

■ **SQL_NULLABLE**
Special columns that can contain NULL values should be included in the result data set produced by this function.

Description   The **SQLSpecialColumns()** function is used to retrieve unique row identifier information (that is, primary key or unique index information) for a specified table. The information returned by this function is placed in a result data set, which can be processed by using the same CLI functions that are used to process result data sets generated by SQL queries. Table 14–7 lists the columns in this result data set.

Table 14–7   Result Data Set Returned by **SQLSpecialColumns()**

Column Number	Column Name	Data Type	Description
1	SCOPE	SMALLINT	The duration for which the name in **COLUMN_NAME** is guaranteed to point to the same row. Valid values for this column are:
			SQL_SCOPE_CURROW: The unique row identifier is guaranteed to be valid only while positioned on that row.
			SQL_SCOPE_TRANSACTION: The unique row identifier is guaranteed to be valid for the duration of the current transaction.
			SQL_SCOPE_SESSION: The unique row identifier is guaranteed to be valid for the duration of the current connection.
2	COLUMN_NAME	VARCHAR(128) NOT NULL	The name of the column that is either the table's primary key or part of the table's primary key. This column contains an empty string (" ") for columns without a name.

Table 14–7 Result Data Set Returned by **SQLSpecialColumns()** (Continued)

Column Number	Column Name	Data Type	Description
3	DATA_TYPE	SMALLINT NOT NULL	The SQL data type of the column identified in the **COLUMN_NAME** column. Valid values for this column include:

SQL_CHAR		SQL_VARCHAR
SQL_LONGVARCHAR		SQL_DECIMAL
SQL_NUMERIC		SQL_SMALLINT
SQL_INTEGER		SQL_REAL
SQL_FLOAT		SQL_DOUBLE
SQL_BIT		SQL_TINYINT
SQL_BIGINT		SQL_BINARY
SQL_VARBINARY		SQL_LONGVARBINARY
SQL_TYPE_DATE		SQL_TYPE_TIME
SQL_TYPE_TIMESTAMP		SQL_GRAPHIC
SQL_VARGRAPHIC		SQL_LONGVARGRAPHIC
SQL_BLOB		SQL_CLOB
SQL_DBCLOB		

For datetime and interval data types, this column contains the concise data type (such as **SQL_TYPE_DATE** or **SQL_INTERVAL_YEAR_TO_MONTH**, rather than the non-concise data type such as **SQL_DATETIME** or **SQL_INTERVAL**).

Column Number	Column Name	Data Type	Description
4	TYPE_NAME	VARCHAR(128) NOT NULL	The data source-specific character representation of the SQL data type name identified in the **DATA_TYPE** column. Valid values for this column include:

"CHAR"		"VARCHAR"
"LONG VARCHAR"		"DECIMAL"
"NUMERIC"		"SMALLINT"
"INTEGER"		"REAL"
"FLOAT"		"DOUBLE PRECISION"
"BIT"		"TINYINT"
"BIGINT"		"BINARY"
"VARBINARY"		"LONG VARBINARY"
"DATE"		"TIME"
"TIMESTAMP"		"GRAPHIC"
"VARGRAPHIC"		"LONGVARGRAPHIC"
"BLOB"		"CLOB"
"DBCLOB"		

Column Number	Column Name	Data Type	Description
5	COLUMN_SIZE	INTEGER	The maximum number of bytes needed to display the column data in character form. For numeric data types, this is either the total number of digits, or the total number of bits allowed in the column. For character or binary string data types, this is the size of the string (string length), in bytes.

Table 14–7   Result Data Set Returned by **SQLSpecialColumns()**   (Continued)

Column Number	Column Name	Data Type	Description
			For date, time, and timestamp data types, this is the total number of characters required to display the value when it is converted to a character string.
			For graphic data types, this is the total number of double byte characters used.
6	BUFFER_ LENGTH	INTEGER	The maximum number of bytes needed for the associated C application variable (buffer) to store data from this column if the value **SQL_C_ DEFAULT** is specified for the *CDataType* parameter of the **SQLBindParameter()**, **SQLBindCol()**, or **SQLGetData()** function. This length does not include the NULL-terminator character used by NULL terminated strings.
			For numeric data, this column may contain a number that is different from the actual size of the data stored in the data source.
			For character or binary data, this column contains the same value as the **COLUMN_SIZE** column.
7	DECIMAL_ DIGITS	SMALLINT	The total number of significant digits to the right of the decimal point.
			If the **DATA_TYPE** column contains **SQL_TYPE_TIME** or **SQL_TYPE_TIMESTAMP**, this column contains the number of digits in the fractional seconds component of the time value.
			For data types in which decimal digits are not applicable, this column is set to NULL.
			For all other data types, this column contains the decimal digits of the column on the data source.
8	PSEUDO_ COLUMN	SMALLINT	Indicates whether the column is a pseudo-column. Valid values for this column are:
			SQL_PC_NOT_PSEUDO: The column is not a pseudo-column
			For maximum interoperability, pseudo-columns should not be quoted with the identifier quote character returned by the **SQLGetInfo()** function.

(Adapted from table 172 on pages 609–610 of *IBM DB2 Universal Database Call Level Interface Guide and Reference*.)

If multiple ways exist to uniquely identify any row in the specified table (for example, if there are multiple unique indexes defined for the specified table), this function retrieves the best set of row identifier column data, based on the data source's internal selection criteria.

The **SQLColumns()** function, which is used to return a variety of information on table columns, does not necessarily return columns that uniquely identify each row or columns that are automatically updated when any value in the row is updated by a transaction. Therefore, some columns returned by the **SQLColumns()** function cannot be used in a select-list or **WHERE** clause. When the **SQLSpecialColumns()** function is called, all column(s) returned can be used in a select-list or **WHERE** clause.

Return Codes SQL_SUCCESS, SQL_SUCCESS_WITH_INFO, SQL_STILL_EXECUTING, SQL_INVALID_HANDLE, SQL_ERROR

SQLSTATEs If this function returns **SQL_SUCCESS_WITH_INFO** or **SQL_ERROR**, one of the following SQLSTATE values may be obtained by calling the **SQLGetDiagRec()** function:

08S01, **24000**, **40003**, **HY001**, **HY008**, **HY009**, **HY010**, **HY014**, **HY090**, **HY097**, **HY098**, **HY099**, **HYC00**, or **HYT00**

Refer to Appendix B for detailed information about each SQLSTATE value that can be returned.

Comments
- Because this function, in many cases, maps to a complex—and therefore, expensive query against a data source's system catalog tables, it should be used sparingly. If the result data set produced is to be used more than once, it should be saved, rather than be regenerated each time it is needed.

- An empty string (" ") can be stored in the memory location the *SchemaName* parameter refers to for schemas without names.

- The *TableName* parameter cannot contain a NULL pointer.

- If the **SQL_ATTR_METADATA_ID** attribute for the statement handle specified is set to **SQL_TRUE**, the values specified for the *CatalogName*, *SchemaName*, and *TableName* parameters are treated as identifier values and their case is insignificant. However, if the **SQL_ATTR_METADATA_ID** attribute is set to **SQL_FALSE**, the values specified for the *CatalogName*, *SchemaName*, and *TableName* parameters are treated literally, and their case is significant. Refer to the "Parameters (Arguments) Used In Catalog Functions" section earlier in this chapter and to the **SQLGetStmtAttr()** function for more information.

- If the *RowIdentifier*, *Scope*, or *Nullable* parameters specify characteristics that are not supported by the data source, this function returns an empty result data set.

- If no unique row identifier information exists (that is, no primary key or unique index has been defined) for the table specified, this function returns an empty result data set.

- The result data set returned by this function is ordered by **SCOPE**.

- The duration for which a unique row identifier value is guaranteed to be valid is dependent on the isolation level being used by the current transaction. Refer to Chapter 2, "Database Consistency Mechanisms," for more information about transaction isolation levels.

■ The columns returned in the result data set produced by this function can be used by applications that need to scroll forward and backward within a result data set to retrieve the most recent data from a set of rows. This is because the column or columns of the row identifier are guaranteed not to change while the cursor is positioned on that row.

■ The column or columns of a row identifier may remain valid even when the cursor is not positioned on a row. An application can determine how long a row identifier remains valid by checking the **SCOPE** column in the result data set produced by this function.

■ An application can use the columns returned in the result data set produced by this function to reselect a row within the defined scope. A **SELECT** SQL statement is guaranteed to return either no rows or one row. If an application reselects a row based on the row identifier column or columns and the row is not found, the application can assume the row was deleted or the row identifier column(s) were modified. The opposite is not true—even if the row identifier column(s) have not been modified, other columns in the row may have changed.

■ The actual amount of memory needed to store the value found in each **VARCHAR** column in the result data set that is produced by this function is dependent on the data source. An application can choose to set aside 128 characters (plus the NULL-terminator) for **VARCHAR** columns (to be consistent with the SQL92 standard limits), or alternatively, to allocate the actual amount of memory required by first calling the **SQLGetInfo()** function with the *InfoType* parameter set to **SQL_MAX_COLUMN_NAME_LEN** to determine the actual length of the **COLUMN_NAME** column that is supported by the current data source.

Prerequisites   There are no prerequisites for using this function call.

Restrictions   There are no restrictions associated with this function call.

See Also   SQLColumns(), SQLTables(), SQLStatistics()

Example   The following Visual C++ program illustrates how to use the **SQLSpecialColumns()** function to obtain information about the unique row identifier columns that exist in a data source.

```
/*------------------------------------------------------------------*/
/* NAME:     CH14EX5.CPP                                            */
/* PURPOSE: Illustrate How To Use The Following CLI API Function    */
/*          In A C++ Program:                                       */
/*                                                                  */
/*              SQLSpecialColumns()                                 */
/*                                                                  */
/* OTHER CLI APIs SHOWN:                                            */
/*          SQLAllocHandle()              SQLSetEnvAttr()           */
/*          SQLConnect()                  SQLBindCol()              */
/*          SQLFetch()                    SQLDisconnect()           */
/*          SQLFreeHandle()                                         */
/*                                                                  */
/*------------------------------------------------------------------*/
```

```cpp
// Include The Appropriate Header Files
#include <windows.h>
#include <sqlcli1.h>
#include <iostream.h>

// Define The CLI_Class Class
class CLI_Class
{
    // Attributes
    public:
        SQLHANDLE    EnvHandle;
        SQLHANDLE    ConHandle;
        SQLHANDLE    StmtHandle;
        SQLRETURN    rc;

    // Operations
    public:
        CLI_Class();                                // Constructor
        ~CLI_Class();                               // Destructor
        SQLRETURN  ShowSpecialColumnInfo();
};

// Define The Class Constructor
CLI_Class::CLI_Class()
{
    // Initialize The Return Code Variable
    rc = SQL_SUCCESS;

    // Allocate An Environment Handle
    rc = SQLAllocHandle(SQL_HANDLE_ENV, SQL_NULL_HANDLE, &EnvHandle);

    // Set The ODBC Application Version To 3.x
    if (rc == SQL_SUCCESS)
        rc = SQLSetEnvAttr(EnvHandle, SQL_ATTR_ODBC_VERSION,
                 (SQLPOINTER) SQL_OV_ODBC3, SQL_IS_UINTEGER);

    // Allocate A Connection Handle
    if (rc == SQL_SUCCESS)
        rc = SQLAllocHandle(SQL_HANDLE_DBC, EnvHandle, &ConHandle);
}

// Define The Class Destructor
CLI_Class::~CLI_Class()
{
    // Free The Connection Handle
    if (ConHandle != NULL)
        SQLFreeHandle(SQL_HANDLE_DBC, ConHandle);

    // Free The Environment Handle
    if (EnvHandle != NULL)
        SQLFreeHandle(SQL_HANDLE_ENV, EnvHandle);
}

// Define The ShowSpecialColumnInfo() Member Function
SQLRETURN CLI_Class::ShowSpecialColumnInfo(void)
```

```cpp
{
    // Declare The Local Memory Variables
    SQLCHAR  ColumnName[129];

    // Allocate An SQL Statement Handle
    rc = SQLAllocHandle(SQL_HANDLE_STMT, ConHandle, &StmtHandle);
    if (rc == SQL_SUCCESS)
    {
        // Retrieve Information About The Special Columns Associated
        // The EMPLOYEE Table In The Data Source
        rc = SQLSpecialColumns(StmtHandle, SQL_BEST_ROWID, NULL, 0,
                    NULL, 0, (SQLCHAR *) "EMPLOYEE", SQL_NTS,
                    SQL_SCOPE_CURROW, SQL_NULLABLE);
        if (rc == SQL_SUCCESS)
        {
            // Bind A Column In The Result Data Set Returned To
            // An Application Variable
            rc = SQLBindCol(StmtHandle, 2, SQL_C_CHAR, (SQLPOINTER)
                    &ColumnName, sizeof(ColumnName), NULL);

            // Display A Header
            cout << "Special Columns For The Employee Table :";
            cout << endl << endl;

            // While There Are Records In The Result Data Set
            // Generated, Retrieve And Display Them
            while (rc != SQL_NO_DATA)
            {
                rc = SQLFetch(StmtHandle);
                if (rc != SQL_NO_DATA && rc != SQL_ERROR)
                    cout << ColumnName << endl;
            }
        }

        // Free The SQL Statement Handle
        if (StmtHandle != NULL)
            SQLFreeHandle(SQL_HANDLE_STMT, StmtHandle);
    }

    // Return The CLI API Return Code To The Calling Function
    return(rc);
}

/*───────────────────────────────────────────────────────────────*/
/* The Main Function                                              */
/*──────────────────────────────────────────────────────────────-*/
int main()
{
    // Declare The Local Memory Variables
    SQLRETURN  rc = SQL_SUCCESS;

    // Create An Instance Of The CLI_Class Class
    CLI_Class  Example;
```

```
                         // Connect To The DB2 Sample Database
                         if (Example.ConHandle != NULL)
                         {
                             rc = SQLConnect(Example.ConHandle, (SQLCHAR *) "SAMPLE",
                                     SQL_NTS, (SQLCHAR *) "userid", SQL_NTS,
                                     (SQLCHAR *) "password", SQL_NTS);

                             // Call The ShowSpecialColumnInfo() Member Function
                             if (rc == SQL_SUCCESS || rc == SQL_SUCCESS_WITH_INFO)
                                 Example.ShowSpecialColumnInfo();

                             // Disconnect From The DB2 Sample Database
                             rc = SQLDisconnect(Example.ConHandle);
                         }

                         // Return To The Operating System
                         return(rc);
                     }
```

SQLStatistics

COMPATIBILITY

X/OPEN 95 CLI	ISO/IEC 92 CLI	DB2 CLI 5.2	DB2 CLI 2.0	ODBC 3.x
☑	☑	☑	☑	☑

ODBC API CONFORMANCE LEVEL   CORE*

*IN ODBC 2.0, THIS FUNCTION WAS A LEVEL 2 API CONFORMANCE LEVEL FUNCTION

Purpose   The SQLStatistics() function is used to retrieve statistical information about a specified table and its associated indexes.

Syntax

```
SQLRETURN    SQLStatistics    (SQLHSTMT        StatementHandle,
                               SQLCHAR         *CatalogName,
                               SQLSMALLINT     CatalogNameSize,
                               SQLCHAR         *SchemaName,
                               SQLSMALLINT     SchemaNameSize,
                               SQLCHAR         *TableName,
                               SQLSMALLINT     TableNameSize,
                               SQLUSMALLINT    IndexType,
                               SQLUSMALLINT    Accuracy);
```

Parameters   *StatementHandle*   An SQL statement handle that refers to a previously allocated SQL statement information storage buffer (data structure).

CatalogName   A pointer to a location in memory where the catalog qualifier portion of a three-part table name is stored. Since DB2 CLI does not support three-part names, this parameter must contain either a NULL pointer or a zero length string.

CatalogNameSize   The length of the catalog qualifier name value stored in the *CatalogName* parameter. Since DB2 CLI does not support three-part names, this parameter must be set to **0**.

SchemaName   A pointer to a location in memory where the schema portion of a three-part table name is stored.

SchemaNameSize   The length of the schema name value stored in the *SchemaName* parameter.

TableName   A pointer to a location in memory where the table name portion of a three-part table name is stored.

TableNameSize   The length of the table name value stored in the *TableName* parameter.

IndexType   Specifies the type of index information that is to be returned by this function. This parameter must be set to one of the following values:

■ **SQL_INDEX_UNIQUE**
  Only information pertaining to unique indexes is to be retrieved and stored in the result data set produced by this function.

■ **SQL_INDEX_ALL**
  Information about all indexes is to be retrieved and stored in the result data set produced by this function.

Accuracy   Specifies whether the **CARDINALITY** and **PAGES** columns in the result data set produced by this function are to contain the most current information. This parameter must be set to one of the following values:

■ **SQL_QUICK**
  Only information that is readily available at the database server is to be retrieved and stored in the result data set produced by this function.

■ **SQL_ENSURE**
  The most up to date information available is to be retrieved and stored in the result data set produced by this function. **New applications should not use this value.**

Description   The **SQLStatistics()** function is used to retrieve statistical information about a specified table and its associated indexes. When invoked, this function returns two types of information:

■ Statistical information about the table itself (if it is available), such as:

■ The number of rows in the table.

■ The number of pages used to store the table.

■ Statistical information about each index defined for the specified table, such as:

■ The number of unique values in an index.

■ The number of pages used to store the table's indexes.

The information returned by this function is placed in a result data set that can be processed by using the same CLI functions that are used to process result data sets generated by SQL queries. Table 14–8 lists the columns in this result data set.

Table 14–8   Result Data Set Returned by **SQLStatistics()**

Column Number	Column Name	Data Type	Description
1	**TABLE_CAT**	VARCHAR(128)	The name of the catalog (qualifier) containing the **TABLE_SCHEM** value. Since DB2 CLI does not support three-part table names, this column is always set to NULL.
2	**TABLE_SCHEM**	VARCHAR(128)	The name of the schema containing the **TABLE_NAME** value.
3	**TABLE_NAME**	VARCHAR(128) NOT NULL	The name of the table to which the statistic or index applies.
4	**NON_UNIQUE**	SMALLINT	Indicates whether the index prohibits or allows duplicate values. Valid values for this column are: **SQL_TRUE**: The index allows duplicate values. **SQL_FALSE**: The index values must be unique. **NULL**: The **TYPE** column indicates that this row is an **SQL_TABLE_STAT** row (that is, it contains statistics information on the table itself).
5	**INDEX_ QUALIFIER**	VARCHAR(128)	The character string that would be used to qualify the index name in a **DROP INDEX** SQL statement. If an index qualifier is not supported by the data source or if the **TYPE** column indicates that this row is an **SQL_TABLE_STAT** row (that is, it contains statistics information on the table itself), this column is set to NULL. If a non-NULL value is returned in this column, it must be used to qualify the index name on a **DROP INDEX** SQL statement; otherwise the value in the **TABLE_SCHEM** column should be used.

Table 14-8 Result Data Set Returned by **SQLStatistics()** (Continued)

Column Number	Column Name	Data Type	Description
6	INDEX_NAME	VARCHAR(128)	The name of the index.
			If the **TYPE** column indicates that this row is an **SQL_TABLE_STAT** row (that is, it contains statistics information on the table itself), this column is set to NULL.
7	TYPE	SMALLINT NOT NULL	Identifies the type of information contained in the current row of this result data set. Valid values for this column are:
			SQL_TABLE_STAT: The current row of this result data set contains statistic information on the table itself.
			SQL_INDEX_CLUSTERED: The current row of this result data set contains information on a clustered index.
			SQL_INDEX_HASHED: The current row of this result data set contains information on a hashed index.
			SQL_INDEX_OTHER: The current row of this result data set contains information on some other type of index.
8	ORDINAL_ POSITION	SMALLINT	The column's (whose name is stored in the **INDEX_NAME** column) sequence number in the index. The first column in the index is number 1, the second column is number 2, and so on. If the **TYPE** column indicates that this row is an **SQL_TABLE_STAT** row (that is, it contains statistics information on the table itself), this column is set to NULL.
9	COLUMN_NAME	VARCHAR(128)	The name of the column in the index.
			If the **TYPE** column indicates that this row is an **SQL_TABLE_STAT** row (that is, it contains statistics information on the table itself), this column is set to NULL.
10	ASC_OR_DESC	CHAR(1)	The sort sequence used to order the column's data. Valid values for this column are:
			'A': The column's data is sorted in ascending order.
			'D': The column's data is sorted in descending order.

Table 14–8 Result Data Set Returned by **SQLStatistics()** (Continued)

Column Number	Column Name	Data Type	Description
			NULL: The **TYPE** column indicates that this row is an **SQL_TABLE_STAT** row (that is, it contains statistics information on the table itself).
11	**CARDINALITY**	**INTEGER**	The number of unique values in the table or index.
			If the **TYPE** column indicates that this row is an **SQL_TABLE_STAT** row, this column contains the number of rows in the table. Otherwise, this column contains the number of unique values in the index
			If this information is not available from the data source, this column is set to NULL.
12	**PAGES**	**INTEGER**	The number of pages needed to store the table or index.
			If the **TYPE** column indicates that this row is an **SQL_TABLE_STAT** row, this column contains the number of pages used to store the table. Otherwise, this column contains the number of pages used to store the index.
			If this information is not available from the data source, this column is set to NULL.
13	**FILTER_ CONDITION**	**VARCHAR(128)**	Identifies the filter condition used if the index is a filtered index. This column contains an empty string (" ") if the filter condition cannot be determined. If the **TYPE** column indicates that this row is an **SQL_TABLE_STAT** row, if the index is not a filtered index, or if it cannot be determined whether the index is a filtered index, this column is set to NULL. Since DB2 CLI does not support filtered indexes, this column is always set to NULL.

(Adapted from table 175 on pages 615–616 of *IBM DB2 Universal Database Call Level Interface Guide and Reference*.)

Return Codes SQL_SUCCESS, SQL_SUCCESS_WITH_INFO, SQL_STILL_EXECUTING, SQL_INVALID_HANDLE, SQL_ERROR

SQLSTATEs If this function returns **SQL_SUCCESS_WITH_INFO** or **SQL_ERROR**, one of the following SQLSTATE values may be obtained by calling the **SQLGetDiagRec()** function:

08S01, **24**000, **40**003, **HY**001, **HY**008, **HY**009, **HY**010, **HY**014, **HY**090, **HY**100, **HY**101, **HY**C00, or **HY**T00

Refer to Appendix B for detailed information about each SQLSTATE value that can be returned.

Comments ■ Because this function, in many cases, maps to a complex—and therefore, expensive query against a data source's system catalog tables, it should be used sparingly. If the result data set produced is to be used more than once, it should be saved, rather than be regenerated each time it is needed.

■ An empty string (" ") can be stored in the memory location to which the *SchemaName* parameter refers to for schemas without names.

■ The *TableName* parameter cannot contain to a NULL pointer.

■ If the `SQL_ATTR_METADATA_ID` attribute for the statement handle specified is set to `SQL_TRUE`, the values specified for the *CatalogName*, *SchemaName*, and *TableName* parameters are treated as identifier values and their case is insignificant. However, if the `SQL_ATTR_METADATA_ID` attribute is set to `SQL_FALSE`, the values specified for the *CatalogName*, *SchemaName*, and *TableName* parameters are treated literally, and their case is significant. Refer to the "Parameters (Arguments) Used in Catalog Functions" section earlier in this chapter and to the `SQLGetStmtAttr()` function for more information.

■ The result data set returned by this function is ordered by `NON_UNIQUE`, `TYPE`, `INDEX_QUALIFIER`, `INDEX_NAME`, and `ORDINAL_POSITION`.

■ The actual amount of memory needed to store the value found in each `VARCHAR` column in the result data set produced by this function is dependent on the data source. An application can choose to set aside 128 characters (plus the NULL-terminator) for `VARCHAR` columns (to be consistent with the SQL92 standard limits), or alternatively, to allocate the actual amount of memory required by first calling the `SQLGetInfo()` function with the *InfoType* parameter set to `SQL_MAX_CATALOG_NAME_LEN`, `SQL_MAX_SCHEMA_NAME_LEN`, `SQL_MAX_TABLE_NAME_LEN`, and/or `SQL_MAX_COLUMN_NAME_LEN` to determine respectively the actual lengths of the `TABLE_CAT`, `TABLE_SCHEM`, `TABLE_NAME`, and `COLUMN_NAME` columns that are supported by the current data source.

Prerequisites There are no prerequisites for using this function call.

Restrictions There are no restrictions associated with this function call.

See Also `SQLColumns()`, `SQLSpecialColumns()`

Example The following Visual C++ program illustrates how to use the `SQLStatistics()` function to obtain information about the indexes that are available in a data source.

```
/*-----------------------------------------------------------*/
/* NAME:     CH14EX6.CPP                                     */
/* PURPOSE: Illustrate How To Use The Following CLI API Function */
/*          In A C++ Program:                                */
/*                                                           */
/*              SQLStatistics()                              */
/*                                                           */
/* OTHER CLI APIs SHOWN:                                     */
/*              SQLAllocHandle()          SQLSetEnvAttr()     */
/*              SQLConnect()              SQLBindCol()        */
/*              SQLFetch()                SQLDisconnect()     */
```

```
/*              SQLFreeHandle()                                    */
/*                                                                 */
/*───────────────────────────────────────────────────────────────*/

// Include The Appropriate Header Files
#include <windows.h>
#include <sqlcli1.h>
#include <iostream.h>

// Define The CLI_Class Class
class CLI_Class
{
    // Attributes
    public:
        SQLHANDLE    EnvHandle;
        SQLHANDLE    ConHandle;
        SQLHANDLE    StmtHandle;
        SQLRETURN    rc;

    // Operations
    public:
        CLI_Class();                            // Constructor
        ~CLI_Class();                           // Destructor
        SQLRETURN   ShowStatisticsInfo();
};

// Define The Class Constructor
CLI_Class::CLI_Class()
{
    // Initialize The Return Code Variable
    rc = SQL_SUCCESS;

    // Allocate An Environment Handle
    rc = SQLAllocHandle(SQL_HANDLE_ENV, SQL_NULL_HANDLE, &EnvHandle);

    // Set The ODBC Application Version To 3.x
    if (rc == SQL_SUCCESS)
        rc = SQLSetEnvAttr(EnvHandle, SQL_ATTR_ODBC_VERSION,
                (SQLPOINTER) SQL_OV_ODBC3, SQL_IS_UINTEGER);

    // Allocate A Connection Handle
    if (rc == SQL_SUCCESS)
        rc = SQLAllocHandle(SQL_HANDLE_DBC, EnvHandle, &ConHandle);
}

// Define The Class Destructor
CLI_Class::~CLI_Class()
{
    // Free The Connection Handle
    if (ConHandle != NULL)
        SQLFreeHandle(SQL_HANDLE_DBC, ConHandle);

    // Free The Environment Handle
    if (EnvHandle != NULL)
```

```cpp
        SQLFreeHandle(SQL_HANDLE_ENV, EnvHandle);
}

// Define The ShowStatisticsInfo() Member Function
SQLRETURN CLI_Class::ShowStatisticsInfo(void)
{
    // Declare The Local Memory Variables
    SQLCHAR  IndexName[129];

    // Allocate An SQL Statement Handle
    rc = SQLAllocHandle(SQL_HANDLE_STMT, ConHandle, &StmtHandle);
    if (rc == SQL_SUCCESS)
    {
        // Retrieve Information About The Indexes Defined For The
        // EMPLOYEE Table In The Data Source
        rc = SQLStatistics(StmtHandle, NULL, 0, NULL, 0,
                (SQLCHAR *) "EMPLOYEE", SQL_NTS,
                SQL_INDEX_ALL, SQL_QUICK);
        if (rc == SQL_SUCCESS)
        {
            // Bind A Column In The Result Data Set Returned To
            // An Application Variable
            rc = SQLBindCol(StmtHandle, 6, SQL_C_CHAR, (SQLPOINTER)
                    &IndexName, sizeof(IndexName), NULL);

            // Display A Header
            cout << "Indexes For The Employee Table :" << endl;
            cout << endl;

            // While There Are Records In The Result Data Set
            // Generated, Retrieve And Display Them
            while (rc != SQL_NO_DATA)
            {
                rc = SQLFetch(StmtHandle);
                if (rc != SQL_NO_DATA && rc != SQL_ERROR)
                    cout << IndexName << endl;
            }
        }

        // Free The SQL Statement Handle
        if (StmtHandle != NULL)
            SQLFreeHandle(SQL_HANDLE_STMT, StmtHandle);
    }

    // Return The CLI API Return Code To The Calling Function
    return(rc);
}

/*----------------------------------------------------------------*/
/* The Main Function                                              */
/*----------------------------------------------------------------*/
int main()
{
    // Declare The Local Memory Variables
    SQLRETURN  rc = SQL_SUCCESS;
```

```
            // Create An Instance Of The CLI_Class Class
            CLI_Class  Example;

            // Connect To The DB2 Sample Database
            if (Example.ConHandle != NULL)
            {
                rc = SQLConnect(Example.ConHandle, (SQLCHAR *) "SAMPLE",
                        SQL_NTS, (SQLCHAR *) "userid", SQL_NTS,
                        (SQLCHAR *) "password", SQL_NTS);

                // Call The ShowStatisticsInfo() Member Function
                if (rc == SQL_SUCCESS || rc == SQL_SUCCESS_WITH_INFO)
                    Example.ShowStatisticsInfo();

                // Disconnect From The DB2 Sample Database
                rc = SQLDisconnect(Example.ConHandle);
            }

            // Return To The Operating System
            return(rc);
        }
```

SQLPrimaryKeys

COMPATIBILITY

X/OPEN 95 CLI	ISO/IEC 92 CLI	DB2 CLI 5.2	DB2 CLI 2.0	ODBC 3.x
☐	☐	☑	☑	☑

ODBC API CONFORMANCE LEVEL   LEVEL 1*

*IN ODBC 2.0, THIS FUNCTION WAS A LEVEL 2 API CONFORMANCE LEVEL FUNCTION

Purpose   The SQLPrimaryKeys() function is used to retrieve the list of column names that make up the primary key for a specified table.

Syntax

```
SQLRETURN   SQLPrimaryKeys  (SQLHSTMT       StatementHandle,
                             SQLCHAR        *CatalogName,
                             SQLSMALLINT    CatalogNameSize,
                             SQLCHAR        *SchemaName,
                             SQLSMALLINT    SchemaNameSize,
                             SQLCHAR        *TableName,
                             SQLSMALLINT    TableNameSize);
```

Parameters   *StatementHandle*   An SQL statement handle that refers to a previously allocated SQL statement information storage buffer (data structure).

CatalogName	A pointer to a location in memory where the catalog qualifier portion of a three-part table name is stored. Since DB2 CLI does not support three-part names, this parameter must contain either a NULL pointer or a zero length string.
CatalogNameSize	The length of the catalog qualifier name value stored in the *CatalogName* parameter. Since DB2 CLI does not support three-part names, this parameter must be set to 0.
SchemaName	A pointer to a location in memory where the schema portion of a three-part table name is stored.
SchemaNameSize	The length of the schema name value stored in the *SchemaName* parameter.
TableName	A pointer to a location in memory where the table name portion of a three-part table name is stored.
TableNameSize	The length of the table name value stored in the *TableName* parameter.

Description The **SQLPrimaryKeys()** function is used to retrieve the list of column names that make up the primary key for a specified table. The information returned by this function is placed in a result data set, which can be processed by using the same CLI functions that are used to process result data sets generated by SQL queries. Table 14–9 lists the columns in this result data set.

Table 14–9 Result Data Set Returned by **SQLPrimaryKeys()**

Column Number	Column Name	Data Type	Description
1	TABLE_CAT	VARCHAR(128)	The name of the catalog (qualifier) containing the **TABLE_SCHEM** value. Since DB2 CLI does not support three-part table names, this column is always set to NULL.
2	TABLE_SCHEM	VARCHAR(128)	The name of the schema containing the **TABLE_NAME** value.
3	TABLE_NAME	VARCHAR(128) NOT NULL	The name of the table containing the primary key.
4	COLUMN_NAME	VARCHAR(128) NOT NULL	The name of the primary key column in the table identified in the **TABLE_NAME** column. This column contains an empty string (" ") for columns without a name.
5	ORDINAL_ POSITION	SMALLINT NOT NULL	The column's sequence number in the primary key. The first column in the primary key is number 1, the second column is number 2, and so on.
6	PK_NAME	VARCHAR(128)	The name (identifier) of the primary key. This column is set to NULL if a primary key name is not applicable for the data source.

(Adapted from table 134 on page 493 of *IBM DB2 Universal Database Call Level Interface Guide and Reference*.)

Return Codes   SQL_SUCCESS, SQL_SUCCESS_WITH_INFO, SQL_STILL_EXECUTING, SQL_INVALID_HANDLE, SQL_ERROR

SQLSTATEs   If this function returns **SQL_SUCCESS_WITH_INFO** or **SQL_ERROR**, one of the following SQLSTATE values may be obtained by calling the **SQLGetDiagRec()** function:

08S01, 24000, 40003, **HY**001, **HY**008, **HY**010, **HY**014, **HY**090, **HY**C00, or **HY**T00

Refer to Appendix B for detailed information about each SQLSTATE value that can be returned.

Comments   ▪ Because this function, in many cases, maps to a complex—and therefore, expensive query against a data source's system catalog tables, it should be used sparingly. If the result data set produced is to be used more than once, it should be saved, rather than be regenerated each time it is needed.

▪ An empty string (" ") can be stored in the memory location the *SchemaName* parameter refers to for schemas without names.

▪ If the **SQL_ATTR_METADATA_ID** attribute for the statement handle specified is set to **SQL_TRUE**, the values specified for the *CatalogName*, *SchemaName*, and *TableName* parameters are treated as identifier values and their case is insignificant. However, if the **SQL_ATTR_METADATA_ID** attribute is set to **SQL_FALSE**, the values specified for the *CatalogName*, *SchemaName*, and *TableName* parameters are treated literally, and their case is significant. Refer to the "Parameters (Arguments) Used in Catalog Functions" section earlier in this chapter and to the **SQLGetStmtAttr()** function for more information.

▪ The *TableName* parameter cannot contain a NULL pointer.

▪ The result data set returned by this function is ordered by **TABLE_CAT**, **TABLE_SCHEM**, **TABLE_NAME**, and **ORDINAL_POSITION**.

▪ The actual amount of memory needed to store the value found in each **VARCHAR** column in the result data set that is produced by this function is dependent on the data source. An application can choose to set aside 128 characters (plus the NULL-terminator) for **VARCHAR** columns (to be consistent with the SQL92 standard limits), or alternatively, to allocate the actual amount of memory required by first calling the **SQLGetInfo()** function with the *InfoType* parameter set to **SQL_MAX_CATALOG_NAME_LEN**, **SQL_MAX_SCHEMA_NAME_LEN**, **SQL_MAX_TABLE_NAME_LEN**, and/or **SQL_MAX_COLUMN_NAME_LEN** to determine respectively the actual lengths of the **TABLE_CAT**, **TABLE_SCHEM**, **TABLE_NAME**, and **COLUMN_NAME** columns that are supported by the current data source.

Prerequisites   There are no prerequisites for using this function call.

Restrictions   There are no restrictions associated with this function call.

See Also   SQLForeignKeys(), SQLStatistics()

Example   The following Visual C++ program illustrates how to use the **SQLPrimaryKeys()** function to obtain information about the columns that comprise the primary keys for a specified table.

```
/*—————————————————————————————————*/
/* NAME:     CH14EX7.CPP                                           */
/* PURPOSE: Illustrate How To Use The Following CLI API Function   */
/*          In A C++ Program:                                      */
/*                                                                 */
/*              SQLPrimaryKeys()                                   */
/*                                                                 */
/* OTHER CLI APIs SHOWN:                                           */
/*          SQLAllocHandle()            SQLSetEnvAttr()            */
/*          SQLConnect()                SQLBindCol()               */
/*          SQLFetch()                  SQLDisconnect()            */
/*          SQLFreeHandle()                                        */
/*                                                                 */
/*—————————————————————————————————*/

// Include The Appropriate Header Files
#include <windows.h>
#include <sqlcli1.h>
#include <iostream.h>

// Define The CLI_Class Class
class CLI_Class
{
    // Attributes
    public:
        SQLHANDLE    EnvHandle;
        SQLHANDLE    ConHandle;
        SQLHANDLE    StmtHandle;
        SQLRETURN    rc;

    // Operations
    public:
        CLI_Class();                              // Constructor
        ~CLI_Class();                             // Destructor
        SQLRETURN  ShowPrimaryKeyInfo();
};

// Define The Class Constructor
CLI_Class::CLI_Class()
{
    // Initialize The Return Code Variable
    rc = SQL_SUCCESS;

    // Allocate An Environment Handle
    rc = SQLAllocHandle(SQL_HANDLE_ENV, SQL_NULL_HANDLE, &EnvHandle);

    // Set The ODBC Application Version To 3.x
    if (rc == SQL_SUCCESS)
        rc = SQLSetEnvAttr(EnvHandle, SQL_ATTR_ODBC_VERSION,
                (SQLPOINTER) SQL_OV_ODBC3, SQL_IS_UINTEGER);

    // Allocate A Connection Handle
    if (rc == SQL_SUCCESS)
        rc = SQLAllocHandle(SQL_HANDLE_DBC, EnvHandle, &ConHandle);
}
```

```cpp
// Define The Class Destructor
CLI_Class::~CLI_Class()
{
    // Free The Connection Handle
    if (ConHandle != NULL)
        SQLFreeHandle(SQL_HANDLE_DBC, ConHandle);

    // Free The Environment Handle
    if (EnvHandle != NULL)
        SQLFreeHandle(SQL_HANDLE_ENV, EnvHandle);
}

// Define The ShowPrimaryKeyInfo() Member Function
SQLRETURN CLI_Class::ShowPrimaryKeyInfo(void)
{
    // Declare The Local Memory Variables
    SQLCHAR  PKeyName[129];

    // Allocate An SQL Statement Handle
    rc = SQLAllocHandle(SQL_HANDLE_STMT, ConHandle, &StmtHandle);
    if (rc == SQL_SUCCESS)
    {
        // Retrieve Information About The Primary Keys Defined For
        // The EMP_PHOTO Table In The Data Source
        rc = SQLPrimaryKeys(StmtHandle, NULL, 0,
                 (SQLCHAR *) "USERID", SQL_NTS,
                 (SQLCHAR *) "EMP_PHOTO", SQL_NTS);
        if (rc == SQL_SUCCESS)
        {
            // Bind A Column In The Result Data Set Returned To
            // An Application Variable
            rc = SQLBindCol(StmtHandle, 6, SQL_C_CHAR, (SQLPOINTER)
                     &PKeyName, sizeof(PKeyName), NULL);

            // Display A Header
            cout << "Primary Keys :" << endl << endl;

            // While There Are Records In The Result Data Set
            // Generated, Retrieve And Display Them
            while (rc != SQL_NO_DATA)
            {
                rc = SQLFetch(StmtHandle);
                if (rc != SQL_NO_DATA && rc != SQL_ERROR)
                    cout << PKeyName << endl;
            }
        }

        // Free The SQL Statement Handle
        if (StmtHandle != NULL)
            SQLFreeHandle(SQL_HANDLE_STMT, StmtHandle);
    }

    // Return The CLI API Return Code To The Calling Function
    return(rc);
}
```

```
/*----------------------------------------------------------*/
/* The Main Function                                        */
/*----------------------------------------------------------*/
int main()
{
    // Declare The Local Memory Variables
    SQLRETURN  rc = SQL_SUCCESS;

    // Create An Instance Of The CLI_Class Class
    CLI_Class  Example;

    // Connect To The DB2 Sample Database
    if (Example.ConHandle != NULL)
    {
        rc = SQLConnect(Example.ConHandle, (SQLCHAR *) "SAMPLE",
                    SQL_NTS, (SQLCHAR *) "userid", SQL_NTS,
                    (SQLCHAR *) "password", SQL_NTS);

        // Call The ShowPrimaryKeyInfo() Member Function
        if (rc == SQL_SUCCESS || rc == SQL_SUCCESS_WITH_INFO)
            Example.ShowPrimaryKeyInfo();

        // Disconnect From The DB2 Sample Database
        rc = SQLDisconnect(Example.ConHandle);
    }

    // Return To The Operating System
    return(rc);
}
```

SQLForeignKeys

COMPATIBILITY

X/OPEN 95 CLI	ISO/IEC 92 CLI	DB2 CLI 5.2	DB2 CLI 2.0	ODBC 3.x
☐	☐	☑	☑	☑

ODBC API Conformance Level   **LEVEL 2**

Purpose   The sqlForeignKeys() function is used to retrieve information about the foreign keys that have been defined for a specified table.

Syntax

```
SQLRETURN    SQLForeignKeys    (SQLHSTMT      StatementHandle,
                                SQLCHAR       *PKCatalogName,
                                SQLSMALLINT   PKCatalogNameSize,
                                SQLCHAR       *PKSchemaName,
                                SQLSMALLINT   PKSchemaNameSize,
                                SQLCHAR       *PKTableName,
```

```
SQLSMALLINT      PKTableNameSize,
SQLCHAR          *FKCatalogName,
SQLSMALLINT      FKCatalogNameSize,
SQLCHAR          *FKSchemaName,
SQLSMALLINT      FKSchemaNameSize,
SQLCHAR          *FKTableName,
SQLSMALLINT      FKTableNameSize);
```

Parameters	*StatementHandle*	An SQL statement handle that refers to a previously allocated SQL statement information storage buffer (data structure).
	PKCatalogName	A pointer to a location in memory where the catalog qualifier portion of a three-part table name of the table containing the primary key is stored. Since DB2 CLI does not support three-part names, this parameter must contain either a NULL pointer or a zero length string.
	PKCatalogNameSize	The length of the catalog qualifier name value stored in the *PKCatalogName* parameter. Since DB2 CLI does not support three-part names, this parameter must be set to 0.
	PKSchemaName	A pointer to a location in memory where the schema portion of a three-part table name of the table containing the primary key is stored.
	PKSchemaNameSize	The length of the schema name value stored in the *PKSchemaName* parameter.
	PKTableName	A pointer to a location in memory where the table name portion of a three-part table name of the table containing the primary key is stored.
	PKTableNameSize	The length of the table name value stored in the *PKTableName* parameter.
	FKCatalogName	A pointer to a location in memory where the catalog qualifier portion of a three-part table name of the table containing the foreign key is stored. Since DB2 CLI does not support three-part names, this parameter must contain either a NULL pointer or a zero length string.
	FKCatalogNameSize	The length of the catalog qualifier name value stored in the *FKCatalogName* parameter. Since DB2 CLI does not support three-part names, this parameter must be set to 0.
	FKSchemaName	A pointer to a location in memory where the schema portion of a three-part table name of the table containing the foreign key is stored.
	FKSchemaNameSize	The length of the schema name value stored in the *FKSchemaName* parameter.

FKTableName	A pointer to a location in memory where the table name portion of a three-part table name of the table containing the foreign key is stored.
FKTableNameSize	The length of the table name value stored in the *FKTableName* parameter.

Description   The `SQLForeignKeys()` function is used to retrieve information about the foreign keys that have been defined for a specified table. The information returned by this function is placed in a result data set, which can be processed by using the same CLI functions that are used to process result data sets generated by SQL queries. Table 14–10 lists the columns in this result data set.

Table 14–10   Result Data Set Returned by `SQLForeignKeys()`

Column Number	Column Name	Data Type	Description
1	PKTABLE_CAT	VARCHAR(128)	The name of the catalog (qualifier) containing the **PKTABLE_SCHEM** value. Since DB2 CLI does not support three-part table names, this column is always set to NULL.
2	PKTABLE_SCHEM	VARCHAR(128)	The name of the schema containing the **PKTABLE_NAME** value.
3	PKTABLE_NAME	VARCHAR(128) NOT NULL	The name of the table containing the primary key.
4	PKCOLUMN_NAME	VARCHAR(128) NOT NULL	The name of the primary key column in the table identified in the **PKTABLE_NAME** column. This column contains an empty string (" ") for columns without a name.
5	FKTABLE_CAT	VARCHAR(128)	The name of the catalog (qualifier) containing the **FKTABLE_SCHEM** value. Since DB2 CLI does not support three-part table names, this column is always set to NULL.
6	FKTABLE_SCHEM	VARCHAR(128)	The name of the schema containing the **FKTABLE_NAME** value.
7	FKTABLE_NAME	VARCHAR(128) NOT NULL	The name of the table containing the foreign key.
8	FKCOLUMN_NAME	VARCHAR(128) NOT NULL	The name of the foreign key column in the table identified in the **FKTABLE_NAME** column. This column contains an empty string (" ") for columns without a name.
8	FKCOLUMN_NAME	VARCHAR(128) NOT NULL	The name of the foreign key column.
9	ORDINAL_ POSITION	SMALLINT NOT NULL	The column's ordinal position in the foreign key. The first column in the foreign key is number 1, the second column is number 2, and so on.

Table 14–10 Result Data Set Returned by **SQLForeignKeys()**   (Continued)

Column Number	Column Name	Data Type	Description
10	UPDATE_RULE	SMALLINT	The action to be applied to the foreign key when an **UPDATE** SQL statement is executed. Valid values for this column are: **SQL_NO_ACTION**: If updating the referenced table's primary key causes a *dangling reference* in the referencing table (that is, rows in the referencing table would no longer have counterparts in the referenced table), then the update is rejected. If updating the referencing table's foreign key introduces a value that does not exist as a value of the referenced table's primary key, the update is rejected. **SQL_RESTRICT**: If updating the referenced table's primary key causes a dangling reference in the referencing table (that is, rows in the referencing table would no longer have counterparts in the referenced table), the update is rejected. If updating the referencing table's foreign key introduces a value that does not exist as a value of the referenced table's primary key, the update is rejected. If this information is not available from the data source, this column is set to NULL.
11	DELETE_RULE	SMALLINT	The action to be applied to the foreign key when a **DELETE** SQL statement is executed. Valid values for this column are: **SQL_CASCADE**: When the referenced table's primary key is deleted, the referencing table's foreign key is also deleted. **SQL_NO_ACTION**: If deleting a row in the referenced table causes a dangling reference in the referencing table (that is, rows in the referencing table would no longer have counterparts in the referenced table), the delete is rejected. If deleting the referencing table's foreign key introduces a value that does not exist as a value of the referenced table's primary key, the delete is rejected. **SQL_RESTRICT**: If deleting a row in the referenced table causes a dangling reference in the referencing table (that is, rows in the referencing table would no longer have counterparts in the referenced

Table 14–10   Result Data Set Returned by **SQLForeignKeys()**   (Continued)

Column Number	Column Name	Data Type	Description
			table), the delete is rejected. If deleting the referencing table's foreign key introduces a value that does not exist as a value of the referenced table's primary key, the delete is rejected.
			SQL_SET_NULL: When one or more rows in the referenced table are deleted, each component of the referencing table's foreign key is set to NULL in all matching rows of the referencing table.
			SQL_SET_DEFAULT: When one or more rows in the referenced table are deleted, each component of the referencing table's foreign key is set to the applicable default in all matching rows of the referencing table.
			If this information is not available from the data source, this column is set to NULL.
12	FK_NAME	VARCHAR(128)	The name (identifier) of the foreign key. This column is set to NULL if a foreign key name is not applicable for the data source.
13	PK_NAME	VARCHAR(128)	The name (identifier) of the primary key. This column is set to NULL if a primary key name is not applicable for the data source.
14	DEFERRABILITY	SMALLINT	Indicates whether constraints are deferred or applied immediately. Valid values for this column are:
			SQL_INITIALLY_DEFERRED: Constraints are deferred initially and applied later.
			SQL_INITIALLY_IMMEDIATE: Constraints are applied immediately.
			SQL_NOT_DEFERRABLE: Constraints cannot be deferred.

(Adapted from table 75 on pages 342–343 of *IBM DB2 Universal Database Call Level Interface Guide and Reference*.)

Return Codes   SQL_SUCCESS, SQL_SUCCESS_WITH_INFO, SQL_STILL_EXECUTING, SQL_INVALID_HANDLE, SQL_ERROR

SQLSTATEs   If this function returns SQL_SUCCESS_WITH_INFO or SQL_ERROR, one of the following SQLSTATE values may be obtained by calling the SQLGetDiagRec() function:

08S01, **24**000, **40**003, **HY**001, **HY**009, **HY**010, **HY**014, **HY**090, **HY**C00, or **HYT**00

Refer to Appendix B for detailed information about each SQLSTATE value that can be returned.

Comments

■ Because this function, in many cases, maps to a complex—and therefore, expensive query against a data source's system catalog tables, it should be used sparingly. If the result data set produced is to be used more than once, it should be saved, rather than be regenerated each time it is needed.

■ An empty string (" ") can be stored in the memory location the *PKSchemaName* parameter refers to for schemas without names.

■ An empty string (" ") can be stored in the memory location the *FKSchemaName* parameter refers to for schemas without names.

■ If the **SQL_ATTR_METADATA_ID** attribute for the statement handle specified is set to **SQL_TRUE**, the values specified for the *PKCatalogName, PKSchemaName, PKTableName, FKCatalogName, FKSchemaName*, and *FKTableName* parameters are treated as identifier values and their case is insignificant. However, if the **SQL_ATTR_METADATA_ID** attribute is set to **SQL_FALSE**, the values specified for the *PKCatalogName, PKSchemaName, PKTableName, FKCatalogName, FKSchemaName,* and *FKTableName* parameters are treated literally, and their case is significant. Refer to the "Parameters (Arguments) Used in Catalog Functions" section earlier in this chapter and to the **SQLGetStmtAttr()** function for more information.

■ If the *PKTableName* parameter contains a valid table name, and the *FKTableName* parameter contains an empty string (" "), this function returns a result data set that contains the primary key for the specified table and all foreign keys (in other tables) that refer to it.

■ If the *FKTableName* parameter contains a valid table name, and the *PKTableName* parameter contains an empty string (" "), this function returns a result data set that contains all the foreign keys for the specified table and all primary keys (in other tables) to which they refer.

■ If both the *PKTableName* parameter and the *FKTableName* parameter contain valid table names, this function returns a result data set than contains the foreign keys in the table specified in the *FKTableName* parameter that refer to the primary key of the table specified in the *PKTableName* parameter. This result data set should contain, at the most, only one key.

■ If the foreign keys associated with a primary key are requested, the result data set returned by this function is ordered by **FKTABLE_CAT, FKTABLE_SCHEM, FKTABLE_NAME**, and **ORDINAL_POSITION**. If the primary keys associated with a foreign key are requested, the result set returned by this function is ordered by **PKTABLE_CAT, PKTABLE_SCHEM, PKTABLE_NAME**, and **ORDINAL_POSITION**.

■ The actual amount of memory needed to store the value found in each **VARCHAR** column in the result data set that is produced by this function is dependent on the data source. An application can choose to set aside 128 characters (plus the NULL-terminator) for **VARCHAR** columns (to be consistent with the SQL92 standard limits), or alternatively, to allocate the actual amount of memory required by first calling the **SQLGetInfo()** function with the *InfoType* parameter set to **SQL_MAX_CATALOG_NAME_LEN, SQL_MAX_SCHEMA_NAME_LEN, SQL_MAX_TABLE_NAME_LEN**, and/or **SQL_MAX_COLUMN_NAME_LEN** to determine respectively the actual lengths of the **PKTABLE_CAT** and `FKTABLE_CAT` columns, the `PKTABLE_SCHEM` and `FKTABLE_SCHEM` columns, the `PKTABLE_NAME` and `FKTABLE_NAME` columns, and the `PKCOLUMN_NAME` and `FKCOLUMN_NAME` columns that are supported by the current data source.

Prerequisites   There are no prerequisites for using this function call.

Restrictions   There are no restrictions associated with this function call.

See Also   `SQLPrimaryKeys()`, `SQLStatistics()`

Example   The following Visual C++ program illustrates how to use the `SQLForeignKeys()` function to obtain information about the columns that comprise the foreign keys for a specified table.

```
/*------------------------------------------------------------*/
/* NAME:     CH14EX8.CPP                                      */
/* PURPOSE: Illustrate How To Use The Following CLI API Function */
/*          In A C++ Program:                                 */
/*                                                            */
/*                 SQLForeignKeys()                           */
/*                                                            */
/* OTHER CLI APIs SHOWN:                                      */
/*          SQLAllocHandle()            SQLSetEnvAttr()       */
/*          SQLConnect()                SQLBindCol()          */
/*          SQLFetch()                  SQLDisconnect()       */
/*          SQLFreeHandle()                                   */
/*                                                            */
/* NOTE: You Must Create A Foreign Key For The EMPNO Column Of The */
/* EMP_PHOTO Table That References The EMPNO Field Of The EMPLOYEE */
/* Table Before This Program Will Return A Value - This Key Is Not */
/* Automatically Created When The DB2 Sample Database Is Installed */
/*------------------------------------------------------------*/

// Include The Appropriate Header Files
#include <windows.h>
#include <sqlcli1.h>
#include <iostream.h>

// Define The CLI_Class Class
class CLI_Class
{
    // Attributes
    public:
        SQLHANDLE   EnvHandle;
        SQLHANDLE   ConHandle;
        SQLHANDLE   StmtHandle;
        SQLRETURN   rc;

    // Operations
    public:
        CLI_Class();                            // Constructor
        ~CLI_Class();                           // Destructor
        SQLRETURN   ShowForeignKeyInfo();
};
```

```
// Define The Class Constructor
CLI_Class::CLI_Class()
{
    // Initialize The Return Code Variable
    rc = SQL_SUCCESS;

    // Allocate An Environment Handle
    rc = SQLAllocHandle(SQL_HANDLE_ENV, SQL_NULL_HANDLE, &EnvHandle);

    // Set The ODBC Application Version To 3.x
    if (rc == SQL_SUCCESS)
        rc = SQLSetEnvAttr(EnvHandle, SQL_ATTR_ODBC_VERSION,
                (SQLPOINTER) SQL_OV_ODBC3, SQL_IS_UINTEGER);

    // Allocate A Connection Handle
    if (rc == SQL_SUCCESS)
        rc = SQLAllocHandle(SQL_HANDLE_DBC, EnvHandle, &ConHandle);
}


// Define The Class Destructor
CLI_Class::~CLI_Class()
{
    // Free The Connection Handle
    if (ConHandle != NULL)
        SQLFreeHandle(SQL_HANDLE_DBC, ConHandle);

    // Free The Environment Handle
    if (EnvHandle != NULL)
        SQLFreeHandle(SQL_HANDLE_ENV, EnvHandle);
}


// Define The ShowForeignKeyInfo() Member Function
SQLRETURN CLI_Class::ShowForeignKeyInfo(void)
{
    // Declare The Local Memory Variables
    SQLCHAR   FKeyName[129];

    // Allocate An SQL Statement Handle
    rc = SQLAllocHandle(SQL_HANDLE_STMT, ConHandle, &StmtHandle);
    if (rc == SQL_SUCCESS)
    {
        // Retrieve Information About The Foreign Keys Defined For
        // The EMP_PHOTO Table That Reference Primary Keys In The
        // EMPLOYEE Table In The Data Source
        rc = SQLForeignKeys(StmtHandle, NULL, 0,
                (SQLCHAR *) "USERID", SQL_NTS,
                (SQLCHAR *) "EMPLOYEE", SQL_NTS,
                NULL, 0, (SQLCHAR *) "USERID", SQL_NTS,
                (SQLCHAR *) "EMP_PHOTO", SQL_NTS);
        if (rc == SQL_SUCCESS)
        {
            // Bind A Column In The Result Data Set Returned To
            // An Application Variable
            rc = SQLBindCol(StmtHandle, 8, SQL_C_CHAR, (SQLPOINTER)
```

```
                                &FKeyName, sizeof(FKeyName), NULL);

            // Display A Header
            cout << "Foreign Keys :" << endl << endl;

            // While There Are Records In The Result Data Set
            // Generated, Retrieve And Display Them
            while (rc != SQL_NO_DATA)
            {
                rc = SQLFetch(StmtHandle);
                if (rc != SQL_NO_DATA && rc != SQL_ERROR)
                    cout << FKeyName << endl;
            }
        }

        // Free The SQL Statement Handle
        if (StmtHandle != NULL)
            SQLFreeHandle(SQL_HANDLE_STMT, StmtHandle);
    }

    // Return The CLI API Return Code To The Calling Function
    return(rc);
}


/*───────────────────────────────────────────────────────*/
/* The Main Function                                       */
/*───────────────────────────────────────────────────────*/
int main()
{
    // Declare The Local Memory Variables
    SQLRETURN  rc = SQL_SUCCESS;

    // Create An Instance Of The CLI_Class Class
    CLI_Class  Example;

    // Connect To The DB2 Sample Database
    if (Example.ConHandle != NULL)
    {
        rc = SQLConnect(Example.ConHandle, (SQLCHAR *) "SAMPLE",
                   SQL_NTS, (SQLCHAR *) "userid", SQL_NTS,
                   (SQLCHAR *) "password", SQL_NTS);

        // Call The ShowForeignKeyInfo() Member Function
        if (rc == SQL_SUCCESS || rc == SQL_SUCCESS_WITH_INFO)
            Example.ShowForeignKeyInfo();

        // Disconnect From The DB2 Sample Database
        rc = SQLDisconnect(Example.ConHandle);
    }

    // Return To The Operating System
    return(rc);
}
```

SQLProcedures

COMPATIBILITY

X/OPEN 95 CLI	ISO/IEC 92 CLI	DB2 CLI 5.2	DB2 CLI 2.0	ODBC 3.x
☐	☐	☑	☑	☑

ODBC API CONFORMANCE LEVEL   **LEVEL 1***

*IN ODBC 2.0, THIS FUNCTION WAS A LEVEL 2 API CONFORMANCE LEVEL FUNCTION

Purpose   The **SQLProcedures()** function is used to retrieve a list of stored procedure names that have been registered in a specified data source.

Syntax

```
SQLRETURN    SQLProcedures    (SQLHSTMT        StatementHandle,
                               SQLCHAR         *ProcCatalog,
                               SQLSMALLINT     ProcCatalogSize,
                               SQLCHAR         *ProcSchema,
                               SQLSMALLINT     ProcSchemaSize,
                               SQLCHAR         *ProcedureName,
                               SQLSMALLINT     ProcedureNameSize);
```

Parameters   *StatementHandle*

An SQL statement handle that refers to a previously allocated SQL statement information storage buffer (data structure).

ProcCatalogName

A pointer to a location in memory where the catalog qualifier portion of a three-part stored procedure name is stored. Since DB2 CLI does not support three-part names, this parameter must contain either a NULL pointer or a zero length string.

ProcCatalogNameSize

The length of the catalog qualifier name value stored in the *ProcCatalogName* parameter. Since DB2 CLI does not support three-part names, this parameter must be set to 0.

ProcSchemaName

A pointer to a location in memory where a schema name search pattern is stored.

ProcSchemaNameSize

The length of the schema name search pattern value stored in the *ProcSchemaName* parameter.

ProcedureName

A pointer to a location in memory where a stored procedure name search pattern is stored.

ProcedureNameSize

The length of the stored procedure name search pattern value stored in the *ProcedureName* parameter.

Description The `SQLProcedures()` function is used to retrieve a list of stored procedure names that have been registered in a specified data source and that match a specified search pattern. A procedure is a generic term used to describe an executable object, or a named entry that can be invoked using input and/or output parameters. The information returned by this function is placed in a result data set, which can be processed by using the same CLI functions that are used to process result data sets generated by SQL queries. Table 14–11 lists the columns in this result data set.

Table 14–11   Result Data Set Returned by `SQLProcedures()`

Column Number	Column Name	Data Type	Description
1	PROCEDURE_CAT	VARCHAR(128)	The name of the catalog (qualifier) containing the **PROCEDURE_SCHEM** value. Since DB2 CLI does not support three-part procedure names, this column is always set to NULL.
2	PROCEDURE_ SCHEM	VARCHAR(128)	The name of the schema containing the **PROCEDURE_NAME** value.
3	PROCEDURE_ NAME	VARCHAR(128) NOT NULL	The name of the stored procedure.
4	NUM_INPUT_ PARAMS (ODBC 2.0)	INTEGER NOT NULL	The number of input parameters defined for the stored procedure. At this time, applications should not rely on the data returned in this column.
5	NUM_OUTPUT_ PARAMS	INTEGER	The number of output parameters defined for the stored procedure. At this time, applications should not rely on the data returned in this column.
6	NUM_RESULT_ SETS	INTEGER NOT NULL	The number of result data sets that will be returned when the stored procedure is executed. At this time, applications should not rely on the data returned in this column.
7	REMARKS	VARCHAR(254)	Descriptive information about the stored procedure (if any exists).
8	PROCEDURE_ TYPE	SMALLINT	Indicates whether the procedure is a stored procedure that does not return a value or a data source-specific function that does return a value. Valid values for this column are: **SQL_PT_PROCEDURE**: The returned object is a stored procedure; it does not return a value. **SQL_PT_FUNCTION**: The object is a function; it returns a value. **SQL_PT_UNKNOWN**: Whether the procedure returns a value or not cannot be determined.

(Adapted from table 140 on pages 505–506 of *IBM DB2 Universal Database Call Level Interface Guide and Reference*.)

Return Codes   SQL_SUCCESS, SQL_SUCCESS_WITH_INFO, SQL_STILL_EXECUTING, SQL_INVALID_HANDLE, SQL_ERROR

SQLSTATEs   If this function returns SQL_SUCCESS_WITH_INFO or SQL_ERROR, one of the following SQLSTATE values may be obtained by calling the SQLGetDiagRec() function:

01S01, 24000, 40003, HY001, HY008, HY010, HY014, HY090, HYC00, or HYT00

Refer to Appendix B for detailed information about each SQLSTATE value that can be returned.

Comments   ■ Because this function, in many cases, maps to a complex—and therefore, expensive query against a data source's system catalog tables, it should be used sparingly. If the result data set produced is to be used more than once, it should be saved, rather than be regenerated each time it is needed.

■ An empty string (" ") can be stored in the memory location the *ProcSchemaName* parameter refers to for schemas without names.

■ If the SQL_ATTR_METADATA_ID attribute for the statement handle specified is set to SQL_TRUE, the values specified for the *ProcCatalogName*, *ProcSchemaName*, and *ProcedureName* parameters are treated as identifier values and their case is insignificant. However, if the SQL_ATTR_METADATA_ID attribute is set to SQL_FALSE, the values specified for the *ProcCatalogName*, *ProcSchemaName*, and *ProcedureName* parameters are treated literally, and their case is significant. Refer to the "Parameters (Arguments) Used in Catalog Functions" section earlier in this chapter and to the SQLGetStmtAttr() function for more information.

■ The values specified for the *ProcSchemaName* and *ProcedureName* parameters can contain the following search pattern values:

   ■ The underscore character (_).
   Any single character can be used in place of the underscore character.

   ■ The percent character (%).
   Any sequence of 0 or more characters can be used in place of the percent character.

   ■ An escape character.
   A driver-specific character used to treat an underscore character, a percent character, and/or the escape character itself as a literal value instead of as a wild card value (that is, % = "%").

■ If this function is to return a list of stored procedures at a DB2 for MVS/ESA (version 4.1 or later) server, the names of the stored procedures must be registered in the server's SYSIBM.SYSPROCEDURES catalog table.

■ If the SQL_LONG_DATA_COMPAT connection attribute has been set to SQL_ID_COMPAT_YES (either by calling the SQLSetConnectAttr() or by setting the LONGDATACOMPAT option in the DB2 CLI initialization file), large object (LOB) data types will be reported as SQL_LONGVARCHAR, SQL_LONGVARBINARY, or SQL_LONGVARGRAPHIC.

- The `SQLGetInfo()` function can be called with the `SQL_ACCESSIBLE_PROCEDURES` information type specified to determine whether a user has the authorization needed to execute any stored procedure found in the result data set produced by this function. If this function is not used to obtain authorization information, an application must be coded in such a way that it can handle situations in which a user attempts to execute a procedure for which they have not been granted the proper authorization privileges.

- The result data set returned by this function is ordered by `PROCEDURE_CAT`, `PROCEDURE_SCHEM`, and `PROCEDURE_NAME`.

- DB2 for Common Servers, Version 2.1 and earlier used a pseudo-catalog table for stored procedure registration. DB2 Universal Database, Version 5.0 and later uses two system catalog tables/views: SYSCAT.PROCEDURES and SYSCAT.PROCPARMS. In order to access information stored in the pseudo-catalog table used by earlier versions, the CLI/ODBC configuration keyword `PATCH1` must be set to `262144`.

- The actual amount of memory needed to store the value found in each `VARCHAR` column in the result data set produced by this function is dependent on the data source. An application can choose to set aside 128 characters (plus the NULL-terminator) for `VARCHAR` columns (to be consistent with the SQL92 standard limits), or alternatively, to allocate the actual amount of memory required by first calling the `SQLGetInfo()` function with the *InfoType* parameter set to `SQL_MAX_CATALOG_NAME_LEN`, `SQL_MAX_SCHEMA_NAME_LEN`, and/or `SQL_MAX_PROCEDURE_NAME_LEN` to determine respectively the actual lengths of the `PROCEDURE_CAT`, `PROCEDURE_SCHEM`, and `PROCEDURE_NAME` columns that are supported by the current data source.

Prerequisites There are no prerequisites for using this function call.

Restrictions If this function attempts to return a list of stored procedures from a DB2 server that does not provide facilities to support a stored procedure catalog, or from a DB2 server that does not provide support for stored procedures, an empty result data set will be returned.

See Also `SQLProcedureColumns()`

Example The following Visual C++ program illustrates how to use the `SQLProcedures()` function to obtain information about the stored procedures that are available in a data source.

```
/*───────────────────────────────────────────────────*/
/* NAME:     CH14EX9.CPP                               */
/* PURPOSE: Illustrate How To Use The Following CLI API Function */
/*          In A C++ Program:                          */
/*                                                     */
/*               SQLProcedures()                       */
/*                                                     */
/* OTHER CLI APIs SHOWN:                               */
/*               SQLAllocHandle()        SQLSetEnvAttr()   */
/*               SQLConnect()            SQLBindCol()      */
/*               SQLFetch()              SQLDisconnect()   */
/*               SQLFreeHandle()                        */
/*                                                     */
```

```
/* NOTE: You Must Create A Stored Procedure For The DB2 Sample    */
/* Database Before This Program Will Return A Value - No Stored   */
/* Procedures Are Automatically Created When The DB2 Sample       */
/* Database Is Installed.                                         */
/*                                                                */
/* You Can Create A Stored Procedure Reference By Issuing The     */
/* Following Command From The DB2 Command Line Processor:         */
/*                                                                */
/*     CREATE PROCEDURE ASSEMBLY_PARTS (IN   ASSEMBLY_NUM  INTEGER, */
/*                                      OUT NUM_PARTS   INTEGER,   */
/*                                      OUT COST        DOUBLE)    */
/*                  EXTERNAL NAME 'parts!assembly'                 */
/*                  RESULT SETS 1 NOT FENCED                       */
/*                  LANGUAGE C PARAMETER STYLE DB2DARI             */
/*                                                                */
/* This Procedure Can Not Be Invoked Unless An External File Named */
/* "parts" Containing An Actual Procedure Named "assembly" is     */
/* created.                                                       */
/*──────────────────────────────────────────────────────────────*/


// Include The Appropriate Header Files
#include <windows.h>
#include <sqlcli1.h>
#include <iostream.h>

// Define The CLI_Class Class
class CLI_Class
{
    // Attributes
    public:
        SQLHANDLE   EnvHandle;
        SQLHANDLE   ConHandle;
        SQLHANDLE   StmtHandle;
        SQLRETURN   rc;

    // Operations
    public:
        CLI_Class();                            // Constructor
        ~CLI_Class();                           // Destructor
        SQLRETURN   ShowProcedureInfo();
};

// Define The Class Constructor
CLI_Class::CLI_Class()
{
    // Initialize The Return Code Variable
    rc = SQL_SUCCESS;

    // Allocate An Environment Handle
    rc = SQLAllocHandle(SQL_HANDLE_ENV, SQL_NULL_HANDLE, &EnvHandle);

    // Set The ODBC Application Version To 3.x
    if (rc == SQL_SUCCESS)
        rc = SQLSetEnvAttr(EnvHandle, SQL_ATTR_ODBC_VERSION,
                (SQLPOINTER) SQL_OV_ODBC3, SQL_IS_UINTEGER);
```

```
        // Allocate A Connection Handle
        if (rc == SQL_SUCCESS)
            rc = SQLAllocHandle(SQL_HANDLE_DBC, EnvHandle, &ConHandle);
}

// Define The Class Destructor
CLI_Class::~CLI_Class()
{
    // Free The Connection Handle
    if (ConHandle != NULL)
        SQLFreeHandle(SQL_HANDLE_DBC, ConHandle);

    // Free The Environment Handle
    if (EnvHandle != NULL)
        SQLFreeHandle(SQL_HANDLE_ENV, EnvHandle);
}

// Define The ShowProcedureInfo() Member Function
SQLRETURN CLI_Class::ShowProcedureInfo(void)
{
    // Declare The Local Memory Variables
    SQLCHAR  ProcedureName[129];

    // Allocate An SQL Statement Handle
    rc = SQLAllocHandle(SQL_HANDLE_STMT, ConHandle, &StmtHandle);
    if (rc == SQL_SUCCESS)
    {
        // Retrieve Information About The Procedures Stored In The
        // Data Source
        rc = SQLProcedures(StmtHandle, NULL, 0, NULL, 0,
                (SQLCHAR *) "%", SQL_NTS);
        if (rc == SQL_SUCCESS)
        {
            // Bind A Column In The Result Data Set Returned To
            // An Application Variable
            rc = SQLBindCol(StmtHandle, 3, SQL_C_CHAR, (SQLPOINTER)
                    &ProcedureName, sizeof(ProcedureName), NULL);

            // Display A Header
            cout << "Stored Procedures :" << endl << endl;

            // While There Are Records In The Result Data Set
            // Generated, Retrieve And Display Them
            while (rc != SQL_NO_DATA)
            {
                rc = SQLFetch(StmtHandle);
                if (rc != SQL_NO_DATA)
                    cout << ProcedureName << endl;
            }
        }

        // Free The SQL Statement Handle
        if (StmtHandle != NULL)
            SQLFreeHandle(SQL_HANDLE_STMT, StmtHandle);
    }
```

```
    // Return The CLI API Return Code To The Calling Function
    return(rc);
}

/*------------------------------------------------------------------*/
/* The Main Function                                                */
/*------------------------------------------------------------------*/
int main()
{
    // Declare The Local Memory Variables
    SQLRETURN   rc = SQL_SUCCESS;

    // Create An Instance Of The CLI_Class Class
    CLI_Class   Example;

    // Connect To The DB2 Sample Database
    if (Example.ConHandle != NULL)
    {
        rc = SQLConnect(Example.ConHandle, (SQLCHAR *) "SAMPLE",
                    SQL_NTS, (SQLCHAR *) "userid", SQL_NTS,
                    (SQLCHAR *) "password", SQL_NTS);

        // Call The ShowProcedureInfo() Member Function
        if (rc == SQL_SUCCESS || rc == SQL_SUCCESS_WITH_INFO)
            Example.ShowProcedureInfo();

        // Disconnect From The DB2 Sample Database
        rc = SQLDisconnect(Example.ConHandle);
    }

    // Return To The Operating System
    return(rc);
}
```

SQLProcedureColumns

COMPATIBILITY

X/OPEN 95 CLI	ISO/IEC 92 CLI	DB2 CLI 5.2	DB2 CLI 2.0	ODBC 3.x
☐	☐	☑	☑	☑

ODBC API CONFORMANCE LEVEL   LEVEL 1*

*IN ODBC 2.0, THIS FUNCTION WAS A LEVEL 2 API CONFORMANCE LEVEL FUNCTION

Purpose   The SQLProcedureColumns() function is used to retrieve a list of input and output parameters, as well as a list of the columns that make up the result data set for a specified stored procedure.

Syntax

```
SQLRETURN    SQLProcedureColumns    (SQLHSTMT        StatementHandle,
                                     SQLCHAR         *ProcCatalog,
                                     SQLSMALLINT     ProcCatalogSize,
                                     SQLCHAR         *ProcSchema,
                                     SQLSMALLINT     ProcSchemaSize,
                                     SQLCHAR         *ProcedureName,
                                     SQLSMALLINT     ProcedureNameSize,
                                     SQLCHAR         *ColumnName,
                                     SQLSMALLINT     ColumnNameSize);
```

Parameters

StatementHandle	An SQL statement handle that refers to a previously allocated SQL statement information storage buffer (data structure).
ProcCatalogName	A pointer to a location in memory where the catalog qualifier portion of a three-part stored procedure name is stored. Since DB2 CLI does not support three-part names, this parameter must contain either a NULL pointer or a zero length string.
ProcCatalogNameSize	The length of the catalog qualifier name value stored in the *ProcCatalogName* parameter. Since DB2 CLI does not support three-part names, this parameter must be set to 0.
ProcSchemaName	A pointer to a location in memory where a stored procedure schema name search pattern is stored.
ProcSchemaNameSize	The length of the stored procedure schema name search pattern value stored in the *ProcSchemaName* parameter.
ProcedureName	A pointer to a location in memory where a stored procedure name search pattern is stored.
ProcedureNameSize	The length of the stored procedure name search pattern value stored in the *ProcedureName* parameter.
ColumnName	A pointer to a location in memory where a column name search pattern is stored.
ColumnNameSize	The length of the column name search pattern value stored in the *ColumnName* parameter.

Description   The `SQLProcedureColumns()` function is used to retrieve a list of input and output parameters, as well as a list of the columns that make up the result data set for a specified stored procedure. This function is typically called before a stored procedure is executed, so information about the parameters used by the procedure and the result data set or sets produced by the procedure (if any) is known in advance by the application. The information returned by this function is placed in a result data set, which can be processed by using the same CLI functions that are used to process result data sets generated by SQL queries. Table 14–12 lists the columns in this result data set.

Table 14–12 Result Data Set Returned by `SQLProcedureColumns()`

Column Number	Column Name	Data Type	Description
1	PROCEDURE_CAT	VARCHAR(128)	The name of the catalog (qualifier) containing the **PROCEDURE_SCHEM** value. Since DB2 CLI does not support three-part procedure names, this column is always set to NULL.
2	PROCEDURE_SCHEM	VARCHAR(128)	The name of the schema containing the **PROCEDURE_NAME** value.
3	PROCEDURE_NAME	VARCHAR(128) NOT NULL	The name of the stored procedure.
4	COLUMN_NAME	VARCHAR(128) NOT NULL	The name of a either a parameter or a column in a result data set that is associated with the stored procedure identified in the **PROCEDURE_NAME** column. This column contains an empty string (" ") for columns without a name.
5	COLUMN_TYPE	SMALLINT NOT NULL	Identifies whether the name identified in the **COLUMN_NAME** column is for a parameter or for a column in a result data set associated with the stored procedure identified in the **PROCEDURE_NAME** column. Valid values for this column are: **SQL_PARAM_INPUT**: The name identified in the **COLUMN_NAME** column is for an input parameter. **SQL_PARAM_OUTPUT**: The name identified in the **COLUMN_NAME** column is for an output parameter. **SQL_PARAM_INPUT_OUTPUT**: The name identified in the **COLUMN_NAME** column is for an input/output parameter. **SQL_RETURN_VALUE**: The name identified in the **COLUMN_NAME** column is for the return code value of the stored procedure. **SQL_RESULT_COL**: The name identified in the **COLUMN_NAME** column is for a column in a result data set produced by the stored procedure. **SQL_PARAM_TYPE_UNKNOWN**: Whether the name identified in the **COLUMN_NAME** column is for a parameter or for a column in a result data set cannot be determined.

Table 14–12   Result Data Set Returned by **SQLProcedureColumns()**   (Continued)

Column Number	Column Name	Data Type	Description
6	DATA_TYPE	SMALLINT NOT NULL	The SQL data type of the parameter/column identified in the **COLUMN_NAME** column. Valid values for this column include: SQL_CHAR SQL_VARCHAR SQL_LONGVARCHAR SQL_GRAPHIC SQL_VARGRAPHIC SQL_LONGVARGRAPHIC SQL_DECIMAL SQL_NUMERIC SQL_SMALLINT SQL_INTEGER SQL_REAL SQL_FLOAT SQL_DOUBLE SQL_BIT SQL_TINYINT SQL_BIGINT SQL_BINARY SQL_VARBINARY SQL_LONGVARBINARY SQL_TYPE_DATE SQL_TYPE_TIME SQL_TYPE_TIMESTAMP SQL_BLOB SQL_CLOB SQL_DBCLOB
7	TYPE_NAME	VARCHAR(128) NOT NULL	The data source-specific character representation of the SQL data type name identified in the **DATA_TYPE** column. Valid values for this column include: "CHAR" "VARCHAR" "LONG VARCHAR" "DECIMAL" "NUMERIC" "SMALLINT" "INTEGER" "REAL" "FLOAT" "DOUBLE PRECISION" "BIT" "TINYINT" "BIGINT" "BINARY" "VARBINARY" "LONG VARBINARY" "DATE" "TIME" "TIMESTAMP" "BLOB" "CLOB" "DBCLOB"
8	COLUMN_SIZE	INTEGER	The maximum number of bytes needed to display the parameter/column data in character format. For numeric data types, this is either the total number of digits, or the total number of bits allowed in the parameter/column, depending on the value in the **NUM_PREC_RADIX** column. For character or binary string data types, this is the size of the string (string length), in bytes. For date, time, and timestamp data types, this is the total number of characters required to display the value when it is converted to a character string. For graphic data types, this is the total number of double byte characters used.

Table 14–12 Result Data Set Returned by **SQLProcedureColumns()** (Continued)

Column Number	Column Name	Data Type	Description
9	BUFFER_LENGTH	INTEGER	The maximum number of bytes needed for the associated C application variable (buffer) to store data for this parameter or from this column if the value **SQL_C_DEFAULT** is specified for the *CDataType* parameter of the **SQLBindParameter() SQLBindCol()**, or **SQLGetData()** function. This length does not include the NULL-terminator character used by NULL terminated strings.
			For numeric data, this column may contain a number that is different from the actual size of the data stored in the data source.
10	DECIMAL_DIGITS	SMALLINT	The total number of significant digits to the right of the decimal point.
			If the **DATA_TYPE** column contains **SQL_TYPE_TIME** or **SQL_TYPE_TIMESTAMP**, this column contains the number of digits in the fractional seconds component of the time value.
			For data types where decimal digits are not applicable, this column is set to NULL.
			For all other data types, this column contains the decimal digits of the parameter/column on the data source.
11	NUM_PREC_RADIX	SMALLINT	The radix value of the parameter/column.
			For approximate numeric data types, this column contains the value **2** and the **COLUMN_SIZE** column contains the number of bits allowed for the parameter/column.
			For exact numeric data types, this column contains the value **10** and the **COLUMN_SIZE** column contains the number of decimal digits allowed for the parameter/column.
			For numeric data types, this column can contain either **10** or **2**.
			For data types where radix is not applicable, this column is set to NULL.
12	NULLABLE	SMALLINT NOT NULL	Indicates whether the parameter/column accepts a NULL value. Valid values for this column are:
			SQL_NO_NULLS: The parameter/column does not accept NULL values.
			SQL_NULLABLE: The parameter/column accepts NULL values.

Table 14–12 Result Data Set Returned by **SQLProcedureColumns()** (Continued)

Column Number	Column Name	Data Type	Description
			SQL_NULLABLE_UNKNOWN: Whether the parameter/column accepts NULL values is not known.
			The value in this column is different from the value in the **IS_NULLABLE** column. The **NULLABLE** column indicates with certainty that a parameter/column can accept NULLs, but it cannot indicate with certainty that a parameter/column does not accept NULLs. The **IS_NULLABLE** column indicates with certainty that a parameter/column cannot accept NULLs, but it cannot indicate with certainty that a parameter/column accepts NULLs.
13	**REMARKS**	**VARCHAR(254)**	Descriptive information about the parameter/column (if any exists).
14	**COLUMN_DEF**	**VARCHAR(254)**	The parameter/column's default value.
			If the default value is a numeric literal, this column contains the character representation of the numeric literal with no enclosing single quotes.
			If the default value is a character string, this column contains that string enclosed in single quotes.
			If the default value is a pseudo-literal, (as is the case for **DATE**, **TIME**, and **TIMESTAMP** columns), this column contains the keyword of the pseudo-literal (for example: **"CURRENT DATE"**) with no enclosing single quotes.
			If the default value is NULL or if no default value was specified, this column contains the word **"NULL"** with no enclosing single quotes.
			If the default value cannot be represented without truncation, this column contains the word **"TRUNCATED"** with no enclosing single quotes.
			The value of this column can be used in generating a new column definition, except when it contains the value **"TRUNCATED"**.
15	**SQL_DATA_TYPE**	**SMALLINT NOT NULL**	The SQL data type of the parameter/column identified in the **COLUMN_NAME** column as it would appear in the **SQL_DESC_TYPE** field of an implementation row descriptor record.
			This column usually contains the same value as the **DATA_TYPE** column, with the following exception:

Table 14–12 Result Data Set Returned by **SQLProcedureColumns()** (Continued)

Column Number	Column Name	Data Type	Description
			For datetime data types, this column contains the non-concise data type (such as **SQL_DATETIME**, rather than the concise data type (such as **SQL_TYPE_DATE**). If this column contains **SQL_DATETIME**, the specific data type can be obtained from the **SQL_DATETIME_SUB** column.
16	**DATETIME_SUB**	**SMALLINT**	The subtype code for datetime and interval data types. For all other data types, this column is set to NULL.
			Valid values for this column are:
			SQL_CODE_DATE **SQL_CODE_TIME** **SQL_CODE_TIMESTAMP**
17	**CHAR_OCTET_LENGTH**	**INTEGER**	Contains the maximum length, in octets (bytes), for a character data type parameter/column. For single byte character sets, this column contains the same value as the **COLUMN_SIZE** column. For all other character sets, this column is set to NULL.
18	**ORDINAL_POSITION**	**INTEGER NOT NULL**	The parameter's sequence number in the procedure call or the column's sequence number in the result data set produced. The first parameter/column is number 1, the second parameter/column is number 2, and so on.
19	**IS_NULLABLE**	**VARCHAR(254)**	Indicates whether the parameter/column is known to be nullable (can contain NULL values), according to the rules in the ISO SQL92 standard. Valid values for this column are: **"YES"**: The parameter/column can contain NULL values. **"NO"**: The parameter/column cannot contain NULL values. (" ") (Empty string): Whether the parameter/column can contain NULL values is not known. An ISO SQL92-compliant DBMS cannot return an empty string. The value returned for this column is different from the value returned for the **NULLABLE** column. (See the description of the **NULLABLE** column for details.)

(Adapted from table 137 on pages 497–499 of *IBM DB2 Universal Database Call Level Interface Guide and Reference*.)

This function can return information on the input parameters, the output parameters, or both the input and the output parameters associated with a stored procedure; however, it cannot return information about the descriptor information that may be associated with any result data sets returned.

Return Codes SQL_SUCCESS, SQL_SUCCESS_WITH_INFO, SQL_STILL_EXECUTING, SQL_INVALID_HANDLE, SQL_ERROR

SQLSTATEs If this function returns SQL_SUCCESS_WITH_INFO or SQL_ERROR, one of the following SQLSTATE values may be obtained by calling the SQLGetDiagRec() function:

08S01, 24000, 40003, 42601, HY001, HY008, HY010, HY014, HY090, HYC00, or HYT00

Refer to Appendix B for detailed information about each SQLSTATE value that can be returned.

Comments ■ Because this function, in many cases, maps to a complex—and therefore, expensive query against a data source's system catalog tables, it should be used sparingly. If the result data set produced is to be used more than once, it should be saved, rather than be regenerated each time it is needed.

■ An empty string (" ") can be stored in the memory location the *ProcSchemaName* parameter refers to for schemas without names.

■ If the SQL_ATTR_METADATA_ID attribute for the statement handle specified is set to SQL_TRUE, the values specified for the *ProcCatalogName*, *ProcSchemaName*, *ProcedureName*, and *ColumnName* parameters are treated as identifier values, and their case is insignificant. However, if the SQL_ATTR_METADATA_ID attribute is set to SQL_FALSE, the values specified for the *ProcCatalogName*, *ProcSchemaName*, *ProcedureName*, and *ColumnName* parameters are treated literally, and their case is significant. Refer to the "Parameters (Arguments) Used In Catalog Functions" section earlier in this chapter and to the SQLGetStmtAttr() function for more information.

■ The values specified for the *ProcSchemaName*, *ProcedureName*, and *ColumnName* parameters can contain the following search pattern values:

   ■ The underscore character (_).
     Any single character can be used in place of the underscore character.

   ■ The percent character (%).
     Any sequence of 0 or more characters can be used in place of the percent character.

   ■ An escape character.
     A driver-specific character used to treat an underscore character, a percent character, and/or the escape character itself as a literal value instead of as a wild card value (that is, % = "%").

■ If this function is to return a list of input and output parameters associated with stored procedures at a DB2 for MVS/ESA server, the names of the stored procedures must be registered in the server's SYSIBM.SYSPROCEDURES catalog table.

■ If the **SQL_LONGDATA_COMPAT** connection attribute has been set to **SQL_LD_COMPAT_YES**, (either by calling the **SQLSetConnectAttr()** or by setting the **LONGDATA_COMPAT** option in the DB2 CLI initialization file), large object (LOB) data types will be reported as **SQL_LONGVARCHAR, SQL_LONGVARBINARY,** or **SQL_LONGVARGRAPHIC**.

■ The result data set returned by this function is ordered by **PROCEDURE_CAT, PROCEDURE_SCHEM, PROCEDURE_NAME,** and **COLUMN_TYPE**.

■ DB2 for Common Servers, Version 2.1 and earlier used a pseudo-catalog table for stored procedure registration. DB2 Universal Database, Version 5.0 and later uses two system catalog tables/views: SYSCAT.PROCEDURES and SYSCAT.PROCPARMS. In order to access information stored in the pseudo-catalog table used by earlier versions, the CLI/ODBC configuration keyword **PATCH1** must be set to **262144**.

■ The actual amount of memory needed to store the value found in each **VARCHAR** column in the result data set produced by this function is dependent on the data source. An application can choose to set aside 128 characters (plus the NULL-terminator) for **VARCHAR** columns (to be consistent with the SQL92 standard limits), or alternatively, to allocate the actual amount of memory required by first calling the **SQLGetInfo()** function with the *InfoType* parameter set to **SQL_MAX_CATALOG_NAME_LEN, SQL_MAX_ SCHEMA_NAME_LEN, SQL_MAX_PROCEDURE_NAME_LEN** and/or **SQL_MAX_COLUMN_NAME_LEN** to determine respectively the actual lengths of the **PROCEDURE_CAT, PROCEDURE_SCHEM, PROCEDURE_NAME,** and **COLUMN_NAME** columns that are supported by the current data source.

Prerequisites   There are no prerequisites for using this function call.

Restrictions   This function does not return information about the attributes of result data sets that may be produced when a stored procedure is executed. If this function attempts to return a list of input and/or output parameters associated with stored procedures from a DB2 server that does not provide facilities to support a stored procedure catalog, or from a DB2 server that does not provide support for stored procedures, an empty result data set will be returned.

See Also   **SQLProcedures()**

Example   The following Visual C++ program illustrates how to use the **SQLProcedureColumns()** function to obtain information about the columns that are associated with the stored procedures that are available in a data source.

```
/*-------------------------------------------------------------------*/
/* NAME:      CH14EX10.CPP                                           */
/* PURPOSE: Illustrate How To Use The Following CLI API Function     */
/*          In A C++ Program:                                        */
/*                                                                   */
/*              SQLProcedureColumns ()                               */
/*                                                                   */
/* OTHER CLI APIs SHOWN:                                             */
/*          SQLAllocHandle()            SQLSetEnvAttr()              */
/*          SQLConnect()                SQLBindCol()                 */
/*          SQLFetch()                  SQLDisconnect()              */
/*          SQLFreeHandle()                                          */
```

```
/*                                                                  */
/* NOTE: You Must Create A Stored Procedure For The DB2 Sample      */
/* Database Before This Program Will Return A Value - No Stored     */
/* Procedures Are Automatically Created When The DB2 Sample         */
/* Database Is Installed.                                           */
/*                                                                  */
/* You Can Create A Stored Procedure Reference By Issuing The       */
/* Following Command From The DB2 Command Line Processor:           */
/*                                                                  */
/*     CREATE PROCEDURE ASSEMBLY_PARTS (IN   ASSEMBLY_NUM  INTEGER, */
/*                                      OUT NUM_PARTS  INTEGER,     */
/*                                      OUT COST         DOUBLE)    */
/*                   EXTERNAL NAME 'parts!assembly'                 */
/*                   RESULT SETS 1 NOT FENCED                       */
/*                   LANGUAGE C PARAMETER STYLE DB2DARI             */
/*                                                                  */
/* This Procedure Can Not Be Invoked Unless An External File Named */
/* "parts" Containing An Actual Procedure Named "assembly" is       */
/* created.                                                         */
/*----------------------------------------------------------------*/

// Include The Appropriate Header Files
#include <windows.h>
#include <sqlcli1.h>
#include <iostream.h>

// Define The CLI_Class Class
class CLI_Class
{
    // Attributes
    public:
        SQLHANDLE   EnvHandle;
        SQLHANDLE   ConHandle;
        SQLHANDLE   StmtHandle;
        SQLRETURN   rc;

    // Operations
    public:
        CLI_Class();                              // Constructor
        ~CLI_Class();                             // Destructor
        SQLRETURN  ShowProcedureColumnInfo();
};

// Define The Class Constructor
CLI_Class::CLI_Class()
{
    // Initialize The Return Code Variable
    rc = SQL_SUCCESS;

    // Allocate An Environment Handle
    rc = SQLAllocHandle(SQL_HANDLE_ENV, SQL_NULL_HANDLE, &EnvHandle);

    // Set The ODBC Application Version To 3.x
    if (rc == SQL_SUCCESS)
```

```cpp
    rc = SQLSetEnvAttr(EnvHandle, SQL_ATTR_ODBC_VERSION,
            (SQLPOINTER) SQL_OV_ODBC3, SQL_IS_UINTEGER);

    // Allocate A Connection Handle
    if (rc == SQL_SUCCESS)
        rc = SQLAllocHandle(SQL_HANDLE_DBC, EnvHandle, &ConHandle);
}

// Define The Class Destructor
CLI_Class::~CLI_Class()
{
    // Free The Connection Handle
    if (ConHandle != NULL)
        SQLFreeHandle(SQL_HANDLE_DBC, ConHandle);

    // Free The Environment Handle
    if (EnvHandle != NULL)
        SQLFreeHandle(SQL_HANDLE_ENV, EnvHandle);
}

// Define The ShowProcedureColumnInfo() Member Function
SQLRETURN CLI_Class::ShowProcedureColumnInfo(void)
{
    // Declare The Local Memory Variables
    SQLCHAR   ColumnName[129];

    // Allocate An SQL Statement Handle
    rc = SQLAllocHandle(SQL_HANDLE_STMT, ConHandle, &StmtHandle);
    if (rc == SQL_SUCCESS)
    {
        // Retrieve Information About The Columns Associated With The
        // Procedures Stored In The Data Source
        rc = SQLProcedureColumns(StmtHandle, NULL, 0, NULL, 0,
                (SQLCHAR *) "%", SQL_NTS, (SQLCHAR *) "%", SQL_NTS);
        if (rc == SQL_SUCCESS)
        {
            // Bind A Column In The Result Data Set Returned To
            // An Application Variable
            rc = SQLBindCol(StmtHandle, 4, SQL_C_CHAR, (SQLPOINTER)
                    &ColumnName, sizeof(ColumnName), NULL);

            // Display A Header
            cout << "Procedure Columns :" << endl << endl;

            // While There Are Records In The Result Data Set
            // Generated, Retrieve And Display Them
            while (rc != SQL_NO_DATA)
            {
                rc = SQLFetch(StmtHandle);
                if (rc != SQL_NO_DATA)
                    cout << ColumnName << endl;
            }
        }
    }
```

```
        // Free The SQL Statement Handle
        if (StmtHandle != NULL)
            SQLFreeHandle(SQL_HANDLE_STMT, StmtHandle);
    }

    // Return The CLI API Return Code To The Calling Function
    return(rc);
}

/*------------------------------------------------------------*/
/* The Main Function                                          */
/*------------------------------------------------------------*/
int main()
{
    // Declare The Local Memory Variables
    SQLRETURN  rc = SQL_SUCCESS;

    // Create An Instance Of The CLI_Class Class
    CLI_Class  Example;

    // Connect To The DB2 Sample Database
    if (Example.ConHandle != NULL)
    {
        rc = SQLConnect(Example.ConHandle, (SQLCHAR *) "SAMPLE",
                   SQL_NTS, (SQLCHAR *) "userid", SQL_NTS,
                   (SQLCHAR *) "password", SQL_NTS);

        // Call The ShowProcedureColumnInfo() Member Function
        if (rc == SQL_SUCCESS || rc == SQL_SUCCESS_WITH_INFO)
            Example.ShowProcedureColumnInfo();

        // Disconnect From The DB2 Sample Database
        rc = SQLDisconnect(Example.ConHandle);
    }

    // Return To The Operating System
    return(rc);
}
```

15

Working with Large Objects

The term large object is used in DB2 to refer to any data value that is larger in size than the largest SQL data type supported by DB2. This chapter is designed to introduce you to DB2 large objects and to the DB2 CLI functions that are used to work with large objects. This chapter begins by examining the three types of large object data types that are recognized by DB2 CLI. This is followed by a discussion about the primary mechanism that is used to manipulate large objects—the large object locator. Finally, a detailed reference section that covers each CLI API function that can be used to work directly with large objects is provided.

Large Objects

By DB2's definition, the term *large object*, and the generic acronym *LOB* refer to any large sequence of bytes that is less than or equal to 2 gigabytes in length.

In DB2, and in DB2 CLI, three different large object (LOB) data types exist:

■ *Binary Large Objects* (BLOB)

Binary large objects are primarily used to hold non-traditional data such as graphic images, audio and video clips, and structured data that is to be used by user-defined data types and user-defined functions. Binary large objects are not associated with any specific character set.

■ *Character Large Objects* (CLOB)

Character large objects are primarily used to store single-byte character or mixed-character based data such as documents written with a single-byte character set. DB2 treats CLOBs as large character strings.

■ *Double-Byte Character Large Objects* (DBCLOB)

Double-byte character large objects are primarily used to store double-byte character based data such as documents written with a double-byte character set. DB2 treats DBCLOBs as large graphic strings.

These three LOB data types are represented symbolically as **SQL_BLOB**, **SQL_CLOB**, and **SQL_DBCLOB**, respectively. Corresponding C/C++ data type identifiers (**SQL_C_BLOB**, **SQL_C_CLOB**, and **SQL_C_DBCLOB**) can be specified with any of the DB2 CLI functions that require or return an SQL data type (such as **SQLBindParameter()**, **SQLBindCol()**, and **SQLDescribeCol()**).

LOB Locators

Because LOB data values can be very large, they are typically transferred between an application and a data source (in pieces) with a data-at-execution sequence. Unfortunately, the data-at-execution sequence can be quite time-consuming when working with a large object value. In addition, the data-at-execution sequence does not provide a way for an application that needs to work with a small portion of a large object value, to load only that portion into memory. The entire value must be transferred from the database to the application. With DB2 CLI, applications can get around these limitations by referencing individual LOB values via *large object locators* (LOB locators).

A LOB locator is a mechanism that allows an application program to manipulate a large object value in an efficient, random access manner. A LOB locator is not a reference to actual LOB data; instead, a LOB locator is a simple token value that represents (references) a single LOB value. Operations performed on a LOB locator has no affect on the original LOB value the locator references. The LOB locator is a run time concept: it is not a persistent data type nor is it stored in the database. Instead, it refers to a LOB data value during a transaction and does not persist beyond the transaction in which it was created. LOB locators are implicitly allocated when:

■ A bound LOB column is fetched into a C/C++ LOB locator variable.

■ An unbound LOB column is retrieved into a C/C++ LOB locator variable with the **SQLGetData()** function.

■ A substring is retrieved into a C/C++ LOB locator variable with the **SQLGetSubString()** function.

■ LOB locators are explicitly freed when the transaction in which they were created is terminated OR when the **FREE LOCATOR** SQL statement is executed.

Using LOB Locators

Just as three different *large object* (LOB) data types exist in DB2 CLI, three different LOB locator types exist:

■ Binary Large Object Locators

■ Character Large Object Locators

■ Double-Byte Character Large Object Locators

Each of these three LOB locator types have their own C/C++ data types. They are: **SQL_C_BLOB_LOCATOR**, **SQL_C_CLOB_LOCATOR**, and **SQL_C_DBCLOB_LOCATOR**, respectively.

LOB locators can, in general, be treated as any other C/C++ data type. There are, however, some important differences:

■ LOB locators are created at the data source when a row is retrieved (fetched) or when the **SQLGetSubString()** function is called to define a LOB locator on a portion of another LOB locator value. Only the LOB locator is transferred to the application; the data to which the LOB locator refers remains on the data server.

■ The value of a LOB locator is only valid within the current transaction. LOB locators cannot be stored for later retrieval (outside the current transaction), even if the cursor that fetches the LOB locator was defined with the **WITH HOLD** attribute.

■ Once a LOB locator is returned from the data source, you can use the **SQLGetSubString()** function to either retrieve a portion of the LOB value or to generate another LOB locator that represents a portion of the LOB value. You can use the **SQLGetPosition()** and **SQLGetLength()** functions with the **SQLGetSubString()** function to define the substring. You can also use the LOB locator value returned from the data source to replace a parameter marker in a SQL statement by using it in a **SQLBindParameter()** function call.

■ A LOB locator does not point to a data source position; rather, it references a snapshot of a LOB value. There is no association between the current position of the cursor position pointer and the row from which the LOB value was extracted. This means that even after the cursor position pointer has been repositioned on a different row, the LOB locator (and thus the value it represents) can still be referenced.

■ A given LOB column in a result data set can be bound to a storage buffer (to hold the entire LOB data value), a LOB locator, or a LOB file reference. The most recent bind column function call determines which type of binding is in effect when the SQL statement is executed. If an application requires the entire LOB data value, it can request direct file input and output. The two CLI API functions that provide LOB direct file access are:

■ `SQLBindFileToParam()`

■ `SQLBindFileToCol()`

The file name provided is either the complete path name of the file (which is recommended) or a relative file name. If a relative file name is provided, it is appended to the current path (of the operating environment) of the client process.

Not all DB2 servers currently have large object support. An application should call the `SQLGetFunctions()` function to determine whether any of the CLI LOB support functions are supported by the current server before attempting to use them.

The CLI Large Object (LOB) Support Functions

Table 15–1 lists the CLI functions that are used to work with large object (LOB) data values.

Each of these functions is described, in detail, in the remaining portion of this chapter.

Table 15–1   CLI Large Object (LOB) Support Functions

Function Name	Description
`SQLBindFileToParam()`	Assigns a LOB file reference to a parameter marker in an SQL statement.
`SQLBindFileToCol()`	Assigns a LOB file reference to a column in a result data set.
`SQLGetLength()`	Retrieves the length of large object data that is referenced by a LOB locator.
`SQLGetPosition()`	Determines the starting position of a substring within a source string that is referenced by a LOB locator.
`SQLGetSubString()`	Creates a new LOB locator that references a substring within a source string that is referenced by a LOB locator.

SQLBindFileToParam

COMPATIBILITY

X/OPEN 95 CLI	ISO/IEC 92 CLI	DB2 CLI 5.2	DB2 CLI 2.0	ODBC 3.x
☐	☐	☑	☑	☐

ODBC API CONFORMANCE LEVEL   **NONE**

Purpose

The `SQLBindFileToParam()` function is used to associate (bind) a parameter marker in a SQL statement to one or more external file references.

Syntax

```
SQLRETURN  SQLBindFileToParm    (SQLHSTMT        StatementHandle,
                                 SQLUSMALLINT    ParamMarkerNum,
                                 SQLSMALLINT     SQLDataType,
                                 SQLCHAR         *FileName,
                                 SQLSMALLINT     *FileNameSize,
                                 SQLUINTEGER     *FileOptions,
                                 SQLSMALLINT     MaxFileNameSize,
                                 SQLINTEGER      *ValueSize_IndicatorValue);
```

Parameters

StatementHandle

An SQL statement handle that refers to a previously allocated SQL statement information storage buffer (data structure).

ParamMarkerNum

Specifies the parameter marker's location in the SQL statement text. Parameter markers are numbered sequentially from left to right, starting with 1, as they appear in the SQL statement.

SQLDataType

The SQL data type of the parameter being bound. This parameter must be set to one of the following values:

  ▪ `SQL_BLOB`

  ▪ `SQL_CLOB`

  ▪ `SQL_DBCLOB`

FileName

A pointer to a location in memory where a file name or an array of file names are stored. File names can be specified as complete (with both path names and file names) or as relative (file name only). This parameter cannot contain a NULL value.

FileNameSize	A pointer to a location in memory where the length of the file name (or an array of file name lengths) referenced by the *FileName* parameter is stored. If this parameter is set to NULL, the length **SQL_NTS** will be used, and the value specified in the *FileName* parameter will be treated as a NULL-terminated string.
FileOptions	A pointer to a location in memory where the file option or an array of file options that are to be used when reading from the file are stored. At this time, only the **SQL_FILE_READ** option is recognized. This option indicates that the file can be opened, read, and closed.
FileNameMaxSize	The maximum size of the file name memory storage buffer (*FileName*), or the maximum size of each element in the file name array.
ValueSize_Indicator	A pointer to a location in memory where a special indicator value (or an array of indicator values) associated with the parameter marker is stored. This indicator value should be set to **SQL_NULL_DATA** if the LOB data value of the parameter is to be set to NULL; otherwise, it should be set to **0**.

Description The **SQLBindFileToParam()** function is used to associate (bind) a parameter marker in a SQL statement to an external file reference or to an array of external file references. This type of binding allows large object (LOB) data stored in an external file to be transferred directly into a LOB column in the data source (when the SQL statement containing the parameter marker is executed).

The LOB file reference parameters (*FileName, FileNameSize, FileOptions*) refer to a file that is physically located within the application program's environment (on the client workstation). The application must ensure that these parameters contain the name of a file, the length of the file name, and the appropriate file processing option (in this case, "Read") before the **SQLExecute()** or **SQLExecDirect()** function is called. The values of these parameters can be changed (if necessary) between each **SQLExecute()** or **SQLExecDirect()** function call.

Return Codes SQL_SUCCESS, SQL_SUCCESS_WITH_INFO, SQL_INVALID_HANDLE, SQL_ERROR

SQLSTATEs If this function returns **SQL_SUCCESS_WITH_INFO** or **SQL_ERROR**, one of the following SQLSTATE values may be obtained by calling the **SQLGetDiagRec()** function:

08S01, **40**003, **58**004, **HY**001, **HY**004, **HY**009, **HY**010, **HY**013, **HY**090, **HY**093, or **HY**C00

Refer to Appendix B for detailed information about each SQLSTATE value that can be returned.

Comments ■ If relative file name(s) are used, DB2 CLI will attempt to locate the file in the current directory path of the running application.

- File name strings stored in the *FileNameSize* parameter should not exceed 255 characters.

- This function must be called once for each parameter marker used in an SQL statement whose value is to be obtained directly from an external file when the SQL statement is executed.

- Valid values must be supplied for the *FileName*, *FileNameSize*, and *FileOptions* parameters before an SQL statement can be executed. When an SQL statement is executed, LOB data is read directly from the referenced file and passed directly to the data source.

- If the **SQL_ATTR_PARAMSET_SIZE** statement attribute indicates that multiple values will be provided for each parameter, the *FileName*, *FileNameSize*, and *FileOptions* parameters must point to arrays of LOB file reference values, and the *MaxFileNameSize* parameter must point to an array of maximum length values that correspond to each file name specified. The *MaxFileNameSize* array is used by DB2 CLI to determine the location of each element in the *FileName* array.

- LOB parameter markers in an SQL statement can be bound to an input file with the **SQLBindFileToParam()** function or to a stored buffer with the **SQLBindParameter()** function. The most recent bind parameter function call used determines which type of binding is in effect when the SQL statement is executed.

Restrictions   This function is not available when you are connected to a data source that does not support large object (LOB) data types. To determine whether or not this function is supported for the current data source connection, call the **SQLGetFunctions()** function with the *FunctionType* parameter set to **SQL_API_SQLBINDFILETOPARAM** and check the value of the *Supported* output parameter.

See Also   SQLBindParameter(), SQLExecute(), SQLExecDirect(), SQLBindFileToCol()

Example   The following C++ program illustrates how to use the **SQLBindFileToParam()** function to bind an external file containing LOB data to a parameter marker in a SQL statement:

```
/*------------------------------------------------------------*/
/* NAME:     CH15EX1.CPP                                      */
/* PURPOSE: Illustrate How To Use The Following CLI API Function */
/*          In A C++ Program:                                 */
/*                                                            */
/*               SQLBindFileToParam()                         */
/*                                                            */
/* OTHER CLI APIs SHOWN:                                      */
/*          SQLAllocHandle()              SQLSetEnvAttr()     */
/*          SQLConnect()                  SQLDisconnect()     */
/*          SQLPrepare()                  SQLExecute()        */
/*          SQLFreeHandle()                                   */
/*                                                            */
/*------------------------------------------------------------*/

// Include The Appropriate Header Files
#include <windows.h>
#include <sqlcli1.h>
```

```cpp
#include <iostream.h>

// Define The CLI_Class Class
class CLI_Class
{
    // Attributes
    public:
        SQLHANDLE   EnvHandle;
        SQLHANDLE   ConHandle;
        SQLHANDLE   StmtHandle;
        SQLRETURN   rc;

    // Operations
    public:
        CLI_Class();                            // Constructor
        ~CLI_Class();                           // Destructor
        SQLRETURN InsertRows();
};

// Define The Class Constructor
CLI_Class::CLI_Class()
{
    // Initialize The Return Code Variable
    rc = SQL_SUCCESS;

    // Allocate An Environment Handle
    rc = SQLAllocHandle(SQL_HANDLE_ENV, SQL_NULL_HANDLE, &EnvHandle);

    // Set The ODBC Application Version To 3.x
    if (rc == SQL_SUCCESS)
        rc = SQLSetEnvAttr(EnvHandle, SQL_ATTR_ODBC_VERSION,
                (SQLPOINTER) SQL_OV_ODBC3, SQL_IS_UINTEGER);

    // Allocate A Connection Handle
    if (rc == SQL_SUCCESS)
        rc = SQLAllocHandle(SQL_HANDLE_DBC, EnvHandle, &ConHandle);
}

// Define The Class Destructor
CLI_Class::~CLI_Class()
{
    // Free The Connection Handle
    if (ConHandle != NULL)
        SQLFreeHandle(SQL_HANDLE_DBC, ConHandle);

    // Free The Environment Handle
    if (EnvHandle != NULL)
        SQLFreeHandle(SQL_HANDLE_ENV, EnvHandle);
}

// Define The InsertRows() Member Function
SQLRETURN CLI_Class::InsertRows(void)
{
    // Declare The Local Memory Variables
    SQLRETURN       rc;
```

```
SQLCHAR        SQLStmt[255];
SQLUINTEGER    Option = SQL_FILE_READ;
SQLINTEGER     Indicator = 0;

// Allocate An SQL Statement Handle
rc = SQLAllocHandle(SQL_HANDLE_STMT, ConHandle, &StmtHandle);
if (rc == SQL_SUCCESS)
{
    // Define An INSERT SQL Statement That Uses Parameter
    // Markers
    strcpy((char *) SQLStmt, "INSERT INTO EMP_RESUME (EMPNO, ");
    strcat((char *) SQLStmt, "RESUME_FORMAT, RESUME) VALUES ");
    strcat((char *) SQLStmt, "('000200', 'ascii', ?)");

    // Prepare The SQL Statement
    rc = SQLPrepare(StmtHandle, SQLStmt, SQL_NTS);

    // Bind The Parameter Marker To An External File
    rc = SQLBindFileToParam(StmtHandle, 1, SQL_CLOB,
             (SQLCHAR *) "RESUME.TXT", NULL,
             &Option, 255, &Indicator);

    // Execute The SQL Statement
    rc = SQLExecute(StmtHandle);

    // Free The SQL Statement Handle
    if (StmtHandle != NULL)
        SQLFreeHandle(SQL_HANDLE_STMT, StmtHandle);
}

// Return The CLI API Return Code To The Calling Function
return(rc);
}

/*------------------------------------------------------------*/
/* The Main Function                                          */
/*------------------------------------------------------------*/
int main()
{
    // Declare The Local Memory Variables
    SQLRETURN  rc = SQL_SUCCESS;

    // Create An Instance Of The CLI_Class Class
    CLI_Class  Example;

    // Connect To The DB2 Sample Database
    if (Example.ConHandle != NULL)
    {
        rc = SQLConnect(Example.ConHandle, (SQLCHAR *) "SAMPLE",
                 SQL_NTS, (SQLCHAR *) "userid", SQL_NTS,
                 (SQLCHAR *) "password", SQL_NTS);

        // Insert A New Resume Record Into The EMP_RESUME Table In
        // The DB2 Sample Database
        rc = Example.InsertRows();
```

```
    if (rc == SQL_SUCCESS)
    {
        cout << "Data from the file RESUME.TXT has been added ";
        cout << "to the EMP_RESUME table." << endl;
    }

    // Disconnect From The DB2 Sample Database
    rc = SQLDisconnect(Example.ConHandle);
}

// Return To The Operating System
return(rc);
}
```

SQLBindFileToCol

COMPATIBILITY

X/OPEN 95 CLI	ISO/IEC 92 CLI	DB2 CLI 5.2	DB2 CLI 2.0	ODBC 3.x
☐	☐	✓	✓	☐

ODBC API CONFORMANCE LEVEL   NONE

Purpose   The SQLBindFileToCol() function is used to associate (bind) an external file reference to a column in a result data set.

Syntax
```
SQLRETURN    SQLBindFileToCol    (SQLHSTMT          StatementHandle,
                                  SQLUSMALLINT      ColumnNumber,
                                  SQLCHAR           *FileName,
                                  SQLSMALLINT       *FileNameSize,
                                  SQLUINTEGER       *FileOptions,
                                  SQLSMALLINT       FileNameMaxSize,
                                  SQLINTEGER        *StringLength,
                                  SQLINTEGER        *ValueSize_IndicatorValue);
```

Parameters

StatementHandle   An SQL statement handle that refers to a previously allocated SQL statement information storage buffer (data structure).

ColumnNumber   Specifies the column's location in the result data set. Columns are numbered sequentially from left to right, starting with 1, as they appear in the result data set.

FileName   A pointer to a location in memory where a file name or an array of file names are stored. File names can be specified as complete (with both path names and file names) or as relative (file name only). This parameter cannot contain a NULL value.

FileNameSize	A pointer to a location in memory where the length of the file name (or an array of file name lengths) referenced by the *FileName* parameter is stored. If this parameter is set to NULL, the length **SQL_NTS** will be used, and the value specified in the *FileName* parameter will be treated as a NULL-terminated string.
FileOptions	A pointer to a location in memory where the file option or an array of file options that are to be used when writing to the file are stored. This parameter must be set to one of the following values:

■ **SQL_FILE_CREATE**
A new file is to be created. If a file with the specified name already exists, **SQL_ERROR** will be returned.

■ **SQL_FILE_OVERWRITE**
A new file is to be created. If a file with the specified name already exists, it will be overwritten.

■ **SQL_FILE_APPEND**
If a file with the specified name already exists, the data is to be appended to any existing data found in it. If a file with the specified name does not already exist, a new file is to be created.

FileNameMaxSize	The maximum size of the file name memory storage buffer (*FileName*), or the maximum size of each element in the file name array.
StringLength	A pointer to a location in memory where this function is to store the size (or an array of sizes), in bytes, of any LOB data that is returned. If this pointer is NULL, no LOB information will be returned by the function.
ValueSize_Indicator	A pointer to a location in memory where DB2 CLI is to store either the size of the LOB data value associated with the column or a special indicator value associated with the column data.
	Any of the following indicator values can be returned to this memory location by DB2 CLI:

■ **SQL_NO_TOTAL**
The size of the column data value is unknown.

■ **SQL_NULL_DATA**
The data value associated with the column is NULL.

Description	The **SQLBindFileToCol()** function is used to associate (bind) an external file reference or an array of external file references to a column in a result data set. This type of binding allows data stored in a LOB column to be transferred directly to a file as each row of a result data set is retrieved (fetched).

The LOB file reference parameters (*FileName*, *FileNameSize*, and *FileOptions*) refer to a file that is physically located within the application program's environment (on the client workstation). The application must ensure that these parameters contain the name of a file, the length of the file name, and an appropriate file processing option ("Create", "Overwrite", or "Append") before the **SQLFetch()** or the **SQLFetchScroll()** function is called to retrieve a row from a result data set. The values of these parameters can remain the same, or they can be changed between each **SQLFetch()** or **SQLFetchScroll()** function call.

Return Codes   SQL_SUCCESS, SQL_SUCCESS_WITH_INFO, SQL_INVALID_HANDLE, SQL_ERROR

SQLSTATEs   If this function returns **SQL_SUCCESS_WITH_INFO** or **SQL_ERROR**, one of the following SQLSTATE values may be obtained by calling the **SQLGetDiagRec()** function:

08S01, **40003**, **58004**, **HY001**, **HY002**, **HY009**, **HY010**, **HY013**, **HY090**, or **HYC00**

Refer to Appendix B for detailed information about each SQLSTATE value that can be returned.

Comments
- If relative file name(s) are used, DB2 CLI will attempt to locate the file in the current directory path of the running application.

- File name strings stored in the *FileNameSize* parameter should not exceed 255 characters.

- This function must be called once for each column in the result data set whose value is to be transferred directly to an external file when a row is fetched from that result data set. LOB data is written directly to the specified file—without any data conversion, and without appended NULL terminators.

- Valid values must be supplied for the *FileName*, *FileNameSize*, and *FileOptions* parameters before data can be retrieved from a result data set. When the **SQLFetch()** or **SQLFetchScroll()** function is called, data for all columns that have been bound to a LOB file reference is written to the file or files pointed to by that file reference. Errors associated with the deferred input argument values of the **SQLBindFileToCol()** are reported at fetch time. The LOB file reference and the deferred *StringLength* and *IndicatorValue* output parameters are updated between each fetch operation.

- If the **SQLFetchScroll()** function is used to retrieve multiple rows of data for a LOB column, the *FileName*, *FileNameSize*, and *FileOptions* parameters must point to arrays of LOB file reference variables, and the *MaxFileNameSize* parameter must point to an array of maximum length values that correspond to each file name specified. The *StringLength* and *IndicatorValue* parameters each point to an array whose elements are updated after the **SQLFetchScroll()** function completes execution. The *MaxFileNameSize* array is used by DB2 CLI to determine the location of each element in the *FileName* array.

- By using the **SQLFetchScroll()** function, you can write multiple LOB data values to multiple files or to the same file, depending upon the file name(s) specified. If multiple LOB data values are to be written to the same file, the **SQL_FILE_APPEND** file option (*FileOption* parameter) should be specified for each file name entry.

- The **SQLFetchScroll()** function only supports column-wise binding of arrays that contain LOB data file references.

Restrictions   This function is not available when you are connected to a data sources that does not support LOB data types. To determine whether or not this function is supported for the current data source connection, call the **SQLGetFunctions()** function with the *FunctionType* parameter set to **SQL_API_SQLBINDFILETOCOL** and check the value of the *Supported* output parameter.

See Also   **SQLBindCol()**, **SQLFetch()**, **SQLFetchScroll()**, **SQLBindFileToParam()**

Example   The following C++ program illustrates how to use the **SQLBindFileToCol()** function to bind a LOB column in a result data set to an external data file:

```
/*──────────────────────────────────────────────*/
/* NAME:    CH15EX2.CPP                           */
/* PURPOSE: Illustrate How To Use The Following CLI API Functions */
/*          In A C++ Program:                     */
/*                                                */
/*                SQLBindFileToCol()              */
/*                                                */
/* OTHER CLI APIs SHOWN:                          */
/*          SQLAllocHandle()        SQLSetEnvAttr()    */
/*          SQLConnect()            SQLBindCol()       */
/*          SQLFetch()              SQLExecDirect()    */
/*          SQLDisconnect()         SQLFreeHandle()    */
/*                                                */
/*──────────────────────────────────────────────*/

// Include The Appropriate Header Files
#include <windows.h>
#include <sqlcli1.h>
#include <iostream.h>

// Define The CLI_Class Class
class CLI_Class
{
    // Attributes
    public:
        SQLHANDLE    EnvHandle;
        SQLHANDLE    ConHandle;
        SQLHANDLE    StmtHandle;
        SQLRETURN    rc;

    // Operations
    public:
        CLI_Class();                        // Constructor
        ~CLI_Class();                       // Destructor
        SQLRETURN GetResults();
};

// Define The Class Constructor
CLI_Class::CLI_Class()
{
    // Initialize The Return Code Variable
    rc = SQL_SUCCESS;
```

```cpp
    // Allocate An Environment Handle
    rc = SQLAllocHandle(SQL_HANDLE_ENV, SQL_NULL_HANDLE, &EnvHandle);

    // Set The ODBC Application Version To 3.x
    if (rc == SQL_SUCCESS)
        rc = SQLSetEnvAttr(EnvHandle, SQL_ATTR_ODBC_VERSION,
                (SQLPOINTER) SQL_OV_ODBC3, SQL_IS_UINTEGER);

    // Allocate A Connection Handle
    if (rc == SQL_SUCCESS)
        rc = SQLAllocHandle(SQL_HANDLE_DBC, EnvHandle, &ConHandle);
}

// Define The Class Destructor
CLI_Class::~CLI_Class()
{
    // Free The Connection Handle
    if (ConHandle != NULL)
        SQLFreeHandle(SQL_HANDLE_DBC, ConHandle);

    // Free The Environment Handle
    if (EnvHandle != NULL)
        SQLFreeHandle(SQL_HANDLE_ENV, EnvHandle);
}

// Define The GetResults() Member Function
SQLRETURN CLI_Class::GetResults(void)
{
    // Declare The Local Memory Variables
    SQLCHAR       EmployeeID[7];
    SQLUINTEGER   Option = SQL_FILE_OVERWRITE;
    SQLINTEGER    Indicator = 0;
    SQLINTEGER    Length;

    // Bind The First Column In The Result Data Set Returned To
    // An Application Variable
    rc = SQLBindCol(StmtHandle, 1, SQL_C_CHAR,
                (SQLPOINTER) EmployeeID, sizeof(EmployeeID), NULL);

    // Bind The Second Column In The Result Data Set Returned To
    // An External File
    rc = SQLBindFileToCol(StmtHandle, 2, (SQLCHAR *) "C:\\_RESUME.TXT",
                NULL, &Option, 255, &Length, &Indicator);

    // Retrieve The First (And Only) Record In The Result Data Set
    // Generated - This Will Produce The File C:\_RESUME.TXT
    rc = SQLFetch(StmtHandle);
    if (rc != SQL_NO_DATA)
    {
        // Display The Employee Information
        cout << "The Resume for employee number " << EmployeeID;
        cout << " has been saved in the file C:\\_RESUME.TXT";
        cout << endl;
    }
```

```
    // Return The CLI API Return Code To The Calling Function
    return(rc);
}


/*————————————————————————————————————————————————————————*/
/* The Main Function                                       */
/*————————————————————————————————————————————————————————*/
int main()
{
    // Declare The Local Memory Variables
    SQLRETURN   rc = SQL_SUCCESS;
    SQLCHAR     SQLStmt[255];

    // Create An Instance Of The CLI_Class Class
    CLI_Class   Example;

    // Connect To The DB2 Sample Database
    if (Example.ConHandle != NULL)
    {
        rc = SQLConnect(Example.ConHandle, (SQLCHAR *) "SAMPLE",
                SQL_NTS, (SQLCHAR *) "userid", SQL_NTS,
                (SQLCHAR *) "password", SQL_NTS);

        // Allocate An SQL Statement Handle
        rc = SQLAllocHandle(SQL_HANDLE_STMT, Example.ConHandle,
                &Example.StmtHandle);
        if (rc == SQL_SUCCESS)
        {
            // Define A SELECT SQL Statement
            strcpy((char *) SQLStmt, "SELECT EMPNO, RESUME FROM ");
            strcat((char *) SQLStmt, "EMP_RESUME WHERE ");
            strcat((char *) SQLStmt, "EMPNO = '000150' AND ");
            strcat((char *) SQLStmt, "RESUME_FORMAT = 'ascii'");

            // Prepare And Execute The SQL Statement
            rc = SQLExecDirect(Example.StmtHandle, SQLStmt, SQL_NTS);

            // Capture The Results Of The SQL Query
            if (rc == SQL_SUCCESS)
                Example.GetResults();

            // Free The SQL Statement Handle
            if (Example.StmtHandle != NULL)
                SQLFreeHandle(SQL_HANDLE_STMT, Example.StmtHandle);
        }

        // Disconnect From The DB2 Sample Database
        rc = SQLDisconnect(Example.ConHandle);
    }

    // Return To The Operating System
    return(rc);
}
```

SQLGetLength

COMPATIBILITY

X/OPEN 95 CLI	ISO/IEC 92 CLI	DB2 CLI 5.2	DB2 CLI 2.0	ODBC 3.x
☐	☐	☑	☑	☐

ODBC API CONFORMANCE LEVEL   NONE

Purpose   The `SQLGetLength()` function is used to retrieve the length of a large object (LOB) value that is referenced by a LOB locator and that was retrieved during the current transaction.

Syntax
```
SQLRETURN    SQLGetLength    (SQLHSTMT        StatementHandle,
                             SQLSMALLINT      LocatorCDataType,
                             SQLINTEGER       Locator,
                             SQLINTEGER       *StringLength,
                             SQLINTEGER       *Reserved);
```

Parameters   *StatementHandle*   An SQL statement handle that refers to a previously allocated SQL statement information storage buffer (data structure).

LocatorCDataType   The C language data type of the LOB locator. This parameter must be set to one of the following values:

■ SQL_C_BLOB_LOCATOR

■ SQL_C_CLOB_LOCATOR

■ SQL_C_DBCLOB_LOCATOR

Locator   The LOB locator variable that references the LOB data.

StringLength   A pointer to a location in memory where this function is to store the length (in bytes) of the information referenced by the locator.

Reserved   This parameter is reserved for later use. For now, it must always be set to NULL.

Description   The `SQLGetLength()` function is used to retrieve the length of a LOB value that is referenced by a LOB locator that was retrieved (as a result of a `SQLFetch()`, `SQLFetchScroll()`, or `SQLGetSubString()` function call) during the current transaction. This function can be used to determine the overall length of the data value referenced by an LOB locator (and thus to choose the appropriate strategy for obtaining some or all of the LOB data).

Return Codes   SQL_SUCCESS, SQL_SUCCESS_WITH_INFO, SQL_STILL_EXECUTING, SQL_INVALID_HANDLE, SQL_ERROR

SQLSTATEs   If this function returns **SQL_SUCCESS_WITH_INFO** or **SQL_ERROR**, one of the following SQLSTATE values may be obtained by calling the **SQLGetDiagRec()** function:

07006, **08**S01, **40**003, **0F**001, **58**004, **HY**001, **HY**003, **HY**009, **HY**010, **HY**013, or **HY**C00

Refer to Appendix B for detailed information about each SQLSTATE value that can be returned.

Comments   ■ The overall length of the LOB data value being referenced by the LOB locator (*StringLength* parameter) is returned in bytes, even if the LOB locator references DBCLOB data.

■ The *Locator* parameter can contain any valid LOB locator that has not been explicitly freed by the **FREE LOCATOR** SQL statement or implicitly freed because the transaction in which the locator was created has terminated.

■ The statement handle used by this function must not be associated with any prepared statements or catalog function calls.

Restrictions   This function is not available when you are connected to a data source that does not support LOB data types. To determine whether or not this function is supported for the current data source connection, call the **SQLGetFunctions()** function with the *FunctionType* parameter set to **SQL_API_SQLGETLENGTH** and check the value of the *Supported* output parameter.

See Also   SQLBindCol(), SQLFetch(), SQLFetchScroll(), SQLGetPosition(), SQLGetSubString()

Example   The following C program illustrates how to use the **SQLGetLength()**, **SQLGetPosition()**, and **SQLGetSubString()** functions to retrieve a retrieve and display portion of a LOB data item:

```
/*------------------------------------------------------------------*/
/* NAME:     CH15EX3.CPP                                            */
/* PURPOSE:  Illustrate How To Use The Following CLI API Functions  */
/*           In A C++ Program:                                      */
/*                                                                  */
/*                SQLGetLength()                                    */
/*                SQLGetPosition()                                  */
/*                SQLGetSubString()                                 */
/*                                                                  */
/* OTHER CLI APIs SHOWN:                                            */
/*                SQLAllocHandle()          SQLSetEnvAttr()         */
/*                SQLConnect()              SQLBindCol()            */
/*                SQLFetch()                SQLExecDirect()         */
/*                SQLDisconnect()           SQLFreeHandle()         */
/*                                                                  */
/*------------------------------------------------------------------*/

// Include The Appropriate Header Files
#include <windows.h>
#include <sqlcli1.h>
#include <iostream.h>
```

```
// Define The CLI_Class Class
class CLI_Class
{
    // Attributes
    public:
        SQLHANDLE    EnvHandle;
        SQLHANDLE    ConHandle;
        SQLHANDLE    StmtHandle1;
        SQLHANDLE    StmtHandle2;
        SQLRETURN    rc;

    // Operations
    public:
        CLI_Class();                              // Constructor
        ~CLI_Class();                             // Destructor
        SQLRETURN ShowResults();
};

// Define The Class Constructor
CLI_Class::CLI_Class()
{
    // Initialize The Return Code Variable
    rc = SQL_SUCCESS;

    // Allocate An Environment Handle
    rc = SQLAllocHandle(SQL_HANDLE_ENV, SQL_NULL_HANDLE, &EnvHandle);

    // Set The ODBC Application Version To 3.x
    if (rc == SQL_SUCCESS)
        rc = SQLSetEnvAttr(EnvHandle, SQL_ATTR_ODBC_VERSION,
                (SQLPOINTER) SQL_OV_ODBC3, SQL_IS_UINTEGER);

    // Allocate A Connection Handle
    if (rc == SQL_SUCCESS)
        rc = SQLAllocHandle(SQL_HANDLE_DBC, EnvHandle, &ConHandle);
}

// Define The Class Destructor
CLI_Class::~CLI_Class()
{
    // Free The Connection Handle
    if (ConHandle != NULL)
        SQLFreeHandle(SQL_HANDLE_DBC, ConHandle);

    // Free The Environment Handle
    if (EnvHandle != NULL)
        SQLFreeHandle(SQL_HANDLE_ENV, EnvHandle);
}

// Define The ShowResults() Member Function
SQLRETURN CLI_Class::ShowResults(void)
{
    // Declare The Local Memory Variables
    SQLCHAR       EmployeeID[7];
```

```
SQLINTEGER    CLOB_Locator;
SQLINTEGER    Length;
SQLUINTEGER   Position;
SQLCHAR       SearchString[10] = "Interests";
SQLCHAR       *Buffer;
SQLINTEGER    BufferSize;

// Bind The Columns In The Result Data Set Returned To
// Application Variables
rc = SQLBindCol(StmtHandle1, 1, SQL_C_CHAR,
          (SQLPOINTER) EmployeeID, sizeof(EmployeeID), NULL);

rc = SQLBindCol(StmtHandle1, 2, SQL_C_CLOB_LOCATOR,
          (SQLPOINTER) &CLOB_Locator, 0, NULL);

// While There Are Records In The Result Data Set Generated,
// Retrieve And Display Them
while (rc != SQL_NO_DATA)
{
    rc = SQLFetch(StmtHandle1);
    if (rc != SQL_NO_DATA)
    {
        // Get The Total Length Of The Resume Record
        rc = SQLGetLength(StmtHandle2, SQL_C_CLOB_LOCATOR,
                CLOB_Locator, &Length, NULL);

        // Get The Starting Position Of The "Interests" Section
        // In The Resume Record
        rc = SQLGetPosition(StmtHandle2, SQL_C_CLOB_LOCATOR,
                CLOB_Locator, 0, SearchString, 9,
                1, &Position, NULL);

        // Allocate A Memory Buffer To Hold The "Interests"
        // Section Of The Resume Record
        Position += 9;
        Buffer = (SQLCHAR *) new char[Length - Position + 1];

        // Copy The "Interests" Section Of The Resume Record
        // Into The Buffer
        rc = SQLGetSubString(StmtHandle2, SQL_C_CLOB_LOCATOR,
                CLOB_Locator, Position, Length - Position,
                SQL_C_CHAR, Buffer, Length - Position + 1,
                &BufferSize, NULL);

        // Display The Employees Interests Information
        cout << "Employee ID : " << EmployeeID;
        cout << "  Interests : ";
        cout << Buffer << endl << endl;

        // Free The Memory Buffer
        delete[] Buffer;
    }
}
```

```
    // Return The CLI API Return Code To The Calling Function
    return(rc);
}


/*————————————————————————————————————————————————————————————*/
/* The Main Function                                          */
/*————————————————————————————————————————————————————————————*/
int main()
{
    // Declare The Local Memory Variables
    SQLRETURN  rc = SQL_SUCCESS;
    SQLCHAR    SQLStmt[255];

    // Create An Instance Of The CLI_Class Class
    CLI_Class  Example;

    // Connect To The DB2 Sample Database
    if (Example.ConHandle != NULL)
    {
        rc = SQLConnect(Example.ConHandle, (SQLCHAR *) "SAMPLE",
                SQL_NTS, (SQLCHAR *) "userid", SQL_NTS,
                (SQLCHAR *) "password", SQL_NTS);

        // Allocate Two SQL Statement Handles
        rc = SQLAllocHandle(SQL_HANDLE_STMT, Example.ConHandle,
                &Example.StmtHandle1);

        rc = SQLAllocHandle(SQL_HANDLE_STMT, Example.ConHandle,
                &Example.StmtHandle2);

        if (rc == SQL_SUCCESS)
        {
            // Define A SELECT SQL Statement
            strcpy((char *) SQLStmt, "SELECT EMPNO, RESUME FROM ");
            strcat((char *) SQLStmt, "EMP_RESUME WHERE ");
            strcat((char *) SQLStmt, "RESUME_FORMAT = 'ascii'");

            // Prepare And Execute The SQL Statement
            rc = SQLExecDirect(Example.StmtHandle1, SQLStmt, SQL_NTS);

            // Display The Results Of The SQL Query
            if (rc == SQL_SUCCESS)
                Example.ShowResults();

            // Free The SQL Statement Handles
            if (Example.StmtHandle1 != NULL)
                SQLFreeHandle(SQL_HANDLE_STMT, Example.StmtHandle1);

            if (Example.StmtHandle2 != NULL)
                SQLFreeHandle(SQL_HANDLE_STMT, Example.StmtHandle2);
        }

        // Disconnect From The DB2 Sample Database
```

```
        rc = SQLDisconnect(Example.ConHandle);
    }

    // Return To The Operating System
    return(rc);
}
```

SQLGetPosition

COMPATIBILITY

X/OPEN 95 CLI	ISO/IEC 92 CLI	DB2 CLI 5.2	DB2 CLI 2.0	ODBC 3.x
☐	☐	☑	☑	☐

ODBC API CONFORMANCE LEVEL   **NONE**

Purpose   The **SQLGetPosition()** function retrieves the starting position of a specified string within a large object (LOB) value.

Syntax

SQLRETURN	SQLGetPosition	(SQLHSTMT	*StatementHandle,*
		SQLSMALLINT	*LocatorCDataType,*
		SQLINTEGER	*SourceLocator,*
		SQLINTEGER	*SearchLocator,*
		SQLCHAR	**SearchLiteral,*
		SQLINTEGER	*SearchLiteralSize,*
		SQLUINTEGER	*FromPosition,*
		SQLUINTEGER	**LocatedAt,*
		SQLINTEGER	**Reserved);*

Parameters

StatementHandle   An SQL statement handle that refers to a previously allocated SQL statement information storage buffer (data structure).

LocatorCDataType   The C language data type of the LOB locator. This parameter must be set to one of the following values:

   ■ **SQL_C_BLOB_LOCATOR**

   ■ **SQL_C_CLOB_LOCATOR**

   ■ **SQL_C_DBCLOB_LOCATOR**

SourceLocator   The LOB locator that references the source LOB data.

SearchLocator   The LOB locator that references the search LOB data. This LOB locator must have the same C language data type as the source LOB locator (*SourceLocator*).

SearchLiteral   A pointer to a location in memory where a search string literal is stored.

SearchLiteralSize	The length of the search string literal value stored in the *SearchLiteral* parameter.
FromPosition	The position (in the source LOB) of the first byte of the source string from which the search is to start.
LocatedAt	A pointer to a location in memory where this function is to store the position (in the source LOB) where the specified string literal was located. If the string literal was not found, this value will be set to **0**.
Reserved	This parameter is reserved for later use. For now, it must always be set to NULL.

Description   The `SQLGetPosition()` function is used to retrieve the starting position of a specified string within a LOB data value. This function is used in conjunction with the `SQLGetSubString()` function to obtain any portion of a LOB data value. In order to use the `SQLGetSubString()` function, you must know the starting position of the substring within the overall LOB data in advance. In situations where you can determine the starting position of a substring by searching the LOB data for the first word(s) or set of characters of that substring, the `SQLGetPosition()` function can be used to perform the search and return the starting position value.

Return Codes   SQL_SUCCESS, SQL_SUCCESS_WITH_INFO, SQL_STILL_EXECUTING, SQL_INVALID_HANDLE, SQL_ERROR

SQLSTATEs   If this function returns **SQL_SUCCESS_WITH_INFO** or **SQL_ERROR**, one of the following SQLSTATE values may be obtained by calling the **SQLGetDiagRec()** function:

07006, **08**S01, **40**003, **0F**001, **42**818, **58**004, **HY**001, **HY**009, **HY**010, **HY**013, **HY**090, or **HY**C00

Refer to Appendix B for detailed information about each SQLSTATE value that can be returned.

Comments   ■ The search string specified can be either a LOB locator value or a literal string.

■ Both the source LOB locator (*SourceLocator*) and the search LOB locator (*SearchLocator*) can be any LOB locator value returned from the data source by a **SQLFetch()**, **SQLFetchScroll()**, or **SQLGetSubString()** function call made within the current transaction.

■ The *SourceLocator* and *SearchLocator* parameters (if used) can contain any valid LOB locator that has not been explicitly freed by the **FREE LOCATOR** SQL statement or implicitly freed because the transaction in which the locator was created has terminated.

■ If a search LOB locator is used, both the *SourceLocator* and the *SearchLocator* parameters must reference the same LOB locator C data type.

■ The statement handle used by this function must not be associated with any prepared statements or catalog function calls.

Restrictions This function is not available when you are connected to a data sources that does not support LOB data types. To determine whether or not this function is supported for the current data source connection, call the `SQLGetFunctions()` function with the *FunctionType* parameter set to `SQL_API_SQLGETPOSITION` and check the value of the *Supported* output parameter.

See Also `SQLBindCol()`, `SQLFetch()`, `SQLFetchScroll()`, `SQLGetLength()`, `SQLGetSubString()`

Examples See the example provided for the `SQLGetLength()` function on page 632.

SQLGetSubString

COMPATIBILITY

X/OPEN 95 CLI	ISO/IEC 92 CLI	DB2 CLI 5.2	DB2 CLI 2.0	ODBC 3.x
☐	☐	☑	☑	☐

ODBC API CONFORMANCE LEVEL   **CORE**

Purpose The `SQLGetSubString()` function is used to retrieve a portion of a large object (LOB) value that is referenced by a LOB locator that was retrieved during the current transaction.

Syntax

```
SQLRETURN    SQLGetSubString    (SQLHSTMT      StatementHandle,
                                 SQLSMALLINT   LocatorCDataType,
                                 SQLINTEGER    SourceLocator,
                                 SQLUINTEGER   FromPosition,
                                 SQLUINTEGER   Size,
                                 SQLSMALLINT   TargetCDataType,
                                 SQLPOINTER    SubString,
                                 SQLINTEGER    SubStringMaxSize,
                                 SQLINTEGER    *SubStringSize,
                                 SQLINTEGER    Reserved);
```

Parameters

StatementHandle An SQL statement handle that refers to a previously allocated SQL statement information storage buffer (data structure).

LocatorCDataType The C language data type of the LOB locator. This parameter must be set to one of the following values:

- ▥ **SQL_C_BLOB_LOCATOR**
- ▥ **SQL_C_CLOB_LOCATOR**
- ▥ **SQL_C_DBCLOB_LOCATOR**

SourceLocator The LOB locator that references the source LOB.

FromPosition The position (in the LOB) of the first byte to be returned by this function.

Size	The length of the string to be returned by this function.
TargetCDataType	The C language data type of the string variable or LOB locator that will be used to store the substring value returned by this function. This parameter must be set to one of the following values:

- **SQL_C_BINARY**
- **SQL_C_BLOB_LOCATOR**
- **SQL_C_CHAR**
- **SQL_C_CLOB_LOCATOR**
- **SQL_C_DBCHAR**
- **SQL_C_DBCLOB_LOCATOR**

SubString	A pointer to a location in memory where this function is to store the substring (or LOB locator) value retrieved.
SubStringMaxSize	The maximum size of the memory storage buffer where this function is to store the substring (or LOB locator) retrieved.
SubStringSize	A pointer to a location in memory where this function is to store the actual number of bytes written to the substring memory storage buffer (*SubString*).
Reserved	This parameter is reserved for later use. For now, it must always be set to NULL.

Description The **SQLGetSubString()** function is used to retrieve a portion of a LOB data value that is referenced by a LOB locator value that was retrieved (as a result of a **SQLFetch()**, **SQLFetchScroll()**, or **SQLGetSubString()** function call) during the current transaction. When any portion of a string that is represented by a LOB locator is retrieved, the result can be placed in an appropriate C string variable, or a new LOB value can be created (on the connected data source) and the result can be placed there via another LOB locator.

Return Codes SQL_SUCCESS, SQL_SUCCESS_WITH_INFO, SQL_STILL_EXECUTING, SQL_INVALID_HANDLE, SQL_ERROR

SQLSTATEs If this function returns **SQL_SUCCESS_WITH_INFO** or **SQL_ERROR**, one of the following SQLSTATE values may be obtained by calling the **SQLGetDiagRec()** function:

01004, **07006**, **08S01**, **0F001**, **22011**, **40003**, **58004**, **HY001**, **HY003**, **HY009**, **HY010**, **HY013**, **HY090**, or **HYC00**

Refer to Appendix B for detailed information about each SQLSTATE value that can be returned.

Comments ▇ You can use this function as an alternative to the **SQLGetData()** function to retrieve data from a result data set. In this case, a column is bound to a LOB locator, which is then used to by the **SQLGetSubString()** function to fetch the LOB value as a whole or in pieces.

■ The *SourceLocator* parameter can contain any valid LOB locator that has not been explicitly freed by the **FREE LOCATOR** SQL statement or implicitly freed because the transaction in which the locator was created has terminated.

■ The statement handle used by this function must not be associated with any prepared statements or catalog function calls.

Restrictions   This function is not available when you are connected to a data sources that does not support LOB data types. To determine whether or not the function is supported for the current data source connection, call the **SQLGetFunctions()** function with the *FunctionType* parameter set to **SQL_API_SQLGETSUBSTRING** and check the value of the *Supported* output parameter.

See Also   **SQLBindCol()**, **SQLFetch()**, **SQLFetchScroll()**, **SQLGetData()**, **SQLGetLength()**, **SQLGetPosition()**

Examples   See the examples provided for the **SQLGetLength()** function on page 632.

APPENDIX A

ODBC Scalar Functions

An ODBC scalar function is an operation denoted by a function name followed by a pair of parentheses enclosing zero or more specified arguments. Because each ODBC scalar function returns a value, scalar functions can be specified in an SQL statement wherever an expression can be used.

Table A–1 describes all the scalar functions that are provided by ODBC. Several functions were added in ODBC 3.0 to align ODBC with the SQL-92 standards. However, it is important to note that ODBC and SQL-92 classify their scalar functions differently. ODBC classifies scalar functions by argument type, whereas SQL-92 classifies them by return value. For example, the function EXTRACT(*argument1* FROM *argument2*) is classified as a time-date function by ODBC, because *argument1* is a datetime keyword and *argument2* is a datetime or interval expression. SQL-92, on the other hand, classifies EXTRACT(*argument1* FROM *argument2*) as a numeric scalar function, because the return value is numeric.

An application can determine which scalar functions a driver supports by calling the SQLGetInfo() function with the appropriate information type specified. Information types are included for both ODBC and SQL-92 classifications of scalar functions; however, because these classifications are different, a driver may only indicate whether it supports some scalar functions if an information type other than an ODBC or SQL-92 scalar function information type is specified. For example, support for EXTRACT(*argument1* FROM *argument2*) in ODBC is indicated by the SQL_TIMEDATE_FUNCTIONS information type. Support for EXTRACT(*argument1* FROM *argument2*) in SQL-92, on the other hand, is indicated by the SQL_SQL92_NUMERIC_VALUE_FUNCTIONS information type.

Each of the functions shown in Table A–1 can be invoked from a DB2 CLI application by using the ODBC vendor escape clause for executing functions (refer to Chapter 6, "SQL Statements and DB2 CLI," for more information about ODBC vendor escape clauses). If an error is encountered while executing any of these functions, SQLSTATE 38552 will be returned, and the text portion of the associated error message will be in the form **SYSFUN:*nn***, where *nn* is one of the following reason codes:

01	Numeric value out of range
02	Division by zero
03	Arithmetic overflow or underflow
04	Invalid date format
05	Invalid time format
06	Invalid timestamp format
07	Invalid character representation of a timestamp duration
08	Invalid interval type (must be 1, 2, 4, 8, 16, 32, 64, 128, or 256)
09	String too long
10	Length or position in string function out of range
11	Invalid character representation of a floating point number

NOTE:　*Users moving from DB2 for Common Servers (Version 2.1.0) to DB2 Universal Database must migrate existing databases before all of these functions will be available.*

Table A–1　ODBC Scalar Functions

Function/Syntax	Description
String Functions	
ASCII(*argument*) (ODBC 1.0)	Returns the ASCII code value of the leftmost character of *argument* as an integer.
BIT_LENGTH(*argument*) (ODBC 3.0)	Returns the length, in bits, of *argument*.
CHAR(*argument*) (ODBC 1.0)	Returns the character that has the ASCII code value specified by *argument*. The value of *argument* should be between **0** and **255**; otherwise, the NULL value is returned.
CHAR_LENGTH(*argument*) (ODBC 3.0)	Returns the length, in characters, of *argument*, if *argument* is a character data type; otherwise, returns the length, in bytes, of *argument* (the smallest integer not less than the number of bits divided by 8). **CHARACTER_LENGTH** is a synonym for **CHAR_LENGTH**
CONCAT(*argument1, argument2*) (ODBC 1.0)	Returns a character string that is the result of concatenating *argument2* to *argument1*.
DIFFERENCE(*argument1, argument2*) (ODBC 2.0)	Returns an integer value that indicates the difference between the sounds of the words in *argument1* and *argument2*, as determined with the **SOUNDEX** function. A value of **0** indicates that the strings sound alike.
INSERT(*argument1, position, size,* *argument2*) (ODBC 1.0)	Returns a character string where **size** characters have been deleted from *argument1* beginning at *position*, and where *argument2* has been inserted into *argument1*, beginning at *position*.
LCASE(*argument*) (ODBC 1.0)	Returns a character string in which all uppercase characters in *argument* have been converted to lowercase.
LEFT(*argument, length*) (ODBC 1.0)	Returns a character string consisting of the leftmost *length* characters of *argument*.
LENGTH(*argument*) (ODBC 1.0)	Returns the length of *argument*, in characters, excluding trailing blanks and the NULL-termination character.
LOCATE(*argument1, argument2* *<, position>*) (ODBC 1.0)	Returns the starting position of the first occurrence of *argument1* within *argument2*. If a *position* is specified, it indicates the character position in *argument2* where the search is to begin. If *argument1* is not found in *argument2*, the value **0** is returned.
LTRIM(*argument*) (ODBC 1.0)	Returns the characters of *argument*, with leading blanks removed.
OCTET_LENGTH(*argument*) (ODBC 3.0)	Returns the length, in bytes, of *argument*. The result is the smallest integer greater than or equal to the number of bits divided by 8.

Table A–1   ODBC Scalar Functions (Continued)

Function/Syntax	Description
POSITION(*argument1* IN *argument2*) (ODBC 3.0)	Returns the position of **argument1** in **argument2**. The result is an exact numeric value with an implementation-defined precision and a scale of **0**.
REPEAT(*argument, count*) (ODBC 1.0)	Returns a character string composed of **argument** repeated **count** times.
REPLACE(*argument1, argument2, argument3*) (ODBC 1.0)	Returns a character string in which all occurrences of **argument2** in **argument1** have been replaced with **argument3**.
RIGHT(*argument, length*) (ODBC 1.0)	Returns a character string consisting of the rightmost **length** characters of **argument**.
RTRIM(*argument*) (ODBC 1.0)	Returns the characters of **argument**, with trailing blanks removed.
SOUNDEX(*argument*) (ODBC 2.0)	Returns a four-character code character string representing the sound of the words in **argument**. The result can be used to compare the sounds of strings.
SPACE(*argument*) (ODBC 2.0)	Returns a character string consisting of **argument** spaces (blanks).
SUBSTRING(*argument, position, length*) (ODBC 1.0)	Returns a character string that is derived from **argument**, starting at the character position specified by **position**, **length** characters in length.
UCASE(*argument*) (ODBC 1.0)	Returns a character string in which all lowercase characters in **argument** have been converted to uppercase.

Numeric Functions

Function/Syntax	Description
ABS(*argument*) (ODBC 1.0)	Returns the absolute value of **argument**.
ACOS(*argument*) (ODBC 1.0)	Returns the arccosine of **argument** as an angle, expressed in radians.
ASIN(*argument*) (ODBC 1.0)	Returns the arcsine of **argument** as an angle, expressed in radians.
ATAN(*argument*) (ODBC 1.0)	Returns the arctangent of **argument** as an angle, expressed in radians.
ATAN2(*argument1, argument2*) (ODBC 2.0)	Returns the arctangent of x and y coordinates, specified by **argument1** and **argument2**, respectively, as an angle, expressed in radians.
CEILING(*argument*) (ODBC 1.0)	Returns the smallest integer value that is greater than or equal to **argument**.
COS(*argument*) (ODBC 1.0)	Returns the cosine of **argument**, where **argument** is an angle expressed in radians.
COT(*argument*) (ODBC 1.0)	Returns the cotangent of **argument**, where **argument** is an angle expressed in radians.
DEGREES(*argument*) (ODBC 2.0)	Returns the number of degrees converted from **argument**, expressed in radians.

Table A–1   ODBC Scalar Functions (Continued)

Function/Syntax	Description
EXP(*argument*) (ODBC 1.0)	Returns the exponential value of **argument**.
FLOOR(*argument*) (ODBC 1.0)	Returns the largest integer value that is less than or equal to **argument**.
LOG(*argument*) (ODBC 1.0)	Returns the natural logarithm of **argument**.
LOG10(*argument*) (ODBC 2.0)	Returns the base-10 logarithm of **argument**.
MOD(*argument1, argument2*) (ODBC 1.0)	Returns the remainder (modulus) of **argument1** divided by **argument2**. If **argument1** is negative, the result is negative.
PI() (ODBC 1.0)	Returns the constant value of **pi** (π) as a floating point value.
POWER(*argument1, argument2*) (ODBC 2.0)	Returns the value of **argument1**, raised to the power of **argument2**.
RADIANS(*argument*) (ODBC 2.0)	Returns the number of radians converted from **argument**, expressed in degrees.
RAND(*<argument>*) (ODBC 1.0)	Returns a random floating-point value using **argument** as the optional seed value.
ROUND(*argument1, argument2*) (ODBC 2.0)	Returns **argument1** rounded to **argument2** places right of the decimal point. If **argument2** is negative, **argument1** is rounded to the absolute value of **argument2** places to the left of the decimal point.
SIGN(*argument*) (ODBC 1.0)	Returns an indicator for the sign of **argument**. If **argument** is less than zero, **−1** is returned. If **argument** equals zero, **0** is returned. If **argument** is greater than zero, **1** is returned.
SIN(*argument*) (ODBC 1.0)	Returns the sine of **argument**, where **argument** is an angle expressed in radians.
SQRT(*argument*) (ODBC 1.0)	Returns the square root of **argument**.
TAN(*argument*) (ODBC 1.0)	Returns the tangent of **argument**, where **argument** is an angle expressed in radians.
TRUNCATE(*argument1, argument2*) (ODBC 2.0)	Returns **argument1** truncated to **argument2** places right of the decimal point. If **argument2** is negative, **argument1** is truncated to the absolute value of **argument2** places to the left of the decimal point.

Date, Time, and Interval Functions

CURRENT_DATE() (ODBC 3.0)	Returns the current date.
CURRENT_TIME(*<argument>*) (ODBC 3.0)	Returns the current local time, using **argument** as the optional seconds precision of the returned value.

Table A–1   ODBC Scalar Functions (Continued)

Function/Syntax	Description
CURRENT_TIMESTAMP(*argument*) (ODBC 3.0)	Returns the current local date and local time as a timestamp value, using *argument* as the optional seconds precision of the returned value.
CURDATE() (ODBC 1.0)	Returns the current date.
CURTIME() (ODBC 1.0)	Returns the current local time.
DAYNAME(*argument*) (ODBC 2.0)	Returns a mixed-case character string containing the data source–specific name of the day (for example, **Sunday–Saturday** or **Sun.—Sat.** for a data source that uses English) for the day portion of *argument*.
DAYOFMONTH(*argument*) (ODBC 1.0)	Returns the day of the month value stored in the month portion of *argument*, as an integer value in the range of **1–31**.
DAYOFWEEK(*argument*) (ODBC 1.0)	Returns the day of the week value stored in the day portion of *argument*, as an integer value in the range of **1–7** (where **1** represents "Sunday" for a data source that uses English).
DAYOFYEAR(*argument*) (ODBC 1.0)	Returns the day of the year value stored in the year portion of *argument*, as an integer value in the range of **1–366**.
EXTRACT(*argument1* FROM *argument2*) (ODBC 3.0)	Returns the *argument1* portion of *argument2* where *argument2* is a datetime or interval expression. *argument1* can be one of the following keywords: **YEAR** **MONTH** **DAY** **HOUR** **MINUTE** **SECOND** The precision of the returned value is implementation-defined. The scale is **0** unless **SECOND** is specified, in which case the scale is greater than or equal to the fractional seconds precision of *argument2*.
HOUR(*argument*) (ODBC 1.0)	Returns the hour value stored in the hour portion of *argument*, as an integer value in the range of **0–23**.
JULIAN_DAY(*argument1*)	Returns the number of days between *argument1* and January 1, 4712 B.C. (the start of the Julian date calendar).
MINUTE(*argument*) (ODBC 1.0)	Returns the minute value stored in the minute portion of *argument*, as an integer value in the range of **0–59**.
MONTH(*argument*) (ODBC 1.0)	Returns the month value stored in the month portion of *argument*, as an integer value in the range of **1–12** (where **1** represents "January" for a data source that uses English)
MONTHNAME(*argument*) (ODBC 2.0)	Returns a character string containing the data source-specific name of the month (for example, **January–December** or **Jan.–Dec.** for a data source that uses English) for the month portion of *argument*.
NOW() (ODBC 1.0)	Returns the current date and time as a timestamp value.

Table A–1 ODBC Scalar Functions (Continued)

Function/Syntax	Description
`QUARTER(argument)` (ODBC 1.0)	Returns the quarter in *argument* as an integer value in the range of **1–4** (where **1** represents January 1 through March 31 for a data source that uses English).
`SECOND(argument)` (ODBC 1.0)	Returns the seconds value stored in the seconds portion of *argument*, as an integer value in the range **0–59**.
`SECONDS_SINCE_MIDNIGHT(argument1)`	Returns the number of seconds in *argument1*, relative to midnight, as an integer value in the range of **0-86400**. If *argument1* includes a fractional seconds component, it will be discarded.

`TIMESTAMPADD(argument1, argument2, argument3)`
(ODBC 1.0)
	Returns a timestamp calculated by adding *argument2* intervals of type *argument1* to *argument3* (where fractional seconds are expressed in billionths of a second). *argument1* can be one of the following keywords:
	
	`SQL_TSI_FRAC_SECOND` `SQL_TSI_SECOND`
	`SQL_TSI_MINUTE` `SQL_TSI_HOUR`
	`SQL_TSI_DAY` `SQL_TSI_WEEK`
	`SQL_TSI_MONTH` `SQL_TSI_QUARTER`
	`SQL_TSI_YEAR`
	
	If *argument3* is a time value and *argument1* specifies days, weeks, months, quarters, or years, the date portion of *argument3* is set to the current date before calculating the resulting timestamp. If *argument3* is a date value and *argument1* specifies fractional seconds, seconds, minutes, or hours, the time portion of *argument3* is set to **0** before calculating the resulting timestamp.

`TIMESTAMPDIFF(argument1, argument2, argument3)`
(ODBC 2.0)
	Returns the integer number of intervals of type *argument1* by which *argument3* is greater than *argument2* (where fractional seconds are expressed in billionths of a second). *argument1* can be one of the following keywords:
	
	`SQL_TSI_FRAC_SECOND` `SQL_TSI_SECOND`
	`SQL_TSI_MINUTE` `SQL_TSI_HOUR`
	`SQL_TSI_DAY` `SQL_TSI_WEEK`
	`SQL_TSI_MONTH` `SQL_TSI_QUARTER`
	`SQL_TSI_YEAR`
	
	If *argument2* or *argument3* is a time value and *argument1* specifies days, weeks, months, quarters, or years, the date portion of *argument2* or *argument3* is set to the current date before calculating the difference between the timestamps. If *argument2* or *argument3* is a date value and *argument1* specifies fractional seconds, seconds, minutes, or hours, the time portion of *argument2* or *argument3* is set to **0** before calculating the difference between the timestamps.

`WEEK(argument)` (ODBC 1.0)	Returns the week value stored in the week portion of *argument*, as an integer value in the range of **1–53**.
`YEAR(argument)` (ODBC 1.0)	Returns the year value stored in the year portion of *argument*, as an integer value in the range of **1–9999**.

Table A–1   ODBC Scalar Functions (Continued)

Function/Syntax	Description
System Functions	
DATABASE() (ODBC 1.0)	Returns the name of the database corresponding to the current connection handle.
IFNULL(*argument1*, *argument2*) (ODBC 1.0)	Returns either ***argument1*** or ***argument2***, depending upon whether or not ***argument1*** is NULL If ***argument1*** is NULL, ***argument2*** is returned. If ***argument1*** is not NULL, ***argument1*** is returned. The possible data type of ***argument2*** must be compatible with the data type of ***argument1***.
USER() (ODBC 1.0)	Returns the user name in the DBMS. This may be different from the login name.
Conversion Function	
CONVERT(*argument1*, *argument2*)	Returns the value of ***argument1*** converted to the data type specified in ***argument2***. Valid values of ***argument2*** are the following keywords:

SQL_BIT	SQL_BINARY
SQL_VARBINARY	SQL_LONGVARBINARY
SQL_CHAR	SQL_VARCHAR
SQL_LONGVARCHAR	SQL_TINYINT
SQL_SMALLINT	SQL_INTEGER
SQL_BIGINT	SQL_DECIMAL
SQL_FLOAT	SQL_REAL
SQL_DOUBLE	SQL_DATE
SQL_TIME	SQL_TIMESTAMP

(Adapted from Appendix E on pages 1,251–1,261 of *Microsoft ODBC 3.0 Software Development Kit & Programmer's Reference*.)

APPENDIX B

SQLSTATE Reference

SQLGetDiagRec() or **SQLGetDiagField()** can be called to retrieve SQLSTATE values generated when a DB2 CLI function returns any return code other than **SQL_NO_DATA** or **SQL_SUCCESS**. The five-character string value returned for an SQLSTATE consists of a two-character class value followed by a three-character subclass value (as defined by *X/Open Data Management: Structured Query Language (SQL)*, Version 2, March 1995).

A class value of **01** indicates a warning and is accompanied by a return code of **SQL_SUCCESS_WITH_INFO**. Class values other than **01** indicate an error and are accompanied by a return code of **SQL_ERROR**. Class values of **HY** have been reserved by X/Open for Call Level Interfaces, which are equivalent to the DB2 CLI 2.0 and ODBC 2.0 **S1** class (DB2 CLI 5.2 and ODBC 3.x drivers also use the **HY** class instead of the **S1** class). In any case, the subclass value 000 indicates that there is no subclass for that particular SQLSTATE.

Table B–1 contains a listing of the SQLSTATE values that can be returned by DB2 CLI functions. DB2 CLI functions can also return driver-specific SQLSTATEs not listed in this table. Refer to the documentation for the driver/data source being used for information about additional SQLSTATE values that may be returned.

> **NOTE:** *Although successful execution of a function is usually indicated by the return code* **SQL_SUCCESS**, *the SQLSTATE **00**000 also indicates success.*

Table B–1 SQLSTATE Cross Reference

DB2 CLI SQLSTATE	Description
01000	General warning. The **SQLGetDiagRec()** function can be used to retrieve a driver-specific informational message (provided one is available).
01002	An error occurred while attempting to disconnect from a data source. The operation was successful; however, **SQL_SUCCESS_WITH_INFO** was returned.
01004	The data stored in one or more DB2 CLI function parameters or returned for one or more result data set columns was longer than the application variable/buffer or column size specified. Because of this data was truncated.
01006	A **REVOKE** SQL statement was specified, and the user did not have the authorization needed to execute it.
01007	A **GRANT** SQL statement was specified, and the user did not have the authorization needed to execute it.
01504	An **UPDATE** or **DELETE** SQL statement that did not contain a valid **WHERE** clause was specified. The operation was successful; however, **SQL_SUCCESS_WITH_INFO** or **SQL_NO_DATA** was returned.
01508	The SQL statement specified was disqualified for blocking for reasons other than storage needs.

Table B-1   SQLSTATE Cross Reference (Continued)

DB2 CLI SQLSTATE	Description
01S00	An invalid keyword or attribute value was specified in the connection string. The connect operation was successful and SQL_SUCCESS_WITH_INFO was returned because one of the following occurred: • The unrecognized keyword was ignored. • The invalid attribute value was ignored, and the default value was used.
01S01	An error occurred while retrieving (fetching) one or more rows from a result data set. The operation was successful; SQL_SUCCESS_WITH_INFO was returned.
01S02	The data source/driver did not support the value specified so it substituted a similar value. The operation was successful; SQL_SUCCESS_WITH_INFO was returned.
01S06	The requested rowset overlapped the start of the result data set OR the application attempted to retrieve (fetch) data from the result data set before the first rowset was returned.
01S07	A fetch operation was performed and, because the data type of the application buffer was not SQL_C_CHAR or SQL_C_BINARY, the data returned to application variables/buffers for one or more columns was truncated. (For numeric C data types, the fractional part of the number was truncated. For time and timestamp, interval C data types containing a time component, the fractional portion of the time was truncated.)
07001	The number of parameters bound to application variables was less than the number of parameter markers coded in the SQL statement specified.
07002	A column number specified while binding columns to application variables was greater than the number of columns found in the result data set.
07005	The SQL statement specified did not produce a result data set.
07006	The data value could not be converted in a meaningful manner to the SQL data type specified—incompatible data conversions are not allowed.
07009	The column number specified exceeded the maximum number of columns in the result data set.
08001	The driver was unable to establish a connection with the data source specified. The connection request may have been rejected because a connection to the data source (via embedded SQL) already exists.
08002	The connection handle specified has already been used to establish a connection to a data source, and that connection is still open.
08003	The connection associated with the connection handle specified is not open. A connection must be established successfully (and the connection must be open) before the DB2 CLI function can be executed.
08004	The data source rejected the attempt to establish a connection.
08007	The connection to the data source failed while the DB2 CLI function was executing. Whether the requested COMMIT or ROLLBACK operation occurred before or after the connection failure occurred cannot be determined.
08S01	The communication link between the driver and the data source failed before the DB2 CLI function completed processing.
0F001	The LOB token variable specified does not currently represent a LOB value.

Table B-1   SQLSTATE Cross Reference (Continued)

DB2 CLI SQLSTATE	Description
21S01	An **INSERT** SQL statement was specified and the number of values provided in the values list did not match the number of columns specified in the table column list.
21S02	A **CREATE VIEW** SQL statement was specified and the number of names provided in the table column list did not match the number of columns in the derived table defined by the query specification.
22001	A character string assigned to a character data type column exceeded the column's maximum length and was truncated. The operation was successful; **SQL_SUCCESS_WITH_INFO** was returned.
22002	A length/indicator variable is required (possibly to indicate that a NULL value is being sent/retrieved) but one was not supplied.
22003	A numeric value assigned to a numeric data type column caused truncation of the whole part of the number, either at the time of assignment or in computing an intermediate result OR the SQL statement specified contained an arithmetic expression that caused a division by zero error to occur.
22005	A value or a literal was incompatible with the data type associated with the parameter.
22007	A datetime value (or the string representation of a datetime value) represented an invalid date.
22008	An arithmetic operation on a date or timestamp value produced a result that was not within the valid range of date or timestamp values.
22011	The starting position specified is greater than the length of the string from which the substring is to be extracted.
22012	An arithmetic expression caused a division by zero to occur.
22015	Assigning an exact numeric or interval C data type to an interval SQL data type OR assigning an exact numeric or interval SQL data type to an interval C data type caused a loss of significant digits.
22018	The C data type was an exact or approximate numeric, datetime, or interval data type, the SQL data type of the column was a character data type, and the value in the column was not a valid literal of the bound C data type OR the SQL data type was an exact or approximate numeric, datetime, or interval data type, the C data type was **SQL_C_CHAR**, and the value in a column was not a valid literal of the bound SQL data type.
22019	The SQL statement specified contained a **LIKE** predicate with "**ESCAPE escape character**" in the **WHERE** clause, and the length of the escape character following "**ESCAPE**" was not equal to **1**.
22025	The SQL statement specified contained "**LIKE pattern-value ESCAPE escape character**" in the **WHERE** clause, and the character following the escape character in the pattern value was not "%" or "_."
22026	The length of character data was set to the data source and the actual length of the long data value sent was smaller than the length specified.
23000	The SQL statement specified was not executed because it would cause an integrity constraint violation to occur.

Table B–1   SQLSTATE Cross Reference (Continued)

DB2 CLI SQLSTATE	Description
24000	The SQL statement specified did not produce a result data set OR a cursor has already been opened for the specified statement handle OR the cursor associated with the specified statement handle is not positioned on a row in the result data set.
24504	The cursor identified in an **UPDATE, DELETE, SET,** or **GET** SQL statement is not positioned on a row in the result data set. This is because results from a previous query are pending on the specified SQL statement handle—or because the cursor associated with the specified SQL statement handle has not been closed.
25000	A transaction is in progress at the data source connection specified. As long as this transaction remains active, the connection cannot be terminated.
25501	A transaction is in progress at the data source connection specified. As long as this transaction remains active, the connection cannot be terminated.
28000	The user ID and/or password specified violated restrictions defined by the data source.
34000	The cursor name specified is invalid or already exists OR a positioned **UPDATE** or a positioned **DELETE** SQL statement was specified and the cursor referenced by the statement is not open.
37000	The SQL statement specified could not be prepared because it contained one or more syntax errors.
37xxx	The specified SQL statement contains one or more of the following: a **COMMIT** SQL statement, a **ROLLBACK** SQL statement, or an SQL statement that the connected data source could not prepare.
40001	The transaction to which the SQL statement belonged was terminated (rolled back if possible) to prevent a deadlock.
40003	The associated connection failed before the DB2 CLI function completed; the state of the transaction cannot be determined.
42000	The user does not have the necessary authorizations to execute the SQL statement specified OR the driver was unable to lock the row, as needed, to perform the requested operation.
42xxx	There are one or more syntax or access problems with the SQL statement specified.
42601	The **PARMLIST** value in the stored procedures catalog table contains a syntax error.
42818	The operands of an operator or function are not compatible, because the length of the pattern specified exceeds 4,000 bytes.
42895	The value of a host variable in an **EXECUTE** or **OPEN** SQL statement cannot be used because of its data type, OR a LOB locator type specified for a bound parameter does not match the LOB data type of the parameter marker, OR a LOB locator type was specified but the corresponding parameter marker is not an LOB data type.
428A1	Unable to access a file that is referenced by a host file variable. This error can be raised for any number of reasons. The following associated reason codes can be used to identify the particular error: **01** (The file name length specified is invalid, or the file name and/or the path has an invalid format).

Table B–1 SQLSTATE Cross Reference (Continued)

DB2 CLI SQLSTATE	Description
	02 (The file option specified is invalid). It must have one of the following values:
	SQL_FILE_READ: Read from an existing file
	SQL_FILE_CREATE: Create a new file for write
	SQL_FILE_OVERWRITE: Overwrite an existing file. If the file does not exist, create it.
	SQL_FILE_APPEND: Append to an existing file. If the file does not exist, create it.
	03 (The file cannot be found).
	04 (The **SQL_FILE_CREATE** option was specified for a file with the same names as an existing file).
	05 (Access to the file was denied. The user does not have permission to open the file);
	06 (Access to the file was denied. The file is in use with incompatible modes. Files to be written to are opened in exclusive mode).
	07 (Disk full was encountered while writing to the file).
	08 (Unexpected end of file encountered while reading from the file); and
	09 (A media error was encountered while accessing the file).
44000	The SQL statement contained a parameter or literal NULL value for a column defined as **NOT NULL** in the associated table column, OR the SQL statement contained a duplicate value for a column constrained to contain only unique values (or some other integrity constraint was violated).
54028	The maximum number of concurrent LOB locator handles has been reached. A new LOB locator cannot be assigned until some other LOB locator is explicitly freed.
56084	LOB columns cannot be selected or updated when connected to a DRDA server (using DB2 Connect or DDCS).
58004	An unexpected system error has occurred. A possible cause is the code page of the environment in which the application is running is not supported by DB2 CLI.
HY000	A general error occurred for which there is no specific SQLSTATE and for which no specific SQLSTATE has been defined. The **SQLGetDiagRec()** function can be used to describe the error and its cause.
	If the **SQLDriverConnect()** function returns this error, the information specified in the connection string was insufficient for making a connect request, and an attempt to display the connection information dialog failed.
HY001	The DB2 CLI Library or the ODBC Driver Manager was unable to allocate the memory needed to support the execution or completion of this DB2 CLI function.
HY002	The column number specified was less than **1** or greater than the maximum number of columns supported by the data source.
HY003	The C data type specified is not a valid C data type for this DB2 CLI function.
HY004	The SQL data type specified is not valid for this DB2 CLI function.
HY007	The SQL statement handle specified is not in the "Prepared" or "Executed" state.

Table B-1 SQLSTATE Cross Reference (Continued)

DB2 CLI SQLSTATE	Description
HY008	**SQLCancel()** was called before the DB2 CLI function completed execution; therefore, the operation was canceled.
HY009	One or more parameter values specified contain a NULL pointer or an invalid value.
HY010	The DB2 CLI function was called while a data-at-execution sequence was running OR the DB2 CLI function was called out of sequence (order).
HY011	The environment, connection, or SQL statement attribute specified cannot be set at this time.
HY012	The value specified was neither **SQL_ROLLBACK** nor **SQL_COMMIT**.
HY013	The DB2 CLI function could not be processed because the underlying memory objects needed could not be accessed, possibly because of low memory conditions.
HY014	The driver-defined limit for the number of handles that can be allocated for the handle type specified has been reached.
HY016	Implementation row descriptors (IRDs) cannot be modified.
HY017	Invalid use of an automatically allocated descriptor handle.
HY018	The server declined the "Cancel" request.
HY021	The descriptor information checked during a consistency check was not consistent.
HY024	An invalid environment, connection, or statement attribute value was specified.
HY090	The value specified for a string or buffer parameter's size exceeds the maximum length allowed OR the value specified for a string or buffer parameter's size is less than **0** and not equal to **SQL_NTS**.
HY091	An invalid descriptor type value was specified.
HY092	The driver does not support the environment, connection, or statement attribute specified.
HY093	The value specified for a DB2 CLI function parameter was either less than **1** or greater than the maximum number of parameters supported by the data source.
HY094	The scale value specified was outside the range of values supported by the data source for the SQL data type specified.
HY096	The information type specified was not valid for the version of DB2 CLI supported by the driver.
HY097	An invalid column type was specified.
HY098	An invalid scope was specified.
HY099	An invalid nullable type was specified.
HY100	An invalid uniqueness value was specified.
HY101	An invalid accuracy value was specified.
HY103	An invalid cursor direction was specified.
HY104	The precision value specified was outside the range of values supported by the data source for the SQL data type specified

Table B–1 SQLSTATE Cross Reference (Continued)

DB2 CLI SQLSTATE	Description
HY105	An invalid parameter type value was specified.
HY106	An invalid fetch type value was specified.
HY107	The row value specified was less than **1**.
HY109	A positioned **UPDATE** or a positioned **DELETE** SQL statement was specified and the cursor was positioned on a row that has been deleted or that could not be retrieved (fetched).
HY110	The driver completion value specified was invalid (that is, not **SQL_DRIVER_PROMPT**, **SQL_DRIVER_COMPLETE, SQL_DRIVER_COMPLETE_REQUIRED,** or **SQL_DRIVER_ NOPROMPT**) OR connection pooling was enabled, and the driver completion value **SQL_ DRIVER_NOPROMPT** was not specified.
HY111	An invalid bookmark value was specified.
HY501	An invalid data source name was specified.
HY503	The specified file name length was less than **0** but was not equal to **SQL_NTS**.
HY506	An error occurred while attempting to close the temporary file generated by DB2 CLI during a data-at-execution sequence.
HY509	An error occurred while attempting to delete the temporary file generated by DB2 CLI during a data-at-execution sequence.
HYC00	The DB2 CLI function recognizes, but the driver does not support, one or more of the parameter or values specified.
HYT00	The timeout period expired before the connection to the data source could be established; before the data source finished processing the DB2 CLI function; or before the data source returned the result data set generated.
S0001	A **CREATE TABLE** or a **CREATE VIEW** SQL statement was specified, and the corresponding table name or view name specified already exists.
S0002	The specified SQL statement referenced a table name or view name that does not exist.
S0011	A **CREATE INDEX** SQL statement was specified, and the corresponding index name specified already exists.
S0012	A **DROP INDEX** SQL statement was specified, and the corresponding index name specified does not exist.
S0021	An **ALTER TABLE** SQL statement was specified, and the one or more column names specified in the **ADD** clause already exist in the base table.
S0022	The specified SQL statement referenced a column name in a table that does not exist.

(*xxx* and *xx* refer to any SQLSTATE within the specified class code. For example, **37***xxx* refers to any SQLSTATE in the **37** class. Adapted from *IBM's DB2 Universal Database Call Level Interface Guide and Reference*, Table 196, pages 667 to 682.)

APPENDIX C

Information Returned By SQLGetInfo()

InfoType Code	Data Type Returned	Description
SQL_ACCESSIBLE_ PROCEDURES	Character string	Indicates whether all CLI/ODBC API procedures returned by the **SQLProcedures()** function can be executed by the application. The following values can be returned for this *InfoType* code: **"Y"** The application can execute all procedures returned by the **SQLProcedures()** function. **"N"**: One or more of the procedures returned by the **SQLProcedures()** function cannot be executed by the application.
SQL_ACCESSIBLE_TABLES	Character string	Indicates whether the current user is guaranteed **SELECT** privileges to all tables returned by the **SQLTables()** function. The following values can be returned for this *InfoType* code: **"Y"**: The user is guaranteed **SELECT** privileges to all tables returned by the **SQLTables()** function. **"N"**: One or more tables returned by the **SQLTables()** function cannot be accessed by the current user.
SQL_ACTIVE_ ENVIRONMENTS	SQLUSMALLINT	Identifies the maximum number of active environments the driver can support. If there is no specified limit, or if the limit is unknown, the value **0** is returned for this *InfoType* code. In some drivers this *InfoType* code has been replaced with the **SQL_MAX_CONCURRENT_ACTIVITIES** *InfoType* code
SQL_AGGREGATE_ FUNCTIONS	SQLUINTEGER bitmask	Identifies the aggregation functions that are supported by the driver. The following values can be returned for this *InfoType* code: SQL_AF_ALL SQL_AF_AVG SQL_AF_COUNT SQL_AF_DISTINCT SQL_AF_MAX SQL_AF_MIN SQL_AF_SUM
SQL_ALTER_DOMAIN	SQLUINTEGER bitmask	Identifies the clauses in the **ALTER DOMAIN** SQL statement that are supported by the data source (as defined in SQL-92).

InfoType Code	Data Type Returned	Description
		When using DB2 CLI, the value **0** will always be returned because the **ALTER DOMAIN** SQL statement is not supported.
		When using ODBC, the following bitmask values can be returned for this *InfoType* code:
		SQL_AD_ADD_DOMAIN_CONSTRAINT: The \<add domain constraint\> clause is supported.
		SQL_AD_ADD_DOMAIN_DEFAULT: The \<alter domain\> \<set domain default\> clause is supported.
		SQL_AD_CONSTRAINT_NAME_DEFINITION: The \<constraint name definition\> clause is supported for naming domain constraints.
		SQL_AD_DROP_DOMAIN_CONSTRAINT: The \<drop domain constraint\> clause is supported.
		SQL_AD_DROP_DOMAIN_DEFAULT: The \<alter domain\> \<drop domain default\> clause is supported.
		The following bits specify the constraint attributes that are supported if the \<add domain constraint\> clause is supported (the **SQL_AD_ ADD_DOMAIN_CONSTRAINT** bit is set):
		SQL_AD_ADD_CONSTRAINT_DEFERRABLE **SQL_AD_ADD_CONSTRAINT_NON_DEFERRABLE** **SQL_AD_ADD_CONSTRAINT_INITIALLY_DEFERRED** **SQL_AD_ADD_CONSTRAINT_INITIALLY_IMMEDIATE**
		If the **ALTER DOMAIN** statement is not supported by the data source, the value **0** is returned for this *InfoType* code.
SQL_ACTIVE_CONNECTIONS	**SQLUSMALLINT**	Identifies the maximum number of active connections available for a single application. If the maximum number of active connections available is dependent upon system resources, the value **0** is returned for this *InfoType* code.
		If the **MAXCONN** keyword in the *db2cli.ini* initialization file OR the **SQL_ATTR_MAX_CONNECTIONS** environment/connection attribute has been used to limit the number of connections available for an application, that limit value will be returned for this *InfoType* code.
		In some drivers this *InfoType* code has been replaced with the **SQL_MAX_DRIVER_CONNECTIONS** *InfoType* code.

InfoType Code	Data Type Returned	Description
SQL_ACTIVE_STATEMENTS	SQLUSMALLINT	Identifies the maximum number of active statements available for a single connection. If the maximum number of active statements available is dependent upon system resources, the value **0** is returned for this *InfoType* code. In some drivers this *InfoType* code has been replaced with the **SQL_MAX_CONCURRENT_ACTIVITIES** *InfoType* code.
SQL_ALTER_TABLE	SQLUINTEGER bitmask	Identifies the clauses in the **ALTER TABLE** SQL statement that are supported by the data source. The following bitmask values can be returned for this *InfoType* code: **SQL_AT_ADD_COLUMN_COLLATION**: The \<add column\> clause is supported, along with the ability to specify column collation. **SQL_AT_ADD_COLUMN_DEFAULT**: The \<add column\> clause is supported, along with the ability to specify column defaults. **SQL_AT_ADD_COLUMN_SINGLE**: The \<add column\> is supported. **SQL_AT_ADD_CONSTRAINT**: The \<add column\> clause is supported, along with the ability to specify column constraints. **SQL_AT_ADD_TABLE_CONSTRAINT**: The \<add table constraint\> clause is supported. **SQL_AT_CONSTRAINT_NAME_DEFINITION**: The \<constraint name definition\> clause is supported for naming column and table constraints. **SQL_AT_DROP_COLUMN_CASCADE**: The \<drop column\> **CASCADE** clause is supported. **SQL_AT_DROP_COLUMN_DEFAULT**: The \<alter column\> \<drop column default\> clause is supported. **SQL_AT_DROP_COLUMN_RESTRICT**: The \<drop column\> **RESTRICT** clause is supported. **SQL_AT_DROP_TABLE_CONSTRAINT_CASCADE**: The \<drop constraint\> **CASCADE** clause is supported. **SQL_AT_DROP_TABLE_CONSTRAINT_RESTRICT**: The \<drop column\> **RESTRICT** clause is supported. **SQL_AT_SET_COLUMN_DEFAULT**: The \<alter column\> \<set column default\> clause is supported. The following bits specify constraint attributes that are supported if specifying column or table constraints is supported (the **SQL_AT_ADD_CONSTRAINT** bit is set):

InfoType Code	Data Type Returned	Description

		`SQL_AT_CONSTRAINT_INITIALLY_DEFERRED`
		`SQL_AT_CONSTRAINT_INITIALLY_IMMEDIATE`
		`SQL_AT_CONSTRAINT_DEFERRABLE`
		`SQL_AT_CONSTRAINT_NON_DEFERRABLE`

`SQL_ASYNC_MODE`	`SQLUINTEGER`	Identifies the level of asynchronous support that is provided by the driver. The following values can be returned for this *InfoType* code: `SQL_AM_CONNECTION`: Connection level asynchronous execution is supported. Either all statement handles associated with a given connection handle execute in asynchronous mode, or all execute in synchronous mode. A statement handle on a connection handle cannot be in asynchronous mode while another statement handle on the same connection handle is in synchronous mode, and vice versa. `SQL_AM_STATEMENT`: Statement level asynchronous execution is supported. Some statement handles associated with a connection handle can be in asynchronous mode, while other statement handles on the same connection handle are in synchronous mode. `SQL_AM_NONE`: Asynchronous execution is not supported, OR if the `ASYNCENABLE` keyword in the *db2cli.ini* initialization file has been set to **0** to disable asynchronous execution.
`SQL_BATCH_ROW_COUNT`	`SQLUINTEGER` bitmask	Identifies how the driver computes and returns row count information. The following bitmask values can be returned for this *InfoType* code: `SQL_BRC_ROLLED_UP`: Row counts for consecutive **INSERT**, **UPDATE**, or **DELETE** SQL statements are rolled into one. If this bit is not set, row counts are available for each SQL statement processed. `SQL_BRC_PROCEDURES`: Row counts, if any, are available when a batch of SQL statements are executed by a stored procedure. If row counts are available, they may be rolled up, or they may be available for each SQL statement processed, depending on the `SQL_BRC_ROLLED_UP` bit. `SQL_BRC_EXPLICIT`: Row counts, if any, are available when a batch of SQL statements are executed directly by calling `SQLExecute()` or `SQLExecDirect()`. If row counts are available, they may be rolled up, or they may be available for each SQL statement processed, depending on the `SQL_BRC_ROLLED_UP` bit.

InfoType Code	Data Type Returned	Description
		When using DB2 CLI, the value **SQL_BRC_ROLLED_UP** will always be returned for this *InfoType* code.
SQL_BATCH_SUPPORT	**SQLUINTEGER** bitmask	Identifies how batch SQL statement execution is supported by the driver. The following bitmask values can be returned for this *InfoType* code:
		SQL_BS_SELECT_EXPLICIT: The driver supports explicit batches that contain one or more result data set generating SQL statements.
		SQL_BS_ROW_COUNT_EXPLICIT: The driver supports explicit batches that contain one or more row count generating SQL statements.
		SQL_BS_SELECT_PROC: The driver supports explicit procedures that contain one or more result data set generating statements.
		SQL_BS_ROW_COUNT_PROC: The driver supports explicit procedures that contain one or more row count generating statements.
SQL_BOOKMARK_PERSISTENCE	**SQLUINTEGER** bitmask	Identifies the operations through which bookmarks persist. The following bitmask values can be returned for this *InfoType* code:
		SQL_BP_CLOSE: Bookmarks are valid after an application calls either the **SQLFreeStmt()** function with the **SQL_CLOSE** option specified, or the **SQLCloseCursor()** function to close the cursor associated with an SQL statement handle.
		SQL_BP_DELETE: The bookmark for a row is valid after the row has been deleted.
		SQL_BP_DROP: Bookmarks are valid after their associated SQL statement handle has been dropped.
		SQL_BP_TRANSACTION: Bookmarks are valid after an application commits or rolls back a transaction.
		SQL_BP_UPDATE: The bookmark for a row is valid after any column in that row has been updated, including key columns.
		SQL_BP_OTHER_HSTMT: A bookmark associated with one statement can be used with another SQL statement. However, unless **SQL_BP_CLOSE** or **SQL_BP_DROP** is returned, the cursor for the first SQL statement must be open.
SQL_CATALOG_LOCATION[1]	**SQLUSMALLINT**	Identifies the position of the catalog portion of a qualified table name. The following values can be returned for this *InfoType* code:

InfoType Code	Data Type Returned	Description
		SQL_CL_START: The catalog portion of a qualified table name is located at the beginning of the name.
		SQL_CL_END: The catalog portion of a qualified table name is located at the end of the name.
		When using DB2 CLI, the value **SQL_CL_START** will always be returned for this *InfoType* code.
		If catalogs are not supported by the data source (see the **SQL_CATALOG_NAME** *InfoType* code), the value **0** is returned for this *InfoType* code.
SQL_CATALOG_NAME	Character string	Indicates whether the data source supports catalog names. The following values can be returned for this *InfoType* code:
		"Y": The data source supports catalog names.
		"N": The data source does not support catalog names.
SQL_CATALOG_NAME_ SEPARATOR[2]	Character string	Identifies the character or characters the data source uses as a separator between a catalog name and the qualified name element that follows or precedes it.
		If catalogs are not supported by the data source (see the **SQL_CATALOG_NAME** *InfoType* code), an empty string (" ") is returned for this *InfoType* code.
SQL_CATALOG_TERM[3]	Character string	Identifies the data source vendor's terminology for a catalog (i.e., the high order part of a three-part name). This string can be in upper, lower, or mixed case.
		Since catalogs are not supported by DB2 CLI, an empty string (" ") is always returned for this *InfoType* code.
SQL_CATALOG_USAGE[4]	**SQLUINTEGER** bitmask	Identifies the SQL statements in which catalog names can be used. The following bitmask values can be returned for this *InfoType* code:
		SQL_CU_DML_STATEMENTS: Catalog names can be used in all Data Manipulation Language SQL statements: **SELECT, INSERT, UPDATE, DELETE, SELECT FOR UPDATE**, (if supported) and positioned **UPDATE** and **delete** statements.
		SQL_CU_PROCEDURE_INVOCATION: Catalog names can be used in the ODBC procedure invocation statement.

InfoType Code	Data Type Returned	Description
		SQL_CU_TABLE_DEFINITION: Catalog names can be used in all table definition statements: **CREATE TABLE**, **CREATE VIEW**, **ALTER TABLE**, **DROP TABLE**, and **DROP VIEW**.
		SQL_CU_INDEX_DEFINITION: Catalog names can be used in all index definition statements: **CREATE INDEX** and **DROP INDEX**.
		SQL_CU_PRIVILEGE_DEFINITION: Catalog names can be used in all privilege definition statements: **GRANT** and **REVOKE**.
		Since catalogs are not supported by DB2 CLI, the value **0** is always returned for this *InfoType* code.
SQL_COLLATION_SEQ	Character string	Identifies the name of the default collation of the default character set used by the data source (for example, "ISO 8859-1" or "EBCDIC").
		If the name of the default collation is unknown, an empty string (" ") will be returned for this *InfoType* code.
SQL_COLUMN_ALIAS	Character string	Indicates whether the data source supports column aliases. A column alias is an alternate name that can be specified for a column in a select list by using an **AS** clause. The following values can be returned for this *InfoType* code:
		"Y": The data source supports column aliases.
		"N": The data source does not support column aliases.
SQL_CONCAT_NULL_ BEHAVIOR	**SQLUSMALLINT**	Identifies how the data source handles the concatenation of NULL valued character data type columns with non-NULL valued character data type columns. The following values can be returned for this *InfoType* code:
		SQL_CB_NULL: The result of the concatenation is a NULL value.
		SQL_CB_NON_NULL: The result of the concatenation is the value of the non-NULL valued column or columns.
SQL_CONVERT_BIGINT **SQL_CONVERT_BINARY** **SQL_CONVERT_BIT** **SQL_CONVERT_CHAR** **SQL_CONVERT_DATE** **SQL_CONVERT_DECIMAL** **SQL_CONVERT_DOUBLE** **SQL_CONVERT_FLOAT** **SQL_CONVERT_INTEGER**	**SQLUINTEGER** bitmask	Identifies whether the specified data type conversion (named in the *InfoType* code) is supported by the data source and the **CONVERT()** ODBC scalar function. For example, to find out if a data source supports the conversion of a **SQL_INTEGER** data type to an **SQL_BIGINT** data type, an application calls **SQLGetInfo()** with the *InfoType* code **SQL_CONVERT_INTEGER** specified. The application then performs an AND operation with the returned value

InfoType Code	Data Type Returned	Description
SQL_CONVERT_INTERVAL_YEAR_MONTH SQL_CONVERT_INTERVAL_DAY_TIME SQL_CONVERT_LONGVARBINARY SQL_CONVERT_LONGVARCHAR SQL_CONVERT_NUMERIC SQL_CONVERT_REAL SQL_CONVERT_SMALLINT SQL_CONVERT_TIME SQL_CONVERT_TIMESTAMP SQL_CONVERT_TINYINT SQL_CONVERT_VARBINARY SQL_CONVERT_VARCHAR		and **SQL_CVT_BIGINT**. If the resulting value is nonzero, the data type conversion is supported. The following bitmask values are used to determine whether conversions are supported: SQL_CVT_BIGINT SQL_CVT_BINARY SQL_CVT_BIT SQL_CVT_CHAR SQL_CVT_DATE SQL_CVT_DECIMAL SQL_CVT_DOUBLE SQL_CVT_FLOAT SQL_CVT_INTEGER SQL_CVT_INTERVAL_YEAR_MONTH SQL_CVT_INTERVAL_DAY_TIME SQL_CVT_LONGVARBINARY SQL_CVT_LONGVARCHAR SQL_CVT_NUMERIC SQL_CVT_SMALLINT SQL_CVT_TIME SQL_CVT_TIMESTAMP SQL_CVT_TINYINT SQL_CVT_VARBINARY SQL_CVT_VARCHAR If the data source does not support any conversions for the specified data, including conversions to the same data type, the value **0** is returned for the *Info-Type* code specified.
SQL_CONVERT_FUNCTIONS	**SQLUINTEGER** bitmask	Identifies the ODBC scalar conversion functions that are supported by the driver and its underlying data source. The following bitmask values can be returned for this *InfoType* code: **SQL_FN_CVT_CAST**: Type casting is supported. **SQL_FN_CVT_CONVERT**: Data conversion is supported. DB2 CLI, Version 2.1 and later supports ODBC scalar conversions between character variables (**CHAR**, **VARCHAR**, **LONGVARCHAR** and **CLOB**) and floating point number variables (**DOUBLE** or **FLOAT**).
SQL_CORRELATION_NAME	**SQLUSMALLINT**	Indicates whether table correlation names are supported by the data source. The following values can be returned for this *InfoType* code: **SQL_CN_NONE**: Correlation names are not supported. **SQL_CN_DIFFERENT**: Correlation names are supported, but must differ from the names of the tables they represent.

InfoType Code	Data Type Returned	Description
		SQL_CN_ANY: Correlation names are supported and can be any valid user-defined name.
SQL_CREATE_ASSERTION	**SQLUINTEGER** bitmask	Identifies the clauses in the **CREATE ASSERTION** SQL statement that are supported by the data source (as defined in SQL-92).
		When using DB2 CLI, the value **0** will always be returned because the **CREATE ASSERTION** SQL statement is not supported.
		When using ODBC, the following bitmask values can be returned for this *InfoType* code:
		SQL_CA_CREATE_ASSERTION: The **CREATE ASSERTION** SQL statement is supported by the data source.
		The following bits specify the supported constraint attribute if the ability to specify constraint attributes explicitly is supported by the data source (see the **SQL_ALTER_TABLE** and **SQL_CREATE_TABLE** *InfoType* codes):
		SQL_CA_CONSTRAINT_INITIALLY_DEFERRED **SQL_CA_CONSTRAINT_INITIALLY_IMMEDIATE** **SQL_CA_CONSTRAINT_DEFERRABLE** **SQL_CA_CONSTRAINT_NON_DEFERRABLE**
		If the **CREATE ASSERTION** statement is not supported by the data source, the value **0** is returned for this *InfoType* code.
SQL_CREATE_ CHARACTER_SET	**SQLUINTEGER** bitmask	Identifies the clauses in the **CREATE CHARACTER SET** SQL statement that are supported by the data source (as defined in SQL-92).
		When using DB2 CLI, the value **0** will always be returned because the **CREATE CHARACTER SET** SQL statement is not supported.
		When using ODBC, the following bitmask values can be returned for this *InfoType* code:
		SQL_CCS_CREATE_CHARACTER_SET **SQL_CCS_COLLATE_CLAUSE** **SQL_CCS_LIMITED_COLLATION**
		If the **CREATE CHARACTER SET** SQL statement is not supported by the data source, the value **0** is returned for this *InfoType* code.
SQL_CREATE_COLLATION	**SQLUINTEGER** bitmask	Identifies the clauses in the **CREATE COLLATION** SQL statement that are supported by the data source (as defined in SQL-92).
		When using DB2 CLI, the value **0** will always be returned because the **CREATE COLLATION** SQL statement is not supported.

InfoType Code	Data Type Returned	Description
		When using ODBC, the following bitmask values can be returned for this *InfoType* code:
		SQL_CCOL_CREATE_COLLATION: The **CREATE** SQL statement is supported.
		If the **CREATE** SQL statement is not supported by the data source, the value **0** is returned for this *InfoType* code.
SQL_CREATE_DOMAIN	SQLUINTEGER bitmask	Identifies the clauses in the **CREATE DOMAIN** SQL statement that are supported by the data source (as defined in SQL-92).
		When using DB2 CLI, the value **0** will always be returned because the **CREATE DOMAIN** SQL statement is not supported.
		When using ODBC, the following bitmask values can be returned for this *InfoType* code:
		SQL_CDO_CREATE_DOMAIN: The **CREATE DOMAIN** SQL statement is supported.
		SQL_CDO_CONSTRAINT_NAME_DEFINITION: The <constraint name definition> clause is supported for naming domain constraints.
		The following bits specify the ability to create column constraints:
		SQL_CDO_DEFAULT: Specifying domain constraints is supported.
		SQL_CDO_CONSTRAINT: Specifying domain defaults is supported.
		SQL_CDO_COLLATION: Specifying domain collation is supported.
		The following bits specify the supported constraint attributes if specifying domain constraints is supported (**SQL_CDO_DEFAULT** is set):
		SQL_CDO_CONSTRAINT_INITIALLY_DEFERRED **SQL_CDO_CONSTRAINT_INITIALLY_IMMEDIATE** **SQL_CDO_CONSTRAINT_DEFERRABLE** **SQL_CDO_CONSTRAINT_NON_DEFERRABLE**
		If the **CREATE_DOMAIN** statement is not supported by the data source, the value **0** is returned for this *InfoType* code.
SQL_CREATE_SCHEMA	SQLUINTEGER bitmask	Identifies the clauses in the **CREATE SCHEMA** SQL statement that are supported by the data source (as defined in SQL-92). The following bitmask values can be returned for this *InfoType* code:
		SQL_CS_CREATE_SCHEMA **SQL_CS_AUTHORIZATION** **SQL_CS_DEFAULT_CHARACTER_SET**

InfoType Code	Data Type Returned	Description
SQL_CREATE_TABLE	SQLUINTEGER bitmask	Identifies the clauses in the **CREATE TABLE** SQL statement that are supported by the data source (as defined in SQL-92). The following bitmask values can be returned for this *InfoType* code: **SQL_CT_CREATE_TABLE:** The **CREATE TABLE** SQL statement is supported. **SQL_CT_TABLE_CONSTRAINT:** The specification of table constraints with the **CREATE TABLE** SQL statement is supported. **SQL_CT_CONSTRAINT_NAME_DEFINITION:** The \<constraint name definition\> clause is supported for naming column and table constraints. The following bits specify the ability to create temporary tables: **SQL_CT_COMMIT_PRESERVE:** Deleted rows are preserved on commit. **SQL_CT_COMMIT_DELETE:** Deleted rows are deleted on commit. **SQL_CT_GLOBAL_TEMPORARY:** Global temporary tables can be created. **SQL_CT_LOCAL_TEMPORARY:** Local temporary tables can be created. The following bits specify the ability to create column constraints: **SQL_CT_COLUMN_CONSTRAINT:** Specifying column constraints is supported. **SQL_CT_COLUMN_DEFAULT:** Specifying column defaults is supported. **SQL_CT_COLUMN_COLLATION:** Specifying column collation is supported. The following bits specify the supported constraint attributes if specifying column or table constraints is supported: SQL_CT_CONSTRAINT_INITIALLY_DEFERRED SQL_CT_CONSTRAINT_INITIALLY_IMMEDIATE SQL_CT_CONSTRAINT_DEFERRABLE SQL_CT_CONSTRAINT_NON_DEFERRABLE
SQL_CREATE_TRANSLATION	SQLUINTEGER bitmask	Identifies the clauses in the **CREATE TRANSLATION** SQL statement that are supported by the data source (as defined in SQL-92). When using DB2 CLI, the value **0** will always be returned because the **CREATE TRANSLATION** SQL statement is not supported.

InfoType Code	Data Type Returned	Description
		When using ODBC, the following bitmask values can be returned for this *InfoType* code: **SQL_CTR_CREATE_TRANSLATION**: The **CREATE TRANSLATION** SQL statement is supported. If the **CREATE TRANSLATION** statement is not supported by the data source, the value **0** is returned for this *InfoType* code.
SQL_CREATE_VIEW	**SQLUINTEGER** bitmask	Identifies the clauses in the **CREATE VIEW** SQL statement that are supported by the data source (as defined in SQL-92). The following bitmask values can be returned for this *InfoType* code: **SQL_CV_CREATE_VIEW** **SQL_CV_CHECK_OPTION** **SQL_CV_CASCADED** **SQL_CV_LOCAL** If the **CREATE VIEW** statement is not supported by the data source, the value **0** is returned for this *InfoType* code.
SQL_CURSOR_ CLOSE_BEHAVIOR	**SQLUINTEGER**	Indicates whether or not locks acquired by a cursor are released when the cursor is closed. The following values can be returned for this *InfoType* code: **SQL_CC_NO_RELEASE**: Locks are not released when the cursor associated with a statement handle is closed. **SQL_CC_RELEASE**: Locks are released when the cursor associated with a statement handle is closed.
SQL_CURSOR_ COMMIT_BEHAVIOR	**SQLUSMALLINT**	Indicates how a commit operation affects cursors and prepared SQL statements within the data source. The following values can be returned for this *InfoType* code: **SQL_CB_DELETE**: Cursors are destroyed and access plans for prepared SQL statements are destroyed. To use the cursor again, the application must reprepare and re-execute the statement. **SQL_CB_CLOSE**: Cursors are destroyed, but access plans for prepared SQL statements are not destroyed. The application can call **SQLExecute()** to re-execute prepared SQL statements without having to reprepare them.

InfoType Code	Data Type Returned	Description
		SQL_CB_PRESERVE: Cursors and access plans for prepared SQL statements remain as they were before the commit operation was performed. The application can continue to fetch data or it can close the cursor and re-execute the SQL statement without having to reprepare it.
		NOTE: In this case, a fetch operation must be performed after a commit operation in order to reposition the cursor before actions such as positioned updates and deletes can be performed.
SQL_CURSOR_ ROLLBACK_BEHAVIOR	**SQLUSMALLINT**	Indicates how a rollback operation affects cursors and prepared SQL statements within the data source. The following values can be returned for this *InfoType* code:
		SQL_CB_DELETE: Cursors are destroyed and access plans for prepared SQL statements are destroyed. To use the cursor again, the application must re-prepare and re-execute the statement.
		SQL_CB_CLOSE: Cursors are destroyed, but access plans for prepared SQL statements are not destroyed. The application can call **SQLExecute()** to re-execute prepared statements without having to re-prepare them.
		SQL_CB_PRESERVE: Cursors and access plans for prepared SQL statements remain as they were before the rollback operation was performed. The application can continue to fetch data or, it can close the cursor and re-execute the SQL statement without having to re-prepare it.
		When using DB2 CLI, the value **SQL_CB_PRESERVE** will never be returned for this *InfoType* code.
SQL_CURSOR_ SENSITIVITY	**SQLUINTEGER**	Identifies how cursors expose changes made to a result data set. The following values can be returned for this *InfoType* code:
		SQL_INSENSITIVE: All cursors on a statement handle show the result data set without reflecting any changes made to it by any other cursor within the same transaction.
		SQL_SENSITIVE: All cursors on a statement handle show all changes made to the result data set by any other cursor within the same transaction.

InfoType Code	Data Type Returned	Description
		SQL_UNSPECIFIED: It is unspecified whether all cursors on a statement handle show the changes made to a result data set by another cursor within the same transaction. Cursors on a statement handle may make none, some, or all such changes made to a result data set by another cursor within the same transaction visible.
SQL_DATA_SOURCE_NAME	Character string	Identifies the data source name used in the *DSName* parameter of the **SQLConnect()** function, or used with the **DSN** keyword in the connection string passed to the driver by the **SQLDriverConnect()** or the **SQLBrowseConnect()** function.
		If the connection string passed to the driver by the **SQLDriverConnect()** or the **SQLBrowseConnect()** function did not contain the **DSN** keyword, an empty string (" ") is returned for this *InfoType* code.
SQL_DATA_SOURCE_ READ_ONLY	Character string	Indicates whether the data source is set to READ ONLY or READ/WRITE mode. The following values can be returned for this *InfoType* code:
		"Y": The data source is set to READ ONLY mode.
		"N": The data source is set to READ/WRITE mode.
		This characteristic only pertains to the data source itself; it is not a characteristic of the driver that enables access to the data source. A driver that is read/write can be used with a data source that is read-only.
		If a driver is read-only, all its data sources must be read-only, and must return **"Y"** for this *InfoType* code.
SQL_DATABASE_NAME	Character string	Identifies the name of the current database in use if the data source defines a named object called "database."
SQL_DATETIME_LITERALS	**SQLUINTEGER** bitmask	Identifies the datetime literals that are supported by the data source (as defined in SQL-92).
		When using DB2 CLI, the value **0** will always be returned because datetime literals are not supported.
		When using ODBC, the following bitmask values can be returned for this *InfoType* code:
		SQL_DL_SQL92_DATE **SQL_DL_SQL92_TIME** **SQL_DL_SQL92_TIMESTAMP** **SQL_DL_SQL92_INTERVAL_YEAR** **SQL_DL_SQL92_INTERVAL_MONTH** **SQL_DL_SQL92_INTERVAL_DAY**

InfoType Code	Data Type Returned	Description

		`SQL_DL_SQL92_INTERVAL_HOUR`
		`SQL_DL_SQL92_INTERVAL_MINUTE`
		`SQL_DL_SQL92_INTERVAL_SECOND`
		`SQL_DL_SQL92_INTERVAL_YEAR_TO_MONTH`
		`SQL_DL_SQL92_INTERVAL_DAY_TO_HOUR`
		`SQL_DL_SQL92_INTERVAL_DAY_TO_MINUTE`
		`SQL_DL_SQL92_INTERVAL_DAY_TO_SECOND`
		`SQL_DL_SQL92_INTERVAL_HOUR_TO_MINUTE`
		`SQL_DL_SQL92_INTERVAL_HOUR_TO_SECOND`
		`SQL_DL_SQL92_INTERVAL_MINUTE_TO_SECOND`

		Note that these are the datetime literals listed in the SQL-92 specification and are separate from the datetime literal escape clauses defined by ODBC.
`SQL_DBMS_NAME`	Character string	Identifies the name of the DBMS product being accessed by the driver (for example, "DB2/2").
`SQL_DBMS_VER`	Character string	Identifies the version of the DBMS product being accessed by the driver. This information is returned in a string that has the format *mm.vv.rrrr*, where *mm* is the major version number, *vv* is the minor version number, and *rrrr* is the release version number (for example, "02.01.0000" would translate to major version 2, minor version 1, release 0). The driver must render the DBMS product version in this format, but it can also append the DBMS product-specific version as well (for example, "04.01.0000 Rdb 4.1").
`SQL_DDL_INDEX`	`SQLUINTEGER`	Identifies whether the the data source supports the creation and destruction of indexes. The following bitmask values can be returned for this *InfoType* code: `SQL_DI_CREATE_INDEX`: Indexes can be created. `SQL_DI_DROP_INDEX`: Indexes can be dropped.
`SQL_DEFAULT_` `TXN_ISOLATION`	`SQLUINTEGER`	Identifies the default transaction isolation level used by the driver or data source. The following terms are used to define transaction isolation levels: **Dirty Read**: Transaction 1 changes a row. Transaction 2 reads the changed row before Transaction 1 commits the change. If Transaction 1 rolls back the change, Transaction 2 will have read a row that is considered to have never existed. **Nonrepeatable Read**: Transaction 1 reads a row. Transaction 2 updates or deletes that row and commits this change. If Transaction 1 attempts to reread the row, it will receive different row values or discover that the row has been deleted.

InfoType Code	Data Type Returned	Description
		Phantom: Transaction 1 reads a set of rows that satisfy some search criteria. Transaction 2 generates one or more rows (either through inserts or updates) that match the search criteria. If Transaction 1 re-executes the statement that reads the rows, it receives a different set of rows.
		If the data source supports transactions, the driver returns one of the following bitmasks:
		SQL_TXN_READ_UNCOMMITTED: Dirty reads, nonrepeatable reads, and phantoms are possible.
		SQL_TXN_READ_COMMITTED: Dirty reads are not possible. Nonrepeatable reads and phantoms are possible.
		SQL_TXN_REPEATABLE_READ: Dirty reads and nonrepeatable reads are not possible. Phantoms are possible.
		SQL_TXN_SERIALIZABLE: Transactions are serializable. Serializable transactions do not allow dirty reads, nonrepeatable reads, or phantoms.
		SQL_TXN_NOCOMMIT: Changes are effectively committed at the end of a successful operation; no explicit commit or rollback is allowed.
		NOTE: This isolation level is only used by DB2 for AS/400.
		If transactions are not supported by the data source, the value **0** is returned for this *InfoType* code.
		In IBM terminology:
		SQL_TXN_READ_UNCOMMITTED = Uncommitted Read
		SQL_TXN_COMMITTED = Committed Read
		SQL_TXN_REPEATABLE_READ = Read Stability
		SQL_TXN_SERIALIZABLE = Repeatable Read
SQL_DESCRIBE_PARAMETER	Character string	Indicates whether the data source can describe parameters. The following values can be returned for this *InfoType* code:
		"Y": Parameters can be described by the data source.
		"N": Parameters cannot described by the data source.

InfoType Code	Data Type Returned	Description
SQL_DM_VER	Character string	Identifies the version number of the ODBC Driver Manager being used. This information is returned in a string with the format *mm.vv.rrrr*, where *mm* is the major ODBC version number (as provided by the constant **SQL_SPEC_MAJOR**), *vv* is the minor ODBC version number (as provided by the constant **SQL_SPEC_MINOR**), and *rrrr* is the ODBC Driver Manager major build number (for example, "03.05.0000" would translate to major version 3, minor version 5, build number 0).
SQL_DRIVER_HENV	SQLUINTEGER	Identifies the driver's environment handle. The driver's environment handle is returned by the DB2 CLI Library or by the ODBC Driver Manager; not by the data source.
SQL_DRIVER_HDBC	SQLUINTEGER	Identifies the driver's connection handle. The driver's connection handle is returned by the DB2 CLI Library or by the ODBC Driver Manager; not by the data source.
SQL_DRIVER_HDESC	SQLUINTEGER	Identifies the driver's descriptor handle. The driver's descriptor handle is determined by the DB2 CLI Library or by the ODBC Driver Manager's descriptor handle, which must be passed as input in the *InfoValue* parameter of the **SQLGetInfo()** function. Note that in this case, the *InfoValue* parameter is both an input and output parameter. The input descriptor handle passed must have been explicitly or implicitly allocated on the connection handle being used. The application should make a copy of the DB2 CLI Library's or the ODBC Driver Manager's descriptor handle before specifying this *InfoType* code to ensure that the handle is not overwritten on output. The driver's descriptor handle is returned by the DB2 CLI Library or by the ODBC Driver Manager; not by the data source.
SQL_DRIVER_HLIB	SQLUINTEGER	Identifies the instance handle (on a Windows platform) or the equivalent (on a non-Windows platform) of the load library returned to the DB2 CLI Library or to the ODBC Driver Manager when the driver DLL was loaded. This handle is only valid for the connection handle specified in the call to **SQLGetInfo()**. The driver's instance handle is returned by the DB2 CLI Library or by the ODBC Driver Manager.
SQL_DRIVER_HSTMT	SQLUINTEGER	Identifies the driver's statement handle. The driver's statement handle is determined by the DB2 CLI Library's or the ODBC Driver Manager's statement handle, which must be passed as input in the *InfoValue* parameter of the **SQLGetInfo()** function.

InfoType Code	Data Type Returned	Description
		Note that in this case, the *InfoValue* parameter is both an input and output parameter. The input statement handle passed must have been allocated on the connection handle being used.
		The application should make a copy of the DB2 CLI Library's or ODBC Driver Manager's statement handle before specifying this *InfoType* code to ensure that the handle is not overwritten on output.
		The driver's statement handle is returned by the DB2 CLI Library or by the ODBC Driver Manager; not by the data source.
SQL_DRIVER_NAME	Character string	Identifies file name of the driver being used to access the data source.
SQL_DRIVER_ODBC_VER	Character string	Identifies the version of ODBC the driver supports. This information is returned in a string with the format *mm.vv*, where *mm* is the major ODBC version number (as provided by the constant SQL_SPEC_MAJOR) and *vv* is the minor ODBC version number (as provided by the constant SQL_SPEC_MINOR) (for example, "03.05" translates to major version 3, minor version 5).
		When using DB2 CLI Version 5.0 or later, the value "03.00" will be returned for this *InfoType* code.
SQL_DRIVER_VER	Character string	Identifies the version and optionally, a description of the driver being used. This information is returned in a string that has the format *mm.vv.rrrr*, where *mm* is the major version number, *vv* is the minor version number, and *rrrr* is the release version number (for example, 02.01.0000 translates to major version 2, minor version 1, release 0). The driver must render the version in this format, but it can append a description to the version as well (for example, "05.02.0000 DB2/2 Driver").
SQL_DROP_ASSERTION	SQLUINTEGER bitmask	Identifies the clauses in the DROP ASSERTION SQL statement that are supported by the data source (as defined in SQL-92).
		When using DB2 CLI, the value 0 will always be returned because the DROP ASSERTION SQL statement is not supported.
		When using ODBC, the following bitmask values can be returned for this *InfoType* code:
		SQL_DA_DROP_ASSERTION: The DROP ASSERTION SQL statement is supported by the data source.
SQL_DROP_CHARACTER_SET	SQLUINTEGER bitmask	Identifies the clauses in the DROP CHARACTER SET SQL statement that are supported by the data source (as defined in SQL-92).

InfoType Code	Data Type Returned	Description
		When using DB2 CLI, the value **0** will always be returned because the **DROP CHARACTER SET** SQL statement is not supported.
		When using ODBC, the following bitmask values can be returned for this *InfoType* code:
		SQL_DCS_DROP_CHARACTER_SET: The **DROP CHARACTER SET** SQL statement is supported by the data source.
SQL_DROP_COLLATION	**SQLUINTEGER** bitmask	Identifies the clauses in the **DROP COLLATION** SQL statement that are supported by the data source (as defined in SQL-92).
		When using DB2 CLI, the value **0** will always be returned because the **DROP COLLATION** SQL statement is not supported.
		When using ODBC, the following bitmask values can be returned for this *InfoType* code:
		SQL_DC_DROP_COLLATION: The **DROP COLLATION** SQL statement is supported by the data source.
SQL_DROP_DOMAIN	**SQLUINTEGER** bitmask	Identifies the clauses in the **DROP DOMAIN** SQL statement that are supported by the data source (as defined in SQL-92).
		When using DB2 CLI, the value **0** will always be returned because the **DROP DOMAIN** SQL statement is not supported.
		When using ODBC, the following bitmask values can be returned for this *InfoType* code:
		SQL_DD_DROP_DOMAIN **SQL_DD_CASCADE** **SQL_DD_RESTRICT**
SQL_DROP_SCHEMA	**SQLUINTEGER** bitmask	Identifies the clauses in the **DROP SCHEMA** SQL statement that are supported by the data source (as defined in SQL-92).
		When using DB2 CLI, the value **0** will always be returned because the **DROP SCHEMA** SQL statement is not supported.
		When using ODBC, the following bitmask values can be returned for this *InfoType* code:
		SQL_DS_DROP_SCHEMA **SQL_DS_CASCADE** **SQL_DS_RESTRICT**
SQL_DROP_TABLE	**SQLUINTEGER** bitmask	Identifies the clauses in the **DROP TABLE** SQL statement that are supported by the data source (as defined in SQL-92). The following bitmask values can be returned for this *InfoType* code:

InfoType Code	Data Type Returned	Description
		SQL_DT_DROP_TABLE **SQL_DT_CASCADE** **SQL_DT_RESTRICT**
SQL_DROP_TRANSLATION	SQLUINTEGER bitmask	Identifies the clauses in the **DROP TRANSLATION** SQL statement that are supported by the data source (as defined in SQL-92). When using DB2 CLI, the value **0** will always be returned because the **DROP TRANSLATION** SQL statement is not supported. When using ODBC, the following bitmask values can be returned for this *InfoType* code: **SQL_DTR_DROP_TRANSLATION**: The **DROP TRANSLATION** SQL statement is supported by the data source.
SQL_DROP_VIEW	SQLUINTEGER bitmask	Identifies the clauses in the **DROP VIEW** SQL statement that are supported by the data source (as defined in SQL-92). When using DB2 CLI, the value **0** will always be returned because the **DROP VIEW** SQL statement is not supported. When using ODBC, the following bitmask values can be returned for this *InfoType* code: **SQL_DV_DROP_VIEW** **SQL_DV_CASCADE** **SQL_DV_RESTRICT**
SQL_DYNAMIC_ CURSOR_ATTRIBUTES1	SQLUINTEGER bitmask	Defines the first subset of dynamic cursor attributes that are supported by the driver (see the **SQL_DYNAMIC_CURSOR_ATTRIBUTES2** *InfoType* code for the second subset of attributes). When using DB2 CLI, the value **0** will always be returned because dynamic cursors are not supported. When using ODBC, the following bitmask values can be returned for this *InfoType* code: **SQL_CA1_NEXT**: The **SQL_FETCH_NEXT** orientation value can be specified with the **SQLFetchScroll()** function when the cursor is a dynamic cursor. **SQL_CA1_ABSOLUTE**: The **SQL_FETCH_FIRST**, **SQL_FETCH_LAST**, and **SQL_FETCH_ABSOLUTE** orientation values can be specified with the **SQLFetchScroll()** function when the cursor is a dynamic cursor. (The rowset fetched is independent of the current cursor position.)

InfoType Code	Data Type Returned	Description
		SQL_CA1_RELATIVE: The **SQL_FETCH_PRIOR** and **SQL_FETCH_RELATIVE** orientation values can be specified with the **SQLFetchScroll()** function when the cursor is a dynamic cursor. (The rowset fetched is dependent on the current cursor position. Note that this is separate from **SQL_FETCH_NEXT** because in a forward-only cursor, only **SQL_FETCH_NEXT** is supported.)
		SQL_CA1_BOOKMARK: The **SQL_FETCH_BOOKMARK** orientation value can be specified with the **SQLFetchScroll()** function when the cursor is a dynamic cursor.
		SQL_CA1_LOCK_EXCLUSIVE: The **SQL_LOCK_EXCLUSIVE** lock value can be specified with the **SQLSetPos()** function when the cursor is a dynamic cursor.
		SQL_CA1_LOCK_NO_CHANGE: The **SQL_LOCK_NO_CHANGE** lock value can be specified with the **SQLSetPos()** function when the cursor is a dynamic cursor.
		SQL_CA1_LOCK_UNLOCK: The **SQL_LOCK_UNLOCK** lock value can be specified with the **SQLSetPos()** function when the cursor is a dynamic cursor.
		SQL_CA1_POS_POSITION: The **SQL_POSITION** operation value can be specified with the **SQLSetPos()** function when the cursor is a dynamic cursor.
		SQL_CA1_POS_UPDATE: The **SQL_UPDATE** operation value can be specified with the **SQLSetPos()** function when the cursor is a dynamic cursor.
		SQL_CA1_POS_DELETE: The **SQL_DELETE** operation value can be specified with the **SQLSetPos()** function when the cursor is a dynamic cursor.
		SQL_CA1_POS_REFRESH: The **SQL_REFRESH** operation value can be specified with the **SQLSetPos()** function when the cursor is a dynamic cursor.
		SQL_CA1_POSITIONED_UPDATE: An **UPDATE WHERE CURRENT OF** SQL statement is supported when the cursor is a dynamic cursor.
		SQL_CA1_POSITIONED_DELETE: A **DELETE WHERE CURRENT OF** SQL statement is supported when the cursor is a dynamic cursor.

InfoType Code	Data Type Returned	Description
		SQL_CA1_SELECT_FOR_UPDATE: A **SELECT FOR UPDATE** SQL statement is supported when the cursor is a dynamic cursor.
		SQL_CA1_BULK_ADD: The **SQL_ADD** operation value can be specified with the **SQLBulkOperations()** function when the cursor is a dynamic cursor.
		SQL_CA1_BULK_UPDATE_BY_BOOKMARK: The **SQL_UPDATE_BY_BOOKMARK** operation value can be specified with the **SQLBulkOperations()** function when the cursor is a dynamic cursor.
		SQL_CA1_BULK_DELETE_BY_BOOKMARK: The **SQL_DELETE_BY_BOOKMARK** operation value can be specified with the **SQLBulkOperations()** function when the cursor is a dynamic cursor.
		SQL_CA1_BULK_FETCH_BY_BOOKMARK: The **SQL_FETCH_BY_BOOKMARK** operation value can be specified with the **SQLBulkOperations()** function when the cursor is a dynamic cursor.
SQL_DYNAMIC_CURSOR_ ATTRIBUTES2	**SQLUINTEGER** bitmask	Defines the second subset of dynamic cursor attributes that are supported by the driver (see the **SQL_ DYNAMIC_CURSOR_ATTRIBUTES1** *InfoType* code for the first subset of attributes).
		When using DB2 CLI, the value **0** will always be returned because dynamic cursors are not supported.
		When using ODBC, the following bitmask values can be returned for this *InfoType* code:
		SQL_CA2_READ_ONLY_CONCURRENCY: A read-only dynamic cursor in which no updates are allowed, is supported. (The **SQL_ATTR_CONCURRENCY** statement attribute can be set to **SQL_CONCUR_ READ_ONLY** for a dynamic cursor).
		SQL_CA2_LOCK_CONCURRENCY: A dynamic cursor that uses the lowest level of locking sufficient to ensure that the row can be updated is supported. (The **SQL_ATTR_CONCURRENCY** statement attribute can be set to **SQL_CONCUR_LOCK** for a dynamic cursor).
		These locks must be consistent with the transaction isolation level set by the **SQL_ATTR_TXN_ISOLATION** connection attribute.
		SQL_CA2_OPT_ROWVER_CONCURRENCY: A dynamic cursor that uses the optimistic concurrency control by comparing row versions is supported. (The **SQL_ATTR_CONCURRENCY** statement attribute can be set to **SQL_CONCUR_ROWVER** for a dynamic cursor).

InfoType Code	Data Type Returned	Description
		SQL_CA2_OPT_VALUES_CONCURRENCY: A dynamic cursor that uses the optimistic concurrency control by comparing values is supported. (The **SQL_ATTR_CONCURRENCY** statement attribute can be set to **SQL_CONCUR_VALUES** for a dynamic cursor).
		SQL_CA2_SENSITIVITY_ADDITIONS: Added rows are visible to a dynamic cursor and the cursor can scroll to the added rows. (Where these rows are added to the cursor is driver-dependent.)
		SQL_CA2_SENSITIVITY_DELETIONS: Deleted rows are no longer available to a dynamic cursor, and do not leave a 'hole' in the result data set; after the dynamic cursor scrolls from a deleted row, it cannot return to that row.
		SQL_CA2_SENSITIVITY_UPDATES: Updates to rows are visible to a dynamic cursor; if the dynamic cursor scrolls from and returns to an updated row, the data returned by the cursor is the updated data, not the original data.
		SQL_CA2_MAX_ROWS_SELECT: The **SQL_ATTR_MAX_ROWS** statement attribute affects **SELECT** SQL statements when the cursor is a dynamic cursor.
		SQL_CA2_MAX_ROWS_INSERT: The **SQL_ATTR_MAX_ROWS** statement attribute affects **INSERT** SQL statements when the cursor is a dynamic cursor.
		SQL_CA2_MAX_ROWS_DELETE: The **SQL_ATTR_MAX_ROWS** statement attribute affects **DELETE** SQL statements when the cursor is a dynamic cursor.
		SQL_CA2_MAX_ROWS_UPDATE: The **SQL_ATTR_MAX_ROWS** statement attribute affects **UPDATE** SQL statements when the cursor is a dynamic cursor.
		SQL_CA2_MAX_ROWS_CATALOG: The **SQL_ATTR_MAX_ROWS** statement attribute affects **CATALOG** result data sets when the cursor is a dynamic cursor.
		SQL_CA2_MAX_ROWS_AFFECTS_ALL: The **SQL_ATTR_MAX_ROWS** statement attribute affects **SELECT**, **INSERT**, **UPDATE**, and **DELETE** SQL statements, and **CATALOG** result data sets, when the cursor is a dynamic cursor.
		SQL_CA2_CRC_EXACT: The exact row count is available in the **SQL_DIAG_CURSOR_ROW_COUNT** diagnostic header record field when the cursor is a dynamic cursor.

InfoType Code	Data Type Returned	Description
		SQL_CA2_CRC_APPROXIMATE: An approximate row count is available in the **SQL_DIAG_CURSOR_ROW_COUNT** diagnostic field when the cursor is a dynamic cursor. **SQL_CA2_SIMULATE_NON_UNIQUE**: The driver does not guarantee that simulated positioned **UPDATE** or **DELETE** SQL statements will affect only one row when the cursor is a dynamic cursor. If a statement affects more than one row, **SQLExecute()** or **SQLExecDirect()** returns SQLSTATE **01**001 (Cursor operation conflict). To set this behavior, an application calls the **SQLSetStmtAttr()** function and sets the **SQL_ATTR_SIMULATE_CURSOR** statement attribute to **SQL_SC_NON_UNIQUE**. **SQL_CA2_SIMULATE_TRY_UNIQUE**: The driver attempts to guarantee that simulated positioned **UPDATE** or **DELETE** SQL statements will affect only one row when the cursor is a dynamic cursor. The driver always executes such statements, even if they might affect more than one row, such as when there is no unique key. If the driver cannot guarantee this for a given statement, **SQLExecute()** or **SQLExecDirect()** returns SQLSTATE **01**001 (Cursor operation conflict). To set this behavior, an application calls the **SQLSetStmtAttr()** function and sets the **SQL_ATTR_SIMULATE_CURSOR** statement attribute to **SQL_SC_TRY_UNIQUE**. **SQL_CA2_SIMULATE_UNIQUE**: The driver guarantees that simulated positioned **UPDATE** or **DELETE** SQL statements will affect only one row when the cursor is a dynamic cursor. If the driver cannot guarantee this for a given statement, **SQLExecute()** or **SQLExecDirect()** returns SQLSTATE **01**001 (Cursor operation conflict). To set this behavior, an application calls the **SQLSetStmtAttr()** function and sets the **SQL_ATTR_SIMULATE_CURSOR** statement attribute to **SQL_SC_UNIQUE**.
SQL_EXPRESSIONS_ IN_ORDERBY	Character string	Indicates whether the data source supports direct specification of expresions in the **ORDER BY** clause list. The following values can be returned for this *InfoType* code: **"Y"**: The data source supports direct expressions in the **ORDER BY** clause list. **"N"**: The data source does not support direct expressions in the **ORDER BY** clause list.

InfoType Code	Data Type Returned	Description
SQL_FETCH_DIRECTION	SQLUINTEGER bitmask	Identifies the cursor fetch direction options supported by the driver and its underlying data source. The following bitmask values can be returned for this *InfoType* code: SQL_FD_FETCH_NEXT SQL_FD_FETCH_FIRST SQL_FD_FETCH_LAST SQL_FD_FETCH_PRIOR SQL_FD_FETCH_ABSOLUTE SQL_FD_FETCH_RELATIVE SQL_FD_FETCH_RESUME SQL_FD_FETCH_BOOKMARK
SQL_FILE_USAGE	SQLUSMALLINT	Identifies how a single-tier driver treats files in a data source. The following values can be returned for this *InfoType* code: SQL_FILE_NOT_SUPPORTED: The driver is not a single-tier driver, therefore files are not supported. SQL_FILE_TABLE: The single-tier driver treats files in a data source as tables. SQL_FILE_CATALOG: The single-tier driver treats files in a data source as a catalog (i.e., as a complete database). When using DB2 CLI, the value SQL_FILE_NOT_SUPPORTED will always be returned for this *InfoType* code because the DB2 CLI driver is not a single-tier driver.
SQL_FORWARD_ONLY_CURSOR_ATTRIBUTES1	SQLUINTEGER bitmask	Defines the first subset of forward-only cursor attributes that are supported by the driver (see the SQL_FORWARD_ONLY_CURSOR_ATTRIBUTES2 *InfoType* code for the second subset of attributes). When using DB2 CLI, the following bitmask values can be returned for this *InfoType* code: SQL_CA1_NEXT: The SQL_FETCH_NEXT orientation value can be specified with the SQLFetchScroll() function when the cursor is a forward-only cursor. SQL_CA1_POSITIONED_UPDATE: An UPDATE WHERE CURRENT OF SQL statement is supported when the cursor is a forward-only cursor. SQL_CA1_POSITIONED_DELETE: A DELETE WHERE CURRENT OF SQL statement is supported when the cursor is a forward-only cursor. SQL_CA1_SELECT_FOR_UPDATE: A SELECT FOR UPDATE SQL statement is supported when the cursor is a forward-only cursor.

InfoType Code	Data Type Returned	Description
		When using ODBC, the following bitmask values (along with all of the previous bitmask values) can be returned for this *InfoType* code:
		SQL_CA1_LOCK_EXCLUSIVE: The **SQL_LOCK_EXCLUSIVE** lock value can be specified with the **SQLSetPos()** function when the cursor is a forward-only cursor.
		SQL_CA1_LOCK_NO_CHANGE: The **SQL_LOCK_NO_CHANGE** lock value can be specified with the **SQLSetPos()** function when the cursor is a forward-only cursor.
		SQL_CA1_LOCK_UNLOCK: The **SQL_LOCK_UNLOCK** lock value can be specified with the **SQLSetPos()** function when the cursor is a forward-only cursor.
		SQL_CA1_POS_POSITION: The **SQL_POSITION** operation value can be specified with the **SQLSetPos()** function when the cursor is a forward-only cursor.
		SQL_CA1_POS_UPDATE: The **SQL_UPDATE** operation value can be specified with the **SQLSetPos()** function when the cursor is a forward-only cursor.
		SQL_CA1_POS_DELETE: The **SQL_DELETE** operation value can be specified with the **SQLSetPos()** function when the cursor is a forward-only cursor.
		SQL_CA1_POS_REFRESH: The **SQL_REFRESH** operation value can be specified with the **SQLSetPos()** function when the cursor is a forward-only cursor.
		SQL_CA1_BULK_ADD: The **SQL_ADD** operation value can be specified with the **SQLBulkOperations()** function when the cursor is a forward-only cursor.
		SQL_CA1_BULK_UPDATE_BY_BOOKMARK: The **SQL_UPDATE_BY_BOOKMARK** operation value can be specified with the **SQLBulkOperations()** function when the cursor is a forward-only cursor.
		SQL_CA1_BULK_DELETE_BY_BOOKMARK: The **SQL_DELETE_BY_BOOKMARK** operation value can be specified with the **SQLBulkOperations()** function when the cursor is a forward-only cursor.
		SQL_CA1_BULK_FETCH_BY_BOOKMARK: The **SQL_FETCH_BY_BOOKMARK** operation value can be specified with the **SQLBulkOperations()** function when the cursor is a forward-only cursor.

InfoType Code	Data Type Returned	Description
SQL_FORWARD_ONLY_ CURSOR_ATTRIBUTES2	SQLUINTEGER bitmask	Defines the second subset of forward-only cursor attributes that are supported by the driver (see the SQL_FORWARD_ONLY_CURSOR_ATTRIBUTES1 *Info-Type* code for the first subset of attributes). When using DB2 CLI, the following bitmask values can be returned for this *InfoType* code: SQL_CA2_READ_ONLY_CONCURRENCY: A read-only forward-only cursor, in which no updates are allowed, is supported. (The SQL_ATTR_CONCURRENCY statement attribute can be set to SQL_CONCUR_READ_ONLY for a forward-only cursor). SQL_CA2_LOCK_CONCURRENCY: A forward-only cursor that uses the lowest level of locking sufficient to ensure that the row can be updated is supported. (The SQL_ATTR_CONCURRENCY statement attribute can be set to SQL_CONCUR_LOCK for a forward-only cursor). These locks must be consistent with the transaction isolation level set by the SQL_ATTR_TXN_ISOLATION connection attribute. SQL_CA2_MAX_ROWS_SELECT: The SQL_ATTR_MAX_ROWS statement attribute affects SELECT SQL statements when the cursor is a forward-only cursor. SQL_CA2_MAX_ROWS_CATALOG: The SQL_ATTR_MAX_ROWS statement attribute affects CATALOG result data sets when the cursor is a forward-only cursor. When using ODBC, the following bitmask values (along with all of the previous bitmask values) can be returned for this *InfoType* code: SQL_CA2_OPT_ROWVER_CONCURRENCY: A forward-only cursor that uses the optimistic concurrency control by comparing row versions is supported. (The SQL_ATTR_CONCURRENCY statement attribute can be set to SQL_CONCUR_ROWVER for a forward-only cursor). SQL_CA2_OPT_VALUES_CONCURRENCY: A forward-only cursor that uses the optimistic concurrency control by comparing values is supported. (The SQL_ATTR_CONCURRENCY statement attribute can be set to SQL_CONCUR_VALUES for a forward-only cursor). SQL_CA2_SENSITIVITY_ADDITIONS: Added rows are visible to a forward-only cursor and the cursor can scroll to the added rows. (Where these rows are added to the cursor is driver-dependent.)

InfoType Code	Data Type Returned	Description
		SQL_CA2_SENSITIVITY_DELETIONS: Deleted rows are no longer available to a forward-only cursor, and do not leave a 'hole' in the result data set; after the forward-only cursor scrolls from a deleted row, it cannot return to that row.
		SQL_CA2_SENSITIVITY_UPDATES: Updates to rows are visible to a forward-only cursor; if the forward-only cursor scrolls from and returns to an updated row, the data returned by the cursor is the updated data, not the original data.
		SQL_CA2_MAX_ROWS_INSERT: The **SQL_ATTR_MAX_ROWS** statement attribute affects **INSERT** SQL statements when the cursor is a forward-only cursor.
		SQL_CA2_MAX_ROWS_DELETE: The **SQL_ATTR_MAX_ROWS** statement attribute affects **DELETE** SQL statements when the cursor is a forward-only cursor.
		SQL_CA2_MAX_ROWS_UPDATE: The **SQL_ATTR_MAX_ROWS** statement attribute affects **UPDATE** SQL statements when the cursor is a forward-only cursor.
		SQL_CA2_MAX_ROWS_AFFECTS_ALL: The **SQL_ATTR_MAX_ROWS** statement attribute affects **SELECT**, **INSERT**, **UPDATE**, and **DELETE** SQL statements, and **CATALOG** result data sets, when the cursor is a forward-only cursor.
		SQL_CA2_CRC_EXACT: The exact row count is available in the **SQL_DIAG_CURSOR_ROW_COUNT** diagnostic field when the cursor is a forward-only cursor.
		SQL_CA2_CRC_APPROXIMATE: An approximate row count is available in the **SQL_DIAG_CURSOR_ROW_COUNT** diagnostic field when the cursor is a forward-only cursor.
		SQL_CA2_SIMULATE_NON_UNIQUE: The driver does not guarantee that simulated positioned **UPDATE** or **DELETE** SQL statements will affect only one row when the cursor is a forward-only cursor. If a statement affects more than one row, **SQLExecute()** or **SQLExecDirect()** returns SQLSTATE **01**001 (Cursor operation conflict). To set this behavior, an application calls the **SQLSetStmtAttr()** function and sets the **SQL_ATTR_SIMULATE_CURSOR** statement attribute to **SQL_SC_NON_UNIQUE**.

InfoType Code	Data Type Returned	Description
		SQL_CA2_SIMULATE_TRY_UNIQUE: The driver attempts to guarantee that simulated positioned **UPDATE** or **DELETE** SQL statements will affect only one row when the cursor is a forward-only cursor. The driver always executes such statements, even if they might affect more than one row, such as when there is no unique key. If the driver cannot guarantee this for a given statement, **SQLExecute()** or **SQLExecDirect()** returns SQLSTATE **01**001 (Cursor operation conflict). To set this behavior, an application calls the **SQLSetStmtAttr()** function and sets the **SQL_ATTR_SIMULATE_CURSOR** statement attribute to **SQL_SC_TRY_UNIQUE**. **SQL_CA2_SIMULATE_UNIQUE**: The driver guarantees that simulated positioned **UPDATE** or **DELETE** SQL statements will affect only one row when the cursor is a forward-only cursor. If the driver cannot guarantee this for a given statement, **SQLExecute()** or **SQLExecDirect()** returns SQLSTATE **01**001 (Cursor operation conflict). To set this behavior, an application calls the **SQLSetStmtAttr()** function and sets the **SQL_ATTR_SIMULATE_CURSOR** statement attribute to **SQL_SC_UNIQUE**.
SQL_GETDATA_EXTENSIONS	**SQLUINTEGER** bitmask	Identifies the common extensions the driver supports for the **SQLGetData()** function. The following bitmask values can be returned for this *InfoType* code: **SQL_GD_ANY_COLUMN**: The **SQLGetData()** function can be called for any unbound column, including those before the last bound column. Note that the columns must be called in order of ascending column number unless **SQL_GD_ANY_ORDER** is also returned. **SQL_GD_ANY_ORDER**: The **SQLGetData()** function can be called for unbound columns in any order. Note that **SQLGetData()** can only be called for columns after the last bound column unless **SQL_GD_ANY_COLUMN** is also returned. **SQL_GD_BLOCK**: The **SQLGetData()** function can be called for an unbound column in any row in a block of data (where the rowset size is greater than 1) after positioning to that row with **SQLSetPos()**.

InfoType Code	Data Type Returned	Description
		SQL_GD_BOUND: The **SQLGetData()** function can be called for bound columns as well as unbound columns. A driver cannot return this value unless it also returns **SQL_GD_ANY_COLUMN**.
		When using DB2 CLI, the value **SQL_GD_BOUND** will never be returned for this *InfoType* code.
		By default, the **SQLGetData()** function is only required to return data from unbound columns that occur after the last bound column; that are called in order of increasing column number; and that are not in a row that's in a rowset.
		If a driver supports bookmarks (either fixed- or variable-length), it must allow the **SQLGetData()** function to be called on column 0. This support is required regardless of what the driver returns for the **SQL_GETDATA_EXTENSIONS** *InfoType* code.
SQL_GROUP_BY	**SQLUSMALLINT**	Identifies the relationship between the columns in a **GROUP BY** clause and the non-aggregated columns in the corresponding select list. The following values can be returned for this *InfoType* code:
		SQL_GB_COLLATE: A **COLLATE** clause can be specified at the end of each grouping column.
		SQL_GB_NOT_SUPPORTED: **GROUP BY** clauses are not supported by the data source.
		SQL_GB_GROUP_BY_EQUALS_SELECT: The **GROUP BY** clause must contain all non-aggregated columns named in the corresponding select list; it cannot contain any other columns. For example, **SELECT DEPT, MAX(SALARY) FROM EMPLOYEE GROUP BY DEPT**.
		SQL_GB_GROUP_BY_CONTAINS_SELECT: The **GROUP BY** clause must contain all non-aggregated columns named in the corresponding select list, however, it can also contain columns not named in the select list. For example, **SELECT DEPT, MAX(SALARY) FROM EMPLOYEE GROUP BY DEPT, AGE**.
		SQL_GB_NO_RELATION: The columns in the **GROUP BY** clause and the columns named in the corresponding select list are not related. For example, **SELECT DEPT, SALARY FROM EMPLOYEE GROUP BY DEPT, AGE**.
		If none of these options are supported, the **GROUP BY** clause is not supported by the data source.

InfoType Code	Data Type Returned	Description
SQL_IDENTIFIER_CASE	SQLUSMALLINT	Identifies the type of case sensitivity used in object identifier names (for example, table names). The following values can be returned for this *InfoType* code: **SQL_IC_UPPER:** Identifiers in SQL are not case-sensitive and are stored in uppercase in the system catalog. **SQL_IC_LOWER:** Identifiers in SQL are not case-sensitive and are stored in lowercase in the system catalog. **SQL_IC_SENSITIVE:** Identifiers in SQL are case-sensitive and are stored in mixed case in the system catalog. **SQL_IC_MIXED:** Identifiers in SQL are not case-sensitive and are stored in mixed case in the system catalog. **NOTE:** Identifier names in IBM DBMSs are not case sensitive.
SQL_IDENTIFIER_QUOTE_CHAR	Character string	Identifies the character that is to be used as the starting and ending delimiter of a quoted (delimited) identifier in SQL statements. (Identifiers passed in ODBC function parameters do not need to be quoted.) This character can also be used for quoting catalog function parameters when the connection attribute **SQL_ATTR_METADATA_ID** is set to **SQL_TRUE**. If the data source does not support quoted identifiers, a blank string (" ") is returned for this *InfoType* code.
SQL_INDEX_KEYWORDS	SQLUINTEGER bitmask	Identifies the keywords in the **CREATE INDEX** SQL statement that are supported by the driver (as defined in SQL-92). The following bitmask values can be returned for this *InfoType* code: **SQL_IK_NONE:** None of the keywords are supported. **SQL_IK_ASC:** The **ASC** keyword (for ascending order) is supported. **SQL_IK_DESC:** The **DESC** keyword (for descending order) is supported. **SQL_IK_ALL:** All keywords are supported.

InfoType Code	Data Type Returned	Description
		If the **CREATE INDEX** statement is not supported by the data source (see the **SQL_DLL_INDEX** *InfoType* code), the value **SQL_IK_NONE** is returned for this *InfoType* code.
SQL_INFO_SCHEMA_VIEWS	**SQLUINTEGER** bitmask	Identifies the views (and their contents) in the **INFORMATION_SCHEMA** that are supported by the driver (as defined in SQL-92).
		When using DB2 CLI, the value **0** will always be returned because views in the **INFORMATIONAL_ SCHEMA** are not supported.
		When using ODBC, the following bitmask values can be returned for this *InfoType* code:
		SQL_ISV_ASSERTIONS: Identifies the catalog's assertions that are owned by a given user.
		SQL_ISV_CHARACTER_SETS: Identifies the catalog's character sets that are accessible to a given user.
		SQL_ISV_CHECK_CONSTRAINTS: Identifies the check constraints owned by a given user.
		SQL_ISV_COLLATIONS: Identifies the catalog's character collations that are accessible to a given user.
		SQL_ISV_COLUMN_DOMAIN_USAGE: Identifies columns for the catalog that are dependent on domains defined in the catalog and that are owned by a given user.
		SQL_ISV_COLUMN_PRIVILEGES: Identifies the privileges on columns of persistent tables that are available to or granted by a given user.
		SQL_ISV_COLUMNS: Identifies the columns of persistent tables that are accessible to a given user.
		SQL_ISV_CONSTRAINT_COLUMN_USAGE: Identifies the columns for the various constraints that are owned by a given user.
		SQL_ISV_CONSTRAINT_TABLE_USAGE: Identifies the tables that are used by constraints (referential, unique, and assertions) and that are owned by a given user.
		SQL_ISV_DOMAIN_CONSTRAINTS: Identifies the domain constraints (of the domains in the catalog) that are accessible to a given user.
		SQL_ISV_DOMAINS: Identifies the domains defined in a catalog that are accessible to a given user.

InfoType Code	Data Type Returned	Description
		SQL_ISV_KEY_COLUMN_USAGE: Identifies columns defined in the catalog that are constrained as keys by a given user.
		SQL_ISV_REFERENTIAL_CONSTRAINTS: Identifies the referential constraints owned by a given user.
		SQL_ISV_SCHEMATA: Identifies the schemas owned by a given user.
		SQL_ISV_SQL_LANGUAGES: Identifies the SQL conformance levels, options, and dialects supported by the SQL implementation.
		SQL_ISV_TABLE_CONSTRAINTS: Identifies the table constraints owned by a given user.
		SQL_ISV_TABLE_PRIVILEGES: Identifies a persistent table's privileges available to or granted by a given user.
		SQL_ISV_TABLES: Identifies the persistent tables defined in a catalog that are accessible to a given user.
		SQL_ISV_TRANSLATIONS: Identifies catalog character translations that are accessible to a given user.
		SQL_ISV_USAGE_PRIVILEGES: Identifies the USAGE privileges on catalog objects that are available to or owned by a given user.
		SQL_ISV_VIEW_COLUMN_USAGE: Identifies the columns on which the catalog's views owned by a given user are dependent.
		SQL_ISV_VIEW_TABLE_USAGE: Identifies the tables on which the catalog's views owned by a given user are dependent.
		SQL_ISV_VIEWS: Identifies the viewed tables defined in the catalog that are accessible to a given user.
SQL_INSERT_STATEMENT	**SQLUINTEGER** bitmask	Identifies how the **INSERT** SQL statement is supported by the data source (as defined in SQL-92). The following bitmask values can be returned for this *InfoType* code:
		SQL_IS_INSERT_LITERALS **SQL_IS_INSERT_SEARCHED** **SQL_IS_SELECT_INTO**
SQL_INTEGRITY[5]	Character string	Indicates whether the data source supports the Integrity Enhancement Facility (in SQL89 and in X/Open XPG4 Embedded SQL).

InfoType Code	Data Type Returned	Description
		The following values can be returned for this *Info-Type* code: **"Y"**: The data source supports the Integrity Enhancement Facility. **"N"**: The data source does not support the Integrity Enhancement Facility.
SQL_KEYSET_CURSOR_ATTRIBUTES1	**SQLUINTEGER** bitmask	Defines the first subset of keyset-driven cursor attributes that are supported by the driver (see the **SQL_KEYSET_CURSOR_ATTRIBUTES2** *InfoType* code for the second subset of attributes). When using DB2 CLI, the value **0** will always be returned because keyset-driven cursors are not supported. When using ODBC, the following bitmask values can be returned for this *InfoType* code: The **SQL_CA1_NEXT** orientation value can be specified with the **SQLFetchScroll()** function when the cursor is a keyset-driven cursor. **SQL_CA1_ABSOLUTE:** The **SQL_FETCH_FIRST**, **SQL_FETCH_LAST**, and **SQL_FETCH_ABSOLUTE** orientation values can be specified with the **SQLFetchScroll()** function when the cursor is a keyset-driven cursor. (The rowset fetched is independent of the current cursor position.) **SQL_CA1_RELATIVE:** The **SQL_FETCH_PRIOR** and **SQL_FETCH_RELATIVE** orientation values can be specified with the **SQLFetchScroll()** function when the cursor is a keyset-driven cursor. (The rowset fetched is dependent on the current cursor position. Note that this is separate from **SQL_FETCH_NEXT** because in a forward-only cursor, only **SQL_FETCH_NEXT** is supported.) **SQL_CA1_BOOKMARK:** The **SQL_FETCH_BOOKMARK** orientation value can be specified with the **SQLFetchScroll()** function when the cursor is a keyset-driven cursor. **SQL_CA1_LOCK_EXCLUSIVE:** The **SQL_LOCK_EXCLUSIVE** lock value can be specified with the **SQLSetPos()** function when the cursor is a keyset-driven cursor. **SQL_CA1_LOCK_NO_CHANGE:** The **SQL_LOCK_NO_CHANGE** lock value can be specified with the **SQLSetPos()** function when the cursor is a keyset-driven cursor.

InfoType Code	Data Type Returned	Description
		SQL_CA1_LOCK_UNLOCK: The **SQL_LOCK_UNLOCK** lock value can be specified with the **SQLSetPos()** function when the cursor is a keyset-driven cursor.
		SQL_CA1_POS_POSITION: The **SQL_POSITION** operation value can be specified with the **SQLSetPos()** function when the cursor is a keyset-driven cursor.
		SQL_CA1_POS_UPDATE: The **SQL_UPDATE** operation value can be specified with the **SQLSetPos()** function when the cursor is a keyset-driven cursor.
		SQL_CA1_POS_DELETE: The **SQL_DELETE** operation value can be specified with the **SQLSetPos()** function when the cursor is a keyset-driven cursor.
		SQL_CA1_POS_REFRESH: The **SQL_REFRESH** operation value can be specified with the **SQLSetPos()** function when the cursor is a keyset-driven cursor.
		SQL_CA1_POSITIONED_UPDATE: An **UPDATE WHERE CURRENT OF** SQL statement is supported when the cursor is a keyset-driven cursor.
		SQL_CA1_POSITIONED_DELETE: A **DELETE WHERE CURRENT OF** SQL statement is supported when the cursor is a keyset-driven cursor.
		SQL_CA1_SELECT_FOR_UPDATE: A **SELECT FOR UPDATE** SQL statement is supported when the cursor is a keyset-driven cursor.
		SQL_CA1_BULK_ADD: The **SQL_ADD** operation value can be specified with the **SQLBulkOperations()** function when the cursor is a keyset-driven cursor.
		SQL_CA1_BULK_UPDATE_BY_BOOKMARK: The **SQL_UPDATE_BY_BOOKMARK** operation value can be specified with the **SQLBulkOperations()** function when the cursor is a keyset-driven cursor.
		SQL_CA1_BULK_DELETE_BY_BOOKMARK: The **SQL_DELETE_BY_BOOKMARK** operation value can be specified with the **SQLBulkOperations()** function when the cursor is a keyset-driven cursor.
		SQL_CA1_BULK_FETCH_BY_BOOKMARK: The **SQL_FETCH_BY_BOOKMARK** operation value can be specified with the **SQLBulkOperations()** function when the cursor is a keyset-driven cursor.

InfoType Code	Data Type Returned	Description
SQL_KEYSET_CURSOR_ ATTRIBUTES2	**SQLUINTEGER** bitmask	Defines the second subset of keyset-driven cursor attributes that are supported by the driver (see the **SQL_KEYSET_CURSOR_ATTRIBUTES1** *InfoType* code for the first subset of attributes).

When using DB2 CLI, the value **0** will always be returned because keyset-driven cursors are not supported.

When using ODBC, the following bitmask values can be returned for this *InfoType* code:

SQL_CA2_READ_ONLY_CONCURRENCY:
A read-only keyset-driven cursor, in which no updates are allowed, is supported. (The **SQL_ATTR_ CONCURRENCY** statement attribute can be set to **SQL_CONCUR_READ_ONLY** for a keyset-driven cursor).

SQL_CA2_LOCK_CONCURRENCY:
A keyset-driven cursor using the lowest level of locking sufficient to ensure that the row can be updated is supported. (The **SQL_ATTR_CONCURRENCY** statement attribute can be set to **SQL_CONCUR_LOCK** for a keyset-driven cursor). These locks must be consistent with the transaction isolation level set by the **SQL_ATTR_TXN_ISOLATION** connection attribute.

SQL_CA2_OPT_ROWVER_CONCURRENCY:
A keyset-driven cursor that uses the optimistic concurrency control by comparing row versions is supported. (The **SQL_ATTR_CONCURRENCY** statement attribute can be set to **SQL_CONCUR_ROWVER** for a keyset-driven cursor).

SQL_CA2_OPT_VALUES_CONCURRENCY:
A keyset-driven cursor that uses the optimistic concurrency control by comparing values is supported. (The **SQL_ATTR_CONCURRENCY** statement attribute can be set to **SQL_CONCUR_VALUES** for a keyset-driven cursor).

SQL_CA2_SENSITIVITY_ADDITIONS:
Added rows are visible to a keyset-driven cursor and the cursor can scroll to the added rows. (Where these rows are added to the cursor is driver-dependent.)

SQL_CA2_SENSITIVITY_DELETIONS:
Deleted rows are no longer available to a keyset-driven cursor and do not leave a 'hole' in the result data set; after the keyset-driven cursor scrolls from a deleted row, it cannot return to that row.

SQL_CA2_SENSITIVITY_UPDATES:
Updates to rows are visible to a keyset-driven cursor; if the keyset-driven cursor scrolls from and returns to an updated row, the data returned by the cursor is the updated data, not the original data.

InfoType Code	Data Type Returned	Description
		SQL_CA2_MAX_ROWS_SELECT: The **SQL_ATTR_MAX_ROWS** statement attribute affects **SELECT** SQL statements when the cursor is a keyset-driven cursor.
		SQL_CA2_MAX_ROWS_INSERT: The **SQL_ATTR_MAX_ROWS** statement attribute affects **INSERT** SQL statements when the cursor is a keyset-driven cursor.
		SQL_CA2_MAX_ROWS_DELETE: The **SQL_ATTR_MAX_ROWS** statement attribute affects **DELETE** SQL statements when the cursor is a keyset-driven cursor.
		SQL_CA2_MAX_ROWS_UPDATE: The **SQL_ATTR_MAX_ROWS** statement attribute affects **UPDATE** SQL statements when the cursor is a keyset-driven cursor.
		SQL_CA2_MAX_ROWS_CATALOG: The **SQL_ATTR_MAX_ROWS** statement attribute affects **CATALOG** result data sets when the cursor is a keyset-driven cursor.
		SQL_CA2_MAX_ROWS_AFFECTS_ALL: The **SQL_ATTR_MAX_ROWS** statement attribute affects **SELECT**, **INSERT**, **UPDATE**, and **DELETE** statements, and **CATALOG** result data sets, when the cursor is a keyset-driven cursor.
		SQL_CA2_CRC_EXACT: The exact row count is available in the **SQL_DIAG_CURSOR_ROW_COUNT** diagnostic header record field when the cursor is a keyset-driven cursor.
		SQL_CA2_CRC_APPROXIMATE: An approximate row count is available in the **SQL_DIAG_CURSOR_ROW_COUNT** diagnostic header record field when the cursor is a keyset-driven cursor.
		SQL_CA2_SIMULATE_NON_UNIQUE: The driver does not guarantee that simulated positioned **UPDATE** or **DELETE** SQL statements will affect only one row when the cursor is a keyset-driven cursor. If a statement affects more than one row, **SQLExecute()** or **SQLExecDirect()** will return SQLSTATE **01**001 (Cursor operation conflict). To set this behavior, an application calls the **SQLSetStmtAttr()** function and sets the **SQL_ATTR_SIMULATE_CURSOR** statement attribute to **SQL_SC_NON_UNIQUE**.
		SQL_CA2_SIMULATE_TRY_UNIQUE: The driver attempts to guarantee that simulated positioned **UPDATE** or **DELETE** SQL statements will

InfoType Code	Data Type Returned	Description
		affect only one row when the cursor is a keyset-driven cursor. The driver always executes such statements, even if they might affect more than one row, such as when there is no unique key. If the driver cannot guarantee this for a given statement,
		SQLExecute() or **SQLExecDirect()** will return SQLSTATE **01**001 (Cursor operation conflict). To set this behavior, an application calls the **SQLSetStmtAttr()** function and sets the **SQL_ ATTR_SIMULATE_CURSOR** statement attribute to **SQL_SC_TRY_UNIQUE**.
		SQL_CA2_SIMULATE_UNIQUE: The driver guarantees that simulated positioned **UPDATE** or **DELETE** SQL statements will affect only one row when the cursor is a keyset-driven cursor. If the driver cannot guarantee this for a given statement, **SQLExecute()** or **SQLExecDirect()** will return SQLSTATE **01**001 (Cursor operation conflict). To set this behavior, an application calls the **SQLSetStmtAttr()** function and sets the **SQL_ ATTR_SIMULATE_CURSOR** statement attribute to **SQL_SC_UNIQUE**.
SQL_KEYWORDS	Character string	A comma-separated list of all keywords recognized by the data source. This list does not include keywords specific to CLI/ODBC or keywords used by both the data source and CLI/ODBC. Instead, this list represents all data source-specific reserved keywords.
		The **#define** value **SQL_ODBC_KEYWORDS** contains a comma-separated list of ODBC-specific keywords.
SQL_LIKE_ESCAPE_CLAUSE	Character string	Indicates whether the data source supports an escape character for the percent character (%) and underscore character (_) in a **LIKE** predicate and whether the driver supports the CLI/ODBC syntax for defining a **LIKE** predicate escape character. The following values can be returned for this *InfoType* code:
		"Y": The data source supports escape characters in a **LIKE** predicate and the driver supports the CLI ODBC syntax for defining a **LIKE** predicate escape character.
		"N": The data source does not support escape characters in a **LIKE** predicate and/or the driver does not support the CLI/ODBC syntax for defining a **LIKE** predicate escape character.
SQL_LOCK_TYPES	**SQLUINTEGER** bitmask	Identifies the lock types supported by the driver and its underlying data source.

InfoType Code	Data Type Returned	Description
		When using DB2 CLI, the value **0** will always be returned—this *InfoType* code is not supported.
		When using ODBC, the following bitmask values can be returned for this *InfoType* code:
		SQL_LCK_NO_CHANGE **SQL_LCK_EXCLUSIVE** **SQL_LCK_UNLOCK**
SQL_MAX_ASYNC_ CONCURRENT_STATEMENTS	**SQLUINTEGER**	Identifies the maximum number of active concurrent SQL statements the driver can support in asynchronous mode on a given connection.
		If there is no specific limit or if the limit is unknown, the value **0** is returned for this *InfoType* code.
SQL_MAX_BINARY_ LITERAL_LEN	**SQLUINTEGER**	Identifies the maximum length (number of hexadecimal characters, excluding the literal prefix and suffix returned by the **SQLGetTypeInfo()** function) that a binary literal in an SQL statement can be. For example, the binary literal 0xFFAA has a length of 4.
		If there is no maximum length or if the length is unknown, the value **0** is returned for this *InfoType* code.
SQL_MAX_CATALOG_ NAME_LEN[6]	**SQLUSMALLINT**	Identifies the maximum length for a catalog name in the data source.
		If there is no maximum length or if the length is unknown, the value **0** is returned for this *InfoType* code.
SQL_MAX_CHAR_ LITERAL_LEN	**SQLUINTEGER**	Identifies the maximum length (number of characters, excluding the literal prefix and suffix returned by the **SQLGetTypeInfo()** function) for a character literal in an SQL statement.
		If there is no maximum length, or if the length is unknown, the value **0** is returned for this *InfoType* code.
SQL_MAX_COLUMN_ NAME_LEN	**SQLUSMALLINT**	Identifies the maximum length for a column name in the data source.
		If there is no maximum length, or if the length is unknown, the value **0** is returned for this *InfoType* code.
SQL_MAX_COLUMNS_ IN_GROUP_BY	**SQLUSMALLINT**	Identifies the maximum number of columns allowed in a **GROUP BY** clause.
		If there is no maximum number or if the limit is unknown, the value **0** is returned for this *InfoType* code.
SQL_MAX_COLUMNS_ IN_INDEX	**SQLUSMALLINT**	Identifies the maximum number of columns allowed in an index.

InfoType Code	Data Type Returned	Description
		If there is no maximum number, or if the limit is unknown, the value **0** is returned for this *InfoType* code.
SQL_MAX_COLUMNS_ IN_ORDER_BY	SQLUSMALLINT	Identifies the maximum number of columns allowed in an **ORDER BY** clause.
		If there is no maximum number or if the limit is unknown, the value **0** is returned for this *InfoType* code.
SQL_MAX_COLUMNS_ IN_SELECT	SQLUSMALLINT	Identifies the maximum number of columns allowed in a select list.
		If there is no maximum number, or if the limit is unknown, the value **0** is returned for this *InfoType* code.
SQL_MAX_COLUMNS_ IN_TABLE	SQLUSMALLINT	Identifies the maximum number of columns allowed in a table.
		If there is no maximum number, or if the limit is unknown, the value **0** is returned for this *InfoType* code.
SQL_MAX_CONCURRENT_ ACTIVITIES[7]	SQLUSMALLINT	Identifies the maximum number of active environments the driver can support.
		If there is no maximum number, or if the limit is unknown, the value **0** is returned for this *InfoType* code.
SQL_MAX_CURSOR_ NAME_LEN	SQLUSMALLINT	Identifies the maximum length for a cursor name in the data source.
		If there is no maximum length, or if the length is unknown, the value **0** is returned for this *InfoType* code.
SQL_MAX_DRIVER_ CONNECTIONS[8]	SQLUSMALLINT	Identifies the maximum number of active connections the driver can support for an environment. This value can reflect a limitation imposed by either the driver or the data source.
		If there is no maximum number, or if the limit is unknown, the value **0** is returned for this *InfoType* code.
		If the **MAXCONN** keyword in the *db2cli.ini* initialization file OR the **SQL_ATTR_MAX_CONNECTIONS** environment/connection attribute has been used to limit the number of connections available for an application, that limit value will be returned for this *InfoType* code.
SQL_MAX_IDENTIFIER_LEN	SQLUSMALLINT	Identifies the maximum length, in characters, for a user-defined name in the data source.

InfoType Code	Data Type Returned	Description
		If there is no maximum length, or if the length is unknown, the value **0** is returned for this *InfoType* code.
SQL_MAX_INDEX_SIZE	**SQLUINTEGER**	Identifies the maximum number of bytes allowed in the combined fields of an index.
		If there is no maximum length, or if the length is unknown, the value **0** is returned for this *InfoType* code.
SQL_MAX_PROCEDURE_ NAME_LEN	**SQLUSMALLINT**	Identifies the maximum length for a procedure name in the data source.
		If there is no maximum length or if the length is unknown, the value **0** is returned for this *InfoType* code.
SQL_MAX_ROW_SIZE	**SQLUINTEGER**	Identifies the maximum length for a single row in a table.
		If there is no maximum length, or if the length is unknown, the value **0** is returned for this *InfoType* code.
SQL_MAX_ROW_SIZE_ INCLUDES_LONG	Character string	Indicates whether the maximum row size returned for the **SQL_MAX_ROW_SIZE** information type includes the length of all **SQL_LONGVARCHAR** and **SQL_LONGVARBINARY** columns in the row. The following values can be returned for this *InfoType* code: **"Y"**: The maximum row size returned for the **SQL_MAX_ROW_SIZE** information type includes the length of all **SQL_LONGVARCHAR** and **SQL_LONGVARBINARY** columns in the row. **"N"**: The maximum row size returned for the **SQL_MAX_ROW_SIZE** information type does not include the length of **SQL_LONGVARCHAR** and **SQL_LONGVARBINARY** columns in the row.
SQL_MAX_SCHEMA_ NAME_LEN[9]	**SQLUSMALLINT**	Identifies the maximum length for a schema name in the data source.
		If there is no maximum length, or if the length is unknown, the value **0** is returned for this *InfoType* code.
SQL_MAX_STATEMENT_LEN	**SQLUINTEGER**	Identifies the maximum length (number of characters, including white space) for a SQL statement.
		If there is no maximum length, or if the length is unknown, the value **0** is returned for this *InfoType* code.
SQL_MAX_TABLE_NAME_LEN	**SQLUSMALLINT**	Identifies the maximum length for a table name in the data source.

InfoType Code	Data Type Returned	Description
		If there is no maximum length, or if the length is unknown, the value **0** is returned for this *InfoType* code.
SQL_MAX_TABLES_ IN_SELECT	SQLUSMALLINT	Identifies the maximum number of tables allowed in the **FROM** clause of a **SELECT** statement.
		If there is no limit, or if the limit is unknown, the value **0** is returned for this *InfoType* code.
SQL_MAX_USER_NAME_LEN	SQLUSMALLINT	Identifies the maximum length for a user name in the data source.
		If there is no maximum length, or if the length is unknown, the value **0** is returned for this *InfoType* code.
SQL_MULT_RESULT_SETS	Character string	Indicates whether the data source supports multiple result data sets. The following values can be returned for this *InfoType* code:
		"Y": The data source supports multiple result data sets.
		"N": The data source does not support multiple result data sets.
SQL_MULTIPLE_ ACTIVE_TXN	Character string	Indicates whether the driver allows multiple active transactions on a single connection. The following values can be returned for this *InfoType* code:
		"Y": Multiple active transactions on a single connection are allowed.
		"N": Only one active transaction at a time is allowed on a connection.
		When using coordinated distributed units of work connections (Type 2 connects), the value **"N"** will be returned (since the transaction or unit of work spans multiple connections).
SQL_NEED_LONG_DATA_LEN	Character string	Indicates whether the data source needs the length of a long data value before that value is sent to it. The following values can be returned for this *InfoType* code:
		"Y": The data source needs the length of a long data value (the data type is **SQL_LONGVARCHAR**, **SQL_LONGVARBINARY**, or a long data source-specific data type) before that value is sent to it.
		"N": The data source does not need the length of a long data value before that value is sent to it.

InfoType Code	Data Type Returned	Description
		When using DB2 CLI, the value **"N"** will always be returned for this *InfoType* code.
SQL_NON_NULLABLE_ COLUMNS	**SQLUSMALLINT**	Indicates whether the data source supports the **NOT NULL** column constraint in **CREATE TABLE** SQL statements. The following values can be returned for this *InfoType* code:
		SQL_NNC_NULL: All columns must be nullable.
		SQL_NNC_NON_NULL: Columns do not have to be nullable (the data source supports the **NOT NULL** column constraint in **CREATE TABLE** statements).
SQL_NULL_COLLATION	**SQLUSMALLINT**	Identifies where NULL values are sorted in a result data set. The following values can be returned for this *InfoType* code:
		SQL_NC_END: NULLs are sorted at the end of the result data set, even if the **ASC** or **DESC** keyword is specified.
		SQL_NC_HIGH: NULLs are sorted at the high end of the result data set, depending on the **ASC** or **DESC** keywords.
		SQL_NC_LOW: NULLs are sorted at the low end of the result data set, depending on the **ASC** or **DESC** keywords.
		SQL_NC_START: NULLs are sorted at the start of the result data set, even if the **ASC** or **DESC** keyword is specified.
SQL_NUMERIC_FUNCTIONS	**SQLUINTEGER** bitmask	Identifies the ODBC scalar numeric functions supported by the driver and its underlying data source. The following bitmask values can be returned for this *InfoType* code:
		SQL_FN_NUM_ABS **SQL_FN_NUM_ACOS** **SQL_FN_NUM_ASIN** **SQL_FN_NUM_ATAN** **SQL_FN_NUM_ATAN2** **SQL_FN_NUM_CEILING** **SQL_FN_NUM_COS** **SQL_FN_NUM_COT** **SQL_FN_NUM_DEGREES** **SQL_FN_NUM_EXP** **SQL_FN_NUM_FLOOR** **SQL_FN_NUM_LOG** **SQL_FN_NUM_LOG10** **SQL_FN_NUM_MOD** **SQL_FN_NUM_PI** **SQL_FN_NUM_POWER**

InfoType Code	Data Type Returned	Description
		SQL_FN_NUM_RADIANS **SQL_FN_NUM_RAND** **SQL_FN_NUM_ROUND** **SQL_FN_NUM_SIGN** **SQL_FN_NUM_SIN** **SQL_FN_NUM_SQRT** **SQL_FN_NUM_TAN** **SQL_FN_NUM_TRUNCATE** **NOTE:** These functions are intended to be used in an ODBC vendor escape sequence.
SQL_ODBC_API_ CONFORMANCE	16-bit **INTEGER**	Identifies the level of the ODBC 2.0 interface that the driver conforms to. The following values can be returned for this *InfoType* code: **SQL_OAC_NONE:** The driver does not conform to any ODBC 2.0 interface level. **SQL_OAC_LEVEL1:** The driver conforms to the ODBC 2.0 Level 1 interface level. **SQL_OAC_LEVEL2:** The driver conforms to the ODBC 2.0 Level 2 interface level.
SQL_ODBC_INTERFACE_ CONFORMANCE	**SQLUINTEGER**	Identifies the level of the ODBC 3.x interface that the driver conforms to. The following values can be returned for this *InfoType* code: **SQL_OIC_CORE:** The driver conforms to the ODBC 3.x Core interface level. This is the minimum level to which all ODBC drivers are expected to conform. This level includes basic interface elements such as connection functions; functions for preparing and executing SQL statements; basic result data set metadata functions; and basic catalog functions. **SQL_OIC_LEVEL1:** The driver conforms to the ODBC 3.x Level 1 interface level. This level provides all Core level functionality, plus support for scrollable cursors; bookmarks; and positioned updates and deletes. **SQL_OIC_LEVEL2:** The driver conforms to the ODBC 3.x Level 2 interface level. This level provides Core and Level 1 functionality, plus advanced features such as sensitive cursors; update, delete, and refresh by bookmarks; stored procedure support; catalog functions for primary and foreign keys and multi-catalog support.

InfoType Code	Data Type Returned	Description
SQL_ODBC_SAG_CLI_CONFORMANCE	**SQLUSMALLINT**	Identifies whether or not the driver is compliant with the *SQL Access Group* (SAG) CLI specification. The following values can be returned for this *Info-Type* code: **SQL_OSCC_NOT_COMPLIANT**: The driver is not SAG CLI compliant. **SQL_OSCC_COMPLIANT**: The driver is SAG CLI compliant.
SQL_ODBC_SQL_CONFORMANCE	**SQLUSMALLINT**	Identifies the SQL grammar level to which the driver conforms. The following values can be returned for this *InfoType* code: **SQL_OSC_MINIMUM**: The driver conforms to the Minimum SQL grammar level. **SQL_OSC_CORE**: The driver conforms to the Core SQL grammar level. **SQL_OSC_EXTENDED**: The driver conforms to the Extended SQL grammar level.
SQL_ODBC_VER	Character string	Identifies the ODBC version that the ODBC Driver Manager conforms to. This information is returned in a string with the format *mm.vv.0000*, where *mm* is the major ODBC version number (as provided by the constant **SQL_SPEC_MAJOR**) and *vv* is the minor ODBC version number (as provided by the constant **SQL_SPEC_MINOR**) (for example, "03.05" translates to major version 3, minor version 5). This information is returned by the ODBC Driver Manager; not by the data source.
SQL_OJ_CAPABILITIES	**SQLUINTEGER** bitmask	Identifies the types of outer joins that are supported by the driver and its underlying data source (as defined in SQL-92). The following bitmask values can be returned for this *InfoType* code: **SQL_OJ_LEFT**: Left outer joins are supported. **SQL_OJ_RIGHT**: Right outer joins are supported. **SQL_OJ_FULL**: Full outer joins are supported. **SQL_OJ_NESTED**: Nested outer joins are supported. **SQL_OJ_NOT_ORDERED**: The column names in the **ON** clause of the outer join do not have to be in the same order as their respective table names in the **OUTER JOIN** clause.

InfoType Code	Data Type Returned	Description
		SQL_OJ_INNER: The inner table (the right table in a left outer join, or the left table in a right outer join) can also be used in an inner join. This does not apply to full outer joins, which do not have an inner table.
		SQL_OJ_ALL_COMPARISON_OPS: The comparison operator in the **ON** clause of the outer join can be any of the ODBC comparison operators. If this bit is not set, only the equals (=) comparison operator can be used in outer joins.
		If the **OUTER JOIN** clause is not supported by the driver or the data source, the value **0** is returned for this *InfoType* code.
		See the **SQL_SQL92_RELATIONAL_JOIN_OPERATORS** *InfoType* code for more information on the support of relational join operators in a **SELECT** statement, as defined by SQL-92.
SQL_ORDER_BY_COLUMNS_IN_SELECT	Character string	Indicates whether the columns in an **ORDER BY** clause must also be in the select list. The following values can be returned for this *InfoType* code:
		"Y": The columns in an **ORDER BY** clause must be in the select list.
		"N": The columns in an **ORDER BY** clause do not have to be in the select list.
SQL_OUTER_JOINS	Character string	Indicates whether outer joins and the ODBC outer join escape sequence are supported by the driver. The following values can be returned for this *InfoType* code:
		"Y": Outer joins and the ODBC outer join escape sequence is supported by the driver.
		"N": Outer joins and the ODBC outer join escape sequence is not supported by the driver.
SQL_PARAM_ARRAY_ROW_COUNTS	SQLUINTEGER	Identifies the driver's properties regarding the availability of row counts when a parameterized SQL statement is executed. The following values can be returned for this *InfoType* code:
		SQL_PARC_BATCH: Individual row counts are available for each set of parameter values provided. This is conceptually equivalent to the driver generating a batch of SQL statements, one for each parameter set in the array. Extended error information can be retrieved by using the **SQL_DESC_ARAY_STATUS_PTR** descriptor header record field.

InfoType Code	Data Type Returned	Description
		SQL_PARC_NO_BATCH: There is only one row count available, which is the cumulative row count resulting from the execution of the SQL statement for the entire array of parameter values. This is conceptually equivalent to treating the SQL statement along with the entire parameter array as one atomic unit. Errors are handled the same as if a single SQL statement were executed.
SQL_PARAM_ARRAY_SELECTS	**SQLUINTEGER**	Identifies the driver's properties regarding the availability of result data sets when a parameterized SQL statement is executed. The following values can be returned for this *InfoType* code:
		SQL_PAS_BATCH: There is one result data set available per set of parameter values provided. This is conceptually equivalent to the driver generating a batch of SQL statements, one for each parameter set in the array.
		SQL_PAS_NO_BATCH: There is only one result data set available, which represents the cumulative result data set resulting from the execution of the SQL statement for the entire array of parameter values. This is conceptually equivalent to treating the SQL statement along with the entire parameter array as one atomic unit.
		SQL_PAS_NO_SELECT: A driver does not allow a result data set-generating statement to be executed with an array of parameter values.
SQL_POS_OPERATIONS	**SQLUINTEGER** bitmask	Identifies the **SQLSetPos()** function options that are supported by the driver and its underlying data source. The following bitmask values can be returned for this *InfoType* code:
		SQL_POS_POSITION SQL_POS_REFRESH SQL_POS_UPDATE SQL_POS_DELETE SQL_POS_ADD
		When using DB2 CLI, the value **0** will always be returned for this *InfoType* code.
SQL_POSITIONED_STATEMENTS	**SQLUINTEGER** bitmask	Identifies the positioned SQL statement options that are supported by the driver and its underlying data source. The following bitmask values can be returned for this *InfoType* code:
		SQL_PS_POSITIONED_DELETE SQL_PS_POSITIONED_UPDATE SQL_PS_SELECT_FOR_UPDATE

InfoType Code	Data Type Returned	Description
SQL_PROCEDURE_TERM	Character string	Identifies the data source vendor's name for a stored procedure (for example, "database procedure," "stored procedure," "procedure," "package," or "stored query").
SQL_PROCEDURES	Character string	Indicates whether the data source supports stored procedures and the driver supports procedure invocation. The following values can be returned for this *InfoType* code: **"Y"**: The data source supports procedures and the driver supports the ODBC procedure invocation syntax. **"N"**: The data source does not support procedures and/or the driver does not support the ODBC procedure invocation syntax.
SQL_QUOTED_IDENTIFIER_CASE	SQLUSMALLINT	Identifies the type of case sensitivity used in quoted identifiers. The following values can be returned for this *InfoType* code: **SQL_IC_UPPER**: Quoted identifiers are not case-sensitive and are stored in uppercase in the system catalog. **SQL_IC_LOWER**: Quoted identifiers are not case-sensitive and are stored in lowercase in the system catalog. **SQL_IC_SENSITIVE**: Quoted identifiers are case-sensitive and are stored in mixed case in the system catalog. **SQL_IC_MIXED:** Quoted identifiers are not case-sensitive and are stored in mixed case in the system catalog.
SQL_ROW_UPDATES	Character string	Indicates whether keyset-driven or mixed cursors maintain row versions or values for all rows fetched. The following values can be returned for this *InfoType* code: **"Y"**: Cursors maintain row versions or values for all rows fetched; therefore, they can detect any updates made to a row since it was last fetched. (This only applies to updates, not to deletions or insertions.) The driver can return the **SQL_ROW_UPDATED** flag to the row status array when **SQLFetchScroll()** is called. **"N"**: Cursors do not maintain row versions or values for fetched rows.
SQL_SCHEMA_TERM[10]	Character string	Identifies the data source vendor's name for a schema (for example, "owner," "Authorization ID," or "Schema."). This string can be in upper, lower, or mixed case.

InfoType Code	Data Type Returned	Description
SQL_SCHEMA_USAGE[11]	SQLUINTEGER bitmask	Identifies the SQL statements in which schemas can be used. The following bitmask values can be returned for this *InfoType* code:
		SQL_SU_DML_STATEMENTS: Schemas are supported in all *Data Manipulation Language* (DML) statements: SELECT, INSERT, UPDATE, DELETE, and, if supported, SELECT FOR UPDATE and positioned UPDATE and DELETE statements.
		SQL_SU_PROCEDURE_INVOCATION: Schemas are supported in the ODBC procedure invocation statement.
		SQL_SU_TABLE_DEFINITION: Schemas are supported in all table definition statements: CREATE TABLE, CREATE VIEW, ALTER TABLE, DROP TABLE, and DROP VIEW.
		SQL_SU_INDEX_DEFINITION: Schemas are supported in all index definition statements: CREATE INDEX and DROP INDEX.
		SQL_SU_PRIVILEGE_DEFINITION: Schemas are supported in all privilege definition statements: GRANT and REVOKE.
SQL_SCROLL_CONCURRENCY	SQLUINTEGER bitmask	Identifies the scrollable cursor concurrency control options supported by the driver and its underlying data source. The following bitmask values can be returned for this *InfoType* code:
		SQL_SCCO_READ_ONLY: A read-only cursor, in which no updates are allowed, is supported.
		SQL_SCCO_LOCK: A cursor that uses the lowest level of locking sufficient to ensure that the row can be updated is supported.
		SQL_SCCO_OPT_ROWVER: A cursor that uses optimistic concurrency control by comparing row versions is supported.
		SQL_SCCO_OPT_VALUES: A cursor that uses optimistic concurrency control by comparing values is supported.
		When using DB2 CLI, the value SQL_SCCO_LOCK will always be returned for this *InfoType* code.
SQL_SCROLL_OPTIONS	SQLUINTEGER bitmask	Identifies the cursor scroll options that are supported by the driver. The following bitmask values can be returned for this *InfoType* code:
		SQL_SO_FORWARD_ONLY: The cursor only scrolls forward.

InfoType Code	Data Type Returned	Description
		SQL_SO_STATIC: The data in the result data set is static.
		SQL_SO_KEYSET_DRIVEN: The driver saves and uses the keys for every row in the result data set.
		SQL_SO_DYNAMIC: The driver keeps the keys for every row in the rowset (the keyset size is the same as the rowset size).
		SQL_SO_MIXED: The driver keeps the keys for every row in the keyset, and the keyset size is greater than the rowset size. The cursor is keyset-driven inside the keyset and dynamic outside the keyset.
SQL_SEARCH_PATTERN_ ESCAPE	Character string	Identifies the character or characters the driver uses as an escape character that permits the use of the underscore (_) and percent sign (%) pattern match metacharacters as valid characters in search patterns. This escape character is only used for those catalog function arguments that contain pattern value parameters. If the driver does not provide a search-pattern escape character, there is no specified limit, or if the limit is unknown, an empty string (" ") is returned for this *InfoType* code. Because this information type does not indicate support of an escape character in the **LIKE** predicate, SQL-92 does not include requirements for this *InfoType* code.
SQL_SERVER_NAME	Character string	Identifies the data source-specific server name associated with the data source. When using DB2 CLI, the value the name of the DB2 Instance (database server) will be returned for this *InfoType* code.
SQL_SPECIAL_CHARACTERS	Character string	Identifies all special characters (that is, all characters except **a** through **z**, **A** through **Z**, **0** through **9**, and underscore (_)) that can be used in an identifier name (for example, a table, column, or index name), on the data source. If an identifier contains one or more of these characters, the identifier must be a delimited identifier.
SQL_SQL_CONFORMANCE	**SQLUINTEGER**	Identifies the level of the SQL-92 SQL standard specification that the driver conforms to. The following values can be returned for this *InfoType* code: **SQL_SC_SQL92_ENTRY**: The driver conforms to the SQL-92 Entry level.

InfoType Code	Data Type Returned	Description
		SQL_SC_FIPS127_2_TRANSITIONAL: The driver conforms to the FIPS 127-2 Transitional level. **SQL_SC_SQL92_INTERMEDIATE**: The driver conforms to the SQL-92 Intermediate level. **SQL_SC_SQL92_FULL**: The driver conforms to the SQL-92 Full level.
SQL_SQL92_DATETIME_ FUNCTIONS	**SQLUINTEGER** bitmask	Identifies the datetime scalar functions that are used by the driver and its underlying data source (as defined in SQL-92). The following bitmask values can be returned for this *InfoType* code: **SQL_SDF_CURRENT_DATE** **SQL_SDF_CURRENT_TIME** **SQL_SDF_CURRENT_TIMESTAMP**
SQL_SQL92_FOREIGN_ KEY_DELETE_RULE	**SQLUINTEGER** bitmask	Identifies the rules for using a foreign key in a **DELETE** SQL statement that are supported by the data source (as defined in SQL-92). The following bitmask values can be returned for this *InfoType* code: **SQL_SFKD_CASCADE** **SQL_SFKD_NO_ACTION** **SQL_SFKD_SET_DEFAULT** **SQL_SFKD_SET_NULL**
SQL_SQL92_FOREIGN_ KEY_UPDATE_RULE	**SQLUINTEGER** bitmask	Identifies the rules for using a foreign key in an **UPDATE** SQL statement that are supported by the data source (as defined in SQL-92). The following bitmask values can be returned for this *InfoType* code: **SQL_SFKU_CASCADE** **SQL_SFKU_NO_ACTION** **SQL_SFKU_SET_DEFAULT** **SQL_SFKU_SET_NULL**
SQL_SQL92_GRANT	**SQLUINTEGER** bitmask	Identifies the clauses in the **GRANT** SQL statement that are supported by the data source (as defined in SQL-92). The following bitmask values can be returned for this *InfoType* code: **SQL_SG_DELETE_TABLE** **SQL_SG_INSERT_COLUMN** **SQL_SG_INSERT_TABLE** **SQL_SG_REFERENCES_TABLE** **SQL_SG_REFERENCES_COLUMN** **SQL_SG_SELECT_TABLE** **SQL_SG_UPDATE_COLUMN** **SQL_SG_UPDATE_TABLE** **SQL_SG_USAGE_ON_DOMAIN** **SQL_SG_USAGE_ON_CHARACTER_SET**

InfoType Code	Data Type Returned	Description
		SQL_SG_USAGE_ON_COLLATION SQL_SG_USAGE_ON_TRANSLATION SQL_SG_WITH_GRANT_OPTION
SQL_SQL92_NUMERIC_ VALUE_FUNCTIONS	SQLUINTEGER bitmask	Identifies the numeric value scalar functions that are supported by the driver and its underlying data source (as defined in SQL-92). The following bitmask values can be returned for this *InfoType* code: SQL_SNVF_BIT_LENGTH SQL_SNVF_CHAR_LENGTH SQL_SNVF_CHARACTER_LENGTH SQL_SNVF_EXTRACT SQL_SNVF_OCTET_LENGTH SQL_SNVF_POSITION
SQL_SQL92_PREDICATES	SQLUINTEGER bitmask	Identifies the predicates of a **SELECT** SQL statement that are supported by the data source (as defined in SQL-92). The following bitmask values can be returned for this *InfoType* code: SQL_SP_BETWEEN SQL_SP_COMPARISON SQL_SP_EXISTS SQL_SP_IN SQL_SP_ISNOTNULL SQL_SP_ISNULL SQL_SP_LIKE SQL_SP_MATCH_FULL SQL_SP_MATCH_PARTIAL SQL_SP_MATCH_UNIQUE_FULL SQL_SP_MATCH_UNIQUE_PARTIAL SQL_SP_OVERLAPS SQL_SP_QUANTIFIED_COMPARISON SQL_SP_UNIQUE
SQL_SQL92_RELATIONAL_ JOIN_OPERATORS	SQLUINTEGER bitmask	Identifies the relational join operators of a **SELECT** SQL statement that are supported by the data source (as defined in SQL-92). The following bitmask values can be returned for this *InfoType* code: SQL_SRJO_CORRESPONDING_CLAUSE SQL_SRJO_CROSS_JOIN SQL_SRJO_EXCEPT_JOIN SQL_SRJO_FULL_OUTER_JOIN SQL_SRJO_INNER_JOIN SQL_SRJO_INTERSECT_JOIN SQL_SRJO_LEFT_OUTER_JOIN SQL_SRJO_NATURAL_JOIN SQL_SRJO_RIGHT_OUTER_JOIN SQL_SRJO_UNION_JOIN **SQL_SRJO_INNER_JOIN** indicates support for the **INNER JOIN** syntax, not for the inner join capability.

InfoType Code	Data Type Returned	Description
SQL_SQL92_REVOKE	SQLUINTEGER bitmask	Identifies the clauses in the **REVOKE** SQL statement that are supported by the data source (as defined in SQL-92). The following bitmask values can be returned for this *InfoType* code: SQL_SR_CASCADE SQL_SR_DELETE_TABLE SQL_SR_GRANT_OPTION_FOR SQL_SR_INSERT_COLUMN SQL_SR_INSERT_TABLE SQL_SR_REFERENCES_COLUMN SQL_SR_REFERENCES_TABLE SQL_SR_RESTRICT SQL_SR_SELECT_TABLE SQL_SR_UPDATE_COLUMN SQL_SR_UPDATE_TABLE SQL_SR_USAGE_ON_DOMAIN SQL_SR_USAGE_ON_CHARACTER_SET SQL_SR_USAGE_ON_COLLATION SQL_SR_USAGE_ON_TRANSLATION
SQL_SQL92_ROW_VALUE_ CONSTRUCTOR	SQLUINTEGER bitmask	Identifies the row value constructor expressions of a **SELECT** SQL statement that are supported by the data source (as defined in SQL-92). The following bitmask values can be returned for this *InfoType* code: SQL_SRVC_VALUE_EXPRESSION SQL_SRVC_NULL SQL_SRVC_DEFAULT SQL_SRVC_ROW_SUBQUERY
SQL_SQL92_STRING_ FUNCTIONS	SQLUINTEGER bitmask	Identifies the string scalar functions that are supported by the driver and its underlying data source (as defined in SQL-92). The following bitmask values can be returned for this *InfoType* code: SQL_SSF_CONVERT SQL_SSF_LOWER SQL_SSF_UPPER SQL_SSF_SUBSTRING SQL_SSF_TRANSLATE SQL_SSF_TRIM_BOTH SQL_SSF_TRIM_LEADING SQL_SSF_TRIM_TRAILING
SQL_SQL92_VALUE_ EXPRESSIONS	SQLUINTEGER bitmask	Identifies the value expressions that are supported by the data source (as defined in SQL-92). The following bitmask values can be returned for this *InfoType* code: SQL_SVE_CASE SQL_SVE_CAST SQL_SVE_COALESCE SQL_SVE_NULLIF

InfoType Code	Data Type Returned	Description
SQL_SQL92_STANDARD_ CLI_CONFORMANCE	**SQLUINTEGER** bitmask	Identifies the CLI standard(s) the driver conforms to. The following bitmask values can be returned for this *InfoType* code:
		SQL_SCC_XOPEN_CLI_VERSION1: The driver conforms to the X/Open CLI Version 1 standard.
		SQL_SCC_ISO92_CLI: The driver conforms to the ISO-92 CLI standard.
SQL_STATIC_CURSOR_ ATTRIBUTES1	**SQLUINTEGER** bitmask	Defines the first subset of static cursor attributes that are supported by the driver (see the **SQL_ STATIC_CURSOR_ATTRIBUTES2** *InfoType* code for the second subset of attributes). The following bit-mask values can be returned for this *InfoType* code:
		SQL_CA1_NEXT: The **SQL_FETCH_NEXT** orientation value can be specified with the **SQLFetchScroll()** function when the cursor is a static cursor.
		SQL_CA1_ABSOLUTE: The **SQL_FETCH_FIRST**, **SQL_FETCH_LAST**, and **SQL_FETCH_ABSOLUTE** orientation values can be specified with the **SQLFetchScroll()** function when the cursor is a static cursor. (The rowset fetched is independent of the current cursor position.)
		SQL_CA1_RELATIVE: The **SQL_FETCH_PRIOR** and **SQL_FETCH_RELATIVE** orientation values can be specified with the **SQLFetchScroll()** function when the cursor is a static cursor. (The rowset fetched is dependent on the current cursor position. Note that this is separate from **SQL_FETCH_NEXT** because in a forward-only cursor, only **SQL_FETCH_NEXT** is supported.)
		SQL_CA1_BOOKMARK: The **SQL_FETCH_BOOKMARK** orientation value can be specified with the **SQLFetchScroll()** function when the cursor is a static cursor.
		SQL_CA1_LOCK_EXCLUSIVE: The **SQL_LOCK_EXCLUSIVE** lock value can be specified with the **SQLSetPos()** function when the cursor is a static cursor.
		SQL_CA1_LOCK_NO_CHANGE: The **SQL_LOCK_NO_CHANGE** lock value can be specified with the **SQLSetPos()** function when the cursor is a static cursor.
		SQL_CA1_LOCK_UNLOCK: The **SQL_LOCK_UNLOCK** lock value can be specified with the **SQLSetPos()** function when the cursor is a static cursor.

InfoType Code	Data Type Returned	Description
		SQL_CA1_POS_POSITION: The **SQL_POSITION** operation value can be specified with the **SQLSetPos()** function when the cursor is a static cursor.
		SQL_CA1_POS_UPDATE: The **SQL_UPDATE** operation value can be specified with the **SQLSetPos()** function when the cursor is a static cursor.
		SQL_CA1_POS_DELETE: The **SQL_DELETE** operation value can be specified with the **SQLSetPos()** function when the cursor is a static cursor.
		SQL_CA1_POS_REFRESH: The **SQL_REFRESH** operation value can be specified with the **SQLSetPos()** function when the cursor is a static cursor.
		SQL_CA1_POSITIONED_UPDATE: An **UPDATE WHERE CURRENT_OF** SQL statement is supported when the cursor is a static cursor.
		SQL_CA1_POSITIONED_DELETE: A **DELETE WHERE CURRENT OF** SQL statement is supported when the cursor is a static cursor.
		SQL_CA1_SELECT_FOR_UPDATE: A **SELECT FOR UPDATE** SQL statement is supported when the cursor is a static cursor.
		SQL_CA1_BULK_ADD: The **SQL_ADD** operation value can be specified with the **SQLBulkOperations()** function when the cursor is a static cursor.
		SQL_CA1_BULK_UPDATE_BY_BOOKMARK: The **SQL_UPDATE_BY_BOOKMARK** operation value can be specified with the **SQLBulkOperations()** function when the cursor is a static cursor.
		SQL_CA1_BULK_DELETE_BY_BOOKMARK: The **SQL_DELETE_BY_BOOKMARK** operation value can be specified with the **SQLBulkOperations()** function when the cursor is a static cursor.
		SQL_CA1_BULK_FETCH_BY_BOOKMARK: The **SQL_FETCH_BY_BOOKMARK** operation value can be specified with the **SQLBulkOperations()** function when the cursor is a static cursor.
SQL_STATIC_CURSOR_ ATTRIBUTES2	**SQLUINTEGER** bitmask	Defines the second subset of static cursor attributes that are supported by the driver (see the **SQL_STA-TIC_CURSOR_ATTRIBUTES1** *InfoType* code for the first subset of attributes). The following bitmask values can be returned for this *InfoType* code:

InfoType Code	Data Type Returned	Description
		SQL_CA2_READ_ONLY_CONCURRENCY: A read-only static cursor in which no updates are allowed is supported. (The **SQL_ATTR_CONCURRENCY** statement attribute can set to **SQL_CONCUR_READ_ONLY** for a static cursor).
		SQL_CA2_LOCK_CONCURRENCY: A static cursor using the lowest level of locking sufficient to ensure the row can be updated is supported. (The **SQL_ATTR_CONCURRENCY** statement attribute can be set to **SQL_CONCUR_LOCK** for a static cursor). These locks must be consistent with the transaction isolation level set by the **SQL_ATTR_TXN_ISOLATION** connection attribute.
		SQL_CA2_OPT_ROWVER_CONCURRENCY: A static cursor that uses the optimistic concurrency control by comparing row versions is supported. (The **SQL_ATTR_CONCURRENCY** statement attribute can be set to **SQL_CONCUR_ROWVER** for a static cursor).
		SQL_CA2_OPT_VALUES_CONCURRENCY: A static cursor that uses the optimistic concurrency control by comparing values is supported. (The **SQL_ATTR_CONCURRENCY** statement attribute can be set to **SQL_CONCUR_VALUES** for a static cursor).
		SQL_CA2_SENSITIVITY_ADDITIONS: Added rows are visible to a static cursor and the cursor can scroll to the added rows. (Where these rows are added to the cursor is driver-dependent.)
		SQL_CA2_SENSITIVITY_DELETIONS: Deleted rows are no longer available to a static cursor, and do not leave a 'hole' in the result data set; after the static cursor scrolls from a deleted row, it cannot return to that row.
		SQL_CA2_SENSITIVITY_UPDATES: Updates to rows are visible to a static cursor; if the static cursor scrolls from and returns to an updated row, the data returned by the cursor is the updated data, not the original data.
		SQL_CA2_MAX_ROWS_SELECT: The **SQL_ATTR_MAX_ROWS** statement attribute affects **SELECT** SQL statements when the cursor is a static cursor.
		SQL_CA2_MAX_ROWS_INSERT: The **SQL_ATTR_MAX_ROWS** statement attribute affects **INSERT** SQL statements when the cursor is a static cursor.

InfoType Code	Data Type Returned	Description
		SQL_CA2_MAX_ROWS_DELETE: The **SQL_ATTR_MAX_ROWS** statement attribute affects **DELETE** SQL statements when the cursor is a static cursor.
		SQL_CA2_MAX_ROWS_UPDATE: The **SQL_ATTR_MAX_ROWS** statement attribute affects **UPDATE** SQL statements when the cursor is a static cursor.
		SQL_CA2_MAX_ROWS_CATALOG: The **SQL_ATTR_MAX_ROWS** statement attribute affects **CATALOG** result data sets when the cursor is a static cursor.
		SQL_CA2_MAX_ROWS_AFFECTS_ALL: The **SQL_ATTR_MAX_ROWS** statement attribute affects **SELECT**, **INSERT**, **UPDATE**, and **DELETE** statements, and **CATALOG** result data sets, when the cursor is a static cursor.
		SQL_CA2_CRC_EXACT: The exact row count is available in the **SQL_DIAG_CURSOR_ROW_COUNT** diagnostic header record field when the cursor is a static cursor.
		SQL_CA2_CRC_APPROXIMATE: An approximate row count is available in the **SQL_DIAG_CURSOR_ROW_COUNT** diagnostic header record field when the cursor is a static cursor.
		SQL_CA2_SIMULATE_NON_UNIQUE: The driver does not guarantee that simulated positioned **UPDATE** or **DELETE** SQL statements will affect only one row when the cursor is a static cursor. If a statement affects more than one row, **SQLExecute()** or **SQLExecDirect()** returns SQLSTATE **01**001 (Cursor operation conflict). To set this behavior, an application calls the **SQLSetStmtAttr()** function and sets the **SQL_ATTR_SIMULATE_CURSOR** statement attribute to **SQL_SC_NON_UNIQUE**.
		SQL_CA2_SIMULATE_TRY_UNIQUE: The driver attempts to guarantee that simulated positioned **UPDATE** or **DELETE** SQL statements will affect only one row when the cursor is a static cursor. The driver always executes such statements even if they might affect more than one row, such as when there is no unique key. If the driver cannot guarantee this for a given statement, **SQLExecute()** or **SQLExecDirect()** returns SQLSTATE **01**001 (Cursor operation conflict). To set this behavior, an application calls the **SQLSetStmtAttr()** function and sets the **SQL_ATTR_SIMULATE_CURSOR** statement attribute to **SQL_SC_TRY_UNIQUE**.

InfoType Code	Data Type Returned	Description
		SQL_CA2_SIMULATE_UNIQUE: The driver guarantees that simulated positioned **UPDATE** or **DELETE** SQL statements will affect only one row when the cursor is a static cursor. If the driver cannot guarantee this for a given statement, **SQLExecute()** or **SQLExecDirect()** returns SQLSTATE **01**001 (Cursor operation conflict). To set this behavior, an application calls the **SQLSetStmtAttr()** function and sets the **SQL_ATTR_SIMULATE_CURSOR** statement attribute to **SQL_SC_UNIQUE**.
SQL_STATIC_SENSITIVITY	SQLUINTEGER bitmask	Identifies how changes made to a static or keyset-driven cursor by the **SQLSetPos()** function or by positioned **UPDATE** or **DELETE** SQL statements are detected by an application. The following bitmask values can be returned for this *InfoType* code:
		SQL_SS_ADDITIONS: Added rows are visible to the cursor, and the cursor can scroll to the added rows. (Where these rows are added to the cursor is driver-dependent.)
		SQL_SS_DELETIONS: Deleted rows are no longer available to a cursor and do not leave a 'hole' in the result data set; after the cursor scrolls from a deleted row, it cannot return to that row.
		SQL_SS_UPDATES: Updates to rows are visible to a cursor; if the cursor scrolls from and returns to an updated row, the data returned by the cursor is the updated data, not the original data.
		Whether an application can detect changes made to a result data set by other cursors, including other cursors of the same application, is dependent upon the cursor type.
SQL_STRING_FUNCTIONS	SQLUINTEGER bitmask	Identifies the scalar string functions that are supported by the driver and its underlying data source (as defined in SQL-92). The following bitmask values can be returned for this *InfoType* code:
		SQL_FN_STR_ASCII SQL_FN_STR_BIT_LENGTH SQL_FN_STR_CHAR SQL_FN_STR_CHAR_LENGTH SQL_FN_STR_CHARACTER_LENGTH SQL_FN_STR_CONCAT SQL_FN_STR_DIFFERENCE SQL_FN_STR_INSERT SQL_FN_STR_LCASE SQL_FN_STR_LEFT SQL_FN_STR_LENGTH

InfoType Code	Data Type Returned	Description
		SQL_FN_STR_LOCATE SQL_FN_STR_LOCATE_2 SQL_FN_STR_LTRIM SQL_FN_STR_OCTET_LENGTH SQL_FN_STR_POSITION SQL_FN_STR_REPEAT SQL_FN_STR_REPLACE SQL_FN_STR_RIGHT SQL_FN_STR_RTRIM SQL_FN_STR_SOUNDEX SQL_FN_STR_SPACE SQL_FN_STR_SUBSTRING SQL_FN_STR_UCASE
		A driver returns the **SQL_FN_STR_LOCATE** bitmask for this *InfoType* code if an application can call the **LOCATE()** function with the **argument1**, **argument2**, and **position** arguments specified (see Appendix A).
		A driver returns the **SQL_FN_STR_LOCATE_2**, bitmask for this *InfoType* code if an application can call the **LOCATE()** function with only the **argument1** and **argument2** arguments specified. A driver that fully supports the **LOCATE()** scalar function returns both the **SQL_FN_STR_LOCATE** and the **SQL_FN_STR_LOCATE_2** bitmask for this *InfoType* code.
SQL_SUBQUERIES	**SQLUINTEGER** bitmask	Identifies the subquery predicates in a **SELECT** SQL statement that are supported by the data source (as defined in SQL-92). The following bitmask values can be returned for this *InfoType* code: **SQL_SQ_CORRELATED_SUBQUERIES**: All predicates supporting subqueries also support correlated subqueries. **SQL_SQ_COMPARISON**: Comparison predicates support subqueries. **SQL_SQ_EXISTS**: **EXISTS** predicates support subqueries. **SQL_SQ_IN**: **IN** predicates support subqueries. **SQL_SQ_QUANTIFIED**: Predicates containing a quantification scalar function support subqueries.
SQL_SYSTEM_FUNCTIONS	**SQLUINTEGER** bitmask	Identifies the scalar system functions that are supported by the driver and its underlying data source (as defined in SQL-92). The following bitmask values can be returned for this *InfoType* code: SQL_FN_SYS_DBNAME SQL_FN_SYS_IFNULL SQL_FN_SYS_USERNAME

InfoType Code	Data Type Returned	Description
		NOTE: These functions are intended to be used in an ODBC vendor escape sequence.
`SQL_TABLE_TERM`	Character string	Identifies data source vendor's name for a table (for example, "table" or "file"). This string can be in upper, lower, or mixed case.
`SQL_TIMEDATE_ADD_INTERVALS`	`SQLUINTEGER` bitmask	Identifies the timestamp interval values that are supported by the driver and its underlying data source for the `TIMESTAMPADD()` ODBC scalar function. The following bitmask values can be returned for this *InfoType* code:

		`SQL_FN_TSI_FRAC_SECOND`
		`SQL_FN_TSI_SECOND`
		`SQL_FN_TSI_MINUTE`
		`SQL_FN_TSI_HOUR`
		`SQL_FN_TSI_DAY`
		`SQL_FN_TSI_WEEK`
		`SQL_FN_TSI_MONTH`
		`SQL_FN_TSI_QUARTER`
		`SQL_FN_TSI_YEAR`

`SQL_TIMEDATE_DIFF_INTERVALS`	`SQLUINTEGER` bitmask	Identifies the timestamp interval values that are supported by the driver and its underlying data source for the `TIMESTAMPDIFF()` ODBC scalar function. The following bitmask values can be returned for this *InfoType* code:

		`SQL_FN_TSI_FRAC_SECOND`
		`SQL_FN_TSI_SECOND`
		`SQL_FN_TSI_MINUTE`
		`SQL_FN_TSI_HOUR`
		`SQL_FN_TSI_DAY`
		`SQL_FN_TSI_WEEK`
		`SQL_FN_TSI_MONTH`
		`SQL_FN_TSI_QUARTER`
		`SQL_FN_TSI_YEAR`

`SQL_TIMEDATE_FUNCTIONS`	`SQLUINTEGER` bitmask	Identifies the scalar date and time functions that are supported by the driver and its underlying data source. The following bitmask values can be returned for this *InfoType* code:

		`SQL_FN_TD_CURRENT_DATE`
		`SQL_FN_TD_CURRENT_TIME`
		`SQL_FN_TD_CURRENT_TIMESTAMP`
		`SQL_FN_TD_CURDATE`
		`SQL_FN_TD_CURTIME`
		`SQL_FN_TD_DAYNAME`
		`SQL_FN_TD_DAYOFMONTH`
		`SQL_FN_TD_DAYOFWEEK`
		`SQL_FN_TD_DAYOFYEAR`
		`SQL_FN_TD_EXTRACT`

InfoType Code	Data Type Returned	Description
		SQL_FN_TD_HOUR SQL_FN_TD_JULIAN_DAY SQL_FN_TD_MINUTE SQL_FN_TD_MONTH SQL_FN_TD_MONTHNAME SQL_FN_TD_NOW SQL_FN_TD_QUARTER SQL_FN_TD_SECOND SQL_FN_TD_SECONDS_SINCE_MIDNIGHT SQL_FN_TD_TIMESTAMPADD SQL_FN_TD_TIMESTAMPDIFF SQL_FN_TD_WEEK SQL_FN_TD_YEAR
SQL_TXN_CAPABLE	SQLUSMALLINT	Identifies the type of transaction support that is provided by the driver or its underlying data source. The following values can be returned for this *Info-Type* code: **SQL_TC_NONE:** Transactions are not supported. **SQL_TC_DML:** Transactions can only contain Data Manipulation Language (DML) statements: **SELECT, INSERT, UPDATE, DELETE**, if supported, **SELECT FOR UPDATE**, and positioned update and delete statements. If a Data Definition Language (DDL) statement (**CREATE_TABLE, CREATE_VIEW, ALTER_TABLE, DROP_TABLE**, and **DROP_VIEW**) is encountered in a transaction, an error occurs. **SQL_TC_DDL_COMMIT:** Transactions can only contain DML statements. If a DDL statement is encountered in a transaction, the transaction will be committed. **SQL_TC_DDL_IGNORE:** Transactions can only contain DML statements. If a DDL statement is encountered in a transaction, it will be ignored. **SQL_TC_ALL:** Transactions can contain DML statements and DDL statements, in any order.
SQL_TXN_ISOLATION_OPTION	SQLUINTEGER bitmask	Identifies the transaction isolation levels that are supported by the driver or data source. The following terms are used to define transaction isolation levels: **Dirty Read**: Transaction 1 changes a row. Transaction 2 reads the changed row before Transaction 1 commits the change. If Transaction 1 rolls back the change, Transaction 2 will have read a row that is considered to have never existed.

InfoType Code	Data Type Returned	Description
		Nonrepeatable Read: Transaction 1 reads a row. Transaction 2 updates or deletes that row and commits this change. If Transaction 1 attempts to reread the row, it receives different row values or discovers that the row has been deleted.
		Phantom: Transaction 1 reads a set of rows that satisfy some search criteria. Transaction 2 generates one or more rows (either through inserts or updates) that match the search criteria. If Transaction 1 re-executes the statement that reads the rows, it receives a different set of rows.
		If the data source supports transactions, the driver returns one of the following bitmasks:
		SQL_TXN_READ_UNCOMMITTED: Dirty reads, nonrepeatable reads, and phantoms are possible.
		SQL_TXN_READ_COMMITTED: Dirty reads are not possible. Nonrepeatable reads and phantoms are possible.
		SQL_TXN_REPEATABLE_READ: Dirty reads and nonrepeatable reads are not possible. Phantoms are possible.
		SQL_TXN_SERIALIZABLE: Transactions are serializable. Serializable transactions do not allow dirty reads, nonrepeatable reads, or phantoms.
		SQL_TXN_NOCOMMIT: Changes are effectively committed at the end of a successful operation; no explicit commit or rollback is allowed.
		NOTE: This isolation level is only used by DB2 for AS/400.
		If transactions are not supported by the data source, the value **0** is returned for this *InfoType* code.
		In IBM terminology:
		SQL_TXN_READ_UNCOMMITTED = Uncommitted Read
		SQL_TXN_COMMITTED = Committed Read
		SQL_TXN_REPEATABLE_READ = Read Stability
		SQL_TXN_SERIALIZABLE = Repeatable Read
SQL_UNION	**SQLUINTEGER** bitmask	Identifies how the **UNION** clause is supported by the data source. The following bitmask values can be returned for this *InfoType* code:
		SQL_U_UNION: The data source supports the **UNION** clause.

InfoType Code	Data Type Returned	Description
		SQL_U_UNION_ALL: The data source supports the **ALL** keyword in the **UNION** clause. (The **SQLGetInfo()** function returns both **SQL_U_UNION** and **SQL_U_UNION_ALL** in this case.)
SQL_USER_NAME	Character string	Identifies the user name used in a particular database (this name can be different from the login name).
SQL_XOPEN_CLI_YEAR	Character string	Identifies the publication year of the X/Open standards specification that the version of the driver being used fully complies with.

(Adapted from the table on pages 759–809 of *Microsoft ODBC 3.0 Software Development Kit & Programmer's Reference*.)

[1]In DB2 CLI 2.0 and earlier, this information type was named **SQL_QUALIFIER_LOCATION**.

[2]In DB2 CLI 2.0 and earlier, this information type was named **SQL_QUALIFIER_NAME_SEPARATOR**.

[3]In DB2 CLI 2.0 and earlier, this information type was named **SQL_QUALIFIER_TERM**.

[4]In DB2 CLI 2.0 and earlier, this information type was named **SQL_QUALIFIER_USAGE**.

[5]In DB2 CLI 2.0 and earlier, this information type was named **SQL_ODBC_SQL_OPT_IEF**.

[6]In DB2 CLI 2.0 and earlier, this information type was named **SQL_MAX_QUALIFIER_NAME_LEN**.

[7]In DB2 CLI 2.0 and earlier, this information type was named **SQL_ACTIVE_ENVIRONMENTS**.

[8]In DB2 CLI 2.0 and earlier, this information type was named **SQL_ACTIVE_CONNECTIONS**.

[9]In DB2 CLI 2.0 and earlier, this information type was named **SQL_MAX_OWNER_NAME_LEN**.

[10]In DB2 CLI 2.0 and earlier, this information type was named **SQL_OWNER_TERM**.

[11]In DB2 CLI 2.0 and earlier, this information type was named **SQL_OWNER_USAGE**.

APPENDIX D

How The Example Programs Were Developed

All of the example programs shown in this book were developed with Visual C++ 6.0 on the Windows NT 4.0 operating system, using the SAMPLE database provided with DB2 Universal Database.

Configuring The Client Workstation

To establish communications between a client workstation and a DB2 Universal Database server, perform the following steps (after installing the DB2 Universal Database *Client Application Enabler* (CAE) and the DB2 Universal Database *Software Development Kit* (SDK) software):

1. Invoke the Client Configuration Assistant by making the appropriate selection from the DB2 for Windows NT Programs menu. The panel shown in Figure D–1 will appear if no database connections have been defined.

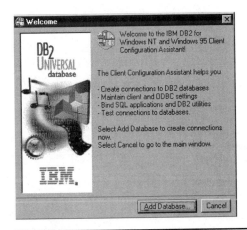

Figure D–1   The DB2 Client Configuration Assistant Welcome Panel

2. When this panel appears, press the *Add Database* push button to start the *Add Database SmartGuide*. The panel shown in Figure D–2 should appear.

3. When the *Add Database SmartGuide* appears, select how you want to set up a connection by choosing the appropriate radio button on the *Source* page. In this example, we will search the network for the desired database (see Figure D–2).

4. When a selection has been made, press the *Next* push button to move to the *Target Database* page of the *Add Database SmartGuide* and select the desired (target) database by traversing the network tree (see Figure D–3).

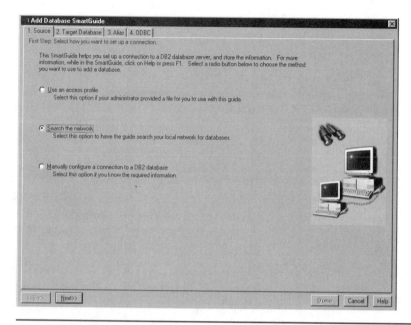

Figure D–2   The Source page of the DB2 Add Database SmartGuide

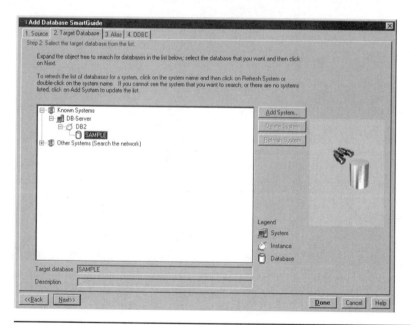

Figure D–3   The Target Database page of the DB2 Add Database SmartGuide

5. Once the database is selected, press the *Next* push button to move to the *Alias* page of the *Add Database SmartGuide* and enter a database alias and description (see Figure D–4).

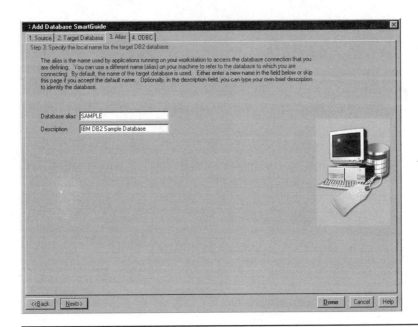

Figure D–4   The Alias page of the DB2 Add Database SmartGuide

6. When an alias and a description have been entered, press the *Next* push button to move to the *ODBC* page of the *Add Database SmartGuide* and specify how the database is to be registered with ODBC (see Figure D–5).

7. Finally, press the *Done* push button to complete the configuration setup. If everything has been entered correctly, the *Confirmation* dialog shown in Figure D–6 will be displayed you can test the connection to make sure it is working properly by pressing the *Test Connection* push button (see Figure D–6).

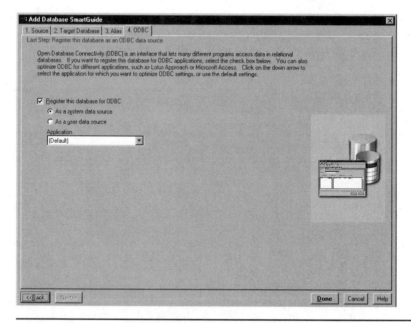

Figure D–5   The ODBC page of the DB2 Add Database SmartGuide

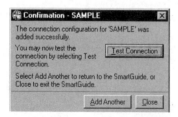

Figure D–6   The configuration confirmation dialog

Testing The Connection

8. After the *Test Connection* push button on the *Confirmation* dialog is pressed, the *Connect To DB2 Database* dialog shown in Figure D–7 will be displayed and you will be prompted for a user ID and password.

9. When this panel is displayed, provide a valid user ID and password and press the *OK* push button. A *DB2 Message* dialog like the one shown in figure D–8 should appear.

10. After the connection has been configured and tested, the *Client Configuration Assistant* panel similar to the one shown in Figure D–9 should replace the *Add Database SmartGuide* and the newly configured database should be listed in the *Available DB2 Databases* list control.

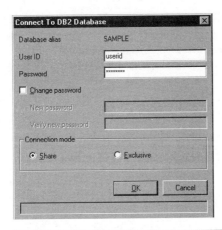

Figure D–7   The DB2 connection information dialog

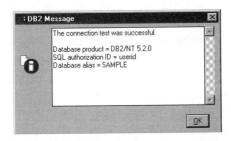

Figure D–8   The "connection test successful" message dialog.

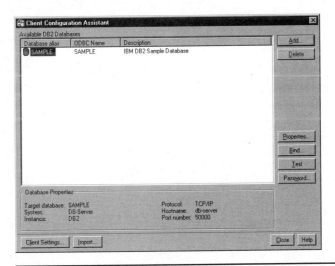

Figure D–9   The Client Configuration Assistant main panel

HOW THE EXAMPLES ARE STORED ON THE DISKETTE   To aid in application development, each of the examples shown throughout the book are provided, in electronic format, on the CD that accompanies this book. This CD contains both a 90 day evaluation copy of DB2 Universal Database Personal Edition and a subdirectory that contains the example programs. This subdirectory (examples) is divided into the following nine subdirectories:

- Chapter_07
- Chapter_08
- Chapter_09
- Chapter_10
- Chapter_11
- Chapter_12
- Chapter_13
- Chapter_14
- Chapter_15

Each of these directories contains the examples that were presented in the corresponding chapters in the book.

HOW TO COMPILE AND EXECUTE THE EXAMPLES   The following steps can be performed to recompile and execute any example program stored on the diskette:

1. Create a directory on your hard drive and copy the example program into it.
2. Invoke the Visual C++ 6.0 Developer Studio.
3. Select *New* from the Visual C++ 6.0 Developer Studio *File* menu.
4. When the *New* panel is displayed, highlight *Win32 Console Application*, enter the appropriate location (hard drive and directory), and a project name that corresponds to the name of the directory that contains the example program (see Figure D–10).
5. When the *Win32 Console Application* wizard is displayed, select the *Empty Project* radio button and press the *Finish* button (see Figure D–11).
6. When the new project is created, select the *Project, Settings . . .* menu item, choose *All Configurations* in the *Settings For:* combo box, and enter the location (path) of the DB2 SDK header files in the *C/C++, Preprocessor, Additional include directories* entry field (see Figure D–12).

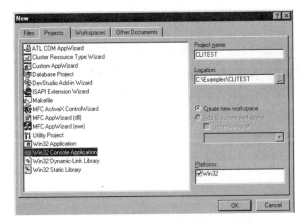

Figure D–10 The New Projects panel of the Visual C++ 6.0 Developer Studio

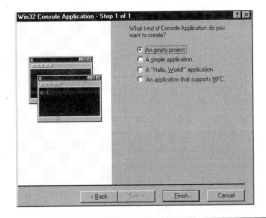

Figure D–11 The first panel of the Win32 Console Application wizard

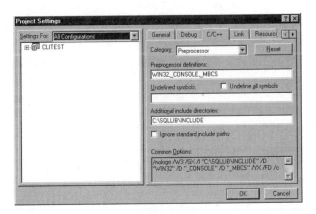

Figure D–12 The C/C++ Project Settings panel of the Visual C++ 6.0 Developer Studio.

7. Next, enter the location (path) of the DB2 SDK library files in the *Link, Input, Additional library path* entry field (see Figure D–13).

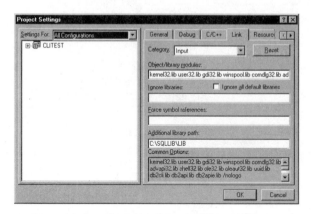

Figure D–13   The Link/Input Project Settings panel of the Visual C++ 6.0 Developer Studio.

8. Then, add the **DB2CLI.LIB** library to the list of library files shown in the *Link, General, Object/library modules* entry field (see Figure D–14).

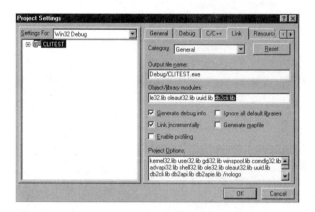

Figure D–14   The Link/General Project Settings panel of the Visual C++ 6.0 Developer Studio.

9. Once the new project settings have been saved, select the *File View* tab in the right-hand window, highlight the *Source Files* project files entry, press the right mouse button to display the pop-up menu, and select the *Add Files to Folder* . . . menu item (see Figure D–15).

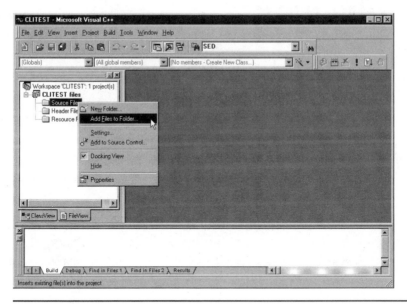

Figure D–15   The Add New Files to Folder . . . menu item

10. Highlight the example file name shown in the *Insert Files into Project* dialog and
press the **OK** push button (see Figure D–16).

Figure D–16   The file selection window.

11. Compile and execute the program.

NOTE: *An appropriate User ID, and Password must be provided in the* `SQLConnect()`
*function calls that are used to connect to the DB2 SAMPLE database. Also, if the user ID
specified is not the same as the user ID of the creator of the SAMPLE database, SQL
statements that interact with tables in the SAMPLE database may have to be qualified. If
this is the case, contact the System Administrator for information about the appropriate
qualifier to use.*

BIBLIOGRAPHY

Date, C.J. with Hugh Darwen. 1993. *A Guide to the SQL Standard, Third Edition.* Reading MA.: Addison-Wesley Publishing Company.

International Business Machines Corporation. 1997. *IBM DB2 Universal Database Administration: Getting Started, Version 5.* S10J–8154-00. IBM Corporation.

International Business Machines Corporation. 1998. *IBM DB2 Universal Database Administration Guide, Version 5.2.* S10J–8157–01. IBM Corporation.

International Business Machines Corporation. 1997. *IBM DB2 Universal Database Call Level Interface Guide and Reference, Version 5.* S10J–8159–00. IBM Corporation.

International Business Machines Corporation. 1997. *IBM DB2 Universal Database Embedded SQL Programming Guide, Version 5.* S10J–8158–00. IBM Corporation.

Joint Technical Committee ISO/IEC JTC 1, and Information Technology Subcommittee SC 21. 1995. ISO/IEC 9075–3 *Information technology—Database languages—SQL—Part 3: Call-Level Interface (SQL / CLI)*, First Edition. Geneva Switzerland. ISO/IEC.

Microsoft Corporation. 1994. *Microsoft ODBC 2.0 Software Programmer's Reference and SDK Guide.* Redmond WA.: Microsoft Press.

Microsoft Corporation. 1997. *Microsoft ODBC 3.0 Software Development Kit & Programmer's Reference.* Redmond WA.: Microsoft Press.

Microsoft Corporation. 1998. *Microsoft ODBC 3.5 SDK RC3 (BETA) On-Line Help (ODBC.HLP).* Redmond WA.: Microsoft Corporation.

The X/Open Company Limited. 1995. *X / Open CAE Specification—Data Management: SQL Call Level Interface (CLI)—Document Number C451.* Reading, U.K..: X/Open Company Ltd.

INDEX

Note: Boldface numbers indicate illustrations.

API INDEX

ABOUT THE AUTHOR

Roger Sanders is an Educational Multimedia Assets Specialist with SAS inSchool™, a division of SAS Institute, Inc. focusing on school technologies. He has been designing and programming software applications for the IBM Personal Computer for more than 15 years and specializes in system programming in C, C++, and 80 × 86 Assembly Language. He has written several computer magazine articles, and he is the author of *The Developer's Handbook to DB2 for Common Servers* and *ODBC 3.5 Developer's Guide*. His background in database application design and development is extensive. It includes experience with DB2 Universal Database, DB2 for Common Servers, DB2 for MVS, INGRES, dBASE, and Microsoft ACCESS.